THE
DEPICTION OF EVICTION
IN IRELAND

For Michael and Sarah
Whose devotion and forbearance have far exceeded
the call of filial duty

* *

THE
DEPICTION OF EVICTION
IN IRELAND
1845–1910

L. PERRY CURTIS, JR

Published by the
UNIVERSITY COLLEGE DUBLIN PRESS
PREAS CHOLÁISTE OLLSCOILE BHAILE ÁTHA CLIATH

2011

First published 2011 by
UNIVERSITY COLLEGE DUBLIN PRESS
Newman House 86 St Stephen's Green, Dublin 2, Ireland
www.ucdpress.ie

ISBN 978-1-906359-57-7 hb
ISBN 978-1-906359-58-4 pb

CIP data available from the British Library

*The right of L. Perry Curtis Jr to be identified as the author of this work
has been asserted by him*

Every effort has been made to trace the owners or copyright holders
of pictures or photographs reproduced in this book, but if any
have been inadvertently overlooked the publishers will be
pleased to make the necessary arrangements
at the first opportunity.

Text design and typesetting
by Lyn Davies
in Adobe Caslon and Bodoni Old Style
Printed in England on acid-free paper
by CPI Antony Rowe,
Chippenham, Wiltshire

Contents

List of Illustrations

Preface

The inspiration for this book came from a painting, Robert G. Kelly's *An Ejectment in Ireland (A Tear and a Prayer for Erin)* (1848) that hangs in the John J. Burns Library at Boston College. Almost a decade ago Professor Rob Savage of the History Department and Irish Studies program there asked me to write a short essay contextualising this picture that occupied a prominent place in the exhibition at the McMullen Museum of Art, Boston College, entitled *ÉIRE/LAND* in 2003.[1]

The rest is – or was – history. To Professor Savage, then, belongs the credit for unintentionally launching me on this *via dolorosa* of eviction. Besides immersing myself in pictorial or graphic images of eviction I perused ballads, poems, and novels as well as the estate papers, government records, and the testimony of so-called experts on the Irish land question. But my principal source comprised the press. Despite all their inherent biases and limitations, the national and provincial newspapers of the Victorian and Edwardian eras served me well as the single most informative source of material pertaining to dispossession in Ireland since the Great Famine. No matter how inaccurate their accounts may have been at times, the vivid details provided by on-the-spot reporters made the painful 'story' of loss well worth the retelling.

Along the way to completion I have incurred huge debts to all those librarians, archivists, and staffers who made these sources available. In particular, the National Library of Ireland furnished me with all kinds of printed and manuscript material with nary a complaint. Kevin Browne, Library Operations Manager, proved a tireless helper and provider of provincial newspapers. In addition, the successive custodians of the Department of Prints and Drawings – Colette O'Daly, Joanna Finnegan, and Honora Faul – kept nourishing my appetite for cartoons and prints relating to this subject. Sandra MacDermott and the National Library of Ireland Society also helped me directly and indirectly from the outset. For permission to reproduce four prints from the Colindale archive I am grateful to the Trustees of the British Library. And for allowing me to publish so many prints and drawings from their fine collection, I am deeply indebted to the National Library of Ireland.

Two steadfast comrades in Dublin, Felix Larkin and Mic Moroney, acted like outriggers that prevented my frail canoe from capsizing in rough weather. Among others who encouraged this project I must count Brendan O'Donoghue, former Director of the NLI, Gerry Lyne, former keeper of manuscripts at the

NLI, Kevin Whelan, Gerard Moran, Ciaran Ó Murchadha, Tim P. O'Neill, Brian Trainor, Margaret MacCurtain, the late James Scully and the late Marcus Bourke. In addition, the director and staff of the National Folklore Collection at UCD proved most helpful in locating reminiscences of famine evictions.

In America I owe many thanks to the Documents Department of the O'Neill Library and to the director and staff of the John J. Burns Library, Boston College as well as the Irish Music Center there. The Baker/Berry Library at Dartmouth College and Peter Harrington of the John Hay Library, Brown University also supplied valuable sources. James S. Donnelly, Jr and J. Bruce Nelson provided both tangible and moral support over the years.

During the long gestation I have benefited from the computer expertise of Susan Bibeau of the Arts and Humanities Resource Center at Dartmouth College and my high-tech son, Michael without whose assistance I would still be bogged down in chaotic word-files. Above all, Barbara Mennell of UCD Press has proved the ideal editor in terms of devotion to content and style as well as patience, wit, and professionalism.

Last but not least, my long-suffering wife, Alison, too often had to compete for my attention with a project that never seemed to end.

L. PERRY CURTIS JR
North Pomfret, Vermont
November 2010

For permission to reproduce paintings, I am grateful to the Crawford Art Gallery (plate 3), the National Gallery of Ireland (plate 2), the National Library of Ireland (plate 4), and the Folklore Department at University College Dublin (plate 39). In addition, Anthony J. Mourek kindly allowed me to reproduce Robert G. Kelly's painting, An Ejectment in Ireland (plate 1).
L. P. C. jr

Abbreviations

AOH	Ancient Order of Hibernians
BL	British Library
BP	*Boston Pilot*
BPP	British Parliamentary Papers
CBS	Crime Branch Special
CDB	Congested Districts Board
CDU	Cork Defence Union
CE	*Cork Examiner*
CJ	*Clare Journal*
CT	*Connaught Telegraph*
DI	*Donegal Independent*
DJ	*Derry Journal*
DPD	Department of Prints and Drawings, National Library of Ireland
DV	*Donegal Vindicator*
EBL	Eblana
FJ	*Freeman's Journal*
GP	*Galway Press*
HC	House of Commons
HWJ	*History Workshop Journal*
ICMRC	Society for Irish Church Missions to the Roman Catholics
ICR	Irish Crime Records
IDI	*Irish Daily Independent*
IGMCR	Inspector General Monthly Confidential Reports
ILPU	Irish Loyal and Patriotic Union
IRB	Irish Republican Brotherhood
IT	*Irish Times*
KO	*Kildare Observer*
KWR	*Kerry Weekly Reporter*
LCE	*Limerick and Clare Examiner*
LRTV	*Limerick Reporter and Tipperary Vindicator*
LS	*Londonderry Sentinel*

MC	*Mayo Constitution*
ME	*Mayo Examiner*
MHCA	*Meath Herald and Cavan Advertiser*
NAI	National Archives of Ireland
NFC	National Folklore Collection
NGI	National Gallery of Ireland
NLI	National Library of Ireland
NW	*Northern Whig*
P/W	*The People (Wexford)*
PDA	Property Defence Association
PIP	*Penny Illustrated Paper*
PMG	*Pall Mall Gazette*
PRONI	Public Record Office of Northern Ireland
RIC	Royal Irish Constabulary
RJ	*Roscommon Journal*
RM	Resident Magistrate
TCD	Trinity College Dublin
Times	*The Times* (of London)
TNA	The National Archives, Kew
UCD	University College Dublin
UI	*United Ireland*
UIL	United Irish League
WDM	*Waterford Daily Mail*
WF	*Weekly Freeman*
WFNP	*Weekly Freeman and National Press*
WI	*Wexford Independent*
WL	William Lawrence Collection of Photographs, National Library of Ireland
WNGA	*Waterford News and General Advertiser*

Introduction

*'The root idea in Ireland has always been
the land and what the land produced, be it corn or cattle.
Back into the remotest antiquity this land factor
is found underlying all Irish history.'*

SIR WILLIAM BUTLER
The Light of the West (Dublin, 1933), p. 156.

*'My father died, I closed his eyes
Outside our cabin door –
The Landlord and the Sheriff, too,
Was there the day before –
And then my loving mother,
And sisters three also,
Were forced to go with broken hearts
From the Glen of Aherlow.'*

'PATRICK SHEEHAN' (1857) *in* GEORGES DENIS ZIMMERMANN
Songs of Irish Rebellion (2002), p. 245

———

Since the 1970s Irish historians have agreed that evictions in the post-famine era affected only a tiny percentage of the 600,000 tenants in Ireland. When compared with the appalling clearances between 1846 and 1854, this conclusion can hardly be faulted. However, the present study is predicated on the assumption that numbers alone do not tell the whole story of rural dispossession even if the majority of landlords were not the predatory or avaricious rent collectors and evictors of nationalist imaginations. In the revisionist rush to acquit landed proprietors of any transgression more serious than selfishness and imprudence it has been all too easy to ignore the impact of even the threat of ejectment on a vulnerable and increasingly politicised populace.

If the old melodrama of villainous or mercenary landlords oppressing an heroic tenantry has been largely discredited, we should be wary of many so-called facts and figures. As Hayden White argued long ago in his *splendidly* subversive essay, 'The Fictions of Factual Representation', the projects of historians and novelists share much in common because both use the same tropes and aspire to 'provide a verbal image of "reality"'. And to quote a distinguished provost of Trinity College Dublin, 'no fallacious argument is so dangerous as that which is based on facts'. Ultra-empirical historians who claim the high ground of objectivity and dismiss or ignore those similarities do so at their peril.[1] No matter how statistically well informed any study of Irish landlord and tenant relations may be, it is bound to involve some stacking of the deck in order to make sense of all the diverse data and arrive at a seemingly plausible conclusion. In short, an exclusively numerical approach to evictions in post-famine Ireland overlooks the importance of their political and cultural role in advancing the cause of both land reform and Home Rule.

When dealing with the land question, moreover, the power of myth, memory, and emotion should never be underestimated. The dispossession of labourers, cottiers and tenant farmers during the reign of Queen Victoria not only helped to fuel the propaganda machine constructed by nationalists and tenant-righters after the famine but also reinforced the growing conviction among Irish Catholics that the land belonged to 'the people' and should therefore be restored to them. Eviction thus became an increasingly political as distinct from an economic and legal issue. Patriotic Irishmen in Greater Ireland overseas responded generously to the appeals of Parnellite MPs for money to support both Home Rule and the victims of the crowbar brigade. As the *Irish Times'* correspondent, James Godkin, wrote in 1870, the age-old conflict between England and Ireland could be reduced to a fight 'over the possession of the soil'. Fear of eviction, he insisted, weighed heavily on the tenantry and the 'crushing' and 'inhumane' land system 'terrorises and dehumanises a people remarkable for their hospitality to the poor'.[2]

According to the revisionist school of history Irish landlords may have been guilty of shortsightedness and incompetence in managing their estates and knew little about conditions beyond their demesne walls, but they were not the predatory or rackrenting 'ogres' and misers of nationalist and anti-revisionist imaginations. Such respected historians as Barbara Solow, W. E. Vaughan, and Cormac Ó Gráda have firmly acquitted them of being rackrenters and evictors after the 1850s. In Vaughan's view they under-rented their land; they failed to 'extract full economic rents' from their tenants; and they spent much more money on luxuries than estate improvements. Far from being the malevolent tyrants of nationalist imaginations they were a self-indulgent and unenterprising elite that had lost its bearings as well as political clout after the famine. Ironically enough, this interpretation was anticipated in 1880 by J. P. Mahaffy, the eminent classical scholar and later provost of Trinity College Dublin that owned more acres than almost any other landlord in Ireland.

According to Mahaffy, who realised the great diversity of this class (while insisting on the racial unity of the primitive Irish Celt), most landlords were socially isolated, complacent, and utterly lacking in 'public spirit'. Addicted to foxhunting and club life, they lacked the unity, enterprise, and courage to organise and confront the 'ruffians' of the Land League. But their greatest failing in his view was their lack of education and reluctance to send their sons to university. Almost a century later Vaughan delivered much the same verdict from within the precincts of Trinity College, arguing that the land war served no useful purpose except to mobilise tenants and their urban allies into a formidable coalition aimed at ending the Union with Great Britain and facilitating the conversion of tenant occupiers into owners of their farms.[3]

If rural evictions were relatively few after the famine, so too were agrarian murders, and yet they both deserve attention. Eviction forms a vital part of the long and troubled story of the struggle for the land. Tim O'Neill has rightly complained that Irish 'evictions are well on the way to being written out of the history of nineteenth-century Ireland'. Noting the tendency of some historians to underestimate the number of famine evictions, he contends that 'the devastation caused by evictions in rural communities is difficult for a modern urban society to appreciate'.[4]

Despite the *de facto* security of tenure enjoyed by the vast majority of tenants and leaseholders after the 1850s, the threat of eviction in hard times for failing to pay the rent and arrears due haunted many occupiers. Land agents often used ejectment writs or notices to quit to squeeze some rent out of tenants in default. In the words of Robert Scally, evictions served as 'the living enactments of the cottier's perennial nightmare, by now the most familiar tableau in nationalist images of the landlords' inhumanity'.[5] During the famine era final evictions not only forced families onto the road or into ditches and lean-tos, if not the dreaded workhouse, but they also transformed the landscape as thousands of small, uneconomic holdings were merged into larger and more productive farms or cattle ranches leaving behind heaps of stones or unroofed cabins – grim reminders of not just dire poverty but also the 'squaring' or 'striping' of estates by their owners in the name of improvement.

Almost half of this study is devoted to the two land wars of the 1880s when the exponential growth in the volume of eviction news galvanised the interwoven campaigns to abolish landlordism and the Union. Spearheaded by *United Ireland* and the *Freeman's Journal*, the Irish nationalist press demonised the landlord class and its backers in Dublin Castle in feature articles and editorials that dwelled on the iniquity and the injustice of eviction. Aware of the sensation value of mass protest meetings and the drama of eviction, newspaper editors assigned 'special correspondents' to record the action and interview the protagonists. London's dailies and weeklies also increased their quotient of Irish eviction news, as did magazines like the *Illustrated London News*, the *Graphic*, and the *Penny Illustrated Paper* that dispatched some of their best artists to sketch these conflicts. At the height of the agitation these illustrated weeklies printed full-page or double-page prints of the contest between unarmed tenants and the well-armed enforcers of the law. The Irish-American press also carried daily or weekly reports of major evictions in the 1880s that were bound to stir even more hatred of Irish landlordism and British imperialism.

Although evictions declined sharply after 1900, the last chapter deals with the third land war, when disputes over the graziers' monopoly of ranch lands and profound disappointment over the failure of the Wyndham act to bring to pass a peasant proprietorship led to anti-rent protests, boycotting, intimidation, and cattle driving. The renewal of the land agitation in the Edwardian era provides the context for a few dramatic evictions as well as the crucial issue of reinstating all the evicted tenants. The so-called ranch wars of 1902–10 had significant repercussions around the country as small farmers and landless men in the west demanded ownership of viable farms. After the Great War, the old hunger for land returned with a vengeance giving rise to not only intimidation of tenants planted on evicted holdings but also some lethal land seizures.

While mindful of the importance of contextualising eviction, I have tried to steer clear of immersion in the 'high politics' or ministerial discussions of Irish questions at Westminster that have received so much attention from political historians since the 1960s. Instead of dwelling at length on rentals, arrears, indebtedness, standards of living, acreage, and land valuations, I have focused instead on contemporary impressions of eviction drawn from newspapers, memoirs, paintings, prints, and photographs as well as poems, ballads, and novels. Of course there are huge gaps in the evidence. If only the testimony of the actual victims of eviction had not been so rare, this study might have been much 'racier of the soil'.

One neglected aspect of this subject is the concerted resistance to eviction that followed the founding of the Land League in October 1879. Long before this pivotal date, of course, some tenants tried in vain to fight off the sheriff and his bailiffs. But they lacked the support of political organisations as distinct from aroused neighbours. All this changed in the 1880s when not even the certainty of defeat and the prospect of imprisonment prevented men and women as well as adolescents, backed by huge crowds, from using non-lethal weapons to 'keep a firm grip on their homesteads'. The palpable threat posed by the landlord and the sheriff to the security, indeed survival, of the family drew whole parishes together in full awareness that the same fate could easily befall any parishioner. As Stephen Ball has shown, menacing crowds turned

out at eviction sites all over the south and west during the first land war to harass and vilify the Crown's forces.[6]

This collective defiance forced Dublin Castle to send forth small armies of
police and soldiers to protect the sheriff's party from harm. The extent of tenant resistance required careful planning and community support in order to
assemble hundreds or thousands of highly vocal protestors who harassed or
impeded the crowbar brigade. Needless to say, nationalist leaders welcomed
the propaganda value of these confrontations with the armed 'myrmidons' of
Dublin Castle and they lavished praise on the heroes and martyrs who emerged
from these trials of strength and will.

Whether explicit or implicit, violence was an inherent part of the eviction
process. Even if the dwelling was not tumbled or wrecked and even if the
occupants offered no resistance, the violence included the smashing of furniture and crockery as the bailiffs threw the movable effects out of the door. The
legality of the notice to quit or ejectment decree did not prevent its victims
from regarding the writ as a grievous injustice. On the purely emotional level
there was no greater wrong in the eyes of the evicted than the loss of the sacred
hearth no matter what the justification. Over the years this violent 'disturbance' energised the rallying cry 'the land for the people'.

To invoke a musical trope, the reality and fear of dispossession runs like a
basso continuo throughout Irish history reaching one major crescendo during
the potato famine and then a more modulated one at the height of the land
wars in the 1880s. During the famine era eviction came to be known as 'extermination' and 'a sentence of death'; and the desire for vengeance sometimes
resulted in ambushes as well as cattle mutilation, arson, threatening letters, and
boycotting. Although the Fenian wing of the nationalist movement had
renounced violence under the so-called New Departure of 1877–9, this did not
stop them from insisting that every Irishman had a right to own a rifle and
defend his homestead against the eviction party.[7] The strength of this conviction makes it all the more amazing that so few of those responsible for eviction
were shot in the line of duty.

No matter how crude, cramped, and fetid a cottier's cabin might be, it represented more than shelter from the elements. The mud-walled and earth-
floored abodes were a far cry from the highly 'romanticised' peasant cottages
depicted by Irish painters since the late eighteenth century that graced the
walls of the Big House or town house owned by wealthy families who wanted
no reminders of rural poverty.[8] Nevertheless, even the poorest peasants, who
shared their living quarters with the livestock and kept a precious midden outside the front door for fertilising the potato bed, were profoundly attached to
their hovels. As John Hinde, the modern impresario of 'high kitsch' postcards

depicting a perpetually sunny and quaint countryside, observed, 'an Irish cottage is like a living thing which grew out of the ground'. Unlike the twentieth-century bungalow that 'sticks out like a sore thumb because it has been imposed', the traditional cottage was 'built by a peasant who lives there, whose grandparents lived there, so close to the ground that they couldn't create something which was out of harmony with it'.[9] Given the force of the old cliché that 'there's no place like home' we may assume that every rafter, stone, nook or cranny as well as stick of furniture meant something special to the occupiers.

Because firsthand accounts by those who suffered eviction are so rare we must rely on the words of observers to gauge their anguish. Even if they could write, few of them were in any position to record their ordeal in a journal or diary. Nevertheless their loss became firmly fixed in the amber of popular songs, ballads, novels, and folklore. On the other hand, as Christopher Morash has observed about the great famine, 'the central motif' of eviction is silence – 'the black hole around which so many narratives of Irish history circled'.[10]

To broaden and enrich this study I have drawn on illustrations of eviction that highlight their pathos and drama. Some Irish art historians have recognised the important connections between graphic images and contemporaneous beliefs and conditions. Thus Brian Kennedy and Raymond Gillespie highlighted the 'specific cultural context' in which works of art were produced in Ireland and have stressed the value of graphic images to historians. 'No image stands by itself; it is always related to other images and to its audience.'[11] In this respect paintings as well as black and white prints, photographs, and even political cartoons can afford insights, however subjective, into the nature and consequences of ejectment. Paintings of eviction are few and far between in large part because few Victorian buyers wanted to hang such painful scenes on their walls. And those who did opted to buy highly sentimentalised renditions of these tragic events. In marked contrast, the woodcut prints and engraved sketches of eviction published in London's illustrated magazines came rather closer to the realities of eviction. In short, Fintan Cullen's call for more 'dialogue … between those who work on visual materials and those in other areas of research' should be heeded.[12]

Unfortunately, we cannot weigh or measure the suffering caused by eviction let alone the impact of these distressing scenes on the myriad eye-witnesses who watched the bailiffs empty house after house and raze some of them on orders from the agent. The images of dispossession presented in these pages – and the countless others that have gone unnoticed – were bound to expose the harsh face of Irish landlordism while tangentially helping to speed the plough of Irish nationalism. Although I have tried to be as comprehensive and inclusive as possible in gathering materials relating to eviction, there is at least one glaring omission – namely, accounts in the Irish language. Any reader fluent in the 'native tongue' is bound to bemoan the absence of such sources. However, this lacuna could prove to be a worthy point of departure for some future scholar.

According to Father Patrick Lavelle, 'the fighting priest of Partry' in County Mayo, 'by far the most heart-rending chapter of modern Irish history is that on evictions, consolidation of farms, and their effects'. Under this 'inhuman policy' an entire people had been exterminated and replaced by livestock. A once 'rich and populous' country had been depopulated and impoverished following the so-called Tudor conquests, the plantation of Ulster, the Cromwellian regime, and the Williamite settlement. English laws had turned Irish landlordism into 'a hideous, heartless thing'.[13] At the outset of his scathing indictment of Irish landlordism and 'English' governance, *The Fall of Feudalism in Ireland* (1904), Michael Davitt, the charismatic ex-Fenian and radical land reformer, denounced eviction as 'social tyranny in its worst form'. 'An eviction', he wrote, 'such as occurs in Ireland, even to-day, is a challenge to every human feeling and sentiment of a man, a citizen, and a Celt. It is the callous expression of the power of profit and of property over the right of a family to live on land without the permission of an individual who controls this natural right.' Such convictions went far to fuel the historic revolt against landlordism led by Davitt and his Land League comrades after 1878.[14]

Exploring the rich variety of images of eviction in newspapers, pamphlets, novels, verse, ballads, government records, and pictures should not blind us to their subjectivity, not to mention the countless pieces of evidence that are missing. Most of the eviction stories in this book derive from newspapers; and the well-known vagaries of journalism place them at one remove, if not further, from the lived reality. In this respect the narrative structure of eviction news brings to mind the film *Rashomon*. Whose version can be trusted? Think of all the possible perspectives: the evicted family, the landlord, the agent, the sheriff, magistrates, parish priests or curates, crowd members, the police and military, bailiffs, the anonymous reporters, and the named 'foreign' observers. Alas, hardly any printed account of forceful dispossession contains more than two of these points of view. Hopefully, the fleeting glimpses of eviction found in the following pages will spur a new generation of historians to explore this painful subject in greater depth.

ONE

DISPOSSESSION AND IRISH LAND LAWS

'If the history of a country is written in its laws, so also the ills of Ireland may be often traced in its statutes.'

DE MOLEYNS AND QUILL
The Landowner's and Agent's Practical Guide
(1877), p. 180.

'There is no crime that can be committed in civilized society so monstrous as that which takes from the poor the shelter and consolations and the refuge of a home.'

MICHAEL DAVITT
speaking at Bodyke, County Clare
24 July 1887.

'Be it ever so humble, there's no place like home.'

JOHN HOWARD PAYNE
Home Sweet Home (1823)

———

The forceful loss of hearth and homestead predates the expulsion of Adam and Eve from the Garden of Eden. But the originating tale of that Biblical banishment could well serve as the iconic starting point for this exploration of rural evictions in nineteenth-century Ireland. As two art historians have pointed out, 'the act of removing people from their present location, their homes, or their homeland through force or threat of force' has inspired countless mythological and religious as well as historical narratives. Ever since the Renaissance, artists have depicted expulsion in paintings beginning with the original 'Fall' and other Old Testament flights. What all these diverse images share in common is the pain and suffering of separation from the cherished comforts of home. For the rural populace eviction also meant loss of livelihood because access to a piece of land, however small, brought food to the table and possibly a tiny profit at the end of a good harvest. As Sir George Nicholls, the noted Irish poor law commissioner, observed about the Irish peasantry, land is 'the great necessary of life' and the occupiers did not hesitate to break the law in order to protect what they deemed their fundamental right to the soil.[1] In fact, the old adage of 'the potatoes for the tenant, and everything else for the landlord' often applied with crushing force to the peasantry until the 1860s.

The long and painful history of eviction is suffused with violence. Even without the deliberate wrecking of the old homestead, the victims of final eviction in rural Ireland experienced the trauma of losing both their home and their primary source of sustenance apart from day labouring. Furthermore, the presence of hundreds of heavily armed police and soldiers to protect the sheriff's party underscored the inherent violence of the deed whether or not they encountered any resistance.

Eviction, in short, deserves to be called one of the major leitmotivs of Irish history – a point not lost on that acute observer of Ireland in the 1830s, Gustave de Beaumont, who wrote that 'confiscation and death had been at the bottom of all the political and religious quarrels from the time of Henry VIII ... [but] how could an entire population be driven from its natal soil? ... How could all be massacred? If not massacred, how were they to live when plundered?' Dispossession, then, was the precondition of colonisation that resulted in clashes of religious, political, and cultural difference that often turned lethal. Whether Anglo-Norman, English, Welsh, or Scottish, the invaders or settlers who arrived with and after Strongbow expropriated the supposedly unclaimed land and reduced most of the indigenous people to mere tillers of the soil or serfs. Backed by the armies of the Tudor and Stuart monarchs, the colonisers did their best to purge so-called rebels or 'wild woodkernes' and install loyalists on the land they had confiscated. Eviction thus became a constant and painful reminder of conquest and remained the dominant grievance of the 'native Irishry'.

At the same time the vast majority of tenants who survived the famine did not suffer eviction during the land wars. As the *Times* (14 April 1881) put it rather too smugly, 'Irish tenants enjoy more privilege, freedom of action, and security of tenure than any in Europe; but exceptional cases are met with of tenants ruthlessly rack-rented and smarting under grievances which the present laws fail to prevent.' As for the ubiquitous problem of arrears, if only tenants who had fallen behind with the rent had read their Burke with care and if only they had been fortunate enough to afford lawyers versed in Terry Eagleton's shrewd interpretation of Burkean 'culturalism', they might have made a stronger case for their 'prescriptive right' to the ancestral homestead. According to Burke, the passage of time rather than a lease or yearly contract determined 'the sacred right of possession.' But how much time was required to seal full title? Many of those evicted could claim that their forebears had worked this particular parcel of land for at least a century if not before the arrival of the Anglo-Irish colonisers. Infusing the Burkean notion of atavistic possession with a dash or two of Freud, Eagleton argues that, like parricide, 'society springs from an illicit source or aboriginal crime ... [or] forcible expropriation from which all of our current titles and estates descend'. Needless to say, actual possession and written titles or deeds, backed by the superior force of British law and Dublin Castle, trumped any such 'moral' or 'historical' claim to ownership.[2]

Whether Anglo-Norman, English, Welsh, or Scottish, the invaders who arrived with and after Strongbow expropriated the supposedly unclaimed land and reduced most of the occupiers to mere tillers of the soil or serfs. Backed by the armies of the Tudor and Stuart monarchs, the colonisers did their best to purge so-called rebels or 'wild woodkernes' and install loyalists on the land they had seized. Eviction thus became a constant and painful reminder of conquest and remained the dominant grievance of the 'native Irishry'.

The leitmotif of dispossession resonates through Irish history, poetry, folk-lore, drama, song, art, and of course, memory. One major consequence of the wholesale appropriation or 'theft' of land in the medieval and early modern era was the decimation of the old Gaelic chieftainships and the 'tribal' system that afforded both protection and land to the plebeian clansmen. After the sixteenth century the so-called New English belonged to an alien religion as well as culture. Backed to the hilt by the armed forces of the English crown, this 'plantocracy' showed little mercy in times of rebellion, wiping out entire districts suspected of harbouring rebels in what deserves to be called a Tudor–Stuart or Cromwellian version of ethnic cleansing.

Reduced to the menial position of rent-paying peasants, few of these tenants at will felt any loyalty to their new masters; and many young sons chose to escape destitution by becoming cannon fodder for the British army and navy. As the enlightened Victorian General Sir William Butler pointed out, evictions undermined Great Britain's imperial mission: 'In pulling down the cabins of those peasants, be they Irish or Scotch ... more was done to weaken the strength of the Empire, to sap the fighting power of the army, and to introduce novel factors into our military history than any enemy of England had ever succeeded in accomplishing.' The Relief Act of 1793 that enfranchised eligible Catholics may have curbed the tendency of Protestant landlords to evict their Catholic tenants in favour of Protestants. Nevertheless, sectarian evictions survived well into the next century under one guise or another albeit on a greatly reduced scale. Thus Colonel Joshua Edward Cooper of Markree Castle, County Sligo, allegedly evicted some Catholic tenants to make way for a deer park and replaced others with Protestant tenants in order to increase his electoral support around Collooney.[3]

Eviction not only severed the taproot of 'home' but also broke up extended families and deprived the occupiers of their only means of existence. Besides the proverbial roof over their heads, evicted tenants had to endure the loss of all their furnishings and crockery inherited or acquired over the years no matter how crude or cracked. As J. M. Synge noted in *The Aran Islands*, 'every piece of furniture' had 'a personality of its own lovingly imparted ... by its maker'. And for that very reason it was all the more cherished.[4]

The observant American journalist and Home Ruler, Hugh Sutherland, had this to say about the ordeal of an evicted couple in Roscommon in the early 1900s:

> Who can measure the grief and shame that burdened this man and woman? It is the ruthless exposure of the home, the brutal turning out in the open of things sacred to the hearth, that seem so cruel. Yet it is all perfectly legal and the most civilised nation on earth quite approves of it.[5]

Of course no description of an eviction can ever do justice to the lived reality. As an Irish reporter observed, it was impossible to appreciate this 'devil's work' unless one happened to be 'on the spot':

> There beyond [the broken furniture] is seated the mother of the family with her young or old...children clustering round her trying to console her, but by their tears only adding more fuel to the fire of her anguish and grief. A short distance away stands the brutal agents [*sic*] of a more brutal tyrant, and as he laughs at the moans of sorrow from the evicted ones as they cling together by the manure heap, perhaps, the glare of the very devil is in his countenance.[6]

In addition, those who were spurred or forced to emigrate by eviction had to contend with all the anxieties, uncertainties, and economic hardships arising from deracination and relocation in a foreign land.

More than thirty-five years ago Barbara Lewis Solow argued in her treatise on the Irish agricultural economy in the late Victorian era that post-famine evictions 'were rare and tenure was in fact secured'. With all the confidence of a latter-day political economist she belittled their significance after the famine era. Ignoring the flaws in police records of evictions, she went on to argue that Lady Butler's highly romantic painting in 1890 of a solitary woman standing next to her ruined cabin on a mountainside in Wicklow gave the wrong impression. Evictions in fact 'were few and far between' and they would merit no more than 'a small chapter' in any history of Irish agriculture after the 1850s. By her reckoning almost half of the 24,675 tenants evicted between 1855 and 1880 were readmitted and only three per cent of the 600,000 tenants in Ireland ever endured final eviction. 'Stories of eviction and rack-renting', she argued emphatically, 'were pressed into service as economic myths ... [that] did yeoman service' for the separatist cause. Her influential study received a ringing endorsement from no less an authority than W. E. Vaughan, who praised her 'breezily iconoclastic approach' and rational conclusions that 'challenged three generations of muddle, exaggeration, and tendentiousness'. At the same time Vaughan admitted that it was hard to exaggerate the emotional impact of evictions in Victorian Ireland.[7]

The Thomas Gradgrind approach to Irish evictions begins and ends with numbers: 'Facts ... nothing but Facts ... Stick to Facts, Sir!' In the wake of Solow's argument most Irish economic historians have stressed the paucity of evictions actually carried out in the post-famine era especially when compared with the myriad notices to quit issued by the courts. Thus Cormac Ó Gráda concludes: 'In reality, post-Famine landlords rarely resorted to eviction, and when they did so it was nearly always for non-payment of rent.' Michael Turner has little to say about evictions after the 1850s except to advise historians to avoid overstating their number and 'pervasiveness'. By ending his monograph on the eve of the land war, Vaughan did not have to deal with the impact of evictions on increasingly politicised rural communities after the founding of the Land League and the onset of feature articles in nationalist newspapers about these operations. After pointing out the marked disparity between the 70,000 families evicted during the famine era with the 30,000 evictions between 1878 and 1887, Vaughan took some of the sting out of eviction by asserting that it 'was not usually different from any of the other debt-collection measures provided by the law'.

Of course numbers matter. So too do their context and the discrete events or instances that contribute to the total. Behind these variables lie the lived experiences of those persons who suffered the consequences of eviction and helped to make up those aggregate and impersonal statistics. In the following pages I have tried to illuminate some of those experiences, even though they constitute a tiny fraction of the total. The focus here falls on the ways in which contemporaries described or represented these traumatic events in both written and pictorial forms. Unlike the highly empirical approach of Solow, Vaughan, and other recent historians of the land question, this book explores the political, social, cultural, and even personal ramifications of eviction.[8]

To utter a truism, final evictions in rural areas mattered deeply to not only the families affected but also the communities to which they belonged whether these comprised a clachan, village, or townland. Besides the obvious tendency of local people to identify with the fate of their dispossessed neighbours, ejectment for any reason served as a painful reminder of the power of the landlord and British land laws. The ruined stone and mud-walled cottages that lay like so many broken teeth along the western littoral after the 1840s bore mute witness to the decimation of a populace and a once thriving Gaelic culture. Irish emigrants, moreover, carried this acute sense of loss overseas and passed tales of eviction on to their children. These indelible memories supplied some of the passion and momentum to the land and nationalist agitations that changed the course of Irish history.

TENANT RIGHT

One chronic cause of disputes between landlord and tenant apart from the rent charged was the custom known as tenant right – most often associated with northeast Ulster. Varying from one estate to another, this diverse practice not only entitled a tenant to occupy his holding so long as he paid the rent but also endowed him with a tangible 'interest' therein. Thus an 'outgoing' tenant vacating his farm could sell this interest or goodwill, composed mainly of the value of any improvements made over the years, to the incoming tenant for amounts ranging up to hundreds of pounds. As Vaughan makes clear, this custom varied widely and did not prevail on every estate in Ulster. Furthermore, some owners or agents discouraged or prohibited the sale of interest by the outgoing tenant because this practice burdened the incoming tenant with a heavy debt in addition to the cost of stocking the farm and paying the rent.[9]

The laws governing eviction during the famine era dated back to the reign of Edward III and boasted an almost Byzantine quality that required serving decrees on everyone with even the most tenuous interest in the holding concerned. When it came to proof of title, moreover, the mechanism could include fictitious or feigned plaintiffs and defendants whose status only solicitors well versed in land laws could understand. Not surprisingly, leaseholders were better protected from capricious eviction than tenants at will or cottiers who could not afford to contest their eviction in a court of law. One compelling reason for the paucity of evictions before 1816 was their cost. Not only did landlords have to apply to a superior court in Dublin for ejectment writs but they also had to pay an average of £18 for each one. If, however, the tenant challenged the suit, then the cost could climb as high as £150. All this changed with the passage of the Ejectment Act of 1816 and its sequels that introduced the civil bill procedure whereby landlords could use local courts to remove tenants after two months whose rent fell below £50 for the price of £2. What nationalists would later call an 'ejectment made easy' act resulted in a slew of evictions in the 1820s on estates where tenants were either in default or suspected of involvement in secret societies or agrarian outrage or where the landlord wished to purge cottiers and squatters. While some wealthy owners continued to apply for writs in the Queen's Bench in Dublin, the majority relied on quarter sessions, civil bill courts, and the assistant barristers' court when proceeding against their tenants. Not until the 1850s, in fact, did the archaic system of ejectment undergo limited reform, but it took years to simplify procedures that would benefit the landlord class.[10]

There is no need to enter here into all the legal intricacies of eviction law and procedures in the 1840s. Suffice to say that a landlord could evict a tenant for non-payment, overholding, or failure to prove entitlement to possession. Eviction on title involved disputes between rival claimants as well as the landlord's declaration that a tenancy had terminated owing to 'time ... death ... breach of condition ... or ... notice to quit'. Besides paying a modest fee, all he had to do was prove that the tenant and everyone else with an interest in or lien on the holding had been served with an ejectment writ or process. The *habere facias possessionem* decree entitled the owner to repossess a holding when or if the occupier or lessee had breached his covenant in some respect. Because an ejectment process affected everyone with the slightest interest in the holding, one writ could result in the expulsion of many families especially when and where the owners wanted to get rid of impoverished sub-tenants or squatters who paid no rent. Thus a Kerry sub-sheriff 'evicted 715 heads of families on foot of 39 habere decrees' in 1847–8; and whole villages were emptied on the strength of just a few such decrees. Final eviction, of course, meant that the landlord had to write off all the arrears as 'irrecoverable'. To avoid this unpleasant and troublesome recourse some landlords tolerated arrears of more than two or three years. Trinity College refrained from disturbing some lessees who had paid little or no rent for years because they were Protestant middlemen with gentry or gentlemanly credentials. On the other hand less indulgent owners used the decree route to scare their tenants into paying up, and this tactic explains why the number of ejectment writs exceeded the police returns for eviction by a wide margin.[11]

While landowners or landlords had a choice of several different courts in which to obtain ejectment decrees, only affluent or resourceful tenants could afford to hire a lawyer to defend their interests. Landlords strapped for cash naturally chose the cheapest route – whether quarter sessions, a civil bill court, or an assistant barristers' court – to obtain notices to quit. In a country so notorious for secret oath-bound agrarian societies like the Rockites, Rightboys, Whiteboys, and Ribbonmen, moreover, some evicted tenants did not have to look far to find men ready and willing to help them uphold 'popular justice' by punishing those responsible for their loss of hearth and home.[12]

In 1860 Parliament passed the milestone Landlord and Tenant (Ireland) Act, known as Deasy's act, that placed the relationship of landlord and tenant on a contractual as distinct from the old customary or feudal basis. Treating land as 'the exclusive property' of the owner, this measure made it much harder for a proprietor to evict without due cause. Before then relations between landlord and tenant had been based on tenure or service rather than contract, enabling the former to eject a yearly tenant at will or a leaseholder for cause. In countless cases, however, evicted tenants went without any compensation for improvements made to their holdings. Under this measure leaseholders were entitled to 'the quiet and peaceable enjoyment of the said lands or tenements' for a stipulated term so long as they paid the amounts set forth in the lease. If they failed to pay on time, the landlord or agent could apply in a superior court for recovery. Or, if the sum owed fell below £100, action could be taken in the nearest civil bill court.[13]

The failure of Deasy's act to guarantee outgoing tenants compensation for improvements moved William Gladstone to preside over the famous Land Act of 1870 (to be discussed in chapter 3) that in theory 'legalised' the Ulster custom throughout the country.[14] However, as A. M. Sullivan, the astute journalist and moderate Repealer, observed, this measure failed to end either 'capricious eviction' or the landlord's 'confiscation' of tenants' improvements that remained two burning grievances.[15]

After 1860 a landlord determined to remove a tenant for non-payment could have him served with a writ or process stating the amount of rent owed. But if arrears were not the problem, then he could obtain a notice to quit within the next six months and follow this with an ejectment order from a civil bill court on the basis of 'overholding'. Whether or not he failed to appear in court, a solvent tenant could forestall his eviction at the eleventh hour by paying arrears and legal costs. The law forbade sub-sheriffs from carrying out evictions before 9 a.m. or after 3 p.m. on any given weekday; and the landlord or agent had to give two days' notice of the pending removal to the local relieving officer.[16]

To avoid delays and costly legal fees landlords relied on a civil bill process, whereby a county court judge granted the all-purpose notice to quit that authorised the seizure or distraint of chattels belonging to the defaulting tenant if not outright eviction. According to one estimate ten such notices were served for every eviction. This route bypassed the time-consuming and costlier proceeding in a superior court in Dublin that gave tenants in arrear a grace period of six months to redeem after being served with a notice to quit. If a landlord wanted to squeeze a defaulting tenant into paying what he owed, he could apply to a county court for both a civil bill process and an ejectment decree for possession. Served simultaneously, these two processes enabled the landlord to seize any chattel while increasing the tenant's legal costs. And, as Vaughan has made clear, the huge discrepancy between the evictions recorded by the police and the number of ejectment decrees obtained by agents in the courts meant that 'the *threat* of eviction was an important part of estate management'.

Tenants in default and served with a writ could prevent the sheriff from executing the dreaded *habere* or civil bill decree for possession by simply paying the money owed. If not, then the sheriff and his bailiffs would proceed to empty the premises of all the occupants and furnishings within a specified time frame. Because landlords expected their tenants to pay the court fees it mattered greatly whether the former applied to a superior court like the Queen's Bench in Dublin, where a writ might cost as much as £17, or to a county court where the cost averaged £2 10s. In the former jurisdiction they could take 'immediate possession'. When the process server handed a tenant a county court writ, the latter had a six months' grace period in which to redeem. As Vaughan reminds us, however, 'ejectment was not a straightforward, mechanical procedure that an agent could apply without compunction'. Reduced to its essentials, it invariably arose out of economic adversity or insolvency.[17]

If close to three-quarters of all ejectment decrees derived from non-payment of rent, many landlords and agents tolerated arrears of at least two years provided that the tenant in default was industrious and had a good excuse. Besides the burden of rent, tenants usually owed money to shopkeepers or the local gombeen man because they could not live without credit. Having to depend on such fickle variables as the weather, the health of livestock, the size of the harvest, and crop prices, even strong farmers struggled at times to make enough profit to pay the landlord and his other creditors.

Adding some insecurity for yearly tenants was the 'hanging gale' that allowed them to pay their half-yearly rent six months 'late' so that they could reap whatever profit from the sale of livestock and produce. Thus a tenant renting a farm in November did not have to make his first payment until the following May. The disadvantage of this system lay in the fact that a yearly tenant could be expelled for non-payment even if the law allowed him to redeem over the next six months. In this respect the hanging gale made it easier for landlords to obtain immediate possession in marked contrast to the notice to quit that allowed a delinquent tenant to stay on for six months before being removed. In either case the landlord could seize any crops or chattel by means of a distraining order and then auction off the tenant's interest in his holding at a sheriff's sale.[18]

Politically motivated ejectments may have been the exceptions to the rule but they mattered enormously to the victims and tenant-right activists. For decades landlords had tried to influence or control the way their tenants voted in parliamentary elections that were notorious for corruption, drunkenness, and violence on a scale rarely seen in Britain. Here and there tenants were threatened with eviction for failing to support their landlords' candidate. Even if such threats were not carried out, their impact on the offending tenants should not be treated as lightly as some revisionist historians are wont to do. Failing expulsion, these tenants might be given a rent hike or denied free slates, timber, or turf. As Theo Hoppen has noted in his learned study of electoral politics in Victorian Ireland, landlords often tried to regulate their tenants' voting habits through cajolery, brow-beating, or threatening to withdraw customary 'favours and indulgences'. Although the number of tenants evicted for disobeying their landlords' wishes remains unknown, Colonel Henry Bruen, Conservative MP for County Carlow, turned out some tenants in 1835 on 'electoral rather than economic grounds' because they had backed the Liberal and Repeal candidate. Furthermore, the resulting criticism angered him. In December 1840, Lord Courtown publicly rebuked those tenants who had voted for a Liberal candidate at the Carlow by-election and forced them to apologise. Admittedly, the electoral influence of landlords faded after the passage of the secret ballot act of 1872 when most Catholic tenants voted according to the wishes of their priests rather than their landlords.[19]

Leaseholders may have enjoyed much greater security of tenure than tenants at will but they too could be evicted if their landlord refused to renew the lease upon expiration. When the last of three named lives died or when the 21 or 31-year stipulated period had elapsed, the owner could install a new tenant, even when the incumbent agreed to pay the higher rent.

The favourite tactic used by agents to squeeze rent or arrears out of tenants involved a court-ordered 'distress' or distraint authorising the seizure of live-stock, crops, or chattels that would be impounded 'as a pledge for payment of the rent due'. Tenants had eight days in which to redeem. Failing payment the land-lord had the right to sell these assets at a sheriff's auction. The seizure of livestock proved more than difficult when farmers scattered or concealed their animals. To stop tenants in default from removing their cattle or crops some landlords hired 'grippers' and 'keepers' to keep an eye on the writted tenants. But wily farmers often circumvented the law enforcers. As Thomas de Moleyns noted in his handy guide to estate management, 'a chronic warfare appears to have raged between Irish landlords and their tenants on the subject of distress'. Forced sales often led to raucous protests as the contesting parties backed by crowds traded insults and threats while the auctioneer struggled to be heard above the din.

The cost and complications surrounding distraint and forced sales discouraged some landlords and agents from pursuing this course of action. [20]

Failing distraint of goods the landlord or his agent would apply in a county court for a writ or notice to quit that set the wheels in motion. No eviction could take place in less than a month and not until the delinquent occupier had been decreed or served with a writ by a so-called process server. Tenants deemed unreliable or destitute by the agent would receive 'a writ of summons and plaint in ejectment' under the Common Law Procedure Act (16 & 17 Vict. c. 113). In the words of Vaughan the notice to quit was a handy 'administrative maid-of-all-work, offering a quick, effective means of settling disputes'. It could also be used like a Damocletian sword held over the heads of wayward, feckless, or quarrelsome occupiers. Receiving a notice to quit induced many tenants to pay most of the rent due. But if this tactic failed, then the agent might obtain a civil bill to recover a debt or one year's arrears. The obvious advantage of an ejectment writ over a distress or distraint was that the tenant could not hide his acres as easily as his chattel or crops. In the post-famine era, however, owners and agents of estates where tenants' arrears exceeded two or three years' rent were either inefficient or reluctant to execute a notice to quit for reasons ranging from sentiment to fear of litigation or some other form of retaliation. [21]

Because any legal step cost money, landlords tried to pass the fees onto the defaulting tenant. The price for serving an ordinary ejectment writ was £2 10s 0d whereas entering a judgment against a tenant usually cost £5 6s 0d. Proceedings in a Dublin superior court were obviously more expensive than those in the county courts where the judges required only the agent's word that the tenant owed so many arrears. In later years when a litigious tenant hired a lawyer and challenged a writ, the landlord might have to pay as much as £30 depending on the length of the hearing and his lawyers' fees. The great advantage for land-lords in choosing the superior court route was volume and cost. A single writ would allow them to sweep away all the tenants and squatters in a townland or parish, whereas the county court or petty sessions procedure required individ-ual writs for each defaulting tenant. The former course also enabled the agent to sort out which 'bad' tenants among all those 'decreed' deserved removal and which 'good' ones should be relocated on enlarged farms after the rundale sys-tem had been abolished and the estate 'squared'. The superior court writ, in short, facilitated the notorious famine clearances. [22]

As for civil bill procedures in a county court, the owner or agent had to notify the judge or magistrate of the amount owed and other particulars before the ejectment order could be granted. Above and beyond non-payment the reasons for obtaining writs ranged from personal misconduct to overholding, poaching, poor farming, or sub-letting. For obvious reasons prudent landlords held on to their most industrious (and profitable) tenants whose good behaviour was duly recorded by the agent in his notebook during tours of inspection.[23] Tenants thus decreed in the post-famine era had twelve days to make their case for non-removal. Failing an appeal, the judge would authorise the sheriff and his bailiffs to execute the order. Until the advent of the Land League only the wiliest or boldest tenant would lodge a counter-claim in the hope of delaying the proceedings.[24]

After the 1860s Irish newspapers began to publish more details of rural evictions including on special occasions the names of the tenants, the size and valuation of the holding, and the amount of rent and arrears owed. Compared with the dense coverage of evictions during the land wars, they paid minimal attention to the tens of thousands of tenants forced out during the famine years. Of course, nationalist spokesmen exaggerated the number of final evictions just as the unionist or landlord lobby ignored or belittled them. Thus Father Thomas Meagher declared that 4.5 million individuals (or half of the Irish population in 1845) lost their homes between 1836 and 1886; and Michael Mulhall, who produced a popular and unreliable *Dictionary of Statistics* in 1883, contended that 363,000 families had lost their homes since 1849. By contrast, police returns for the period 1849–80 placed the number of evicted families at 68,767 or 344,711 individuals. Annual eviction rates fluctuated widely, peaking during the famine era and then plunging between 1865 and 1877. The numbers rose steadily during the agricultural depressions of the early 1860s, and from 1879 to 1886, when prices plunged, arrears soared, and yields per acre declined. For the period 1854–78 final evictions averaged between 700 and 800 annually, providing ample proof that the vast majority of agricultural tenants enjoyed *de facto* security of tenure.[25]

READMISSIONS

Ambiguities continue to swirl around the number of final evictions in rural Ireland. According to one constabulary count, 19.4 per cent of the 115,604 families evicted between 1849 and 1887 were readmitted as either caretakers or as tenants upon payment of a token or nominal sum. Relying on police data, Solow arrived at the figure of 23.7 per cent for the readmission as caretakers of the 90,107 families evicted in the period 1849–80. Drawing on Dublin Castle figures for 1880–1, she estimated that half of the 1,065 evictions ended in readmission.[26]

Quite apart from the imperfections of the official data, these estimates ignore the salient fact that most caretakers re-entered their premises on the landlord's sufferance and could be ousted within six months without a formal court hearing. How many or few of those readmitted were turfed out within a year for failing to redeem during the grace period? The percentage of readmissions is thus deceptive because the official returns do not mention the duration of those reoccupations. How long did they last beyond the time allowed for redemption? In addition, the police failed to record the number of evicted tenants who returned to their dwellings illegally after the sheriff's party had left and lived there until evicted once and for all. Eviction data should therefore be treated with care. The monthly reports of district and county inspectors sent to the Inspector General of the Royal Irish Constabulary in Dublin Castle varied in accuracy and in some cases excluded cottiers and town tenants not to mention squatters. [27]

Besides the chronic fear of bad weather and poor harvests, the tenant farmer's main concern was the possibility of rent increases in the wake of any improvements he or she may have made to the farm. While landlords insisted that their rents were low or reasonable, many of their tenants – not to mention tenant right activists and nationalist politicians – complained about 'rackrenting' or exorbitant rents. The endless controversy surrounding what constituted a 'fair rent' bedevilled not only landlord and tenant relations but also officials, economists, and solicitors learned in the laws pertaining to the tenure of land.

Even if proprietors did under-rent their farmland as its value appreciated after the 1850s, enough landlords raised rents following tenant improvements to expose the entire class to the polemical charge of rackrenting that loomed so large during the land wars. Thus the overbearing third Earl of Leitrim pursued this policy on his Donegal and Leitrim estates; and his brutal murder along with two retainers in April 1878 guaranteed him a permanent place in not only history books but also the nationalist hall of infamy. Over the years he kept his tenants on a tight rein with frequent rent raises and threats of eviction for disobedience. To take one example, the estate accounts for 1856–7 reveal that rents were raised on 53 holdings and reduced on only two; and seven tenants were expelled in 1855 for arrears of over £70.[28]

As for capital investment in estates, Vaughan has given the landlord class a failing grade, arguing that most proprietors spent only a small fraction of their income on improvements. Here and there some owners obtained government loans to carry out drainage works, while others supplied timber, slate, and other materials to tenants for cottage construction. Rarely, however, did even the richest landlords invest more than five per cent of their annual receipts on agricultural improvements in the 1860s and 1870s. They were much more likely to spend disposable income on enhancements to the Big House and the pleasure grounds, hunting, fishing, shooting, and yachting, and making the social rounds in Dublin, London, and on the Continent.[29]

If sensible agents – including land management firms in nearby towns –

avoided evicting reliable or industrious tenants when they ran into hard times or a family crisis, they did not suffer drunken, improvident, or 'uppity' tenants gladly. As the venerable Irish land valuer, Sir Richard Griffith, once observed, a wise landlord did his best to keep 'a good tenant whenever he finds him'.[30] Although average annual evictions after 1855 'amounted to less than a quarter of a percent of all agricultural tenants', and the number of net evictions may have come close to 17,841 between 1861 and 1880, tenant-right advocates accused landlords of evicting without cause in order to strengthen their case for legislation to curb landlord rights. The learned legal historian at Trinity College Dublin, Professor Alexander Richey, asserted 'every notice to quit brought home to the tenant the power of the landlord to evict him'. In general, evictions on well-managed estates remained rare between 1855 and 1879. Only eight evictions took place on the Draper's Company property in County Londonderry (1857–62); three occurred on Lord Portsmouth's Wexford property (1843–80); while thirty families were ousted on Lord Lansdowne's 121,000 acres in six different counties during the 1870s. And in the prosperous county of Kildare only 23 evictions took place between 1877 and 1880 out of almost 9,000 agricultural holdings. After a brief spell of prosperity from the mid-1860s to the late 1870s, the agricultural crisis of 1879 profoundly altered the political as well as economic landscape.[31]

The security of tenure enjoyed by most tenants after the famine did not relieve them altogether of the fear of losing their holding owing to the threat of eviction if they failed to reduce their arrears. Agents often placed an asterisk or red-ink mark in the ledger next to the names of tenants deemed in need of warning about their arrears or misbehaviour. One can only imagine the stress and strain such threats caused the families concerned.[32]

RESISTING EVICTION

Executing an ejectment decree carried its own set of problems for all concerned. Even during the famine the possibility of resistance was not far from the minds of the sheriff and his bailiffs who tended to exaggerate the danger during and after the rebellions of 1848. Given the prevalent stereotype of the wild Irish peasant ready and willing to fight at the least provocation, most sub-sheriffs did not embark on eviction without a protection force of police and soldiers. As Vaughan has made clear, agrarian violence came in all shapes and sizes and involved a wide range of victims. Few of the latter belonged to the landlord class although many were in their employ. According to his calculations no more than a 'mere handful' of the 113 homicides recorded by the police between 1857 and 1878 involved landlords. From 1848 to 1880, however, almost one-third of all agrarian outrages – as distinct from murders – involved landlords and agents. This was not an insignificant figure given their small percentage of the rural populace. During the first land war only around six landlords, most of them small proprietors tainted by eviction, were murdered. In general the principal targets of rural violence were process servers, bailiffs, labourers, and tenant farmers caught up in disputes over land or property. Resentment over eviction or distraint of goods often boiled over into attacks on the so-called offending party.[33]

After 1879, as we will see, organised resistance to eviction became one of the Castle's biggest headaches as the Land League encouraged tenants to defend their houses with stones, sticks, pitchforks, and other non-lethal weapons. The resisters were often supported by raucous and menacing crowds numbering in the hundreds if not thousands. By contrast, tenants during the famine era were usually too weak from hunger and disease as well as too unorganised and demoralised to do more than curse or revile the sheriff and his bailiffs. Only on rare occasions did serious rioting erupt.

No eviction was complete, of course, until the bailiffs had removed every inhabitant, stick of furniture, and animal from the premises. As the American observer, William Hurlbert, noted in 1888, 'To make an eviction complete and legal here, everything belonging to the tenant, and every live creature must be taken out of the house. A cat may save a house as a cat may save a derelict ship. Then the Sheriff must "walk" over the whole holding.'[34] Once the premises had been emptied, the sub-sheriff would fasten the door to prevent re-entry and snatch a wisp of straw or piece of sod from the roof that he handed to the agent as the final ritual in the dispossession process.

HOUSE LEVELLING

The law allowed proprietors to unroof or destroy the abodes of evicted tenants without any permit. As a result thousands of tenants lost their homes along with the holding. In most instances the landlord or his agent would order the levelling of an abode in order to prevent re-entry and facilitate the consolidation of smallholdings into large farms or pasturage. At the height of the famine the task of house-wrecking kept many jobless young men from the towns gainfully employed. Whatever the owner's motive the 'slaughter' of houses added another layer of opprobrium to the already tarnished reputation of the landlord class.

In 1848 the Whig government passed a magnanimous act that prohibited house-razing if any human beings were still inside. After the 1850s the public outcry provoked by this wanton destruction finally brought the numbers down. Between 1846 and 1849 some 44 per cent of all evicted houses – mostly fourth-class housing – were levelled. But for the decade 1850–9 this figure declined to 33 per cent and then reached a mere 12 per cent for the 1860s. With some notorious exceptions in the mid-1880s landlords shied away from house destruction given the reporters present and their distaste for adverse publicity.[35]

As for estate management the practices pursued on many an Irish property fell somewhere between those of Sir Condy Rackrent and Lord Leitrim. Only the most obstinate or impecunious landlords failed to heed the advice of professional agents who knew the lay of the land and visited tenants on a regular basis. Weighed down with family charges and other incumbrances, landowners who survived the famine tended to exercise their powers and privileges more judiciously than their forebears until they faced a full-fledged tenant rebellion in the 1880s. The trusts created by strict family settlements, moreover, forced them to defer to the trustees when it came to mortgaging and selling land.

THE VANISHING MIDDLEMAN

Landlords and agents did not just target the poorest tenants when it came to removal. They also had to deal with middlemen holding leases of 21 or more years' duration who sub-let farms to sub-tenants at exorbitant rents. Under the old system, both Protestant and Catholic middleman – whether jumped-up gentry, squireens, or improving head tenants – had held hundreds of acres at a relatively low rent; and they made a hefty profit from their sub-tenants who paid much more per acre. Well before the famine, enterprising landlords began to remove these middlemen by refusing to renew their leases and replacing them with yearly tenants over whom their agents held sway. The slow increase in the value of land led to rising rentals of these holdings.

The label often attached to middlemen – 'land-jobbers' – says something about the low regard in which they were held even though some spent money on improvements. By the 1840s most of them had emigrated, faded away, or joined the class of leaseholders for three lives or 33 years. On the other hand, two of the largest landlords in the country – Trinity College Dublin and the livery companies of London – operated their vast properties through middlemen, some of whom were aristocrats and gentry. Trinity College's inconsistent and hands-off management of its diverse properties meant that in some cases large arrears were tolerated and few leaseholders were evicted. However, rent increases rendered some of these lessees insolvent. (Perpetuity leases made compulsory by an act of 1851 eventually proved their worth as the college's rental income virtually doubled between 1850 and 1900.) As Donnelly has pointed out, middlemen found themselves 'ground into dust between the upper and nether millstones' of heavily indebted landlords and their own hard-pressed tenants. The Great Famine accelerated the extinction of this class and few mourned its passing.[36]

Words can never convey the impact of eviction on its victims. Terms like devastation, despair, and misery fail to do justice to the trauma of separation from home, farm, and landscape. The toll on those who suffered this fate did not escape Vaughan's notice: 'It would be hard to exaggerate the emotional significance of evictions in nineteenth-century Ireland. The family thrown out of its home in bad weather, with no refuge but the workhouse, was well depicted in prose and verse, in paintings, and in magazines like the *Illustrated London News*.'[37] The reporting of evictions increased exponentially after the founding of the Irish Land League in 1879. Partisan reporters flocked to remote sites to record the proceedings and send back heart-rending stories to editors in county towns or Dublin and London where the politicisation of eviction was vividly reflected in headlines and feature articles. Across the Irish Sea Fleet Street's illustrated weeklies produced some sensational prints of burning cabins and homeless tenants surrounded by grim police cordons and howling mobs. Such vivid images were bound to move viewers to question the efficacy, if not the morality, of Irish landlordism.

Deprived of access to crops and livestock, homeless families had good reason to consider eviction a 'sentence of death'. And their advocates made frequent use of this phrase. One obvious consequence of a final eviction was the break-up of the nuclear family. More often than not younger people emigrated while their elderly parents or grandparents stayed behind. The resulting exodus moved the moderately conservative *Clare Journal* to wonder in 1854 just who would be left to 'represent the Celt on his native soil' and exploit the rich resources of the country.[38]

On both the county and national levels evictions proved a powerful stimulant for the reform of the land laws and the demand for tenant-right. Eviction thus imparted a powerful thrust to the popular slogan, 'the land for the people'. In the words of Kevin Whelan, 'Haunted by the ubiquity of displacement and family disintegration, the Irish popular mentality nurtured as a counterpoise a fierce sense of place, home and family. Any forces which threatened this trinity destabilised the equanimity of the popular imagination.' Eviction then became 'a highly charged political weapon, wielded with consummate rhetoric and force during the Land League period as a stick with which to beat the landlords'.[39]

Eviction also inspired the desire for revenge. As Tim O'Neill has observed, 'The brutality of many evictions ... destabilised rural society' and led directly or otherwise to agrarian crimes ranging from murder to arson and mutilated cattle. Although relatively rare in number, more than a handful of landlords, agents, and bailiffs lost their lives to vengeful tenants after 1845. For example, two of the six men sentenced to death for murder in January 1848 in County Limerick had been driven to kill by eviction and two others had murdered a bailiff for having served a notice to quit and a writ for distraint of goods.[40]

William Mulchinock evoked some of the pain and suffering arising out of eviction in his romantic 'Song of the Ejected Tenant':

I leave thee on the morrow, my old accustomed home,
In sadness and in sorrow the hollow world to roam:
Too bold to be a ranger, with heart too full of pride
To crouch unto the stranger whom I have oft defied.
Tis hard links should be riven that time and friendship wove;
'Tis hard when death is near me with certain step, though slow –
When naught is left to cheer me, 'tis hard from home to go.

I leave the chimney-corner, the old familiar chair,
To lay before the scorner my aged bosom bare,
To stand at every dwelling, to catch the rich man's eye,
And with a heart high swelling, for small pittance sigh.
My hope of joy is broken, my happiness is o'er.
The words of fate are spoken – 'beg thou for evermore.'
Would that my life were over, my weary life of pain!
Would that the green grave's cover my aged form might gain!

Over the mighty mountain, and by the lone sea shore,
By ice-bound stream and fountain we'll wander evermore;
To us, like a lamb that ranges along a bleak hillside,
From all the season's changes a shelter is denied.
I will not wish disaster to him that did me wrong,
I leave him to a Master that's merciful as strong;
And when the dawn is breaking upon the land and sea,
I'll say, with bosom aching: 'Farewell, old home, to thee.'[41]

Comprehending the significance of eviction in the course of Irish history requires both empathy and imagination. Besides depriving so many people of their homes and livelihood the 'story' of eviction includes the armed might of Dublin Castle at some evictions and the huge crowds that protested the bailiffs' task and shouted words of encouragement to their ill-fated neighbours. Poor cottiers living on rocky or boggy holdings in the west had every reason to dread a visit from the sheriff and his posse should their potato crop fail and agricultural prices plummet. In the heyday of the Land League evictions became both public spectacle and political theatre as hundreds and even thousands of people gathered from miles around to bear witness and curse the sheriff's party protected by the constabulary and the military. If concerted resistance was relatively rare before 1879, tenant families had long devised ways to defy or impede the forces of law and order. If those who fought the crowbar brigade with shillelaghs and pitchforks lost the struggle to save their homes, their individual acts of resistance strengthened communal solidarity and eventually promoted the interlocking causes of Home Rule and tenant right as well as peasant proprietorship.

TWO

THE FAMINE EVICTIONS

*'One such act [of eviction] suffices to make a human
monster – a multitude of them, a political economist.'*
MICHAEL T. SADLEIR
Ireland, Its Evils and Their Remedies (1826), p. 142.

'Irish landlords are not all monsters of cruelty.'
JOHN MITCHEL
History of Ireland, p. 213.

'Exterminate all the brutes!'
MR KURTZ *in* JOSEPH CONRAD'S
Heart of Darkness.

*'They [the Irish] ought to have been exterminated long ago,
but it is too late now.'*
GERALD BALFOUR
Wilfrid Scawen Blunt, *My Diaries, Part One: 1888 to 1900*
(London, 1919), p. 85.

———

Ever since the 1980s Irish historians have tried to atone for the long neglect of the Great Famine with a plethora of studies of the economic, demographic, social, cultural, biological, and medical aspects of what Michael Davitt called the 'holocaust of humanity'. This 'greatest calamity that had befallen Ireland since the Cromwellian extermination', as he put it, resulted in over one million 'excess deaths' and has inspired countless books and articles as well as moving memorials at home and abroad. Lady Gregory's moving testament in 1926 still rings true today: 'The Hunger, there's a long telling in that, it is a thing that will be remembered always.'

The plethora of famine studies has highlighted the continuing disagreement among historians over the number of final evictions as well as deaths arising from this catastrophe. Among modern historians the more plausible estimates range from 250,000 persons (W. E. Vaughan) to more than 500,000 (J. S. Donnelly). Dublin Castle estimated that the number of families evicted between 1849 and 1856 amounted to 68,369 with a quarter of these readmitted as tenants not caretakers. Multiplying the net figure by five – roughly the average size of a peasant family – we arrive at a total of over 340,000 individuals rendered homeless. Tim O'Neill's use of local court, police, and shrieval records has led him to estimate that between 579,000 and 724,000 persons were evicted in 1849–54.[1] To the vagaries of police estimates must be added not only the difficulty of counting cottiers and labourers who were expelled without formal notice but also the perennial ambiguity surrounding readmissions. Furthermore, some historians have conflated total 'evictions' with evicted families or individuals. Needless to say, ardent nationalists have always embraced the highest figures with Davitt plumping for a total of 190,000 families or almost one million people driven out in 1849–51 alone.[2]

Whatever the margin of error might be, numbers on this scale are hard to comprehend let alone excuse. No amount of description or analysis, moreover, can possibly convey the extent of suffering. As two historians have noted, 'Symptomatically wavering between silence and speech, forgetting and remembering, the Famine exemplifies history as trauma .... Recrudescent and unnerving, traumatic history cannot be comfortably accommodated: it lodges disruptively in the present.'[3] Partial failures of the potato harvest had a long history in Ireland, and thousands of evictions had occurred during the run-up to the arrival of the fatal blight. As Raymond Crotty has observed, 'had landlords single-mindedly pursued the maximising of their rental incomes they would have cleared more than 1½ million more people off the land before 1845'. But they were not 'captains of industry'; nor were they as ruthless as their adventurer or conquering forebears. In his view they were 'no braver' nor more selfish and harsh than 'any other cross-section of humanity'. Revisionist historians, moreover, have played down the failures of famine relief and dwelled on the 'false ideology' of John Mitchel and his admirers who accused everyone from the prime minister and cabinet down to Irish landlords, agents, strong farmers, corn dealers, and land grabbers of complicity in a plot or scheme to rid Ireland of its 'surplus' population.[4]

The new and deadly fungus, *Phytophthora infestans*, that spread westward on winds blowing from the Continent during the summer of 1845 destroyed the 'lumper' potato crop on which Irish peasants and their livestock completely depended. Wet and humid weather also helped to spread this deadly blight or murrain that ushered in so much hunger, disease, eviction, and death. A. M. Sullivan, editor of the *Nation*, described the 'stupor' that beset cottiers in County Cork when they found their staple food rotting in the ground:

It was no uncommon sight to see the cottier and his little family seated on the garden fence gazing all day long in moody silence at the blighted plot that had been their last hope. Nothing could arouse them. You spoke; they answered not.[5]

Successive crop failures devastated the pauperised poor on their tiny plots of land. Roughly a third of the cottier and labouring classes lived in one-room and earthen-floored hovels that they shared with the pig or cow, and they now paid the heaviest price for having multiplied too fruitfully and indulged in too much subdivision of marginal land. In western Munster and Connacht the death toll from famine-related fevers soared dramatically. Whether the pauperised hordes feared disease more than starvation, eviction, or the poor house remains a moot question. In fact countless peasants had to contend with all four horrors at one point or another.

The exodus of over two million people between 1845 and 1855 drained the country of tens of thousands of young and potentially productive people. From a peak of roughly 8.5 million in 1845 the population plummeted to 5.2 million in 1881. Today Ireland remains the only modernised country whose population is half what it was in 1845.

Cecil Woodham-Smith's *The Great Hunger* (1962) is unlikely to be surpassed as the master narrative of this disaster. Apart from statistical squabbles over the number of famine related deaths, controversy continues to swirl around the vexed issue of blame. Clearly, both the government and private charities could have done much more to prevent many of the million or so deaths from hunger and disease between 1846 and 1851.[6] Clad in rags, the near skeletal victims of cold, hunger, and 'famine fever' often walked miles to the nearest poor house and then endured, if they were 'lucky', the appalling conditions inside those prison-like buildings. Many begged for admission to the workhouse simply because they preferred burial in a plain pine coffin to having their remains wrapped in a shroud and thrown into a pit. The streets of western towns soon grew crowded with the homeless begging for handouts or trying to seize cartloads of bread.[7]

THE GREGORY CLAUSE

Much of the anger over the government's response to this crisis arose from Parliament's approval in June 1847 of a Whig amendment to the Irish poor law that made Irish landlords and other owners of property responsible for the welfare of their poorer tenants. The landed elite that dominated Westminster promptly passed an amending clause proposed by William Gregory, a Tory squire from Galway, that made occupiers of more than a quarter acre (one

rood) ineligible for relief. Following on the Whigs' decision to shut down most
public works, the notorious 'quarter-acre' clause opened the sluice gates of
mass evictions by forcing tens of thousands of subsistence tenants to abandon
their holdings. This measure also reflected the conviction of the new and hard-
line lord lieutenant, the Earl of Clarendon, that the only way to eliminate
chronic Irish poverty was to 'sweep Connaught clean' of all its paupers or 'surplus'
people. Desperate for food, cottiers and labourers surrendered their small homesteads in order to qualify for admission to the workhouse. Although modified
later, the Gregory clause seriously aggravated the crisis and raised even shriller
outcries against the government's relief efforts. With good reason the *Freeman's
Journal* attributed this measure to 'avarice, cupidity, or inhumanity'. [8]

The combination of famine, disease, eviction, and emigration wiped out
countless clachans or small Irish-speaking settlements where communal support or neighbourly charity had prevailed for generations. Operating on the
old rundale system whereby families cultivated dispersed strips of land on a
rotation basis each year, these scattered clusters depended on the lumper potato for survival. In the course of a few years these once thriving settlements were
dying or dead leaving behind only roofless stone cabins. [9]

Multiple evictions soon followed on the heels of the lost potato crops as
pauperised tenants were driven out throughout the south and west. The reaction of the provincial press to these clearances tended to run along party lines.
Thus the pro-landlord *Clare Journal* exonerated the Rev. Massy-Dawson from
any blame after he had ordered the removal of 500 tenants at Toomevara, near
Nenagh, County Tipperary in the spring of 1849. Claiming impartiality this
paper also published the self-serving letters of the notorious land agent,
Marcus Keane, and criticised its rivals for labelling his handiwork 'Awful
Exterminations'. However, even Dublin's pro-Repeal paper, the *Freeman's
Journal* that cultivated a Catholic middle-class urban readership devoted more
space to the assizes and poor law administration than to evictions, preferring
to blame the land laws rather than individual landlords for evictions. [10]

Running true to form, many British newspapers attributed Ireland's subsistence crisis to flaws in the Irish national or racial character that stressed 'Paddy's'
proverbial laziness, ignorance, and contempt for the law. Highly racialised
images of the feckless or unstable Celt as well as Protestant biases against popery and the 'tyranny' of the Roman Catholic priesthood meant that Paddy
could never escape from his miserable existence and unstable character unless
he somehow became 'Anglicised' or 'civilised'. As Michael de Nie has made
clear in his rigorous study of images of the Irish in the British media, a potent
mix of racial and religious prejudices resulted in placing most of the blame for
this 'great calamity' on the victims. Thus 'Paddy's' moral failings and lack of

(Anglo-Saxon) 'character' accounted for the severity of this crisis. Reinforcing the arguments of Anglo-Saxonist 'moralists' about the hereditary character flaws in the Irish 'race', English and Scottish political economists argued that culling the hordes of 'feckless' peasants would turn Ireland into a prosperous, self-reliant, and therefore governable country. To add to the burdens borne by the Irish people, British providentialists and evangelicals believed that God had sent the blight to punish or test the faith of the Irish people. Even the *Illustrated London News*, whose stark prints and reports of widespread suffering in 1846–7 must have left an indelible impression on readers, changed its tune a year later by declaring that clearances were a painful but necessary remedy for all the country's social and economic ills. Eviction, in short, was not just 'a legal but a natural process' that would pave the way for the efficient farming practised in Britain.[11]

Never one to mince words, the rebel Young Irelander John Mitchel called government relief efforts not only 'confused and wasteful' but also tantamount to mass murder. Parliament's adherence to a 'Code of Cheap Ejectment', the export of home-grown food to English markets, and showers of eviction decrees, he contended, had allowed the landlords to 'exterminate' the poorest Celts in order to make the country less rebellious and more Anglo-Saxon.[12] In the undying quest for blame the British government has come in for the heaviest opprobrium, with Charles Trevelyan, the Treasury official largely responsible for famine relief, cast as the leading villain. Treasury parsimony, laissez-faire convictions, and bureaucratic red tape cannot, however, be blamed entirely for all the failures of famine relief. After all Trevelyan was not just a classical Whig political economist. Like some of his cabinet colleagues he regarded the famine as God's way of punishing the Irish peasantry for overdependence on the potato, reckless breeding habits, excessive subdivision of land, and lack of industriousness. 'The great evil with which we have to contend', he insisted, '[is] not the physical evil of the famine, but the moral evil of the selfish, perverse and turbulent character of the people.' The trouble with the Irish, he might just as well have said, was that they were not sufficiently English. Admittedly, a few devout Catholic commentators justified the waves of emigration or the Irish diaspora as God's way of propagating the faith abroad.[13] On the other side of this impassioned debate, Father Patrick Lavelle, the fervently patriotic priest of Cong, called the famine 'the most melancholy chapter of modern history' and denounced the landlords as 'exterminators', whose endless war against their tenants had resulted in 'mutual murder'.[14] Leaving aside Lavelle's penchant for hyperbole, the fact remains that the government's response fell far short of what the richest empire in the world could have afforded even if food imports into Ireland greatly exceeded exports.

During the 1840s half the estimated wealth of the countryside lay in the hands of the 2,553 owners of estates valued at over £1,000. Some 3,318 other estates fell into the cohort of £500 to £1,000 in valuation. Because so many owners were heavily incumbered with family charges the poor law valuation of their estates bore little relationship to either their annual income or net profit. Resident landlords like the Marquess of Sligo, Sir Robert Lynch-Blosse, and Colonel Vaughan Jackson fed their pauper tenants soup and bread from the back door of the Big House; and they donated sums to the workhouses in their poor law unions. But once the demand for food became overwhelming, the hand-outs stopped. Among the few landlords who managed to keep their good reputations at least for a time were the Duke of Leinster, the Earls of Kingston and Shannon, Lord Stopford, and the Leslies in Monaghan.[15] Too many English and Irish peers, however, deplored the rampant lawlessness in Ireland. Ignoring the surge in evictions, they regarded that sister kingdom as the one indelible 'blot' on the British imperial escutcheon. To his credit the leading liberal Whig, Earl Grey, blamed Ireland's wretched condition on misgovernment rather than national character.[16] While Lord Clancarty urged poor law reform, Lord Westmeath complained that he could not find good tenants to replace those he had expelled, and Lord Clanricarde worried much more about homicides and his rental income than the rampant hunger and disease.[17]

'THE HORROR'

Accounts of the great hunger can never be complete without horror stories many of them related in one way or another to the involuntary 'surrender' of holdings. Apart from sheer starvation, what was generically called 'famine fever' ranging from typhus to dysentery decimated the populace and shattered communal solidarity as family members and friends often kept away from the infected.[18] Cabins containing the victims of fever were sometimes set on fire. During the 'Black '47' countless bodies were wrapped in shrouds and thrown into deep pits or shallow graves without benefit of clergy. Carpenters built deal coffins with hinged or trapdoors for repeated use. Many of the survivors lacked the strength to bury their beloved ones before heading towards the overcrowded and disease-ridden workhouse. Skibbereen in southwest Cork earned lasting fame or notoriety for a mass grave into which hundreds of corpses were thrown. In Kenmare the bodies of homeless paupers who had died were burned at night. Starving families were reduced to eating tainted horsemeat as well as turnip tops and cabbage stalks left in the field. Hungry dogs and rats competed for corpses lying indoors or outdoors. Because some desperate fathers were willing to risk life and limb to feed their families, many farmers resorted to shotguns to ward off any would-be thieves.[19]

Two fervent evangelicals – the aristocratic philanthropist, the Rev. Sidney Godolphin Osborne, and the democratic New England bible monger, Asenath Nicholson – bore witness to the horrendous effects of hunger and disease. On visits to the west in 1849 and 1850 Osborne was torn between respect for law and order and shock at the sight of so much sickness and death. Appalled by the starving hordes, he wrote long letters to the *Times* urging property owners to provide more food. The nightmarish conditions inside workhouses did not, however, stop him from defending the poor laws. He railed against the clearances and the 'slaughter' of houses and blamed the high mortality rates on 'pure tyranny' because so much cheap food seemed to be available. [20]

During her four-year sojourn in Ireland Asenath Nicholson tried to relieve famine victims by handing out both food and bibles. Blending Christian charity with the principles of political economy, she accused the 'masters of the soil' of forcing paupers to surrender their holdings and then imprisoning them in the workhouse. She could not forget the 'living, shivering skeletons' seen squatting in Westport. On Arranmore island, off the coast of Donegal, she noticed the full-bellied dogs prowling around a deserted village and asked: 'How can the dogs look so fat and shining here where there is no food for the people?' When the boat pilot hesitated to reply, the ugly truth dawned: 'Reader, I leave you to your thoughts', she wrote, 'and only add that the sleek dogs of Arranmore were my horror, if not my hatred, and have stamped on my mind images which can never be effaced'. [21]

An anonymous poet was less reticent on this grim subject:

On highway side, where oft was seen
The wild dog and the vulture keen
Tug for the limbs and gnaw the face
Of some starved child of our Irish race. [22]

In vain the radical land reformer, James Fintan Lalor, called for a social revolution and a 'moral insurrection' that would undo both the Act of Union and the English conquest. The 'robber landlords' who made up the English 'garrison' in Ireland had no right to the land that rightly belonged to everyone who had created value from its cultivation. Only a nationwide rent strike and resistance to ejectment, he contended, would produce a truly Irish nation. [23]

Another stern critic of government assistance was the Quaker philanthropist from York, James Hack Tuke, whose travels through Donegal, Sligo, and Mayo in December 1846 exposed him to destitute and half-naked families lying inside sod-roofed huts, bogholes or scalpeens uttering groans and 'demoniac yells'. At Belmullet he saw beggars eating boiled seaweed. In 1848 Tuke nearly died from 'famine fever' and the effects lasted a lifetime.[24] Some families afflicted with fever simply shut their doors and lay down to die before the bailiffs could 'smash the walls upon our mould'ring bones'. After doing his sums, Tuke reckoned that death, eviction, and emigration had reduced the number of families in Mullaroghe, Clogher, and Tiraun from 184 to only 38.[25]

THE CLEARANCES

In pre-famine Ireland most evictions came and went with little or no outcry beyond the boundaries of the parish or townland unless accompanied by eruptions of violence. But during the latter 1840s, the purging of pauper tenants on huge tracts of land attracted increasing notice in some newspapers. Driving cottiers out of their cabins gave Repealers and tenant-righters all the ammunition they needed to denounce the land tenure system along with landlord avarice. During the 1820s and 1830s mass evictions had been less frequent in the west than in Leinster where improving landlords and middlemen expelled cottiers or undertenants after their leases had expired in order to consolidate these smallholdings into larger farms or pasturage. Typical of this 'squaring' process was the conversion in 1844 of 600 acres owned by Lady Boyle near Kanturk into 'compact farms of thirty to forty acres'. The impoverished occupiers were replaced by twenty 'industrious' tenants. Between 1836 and 1843, hundreds of similar evictions occurred in Queen's County and Meath as well as Mayo – all in the name of improvement.

These improvements may have pleased political economists but in Ireland they often resulted in death notices and physical violence wherever agrarian 'bandits' or rebels flourished. For years the Peep O' Day Boys, Rightboys, Whiteboys, Caravats, Shanavests, Rockites, and Ribbonmen had punished landlords and middlemen who raised the rent, evicted, or served ejectment decrees. Any farmer who had taken over an evicted holding – known as land canters, land jobbers, and, later, land grabbers – did so at some risk to life and limb. Long before the famine, notices to quit had proved a dangerous undertaking for anyone connected with the enforcement of the law in districts where secret agrarian societies thrived. As James Donnelly's exhaustive study of Captain Rock's disciples makes clear, many of the death threats circulating in the early 1820s were far from empty. Excluding ambushers who missed their targets, the fact that some 93 people met violent deaths at the hands of Rockites in only six counties (most of them in Tipperary, Limerick, and Cork) during 1821–4 speaks volumes about the extent of agrarian outrage. Indeed, the axe-murders of several middlemen in 1823 sent a chilling message to anyone contemplating eviction thereabouts.[26]

Agrarian violence was a two-way street. When Robert King, 2nd Viscount Lorton replaced some Catholic tenants on his Longford estate with Protestants in 1835, Ribbonmen killed one of the newcomers and maimed eight others. Lorton then announced that unless the perpetrators were brought to justice he would raze the entire village of Ballinamuck. True to his word, he carried out this threat and hostilities lasted for years. Apparently, the second Earl of Bandon had little difficulty in 1837 when he expelled all the Catholic tenants on his Kinneigh property in County Cork after the expiration of a middleman's lease and then replaced them with Protestants.[27] In the early 1840s tenants uprooted by the wealthy Evelyn John Shirley of Lough Fea, County Monaghan, formed a secret society, the Molly Maguires, taking this name from a mythical widow who had defied her landlord. Emulating the Ribbonmen, they disguised themselves by wearing dresses and blackening their faces before assaulting grippers, landgrabbers, gamekeepers, and process servers. During a riot on 4 June 1843 at Magheracloone, soldiers opened fire killing one boy and adding another burning grievance to the Mollies' long list. This incident taught Shirley's shrewd agent, William Steuart Trench, the advantage of diplomacy over eviction; and in 1844 he persuaded 180 impoverished tenants to emigrate. But his master disapproved of such leniency and replaced Trench with a tougher agent who drove out 317 families and destroyed their cottages.[28]

Official eviction data are lacking for the years 1845–6 but Dublin Castle estimated that final evictions rose from 3,500 in 1846 to 9,657 in 1848. In March 1846 the Whig leader and Irish landlord, Lord John Russell, declared in Parliament that some fifty thousand families had been 'turned out of their wretched dwellings without pity and without refuge' making Ireland 'the most degraded and the most miserable country in the world'. At this point the full extent of the catastrophe lay well ahead. Deploring mass evictions, he also worried about the lack of compensation for farmers who had improved their holdings. Anxious to soften the blow of a new coercion bill and to stop landlords from indulging in mass evictions, he stated in March 1848: 'if we put down assassins we ought to put down the Lynch Law of the landlord'. Sir James Graham, who remained loyal to Peel during this crisis, condemned the multiple evictions by Roscommon landlords who 'will neither learn prudence, nor exercise forbearance towards their tenantry'. The dozen or so bills introduced in Parliament between 1845 and 1857 aimed at compensating tenants for their 'disturbance' and improving landlord and tenant relations died before reaching the House of Lords. In the meantime landlords continued to get rid of the occupiers of unprofitable holdings. In all some 48 clearances – defined as the eviction of more than 40 families at one fell swoop – took place forcing thousands of desperately poor families out of their homes.

In the summer of 1851 Trinity College evicted some 753 families in Kerry before readmitting 502 of them. Declaring that he 'would not breed paupers to pay priests', the irascible and domineering 3rd Earl of Lucan, who owned 60,000 acres around Ballinrobe and Castlebar, County Mayo, earned the epithet of 'the Exterminator' by expelling hundreds of cottiers before the famine and consolidating their wretched holdings. After 1846 he ordered the levelling of hundreds of cabins and the expulsion of as many as 4,000 persons in his relentless pursuit of profit – all in the name of 'improvement'. Around one-tenth of those evicted were retained as cottars or labourers, while the squared and stocked farms were let to strong farmers or small-time graziers. When asked what had happened to all the homeless, his Scottish head steward replied: 'I think they are vara much iprovit.' Lucan's equally land-rich neighbour, the 3rd Marquess of Sligo, purged over a thousand individuals on the grounds that he faced a choice between evicting and being evicted. He also chided 'indulgent' landlords for not clearing away 'the idle and dishonest' occupiers who would have to go sooner or later. In Mayo alone more than eleven clearances took place between 1850 and 1853 depriving 771 families of their homesteads.

In the span of two years the agent of the absentee owner, the Rev. Maurice F. Townsend, cleared this west Cork estate of 154 families or some 850 individuals. Even if one-fifth of all the dispossessed were readmitted as caretakers or tenants, this reprieve was only temporary because they lived on the sufferance of their landlords and could be evicted finally within a few months. Many other western landlords followed suit by driving out countless cottiers, squatters, and labourers and replacing them with solvent tenants. Concomitantly, the number of fourth-class dwellings or hovels fell by two-thirds from 491,127 in 1841 to 135,589 in 1851 and holdings of one acre and below fell sharply from 73,016 in 1847 to 37,728 in 1851. The highest eviction rates prevailed in western Connacht and Munster running along a wide swathe west from Youghal, north from Skibbereen to Malin Head in Donegal, and then down through Roscommon and Leitrim to Tipperary.[29]

During these grim years some 200,000 smallholders surrendered their plots of land 'voluntarily' in order to qualify for poor relief or assisted emigration. Many of those who could not bear to leave huddled nearby in scalps and scalpeens or *bothógaí* dug into a ditch and covered with a roof made of sod and sticks. Others built crude lean-tos inside their broken walls that afforded scant protection from the cold and rain.[30]

A series of 'fearful' evictions took place at Ballinglass near Mount Bellew, County Galway on 13 March 1846 even though some of the dispossessed had offered to pay their rent. The evictor was an absentee landlord, Mrs John G. Gerrard, who lived at Gibbstown, County Meath and was determined to 'thin' her lands to make room for 'fat bullocks'. The *Freeman's Journal* reporter

stressed the 'truly painful character' of these expulsions as 61 sobbing or howling families were driven out of hovels that were immediately demolished.
When some 'wretches' built lean-tos inside the ruins, the bailiffs quickly tore
them down. The few tenants left in place were warned not to give shelter to the
homeless unless they wanted to share the same fate. These Irish-speaking victims sought refuge in ditches into which they carried crockery and a few sticks
of furniture. One old man scratched up some dung outside his door to fertilise
his few potato plants, while two young girls wailed outside their tumbled cottage. A disgusted head constable complained that 'more than FOUR THOUSAND'
people had been driven out over the past three years. In short, this once thriving
village had been 'Gerrardised'. A local innkeeper, who was distantly related to
Mrs Gerrard, called her 'the greatest exterminator of the tenantry'. Even Lord
Londonderry was shocked by these 'scandalous' and 'frightful' evictions that
made him realise why so much lawlessness prevailed and 'assassins walked
abroad'. When a reporter asked her how she felt about these evictions, Mrs
Gerrard replied: 'Thank you, I am well, thriving, and getting fat on the curses of
the wretches.' Evidently, her husband had a different version. When asked the
same question, he allegedly answered that his bullocks 'were fattening on the
lands and thriving on the curses of the wretches'. [31]

Like Lord Lucan, the heavily incumbered Sir Roger Palmer and Sir Samuel
O'Malley purged countless cottiers and conacre tenants from their rocky and
boggy holdings in the uplands of Mayo after ranting for years against the reckless sub-division of smallholdings. Another mass evictor was the Law Life
Assurance Company that held huge mortgages on the Martin and O'Malley
estates and had bought and sold thousands of acres in the Incumbered Estates
Court. After taking over the insolvent Archer estate, this company ejected
some 600 tenants, consolidated their smallholdings into 209 farms, and hired
some of the former occupiers as labourers. These clearances also took their toll
on shopkeepers in the west who complained that they had lost rich and poor
customers alike including insolvent landlords. [32]

Small wonder then that the militant Father Lavelle played fast and loose with
the numbers by accusing Lords Lucan and Sligo of destroying 270,000 houses
between 1841 and 1861 and driving 1.3 million people to 'the workhouse, exile, or
death'. By his reckoning the population of Louisburgh parish fell from 2,200
in 1846 to 700 in the 1860s. Apparently, Lord Lucan and his bailiffs wanted to
make sure that the only living creatures left on the estate were cattle and sheep
branded with a large 'L'. Lavelle continued his impassioned indictment:

> How the spirits of the thousand human beings who once trod and tilled those
> fields must look down today on this beastly substitute thus made for themselves!!
> How the sons and daughters of those banished, murdered sires, must look back

across the wide wave, and traverse, in spirit, those consolidated fields again, and with clenched fist and set teeth, and seething soul, renew their vow that, one day or other, the beast must retire, and they, the children of the disinherited, recover their rightful own again! [33]

In mid-Ulster some evictions were tainted by sectarianism as Protestant landlords and agents replaced Catholic tenants with farmers of their own religious persuasion on the vacant farms.[34]

KILRUSH, CLARE

Clearances in County Clare took on a life of their own as landlords and agents competed to see who could expel the most peasants in the shortest amount of time. Marcus Keane of Beechwood, the masterful agent for a dozen large properties, depopulated many of the 140,000 acres under his control. With all the zeal of Patrick Sellar, the notorious Scottish factor who had destroyed so many crofters' cottages on the Sutherland estate to make way for sheep, Keane's expulsions of pauperised tenants earned him the sobriquet of 'the Exterminator General of Clare'. As one of his many enemies put it, he seemed 'unhappy only when not exterminating'. The meticulous studies of these clearances by James Donnelly and Ciarán Ó Murchadha obviate the need to linger over the depressing details. Suffice to say that between November 1847 and June 1848 some six thousand notices to quit were obtained in a county that could lay claim to having the highest ratio of evicted persons (97.1 per 1,000 inhabitants) in the country. By 1850 at least 17 per cent of the populace of Kilrush union had disappeared. The fatal triad of hunger, disease, and eviction turned much of this district into a wasteland because the landlords feared being 'swamped by pauperism'.[35]

Besides extensive coverage of the state trial of the Young Ireland rebels, the pro-Repeal press railed against these clearances and the abysmal shortcomings of government relief. Thus the *Limerick and Clare Examiner* denounced Keane's destructive handiwork for absentee landlords who were living in luxury abroad on money squeezed out of the very tenants they were now expelling. Keane responded by accusing his critics of grossly exaggerating the number of evicted tenants and ignoring all the unpaid rent and arrears. Most of these tenants, he added, had left of their own free will and some had even offered to raze their own abodes.[36]

Castigating Keane for having 'thinned' so many estates, the *Limerick and Clare Examiner* charged this 'evil genius of Landlord and Tenantry' with expelling 185 individuals from the Westby estate in a single week. On Lord Conyngham's property at Meelick, Patrick Hickie (or Hickey) and his family had suffered eviction.

Both parents and three children had died and the two surviving siblings ended up in Limerick fever hospital. In the words of the *Examiner* Keane personified 'that pestilent sore – Agency – in its most repulsive form'. By 14 February 1849, some 1,416 more ejectment decrees had been granted in Clare meaning that almost seven thousand more people faced expulsion. Relying on the findings of Captain Arthur Kennedy, the able inspector for Kilrush poor law union, the *Examiner* reckoned that 16,000 people had been driven out between 1847 and 1850. The combative Keane then sent a formal petition to Parliament justifying all his actions and accusing Kennedy of gross exaggeration. While the pro-landlord *Clare Journal* published Keane's self-serving letters and refused to take sides in this dispute, the *Examiner* backed Kennedy's figures and continued to condemn Keane. [37]

The English humanitarian and radical George Poulett Scrope MP, who led a select committee of inquiry in the summer of 1850, confirmed Kennedy's tabulations. Instead of blaming the landlords, however, Scrope faulted the government for 'exterminating' pauper tenants so as to enhance the value of land and save the owners from ruin. While visiting west Clare he had seen the 'blackened and skeleton frames' of ruined houses and heaps of stones and dirt where 'a comfortable hamlet' had once stood. 'At times a whole street in a village had been destroyed. I seemed to be tracking the course of an invading army.' Testifying before the Scrope committee, Keane defended his actions by declaring that had he not evicted unprofitable tenants, complete ruin would have befallen the country.[38] In response to this testimony the *Examiner* wondered whether all the deaths arising from eviction constituted mass murder or merely manslaughter.

In the meantime the narrow streets of Ennis, Ennistymon, and Scariff were clogged with homeless and starving paupers begging for food and shelter. Deploring the loss of one-third of Kilrush's population since 1846, the editor scoffed at the Whigs' opposition to more government interference. Given the hordes already 'unhoused' around Kilrush this paper predicted many more deaths would occur because the 14,000 people on indoor and outdoor relief lacked food and the local workhouse was running out of turnips and parsnips. Emigration, moreover, offered no solution. An editorial entitled 'THE EXTERMINATORS AGAIN' despaired of any end to these 'horrible' evictions. 'Oh! Whigs, Whigs! Heaven's malediction will be on you if you sanction it further. Do you not see it? Do you not know it? Are your ears closed against the shrieks of the people?'[39]

VENTRY/DINGLE

The 'exterminators' were also busy on Lord Ventry's estate on the Dingle peninsula where hundreds of families were driven out in 1847–8. Whereas the pro-landlord *Kerry Evening Post* defended his lordship and accused the

Limerick and Clare Examiner of 'treason' and 'hostility' for disparaging the landlords, the *Cork Reporter* condemned the evictions and mocked this noble family for having changed their name from Mullins to De Moleyns. Charges of proselytising by his ardently Protestant agent did not enhance Lord Ventry's reputation.[40] Sectarian animus also poisoned relations on the Ormsby estate at Birdhill, County Tipperary where the zealous agent, George Twiss, seized the Catholic chapel with the help of police, expelled the priest, and tried to convert Catholic tenants by means of a Protestant bible school and a kitchen dispensing watery soup known as 'stirabout'. Instead of holding the landlords accountable for the famine horrors, the *Limerick and Clare Examiner* blamed them on callous agents like Marcus Keane as well as British ministers who flouted Christian charity and constitutional principles.[41]

In the 1860s Thomas Madigan honoured the victims of clearances with a moving song about the bodies buried in a common grave at Shanakyle near Kilrush:

> Far far from the isle of the holy and grand
> Where wild oxen fatten and brave men are banned
> All lowly and low in a far distant land
> Do I wander and pine for poor Erin.
>
> Sad, sad is my fate in weary exile
> Dark, dark are the night clouds round lone Shanakyle.
> Your murdered sleep silently pile upon pile
> In the coffinless graves of poor Erin.
>
> I am watching and praying through the length of the night
> For the grey dawn of freedom my signal to fight.
> My rifle is ready my sabre is bright
> For to strike once again for poor Erin.[42]

A. M. Sullivan also tried to convey the trauma of ejectment:

> An Irish eviction … is a scene to try the sternest nature. …The anger of the elements affords no warrant for respite or reprieve. In hail or thunder, rain, or snow, out the inmate must go. The bed-ridden grandsire, the infant in the cradle, the sick, the aged, and the dying, must alike be thrust forth, though other roof or home the world has naught for them, and the stormy sky must be their canopy during the night at hand.

The Catholic Bishop of Meath witnessed the expulsion of 700 people in a single day and found it hard to forget 'the wailing of women, the screams, the terror, the consternation of children, the speechless agony of men.' When a sheriff discovered the victims of typhus fever lying dead inside their abodes, he ordered his men to cover them with 'a winnowing sheet' and then pull down the roof. The sight of so many homeless people and so much house wrecking 'wrung tears of grief' from bystanders, and even a few policemen cried 'like children'. [43]

Feelings of despair and helplessness inspired fantasies of retribution. In one such scenario, recorded by a folklorist, an agent presided over the eviction of a poor widow on Christmas Eve and then refused her request to take refuge next to the cottage wall until after Christmas. When he ordered the bailiffs to knock down the dwelling, the local priest warned the agent: 'You can look your last on B—lough as you're passing through it on your way home.' And lo and behold, the agent suffered a fatal stroke before he reached the lough. [44]

Wracked by hunger, fatigue, and disease, few families had the will let alone the strength to resist the crowbar brigades. Apart from a good deal of jeering, cursing, and shoving, most of the evicted submitted meekly to their fate. In the words of Poulett Scrope they suffered from 'the unresisting apathy of despair' and silently waited for the arrival of the sheriff's wrecking crew. Demoralised and unorganised they also feared losing their eligibility for relief. The passivity of this exodus was a far cry from the violent reprisals of the Rockites and other agrarian rebels during the anti-rent and anti-tithe upheavals of the early 1820s and 1830s. Nevertheless the authorities feared riotous mobs and the slightest resistance to eviction during the famine years even though they rarely had to contend with anything more serious than hearty curses and the occasional blow of a shillelagh. [45]

Robert Scally's probing study of Ballykilcline, County Roscommon during and after the famine delves into 'the arsenal of peasant resistance' to eviction in 1844, when some of Major Denis Mahon's tenants defended their homesteads after endless disputes over rent and tenure. Although their protests usually involved more smoke than fire, local authorities were wont to panic. When four families reoccupied their houses illegally after the sheriff had left, the magistrates called this a 'jacquerie' and a 'rebellion' and sent for police reinforcements. [46] Despite their anger the crowd refrained from violence while a frightened crown bailiff nailed the doors of the cabins shut. Some bystanders swore they would return and kill anyone who got in their way. The 'caretakers' hired to guard these houses against re-entry heard these threats and promptly left. But when the Crown agent, George Knox, returned three weeks later without a police escort to post ejectment notices, some hostile tenants forced him to flee to the nearest police barracks. A brutal baton charge by the police soon drove his persecutors away. What the authorities called a riot by 'landless banditti' resulted in more arrests.[47]

Early in 1847 Major Mahon and his agent announced that any tenant who refused to emigrate at the Crown's expense faced ejectment. For want of a parliamentary reprieve 217 families or 490 individuals quit their homesteads on 26 May in return for a few pounds of travel money and their cottages were levelled. Eventually, almost 3,000 people were paid a total of £14,000 to leave. Then on 2 November the major was shot dead in an ambush near Doorty shortly after the parish priest of Strokestown had denounced him at Sunday mass. Whether or not the shooters were inspired by the clearances or the false rumour that he had hired a 'coffin' ship that sank with all hands on board, the fact remained that Mahon was no more; and his murder became headline news. The shock waves from this assassination reverberated through Parliament where the law and order lobby called for more coercive measures. A year later 139 more tenants set out from Strokestown on the long journey to Dublin and Liverpool. Some dropped out along the way and the others eventually sailed to America.[48]

Apart from ambushes the police were most afraid of riotous crowds at eviction sites. On Sir Capel Molyneux's estate near Castleconnell, County Limerick, 1,200 people assembled to protest the serving of ejectment decrees in mid-January 1846. Armed with shovels, pitchforks, and a few guns, these 'insurgents' refused to decamp. Finally, two regular army companies and a squad of police appeared; and after the riot act had been read three times the 'rioters' withdrew. Three men were arrested for inciting a riot, but no blood was shed.[49]

Back at Kilrush one family managed to obstruct the eviction party led by Marcus Keane's mentally unstable younger brother, Henry, in mid-February 1849. When the sheriff reached the Kinnavane farmhouse at Meelick Cross on the Conyngham estate, three muscular men sallied forth to defend their aged mother who lay dying inside. Brandishing blackthorns, they cried: 'Come on ye cowardly ruffians and we will see it out with you.' A few hard blows from the brothers put the would-be levellers to flight. Equally enraged and mortified, Henry, otherwise known as 'Marcus Secondus', pulled out his pistol and aimed it at the retreating bailiffs while repeating the phrase, 'I am the poor man's friend.' He then threatened to evict many more tenants if the reporter present dared to publicise this rout. Even more bizarre was his decision to spend the whole night inside the cabin. On the following day he told the reporter that he would serve three hundred ejectment notices if his newspaper mentioned either himself, his brother, or Lord Conyngham. Insisting once again that he was 'the poor man's friend', he announced: 'I am the man that's Cane [*sic*] to the backbone, and I won't be conquered; I was never conquered.' A day or two later Henry returned with the police, forced the family out, and ordered the cabin's destruction.[50]

In September 1853 over 400 enraged men and women confronted the constabulary at Kilcoosh, County Galway, on the property of John Gerrard, whose wife had already achieved so much notoriety. After 42 families scheduled for ejectment refused to leave once they had harvested their crops, the agent gave the order to destroy their abodes. But the menacing crowd forced the sheriff's party to withdraw. They returned a fortnight later backed by one hundred policemen and soldiers and the crowbar gang emptied another 31 houses.[51]

One folk tale about resistance involved Paddy Scally's refusal to quit his farm at Carna, County Westmeath. Confronting his Catholic landlord, Sir Richard Nagle, he allegedly threw two pistols down on the floor of the drawing room and challenged him to a duel saying, 'Take your pick now, Sir Richard, and let us settle it here and now. Let the best man win.' Instead of accepting this challenge, Nagle wisely allowed the Scallys to stay.[52]

HOUSE RAZING

The systematic unroofing and levelling of cabins was one of the cruellest and most common features of the famine evictions. When some families were driven by hunger to enter the poor house for a spell to obtain food, they often returned home to find their cabin in ruins. Bereft of their home they faced a stark choice between begging, emigrating, or hunkering down in a scalpeen to await death. To consolidate smallholdings and prevent re-entry, agents hired gangs of 'drivers' or 'levellers' from nearby towns, who had no qualms about wrecking the cottages of fellow Catholics. Desperate for cash, these tough young men used to fortify themselves with whiskey before tackling their destructive task. In one hour they could easily raze ten cabins depending on the distance they had to travel. The *Limerick and Clare Examiner* likened them to 'banditti of roving Arabs' who seemed to enjoy their 'revolting duty'.

In April 1846 some 46 houses were tumbled on the Marquess of Waterford's estate rendering 277 people homeless. Each evicted family received £2 to leave. Baron Dunsandle's agent ordered the razing of 24 out of 26 houses near Brokeen Cross, County Galway in 1850. Apparently, the only two houses left standing belonged to two 'pretty girls'. Later forty more houses were emptied and then levelled. In vain Dunsandle tried to justify his actions: 'They will never stop breeding beggars in this country.' According to local folklore an elderly female victim accosted him and uttered a dire curse: 'You will be found on the side of the road yet eating dust.' Some agents paid tenants to tear down their own hovels. Thus Francis Carey accepted £5 from Keane to wreck his own house watched by his pregnant wife. At least half of all the 'actual' evictions between 1846 and 1849 ended in demolition that scarred not only the landscape but also the minds of the victims.[53]

The need for a more efficient method of house wrecking prompted William Scully, the notorious landlord of Ballycohey, County Tipperary, to invent an apparatus of 'massive iron levers, hooks, and chains' that was attached to the rafters or the coign of a wall and then hooked up to a horse. When whacked with a stick, the horse would lunge forward and the roof beams would collapse. Evidently, two such appliances could destroy ten times as many houses in a day as fifty crowbar-wielding men. Whether Scully's invention was deployed elsewhere is not known. The sight of so many tumbled cabins deeply disturbed Poulett Scrope who toured Galway in 1849 and described one district where several thousand families had been evicted as 'an enormous graveyard – the numerous gables of the unroofed dwellings seemed to be gigantic tombstones'. And in August 1852, Sir Francis Head, the former poor law commissioner from England, was appalled by the number of unroofed cabins he saw along the road from Tuam to Ballinrobe and thence to Connemara. 'Pointing to heaven, were the stark, stiff, rugged gables of a small evicted village, of which not a human being had been spared. All were gone, and rank weeds were here and there flourishing on the very floors on which probably several generations of honest people had slept.'[54]

As a boy of twelve William Butler, who became a much-decorated British army general, had watched a 'crowbar-brigade … composed of the lowest and most debauched ruffians' tear down a cottier's cabin. Years later he wrote: 'I think if a loaded gun had been put into my hands I would have fired into that crowd of villains, as they plied their horrible trade by the ruined church of Tampul-da-voun.' His friend, Captain (later Sir) Arthur Kennedy, the poor law commissioner in charge of relief in West Clare during the famine, felt the same revulsion. While staying at Highclere, the castellated seat of Lord Carnarvon, in the 1870s he confessed that after seeing so much hunger and misery he became 'so maddened … that I felt disposed to take the gun from behind my door and shoot the first landlord I met.' To this comment Carnarvon replied: 'Strong words, Sir Arthur.' And Kennedy answered: 'Not stronger, my lord, than were my feelings at that time.'[55]

As for the impact of eviction on the rate of agrarian crime, Dublin Castle played down any such linkage pointing out the great disparity between the 5,277 outrages and the 53,479 families evicted during the 1850s.[56] In 1852 an eviction of historic import took place in the village of Straide, County Mayo where the Davitt family lost their homestead and wound up in Lancashire where father and son worked in a textile mill. Michael Davitt was only five years old when the evictors arrived and he never forgot this harrowing experience. Six years later he lost an arm in a carding machine accident. Like so many victims of eviction he nursed a burning grievance against the landlords and devoted his life to dispossessing the hereditary enemy and returning the land 'to the people'. Looking back on the famine in the twilight of his life, he accused 'landlordism and English rule' of forcing the Irish people to pay 'pagan homage to an inhuman system'. It was nothing short of blasphemy, he declared, to blame Providence for the famine horrors because the prime culprits were the landlords together with the government and the Catholic Church. He also denounced the export of food worth £45 million in a single year while a million people were dying of hunger.[57]

The famine death toll and the clearances so incensed John Mitchel that he accused the British state of 'peacefully' murdering a million and half people by means of the Gregory clause, the poor law system, incompetent officials, and self-ish landlords. In his view the government's relief efforts were 'contrivances for slaughter' and the export of cereal crops to feed the British populace constituted the kind of crime that would later be labelled genocide. 'Agents, bailiffs and the police [had] swept whole districts with the besom of destruction.' If perchance God had sent the potato blight, then 'the English created the famine'.[58]

Despite all the hostility remarkably few landowners and agents were shot during the famine. However, they did not all escape ambush. In the bleak winter months of 1847–8, some sixteen landlords, agents, and middlemen suffered violent deaths while the landgrabber remained the chief target of those seeking revenge.[59]

PICTORIAL IMAGES OF EVICTION

On the eve of the famine Thomas Davis urged Irish artists to produce work that celebrated the nation's most historic events and heroes. He called on them to produce a 'pictorial history of our houses, arts, costume, and manners' that would give the Irish people something to revere as their unique heritage. Beyond being a 'register of fact' art should also be 'biography, history, and topography taught through the eye' on a grand scale. Convinced that painters should focus on the beautiful and sublime and avoid unpleasant or sordid subjects, Davis would not have approved of 'realistic' pictures of eviction not to mention starving or dying beggars.[60]

Under the influence of the Flemish school and David Wilkie, a number of Irish painters combined portraiture with scenes of peasants dancing, drinking, and eating merrily in clean and decent dwellings – a far cry from the dirty and foul-smelling cottages of the cottiers and labourers. If artists trained in Cork came closer than their Dublin counterparts to depicting the realities of rural life, they knew full well that images of skeletal bodies and ravaged features would never sell. For this reason they left the horrors of the famine to the pen and pencil artists working for the *Illustrated London News* and focused instead on scenes of domestic bliss or merriment in the midst of relative or even absolute poverty.[61]

Nevertheless a few mid-Victorian painters braved the conventions of the day by trying to convey the consequences of Irish evictions. Trained in the art schools of Cork, Dublin, London, Glasgow, and Edinburgh, they eschewed the idyllic thatched cottage of a happy-go-lucky peasantry even though aware that paintings of dire distress might ruffle the feathers of the landed gentry. Relying on artistic licence, they portrayed homeless, if handsome and well-dressed, evicted tenants huddling together on the road to nowhere with their empty homes in the background. Hardly any of these idealised victims showed signs of starvation although their faces were lined with despair. Thus George F. Watts's *The Irish Famine* (1849–50) formed part of a series devoted to rural poverty. In this studio production he tried to encapsulate the pain of ejectment as the wife and husband – reprising the Holy Family – sit on a pile of stones in the midst of a treeless landscape. To emphasise the calamity, the young mother holds her dying or dead infant in her lap.[62] At the same time Frederick G. Goodall, best known for his Orientalist and biblical pictures as well as landscapes, produced *An Irish Eviction* wherein a muscular farmer stands outside his cabin with a hat and stick in hand while his sorrowful wife sits with her head between her hands next to her little child crawling on the ground. The two older children huddle together on the thatched roof of a small barn. The absence of any furniture tossed outside serves to reinforce their utter destitution.[63]

A much more eloquent statement about the violence underlying eviction appears in Robert George Kelly's *An Ejectment in Ireland (A Prayer and a Tear for Erin)* (1848) (Plate 1). This genre painting reverberates with both pathos and defiance as the strong and handsome young man struggles against arrest by a constable for having beaten the man – possibly a bailiff – who lies in the road near an empty cart in the background. Here the police accost a respectable farming family just forced out of the house behind them. With his arm raised towards heaven the priest on the right consoles the kneeling woman with her infant. The older woman on the left also kneels in supplication and implores a constable to release her son who holds a cudgel while his brave little son tries to push the other policeman away. The old man in the centre gazes sorrowfully at the priest, and his pretty granddaughter pathetically cradles the lamb of innocence. On the far right an untethered goat, signifying temptation or desire, grazes. Far down the winding road in the distance red-coated cavalrymen march to another eviction site. Some English critics apparently found this picture too 'political' even though Kelly had no such intention.[64]

The gifted Scottish artist, Erskine Nicol, struck a more despairing note in *An Ejected Family* (1853) (Plate 2) that overlays any element of realism with a heavy coating of sentimentalism. He toured Connacht during the famine years but steered clear of depicting the acute suffering encountered along the way. In sharp contrast to the playful and droll 'Paddies' who populate many of his other Irish pictures this painting underscores the plight of the homeless by evoking the expulsion of the Holy Family. Apart from the stooped old man, the robust appearance of this three-generation family elides any signs of starvation. As if to signal a little ray of hope, the black, rain-swept cloud overhead is broken by a brighter sky on the left. Nicol's picture turned the hardship of one evicted family into an icon of the national tragedy.[65]

As Catherine Marshall has noted, the healthy appearance of these famine victims belies the realities of skeletal bodies, gaunt faces, or ragged clothes that appeared in the *ILN*'s prints. She attributes this discrepancy to the schooling of artists in the Greco-Roman tradition that 'idealise[d] and ennoble[d] the human figure, juxtaposing the best parts to arrive at a perfect whole'. [66] At the same time these painters had to bear the sensibilities of their clientele in mind.

Daniel MacDonald's poignant painting *The Eviction* (c.1850) also highlights the trauma of loss by another three-generation family forced out of their humble cottage. This handsome tenant hands the door key to the agent or landlord who is protected by two soldiers. Two mothers with children bemoan their fate, and an old woman kneels in the traditional posture of maternal misery and supplication. The posture of the man on the far right suggests anger or resentment. The broken furniture in the foreground attests to the bailiffs' destructive handiwork.[67] However, no artist at this time seems to have depicted an eviction in progress with the police and military restraining hostile crowds.

BLACK AND WHITE PRINTS

Unlike oil paintings the images of the famine found in the *ILN* and the *Pictorial Times* are noteworthy for their lack of sentimentality as well as their immediacy and starkness. Although lithography still dominated the British printing trade in the 1840s, the new illustrated weeklies were turning to the wood-block made of close-grained boxwood that provided sharper detail and expedited production.[68]

According to Walter Benjamin the *ILN* 'brought graphic art to the masses' and gratified their desire for images to which they could relate. Peter Sinnema has credited the *ILN* with seeking 'to mediate the temporal and physical distance between readers and "original" objects (for example a cottage interior)'. Keen to promote circulation while manifesting some concern for the victims of famine and disease, the editors combined pictures and words in ways that 'allow[ed] meaning to be produced linguistically and visually'.[69]

Aspiring to verisimilitude, the artists employed by these magazines never-theless played down the full horrors of the famine. Of the roughly forty prints in the *ILN* dealing with the famine between 1846 and 1850, the majority focused on the profound misery of the rural populace but avoided images of skeleton-ised or dead bodies lying by the roadside. Instead they filled their sketches with despairing mothers and children, roofless dwellings, and deserted villages. Although graphic depictions of eviction were few and far between, an invisible cloud of homelessness hovered over the heads of the starving hordes.

As Margaret Crawford has pointed out, the *ILN*'s artists endowed the fam-ine victims with relatively strong limbs no matter how forlorn their facial expressions. During the *annus horribilis* of 1847 the Cork trained watercolorist and illustrator, James Mahony (or Mahoney), toured his native county in search of the human scars of this social and demographic disaster. He illus-trated his two-part article on the conditions around Skibbereen and Clonakilty with a dozen pictures of rotting potato beds, hungry families, food riots, barren landscapes, tumbled houses, and weeping emigrants. At one point he came across four dead bodies inside a cabin with a fifth occupant dying on the threshold – a sight he would never forget. For sheer desolation it would be hard to surpass his rendering of the once thriving but now deserted clachan of Moveen near Kilrush.[70]

Mahony's iconic image of starvation, 'Woman in Clonakilty begging for money to bury her dead child', features a Madonna-like mother wearing a hooded mantle and holding her dead or dying infant in one hand and a beg-ging bowl in the other. Her gaunt features highlight what Margaret Kelleher has called 'a primordial breakdown' in the social order because death has invad-ed the potato crop – the very staff of life. Also suffused with morbidity is the 1849 image of the emaciated and dishevelled but still beautiful Bridget O'Donnell with her two daughters clad in rags in Kilrush union. This barefoot trio exemplifies Margaret Kelleher's concept of the 'the feminisation of famine' by artists and writers alike.[71]

Peter Murray's contention that these famine pictures 'helped change public opinion in Britain and resulted in increased government assistance' may sound plausible but is hard to prove. Certainly, the *ILN*'s initial denunciation of Irish landlords as 'extremely selfish, ignorant, negligent, profligate, and reckless' did not enhance their reputation. Mahony's print of the roofless and empty village of Tullig in the townland of Kilrush serves as an epitome of the harsh measures taken by Marcus Keane and other agents to get rid of the 'surplus' population of paupers (Figure 2.1).[72]

2.1 The roofless village of Tullig, Kilrush. James Mahony captures the devastation caused by the famine clearances as well as disease and emigration in this sketch of the empty clachan of Tullig, near Kilrush, County Clare. (*ILN*, 15 Dec. 1849)

2.2   C. W. Cole, 'Eviction: The Last Look – A Life's Adieux'. A respectably dressed tenant and his family bid farewell to their beloved cottage in this sketch. The agent on horseback and several constables hover near the dwelling. (NLI, 2196 TX)

Besides depicting ruined potato crops, the *Pictorial Times* also carried small images of emaciated peasants, deserted villages, and evicted families surrounded by their broken furniture. C. W. Cole limned the abject despair of an evicted family in 'Eviction: The Last Look – A Life's Adieux' wherein respectably dressed tenants take a last look at their cottage while the agent sits astride his horse next to several constables (Figure 2.2).[73]

Shortly before Christmas in 1848 the Irish artist Edmund Fitzpatrick drew a rare before-and-after eviction scenario for the *ILN*. In his action-filled 'Ejectment of Irish Tenantry' (Figure 2.3), the bailiffs are hard at work emptying the cabin, distraining chattel, and stripping the sod roof while an angry bystander on the left scowls. In vain the unresisting tenant implores the sheriff or agent on horseback for a reprieve. And in the sequel, 'The Day After the Ejectment' (Figure 2.4), the forlorn cottier stands outside a crude lean-to made of logs and thatch while his wife cuddles her infant and their daughter points to the former home in the distance. The almost leafless tree and the barren landscape underscore their loss. The accompanying article contains an excerpt from the *Tipperary Vindicator* asserting that a conspiracy 'to uproot the 'mere Irish' has turned the country into a 'Great Desert' and made a 'mockery of the eternal laws of God' on the eve of Christmas. According to this writer, 'the agonies' of the Irish people 'are far more poignant than the imagination could conceive, or the pencil of a Rembrandt picture'.[74]

2.3   Edmund Fitzpatrick, 'The Ejectment'. In this print bailiffs protected by police empty a cottage and strip the thatched roof, while the tenant and his daughter implore the agent for a reprieve. On the left a local man raises his blackthorn in anger. (*ILN*, 16 Dec. 1848)

2.4   Edmund Fitzpatrick, 'The Day After the Ejectment'. In the sequel Fitzpatrick reveals the evicted cottier standing outside his lean-to or scalpeen and his wife cradling their infant inside. On the right a barefoot daughter points to their ruined cottage in the distance. (*ILN*, 16 Dec. 1848)

EMIGRATION

If Irish landlords and their adversaries, the political economists, ever agreed on anything, it had to do with their conviction that evictions were not the cause of the sharp rise in emigration because pauperised tenants could not wait to exchange their miserable existence for a prosperous life overseas. Ireland's greatest problem, both believed, was the huge 'surplus' population that had no fertile land, no money, and no prospects for gainful employment. Lord Dufferin, a keen student of the land question, asserted that evicted persons constituted only five per cent of those who left the country between 1856 and 1865; and the economist William Neilson Hancock denied that landlords were guilty of callous evictions because only 14 per cent of all the emigrants between 1849 and 1862 had suffered that fate. Heavily indebted landowners could not possibly support their 'wretched peasants' without bankrupting themselves and by culling the hordes they hoped to make their estates more profitable.[75] Despite the arguments of political economists the fact remains that eviction rates soared during the famine years while more than two million people – or almost a quarter of Ireland's population – had left their 'doomed land' by 1855. Driven by force, panic, and the lure of a better life overseas, the vast majority headed for North America while 300,000 landed in Australia, and a similar number ended up in Great Britain. By 1852, there were more Irish-born people living in London than in Dublin. Although many of the new arrivals in North America were respectable and hardworking, the influx of so many impoverished, unwashed, and Catholic plebeians did not exactly delight the largely Protestant and nativist citizenry.[76] All told, between 1845 and 1914 almost four million people bid farewell to Ireland in an exodus that some nationalists labelled the 'extermination of the Irish race'.

ASSISTED EMIGRATION

Before, during and after the famine, a number of landlords paid their poorest tenants to surrender their holdings and emigrate. Exasperated by the lack of any income from cottiers and squatters, they were not unlike the helmsman of an overloaded lifeboat on the verge of foundering unless one-third of the passengers were tossed overboard. Keen to consolidate the smallholdings on their properties, these proprietors looked first to the state for help. But when the parsimonious government refused to help paupers to emigrate, solvent landlords spent thousands of pounds on so-called voluntary transportation. In the 1820s Peter Robinson and other 'reformers' like William Horton and Thomas Spring Rice had proposed schemes to export 'surplus labour' – not to mention lawless and rebellious young men – abroad. After 1845, however, 'assisted emigration' became the method of choice for wealthier landlords who wanted to get rid of unprofitable tenants without incurring the stigma of eviction. Over the course of the nineteenth century at least 250,000 individuals in Ireland received small subsidies to embark for Canada and the United States – admittedly a tiny fraction of all those Irish people who sailed overseas. From 1846 to 1855 upwards of 80,000 tenants and their families or roughly 4.5 per cent of all the emigrants received some assistance from their landlords exclusive of grants from family and friends.

As Gerard Moran has pointed out, this exodus engendered much criticism from Irish shopkeepers and moneylenders who feared losing all the money they were owed by the leavers. In addition, the Catholic hierarchy and many priests deplored the erosion of the old faith that was bound to result from the relocation of their parishioners in largely Protestant, if not godless, parts of North America and Australia. Repealers or nationalists, moreover, condemned not just the depopulation of townlands but also the 'extermination' – their term – of potential or actual supporters through eviction and emigration.

Of course, landlords committed to this form of deportation convinced themselves that it was wholly voluntary. However, one must ask what fate awaited destitute tenants who refused to leave. In short, the line between voluntaryism and involuntaryism was exceedingly fine; and as Moran has put it, assisted emigration amounted to 'a more humane form of clearance'. Most of the assisted emigrants received between £2 and £5 in passage money and local boards of guardians or poor law unions sometimes covered the cost of clothing and travel to the nearest port. [77]

One prominent practitioner of this culling process was the 5th Earl Fitzwilliam whose agents used both the 'carrot' of money and the 'stick' of ejectment to induce thousands of the poorest tenants to surrender their holdings around Coolattin in County Wicklow. After closing their doors for the last time, they made the long and arduous trek to New Ross whence they embarked for Canada. At the height of the subsistence crisis Lord Palmerston's agent hired over a dozen ships to transport several thousand tenants to New Brunswick where local citizens recoiled from the intrusion of so many destitute, sickly, and half-naked women and children.[78] Paupers were also purged on the Kerry estate of Lord Lansdowne whose mortgage loans amounted to some £300,000. Not even this wealthy Anglo-Irish proprietor could afford to support all the destitute people begging for food around Kenmare. On the advice of his shrewd agent, William Steuart Trench, he spent some £17,000 on uprooting 14,000 people on the Glanarought estate. Relieved of arrears, they surrendered their holdings and walked up to eighty miles to Cobh where they embarked for Liverpool and thence North America. Trench supervised every detail of this operation and took credit for saving countless lives without acknowledging the help of local relief committees. Another 668 Kenmare tenants pulled up stakes and emigrated in the 1860s with the aid of a few pounds handed out by the agent. As Gerry Lyne has judiciously observed, 'while some might regard these removals as evictions in all but name, the odium and overt violence associated with full eviction was, at least, avoided'. [79]

Well before the famine, Sir Robert Gore Booth had exported some marginal tenants from his 32,000-acre estate in western Sligo, where smallholders on 800 acres around Ballygilgan or the Seven Cartrons were driven out to make room for cattle. When given a choice between farming undesirable holdings elsewhere or emigrating, some 52 families accepted the offer of free passage overseas. According to long cherished local legend the 'coffin ship' he hired for this purpose, the *Pomona*, foundered with all hands on board lost. The absence of any proof of a conspiracy to scuttle the vessel did not stop Gore Booth's enemies from accusing him of cold-blooded murder. In fact a ship by that name continued to ply the seas long after the alleged sinking. Evidently, Sir Robert and his agent provided food and relief work for many tenants. Not only did they inspect the three ships chartered to convey them across the Atlantic but they also ensured that all 1,500 passengers passed a medical exam before embarking. Nevertheless, the story of the doomed *Pomona* cast a pall over the family's reputation for generations. By way of contrast, assisted emigration took a heavy toll on Denis Mahon's Roscommon property. Over half of the 464 tenants who shipped out on the *Naomi* and *Virginius* died en route to North America. If this high mortality was exceptional, it left a lasting impression. [80]

Inspired more by self-interest than altruism, assisted emigration under these dire circumstances was bound to compromise seriously the concept of voluntaryism. Even if the agent only hinted at eviction, this veiled threat hung over the heads of cottiers heavily laden with arrears. In the realm of ideology both lay and clerical nationalists insisted that eviction and emigration went hand in glove and served to prove the existence of a sinister Sassenach plot to rid the country of its so-called surplus and Gaelic populace. In his monumental study of the forces behind the great Irish exodus and diaspora, Kerby Miller contends that Catholic nationalists 'stigmatised Famine emigration as forced exile' and this conviction fomented their 'savage hatred' of the English government and its landlord 'garrison' in Ireland whom they held responsible for the disastrous haemorrhaging of the native population. [81]

Of course the landlords defended assisted emigration on the grounds of both benevolence and their own survival. Insisting that they had no choice if they wished to retain their estates intact, they pointed out repeatedly that their former tenants had found a new and prosperous life overseas instead of starving to death at home. Here and there some proprietors took steps to ensure that their departing tenants were free of disease and reached their destinations safely clad in decent clothing rather than rags or workhouse uniforms.

Whatever the push and pull factors involved in the decision to leave their holdings there could be little doubt about the deleterious impact of this exodus on the social and cultural fabric of Munster and Connacht. In the long run, however, not even the hardships of the transatlantic passage and the sadness of leaving home could efface the fact that tens of thousands of families avoided an untimely demise or enduring misery by starting a new life overseas. No doubt they were much envied by all those other emigrants who struggled to find the fare needed to escape from pauperism and premature death at home. At the very least assisted emigration enabled landlords to dodge the charge of eviction and claim the high moral ground of paternalism as their former tenants made better lives for themselves in the new world.[82]

Those who survived the 'great hunger' as well as travellers through the western provinces had good reason to repeat Thomas Davis's haunting question: 'Where – oh where – are the children?' Empathy for the victims of eviction and hunger suffuses his poem written shortly before his death about arriving at a sylvan beauty spot to find that an old cabin had vanished.

> And the trees, like mourners, are watching the spot,
> And cronauning with the breeze,
> And the stems are bared with the children's play:
> But the children – where – oh, where! – are they?
> But the typhus came, and the agent too,
> Ah! need I name the worse of the two?
> Their cot was unroofed, but they strove to hide
> 'Midst the walls till the fever was passed.
> Their crime was found out, and the cold ditch side
> Was their hospital at last.
> Slowly they went to the poorhouse and grave.[83]

It took the genius of James Clarence Mangan to evoke the anguish arising out of the lost potato crops. In his poem, 'The Famine' (1849), written shortly before his death, he described the shift from an Edenic country filled with 'joy and revelry' to a virtual wasteland:

> Despair? Yes! For a blight fell on the land –
> The soil, heaven-blasted, yielded food no more –
> The Irish serf became a Being banned –
> Life-exiled as none ever was before.
> The old man died beside his hovel's hearth,
> The young man stretched himself along the earth,
> And perished, stricken to the core!
>
> .   .   .   .

Ye True, ye Noble, who unblenched stand
Amid the storms and ills of this dark Day,
Still hold your ground! Yourselves, your Fatherland,
Have in the Powers above a surest stay!
Though Famine, Pest, Want, Sickness of the Heart,
Be now your lot – all these shall soon depart –
And Heaven be yet at your command. [84]

Aubrey De Vere, the gentry poet of Curragh Chase, Adare, and a devoted convert to Catholicism, alluded in passing to eviction in his deeply spiritual poem, 'The Year of Sorrow – Ireland –1849' (dedicated to Cardinal Newman). Dwelling on the devastation wrought by the unrelenting famine, he wrote:

From ruined huts and holes come forth
Old men, and look upon the sky!
The Power Divine is on the earth:
Give thanks to God before ye die!

And ye, O children worn and weak!
Who care no more with flowers to play,
Lean on the grass your cold, thin cheek,
And those slight hands, and, whispering, say

'Stern mother of a race unblest,
In promise kindly, cold in deed, –
Take back, O Earth, into thy breast,
The children whom thou wilt not feed.'

   .   .   .   .   .   .

The roof-trees fall of hut and hall;
I hear them fall, and falling cry,
'One fate for each, one fate for all;
So wills the Law that willed a lie.' [85]

The myriad memories and images of skeletal beggars, ruined cabins, over-crowded and disease-ridden workhouses, and deserted clachans combined to form a massive and enduring grievance. The collective bitterness arising from the failures of both the landed elite and the government to save more lives and arrest the depopulation of the countryside only increased in intensity with the next generation of nationalists who conflated landlordism with eviction – a connection that paid large dividends during the subsequent land agitations. As Tim O'Neill points out, myths do matter, even if they lack any empirical basis. Even though some altruistic landlords strained their dwindling resources to serve stirabout and bread to the starving hordes that 'invaded' the demesne, the clearances shattered the last remnants of faith in landlord paternalism and hastened the decline and fall of the Irish gentry by creating 'a new political agenda'.[86]

In his fluently revisionist survey, *Modern Ireland* (1988), R. F. Foster has remarkably little to say about famine evictions. In fact the words eviction and clearance barely surface in his chapter on the origins and consequences of the famine. There is no mention of the 20,000 dwellings razed between 1849 and 1868. Furthermore, he denies that this disaster constitutes a significant 'watershed' in nineteenth century Irish history, selecting instead the economic crisis following the end of the Napoleonic wars. By the same token Joel Mokyr's cliometric study of the Irish economy on the eve of the famine, *Why Ireland Starved*, is curiously silent on the subject of evictions before 1845. The prevalence of long leases before the famine, he contends, protected the tenantry from any 'predatory behaviour' by their landlords. Nevertheless he concedes that 'tenant insecurity' contributed to 'prefamine poverty'. For good measure he adds that most tenants at will 'fully trusted' their landlords not to raise the rents after improvements. This rosy scenario may have prevailed among strong farmers on prosperous and well-managed estates in Leinster and Ulster but it hardly applied to cottiers and conacre tenants on sprawling estates in Munster and Connacht. Far more convincing is Tim O'Neill's contention that the efforts of Irish historians to minimise the effects of the famine and the role of evictions in alienating the masses cannot help to 'reconcile ancestral antagonisms'.[87]

In Great Britain the famine confirmed the belief of those who took such inordinate pride in their Anglo-Saxon heritage and character that the Celtic or Gaelic and Catholic people of Ireland belonged to a different, unruly, and feminine race. Michael de Nie's trawling through British newspapers has shown that Anglo-Saxonists were convinced that the two 'races' would never be able to live in harmony or mutual understanding unless or until 'Paddy' had been thoroughly Anglicised – a process bound to take generations if not centuries. As for the political fallout from the famine the decimation of the rural population strengthened the resolve of Repealers, Home Rulers, tenant-righters, and republican separatists to restore the land to 'the people' once independence had been won. Searing memories of the clearances in short galvanised not only Fenianism and the Home Rule movement but also the land wars after 1879.

THREE

INTERLUDE
1855–78

'NO MAN MADE THE LAND ... *It is the original
inheritance of the whole species. Its appropriation
is a question of general expediency.'*

FATHER PATRICK LAVELLE
The Irish Landlord Since the Revolution
(Dublin, 1870), pp. 43–4.

'*The Irish landlords in their dealings with the tenants
have been little better than skilful thieves.'*

JAMES ANTHONY FROUDE
Quoted in L. Paul-Dubois, *Contemporary Ireland*
(Dublin, 1908), p. 97

———

Apart from the high mortality rate, two significant fallouts from the famine clearances were the sharp decrease in the number of holdings under one acre and the growth of commercial cattle ranching on the cleared lands. While the category of farms between one and thirty acres constituted over 60 per cent of all holdings between 1850 and 1900, the number of holdings of less than one acre never rose above ten per cent. As David Jones has shown in his insightful study of the grazier economy and culture, the livestock trade in the plains or broad valleys of eastern Connacht and Munster grew by leaps and bounds. Prosperous proprietors like Henry Bruen of Oak Park, County Carlow, converted much fertile land from tillage to pasturage owing to the scarcity and expense of labourers and the desire for more income. The number of dry cattle doubled in this half-century and exports of livestock from Ireland to Britain rose from an annual average of 202,000 in 1851–5 to 682,000 in 1876–80. The chief beneficiaries of this seismic shift from corn to horn were graziers who leased hundreds of acres on the eleven-month system and remained almost immune from eviction. The countryside thus grew 'greener' with the conversion to pasturage for both dry and milch cattle. Out of the demographic and economic disaster of the famine emerged a prosperous and socially ambitious 'rural bourgeoisie', the graziers, who made more enemies than friends wherever they held sway.[1]

The cottiers and small farmers who escaped eviction and emigration, not to mention death, during the famine usually kept one or two cows on their tiny holdings to provide milk for the family. Most of these cattle were the hardy and high yielding 'Irish cottar's cow' or Kerry, that also produced precious manure for the potato bed. Larger farmers went in for the Dexter or the horn-less Moil, the Longhorn, and the Shorthorn. The appeal of the once humble Kerry and its Dexter offshoot soared after aristocrats like the Knight of Kerry and the Duke of Leinster (not to mention King Edward VII) began to breed and exhibit pedigree herds.[2]

If evictions did not stop with the recovery of the potato crop after 1855, they declined sharply. On Lord Leitrim's Donegal estate, for example, only seven tenants were evicted in 1856–7 and arrears amounting to £141 were written off.[3] Across the country final evictions for the decade 1855–64 dropped down to 9,733 and then fell further to 4,866 for the years 1865–74. The depression of 1861–4 took its toll, accounting for a quarter of all evictions between 1855 and 1880. However, roughly one-fifth of the 9,477 families evicted in 1857–64 were readmitted as tenants. In Queen's County a net total of 111 final evictions (yielding an annual average of 8.7) occurred between 1864 and 1878 compared with 187 for the five years 1879–83.[4]

The drop in evictions and the return of tranquillity to the Irish countryside did not prevent the *Times* and other London papers from highlighting agrarian crime to the point where readers must have assumed that assassins were lying in wait behind every other hedgerow. One company refused to insure the life of Lord Gosford's agent in 1852 owing to fears that this investment would be too risky. In fact, rural Ireland in the three decades following the famine was no more dangerous than rural England and Wales. Only nine landlords, one agent, and seven bailiffs were murdered in Ireland between 1857 and 1878, while ten employees or servants of landlords suffered this fate. Like the media today, the Victorian press went out of its way to sensationalise any crime or scandal involving persons of elite status.[5]

No matter how large their arrears the removal of tenants from farms held for generations never failed to inspire tears and raise the hackles of those most directly affected. During especially hard times Catholic landlords, who consti-tuted around 43 per cent of this class, were just as likely to evict their poorest Catholic tenants as were their Protestant counterparts once arrears had sur-passed the two-year mark and local moneylenders or gombeen men refused any more credit.[6] On the Lansdowne estate around Kenmare solvent tenants did not have to worry about ejectment. But the masterful agent, W. S. Trench, held that threat over the heads of anyone who violated estate rules or fell behind with the rent. During the mid-1850s he expelled more middlemen along with their impoverished under-tenants, paid the latter to emigrate, and found industrious tenants to take on the newly squared farms. His reputation for harshness grew by leaps and bounds in 1855 when he levelled a dozen houses and drove the seventy occupants out into a snowstorm. One husband carried his paralysed wife in a basket on his back through the mountains only to see her die at the end of this harrowing journey. Trench also ordered the bailiffs to stop evicted tenants from building lean-tos inside their ruined abodes. When a troublesome tenant-caretaker, Jerry Sullivan, was turned out in July 1864, the local press took note but did not print the curses hurled by his wife at the evictors. At least Trench compensated most of the outgoing tenants for their improvements.[7]

POLLOCK/GALWAY

One of the new investors in Irish land after the famine was an ambitious timber merchant and land speculator from Glasgow and Renfrewshire named Allan Pollock (or Pollok). This foolhardy businessman dreamed of turning the 25,000 acres of land in County Galway bought in the Incumbered Estates Court for £212,460 into a profitable enterprise. Seeking to modernise this property along Lowland lines, he converted cottiers and graziers, whom he considered feckless, into waged labourers, after obtaining hundreds of notices to quit. Offered the choice between assisted emigration and the life of a landless labourer, many chose to stay. But their response to his 'commercial' scheme anticipated the land war of the 1880s, what with attacks on process servers, the arrival of police reinforcements, and angry mobs stoning the evictors. During the summer of 1853 almost 600 people were driven out, half of whom were readmitted presumably as labourers while the remainder left. During 1855–6 the districts around Creggs, Glinsk, and Lismany grew so turbulent that a hundred extra police were assigned to protect the eviction party. Pollock let the newly squared farms to cattlemen who reared young stock before sending them to east Leinster for final fattening. His labourers toiled in fields devoted to turnips and other kinds of fodder and nursed their wrath at the prosperous graziers. In 1854 Pollock lost his mansion to arsonists. Backed by their parish priest and curate, some 1,400 tenants signed a petition to Parliament protesting the purges. But notoriety did not faze Pollock, who had the gall to boast that he had never forced a single tenant out of his holding.[8]

The consolidation of small farms continued during the 1860s as some landlords relied on eviction and assisted emigration to sweep away unprofitable tenants. The *Pall Mall Gazette* welcomed the end to clearances, even though land speculators like Pollock had no qualms about thinning their newly acquired properties.[9] The editors of nationalist or Repeal papers continued to rant against evicting landlords and equated assisted emigration with 'extermination'. Thus the *Nation* warned landlords in 1860 to avoid the 'extremely harsh and cruel proceedings' pending in Meath, Louth, and Mayo because they were not 'morally entitled to clear off the peasantry as if they were vermin'. God had not given them a monopoly in the land; and no other people in the world would 'tolerate ... the system of eviction which is so incessantly worked in this country'. The *Galway Press* condemned evictions as a death sentence because 'a damnable murderous law is killing off our people with unerring certainty'. [10] Nevertheless, few tenants facing eviction resorted to physical force when the sheriff's party arrived. Apart from ripe curses and fist-shaking most of them left their premises without a fight. No doubt some acts of resistance escaped the notice of reporters; but almost all the violence emanated from the bailiffs and police.

SOUPERISM

The fusion of religion and popular politics in the post-famine era owed much to Daniel O'Connell's recruitment of the Catholic clergy to help promote his two great campaigns – Catholic emancipation and Repeal. After 1850 the politicisation of the parish priests, canons, and their parishioners was fast becoming a *fait accompli*. Apart from such obvious exceptions as Davis, Mitchel, Butt, and Parnell, the vast majority of nationalists in this era were Catholic. By the same token the identification of Protestants with the Act of Union and unswerving loyalty to Westminster was constantly reinforced by the sectarian bigotry flowing out of the Orange Order since its founding in the mid-1790s. Shortly after the end of the Napoleonic wars, Protestant missionaries arrived in the western provinces bent on converting the 'heathen peasantry' to the one and only Christian faith. As Donnelly has shown, the Rockite rebellion of the early 1820s was in part a sectarian as well as Catholic millenarian response to the evangelical clergymen and schoolmasters armed with English and Irish bibles who were roaming the southwest during 1821–4. Some of the Rockite violence then was aimed directly at Protestant proselytisers keen to lure their co-religionists away from the 'true' faith and their beloved priests.[11]

During and just after the famine a new generation of Protestant zealots reached Ireland armed with Irish-language bibles and money in quest of converts or 'jumpers'. The Archbishop of Tuam, Power Le Poer Trench, along with William Magee, Archbishop of Dublin, spearheaded this crusade, aided and abetted by such dynamic apostles as the Reverends William Baker Stoney, Edward Nangle, and Alexander R. C. Dallas. These religious fanatics were fond of pointing to the number of 'public recantations of the errors of Romanism' in Ireland; and after 1847 they founded dozens of small Protestant colonies at Dingle, Doon, and Achill that incensed the eminent Catholic Archbishop of Armagh (and later Cardinal), Dr Paul Cullen. Building on the legacy of Nangle, who claimed to have converted at least 372 people on Achill Island, these English bible thumpers targeted the poor peasants of western Connacht and Donegal whom they regarded as pagans. One of these crusaders, the Rev. William Allen Fisher, worked long and hard to feed the starving hordes around Killmoe in southwestern Cork during the famine. Hundreds of poor souls flocked to his church to obtain food and confess their sins to this high church priest. After the famine over half the population had disappeared through death and emigration and the converts reverted to the old faith. For all his good works he was accused of having evicted tenants because they had refused to join his flock, thereby forcing others to 'turn' in order to save their farms. Although funds from Anglican parishes in England were dwindling, both Dallas's Society for Irish Church Missions to the Roman Catholics (ICMRC), based in London's Exeter Hall, and the Church of Ireland promoted this brand of salvationism. Besides providing stirabout soup and clothing, these missionaries offered to educate local children in new Protestant schools.[12]

The epitome of the second Protestant reformation in Ireland, Alexander Dallas had left his Hampshire parish in 1847 to spread the gospel in Munster and Connacht. Known variously as the 'Protestant Loyola' and a 'latter-day Oliver Cromwell', he raised funds and sent preachers into the hinterland equipped with Irish language bibles and tracts to 'Christianize… a rude uncivilised race'. Offering hot porridge and good schooling, and holding out the prospect of certain salvation, the emissaries of the ICMRC worked tirelessly to pry the peasantry away from their priests and creed. According to the profoundly anti-clerical English traveller, Sir Francis Head, these missionaries were bringing civilisation to the physically and morally degraded peasantry of the west; and he hailed the recent construction of eight Protestant churches in the parish of Westport alone. Not only did the proselytisers become the real 'visitation of God' during the famine but they also set in motion a counter-crusade by Catholic prelates and priests who despised every form of 'stirabout religion'.[13]

Charges of souperism were often heard before, during, and long after the famine. As Lord Brougham once declared, 'Of all the curses that could afflict a country, the mixing of religious matters with the performance of charitable duties was the greatest.'[14] Part myth and part reality these evangelical seducers enjoyed a long life in local folklore. Tales of Catholic peasants 'jumping' or converting during the famine years reverberated for over a century and kept the home fires of sectarian animosity burning brightly.[15]

PLUNKET AND PARTRY, 1860

Arguably the most notorious proselytiser of the post-famine era was Thomas, 2nd Baron Plunket, the Protestant Bishop of Tuam, Killala, and Achonry. In 1854–5 this aristocratic divine bought ten thousand acres around Tourmakeady and Partry in southwest Mayo, where his whiggish father owned a shooting lodge. The great famine had decimated the parish killing off 1,300 persons out of a population of 6,000 in one year.[16] At the end of November 1860 Plunket embarked on a small eviction campaign following a long-simmering sectarian conflict. As Lyne has observed, 'the Famine crisis provided the backdrop to a bitter contest between the two sides for custody of the immortal souls of a horde of starving wretches'. At the height of the famine, in fact, the wealthy Rev. Denis Mahony of Dromore Castle had tried to spread his ultra-Protestant dogma around Lord Lansdowne's Kenmare estate. Besides bible readings he attracted hundreds of desperately poor people with offers of food and clothing. But in 1850 his campaign backfired badly when a rowdy mob, stirred up by the parish priest, assaulted Mahony who died six months later.[17]

Plunket's missionary zeal around Partry culminated in a 'war' for the hearts and souls of the inhabitants. Not only did he endorse Dallas's crusade but he also promoted Nangle's mission by subsidising five Protestant schools and offering rewards to any converts. His hot and heavy pursuit of Catholic souls inspired a worthy adversary or nemesis in the person of Father Patrick Lavelle, curate and 'administrator' of Partry. Trained at the Irish College in Paris, this combative priest soon crossed swords with Plunket by launching a spirited counter-offensive against both proselytism and landlordism.

Lavelle's Fenian sympathies nettled Cardinal Cullen as well as the Vatican but not even a stern primatial reprimand could stop him from fighting on behalf of his beloved parishioners. An admirer of John Stuart Mill for his commitment to peasant proprietorship, Lavelle insisted that God had made the land but not the land laws that entitled owners to 'claim every morsel of earth, stone, sand, fish, game, minerals' in perpetuity. And he never gave up fighting against the landlords' 'power of life and death over the many'.[18]

As soon as he took over the parish of Partry, Father Lavelle denounced 'jumpers' and forbade his parishioners from sending their children to Protestant schools. He also told them to defy Plunket's ban on conacre, burning fields after the harvest, and turbary rights. The pressure to convert accompanied by veiled threats of eviction moved some tenants to hide whenever they saw the bishop's acolytes or his equally evangelical sister approaching. According to a visiting English lawyer Plunket had urged Catholic children to attend his schools and had warned their parents not to criticise the Irish Church Mission Society. By December 1857 some twenty tenants had converted and several bible readers had been assaulted. Local resentment mounted rapidly after some cattle were impounded and several farmers were prosecuted for burning their fields in defiance of estate rules.

Charges and counter-charges of harassment and gross misconduct fuelled the fires of sectarianism. Father Lavelle went so far as to accuse a Protestant minister of trying to shoot him during an altercation but later withdrew the charge. He also sued the proprietor of the pro-Plunket paper, the *Mayo Constitution*, for six allegedly libellous articles that called him a vain busybody, a 'mountebank', and a 'Frenchified … pugilist'. The trial in a Galway court ended in a hung jury. Seeking to make peace, Archbishop MacHale of Tuam elicited a formal apology from the tenantry for their protests (known as the Castlebar Settlement). Plunket's ire reached new heights after a Protestant ploughman was murdered and rumours circulated about his wife's infidelity. In a highly publicised incident two scripture readers entered Pat Lally's house whereupon one of them called Mrs Lally's scapular a 'dirty rag' associated with the devil. When he tried to remove this cloth, she lashed out with a candlestick and her son thrashed both intruders. Plunket retaliated by charging the family with 'outrage, conspiracy, incendiarism, perjury, and murder'. He also ordered their eviction even though they had paid their rent. The *Mayo Constitution* approved Plunket's conduct, supported the charge of a criminal conspiracy, and denounced Lavelle. 'A few more evictions, such as that of Partry', the editor declared, 'will do more to promote peace in the country than all the machinery of Arms Acts, and Proclamation and additional Police.' Needless to say, all these accusations, recriminations, assaults, and trials poisoned the wells of a once tranquil community.[19]

Despite the threat of eviction, Catholic parents refused to allow their children to attend Protestant schools, while Plunket insisted that sectarianism played no role in the ejectments that he attributed to breaches of contract and his need to 'stripe' or square the farms in question. Lavelle fired back that the farms had already been striped and that no Catholic tenant whose children attended a Protestant school had ever been evicted.

To prevent rioting the Castle reinforced the local police, many of whom were Catholics, with several hundred soldiers and cavalry. Partry soon resembled an armed camp as the evictions loomed near. On 21 November 1860 Colonel Knox, High Sheriff of Mayo, led his expeditionary force to Tourmakeady, where the bailiffs drove out five families. Despite Lavelle's call for resistance the tenants left quietly in the pouring rain and watched their houses being levelled. Knox returned the next day with only 25 police but sent for reinforcements as soon as he saw Lavelle at the head of a menacing crowd. Seven more houses were then emptied. In all a dozen families or almost 70 people were driven out and spent several miserable nights in the rain before finding shelter.[20]

Seated on a knoll above one eviction site, the *Morning Post's* reporter jotted down the events unfolding before his eyes:

> While I write the sound of Bishop Plunket's crowbar brigade rings in my ears. Three houses have already fallen, and the house of John Boyle is this moment coming down with a crash … It would wring the heart of the veriest pagan, the sight presented at this moment – just ten minutes a beautiful house, now a mass of ruins. One man made an attempt at resistance, but of course, in vain. He and his wife were dragged like beasts out of their neat and comfortable house, the abode of their fathers for several generations. The representatives of the Christian bishop seem to take a kind of fiendish pleasure in the agonising business: you may see them going about as merrily as if at a wedding feast.[21]

Father Lavelle arrived on horseback and took copious notes, while the sullen crowd prayed and cursed in Irish. Surprisingly, he did not protest when several bailiffs seized Tom Lally's wife by the head and shoulders and hauled her outside. He observed that 'her bosom' was 'exposed' and her hair dishevelled. Four men then dragged Lally out 'like a butchered calf' and 'flung' him on the dunghill. As he gasped for breath, his wife exclaimed: 'Thank God, they cannot turn us out of heaven.'

On the second day the bailiffs carried on evicting the young and the old, including a mother with a baby in a cradle. Amidst tears and wails more houses were razed. James Henaghan and his pregnant wife, who had been accused of assaulting a scripture-reader, spent the night outdoors in freezing rain. As Lavelle recalled,

> I saw an old man, 80 years of age, and his wife, 74, tottering out of a house which had seen their great grandparents, and standing by with streaming eyes, amid torrents of sleet and rain, as the venerable roof and walls crumbled to the ground. I saw the young mother, and the babe at her bosom, linger on the threshold they were never to cross again. I saw the cradle, in which slept the happily unconscious child, carried out by the father, the rain beating with fury on the innocent brow. I saw the pot of potatoes intended for the morning's meal, taken off the fire and flung on the dung-heap. In one word, sir, I saw extermination in its worst of forms, carried out by 'the Bishop of Tuam and Peer of Ireland', and that under the aegis of her majesty's police and military.[22]

After these evictions the bishop sued Lavelle for installing a subtenant on his land without his consent. In Ballinrobe courthouse the priest's attorney grilled Plunket relentlessly, but the judge ruled against the priest, and the *Mayo Constitution* hailed this outcome. In public letters and a pamphlet, *The War in Party* (1860), Lavelle scoffed at 'the Bishop Burglar's' denial that religion had anything to do with the evictions and he stressed the absurdity of accusing tenants of committing felonies without a shred of evidence.[23]

If these evictions did not amount to a clearance, their notoriety drew reporters from London as well as Dublin who relished this melodramatic contest between two men of the cloth. One Catholic priest accused Plunket of having cleared every soul off four townlands because he wanted to enclose them 'for himself, his game, and his bullocks'. Although the *Illustrated London News* published no prints of the Partry evictions, Lavelle made up for this pictorial neglect by publicising them in letters and speeches that reached a wide audience. Plunket's defenders on the other hand denounced the priest as a rabble-rouser and called 'the poor peasantry of the Mayo mountains …very ignorant and very excitable'.[24]

The *Times*' longstanding sympathy for the landed elite did not prevent it from condemning the Partry evictions as a 'hideous scandal'; and an editorial (27 November) described the sickly stench emanating from Plunket's estate. No prince of the church, the editor observed, should be punishing innocent 'old men, women, and children' by emptying and destroying their homesteads. 'We avow an honest prejudice against the use of a pickaxe and a crowbar by a successor of the Apostles.' Granted that even prelates had a legal right to evict tenants for non-payment, Plunket should be applying 'an open palm and a gentle pressure – not a heave at the crowbar, followed by falling thatch, and crumbling masonry'. Instead of lavishing thousands of pounds on demesne improvements, he should be spending a few hundred pounds to help his poorest tenants. The *Galway Press* endorsed the *Times*' stance and demanded an end to the soupers' 'game of religious humbug'. Plunket's insistence that he harboured no bias against Catholics rang hollow and only heightened tensions.[25]

The fallout from Partry crossed the Irish Sea as well as the English Channel. In France the wife of Marshal MacMahon and the Duchess of Hamilton persuaded the Bishop of Orleans to preach a sermon on behalf of the victims and collect funds for their relief. Responding to the charges of sectarianism, Plunket sent a public letter to the British ambassador in Paris blaming the evictions on 'persistent provocation' by some tenants. Disavowing once again any religious bigotry, he pointed out that almost all of his tenants were Catholic and remained on their farms even though none of their children attended Protestant schools. Perhaps it was only a coincidence that Erskine Nicol completed his grim painting, *Notice to Quit*, two years later. Here a dour official accompanied by his bulldog serves an impoverished Catholic family with the dreaded eject-ment decree. The seated father tries to console his kneeling wife while holding a staff in his hand. And on the far left an angry old woman raises her right arm in defiance next to a sickly child lying in the nearby bed. [26]

At length all the turmoil, litigation, and adverse publicity arising from this conflict drove Plunket to sell the Partry estate in 1863 to two English industri-alists and he retreated to the safe and peaceful haven of the archbishop's palace in Tuam. [27]

In his polemical memoir Father Lavelle ended one chapter by quoting two passages from Oliver Goldsmith's 'Deserted Village' including:

Ill fares the land, to hastening ills a prey,
Where wealth accumulates, and men decay.
Princes and lords may flourish, or may fade –
A breath can make them, as a breath has made;
But a bold peasantry, a nation's pride,
When once destroyed, can never be supplied.[28]

This religious and personal conflict elevated Lavelle onto the national stage where he championed the cottiers' cause and served as a role model for a new generation of priests who joined the next round of struggles against high rents, proselytism, and eviction.

Partry inspired at least two novels wherein eviction played a central role. Written by Irish-American women, these romances or melodramas featured innocent young women menaced by lecherous landlords, agents, or money-lenders who were given to intrigue and even murder. In Mary Meaney's *The Confessors of Connaught* (1865), the 'imperious' Lord Bishop Woolcut (Plunket) seeks to lure Mayo peasants away from 'the superstitions of Popery' with soup and bibles. As one good Catholic puts it, 'Papists are at least Christians'. To punish the tenants for spurning his bribes Woolcut evicts them amidst curses and tears. After the distraint and impounding of their cattle in a Catholic cem-etery, the infuriated people storm the pound and release their animals. Woolcut then sends for more police and seizes more livestock. At the end sixty families pull up stakes and move to another parish, while a young Protestant clergy-man, whom the bishop had dismissed for being too liberal, converts to Catholicism, returns to England, and raises money for the evicted tenants.[29]

Also filled with sectarian strife, evictions, and sinister schemers is Alice Nolan's novel, *The Byrnes of Glengoulah* (1869). However, the action takes place not in Partry but in the beautiful vale of Avoca, County Wicklow; and the arch villain is the Rev. Samuel W. Biggs DD, an ugly anti-Catholic and lower-middle-class English clergyman. His nemesis or antithesis is a handsome curate, Father O'Tool, the mirror image of Lavelle. The benevolent and elderly Catholic agent, Charles De Courcy, resigns over Biggs's insistence on raising the rent, and his successor is a hard-driving Scot named Jacob 'Jab' Margin who resembles the unscrupulous Jason Quirk in *Castle Rackrent*. Elevated to a bishopric, Biggs embarks on an eviction campaign aided and abetted by thuggish bailiffs from Dublin. After half a dozen tenants die from shock and exposure, a secret agrarian society sentences him to death. Driven mad by eviction, a young woman curses the bishop, and dies from exposure on the stone steps of his mansion. Biggs barely survives an ambush; and an innocent tenant is falsely accused, convicted, and executed for this crime. But all is not lost. In the almost obligatory 'happy' ending for such novels the bishop loses his mind and winds up in an English insane asylum; and a kindly new owner arrives to reinstate the evicted tenants.[30]

On 22 November 1860, several evictions occurred on the estate of the Irish Lord Chancellor, John, 1st Baron Campbell, at Moycullen in County Galway. The victims were three destitute families living in the townland of Ballyquirk with 24 children between them. Comprising 'twenty half-starved creatures' from Barna, the crowbar gang reduced the abodes to rubble watched by the rain-soaked former occupants. The sheriff reprieved Mary Ryan, a respectable widow, on the grounds of poor health, but she disappeared. As the *Galway Press* put it, Lord Campbell had emulated Plunket by flourishing the crowbar with as much 'deadly effect' as his claymore-wielding Scottish forebears because his priority lay with 'legalised spoliation'.[31]

ADAIR/DERRYVEAGH

Partry was soon followed by the equally notorious evictions at Derryveagh, also known as Glenveagh (the Glen of Silver Birches), in a remote and scenic corner of northwest Donegal. The owner was a wealthy land speculator and developer, John George Adair, the scion of a minor gentry family in Queen's County, who was related by marriage to William Steuart Trench. Just as obsessed with profit as Pollock, Adair sought to enhance his social status and income from sheep ranching. He evolved from an advocate of tenant right to a rigid enforcer of landlord rights. Romantic inclinations combined with sporting interests moved him in 1857–8 to buy 42,000 acres of mountainous pasture along with several large lakes. Like Lord George Hill, he abolished rundale and squared farms through eviction and house wrecking in order to make way for Scottish sheep.

Adair's 'improvements' included the hiring of some shepherds from Scotland who were bitterly resented. In less than a year several hundred sheep disappeared – whether through neglect or theft is not clear. Blaming the tenants for this loss and other so-called offences, Adair made sure that local ratepayers bore the cost of his reimbursement. The poisoning of two beloved foxhounds was followed by the murder of his Scottish farm steward or head shepherd, James Murray, in November 1860. With malice aforethought Adair ordered the eviction of 47 families or 244 individuals (159 of whom were children) on the grounds that they either knew or were harbouring Murray's murderers. Even neighbouring landlords as well as Castle officials deplored this collective punishment for a crime that went unsolved. As A. M. Sullivan observed in his account of these melancholy events, it was 'an evil day for the mountaineers when Mr Adair first set eye on their home'. [32]

On Monday morning, 8 April 1861, the keening of women broke the silence of Derryveagh valley as the sheriff's party, escorted by 200 police, carried out their orders and razed 28 of the 47 empty houses. The widow McAward and her seven children walked out and into the rain uttering 'terrifying cries' and fell to the ground in despair while their cabin was being demolished. As the keening intensified, many onlookers shed 'tears of sympathy'. On the way out an eighty-year-old man 'reverently kissed the doorposts with all the impassioned tenderness of an emigrant leaving his native land'. Without any resistance the evictors completed their task in three days and then rounded up and impounded the livestock. A few families were readmitted as caretakers or tenants but the others had to spend several days and nights near their ruined hovels shivering from the cold and rain. [33] One old man was apparently driven mad by this ordeal. Those who accepted the offer of free passage to the antipodes travelled by train to Dublin escorted by a young clergyman, Father James McFadden, who would later achieve fame as the rebel priest of Gweedore. Sullivan arranged a banquet in their honour in town before they embarked for Liverpool and thence Australia. [34]

The Derryveagh evictions provoked indignant editorials and letters to the editor at home and abroad. Among other papers the *Galway Press*, *Morning Star* (London), and *Western Daily Mercury* (Plymouth) denounced this 'ghastly, horrifying' atrocity as well as the laws that allowed men like Adair to 'exterminate 280 Donegal peasants'. One leader writer condemned the insecurity of tenants-at-will and accused 'the English empire' of harbouring a 'diabolical hatred of the Irish race'. The *Cork Examiner* called Adair 'a poor, erring worm' devoid of common sense and humanity, who had sentenced his tenants to 'beggary and degradation' if not death out of 'blind, stupid, brutal, wicked' vengeance. The *Freeman's Journal* exonerated the tenants from any role in Murray's murder and deplored the laws that enabled Irish landlords to wipe out the peasantry. All this publicity inspired some Protestants as well as Catholic members of the Donegal Celtic Relief Committee in Australia to send money for the relief of Adair's victims.[35]

Like Lord Bishop Plunket, Adair seemed impervious to odium. However, he did take death threats seriously and imposed the cost of extra police and their barracks on the ratepayers. In Parliament Vincent Scully, MP for County Cork and brother of the notorious evictor, William Scully of Ballycohey, questioned Adair's fitness to serve as a magistrate given the harsh treatment of his tenants. On the other hand, the American journalist, W. H. Hurlbert, who toured Ireland twenty-five years later, called these evictions 'a blessing in disguise' because the descendants of these tenants were now relatively happy and prosperous in their new environs overseas.[36] Once again, as with Partry, the *Illustrated London News* missed a golden opportunity to depict an Irish eviction preferring instead to portray Garibaldi's campaign in Italy, British royalty, naval manoeuvres, shipwrecks, cathedrals, and the civil war in America. Two years later another unsolved homicide in Derryveagh added more notoriety to this estate.

In 1870 an Irish-American journalist, Patrick Sarsfield Cassidy, a native of Derryveagh, published a sensation novel, *Glenveigh, Or the Victims of Vengeance*, that was serialised in the *Boston Pilot*. Based on intimate knowledge of the district, this tale featured a villain named Adams –and his son Bob – who conspire to murder a Scottish shepherd (Murray) whose farm they coveted for the purpose of sheep ranching. After 'sweep[ing] the scum of wretched animals' or profitless tenants off the land, the social climbing Adams derives pleasure from pulling down the cottages by means of oxen and thugs hired from Glasgow's docklands while 500 police stand guard. The victims submit meekly to their fate but curse this 'grasping, grinding' Scottish tyrant as 'begot between the Devil and one of the old Highland witches'. Brutal arrests follow Murray's murder. One old man kneels down and kisses the doorposts before quitting his hovel; a young girl is beaten senseless by a bailiff; and the evicted tenants emigrate to North America.[37]

The Derryveagh evictions also inspired at least four epic poems or ballads quoted by Liam Dolan at the end of his account. These ranged from Thomas Nielson Underwood's ballad quoted at the outset of Cassidy's novel to Dominic O'Ceallaigh's centenary tribute in 1961. Underwood's verses dwelled on the 'the heart of hate' that uprooted a 'happy, harmless race…by rude and reckless men'. 'The wrecker and the sheriff, and the throng of armed slaves', he wrote

> Moved on in desolation, like wreck divided waves;
> From house to house they passed along and razed them to the ground,
> Till all along the mountains' sides no standing cot was found.

. . . .

'Twere nobler far for men to die in freedom's glorious fray,
Than crouch in fear and wait the fate that wildernessed Glenveigh.

·   ·   ·   ·   ·   ·   ·   ·   ·

Think, think, the Desolator has his eyes upon your home, –
Fix the day for your redemption, or his force and greed will come! [38]

ORMONDE/COOLNAGHMORE

In the spring of 1861 a remarkable eviction took place on the Ormonde estate in County Kilkenny where a form of tenant right supposedly prevailed. At the expiration of her lease, a young and recently married woman named Cormack received a notice to quit her farm at Coolnaghmore in the parish of Callan even though she had offered to pay a higher rent for renewal. The Catholic agent, John Walsh, and his employer, the English-born Marchioness of Ormonde (a Paget) stood firm. The Cormacks were no ordinary tenants. In fact, they were highly respectable farmers living in a substantial house. Over the course of two centuries they had reclaimed many acres of bogland or swamp and had invested at least £1,500 in housing thereby enhancing the value of the premises. Apparently, they had long enjoyed the friendship of the Butler family. According to Daniel Welply, the Cormack's well-to-do relative and trustee, two family members had apparently saved the lives of two marquesses. In the first case Lord Ormonde had sent for 'his trusty friend' Cormack who helped to repel a lethal attack by Whiteboys. And in the second case, a Mrs Cormack, kinswoman of the Butlers, took in the sickly young heir to the title and nursed him through a virulent septic infection.

Evidently the Cormacks' record of loyalty did not impress her ladyship who denied that they had done much to improve their farm and seemed determined to lease the premises to a Protestant. While the Partry evictions were taking place, the sub-sheriff of Kilkenny led a company of Royal Artillerymen towards Coolnaghmore house. Because no bailiffs were willing to do the dirty work, the agent hired a few deferential tenants to empty the house. The editor of the *Cork Examiner* called this a 'sad – almost savage case' that would never have been tolerated in England. Reluctantly, Welply who was also an auctioneer, sold off the Cormacks' furniture. On the same day, the young bride's former coachman arrived at her temporary home to serve another ejectment writ for a small farm held nearby.

Within a month of her eviction the former Miss Cormack was dead – allegedly from 'a broken heart'. As the *Galway Press* put it, she had gained 'possession of the land of her forefathers' and not even the great house of Ormonde could take this away from her. 'Miss Cormack is free from the strife of life.

Landlord law cannot reach her now.' However exceptional, this case received much notice in the local press and damaged the reputation of the most noble house of Butler. In a long letter to the *Cork Examiner*, Welply, who quoted Bentham at one point, ranked this callous deed alongside the evictions at Derryveagh and Partry. At least Adair and Plunket deserved some credit, he added, for trying to justify their conduct. One can only wonder how long it took for the blot of Miss Cormack's eviction and death to fade from the Ormondes' ancient escutcheon. [39]

SCULLY/BALLYCOHEY

If obstructing the evictors was rare during the 1860s, some of William Scully's tenants proved the exception to the rule. The youngest son of a wealthy Catholic gentry family from Tipperary, he plunged into land speculation in both Ireland and America while still in his twenties after his older brother, James, had been murdered in 1842. Consumed by the profit motive, he antagonised the tenants around Ballycohey by demanding more industry and higher rents. In 1849 a jury acquitted him of the charge of shooting two young sons of an evicted tenant. But in May 1865 he attained much more notoriety by being found guilty of assaulting Bridget Teahan while serving a writ in the middle of the night. She accused him of striking her with a stick in a fit of anger. At the end of a sensational trial the judge ordered him to pay the plaintiff £80 in damages and spend a year in jail. This stern and unbending landlord demanded that his Irish tenants sign a 'despotic' lease that gave him the power to evict with only 21 days' notice. In addition, they were required to pay the rent six months in advance thereby eliminating the hanging gale.[40]

On rent collection day Scully would sit at his desk between two loaded revolvers with a constable standing nearby. Infuriated that so few tenants turned up to sign the new lease, he set out on 14 August 1868 to make an example of one holdout, Michael O'Dwyer, and serve more notices to quit. Warned of the danger, he armed himself 'like Robinson Crusoe in the neighbourhood of the Cannibals'. Arriving at O'Dwyer's farm he led a squad of bailiffs and police in an assault on a fortified barn. Suddenly the defenders opened fire from the loft killing one constable as well as a promising young man named Darby Gorman. Several bullets struck Scully in the jaw and neck. (Both local legend and A. M. Sullivan attributed his survival to a chain-mail vest, described as 'a helmet on his stomach'. But Scully denied this rumour.) Despite his non-fatal wounds Scully blazed away with his rifle and revolver but the fourteen defenders escaped through a hole in the roof and scattered. Although their identity was well known, they eluded the police. Vigorously defending his actions, Scully insisted that he had treated his tenants in a 'legal … equitable and just' manner. After his wounds healed, he sold the property and headed for America where he amassed a fortune through shrewd land investments. All told he bought some 250,000 acres in four Midwestern states and made almost as many enemies in America as he had back home.

What came to be known as 'Scullyism' meant high rents and stringent rental agreements that did nothing to enhance the reputation of Irish landlords as a class. But it did inspire one ballad about 'Rory of the Hill' swearing vengeance on Scully for having evicted his mother. A poem by J. J. Finnan celebrated the shooters at Ballycohey, who had fought against Scully, the 'black livered Nero'.

> If Irishmen all had their faith and reliance
> If Irishmen showed their bold front of defiance
> Our land they could wrest from the big Saxon bully
> And smash him the same as these heroes did Scully.

The Ballycohey 'ambuscade' became 'the sensation of the day' in nationalist newspapers. However, the *Freeman's Journal* blamed this 'fearful tragedy' on the land laws rather than Scully who was 'only playing out the landlord game'. And the *Cork Examiner* opined that 'insecurity' of tenure was the 'giant evil' that made men 'reckless, idle, desperate'. This 'horrid slaughter' should remind everyone that peace would never come to Ireland 'until the tiller of the soil is adequately protected from caprice and tyranny'. Around this part of Tipperary the heroism of O'Dwyer and his thirteen comrades was not forgotten and in 1968 a stone column was erected in a cemetery near Ballycohey to commemorate their 'Fight Against Landlordism'.[41]

IRISH LAND ACT, 1870

The decade drew to a close with the Liberal Party's electoral victory in 1868, the disestablishment of the (Anglican) Church of Ireland, and the drafting of the Landlord and Tenant (Ireland) Act of 1870 that extended the so-called Ulster custom to the rest of the country. In effect, Gladstone's labyrinthine measure allowed tenants who had been arbitrarily forced out or 'disturbed' for reasons other than non-payment of rent to apply to an arbitration court for compensation to cover their improvements. Although the custom was not confined to Ulster and varied widely from one estate to another, it usually granted an outgoing tenant the right to sell his 'interest' and 'goodwill' in the holding – based on improvements made during his occupancy – to the highest bidder with or without the agent's consent. As James Godkin put it rather floridly, Ireland had long suffered from a serious wasting 'disease' caused by the Saxon oppression of the Celts and Gladstone was the 'great physician' who could cure this long suffering patient. The Ulster custom did not 'guarantee' fixity of tenure if the tenant failed to meet his rent obligations.

The Land Act did not define the custom clearly let alone distinguish it from other forms of tenant right; and only solicitors steeped in land law fully understood all the provisions that ranged from 'away-going crops' to quit rents. Designed to force landlords to pay outgoing tenants for improvements, this measure made it much harder for them to evict if a court deemed the rent exorbitant. Tenants on holdings valued at more than £15 could not be removed for less than one year's arrears but those in arrear were ineligible for compensation if evicted. While the act protected many tenants from arbitrary eviction, some agents promptly drew up leases that nullified some of the crucial provisions and then gave tenants a choice between signing and ejectment. Beyond a modest clause that enabled affluent tenants to buy their holdings, this measure also offered minor benefits to leaseholders. As a result, roughly one-third of the 3,625 tenants evicted during 1871–6 received an average compensation of £86.

Deploring all the denunciations of landlords in 'the cheap popular papers' as tyrants and rent-extortioners, Peter Fitzgerald, the well-intentioned Knight of Kerry, took advantage of this act in 1872 to notify some of his tenants on the island of Valencia of his plan to square farms in order to make them more productive. Improving tenants would be assigned to take over the new holdings, but the others would have to leave. However, to spare the latter any undue 'pain and suffering' he promised to compensate them for their 'disturbance'. Few tenants could afford to take their landlords to court unless subsidised by the League. In short, Gladstone's Land Act failed to stop either evictions or the serving of 21,572 notices to quit between 1875 and 1880. Not surprisingly, the rising star of conservative Toryism, Lord Salisbury, accused this measure of setting a bad precedent by 'bribing one class and plundering another'.[42]

PORTRAYING EVICTION

One painting of an Irish eviction dating from the famine aftermath originated in America, where the well-known Cincinnati artist William Henry Powell produced *The Eviction (A Scene From Life in Ireland)* (Plate 4).[43] Reminiscent of Robert George Kelly's *An Ejectment in Ireland*, this picture (and the colour lithograph derived therefrom in 1871) portrays a dying man lying on a bed of stones with a crucifix on his chest surrounded by a semi-circle of grieving friends and relations. His white jacket or blouse suggests both innocence and a shroud. Near him a woman balances a bundle of household goods on her head in the manner of a Native American squaw rather than an Irish peasant woman. The priest raises his eyes heavenward while administering the last rites. In the centre the soldier son, recently returned from the Crimean war minus an arm, makes a vengeful gesture with his other arm. The farmer on the left wields a pitchfork defiantly near two mounted constables. On the far right a mother holds her dead infant next to a small coffin. A Madonna-like mother cradling a baby stands above them. In the rear a second eviction is unfolding. A stricken man lies near his swooning wife as the sheriff and the agent sit astride their horses beneath a large umbrella calmly surveying the scene. The twenty stanzas accompanying the print describe an all too familiar event that resonates with loss, despair, and resentment.[44]

MORE EVICTION FICTION

Several melodramatic novels highlighted eviction in this period. Their plots are driven by the usual assortment of wicked landlords, sinister agents, and scheming solicitors who lust after not only land but also the nubile women whose parents they have wronged or evicted. The English writer, J. G. Barrett ('Erigena'), set *Evelyn Clare* (1870) in the west of Ireland at the height of the penal laws. The eponymous heroine is an Anglo-Irish heiress, whose fiercely anti-Catholic mother wants her to marry a dour Protestant parson. Evelyn recoils from this suitor and falls in love with a handsome, young French general named Louis DeVoy, who is a devout Catholic. The absentee landlord, Lord Ironhoof, whose estate lies nearby, orders his agent to evict a kindly tenant, Richard O'Shea, for having harboured a priest. After performing the last rites for O'Shea's dying daughter, Father Dwyer tries and fails to prevent the sheriff's men from emptying the house wherein the dead girl lies. In vain O'Shea fights off the evictors with an iron pike but is felled by a pistol butt. Dumping the daughter's corpse in the snow, the bailiffs burn down the house as the crowd cries for revenge. Evelyn, who is 'at heart' a Catholic, elopes with DeVoy to France where they marry in Notre Dame Cathedral. On their voyage back to Ireland the boat founders in a storm. The pregnant Evelyn is rescued, but her husband is presumed to have drowned. She gives birth to a son and spurns Lord Ironhoof's marriage proposal. The villainous land agent and magistrate Hogg then hires two thugs to murder Mrs O'Shea and her children because he covets their land. But her young son Richard slays the would-be assassins. Hogg betrays Lord Ironhoof by covertly selling his land but his plot to murder his master fails. DeVoy turns up alive and well, embraces his wife and infant son Gerald, and discovers that his mother is a local woman who had given him up for adoption. In yet another felicitous closure, the DeVoys become exemplary landlords and live long enough to see the penal laws repealed. [45]

In William Upton's novel, *Uncle Pat's Cabin* (1882), Davey McMahon and his family are evicted in 1863 from their farm at Gourbawn in County Limerick by a landlord named Pakenham. The evil landgrabber, Tom Cassidy, takes over the farm and bungles not only a burglary but also an attempt to kill Davey's daughter, Kathleen, because she has spurned his advances. She emigrates to America; her parents die homeless and heartbroken; and the son, Johnny, ambushes Cassidy, who dies of fright. Once again the novelist reassures readers that the victims of eviction will sooner or later be avenged. [46]

Mrs Lorenzo Nunn's novel, *Heirs of the Soil* (1870), begins with the expulsion of several families by a landlord named Ormsby during the Fenian era. While the sheriff's party storms the house of Terry and Tom McGwire, the enraged crowd throws stones at the police and soldiers, who charge the protesters. To avert a fusillade old Terry walks out cursing the landlord, the agent, and every Sassenach law. Although reinstated as caretaker, he dies of a broken heart before dawn. Fenian skirmishes and Ribbonmen conspiracies provide the context for a love story involving the beautiful May Langley, whom Ormsby wants to marry. But the dashing hero Hugh Dudley wins her hand and the evicting landlord dies at the hands of Ribbonmen. [47]

VERSIFYING EVICTION

The Great Famine and its aftermath challenged poets, balladeers, and songwriters to convey the consequences of eviction and exile. As Georges Zimmermann has pointed out, these 'enduring grievances' were not confined to Ireland but there they attained 'great intensity' and often 'shade[d] into the political'. [48] Besides lamenting the loss of hearth and farm, these songs and poems paid tribute to the heroes and martyrs of the struggle for independence and demonised evicting landlords. A good example of the ex-tenant's profound nostalgia for the hills and valleys of home is 'The Emigrant's Farewell to Donegal' wherein he bids a tear-stained adieu to 'dear Erin' because five poor acres could not support the family. 'Banished' from his 'native land', he crosses the ocean and enters the 'land of liberty' with fond hopes that his true love will join him. At least the absence of 'rents or taxes' eases his anguish at leaving 'my native and old Donegal'. [49]

One eviction song, 'The Irish Tenant Farmer's Lament', begins with the loss of the old homestead owing to rack rents and high taxes. Pat Roe's arrears have reached the point of no return and his 'grief and woe' spill over when the sheriff's party arrives:

When I saw my cabin level'd where first I drew my breath
And my children crying round me unto me it was second death
My brain it reel'd I stagger'd fell & crye'd where will you go
For shelter with your family now poor Pat Roe.

Wandering without food or shelter, the family is forced to enter the work-house where:

My wife died broken-hearted when she found we were exile'd
When I think of her departure with greif [*sic*] I near go wild
And often down my furrowed cheeks the briny tears do flow
For her that's dead who in youth was
Wed to por [*sic*] Patt Roe.

Poor Pat does not live to see the day when 'the struggling tenant farmer' would own his house and land and the peasantry would 'neither want or [*sic*] misery know'.[50]

While languishing in prison, the Fenian writer, Charles J. Kickham, wrote a famous song in 1857 about eviction:

My name is Patrick Sheehan,
My years are thirty-four;
Tipperary is my native place –
Not far from Galtymore;
I came of honest parents –
But now they're lying low –
And many a pleasant day I spent
In the Glen of Aherlow.

My father died; I closed his eyes
Outside our cabin door;
The Landlord and the Sheriff, too
Were there the day before –
And then my loving mother,
And sisters three also,
Were forced to go with broken hearts
From the Glen of Aherlow.

For three long months, in search of work,
I wandered far and near;

I went unto the Poorhouse
For to see my mother dear –
The news I heard nigh broke my heart;
But still in all my woe
I blessed the friends who made their graves
In the Glen of Aherlow.

Bereft of home, and kith and kin –
With plenty all around –
I starved within my cabin,
And slept upon the ground!
But cruel as my lot was,
I ne'er did hardship know,
Till I joined the English army,
Far away from Aherlow.

The poem ends with Sheehan's rapid decline and fall after the siege of Sebastopol. Blinded by a shell burst, he will never see his 'own sweet Aherlow' again. Back in Ireland his army pension runs out and he becomes a beggar who lands in 'Dublin's dreary jail'. The moral of this sorry tale is all too clear:

For if you join the English ranks,
You'll surely rue the day.[51]

One dramatic contest between an aggrieved tenant and his agent produced a capital crime, a great escape, and a memorable ballad. At the end of July 1862 Michael Hayes, a 61-year-old bailiff who was reviled as 'Black Mick' for all the evictions he had carried out on orders from the Munster agent and attorney, John Walter Braddell, showed up at Dobbyn's Hotel in Tipperary town. Entering a room used by Braddell as an office, he tried to pay the rent on the twelve-acre farm at Carrigmore, County Limerick, from which he had been evicted. The harsh agent of a harsh Limerick landlord named Colonel Hare, Braddell had made good use of Hayes's strong-arm methods for years and they remained close friends until the former decided to replace him with a younger man. For dismissing and then evicting Hayes, Braddell was asking for trouble because the tenant and his sons were violent men. After Hayes's offer to pay his rent had been rebuffed for the third time, he pulled out a pistol and shot the agent in the stomach before escaping through a rear window. The mortally wounded Braddell staggered outside and died shortly after making a sworn statement identifying his assailant. For months the police pursued the shooter far and wide. The elusive Hayes first fled west and then north taking refuge with local people who now regarded him as a hero for having dispatched a despised agent. Despite the allure of reward money totalling £500 and a media blaze of apparent sightings, he eluded his pursuers from Limerick to Galway and beyond. According to legend he survived on the strength of his wits and new-found celebrity. After some island-hopping off the coast of Connemara, he spent six months on Inishboffin before heading for Scotland and thence New York City where he died in obscurity.

Besides countless newspaper articles Hayes inspired an Aesopian ballad, 'The General Fox Chase' (1862), about the hunt for this villain turned hero. According to one version, Hayes punished Braddell – a 'fool and knave' – for having evicted him from his ancestral home. After stealing his oppressor's ducks and geese and 'murdering all his drakes', he took to his heels. Transformed into a 'bold and undaunted fox' he eluded the relentless hounds who sought him from Tipperary to Wexford and then Kerry and Clare. Hounded into Galway and then Mayo, the weary fox paused at Swinford town to catch his breath and drink a dram. While inside the pub, he heard the 'dreadful cry' of horses. Bereft of den or covert he slipped away in the dark to Castlebar and then sailed to 'a foreign clime'. Safely arrived in 'the land of liberty', he cared not 'a fig for all my foes'. In this way the wily Hayes redeemed himself and became a champion of tenant right far beyond Carrigmore. Thanks to sung performances of this ballad and a well-informed Irish television documentary made in 2005, the saga of Hayes the evicting bailiff or evicted farmer lives on to this day.[52]

One anonymous poem dwells on the plight of a young mother facing eviction:

> Pity! Oh, pity! a little while spare me;
> My baby is sick – I am feeble and poor;
> In the cold winter blast, from my hut if you tear me,
> My lord, we must die on the desolate moor.
>
> 'Tis vain, for the despot replies but with laughter,
> While rudely his serfs thrust her forth on the wold;
> Her cabin is blazing, from threshold to rafter,
> And she crawls o'er the mountain, sick, weeping, and cold.
>   .   .   .   .
> Vainly she tries in her bosom to cherish
> Her sick infant boy, 'mid the horrors around,
> Till, faint and despairing, she sees here babe perish;
> Then lifeless she sinks on the snow-covered ground.[53]

A long and prosaic poem about landlord and tenant relations came from the pen of William Allingham born in Donegal whose job as a custom-house officer gave him ample time to write poetry and edit works as well as travel and consort with illustrious authors.[54] Written shortly after the Partry and Derryveagh evictions, *Laurence Bloomfield or Rich and Poor in Ireland* was serialised in *Fraser's Magazine* in 1862–3. Dedicated to Samuel Ferguson, this ballad is populated with images of 'Paddies, Priests, And pigs, those unromantic beasts, Policemen and Potatoes!' James Pigot the callous agent is a profit-driven social climber who evicts tenants right and left. His nemesis or antithesis, Bloomfield, is the classic 'good landlord'. An enlightened, compassionate, Cambridge-educated landowner and Irish patriot – 'Irish born and English bred' but nursed by 'a Keltic peasant' – he seeks to relieve the suffering of his tenants. He refuses to betray the names of local Ribbonmen or evict the hard-working 'Paddies'. When Pigot orders the clearance of Ballytullagh hamlet,

> Soon from house to house is heard the cry
> Of female sorrow, swelling loud and high,
> which makes the men blaspheme between their teeth.
> Meanwhile, o'er fence and watery field beneath
> The little army moves through drizzling rain;
> A 'Crowbar' leads the Sheriff's nag; the lane
> Is enter'd, and their plashing tramp draws near;
> One instant, outcry holds its breath to hear;
> 'Halt!' – at the doors they form in double line,
> And ranks of polish'd rifles wetly shine.
>
> The Sheriff's painful duty must be done;
> He begs for quiet – and the work's begun.
> The strong stand ready; now appear the rest,
> Girl, matron, grandfather, baby on the breast,
> And Rosy's thin face on a pallet borne;
> A motley concourse, feeble and forlorn.
> One old man, tears upon his wrinkled cheek,
> Stands trembling on a threshold, tries to speak,
> But, in defect of any word for this,
> Mutely upon the doorpost prints a kiss,
> Then passes out for ever. Through the crowd
> The children run bewilder'd, wailing loud;
> Where needed most, the men combine their aid.

The evicted peasants wander down the road vowing they will never enter the workhouse. After a woman lays a curse on Pigot, a Ribbonman shoots him dead. In the happiest of endings Bloomfield uses his initiative, ecumenicism, and money to make the estate prosper.[55]

In his poem, 'The Eviction' (1868), Robert Burke pilloried a landlord who has driven out 'the white-haired father ... the shrivelled mother ... the stalwart son ... the youthful widow' as 'a long wild cry, a mournful moan/Came though the leafless trees'. The houses are tumbled and the victims lose 'all they loved in life'. Whereas the family members who emigrated to America were able to 'gaze on Freedom's sky', those who stayed behind were hired to level the houses of their kith and kin. All was not lost, however, because one fine day 'the tyrant lord' was found lying 'stark and dead within his pillared hall!' The familiar yearning for vengeance or retributive justice remained foremost in this poet's imagination.[56]

Last but not least, Jeremiah O'Donovan Rossa reinscribed the sad fate of so many young Irishmen driven out of their homes. Following expulsion they enlisted in the British army, served overseas, returned to Ireland, and embraced Fenianism. Several stanzas in 'A Fenian Ballad' convey the consequences of the famine clearances:

> The Bailiff with the 'notice' came – the bit of ground was gone –
> I saw the roof-tree in a flame – the crow-bar work was done.
> With neither house nor bed nor bread, the Workhouse was my doom,
> And on my jacket soon I read: 'The Union of Macroom'.
>
>   .   .   .   .
>
> My mother died of broken heart; my uncle from the town
> Brought for her a horse and cart and buried her in Gleown.
> I joined the 'Red Coats' then – mo léir! What would my father say?
> And I was sent in one short year on service to Bombay.
> With famous Captain Billy O, I joined the Fenian band.
> And swore, one day, to strike a blow to free my Native Land.
>
>   .   .   .   .
>
> Back in this sinking isle again, where vultures drink our blood,
> Friends are scattered, starved or slain – I'm told I'm cursed by God,
> That I could swear my life-long days to serve from Pole to Pole
> In any other cause but this, with safety to my soul.
> How can it be by God's decree I'm cursed, outlawed and banned
> Because I swore, one day, to free my trampled Native Land.[57]

FOUR

THE FIRST LAND WAR
1879–83

'I'll never lave myself be evicted from the farum that
we reclaimed from the wild, naked mountain.
I don't care what'll become of me. Oh! my poor wife and
childhre, what'll ye do athout house or home now?'

WILLIAM C. UPTON
Uncle Pat's Cabin or Life Among the Agricultural Labourers
(Dublin, 1882), p. 1

'Tenants will do anything rather than be evicted. They have
no occupation to turn to. Disturbance is ruinous to them.'

Times, 1 January 1881

'The people ... cling to their inhospitable mountains
as a woman clings to a deformed or idiot child.'

BERNARD BECKER
Disturbed Ireland (London, 1881), p. 37.

'I have never known a man leave a farm unless compelled.'

SAMUEL M. HUSSEY
Reminiscences of An Irish Land Agent, p. 204.

———

From 1865 to 1877 landlords and agents along with strong farmers, moneylenders, and shopkeepers enjoyed a welcome burst of prosperity. One telling sign of the economic recovery was the sharp decline in arrears as well as evictions for non-payment on well-managed properties. A small sample of ten estates located mainly in Leinster reveals that combined arrears fell from £21,786 in 1863 to just under £9,000 in 1870. During this period many landlords lavished thousands of pounds on their Big Houses and pleasure grounds; and a few even invested a little money in draining wetland and other capital improvements. Moreover, some consolidated and refinanced their debts or family charges through mortgage loans at seductively low interest rates from such friendly lenders as the Church of Ireland, St Patrick's College, Maynooth, and British insurance companies. This borrowing and spending spree made them all the more reluctant to lower rents after 1879.

The agricultural boom came to a jarring halt after 1878 when prolonged cold, wet weather ruined harvests and cheap imports depressed crop and cattle prices. The value of the potato crop soon fell by some £7 million. The severe depression led to a tight credit squeeze that crippled the ability of smallholders to pay not only rent but also the interest on debts to shopkeepers or money-lenders. The economic downturn also strained the resources of small to middling tenant farmers, who flooded estate offices with requests for abatements. By the end of 1881 arrears on those ten estates had soared to £26,000; and tensions between landlords and tenants had erupted into widespread and at times open conflict.[1]

Robert Kirkpatrick's sterling study of landed estates in mid-Ulster in the early 1880s argues convincingly that southern and western landlords were not alone in suffering financial reverses and acute strife with their tenants. The tactics adopted to cope with this crisis varied according to personalities, politics, agents' advice, and local conditions. Great estates often bred great arrears. Lenient proprietors like Lords Erne and Gosford, the Duke of Abercorn, and Trinity College Dublin had tolerated large arrears for years and seemed reluctant to obtain notices to quit except in hopeless cases. On the Duke of Manchester's property in Armagh arrears rose from half of the £18,000 rental in the mid-1870s to 80 per cent or £14,397 by the end of 1879. Arrears on the Duke of Abercorn's 63,500-acre estates in Donegal and Tyrone had averaged around £40,000 before 1880. But by 1881 these had soared to £58,000. The amount of unpaid rent on the Belmore and Gosford estates in Fermanagh and Tyrone as well as Cavan and Armagh respectively increased fivefold between 1879 and 1880. One exception to this rule was Sir Victor Brooke's well-managed Colebrooke estate in Fermanagh where arrears came to a mere £94 in 1878 on a rental of £15,000 and then increased to only £1,633 in 1881. When it came to rents received, the landed magnates of Ulster fared much better than their counterparts in western Munster and Connacht. On Lord Kenmare's estate at Killarney arrears reached 89 per cent of the rental by 1882, while those on the Cosby estate at Stradbally, Queen's County rose tenfold between 1876 and 1881. Of course, landlords strapped for cash were less indulgent and more likely to threaten or obtain decrees for non-payment after 1879, as the correspondence of Trinity College's board of estate management amply reveals.

As arrears piled up, so too did the requests, pleas, and demands for substantial abatements. The landowning elite was deeply divided over the necessity or wisdom of reducing rents at this critical juncture. Some argued that the distress of 1879–80 was not as severe as their tenants made out and that since rents had not been raised in good times, they expected their tenants to weather this storm on their own. More generous or prudent landlords, on the other hand, granted temporary reductions that ranged between 10 and 40 per cent based on a sliding scale with the more affluent occupiers receiving the smallest concessions. On estates where no such concessions were forthcoming more and more tenants joined the new Land League and withheld much of their rent. Notices to quit as well as eviction parties soon followed in short order.

After the summer of 1879, remittances received by landlords plunged along with their bank balances. In this vicious circle agents obtained many more ejectment decrees in the hope of squeezing some money out of tenants unable or unwilling to pay the full fare. Thus Sir William Verner's agent, James Crossle, informed him in May 1880 that he had only £600 left in his bank account and the bills were steadily mounting. Soon the payments to Verner's family dependants had to be suspended. At least this agent could derive some satisfaction from having 'quietly' evicted 23 tenants for non-payment with minimal publicity. Lord Belmore's agent boasted that only one tenant had been ejected on the Tyrone property during the 1870s, but he had to press tenants hard for payment because his master was strapped for cash. During 1879 a dozen tenants were served with ejectment decrees for two years' arrears and half of these were executed. Although evictions in Ulster had been the lowest of the four provinces, they soon trebled and in 1881 they actually exceeded those in Munster and Connacht. Economic adversity, moreover, was no respecter of religious denominations. On some estates in the north, Protestant tenants were just as likely to denounce their Protestant landlords and agents and join the Land League as were their Catholic counterparts even when they enjoyed the Ulster custom.[2]

Hard times forced landlords to make hard choices. They could grant abatements and watch their income decline further and their debts to merchants and banks steadily increase. Or they could evict tenants with outstanding arrears and drive them into the waiting arms of local Land League leaders. In extreme cases they could close up the Big House, dismiss all the servants, and save some money by staying in London or on the Continent. In fact, some landlords chose all three options. By contrast, the Knight of Kerry, whose family had resided on the 4,230-acre Valencia estate for five centuries, offered to grant abatements to his 'good friends' – the tenants – if their rents had been set in the 'fat' years when prices were considerably higher than those prevailing in the autumn of 1879. Those whose rents dated from the 'lean' years would receive nothing. Denying all the accusations that they were 'rack-renters', most landlords and their agents at some point threatened ejectment or distraint to obtain long overdue rent while hoping (in vain) to deter tenants from joining the League. Lord Belmore's agent told the Bessborough Commission that this was an effective way to increase receipts on gale days. Lord Howth's agent prised some rent out of several tenants in May 1879 by serving them with decrees while extending the grace period to redeem. In many cases the threat of eviction soon turned into reality. Thus nine of Captain Mervyn Archdale's tenants in Fermanagh were turned out for having failed to pay arrears in excess of 18 months.[3]

As the depression deepened in 1880–1, landlords faced even more pressure to lower their rents. Again their responses to League-backed demands for abatements varied. Besides granting reductions of up to 40 per cent, generous owners in mid-Ulster and elsewhere provided tenants in dire need with seed potatoes, fuel, and clothing. At the opposite end of the spectrum, however, landlords refused abatements on the grounds that their rents already came close to Griffith's valuation and had not been raised for years.

It took more than impersonal factors and landlord intransigence to ignite a national agitation for both Home Rule and the abolition of landlordism. What brought about the land war was not just the economy but also the confluence and co-operation of three outstanding political leaders – the plebeian and Catholic Davitt, the aristocratic Protestant, Charles Stewart Parnell, and the resourceful Irish-American republican, John Devoy. Parnell was much more than a charismatic and practical politician. His deep roots in the County Wicklow gentry with all its privileges did not prevent him from acquiring an impressive if not profound grasp of the issues surrounding Irish land tenure. Although no political economist, he insisted, as Liam Kennedy points out, that the real value of any farm came mostly from the improvements made by the occupier who was therefore entitled to a major share of any proceeds. To the surprise of the political pundits and the general public Davitt, Devoy, and Parnell managed to submerge their profound differences of class, religion, and life experience to build an improbable but effective alliance.[4]

Parnell's willingness to shed the convictions and biases of his class and slowly but surely join in the ambitious effort to abolish landlordism was no less remarkable than Davitt's willingness to turn the sword of Fenianism into the ploughshare of peasant proprietorship. Over the course of five years these leaders arrived at a momentous agreement known as the New Departure that fused the physical force commitment of Fenianism with the moral force imperatives of the 'constitutionalists' designed to deliver Ireland from both landlordism and the Act of Union. As Devoy explained, every rebellion in Ireland had contained 'an agrarian character' and the new agitation to drive the foreign 'tyrants' or landlords back to England was intended as much to spur Irish farmers and labourers to join in 'revolutionary conspiracies' as to provide them with the benefits of 'national self-government'. According to Paul Bew the New Departure sought to 'smash' not only landlordism but also 'the British link', and to achieve the ultimate goal of occupier ownership the landlords would have to sell their tenanted land. Realising the futility of 'the armed struggle', this triumvirate sought to harness the power of a mobilised tenantry and their urban allies to the quest for Home Rule. Taking advantage of the agricultural crisis and building on the land agitation launched in County Mayo, they embarked on an historic campaign to return 'the land to the people' and restore Ireland's parliament.

THE LAND LEAGUE AGITATION

Not even the most aggrieved tenant farmer or the most reactionary landlord could have predicted at the outset of 1878 the eruption of an agrarian agitation over a year later that would consume the countryside and command the attention of officials in Dublin Castle as well as politicians at Westminster. Historians from T. W. Moody and F. S. L. Lyons to James Donnelly, Paul Bew, Sam Clark, Margaret O'Callaghan, Philip Bull, and Fergus Campbell have explored the vital connections between the Home Rule movement and the land question during and after 1879. If they disagree here and there about the immediate and long-term causes of the land war, there is much merit in both Donnelly's emphasis on the impact of the depression on the 'rising expectations' of both the tenantry and their landlords, and Bew's verdict that the deep rift in rural society between the landlords and tenants made 'it likely that an agricultural setback would bring in its wake an increase in dissatisfaction with the land system'. While revisionists like Vaughan embrace the concept of a politically and morally, if not quite financially, bankrupt but non-predatory landlord class, anti-revisionists have hewed closer to the view that such long-standing grievances as so-called rack rents and eviction as well as bitter memories of the famine clearances drove them to rebel after their pleas or demands for substantial abatements of rent had gone unheeded. In fact a constellation of political, social, economic, and climatic factors culminated in the creation of a popular front movement in the autumn of 1879 with a hard core consisting of large and small farmers and their urban allies bent on achieving 'fair rents' and security of tenure. Backed by their politicised priests, they dreamed of restoring 'the land to the people' by dispossessing the landlord class. As for government reactions to the political crisis in Ireland, Margaret O'Callaghan (a disciple of the Cambridge school of 'Cabinet history' that follows the gospel of Gilbert Pinfold whereby politicians 'seek a policy' that will earn them power) has argued that both the Liberal and Tory parties were much more concerned about 'political manoeuvres' at Westminster designed to achieve or hold on to office rather than serve the best interests of Ireland.[5]

The Irish National Land League emerged out of several militant tenants' associations inspired by radical tenant-righters and ex-Fenians. By the spring of 1879 central and western Mayo had become a hotbed of agrarian unrest in large part because four of the biggest landowners, whose combined acreage came close to 275,000, refused to grant significant abatements. Over the summer James Daly, John O'Connor Power, Matt Harris, John Louden, Davitt, and their former Fenian followers joined forces to found the Land League of Mayo that sought to abolish both landlordism and Castle rule. Their immediate and more realistic objective was to lower rents and stop evictions deemed utterly unjust.[6] To achieve these goals members were urged to withhold rent until the sheriff and his bailiffs came knocking on the door with their notices to quit. Tenants and townsmen alike were urged to join forces in a 'challenging collectivity', to use Clark's apt phrase, that would agitate for the radical reform of landlord and tenant relations. At rallies around the county tenant-righters carried banners inscribed with such slogans as 'The Land for the People' and 'Down with the Landlords – Down with the Bailiffs' and they cheered for the French revolution, the Irish republic, and the Zulu nation. Coming out of semi-retirement, Father Patrick Lavelle of Cong deplored the failure of the Land Act of 1870 to curb the landlords' power to raise rents and evict.

Within a few months bad weather, potato crop failures, and the refusal of many landlords to grant significant abatements enabled the Mayo organisation to metastasise into the Irish National Land League with headquarters in Dublin. As Bull points out, by this time many tenants were questioning the legitimacy of rent owed to landlords whose claim to ownership rested on the hollow foundation of conquest and confiscation. League branches soon sprouted up all over the country outside northeast Ulster with parish priests often playing prominent roles and helping to restrain the extremists. Nevertheless some local League leaders clung to their Fenian ideals and rigidly opposed any reconciliation between tenants and landlords.[7]

While Solow considered the land war 'unnecessary', Vaughan has called it a 'fluke' with no winners. Most historians would agree, however, that the principal causes included resentment over the famine evictions, tenant-right associations, Fenian convictions, Isaac Butt's plans for land tenure reform, atrocious weather, the downturn in the agricultural economy, the 'rising expectations' of tenants and landlords alike, and the determination of political and agrarian activists to achieve both Home Rule and land reform by non-violent means.[8]

From the outset the Land League's executive pursued a low-rent campaign by exhorting tenants to pay no more than Griffith's valuation of their holdings – a figure based on an assessment by government valuers made years previously and designed for the purpose of taxation. In practice this valuation hovered around four-fifths of the gross rental. Tenants who complied with the League's dictum were urged to 'pay only at the point of a bayonet' or when the sheriff's party or the distrainers arrived at their door. The rapid spread of League branches across the country exemplified the refusal of this post-famine generation to submit to the awesome forces of landlordism and Dublin Castle. As much as Liberal ministers might deplore 'unreasonable' or 'harsh' evictions, they shared Chief Secretary William Forster's view that any resistance by tenants was 'in nine cases out of ten, a clear attempt at robbery'. Absentee landlords who indulged in multiple evictions may have been the bane of Liberal and Radical MPs but the Castle's responsibility for law and order could not be compromised.

Beyond the avowed aims of fair rents, compensation for improvements, and an end to eviction the League's ultimate goal was occupier-ownership. As David Haire has shown, to achieve these ambitious goals, Land Leaguers kept the Royal Irish Constabulary and British soldiers – not to mention all the civilian officials involved in law enforcement – more than busy. During the turbulent years 1881–2 regular army units reinforced the police at evictions; and even though they did not join the constabulary in besieging barricaded houses, their presence was bound to affect the resisters and their myriad supporters. On several occasions when defenders were repelling the police, army commanders gave orders to load rifles and take aim at those inside and only priestly intervention forestalled serious bloodshed. No matter how repugnant or boring the military might find eviction duty, they played a prominent role in ensuring that the full weight of the law or Dublin Castle was brought to bear on tenants resisting ejectment.[9]

The massive outpouring of nationalist support for the New Departure (an ostensibly non-violent or 'constitutional' mixture of Parnellism, Davittism, and Fenianism) at home and abroad moved the *Freeman's Journal* and other Parnellite newspapers to increase their coverage of evictions, agrarian crimes, Land League meetings, and government prosecutions for 'incendiary' speeches. In July 1881 Parnell asked the young and outspoken journalist, William O'Brien, to become editor of *United Ireland* that served as the League's organ. Reports of tenants defending their homesteads and clashing with the police made scintillating news; and this paper regaled readers with bold headlines and vivid accounts of evictions and boycotting around the country. Provincial papers of a Home Rule hue like the *Connaught Telegraph*, edited by the radical James Daly, filled their pages with reports of League meetings, outrages, evictions, and abatement-granting landlords.[10]

If the landlords were not the predatory rack renters and evictors of nationalist imaginations, the notable exceptions to this rule – men like Scully, Adair, Pollock, Lord Leitrim, and the 2nd Marquess of Clanricarde – made life difficult for other members of that class who rarely indulged in final evictions. According to Vaughan, the landlords as a class had long under-rented their farms thereby enabling strong farmers – notably leaseholders – to reap the benefits of the economic upturn.[11] Ironically, the *Times* of London (30 May 1881), that bastion of Unionism and property rights, anticipated the modern revisionist line by dismissing the nationalist outcry over evictions on the grounds that they were few and that the landlords were fully justified in claiming what was 'fairly due' to them.

The Land League's clarion call for permanent abatements meant that arrears soon doubled or tripled wherever tenants heeded that appeal or simply lacked the money to pay in full. Here and there landlord concessions kept the forces of popular resentment at bay. Thus Lord Dillon announced abatements of between 20 and 30 per cent on his 89,000-acre estates in Mayo and Roscommon in September 1879; and this sign of largesse elicited testimonials of 'the liveliest gratitude for your [lordship's] timely ... noble and generous... [and] benevolent reduction'. The tenants' spokesmen sang the praises of the agent, Charles Strickland, and wished Lord Dillon 'every blessing and happiness and a long life to preside over us auspiciously as you have done heretofore'. They also pledged their 'fidelity, love, respect, and veneration towards your Lordship'.[12] However, such glowing sentiments were short-lived and did not exist wherever the demand for abatements fell on deaf ears.

Representing strong farmers and cattle graziers, the Central Tenants' Defence Association also joined the demand for land reform. In the far west many small farmers directed some of their hostility towards the well-off graziers whose fertile grasslands they coveted. 'Dead set' against these ranchers League members would mutilate their livestock and set fire to buildings or hayricks. Hard times hardened the resolve of men on both sides of law. By the end of this year tenants had abandoned their deferential language and posturing in favour of open defiance when and where their landlords refused to grant abatements. Gone were the florid or fawning memorials and letters from tenants filled with profuse thanks for reductions. In their place came endless requests if not demands for abatements of at least 10 or 20 per cent and the remission of arrears.[13]

Lurking in the background or on the hillsides were Fenian veterans and self-styled 'moonlighters' who yearned to take up arms to free Ireland from the British yoke. However, Parnell remained hostile towards these extremists who threatened to upset the New Departure. Speaking to a huge rally of six thousand people in rainswept Westport on Sunday 8 June 1879, he echoed Bentham, Mill, and Henry George by insisting that landlordism was not 'a natural institution' and benefited only one small class. He hailed the spread of peasant proprietorship throughout France, Belgium, Prussia, and Russia and called for the abolition of landlordism through land purchase because this would benefit the greatest number of people and make the country prosperous. Refusal by the landlords to grant abatements would result in a repetition of the calamity of 1847–8. The time had come, he urged, to break down class barriers through a united effort. 'You must show the landlords that you intend to hold a firm grip of your homestead and lands. You must not allow yourselves to be dispossessed as you were ... in 1847.'[14]

In a speech at Milltown, County Galway, Davitt announced that the League's slogan should be 'Down with landlordism [and] death to eviction'; and at Claremorris he invoked Mill's argument that landlords had no right to receive rent or 'surplus profit' from the soil when all the labour and investment came from their tenants. There was no reason why the latter should have to pay 'exorbitant' rents. Although he dreamed about an armed uprising, he had no illusions about victory and quoted Hamlet to the effect that 'conscience makes cowards of us all'.[15] Davitt's young acolyte, John Dillon, son of the famous Young Irelander, John Blake Dillon, and grandson of an evicted tenant, condemned all landlords as potential or actual evictors. A reluctant convert to 'constitutional agitation', he so despised landlords that in his youth he fantasised about resorting to physical force. If he were 'an Irish peasant', he declared in the House of Commons, he would not hesitate to 'shoot as many' bailiffs or evictors as possible because 'the people' would never regain their land without force as well as unity. And he added for good measure that Irish tenants had just as much right to bear arms as any landlord. That ardent conciliator and co-operativist, Sir Horace Plunkett, regarded Dillon as 'so narrow that he might be honest. I never knew a mind so dominated by its inherited prejudices.' Speaking at Loughrea in March 1881, Dillon opposed the use of arms in resisting eviction but insisted that the League had an obligation to teach landlords that 'eviction was not a paying but a losing game'. In fact, he devoted much of his career to 'fighting the Evictors' and their cherished Act of Union. Another hardcore Land Leaguer, Michael O'Sullivan, declared that free men had an inherent right not only to vote but also to carry a gun and he urged audiences to take up target practice.[16]

At mass meetings all over the south and west, Home Rule MPs and League leaders called for rent reductions and resistance to eviction. They also lobbied for government grants to stimulate rural industries. Funds from Irish-American supporters poured into the coffers of the Land League whose spokesmen at Irishtown, Westport, Ballinasloe, Swinford and elsewhere ranted against evicting and rackrenting landlords and warned that the spectre of the famine clearances would return if the people failed to fight the hereditary foe. They also demanded a state-assisted land purchase scheme that would enable tenants to buy their farms at a fair price. If anything the government's decision to outlaw the Land League and arrest its national leaders on 20 October 1881 gave rise to much more violence against the agents of Dublin Castle and all those connected to 'landlordism'. By the latter term Parnell, Davitt, and their followers meant a system of land tenure characterised by profound social injustice, foreign rule, and eviction – what Davitt called that 'dark, dread shadow which almost always loomed over three or four hundred thousand households'. One harbinger of this rebellion was the assault in December 1879 on Lord Fermoy by a shillelagh-wielding evicted tenant named O'Shea. This attack was all the more brazen for having taken place on the porch of the Limerick County Club, where the 'ruffian' knocked Fermoy unconscious before he was subdued by two club members and handed over to the police.

To escape the dangers of the land agitation some landowners temporarily abandoned the Big House and took their families to London, the continent, and the Mediterranean in an aristocratic exodus. In the autumn of 1881 Lord Annesley embarked on a long cruise on board his yacht, the *Seabird*. From Nice he informed his agent that he would 'stand no nonsense' from any tenants who refused to pay their rent. Unless they were genuinely distressed, anyone who withheld rent, or who showed 'the slightest disrespect', or who belonged to the Land League should be evicted. 'A few sharp examples', he declared, 'will do a world of good & will bring the people to their senses.' From Corfu he wrote in March: 'Your business is to fight my former tenants, but present enemies, by every means in your power assisted by my lawyer.' He would not be satisfied 'until legal steps have been taken against every defaulter on the Down estate'. The outlook was bleak: 'The days of [sentiment?] are ... past. There is no doubt that every Agent in Ireland will pass the rest of his life, or so long as he is an Agent, in fighting with the tenants.'

Another Ulster landlord, the virulently anti-clerical and disgruntled Earl of Charlemont, spent November and December 1880 touring Italian cities. Writing to his agent from Florence, he blamed his exile and poor health on the 'Papist Leaguers' and their priests whom he hated with a passion. Ireland, he insisted, should be put under martial law, Habeas Corpus suspended, and all juries abolished. Moreover, the 'surplus population' of unprofitable smallholders should be forced to emigrate. Both Ireland and India in his opinion were afflicted by overpopulation. For want of government subsidies only 'Providence in the shape of cholera, typhus or starvation' would solve this problem. After this choleric outburst, he advised his agent to buy arms and fortify his premises against the forces of anarchy.[17]

One noteworthy but obscure victim of League persecution was Mrs Caroline Blake of Renvyle House, Letterfrack, County Galway, who faced penury because her tenants had withheld the rent and imposed a boycott. With her estate in chancery she was forced to borrow money from local friends. When her straits became known through press reports, the public subscribed over a thousand pounds in 1893. Only by converting her handsome house into a hotel did she and her daughter manage to hold on. The League also targeted Sir William Gregory who had granted a mere ten per cent abatement in 1879. In a compelling simile he lamented that a no-rent protest was 'creeping on like lava, filling every cranny' on the Coole estate.[18]

Although intimidation during the land war proved to be more covert than overt, there was no lack of non-lethal physical force to punish the League's enemies. The favourite instrument of discipline or control at the local level was the threatening letter that had such a long and rich history in Ireland. In the time-honoured tradition of plebeian intimidation death notices soon littered estates around the country. Just as the followers of Captain Rock, the Caravats, the Carders, Hearts of Steel, and other agrarian rebels had warned their enemies to behave or face the lethal consequences, so too in the early 1880s anonymous writers warned landlords, agents, and bailiffs to obey the League's will or run the risk of death. Any tenant who paid his rent covertly or took over an evicted holding was likely to receive such a threat to his life and property. Landowners and their 'loyal tenants' thus faced an ominous 'conspiracy' designed to deprive them of the 'rights' or powers and privileges they had so long enjoyed. Besides requesting more protection from the police, hundreds of proprietors decided to mount their own counter-offensive by joining such anti-League and anti-Home Rule organisations as the Orange Emergency Committee, the Land Corporation, and the muscular Property Defence Association (PDA). These well-financed landlord combinations often recruited strong-arm Protestants in Ulster – otherwise known as emergency men – to thwart the boycotters and protect 'loyal' tenants from reprisals.[19]

Boycotting, shunning, or exclusive dealing had a long history in Ireland. And the results of such social and economic ostracism often wrecked the lives of the victims. Acts of vandalism and other forms of intimidation were also directed against those who defied the communal will. According to Dublin Castle estimates, agrarian crimes or 'outrages' rose from 301 in 1878 to 863 in 1879 and then to 2,585 in 1880 before peaking at 4,439 in the following year and then declining to 3,433 in 1881. Almost half of these offences consisted of threatening letters, but many of them involved arson and shooting into houses. Some 70 per cent of the 7,808 outrages recorded in 1881–2 took place in Munster and Connacht. An unknown number of these offences arose out of personal feuds or vendettas that stemmed from land disputes and were carried out under the umbrella of the land war. However, in some mid-Ulster counties outrages often followed evictions, whereas in the southwest they occasionally preceded the sheriff's arrival. Despite the ostensibly non-violent nature of the Land League agitation some 69 homicides were classified as agrarian, 49 of which took place in 1881–2, when agrarian offences made up roughly 58 per cent of all recorded crimes. Dublin Castle came to rely heavily on British army units to reinforce the police in dealing with agrarian unrest. Not only did the League's executive lack the ability to control all its branches – let alone Captain Moonlight's marauders – but also, as Parnell once overstated the case, 'moonlighting is our only preventive against eviction'. [20]

Evictions exclusive of readmissions climbed steadily from 834 in 1878 to 1,893 in 1880 and then up to 5,003 in 1882. In Ulster, where evictions had averaged 120 families a year in the 1870s, they reached 497 in 1880 and then peaked at 1,219 a year later. However, almost half of these tenants were readmitted as caretakers or tenants – a figure much higher than in the south and west even though readmission did not guarantee anything like fixity of tenure. Evictions in Ulster amounted to 15 per cent of the national total in 1879 and then climbed to 36 percent in 1881. By contrast, evictions in Munster fell from 33 per cent of the national total in 1879 to 20 per cent in 1881 before rising to 36 per cent in 1883. Over half (52 per cent) of the 8,224 evictions in the country in 1881–2 occurred in Munster and Connacht. In the hope of suppressing some of the unrest and turmoil arising from the growing revolt of the tenantry and their urban allies, the Liberal government resorted to the familiar Peelite formula of the stick and the carrot by mixing coercion with land reform. [21]

When and where tenants hesitated to join the League, it took only a few evictions to change their minds. The ejectment of Malachy Kelly, a strong farmer on the Borrowes estate near Bushfield in Queen's County on 7 February 1880, led to a protest meeting at which Davitt called for a united front to fight the hereditary enemy. Local Leaguers blacklisted Kelly's farm and the caretakers installed there stood in constant fear of a visitation from the nocturnal marauders known as Captain Moonlight or 'Rory of the Hills'. [22]

While the League was composed primarily of Catholic tenants and their urban middle-class allies, many Protestant farmers in mid-Ulster also joined the movement. The latter remained loyal to the League until the Home Rule agitation took precedence after 1883 and raised the spectre of a Catholic-dominated parliament in Dublin. Besides the tenantry, a number of agricultural labourers enrolled in the League even though their agenda conflicted with that of farmers over the issue of wages. The discontent of these rural plebeians led them to form clubs and leagues in the early 1880s culminating in the launch of the Irish Labour and Industrial Union in August 1882. The Land League's executive could not afford to ignore the Union, and Parnell prudently accepted the presidency. But within a year this organisation was swallowed up by the National League. [23]

Subsidised by donors in Greater Ireland and led by resourceful organisers, the League posed a formidable threat not just to landowners but also to Dublin Castle. All over the country branches acted like 'committees of public safety' approving the boycotting and intimidation of anyone who violated their rules. Tenants who paid the full rent due in League-dominated districts ran the risk of being beaten or shot. Other punishments included the mutilation of livestock and the burning of hayricks. 'Land-grabbers' or 'land-jobbers' who took over evicted holdings were rigorously ostracised and only police protection spared many from serious injury or death.

In some respects the agrarian violence of the 1880s echoed the Rockite revolt against landlords, middlemen, distrainers, evictors, and landgrabbers in the southwest during the depression of 1821–4 that James Donnelly has explored so shrewdly and fully in *Captain Rock*. Of course there were differences between the Rockites not to mention the members of all the other agrarian societies that flourished before the famine. Unlike the Rockites the nocturnal marauders of the 1880s did not suffer unduly from Catholic millenarianism and anti-Protestant bigotry; their punishments were less horrific with more firing into houses than persons and no recorded incidents of rape. But then the Leaguers were spared the hated tithes and Orange-hued yeomanry. Also, there were no Protestant middlemen in the 1880s intent on enlisting their subtenants in the anti-rent protest. Not only did the Moonlighters operate well beyond the confines of Cork, Limerick, Tipperary, and adjacent counties, they were also much more politicised, not to say nationalist, than their rebellious precursors owing to the Home Rule movement and the New Departure. And they enthusiastically supported the League's favourite non-violent weapon of communally based boycotting.

Nevertheless, both these agrarian rebellions emerged out of a severe economic crisis aggravated by crop failures that brought together a varied rural populace that ranged from impoverished cottiers to prosperous farmers. With or without the Land League's disapproval, Captain Moonlight's 'knight errants' often indulged in acts of purposeful and vindictive violence. Classic examples of déjà vu included attacks on rent drivers, agents, stewards, process servers, land grabbers, informers, and distrainers of crops and livestock not to mention their addiction to death threats. All of these offences echoed Rockite activities sixty years earlier and reflected the visceral response of tenants made desperate by rising eviction rates in the midst of a profound economic crisis that threatened to ruin them and their families. Like the Rockites the Moonlighters struck hard at 'soft' or unarmed targets with every weapon from stones and pitchforks to firearms and arson. Last but not least, both the older and newer agrarian rebels regarded eviction as the most heinous of all crimes because it not only hurt 'the people' but also offended the Almighty.[24]

Resident landowners with military experience shrugged off the death threats as a minor nuisance, convinced as they were that any ambushers would miss their target or run away at the mere sight of a firearm. Some taught their wives and daughters how to shoot, and few were foolhardy enough to leave the demesne without a loaded weapon or a police escort. Attacks on 'loyal' tenants caused special dismay in Big Houses if only because unlike the landed elite these victims could not leave the district or receive police protection. On the Earl of Kenmare's 91,000 acre estate around Killarney evictions had numbered only around two per thousand tenants between 1878 and 1881, and the owner had spent £33,645 on abatements and improvements. But the receipt of a death threat in November 1880 bothered him far less than the shooting of several tenants in the arms and legs because they had paid the full rent due. This outrage so perturbed the gourmandising Lord Kenmare that he shut down his 'establishment' and took his family to London, thereby depriving estate workers of £480 in weekly wages. The brilliant comic artist, George Cruikshank, once mocked the proverbial threat of violence in the Irish countryside by listing the national sports as 'Throwing the Hatchet, Drawing the Long Bow, Shooting the Moon, And (in effigy out of consideration for Saxon prejudices) Shooting the Landlord.'[25]

The surge in agrarian crime spurred Gladstone's government to charge the League's executive with criminal conspiracy and incendiary speechmaking. The arrest of Davitt in November 1879 along with two other League leaders from Mayo – James Daly and James Killen – had triggered fierce protests around the country. Home Rule papers railed against coercion, rackrenting landlords, and police brutality; and Daly, who edited the influential *Connaught Telegraph*, urged his readers to resist eviction and stop cowardly 'land robbers' from taking over vacant farms.[26] The subsequent show trial of fourteen League leaders including Parnell in December 1880 attracted a huge amount of publicity but ended with an acquittal after the jury failed to agree on a verdict. Nationalists all over the country rejoiced over this outcome. In the meantime British as well as Irish newspapers faithfully reported shootings, cattle maiming, boycotting, and arson attacks – not to mention the rumoured eviction of a nearly naked woman near Kinsale in June 1881. A stone-throwing crowd at Skibbereen led to a serious skirmish with the forces of law and order. As the alarmist *Times* put it, the Irish constabulary were involved in 'a life and death struggle with the anarchists'. On the eve of Dillon's arrest in June the Castle was so fearful of rioting that it proclaimed all of Dublin under the new crimes act.[27]

One Land League song exemplified the defiant stance of this new coalition:

Cheer up your hearts, you tenant farmers, the land you nobly till,
Pay no rent, and keep the harvest, it's posted upon every bill.
If from your homestead you're evicted and on the roadside must lie,
Be advised by Michael Davitt, or in the poor-house you will die,
Pay no rent and keep the harvest, this I am sure is Land League law,
And if the landlord asks you for it give to him an oaten straw.[28]

Desperate to curb this revolt, some landlords evicted the League activists on their estates and seized their chattel if they were in default. Once the local court had approved the ejectment decree, the agent would move to auction off the tenant's interest in his farm – a sum that could reach ten or twenty times the annual rental for an improved holding. Under the Land Act of 1881, however, tenants marked for eviction could redeem within six months provided they paid enough rent to satisfy the agent. At the 'execution sale' of the interest or chattel of a foreclosed farm, angry League supporters would gather to prevent local people from submitting bids thereby forcing the agent to buy the assets for a pittance. [29]

While civil bill decrees rose from 6,738 in 1877 to 22,706 in 1883, less than a quarter of these were actually executed. In Queen's County, writs more than doubled in the next two years, and net evictions soared eightfold to an annual average of 65 between 1879 and 1883. As arrears mounted around the country after 1880, so too did the number of homeless families. Overall the police tallied 980 (gross) evictions in 1878, 2,110 in 1880, and 5,201 in 1882, while readmissions for these years came to 561 or 6.8 per cent of the whole. In mid-Ulster, evictions also rose but over half of the tenants involved were reinstated.[30] In some cases decrees had the desired effect and tenants who could afford to do so paid up. But those burdened with over two years' arrears experienced the threat or reality of eviction that occasionally triggered mild or severe agrarian outrages. [31]

By the spring of 1881 League branches had tightened their grip all over the south and west; and partial failures of the potato crop were causing widespread misery. Most of the goodwill among the tenantry in the 1870s had vanished along with the traditional deferential posturing. Tenants were now demanding an abatement of at least 25 per cent as well as the release of political prisoners – a sure sign of how far grievances over rent and arrears had become entangled with national political issues. In June 1881 Lord Dillon's agent reported that Ballaghadereen was in 'an extremely excited state' and tenants were refusing to pay any rent owing to fear of reprisals. In March 1882 an anonymous tenant in Mayo informed the agent: 'I think that some does not think they will pay rent at all.' The shooting of two men at Kiltullagh 'has fear put in a great deal of the tenants to pay any rent … they want reduction …. I think they mean to have done with Landlords altogether if they can.' Aware that threats of eviction did 'more harm than good', Strickland expressed concern about his master's loss of income and told the estate bailiffs to press the tenants to pay. By the end of 1881 arrears on the estates were approaching £4,000. The *Times'* Irish correspondent noted that poorer tenants were struggling to pay even moderate rents let alone reduce their arrears. Whether threatened or executed, the notice to quit invariably boosted support for the League. All told some 31,000 evictions occurred in the decade 1878–87. Assigning an average of five persons to each family, these numbers translated into 155,000 men, women, and children.[32]

Although this number could not hold a candle to the totals during the famine era, when it came to publicity and political significance, evictions in the 1880s emerged as clear winners. Thanks to the Land League, the Parnellite party, and the nationalist press, evictions became highly politicised events that seriously undermined both landlordism and the Union. Even Fleet Street helped to elicit sympathy for the victims of eviction and antipathy towards their landlords by sending correspondents to remote parts of the country to report on the fate of families who could not or would not pay the rent due and were being driven out into the cold and the rain.

EVICTION CROWDS

Besides boycotting and intimidation, the Land League's revolt involved mobilising huge crowds at eviction sites and wherever process servers and distrainers were at work. Hundreds and even thousands of men and women of all ages would flock from miles around marching to the lively music of brass bands and singing patriotic songs. Local notables mounted on horseback led these boisterous processions wearing green ribbons or bearing banners emblazoned with harps and shamrocks and slogans like 'The Land for the People' and 'Those Who Toil Must Own the Soil'. Some protesters brandished replica pikes and swords. Fiery orators would rant about rack rents, evictions, police brutality, and the Act of Union. Even the aging Father Lavelle came out of semi-retirement to attend a protest meeting near Ballinrobe. What mattered was not just the size of these crowds but their dynamism or readiness to take on the police with fists, cudgels, and stones when the baton charges had exhausted their patience. In late 1880 rumours of a possible uprising in the west prompted nervous officials in Dublin Castle to put the military on stand-by, arrange barrack facilities, and procure thousands of rounds of buckshot to deal with any such outbreak.[33]

Both Samuel Clark and Stephen Ball have emphasised the composite nature of these crowds that contained not only large and small farmers but also publicans, shopkeepers, and artisans. Local circumstances determined whether they became more proactive than reactive. Catholic priests and canons or curates often stood in the front ranks trying to discourage violence. If they did not relish arrest, many of them were ready and willing to risk imprisonment on behalf of their parishioners. These so-called indignation meetings celebrated local identity and served as a form of political theatre acted out dramatically in scenarios all too familiar to the police, magistrates, and Castle officials who had to cope with the consequences.

As for graphic images of Land League demonstrators or activists, Aloysius O'Kelly captured their anger and resolve in a number of striking prints published in 1881–2. In her definitive biography of O'Kelly, Niamh O'Sullivan points out that this talented and versatile artist, draughtsman, and illustrator was also a keen nationalist who shared Fenian convictions with his three brothers. In fact, his picaresque brother, James J., had sat on the Supreme Council of the Irish Republican Brotherhood before joining the Parnellite party and representing North Roscommon in the mid-1880s. The son of a Dublin artisan the enterprising O'Kelly studied under the charismatic J. L. Gérôme in Paris and spent several summers in Brittany along with dozens of other painters who were captivated by the qualities and attire of Breton peasants. By the early 1880s he had developed an eclectic style that ranged from realism to Orientalism. His black and white images of political conflict in Ireland and lush paintings of people and landscapes in Egypt and Morocco attracted many admirers including Vincent van Gogh. Having landed the prestigious position of 'Special Artist' for the *Illustrated London News*, he applied his skills to limning the hardships of the newly politicised peasantry during the first land war. Sympathy for a defiant peasantry made him in O'Sullivan's words 'the most radical Irish artist of his era'.

The subversive nature of his interpretations of the land war emerges clearly in the physiognomies he bestowed on members of Land League crowds. Instead of the frightening Paddy stereotype found in English and American comic magazines of the time, marked by acute prognathism, a high upper lip, and snub-nose, virtually all of O'Kelly's rebellious peasants possess handsome, even aquiline, features that convey both dignity and honesty. In short he went 'against the grain' – to use O'Sullivan's apt phrase – by refusing to demonise or simianize the supporters of the Land League. Given the *ILN*'s role as the leading graphic purveyor and promoter of British imperial might and majesty, this was a significant deviation from the anti-nationalist norm along Fleet Street.

Two examples of O'Kelly's affirmative depiction of Irish agrarian rebels may be cited. In *The State of Ireland: A Sheriff's Sale of Cattle to Pay the Rent* (*ILN*, 18 June 1881), none of the men protesting the forced sale of distrained cattle bears the stigmata of Paddy. Similarly, there is little difference between the facial features of the defiant stone-throwers standing on a cliff in "The State of Ireland: The Affray at Belmullet, County Mayo" (*ILN*, 12 November 1881) and those of the attacking Royal Irish Constabulary. If somewhat idealised, O'Kelly's Land Leaguers could not have been further removed from the menacing monsters that populated Irish political cartoons in *Punch, Judy,* and comparable comic periodicals.[34]

Both the national and local leaders of the Land League deserve credit for organising these displays of communal hostility towards the enforcers of law and order and the functionaries of landlordism. According to Ball, some 25 mass gatherings were held each month during 1880–1 and another four hundred took place over the next four years amounting in all to more than a thousand meetings. Crowds would also turn out to hail a visiting Parnellite MP or welcome a martyr just released from jail. No matter how remote the district they would foregather to protest an eviction or the distraint and forced sale of livestock. Depending on advance notice some protests were highly organised while others were more spontaneous. In the timeless response of tight-knit communities to the 'invasion' by shrieval forces, lookouts would summon crowds with horns, church bells, and word of mouth in order to impede or harass the authorities. A small *ILN* print (Figure 4.1) revealed the primitive but effective early warning system used by villagers near Derrybeg, County Donegal.

Of course, the arrival of the sheriff's party the night before in search of lodging was another sure sign of imminent evictions. Quite rightly, Ball contends that 'popular resistance to eviction was an integral part of Land League strategy' and 'the most prominent example of civil disobedience' during the first land war. These protests, he maintains, were 'part of a wider social and political movement which was progressive and forward looking' and inseparable from the campaign for Home Rule. League activists were convinced that every dispute with a landlord over rent and tenure was the product of brutal conquest and the time had come to undo all the confiscations by an alien elite and restore the land to the 'native Irishry'. Resistance to process serving and eviction not only hampered the sheriff and his men but also severely tested the forbearance of the RIC who were warned about the dire consequences of opening fire on their stone-throwing tormentors. Despite the ever-present threat of physical force, mortal injuries were rare. Remarkably, no more than five people and one constable were killed during all the protest meetings in the early 1880s – a testament to the restraint shown by both sides during these confrontations.[35]

Janet TeBrake has stressed the prominent role played by peasant women to impede the evictors and boycott the League's enemies. Indeed, there was nothing quite like an eviction to break down the traditional 'separation of spheres'; and well

4.1 'Sketches of the Eviction Campaign in Ireland ... Sounding Alarm in a Village on Approach of Eviction Party'. A young boy blows a horn to alert villagers armed with pitchforks to the approach of the sheriff's party. (*ILN*, 27 Nov.1886)

before the launch of the Irish Ladies Land League in January 1881, many women took the lead in stoning or assaulting process servers, bailiffs, and the police.[36]

If the Ladies Land League accepted as members only women who held farms in their own name, most of them being widows, thousands of ordinary tenants' wives and daughters took part in agrarian protests. They brazenly defied the police and helped evicted families to reoccupy their homes illegally. For such transgressions some were arrested and spent time in prison. Peasant women certainly did not require middle-class leadership when it came to repelling the process servers and bailiffs. Davitt, as we will see, was dismayed to see women fighting harder than their menfolk in repelling the evictors and the process servers. At Gweedore, County Donegal, the police arrested 75 disturbers of the peace in May 1881. Twenty of them were women accused of stone throwing or assault. By contrast only three of the 55 men on trial were charged with having thrown stones. During the second land war, moreover, some women showed more courage than the men in defending their homes.[37] Whether or not the League's tacticians assigned women to stand in the forefront of crowds, knowing that the police would be reluctant to baton them, the fact remains that men and women commingled in these communal protests.

While the provincial press carried reports of League rallies and evictions, newspapers in Dublin and London sent special correspondents to provide feature articles about any dramatic events. In fact, the volume of eviction news soared after 1879 accompanied by sensational headlines. As Ball asserts, 'the radical press fostered a spirit of solidarity' among agrarian activists all over the country.[38] So, too, did eviction. Of course, the size and behaviour of crowds varied from one site to another but most of them assembled under the auspices of the local League branch. The standard scenario began with thunderous jeering, groaning, and cursing of the sheriff's party. Threatening gestures like clenched fists and the brandishing of blackthorns were an essential part of the ritual. Whether stones flew depended on the temper of the crowd and the ability of the local clergy to discourage this activity. Quite apart from the overheated rhetoric of speakers about British tyranny and avaricious landlords, an air of menace hovered around these gatherings as hardcore activists directed their anger at the sheriff, the crowbar brigade, and the agent who invariably carried a rifle or revolver.

Seeking turnouts of at least five hundred people, League activists took steps to ensure that friends and neighbours showed up to jeer, curse, and if possible impede the bailiffs in the execution of their duty. The League's national leaders urged tenants to avoid violence in the knowledge that even peaceful protests made good propaganda for their cause. Nationalist newspapers obliged with feature articles about these defiant crowds. Although the fortification of cottages or houses and other siege warfare tactics lay a few years ahead, resistance to eviction usually involved shillelaghs and stones as well as the occasional pitchfork or slane. Volleys of stones or sods of grass may have bruised or discomfited the forces of law and order, but they failed to deter the evictors from completing their mission. Unable to arrest all but a few stone throwers, the police would seize the organisers and speakers at gatherings banned under one coercion act or another.

Whenever a district magistrate feared serious danger to the men under his command, he would read the riot act, and if this step failed to subdue the crowd, then the presiding police officer would order a baton or bayonet charge. Needless to say, most of the ensuing blood flowed from the civilians in the front ranks. On the whole, however, the RIC exercised much more restraint than had been used by their predecessors during the tithes war. And despite much provocation they inflicted fewer casualties on their assailants during the early 1880s than in the Plan of Campaign era.

Near Pallas Station in the Golden Vale, disputes over rent boiled over into ugly confrontations between the police and howling crowds. A rent strike was followed by a boycott of the police; and when one brave tenant 'committed the unpardonable crime' of paying his rent, someone fired a bullet through his front door. Nearby another crowd blocked the transport of an iron police guard hut from the railway station to an evicted farm occupied by a bailiff or caretaker who had also been the target of gunfire. The ensuing trial of strength between the League's 150 hard-core supporters and a massive force of 350 constables, soldiers, cavalry, and artillery men ended with a victory for the Castle as the crowd backed off at the sight of all this armed might and at the sound of Father Ryan's urgent appeals for restraint. To avoid fatalities the chief secretary arranged for the police to carry buckshot instead of the more lethal ball cartridge. However, in October 1881 several volleys of buckshot failed to deter a crowd of four hundred people from throwing stones at Graghill, County Mayo. After two riflemen loaded their carbines with bullets and fired, two women died. The growing militancy of crowds moved Dublin Castle to reinforce the police escorts at evictions and protest rallies with units of the regular army.[39]

The objectives of these crowds were twofold: to 'protect members of the local community from destitution' and to promote radical land reform. While most of these meetings were orderly, the police could not predict the outbreak of violence. And as League branches increased in numbers, confidence, and militancy, Dublin Castle assigned ever-larger contingents of police and soldiers to protect the sheriff's party and minimise the chance of a riot. The odds in favour of a clash with the police invariably rose when and where evictions were in the offing.[40]

CONFRONTATIONS AT BALLA AND CARRAROE

In one of the earliest mass protests against eviction during the first land war several thousand people gathered at Loonamore near Balla, County Mayo on the estate of Sir Robert Lynch-Blosse on 22 November 1879 to hear Davitt and other speakers denounce the imminent eviction of Anthony Dempsey and his family of eight. Illness in the family prompted the sheriff to postpone the eviction for a week. However, Davitt's arrest on the 19th spurred Parnell to fill the breach and he travelled by train from Dublin in the company of Dillon. Upon arrival they were greeted by hundreds of men carrying shillelaghs as well as banners with such slogans as 'Stick to Your Homesteads' and 'No Surrender'. At Dempsey's farm the crowd had swelled to almost 8,000 people who, as William O'Brien recalled, surrounded the 100 police constables in a pincer movement akin to the favourite tactic of Zulu warriors. Fearing encirclement the police looked to their rifles. At this point Parnell sprang into action by beating some of the protesters back with his umbrella thereby heading off any fusillades from the police. The sheriff wisely withdrew his paltry force. At a subsequent 'indignation' meeting several Mayo Land Leaguers joined Parnell in condemning rack rents and evictions as well as the Union. A fortnight later the sheriff returned with a larger escort and drove out the family peacefully. But when a four-year-old boy dashed back inside screaming and crying and hugging a wall, the bailiffs had to haul him out. The agent warned the neighbours against sheltering the Dempseys so they had to spend all day shivering on the roadside before lodging in a hotel.[41]

A much more serious collision took place at the outset of 1880 at Carraroe, lying west of Spiddal in Connemara, where a hated process server named Fenton drew a hostile crowd while serving writs. Fearing for his life, he sought refuge in a house along with his small police escort. Davitt witnessed the fracas and his account rings with a mixture of authenticity and passion. When Fenton and his guards made a dash for the police barracks, they were pursued by a howling horde. In the meantime some local men cornered Fenton's son inside the chapel and forced him to kneel and swear at the altar that neither he nor his father would serve any more writs.

Fenton foolishly ignored this threat and tried to resume his operation on 3 January, when some 500 'mountaineers' came down from the hills to stop him. They were reinforced by over 500 equally angry protestors. Wearing 'bawneens and red petticoats', the women eyed Davitt with suspicion until they recognised him as the League's distinguished leader. Someone had dug a trench across the road to Carraroe and the local people were spoiling for a fight. Davitt sat on a rock overlooking the field of combat taking notes diligently while women and boys kept up a steady barrage of stones and sticks. Fenton foolishly emerged from the barracks to serve more writs; the crowd attacked; and the police charged with fixed bayonets. At least one woman received 'a fearful' cut on her neck. At this point the hitherto passive men in the crowd decided to join the fray. Exposed to volleys of stones, the police panicked and fired shots over the crowd before retreating to the barracks with the terrified Fenton in tow.

The arrival of police reinforcements did not deter the rioters whose numbers had now swollen to two thousand. Wielding blackthorns and hurling stones, they besieged the barracks and dared the 'woman-beaters' to come out and fight. But the police remained holed up for another day or two. At length Fenton 'threw up the sponge' and resigned his post. Because the time limit for serving writs had expired a truce ensued and the police sailed back to Galway, leaving behind a token force that had to endure a total boycott. The pusillanimous conduct of the police at Carraroe moved the under-secretary to deplore their display of 'the white feather'. According to Bew this kind of resistance was not at all typical of League tactics. However, this clash taught the police about the folly of not dividing their forces into small skirmishing parties in order to deal with the roving bands of protestors.[42] Although the Castle was soon providing shrieval escorts of up to three hundred constables at some evictions, the League's clever tactics and the Castle's obvious desire to avoid massacring civilians rendered the RIC's firepower virtually useless.

Fear of retaliation may have curbed the appetite of some landlords for eviction but they soon resumed sending out notices to quit with the result that 11,758 families were ousted in the second half of 1881. From 1883 to 1885 evictions averaged 3,650 per year. During the second land war, moreover, crowds behaved even more aggressively towards the evictors and their police escort. And just as in 1880–2 so too in 1885–7 the mass protests of Irish National Leaguers involved more than defending homes. They were proactive in the sense that the leaders would often use this opportunity to negotiate with the agent in the hope of reaching a compromise that would enable the defaulting tenants to re-enter their abodes upon a nominal payment. If the agent spurned any settlement, this was not for want of trying by the League's local leaders who were determined, as Ball contends, to challenge laws that were considered utterly unjust. In this respect 'collective resistance ... formed part of a wider progressive movement' that questioned the entire edifice of landlordism and put enough pressure on Parliament to pass a land act that benefited many tenants and some leaseholders.[43]

THE WAR ON PROCESS SERVERS

The League's official rejection of physical force did not prevent countless members – not to mention Moonlighters – from threatening their enemies with death. If few of these threats ended in fatal injuries, they could not be entirely ignored. Landowners and agents suffered only around a dozen violent deaths in the early 1880s. But this number would have been higher had the ambushers been more accurate with their rifles or shotguns and had the intended victims not returned fire or benefited from police protection. Besides landgrabbers and evicting bailiffs those at greatest risk were process servers who had to visit remote areas without a police escort. The process server was the lynch pin of the eviction process because a decreed tenant had to be served with the notice to quit. If no one was home or the door was locked, he would nail the document to the door providing that a hostile mob did not stand in his way. Tenants who had not been served could remain in place until the civil bill court reconvened several months later. In the previous century the demise of these hated officials had inspired one Munster poet to satirise a 'devilish bum-bailiff' from Cork who ended up hanging from a 'gallows-tree' with hell in the offing. A more prosaic comment came from H. O. Arnold-Forster, nephew of Matthew Arnold, who opined in 1882 that 'crime follows the Land League and not the process-server'.[44]

Determined to throw a spanner into the legal machinery of eviction, League branches declared war on process servers or 'rent warners'. Many of these 'detested instrument(s) of landlord oppression and of English law', as Davitt called them, were severely punished by families or mobs. Besides harassment they suffered beatings while a few were shot. Here and there crowds prevented them from getting near the tenant's abode. Such attacks grew so frequent and vicious that the Castle assigned scores of constables to protect them. Near Abbeyfeale, County Limerick, process servers managed to nail seven writs to doors in January 1880 but only because 400 policemen stood guard. On 1 September, three men beat and kicked a process server near Balllymore in Tipperary and tore up his writs as he pleaded for his life. At Brosna in County Kerry a crowd of 500 ignored the fourteen police who threatened to open fire and forced the process server to tear down his writs. On the Skerritt estate near Headford, County Galway, thirty police could not save one such official from being cursed and pelted with excrement by the tenant's wife. Elsewhere screaming women threw faecal 'mud' at the bailiffs and their escort. In the summer of 1881 mobs almost killed three process servers with stones and sticks in Sligo and west Cork. At Banagher in King's County a crowd drove the sheriff's posse away and impaled a bailiff's dog on a pitchfork to warn of the fate awaiting him should he serve any more writs. On another estate 'ruffians' with blackened faces held a bailiff over a fire scorching his flanks. The dwellings of some process servers were set on fire. One bailiff was beaten with his own blackthorn and then thrown into a pond from which he emerged to spend the night shivering in a pigsty.[45]

A lethal mêlée broke out on 2 April 1881 at Clogher near Lough Gara in south Sligo where angry protestors threw stones at police protecting an armed process server named James Broder. During a baton charge one constable named Armstrong suffered a severe beating and his alarmed comrades opened fire killing two men and wounding thirty. Armstrong died later from his injuries. The coroner's jury found three policemen, including Armstrong, as well as Broder guilty of murder.[46] One process server was forced to kneel while a dog bit him repeatedly until he swore that he would never return; and another man in County Limerick was stripped down to his breeches and made to walk five miles. A bailiff died after being hit by stones and another one ran into some angry women who tried to dunk him in the village fountain. Many others were boycotted or lost their homes to arson. Small wonder that they refused to work without more protection and a pay rise.[47]

On the Brasier estate near Emly, County Limerick, where good relations had once prevailed, the estate bailiff refused to serve any more writs and the agent had to hire an outsider. Summoned by horns, 3,000 people assembled on

7 May 1881 to harass this man. They besieged the police barracks at Kilross where he had taken refuge and dared him to show his face. Some of the protestors danced jigs and reels to the tunes of a fiddler, but the mood turned ugly as soon as stones began to fly wounding several constables. After more police arrived, three priests tried to restore peace. But a vicious baton charge resulted in many bruises and arrests. At Rathduff, County Westmeath, a process server named Foley was stripped naked while a hundred women screamed and jeered – a humiliating experience he was unlikely to forget. After flogging him with furze bushes, the assailants threw him into a river.[48]

At the end of December 1881, a bailiff named Joseph Huddy and his nephew disappeared while serving writs on Lord Ardilaun's estate in Joyce's country, County Galway. A month passed before their corpses were found at the bottom of Lough Mask. They had been shot and their bodies stuffed into bags weighted with stones before being dumped in the water. Local people showed little remorse about these murders. Several months later the young son of a gamekeeper and his mother were waylaid outside Clonbur. The lad died from a fractured skull and his mother was seriously injured.[49]

In the first six months of 1880 over 500 cases of attacks on process servers were recorded. Dublin Castle responded to this threat by assigning 6,000 constables to protect these officials in Galway, Mayo, Sligo, and several other counties. The police also changed their tactics. Instead of approaching a hostile throng in a solid phalanx they formed flying squads ready to peel off and protect their flanks while the advance guard encircled the process server.[50]

Underscoring the hazards of the process server's occupation and the pursuit of rent by landlords who could find no one willing to risk his life for this purpose, Aloysius O'Kelly sketched a revolver-toting landlord, backed up by his armed retainer, handing the dreaded writ to a well-dressed tenant near Claremorris, County Mayo (Figure 4.2). Behind the tenant stand his apprehensive wife cradling a baby and their daughter, while chickens peck away on the earthen floor.[51] In a much more dramatic print, 'The Irish Land League Agitation: Attack on a Process Server' (Figure 4.3), O'Kelly conveyed the depth of communal solidarity as an angry mob pursues a process server through a field. The barefoot woman in front is poised to throw a stone at this despised official. Once again the features of these plebeian Land Leaguers betray no signs of Paddy-like prognathism.[52]

To save lives and limbs the government adopted the pre-famine expedient of 'substitution of service', whereby a court would approve the posting of writs on public buildings in the nearest town. Almost every day the *Freeman* and other papers published the number of requests by agents for ejectment decrees and their approval or denial by county court judges. On the other hand the

Castle could not possibly afford protection for all the other petty officials responsible for enforcing the laws of real property including distrainers of live-stock and keepers of animal pounds or seized crops. Needless to say, the mobi-lising, transporting, and accommodating of hundreds of police and soldiers to

ABOVE
4.2   Aloysius O'Kelly, 'The Irish Land League Agitation: Mr Walter Bourke Serving Writs on His Tenants' (*ILN*, 14 May 1881). O'Kelly depicts a landlord armed with a revolver accompanied by a retainer handing an ejectment decree to a tenant near Claremorris, County Mayo because he cannot find a process server. The tenant's wife clutches her baby in alarm. (*ILN*, 14 May 1881)

LEFT
4.3   Aloysius O'Kelly, 'The Irish Land League Agitation: Attack on a Process Server'. A vengeful mob pursues a process server through a field in this print by O'Kelly. In the front a barefooted woman aims a stone at her quarry. (*ILN*, 21 May 1881)

contend with all this agrarian unrest cost the government thousands of pounds; and doubtless the Land League's executive was delighted over the expenditure of so much money and manpower in response to their activities.

COMPENSATION FOR DISTURBANCE

In response to the Parnellite demand for a two-year suspension of evictions and anxious to allay agrarian unrest, Gladstone's government tried to take some of the sting out of eviction by means of the Compensation for Disturbance bill. Launched in the spring of 1880, this measure would have reimbursed tenants ejected from holdings valued at £30 and under, provided that they could prove that their insolvency arose out of ruinous harvests. Worried lest surging arrears result in clearances, Chief Secretary Forster worked hard to steer this controversial measure through the Commons where fierce criticism forced him to water down some provisions. Early in August, however, the House of Lords rejected it soundly. This Liberal effort at conciliation divided the Parnellite party over such issues as exorbitant rents and the amount of compensation, while landowners denied that evictions were so numerous and harsh as to justify this relief. The bill's demise deprived the government of a valuable chance to strengthen the hand of moderate Home Rulers but gratified radical Land Leaguers who welcomed another excuse to agitate. More tenants joined the League and more evictions ensued. In fact evictions rose from 490 in the first quarter to 629 in the third quarter of 1880. In the meantime some Conservatives made light of both this measure and its author by bestowing on Gladstone the sobriquet 'Disturbance Bill'.[53]

THE LAND ACT OF 1881

The defeat of the Compensation for Disturbance bill and increasing unrest soon prompted the Gladstone government to produce a watershed measure – the Irish Land Act of 1881. Besides instituting the famous 'Three Fs' – fair rents, fixity of tenure, and the tenant's freedom to sell the interest in his holding – this measure created a powerful state agency, the Irish Land Commission, presided over by a high court judge and staffed with assistant commissioners as well as land courts to adjudicate rents around the country. This new authority enabled yearly tenants – but not leaseholders – to receive a judicial rent if their applications for reduction were approved. The act also ensured compensation for improvements made by the outgoing tenant. After the passage of fifteen years these judicial rents would be revised. Although endless controversy swirled around the criteria of what constituted a fair rent, the land courts were soon overwhelmed with petitioners. By 1916 the Land Commission had received almost half a million applications for judicial rents including those withdrawn or dismissed and 381,687 first-term rents were reduced by an average of 20.7 per cent.[54]

This innovative measure infuriated the landlord class by creating what was called 'dual ownership' owing to the official recognition of the tenant's 'interest' in his or her holding. Reeling from the League's efforts to prevent his beloved horses and hounds from foxhunting around Curraghmore, Lord Waterford deplored 'the frightful anarchy' in Ireland and predicted that the Land Act would bankrupt half the landlord class. As Philip Bull points out, the act seemed to 'vindicate' the tenants' 'longstanding [and] deeply held' belief 'in their proprietary rights in the land' despite the fact that the famous 'Three Fs' did not add up to full partnership let alone half ownership of the farm. Nevertheless Parnell firmly believed, as Liam Kennedy contends, that 'the tenant was entitled to co-ownership rights in the land he worked' and that a 'fair rent' meant the receipt by the tiller or minder of the soil of the full value of his improvements. In both theory and practice the land, he argued, ought to be let at close to the poor law valuation or roughly 25 per cent less than the average rental. By Parnell's criteria, at least three quarters of the tenantry were being either rack-rented or charged 'very exorbitant rents'. Those who championed dual ownership, however, overlooked the fact that the landlord retained the power of ejectment for non-payment or any other breach of contract.[55]

What many farmers regarded as their 'Magna Charta [*sic*]' radical Leaguers regarded as 'too little, too late'. Predictably, most landowners condemned the measure as 'an unjustifiable invasion' of their 'sovereign right' to control the terms of rent and tenure and some circumvented the fair rent clauses by leasing large tracts of land to graziers on the eleven-month basis thereby enabling them to avoid the land courts altogether. In short, full market value rather than the verdict of a sub-commissioner determined the rent of these pasture lands.[56] Initially, the land act failed to allay agrarian violence and unrest because Parnell and his lieutenants advised their followers to steer clear of the Land Commission on the grounds that the sub-commissioners were biased in favour of the landlords. But when the land courts approved reductions of at least twenty per cent, thousands of yearly tenants looked to this agency for their financial salvation.

When it came to eviction, tenants in arrears faced a hard choice between obstructing the sheriff and risking arrest and imprisonment on the one hand and surrendering their homes meekly on the other. The price of resistance was not just jail time but inability to support the family for several months. At mass rallies some ex-Fenians and radical tenant-righters used the language of menace by alluding to the necessity of firearms in defence of the homestead. Thus Matt Harris MP told a Galway audience in February 1881 that he would lose no sleep if landlords 'were shot down like partridges'. But in the very next sentence he admitted his abhorrence of bloodshed. Davitt's Fenian origins and his harsh treatment in Dartmoor prison drove him at times to fantasise about a 'good clean fight' against the British state even though he knew that any such rising was doomed to fail. The hard-line Fenian, Jeremiah O'Donovan Rossa, not only declared war on all evictors but also warned that the revolutionary republican organisation, Clan na Gael, founded in New York City and backed by the entire Irish race, would track down any landlord who carried out sentences of death through eviction on the people. The time was not far distant, he warned, when 'the avenging angel' would eliminate every such 'murderer'.[57]

Such bombast or wishful thinking could not disguise the fact that almost fifty agrarian murders occurred between 1879 and 1883. Less than a dozen of the victims belonged to the landed elite. Three lethal attacks on landlords attracted almost as much press notice as the murder of Major Denis Mahon back in November 1847. In mid-September 1880 ambushers shot and killed the insolvent 5th Viscount Mountmorres near Clonbur, County Galway. Because no local man dared to touch the body it lay in the middle of the road for several hours. At the end of March 1882 an assassin waylaid a small agent and landlord named Arthur E. Herbert near Castleisland, County Kerry and left his bullet-riddled body in the road. Recently he had carried out some evictions and many locals resented his harsh and overbearing behaviour. A week later Mrs William Barlow Smythe of Barbavilla House, near Collinstown, County Westmeath and Fitzwilliam Place, Dublin, was the victim of buckshot intended for her absentee landowning husband while they were returning from Sunday service. In each case evictions hovered in the background and probably contributed to their demise. But these were the exceptions. Most victims of agrarian homicide were plebeian: landgrabbers, bailiffs, process servers, and tenants who had defied the League branch by paying their rent on the sly. Needless to say, many more murders would have occurred had the ambushers learned how to shoot straight and had not apprehensive landlords like the Earl of Kenmare and his fellow peers in Ulster decided to forsake their beleaguered demesnes in favour of the delights of London or a European spa – a luxury denied to their agents.[58]

The surge in boycotting and intimidation moved many landowners to press Dublin Castle for more police protection. In October 1880 over one hundred landlords and agents met in Dublin to deplore the 'lawless' condition of the country and they sent a delegation to the Castle to plead for more stringent measures. By 1882 the Liberal government had passed not one but two coercion acts that facilitated the banning of meetings and the arrest and conviction of anyone inciting a riot or promoting a boycott. Hundreds of arrests and jail terms, however, did not discourage League speakers from holding their rallies elsewhere. Not even Catholic landlords were spared the people's wrath if they tried to 'disturb' their tenants. Because George Louden, brother of the president of the Land League of Mayo, could find no one to serve writs on his small property in western Mayo, he took on this task himself. Threatened by some ruffians, he fled to a nearby hut and held them off with his rifle until rescued by the police.[59]

During the 1880s many Big Houses were, as Yeats put it succinctly, 'shaken by the land agitation'. Although a few Protestant gentry like Lady Gregory supported Home Rule, they had little time for the Land League's denunciation of landlordism. Shortly after their arrest on 13 October 1881, Parnell and other leading Leaguers issued the famous 'No Rent Manifesto' from their new headquarters inside Kilmainham jail. Drafted by William O'Brien, this edict proclaimed a national strike against 'rack rents' until such time as 'the Government relinquishes the existing system of terrorism and restores the constitutional rights of the people'. The League's executive told members to ignore threats of 'military violence' and eviction and subvert landlordism as well as 'English tyranny'. This manifesto seriously hampered rent collections around the country. Gladstone's Arrears of Rent Act of 1882 relieved tenants of some £1.76 million in unpaid rent of which less than half went to the landlords. After the Kilmainham treaty and Parnell's release on parole on 10 April 1882, many more tenants applied to the land courts for judicial rents.[60]

During 1882 – the year of the notorious murders of the newly appointed Irish chief secretary and his under-secretary in Phoenix Park – League spokesmen continued to exaggerate the number of evictions. Thus the versatile journalist and Home Rule MP, T. P. O'Connor, declared that almost 17,641 people had been 'absolutely thrown on the roadside' in the previous year.[61] By this time the leading nationalist papers were publishing the names, location, acreage, valuation, rent, and arrears of tenants marked for eviction along with the speeches of Parnellite MPs and supporters from America. At a League meeting in Cobh on the eve of a fund-raising trip to America, the ardent American Home Ruler James Redpath accused '7,000 irresponsible rural despots called landlords' of having oppressed the Irish people for three centuries. They had 'robbed you of your food and clothing; they have confiscated your ancestral lands and levelled your ancestral homes. They have banished you by the million, and by the million they sentenced you to death by starvation.' Paraphrasing Pope's *Essay on Man*, he added that Irish landlordism, 'like a fiend, is a mad monster of 'such hideous–mien, As to be hated needs but to be seen.' Eviction for Redpath epitomised the Gall's ruthless confiscation of the Gael's birthright.[62]

Famine memories and anger or shame over the failure of so many victims of eviction to resist continued to inspire Land Leaguers and their American supporters who were determined to avoid any repetition of that disaster. In New York City an illustrated Land League booklet, *Parnell's Land League Songster* (1880), served up lashings of rhetorical violence by exhorting the Irish people to rise up like the men of '98 and fight for freedom from Anglo-Saxon enslavement. 'Forth from the scabbards flash your swords! ... Rise in armed might / And fling your Green Flag to the air. . . . Till you are victor in the fight!' Prayers alone would never impress 'the despot'. Therefore the time had come to try 'the eloquence and power of steel' even if this meant slaying and being slain: 'Be men, no longer kneel and sue!'[63] A recurrent theme in this songbook was nostalgia for 'My Beautiful Erin' following the forced departure for the new world. From 'Poor Pat Must Emigrate' came the following verses:

> If they'd leave us in our cabins
> Where our fathers drew their breaths;
> But when they'd come upon rent day
> And you have no half-pence for to pay,
> Faith, they'd drive you out of house and home
> To beg or starve to death.
> What kind of treatment, boys, was that,
> To give poor, honest, Irish Pat?
> To drive his family to the ditch
> To beg or starve to death!
> But I rose up with heart and hand,
> And sould [sic] my little spot of land;
> That's the reason, boys, I'll tell you now,
> I was forced to emigrate.

Two prints in this songbook limned the prelude to eviction. In 'The Cruel Landlord's Agent Serving a Notice to Quit' (Figure 4.4), the villainous agent hands the writ to a haggard woman uttering the words: 'Pay Up or Git'. Second, an impoverished family carries an old kettle and clock into the shop of a palpably Jewish pawnbroker in 'Pawning the Furniture to Pay the Rent' (Figure 4.5).

A third and tear-inducing sketch conveys the consequence of eviction – the loss of hearth and home. In 'Made Homeless by the English Landlord' a little boy holds his sister in his arms (Figure 4.6). [64]

Lastly, echoes of the famine clearances resound through the classic song, 'Skibbereen':

It's well I do remember that bleak December day
The landlord and the sheriff came to drive us all away,
They set my roof on fire with their demon yellow spleen,
And that's another reason why I left old Skibbereen.

.   .   .   .

Oh, Father dear, the day will come when vengeance loud will call,
And we will rise with Erin's boys and rally one and all,
I'll be the man to lead the van beneath our flag of green,
And loud and high we'll raise the cry: 'Revenge for Skibbereen!'[65]

MITCHELSTOWN/KINGSTON

Major conflicts arising out of eviction took place on the 24,400-acre estate of
Anna, dowager Countess of Kingston around Mitchelstown, County Cork.
She had married into a family well known for both unsound minds and finances.
(Her late husband's older brother, the 4th Earl, had been declared a lunatic
after years of 'eccentric' behaviour.) Conflicts over rents, arrears, and abatements
culminated in a partial rent strike followed by the serving of over 200 ejectment writs in mid-April 1881. Actual evictions came in three main waves – late
May, early July, and mid-August – each of which drew vast crowds. Rioting
erupted on 27 May, after the sub-sheriff of Cork and his bailiffs with an escort
of 250 police and a troop of dragoons marched out of the castle grounds to evict
three poor tenants. Chapel bells tolled, shops were shuttered, and three brass
bands played patriotic tunes until the police smashed their instruments.

The Kingston tenantry mounted a vigorous resistance by blocking the
approach roads with trees and boulders. They barricaded their homes with
prickly brush and timber, and stockpiled stones and other missiles. But the
eviction party was spared the pain of storming every abode because most of the
tenants paid up at the last moment and were allowed to re-enter. Nevertheless
crowds of up to ten thousand converged from miles around to harass the enemy
with curses and stones. Magistrates read the riot act and the police charged
with batons and fixed bayonets inflicting many minor injuries. Had it not been
for Father O'Connell's calming influence and the restraint shown by the sheriff
and his army gunfire might well have erupted. When the evictors marched
through Mitchelstown on 27 May, they were bombarded with stones and eggs.
The police and cavalry charged and inflicted over forty casualties. The protesters
rolled barrels between the horses' legs causing them to stumble and fall and
one horse expired after being hit by a large stone. On the following morning

LEFT
4.4   'The Cruel Landlord's Agent Serving a Notice to Quit'. In this print by an anonymous Irish-American artist a sinister-looking agent serves a distressed woman with the dreaded notice to quit. (*Parnell's Land League Songster*, New York, 1880)

BELOW LEFT
4.5   'Pawning the Furniture to Pay the Rent'. Three pathetic children carry their parent's mantelpiece clock and a kettle to the pawnshop in the hope of obtaining the rent money. (*Parnell's Land League Songster*)

BELOW
4.6   'Made Homeless by the English Landlord'. A young boy cradles his sister in this heart-rending picture of the consequences of eviction. (*Parnell's Land League Songster*)

someone cut off its head and stuck it on a pole set in the ground. The message placed in its mouth read: 'Webber, here's your rent'. (William Downes Webber was the countess's agent and husband.) Women and children surrounded this gruesome symbol and cheered until a constable took it away. All this turmoil delayed proceedings. One tenant, John Donoghue of Pollardstown, watched the bailiffs toss his furniture outside before paying his rent and being readmitted. Wherever final evictions occurred the sheriff installed an emergency man guarded by half a dozen constables. On their way back to town the sheriff's party had to endure more stones, 'dirty water', and rotten eggs.[66]

Multiple evictions resumed on 10 August when an army of 300 police and 700 soldiers invaded the district. But not even this massive show of force could prevent stone throwing and baton charges. One prominent visitor was Parnell's sister, the high-spirited and energetic Anna, who joined her sister, Fanny, as a leader of the Ladies Land League founded in America in the autumn of 1880. When the Land League was proclaimed in October 1881 and the leaders were imprisoned, the Irish Ladies League sprang into action. They organised protests, compiled data in a modern 'Domesday' book about estates, and promoted resistance to both rent and eviction. They also raised funds to support and house evicted tenants. To achieve even a few of these goals they spent money lavishly and their extravagance as well as resentment of the Land League so antagonised their male counterparts that Parnell shut them down in the summer of 1882 thereby permanently alienating brother and sister. At Mitchelstown Anna Parnell consoled evicted families and berated the police for beating innocent bystanders. Several troopers used their horses to block her approach to eviction sites. On the night of 13 August she joined her brother as well as Davitt and Dillon in a huge rally illumined by bonfires where speakers praised the League and damned police violence.

On 15 August over a dozen tenants were driven out before paying up and returning. One distraught woman punched a bailiff and then struck a constable with a piece of wood. An old woman, Mrs Barry, died from 'fright' two days after being ousted. On the following day the sheriff dealt with a dozen town park tenants who had put up posters with slogans like 'Down with landlordism', 'No surrender', 'God save Ireland', and 'Closed for the death of the landlord'. The bailiffs tore down porches and smashed doors to gain entrance. Pat Flavin had blocked his windows and door with thorn branches interlaced with logs. He also heated up an anvil that burned the hands of the bailiff who tried to remove it. Over the next few days the sheriff's party tackled sixteen more barricaded cottages while keeping Anna well away from the action. More stone throwing and baton charges accompanied these proceedings. In the end the agent collected a mere fraction of the rent due from tenants who were following the League's order to pay nothing except 'at the point of a bayonet'.

The Mitchelstown evictions gained both local and national notoriety in newspapers. One piece of doggerel inscribed on the wall of Johanna Meagher's house (her son was a prominent Land Leaguer) conveyed the tenants' resolve to resist:

I'll nobly fight and proudly wait;
I'll toil, join, and educate.
Man is master of his fate;
I'll have my home again.

These evictions also inspired some verses by Mary Lonergan, sister of the
secretary of the Mitchelstown Ladies Land League, who left a message for the
sheriff's party on the door before vacating her abode:

Landlords did always frown
On us poor farmers round Mitchelstown;
Their power to hell we have now hurled,
And o'er hill and dale our flag unfurled.[67]

As evictions multiplied, the *Freeman's Journal* accused some landlords of
imposing death sentences on their tenants: 'It looks an unfair match to find the
Earl of Charlemont pitted against Bridget Quinn, or the Bishop of Derry
against Pat Harkin, or the Lord Chamberlain of Her Majesty's Household
(Lord Kenmare) against Corny Flynn.'[68]

BODYKE/O'CALLAGHAN

Shortly after the opening round of the Mitchelstown evictions, gunfire erupted
at Bodyke, County Clare where Lieutenant Colonel John O'Callaghan JP had
denied his tenants' demand for an abatement. Besides backing a rent strike the
local League branch had imposed a boycott that forced the colonel's wife to
drive three miles to collect her mail armed with a revolver and an 'express rifle'.
O'Callaghan retaliated by obtaining 26 ejectment decrees. When the process
server showed up on 1 June backed by 150 police, the chapel bells summoned a
crowd armed with cudgels, shovels, and pitchforks. Foolishly, the bell-ringers
unloosed two beehives in the hope of driving the sheriff's party away, but the bees
stung indiscriminately. Although no stones were thrown, a county inspector
ordered six mounted constables to charge the crowd. John Moloney, a local
farmer, was trying to save a friend from arrest when a policeman struck him
twice in the head with his rifle butt fracturing his skull. Carried to a nearby
pub, he died several hours later.

At the first house on the sheriff's list Father Peter Murphy had a hard time
restraining the angry crowd. After some hillside snipers opened fire, the panic-
stricken landlord shouted: 'We are all shot.' More bullets flew and several
police riflemen ran up the hill. All they found were three young women sitting

on a wall because the gunmen had slipped away. To deter further sniping the police rounded up twenty hostages and took them as a human shield to each house marked for eviction. On their way back to town they came under fire again but the only fatality was a police horse. The 'battle of Bodyke' ended with a rowdy protest rally at Tulla on 5 June when Anna Parnell's tirade thrilled her many admirers. At the Moloney inquest the coroner's jury returned a verdict of wilful murder by an unknown policeman.[69]

As the agitation intensified, sub-sheriffs routinely requested armed escorts of several hundred police and soldiers – the latter being drawn from the 25,000-strong British army garrisons around the country. The Castle had already sent an extra 200 soldiers and officers to Galway; and in October 1880 the RIC's inspector general requested 67,000 additional rounds of buckshot cartridges – hence the epithet applied to the chief secretary, 'Buckshot Forster'.[70]

Hoping to avoid rioting and rifle fire, Castle officials dispatched large escorts of police and military wherever large crowds and resistance were expected. To cite only two examples, one hundred constables attended the eviction of thirteen poor families near Ballina, County Mayo at the end of March 1881. No injuries were reported. But because the occupiers carried away their doors, presumably to build scalpeens, the bailiffs had to block the entrances with stones. And in June 1881, the rumoured arrest of Father Murphy, parish priest of Skull (Schull), incited several thousand people to arm themselves with scythes and pitchforks before blocking roads and cutting telegraph wires around Ballydehob. After breaking the windows of the police barracks, they forced 50 marines to retreat to their gunboat in Bantry Bay. In general, the crowds at evictions showed much more hostility towards the police than the military – even though both carried rifles and bayonets – because the latter were there to overawe and unlike the RIC they had no batons with which to beat those who hurled curses and stones.[71]

NEW PALLAS/HARE

Evictions ordered by Colonel the Honourable Richard Hare at New Pallas, County Limerick, earned headlines at the end of May 1881 owing to the so-called 'siege of [Tim] Quinlan's castle'. The activity of moonlighters and Land Leaguers on this property moved Dublin Castle to provide the sheriff's party with enough armed men to discourage any resistance. Some 400 soldiers of the Coldstream Guards and Royal Scots Fusiliers along with assorted engineers and ambulance men joined 200 constables at New Pallas to protect Sub-Sheriff Naish's bailiffs or emergency men. Recruited in the north by the PDA, these tough plebeian Protestants carried revolvers as well as the usual paraphernalia of their trade. They were notorious for their aggressive, at times brutal, treatment of Catholics who refused to show them respect and they were often accused of being drunk on duty.[72] On May 21 the eviction party headed for Doon to oust six tenants who had refused to pay more than Griffith's valuation. Delayed by broken bridges this task force had to walk single file across one of them. Signal fires and bugles drew a crowd of several thousand who jeered and cursed the invaders until the police dispersed them with batons. Among those beaten was the *Freeman*'s reporter.

There are at least two wholly different versions of what transpired at Quinlan's farm. According to the *Times* the defiance of the law displayed at New Pallas resembled an insurrection albeit without bloodshed. The farmer and his comrades occupied a nearby castle and for several days stood their ground hurling stones from the battlements on the besiegers below. They also used scythes and pitchforks to drive back the constabulary from the narrow entrance. After the magistrate read the riot act, the police set up a cordon around the castle to prevent any food from reaching the garrison. When an officer ordered some riflemen to aim their weapons at the defenders, three priests rushed forward to avert a bloodbath. The defenders fought hard up to nightfall and then surrendered in the morning after running out of ammunition and water.[73]

At first both the *Cork Examiner* and *Freeman's Journal* confirmed this version of events. Thus on 23 May the *Freeman*'s special correspondent described the shower of stones descending from the battlements and a near miss by a rifle bullet as Colonel Hare stood near a wall. One constable suffered a skull fracture; a baton charge by the police injured numerous bystanders; three local priests headed off a serious riot; a young boy named Quinlan was arrested; and the *Freeman*'s reporter was assaulted and insulted by a constable. By 4 June, however, this reporter had completely changed his tune. The siege of Quinlan's castle was an 'unadulterated figment'. There was no fortress – only 'three naked walls of a ruined castle'. Quinlan himself was a 'magnificent' middle-aged man of 'unblemished character' – the very ideal of a yeoman, whose rent had been doubled between 1852 and 1873. Instead of confronting a well-armed and entrenched garrison, however, the evictors had faced some boyish scamps who threw stones from behind the low walls of a 'fortalice'. Another long article entitled 'Guards on the Warpath' lampooned the 'noble warriors' whose forebears had won honours at Waterloo. The civilian officials also came in for some heavy ribbing. The *Freeman*'s editor compared the whole affray to the greatest sieges in history – from Troy, Rome, and Athens to Orleans and Derry – and mocked the fact that this 'siege' had made headlines around the world. The Queen's own guardsmen had scored no victory because this was a 'castle in the air'.

A British army was engaged near Doon to-day in the most inglorious exploit that ever stained its banners. The Guards have had active service just three times in this century. They have been at Waterloo, in the Crimea, and at Tim Quinlan's Castle; and Tim Quinlan – what neither Napoleon nor Menchikoff did – has sent the Guards home baffled and ridiculous.

To make the operation even more ludicrous, Quinlan had evidently returned home and was now 'sleeping snugly under his own roof'. The editor also took the government to task for enforcing evictions made unjust by the tenants' inability to pay exorbitant rents. Alluding to the ongoing conflict in South Africa, the *Cork Examiner* called the standoff an 'Irish Transvaal'. By contrast, John Gorst, the prominent Tory MP, suggested in the House of Commons that Quinlan's defenders might be guilty of high treason by waging war against Her Majesty's forces. Parnell elicited some laughter by pointing out that the only occupant of the castle was an old woman who had built a cabin inside the walls long ago. Dublin Castle stood by the official version, of course, if only to justify having sent such a huge task force to New Pallas. Several more families were driven out in early June near Kilteely where the police batoned protesters. On 4 June, Naish's little army boarded the train to Dublin 'without firing a shot or drawing a bayonet after all their trouble'. [74]

The *Times*' reporter used this 'siege' as an excuse to repeat the age-old stereo-type of the Irishman's hereditary love of fighting:

It is the nature and habit of the people to fight. A fierce and furious combat seems to them only a healthful exercise or a pleasant pastime. They enter into it con amore, and do not wait to consider what is the cause of the fray or what the object to be gained if only an opportunity of indulging their national propensity presents itself. From the moment they are able to grasp a blackthorn they feel an irrepressible desire to use it, and are ready to follow the advice given by a veteran of the warlike 'three-year olds' to his son on entering a fair, 'Wherever you see a head, hit it.'[75]

Also at the end of May, pending evictions on Arranmore provoked T. P. O'Connor to question the legality of using a naval gunboat, HMS *Goshawk*, to convey the sheriff's party and police from Gweedore. In response Gladstone declared that the royal navy had every right to transport this force but was not allowed to take part in the actual eviction. Set on recapturing the common grazing ground taken away by their landlord, the League-backed islanders rounded up all their donkeys. After an hour of raucous braying these beasts broke through a gate and began to devour the grass denied them for so long.[76]

AGHABOE/STUBBER

The eviction of Mary Dowling, a young orphan, on Robert Hamilton Stubber's estate in Queen's County on 28 May 1881 caused quite a stir and enabled a League branch to orchestrate a major protest against this 'vile' proceeding. Responsible for four younger siblings, the twenty-year-old orphan could not afford the rent increase on her farm. Nevertheless, upon the expiration of her lease she offered to pay the rent and arrears due. Apparently Stubber coveted her farm and set the wheels of ejectment in motion without giving any notice until the night before. Word of his intentions spread like wildfire and no fewer than eleven priests along with one thousand parishioners greeted the sheriff's party with its escort of 100 police and soldiers at Aghaboe to protest the seizure of 75 cattle. The noise of the crowd and three brass bands prompted a stampede and the bailiffs had a hard time rounding up the livestock. Not even the threat of a baton charge stopped the crowd from surrounding an empty herdsman's hovel barricaded by Miss Dowling and her supporters. To gain entry the sheriff had to employ a scrawny local 'character' who wriggled through the narrow gap made by a stone wall inside the front door. After this entry the sheriff handed possession to the agent. At a post-eviction rally Canon Matthew Keeffe denounced Stubber's 'vile action' and praised Mary Dowling's refusal to be crushed by her tyrannical landlord. Speaking softly from the platform, she called the eviction 'harsh, barbarous and capricious'. For reasons best known to himself Stubber relented, readmitted two sub-tenants, and allowed Mary Dowling to graze her cattle on the repossessed farm.[77]

Many more ejectments took place during the bleak winter of 1881–2 as landlords ran out of patience and tenants ran out of cash. Dublin Castle's reputation for repression was enhanced when word leaked out that County Inspector Major Clifford Lloyd of Clare had sent out a circular in April 1882 authorising his men to shoot on sight any suspects with firearms. Needless to say, the nationalist camp had a field day with this disclosure. In Parliament T. P. O'Connor defended the right of tenants to assemble and protest eviction on the grounds that they were fighting to defend their cabins, fields, and children. The cause of such protests, he added, 'lay deep in the social conditions of the Irish people' and was not the result of blind obedience to the dictates of the Land League. Not only were these evictions unjust but also the real 'originators of disturbance' were the evictors who should be held responsible for any criminal acts that might follow their actions.[78]

Returning to Galway in February 1882, J. H. Tuke was struck by the stark contrast between the beauty and tranquillity of Connemara and the despair of its inhabitants. The eviction of seventy families on the Berridge estate at Carna just after Christmas had driven many large families into scalps or lean-tos with sod roofs and doors, old dressers or tables serving as walls. Whether they chose the workhouse or emigration, the homeless faced a grim future. Tuke shuddered at the sight of 'strong men' crouching by a tiny fire, despairing of finding even menial work, and preferring death to the poor house. Heeding the calls to reduce the chronic distress of cottiers in the west, Tuke, along with H. L. Vere Foster, the Duke of Bedford, and other philanthropists helped to raise almost

4.7   R. Caton Woodville, 'The State of Ireland: Serving a Process Near Headford, Galway' (*ILN*, 7 Feb. 1880). A bent old man stands next to his little granddaughter with a stick in hand while the evicted tenant clenches his fist in anger at the constable guarding the process server. Other policemen with fixed bayonets keep the onlookers away.

£70,000 for assisted emigration. In addition the government spent over £150,000 on the emigration of roughly 50,000 smallholders in the west to North America.

What Tuke did not address was the fighting spirit of some tenants well after the Land League had been outlawed. Not only was intimidation widespread in parts of the west but the votaries of Captain Moonlight continued to threaten death to any landlord or agent who defied the League's will. According to the French aristocrat, Baron Edmond De Mandat-Grancey, who toured 'Paddy's' country in search of the causes of the land war, a fierce rent dispute had broken out on the 5,137-acre Limerick estate of Valentine Lawless, Baron Cloncurry, in 1884. Led by their priest the tenants had demanded a ten per cent reduction on both rent and arrears. The agent replied that abatements would have

to be made on an individual basis. A prosperous cattle-rancher and keen sportsman, Lord Cloncurry of Lyons, Hazlehatch, County Kildare, flatly rejected any across-the-board reduction. Some seventy tenants refused to pay and notices to quit followed in due course. On the appointed day a restive crowd greeted the sheriff and his armed escort with mud and stones. After this routine barrage, the families scheduled for eviction apparently lay down on the floors of their cottages. Two policemen entered each abode, hauled out the men, women, and children, and 'gently deposited them on the manure heap'. All the furniture was then removed. During this operation a National League spokesman appeared and announced that the estate would be boycotted. He then pointed to a group of carts that had just arrived. They were loaded with wooden frames and boards that soon turned into huts erected along the road nearby. When De Mandat-Grancey visited the estate in 1886, the evicted tenants were still living in these shelters and receiving allowances from the League. Boycotting was widespread, policemen were patrolling the grounds, and Cloncurry's 'cows' were grazing peacefully in the fields. Because rent receipts on this turbulent property fell by almost one half during this period the owner wanted to sell it, but the tenants considered his purchase price exorbitant.[79]

PORTRAYING THE LAND WAR

Determined to produce a visual record of the land war, the *ILN*, *Graphic*, and *Penny Illustrated Paper* sent a raft of artists to Munster and Connacht to sketch sensational or newsworthy scenes. Besides O'Kelly these gifted illustrators included Amedée Forestier, R. Caton Woodville, Jr, Claude Byrne, S. T. Dadd, and W. H. Overend all of whom supplemented their incomes by painting as well as illustrating serialised novels and short stories in magazines. As O'Sullivan points out, they collaborated at times in turning sketches from the actual sites of agrarian conflict into beautifully detailed prints to meet the high standards of the *ILN*.[80] Thus, on 7 February 1880, the *ILN* carried Woodville's image of a process server nailing a writ to the door of a hovel. In 'Serving a Process Near Headford, Galway', a bent old man and his granddaughter stand next to the tenant who clenches his fist in anger while several policemen with fixed bayonets watch the crowd (Figure 4.7).[81]

On 7 January 1882 the *Graphic* published four arresting sketches about the effects of eviction. These images include the interior of a cottage in Castleisland, County Kerry, empty, of furnishings but riddled with rats, a homeless but well-dressed family sheltering under a makeshift tent in a ditch, and a cabin built by Land Leaguers for evicted tenants at Derhee (Figure 4.8).[82] This six-penny periodical had been launched in 1869 by two wood-engraver brothers, William Luson and George Housman Thomas, who had worked for the *ILN* and decided to start a rival weekly. The magazine owed much of its success to several outstanding artists and the editor's sensitivity to reader tastes.[83] Like those of the *ILN* the *Graphic*'s artistic staff moved effortlessly between wood-block prints and oil paintings as well as between the two magazines. Well-versed in the art of combining realism and sentimentalism, Luke Fildes and the Frenchman Charles Paul Renouard also produced haunting images of pauperism in the

4.8   Anon, 'Within and Without – Results of the "No Rent" Policy, Castleisland, County Kerry'.
These multiple images reveal the interior of a cottage in Castleisland, County Kerry. Rats scurry about
the empty room and the homeless family huddles under a tent in a ditch. Also pictured is a Land
League cabin built for evicted tenants at Derhee. (*Graphic*, 7 Jan. 1882)

slums of London akin to Gustave Doré's classic portrayal of the nether world
in *London – A Pilgrimage* (1872).[84] The *Graphic* rivalled the *ILN* with its dramatic prints of newsworthy events along with full-page 'portraits' of the leading lights of church and state, the army, and the navy. Apart from scenes of
agrarian conflict in Ireland both weeklies offered middle-class readers a pot-
pourri of images ranging from royalty to ironclad ships, military manoeuvres,
foreign wars, volcanic eruptions, African and Arctic explorations, train wrecks,
and natural disasters.

A cloying sentimentalism pervades O'Kelly's 'An Eviction in the West of
Ireland' (Figure 4.9), wherein a compassionate constable escorts a stooped old
man out of his hovel while a police officer stands nearby and the sub-sheriff or
agent sits astride his horse. On the far right policemen keep a sharp eye on the
menacing crowd with its quotient of grief-stricken women and children.[85] In
much the same vein, Woodville's 'The State of Ireland – Evicted: A Sketch on

4.9   A. O'Kelly, 'An Eviction in the West of Ireland'. A kindly constable helps an old man out of his hovel in this romantic print by O'Kelly. The sub-sheriff or agent sits impassively on his horse while the police cordon keeps the crowd away. (*ILN*, 19 Mar. 1881)

the Road in Connemara' (Figure 4.10) features another three-generation family in the depths of despair after being stranded on a snowy road in the back of beyond. The old nag has collapsed in its traces after pulling the cart filled with furniture, and there is no shelter in sight for these victims. [86]

Occasionally, the Irish land war earned notice in the French press. Thus *Le Monde illustré* published a print by Charles A. Loye, who used the penname G. Montbard, limning a bailiff nailing a writ to a cabin door while the distraught family bemoans their fate. In his print, 'Irlande – La land-league – Expulsion d'un fermier par la police anglaise' (Figure 4.11) half a dozen 'English' constables restrain the crowd, while a despairing old woman sits beside a wicker basket filled with her few worldly goods. [87]

Rarely did any comic note creep into evictions. But on the Cloghan estate in King's County in December 1881 an emergency man picked up a young pig whose loud squeals provoked laughter from the police and the crowd. After the bailiffs had carried 'rags and rickety furniture and old trumpery' out of another house, members of the Ladies Land League cheered and jeered. When the bailiffs tried to catch several donkeys in an adjoining field, the animals gave

4.10   R. Caton Woodville, 'The State of Ireland – Evicted: A Sketch on the Road in Connemara'. This engraving by R. Caton Woodville conveys the deep despair of a three-generation family stranded on a snowy road with no relief in sight after their cart-horse has collapsed from fatigue. (*ILN*, 20 Mar. 1880)

4.11   Montbard (C. A. Loye), 'Irlande - La land-league – Expulsion d'un fermier par la police anglaise'. A bailiff nails a writ to the door of a cabin in Montbard's print while the distraught family bemoans their fate and 'English'[*sic*] constables restrain the angry tenant. (*Le Monde illustré*, 11 Dec. 1880)

them a merry chase 'to the intense amusement of the vast crowd' that included the notable American socialist Henry George. As the *Freeman* reported,

> The scene changes once more, and out of the town the black battalions march, weighed down to the very ground with rounds of buckshot. The families to be evicted live up a lane, which was chokeful of dreadful slush. It was a picture for a painter to see the sheriff picking his steps through it.[88]

Assaults on landgrabbers multiplied as rapidly as evictions. Heartily denounced at Land League rallies, these despised 'creatures' ranked just below the informer or traitor in nationalist eyes. O'Brien wanted to see them completely isolated in every community. Tim Healy declared that boycotting was a much better punishment than shooting them. Any man who took an evicted holding could expect to be treated like 'social vermin' or a leper. A 'black cloud' would hang over his farm and he would be taunted with shouts of 'grabber' on his way to market or fair. Like process servers these 'planters' had to endure ostracism, ambushes, cattle maiming, and arson.[89]

Although songs and ballads about eviction were less numerous than those celebrating rebellion and the struggle for Irish freedom, several Land League songbooks invoked the cherished goal of restoring the land to its rightful owners. As one broadside put it, the Irish people

> fought for freedom's glory, to let every farmer see
> The land that God had given them it should be free.
>
> *Chorus*
> Yes! their land it must be free,
> Yes! their land it must be free,
> No more rack-rents or evictions,
> For the tenants must be free.[90]

Another ballad commemorated a Kerry farmer named McMahon who has been served with a notice to quit after failing to make the rent. Surrounded by soldiers and police, the agent demands possession. With tears in his eyes McMahon pleads for mercy:

> For God's sake, let us stop, sir, for we've got no place to go!
> I'm sure you wouldn't turn us out in all that blinding snow.
> Ah, look at those poor children, sir, they'll soon be left alone;
> For God's sake, don't evict us from our little Irish home!

It was in that little cabin, sir, those children first saw the light;
It was there their poor old mother died only last Christmas night.
I've always paid my rent, you know, until this sorrow came,
Here I stand, God help me now, with nothing to my name;
But if you'll let me stop, sir, for just a week or two,
I'll try my best to get the rent, and I will pray for you.
Just then they brought McMahon's sick child out on the road to die,
He knelt himself down in the snow, again I heard him cry:
The Agent he stood coldly by, he didn't heed the plea,
The gold was all he wanted, for to satisfy his greed;
But if you let us stop, sir, your heart's not hard I know…
But then his scanty furniture they threw out in the snow.
Then, with a cry of anguish, he sinks upon the ground,
While tears are being freely shed by everyone around;
A neighbour then came from the crowd, and gently raised his head –
His trouble's past, he'll speak no more, for poor McMahon was dead. [91]

In the realm of folklore heroic tenants avenged themselves on wicked evictors and landgrabbers with impunity. Thus one Tipperary man told the tall tale of a strong farmer named Quinlan who vowed to shoot everyone responsible for his eviction. Endowed with magical powers he killed seven men including the man who took over his farm. And whenever he landed in jail Quinlan always managed to escape. [92]

MORE FICTIONS OF EVICTION

Evictions also figured prominently in several novels wherein repacious or lecherous landlords and dishonest agents menace young lovers or innocents. In W. G Lyttle's melodrama, *Sons of the Sod: A Tale of County Down* (1886), an evil bailiff cum farmer named 'Black Ben' Hanlon evicts the eighty-year-old Corney O'Neill and then plots against his kindly master, Squire Brown, by hiring burglars who almost kill him. But Brown survives the attack and testifies in court that Hanlon has defrauded the tenantry. Love triumphs over hate and the squire's daughter marries Corney's son. [93]

The ejectment of Mat Vaughan and his family by Lord Emervale's agent serves as the defining moment of Ellis Carr's novelette, *An Eviction in Ireland* (1881). Uttering cries of despair, old Mat kisses the doorpost on his way out and then dies on the threshold. Father O'Donnell dissuades the enraged crowd from punishing the evictors. Mat's devoted granddaughter, Molly, tries and fails to kill the hardnosed agent, Blindley. Fleeing to London, she is driven into prostitution and suffers mortal injuries after being run over by a carriage driven by Lord Emervale's son. The contrite landlord visits her in hospital just before her death and returns to Ireland to become a benevolent landlord in search of redemption. [94]

A callous eviction marks the mid-point of Jules Verne's Bildungsroman about an orphan child named Mick whose vicissitudes resemble those of Oliver Twist. *The Extraordinary Adventures of Foundling Mick* (1883) takes place during the first land war when a battered and innocent orphan is adopted by the kindly MacCarthy family of Kirwan's Farm in County Kerry. Nourished with food and love Mick suffers a traumatic blow when the evil sub-agent Herbert, who abhors the Land League, evicts the MacCarthys for non-payment. Bereft of his benefactors Mick returns to the road. However, his precocious business skills enable him to graduate from selling newspapers and stationery in Cork to owning a shop in Dublin, the Boys' Bazaar, that attracts both middle-class and gentry customers. By the age of fourteen his credit at the Bank of Ireland stands at £4,000 some of which he applies to the purchase of Kirwan's Farm. After the MacCarthys have returned from an ill-fated sojourn in Australia, he installs them back in their beloved home.[95]

Last but not least there is the saga of Murty Hynes, whose vicissitudes were enshrined in a ballad based on an episode on Lord Dunsandle's estate at Loughrea, County Galway. In 1880 Hynes took over a farm near Athenry from which Martin Bermingham had just been evicted. Warned by local Leaguers to vacate the premises, Murty promptly left. His successor, Peter Dempsey, had served as head gardener at Moyode castle, Craughwell owned by the prominent Galway landlord and foxhunter, Burton Persse. The industrious Dempsey brushed aside warnings to give up the holding. While walking to mass at Kill on Sunday 29 May 1881, he was ambushed by three men. His murder was all the more appalling because two young daughters watched their father die. Focusing on Murty's redemption, the balladeer explained:

Out upon the roadside poor Bermingham was sent
Because with all his starving he could not pay the rent
To keep up Lord Dunsandle in horses, dogs, and wine
Who comes and takes the holding but foolish Murty Hynes.

When the noble Land League heard of this disgrace
They sent a man to Murty to reason out the case
I own my crime says Murty – but I'll wash out the stain
I'll keep the farm no longer I'll give it up again.

Then Murty wrote a letter and he sent it to the League
Saying for the cause of Ireland I never will renege.
And never more I promise while the heavens above me shines
Would I for land go grabbing says honest Murty Hynes

And when the people heard of it
They gathered in a crowd
The boys brought out their banners
And beat their drums aloud.

And there were songs and speeches
And dancing light and gay
Around the flaming bonfire
That night in Old Loughrea.
Come all ye sons of Erin
Where ever that you be
Come join the celebration
Of this glorious victory.

Whether by Columbian rivers
Or amid Canadian pines
Give three cheers for the Land League
And nine for Murty Hynes.

Avoiding any mention of Dempsey's fate, these verses gave Murty legendary status. Evidently, the prime suspects in the murder were the former tenant Bermingham and his nephew whom the police took into custody that afternoon. With a little bit of help from the Land League Murty learned that landgrabbing did not pay.[96]

Under the heading of the Great Famine remembered A. M. Sullivan joined many others in vowing that the 'horrors of 1847' would never be allowed to recur. A more tangible reminder of the famine clearances surfaced in 1883, when some men broke into the burial vault of Marcus Keane at Kilmaley cemetery in Clare shortly after his demise and removed his mortal remains along with those of a family governess. Apparently they wanted to throw the large lead-lined coffin into the river but it proved so heavy that they buried both coffins in a shallow grave nearby. When the vault was opened a year later, the authorities had no clue about what had happened to Keane's remains. Only in 1891 did some gravediggers stumble upon the purloined coffin and remove it to the new family mausoleum at Beech Park.[97]

In one of the last salvoes of the first land war, the land agent Sam Hussey was jarred awake by a huge explosion at the back of Edenburn House near Tralee on the night of 28 November 1884. Although none of those asleep inside, including three constables, was injured by this dynamite bomb, Hussey took the hint and removed himself and his family to the safety of London for a time.[98]

To sum up, the land war that had begun with so much enthusiasm, solidarity, and defiance of the combined forces of landlordism and Dublin Castle slowly ground to a halt after 1881. What caused this disintegration was not just coercion or the outlawing of the Land League in October 1881, the imprisonment of the leadership, Gladstone's second land act, and the counter-combinations of fighting landlords. The agitation also fell apart because of internal disputes over objectives and tactics as well as quarrels over priorities and dwindling funds. On the other side of the conflict, the land war created lasting bitterness in the Big House. Arthur Kavanagh, the driving force behind some anti-League organisations, felt such anger against his disloyal tenants that he had his younger son buried in a London cemetery in November 1882 rather than bring the body back to Borris to be mourned by 'a crowd of howling hypocrites whose pretended grief would be measured by their hatbands'.[99]

Nevertheless the mobilisation of the tenantry and their urban allies along with the militancy of crowds in the early 1880s set important precedents for the renewal of agrarian conflict in 1886–90 when Castle officials, the RIC, sheriffs, and magistrates faced far more concerted and violent obstruction. What Stephen Ball has observed about the first land war could just as well be applied to the second: 'eviction scenes are the most enduring images' of that conflict.[100]

FIVE

THE SECOND LAND WAR
1886–90

*'It was only by the unlimited application
of British gaols and British bayonets that evictions
could now be carried out in Ireland.'*

P. J. NEILAN
speaking at a National League rally at Kanturk,
County Cork on 16 September 1888.

*'You may evict us from our homes, but you cannot
evict the spirit of nationality from our hearts.'*

THOMAS KENNEDY
speaking to his evictors at Coolgreany,
County Wexford on 7 July 1887.

———

Declining crop prices and tighter credit in 1885–6 sorely afflicted small tillage farmers in the west while cattle dealers and dairy producers fared much better. Elsewhere harvests remained good with the exception of partial potato crop failures in Connacht. According to the *Pall Mall Gazette*, the value of Irish cereal crops fell by at least one-fifth nullifying many of the judicial rents set since 1881. After visiting the vast Clanricarde estate, the legendary editor, W. T. Stead, advocated abatements to prevent serious suffering in the west. And a tour of the islands off the coast of Mayo in February 1886 prompted Davitt to write four articles for the *Freeman's Journal* describing the acute distress and warning about possible starvation.[1]

Renewed recession and distress led to the familiar cycle of more arrears, ejectment writs, attacks on process servers, evictions, agrarian outrages, and protest meetings. As in the past some tenants scheduled for eviction decided to settle at the eleventh hour in order to achieve readmission as caretakers or tenants. From 1880 to 1887 the percentage of readmissions was much lower than in the 1870s with only five per cent of the 29,124 families affected qualifying as compared with 17 per cent for the previous decade. On the well-managed

1   Robert George Kelly, *An Ejectment in Ireland*. In this multi-layered painting, two police constables are arresting a handsome tenant farmer for assault. He and his family have just been evicted from their sturdy house down the road. In the centre a priest tries to console the devastated family by raising his arm towards heaven; and in the distance a troop of cavalry move on to the next eviction site. (From the collection of Anthony J. Mourek on loan to the John J. Burns library, Boston College)

2   Erskine Nicol, *An Ejected Family*.
Another three-generation family rests
on the road to nowhere in this painting
by the well-known Scottish artist, Erskine
Nicol. The anguish of eviction is etched
on their faces. Hinting at the possibility
of better times to come the dark cloud
overhead gives way to a brighter sky on
the left. In the background stands the
substantial thatched cottage now sadly
vacant. (Oil on canvas, 50 × 82 cm.
National Gallery of Ireland collection.
Photo © National Gallery of Ireland)

3   Daniel MacDonald, *The Eviction*
(*c*.1850). In this genre painting,
attributed to Daniel MacDonald, a
respectable tenant farmer holding a
spade in one hand turns over the key to
his cottage to the landlord or agent while
his wife sobs on his shoulder. Two soldiers
stand ready to deal with any trouble. The
evicted family includes the traditional
images of the kneeling old woman with
arms and eyes raised to heaven and a
young mother holding an infant. A
broken spinning wheel, a large iron pot,
and other household goods are strewn on
the ground. (Crawford Art Gallery, Cork)

4   William Henry Powell, *The Eviction: (A Scene From Life in Ireland)* (1871). In this genre painting by the American artist, William Henry Powell, an evicted tenant wearing a white blouse and crucifix lies dying surrounded by friends and relations. In the centre a woman balances a bundle of goods on her head like a Native American squaw. The priest looks heavenward while administering the last rites. The soldier son in uniform has just returned from the Crimean war minus an arm and raises his fist in a vengeful gesture. On the far right a mother holds her moribund infant next to a coffin. In the right background a second eviction is unfolding as another man lies near death next to his swooning wife. Secure in their saddles the sheriff and agent turn their backs on these victims. (By permission of the NLI)

5   'Hut at Present Occupied by Evicted Tenant (10 In Family)': Francis Guy's camera has caught a family of two adults, eight children, and one dog sheltering in a scalpeen after their eviction in County Cork. (NLI, EBL 2659, WL)

6   J. F. O'Hea, 'The Most Noble'. O'Hea's skill at demonising Irish landlords looms large in this caricature of the 2nd Marquess of Clanricarde whose lawyer asks the jury: 'Is my client as black as he is painted?' And the jurors reply unanimously: 'Yes! Blacker!!!' (*WF*, 17 Dec. 1887)

7   J. D. Reigh, 'The Vindication of the Law'. Reigh's cartoon memorialises James Dunne who died of heart and lung failure after being evicted from his hovel near Collon, County Louth in October 1888. The sickly old man had warned the evictors that he would die if removed from his hearth. After exposure to the cold he was carried to a barn and soon expired. The pale blue light of the moon illuminates this scene of death devoid of priest or mourners. (*UI*, 20 Oct 1888)

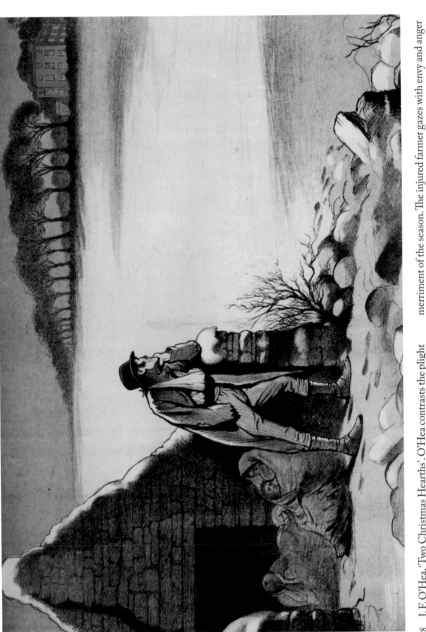

8 J.F. O'Hea, 'Two Christmas Hearths'. O'Hea contrasts the plight of a homeless family shivering in the ruins of their cottage on Christmas eve with the Yuletide festivities inside the Big House in the distance where the landlord and his family enjoy the warmth, comforts, and merriment of the season. The injured farmer gazes with envy and anger across the frozen field at the luxurious lifestyle of those responsible for his family's distress. (*WF*, 18 Dec. 1886)

estate of Robert Ashworth Cosby around Stradbally, Queen's County, a judicious mixture of ejectments, abatements, and the write-off of more than £960 in irrecoverable arrears reduced the latter by half in 1884 and enabled the agent to collect £7,101 in rent two years later. On the Cavan estate of Sir Robert Hodson the agent squeezed some rent out of unwilling tenants by threatening eviction and holding out the prospect of an abatement or cancellation of some arrears if they paid promptly. Like any prudent agent he wanted to avoid final eviction and prevent more tenants from applying to the land court for fair rents.[2]

Agrarian outrages averaged 815 per annum between 1885 and 1889 and then dropped down to an average of 444 between 1890 and 1893. In 1886, 424 of these 1,056 offences consisted of threatening letters. Any surge in crime or crowd aggression taxed the resources of the police and the courts. In mid-Ulster, however, the advent of the Home Rule agitation had divided Protestant and Catholic tenants with the result that the former were much less likely to support the National League after 1885. Touring the southwest in the summer of 1886, the *Times'* reporter blamed boycotting and outrages on 'the iron grasp of the League'; and only the Cork Defence Union had saved some non-compliant farmers from serious harm. The landlords he met were convinced that boycotting and resistance to rent would continue until the League was suppressed.[3]

The defeat of the Home Rule bill in June 1886 demoralised most members of the National League who took little comfort in Gladstone's bold declaration in October that he would some day cut down the tall and 'noxious' tree of Protestant ascendancy. The hard times prompted several leading Parnellite MPs to contemplate reviving the land war in order to bring rents down and sustain morale among the supporters of the New Departure. As more landlords obtained ejectment decrees for non-paying tenants, the war on process servers revived. In October 1885 a Kilkenny family stuffed their notice to quit into the bailiff's mouth. After swallowing one half, he choked on the remnant, which they then burned. Only his 'piteous cries for mercy' and profuse apologies saved him from being buried alive in a bog. In February 1886, near Castlegregory, County Kerry five moonlighters entered the house of a one-armed process server named Roe late at night. After muzzling his wife, one invader sliced off the man's ear with a razor. While serving decrees on Captain Richard Oliver's estate in north Kerry, the agent, Cecil Vandeleur, was ambushed but drove his attackers off with his revolver.[4]

At indignation meetings around the country nationalist speakers including priests railed against 'landlord tyranny' and coercion. John O'Connor MP urged an audience at Gweedore in January 1887 to follow Father McFadden's lead and relight the turf fires in the hearths of evicted homes. Condemning the evictions then taking place at Glenbeigh, he cited a passage from Disraeli's novel, *Vivian*

Grey, wherein the hero lets the light into an evicted house. 'Yes, my friends', he proclaimed, 'landlordism is dying hard. It is on its [*sic*] legs and it is kicking violently. It is doomed to die and it is our duty to hasten its departure.'[5]

Just as in the heyday of the Land League, huge crowds assembled at eviction sites to harass and abuse the sheriff's party with invective if not stones. Compared with the 'monster meetings' of O'Connell's repeal campaign, these protests were smaller but far more confrontational. Summoned by signals, they listened to fiery orators and then howled whenever an evicting landlord or agent was mentioned. At night they attended boisterous rallies and applauded the harangues against 'iniquitous' evictors and the land laws.[6] Nationalist newspapers continued to report the latest numbers of notices to quit as well as the details of evictions and League rallies. 'Special correspondents' from both Dublin and London interviewed the protagonists and noted the names of the evicted families as well as their acreage, rent, valuation, and arrears. Wherever the police encountered resistance, they would set up a cordon in order to keep reporters, priests, and other observers well away.

Exemplifying the emotive force of eviction news was a report in August 1886 by the *Freeman*'s correspondent who described a visit to Captain Arthur Hill's estate near Gweedore, County Donegal:

> If familiarity begets contempt, it is not surprising that the poor people of Gweedore would heartily despise this persistent dangling before them of the strong arm of the law. I cannot conceive anything more supremely silly than a sub-sheriff and half a dozen bailiffs, an R.M., county and district inspectors, a head constable, a number of sergeants, and 100 men marching up a hill to besiege a poor widow and her two daughters in a miserable mountain cabin, with nothing to disturb or alarm them but the rattle of their own accoutrements.

His account of the ordeal of Denis Coll and his family is worth quoting:

> Within, the father, mother, and the rest of the children are in tears. I have not often seen such evidence of deep misery. There is not even a stool in the house; there is but one bed, with only heath and a relief coverlet. The wretched mother holds the infant child in her arms, and some of the children try to hide themselves out of view, which is easily done, as there is not a ray of light except what is admitted through the door. . . . To let this wretched family resume possession for six months ... the poor man has to sign his hand to this form. ... he touches the pen with sobs and tears, and extinguishes the tenancy which his family has held from time immemorial. The entire family are now just outside, and the nakedness and raggedness of the father and mother and the four children become strikingly evident in the glare of

midday light. Even the priest … is surprised and shocked, and he passes some
money into the hands of the old man with emphatic instructions for him to go to
the fair… and buy covering for the children.[7]

Another example of eviction reportage appeared in the *Waterford Mail* on
14 February 1887 when James Rockett, his wife, and their seven children were
expelled at Kilsheelan, County Waterford. Unable to pay the rent, he had been
served with a notice to quit and his feeble effort to barricade the dwelling failed
to thwart the bailiffs. When Father Spratt urged the landlord, Mrs Hayden, to
relent, she 'smote her thigh with a stout cudgel' and exclaimed: 'Not a bit of it!
Not a bit of it!' at which point the reporter called her 'A Fiend in Petticoats'.[8] In
September the agent, Colonel Dopping, rode around the estate guarded by
police serving summons to tenants who had been readmitted as caretakers but
now faced final eviction for failing to pay what they had promised. Dopping
did not escape unscathed, however, because a woman threw a bucket of hot
water in his face. Another woman spent a month in jail for striking a constable's
helmet with a stone.[9]

Reports of growing distress after potato failures in the west moved the government to ship modest amounts of seed potatoes and corn meal to western
islanders in greatest need. As Sir Henry Robinson, the local government board
official pointed out, the islanders often feared the sight of British gunboats
because they did not know whether the vessels were carrying process servers,
bailiffs, and police or food supplies. These relief measures may have prevented
famine but they did not help to pay the rent. As arrears piled up, landlords
rebuffed requests for abatements, and priests instructed their parishioners to
pay only what they could afford. In the spring of 1886 the *ILN's* 'special artist',
Claude Byrne, sailed across Galway Bay on a gunboat carrying meal for the
destitute of Inishmore, Achill, and Inishboffin. One sketch, entitled 'The
Distress in the West of Ireland', depicted Aran islanders escaping an angry sea
and collecting seaweed from the shore as well as officials distributing seed-
potatoes and corn meal to the 'starving' peasants.[10] Another print, 'The Distress
in the West of Ireland: Scene at an Eviction on Clare Island' (*ILN*, 10 April
1886) (Figure 5.1), portrayed a police constable at an eviction site at the mouth
of Clew Bay 'tenderly nursing a child of the disconsolate family' while two
older brothers observe this unusual scene. Rarely did the quotient of pathos in
the sub-genre of eviction art reach such heights. A far cry from nationalist
vilifications of the RIC, this picture may have been partly inspired by a few
Mayo constables who gave some money to the poor families they had just
helped to eject.[11]

One week later Byrne produced a starker image of dispossession in 'All That Is Left: Scene at a Mayo Eviction' (Figure 5.2). According to the caption, the young girl and her family have been 'shut out' of their cottage. Sitting alone on a table in the driving rain, she waits for her family to return from their search for food and shelter. Her 'scanty clothing' suggested to the reporter that 'it is likely that the weaker may perish'.[12]

On 1 May 1886 the *ILN* published O'Kelly's double-page print drawn three years earlier while touring a rocky island in Roundstone Bay, Galway, where a dozen Irish-speaking families had been evicted. The reporter described them vividly as 'squalid' and half-starving mountain-farmers – 'a race of wild people, poorly clad, and living with the cattle in their houses, often lying on the damp ground on hay' like their animals. The nine images in 'On Eviction Duty in Ireland: Sketches in Galway with the Military and Police Forces' (Figure 5.3) run the gamut from the landing of the police and troops in the upper left corner (no. 1) to the teepee built by the mother for her three daughters in the lower right hand corner (no. 9).

In the central image (no. 5) the bailiffs carry out a table watched by the occupants and police in casual repose. No. 6 reveals the sheriff giving formal possession of the premises to the head bailiff by 'handing him a wisp of straw' from the roof.

As the reporter noted, the presence of so many police and soldiers made

5.1   Claude Byrne, 'The Distress in the West of Ireland: Scene at an Eviction on Clare Island'. In this highly sentimental print Byrne portrays a policeman seated outside an evicted hovel at Clew Bay consoling the little girl on his lap while her brothers survey the scene. (*ILN*, 10 Apr. 1886)

5.2   Claude Byrne, 'All That Is Left: Scene at a Mayo Eviction'. Byrne's iconic image of eviction features a thin young girl sitting alone on a table surrounded by the pathetic contents of the cottage. She awaits the return of her family who have gone in search of food and shelter. (*ILN*, 17 Apr. 1886)

5.3   A. O'Kelly, 'On Eviction Duty in Ireland: Sketches in Galway with the Military and Police Forces'. The nine images in O'Kelly's double-page print range from the landing of the police and troops and their march to the eviction sites (nos 1–2, 4, 8) to the crude teepee built by the mother of three girls (no. 9). In the centre (no. 5), the bailiffs carry out a table watched by the former occupants and the police. And in no. 6 the sheriff gives possession of the premises to the head bailiff by handing him a wisp of straw. (*ILN*, 1 May 1886)

these operations resemble a 'military invasion' complete with an army surgeon equipped with medical supplies who examined the sickly or aged occupants to see if they were fit to be removed. Observing one homeless pauper family, a soldier muttered: 'Shame – it's a damned shame!' Some of his comrades felt so much chagrin over their task that they contributed a few pounds to the homeless. These images bear comparison with a photograph taken around 1888 by Francis Guy of Cork who also measured the interior of this *bothóg* and found a 6 by 5 feet floor space with a height of only 4½ feet (Plate 5). Here the evicted tenant, his wife, eight children, and a dog pose forlornly outside their scalpeen.[13]

The travails of land agents increased apace whenever tenants re-entered their old homes illegally after the sheriff's party had left. In many cases the premises were destroyed to prevent re-entry. Two cases of 'forcible possession' were tried in a Gweedore court in July 1887. The tenants of Mrs Ann Stewart had forcibly reoccupied their former abodes, and their attorneys argued that they were more justified in returning to their dwellings than the police had been in forcing them out. While the judge upheld the landlords' right of repossession by decree, some jurors sided with the tenants. Nettled by the hung jury, the judge ordered a second trial that ended with a verdict of guilty.[14]

A contentious dispute over possession involved the Marquess of Ormonde, whose brother, Lord Arthur Butler, held the agency. A tenant named James Fribbs had been expelled from his 40 (Irish)-acre farm in Tipperary, having paid no rent for three years. After moving into a neighbour's house, Fribbs stopped local farmers from grazing his former fields. One grazier, Michael Delany, found his cattle severely beaten, but a magistrate refused to allow him to carry a brace of pistols for self-protection. In August 1880, after Fribbs and his wife had re-entered illegally, he was charged with unlawful trespass. Denied bail, he went to jail and stood trial at the winter assizes in Waterford. To Lord Arthur's dismay the jurors acquitted him on 'the trivial plea' that he had climbed into his former house through an unlocked window and was therefore not guilty of forcible entry. Upon his release Fribbs returned to his old abode and the exasperated agent wrote to Thomas H. Burke, the Irish under-secretary, asking if Lord Ormonde should retake possession by force or through an 'ordinary action for trespass'. Although we do not know Burke's response, Fribbs must have caused the agent a monumental headache.[15]

Reprising their tactics during the first land war, the police often resorted to baton charges and fixed bayonets whenever crowds began to throw stones. On Lord Cork's Dingle estate, however, the sheriff chose to withdraw his task force on 16 February 1887 because they were undermanned. Returning several days later with reinforcements, he ordered his men to charge what the *Times* called 'a howling mob armed with scythes, pikes, iron-shod sticks, and stones'.[16] In the same month the police also ran into resistance on Hugh Montgomery's estate near Drumkerran, County Leitrim. To prevent the ejectment of three farmers their friends and neighbours dug trenches and built stonewalls across the road that held up the sidecars and wagons of the police. When the sheriff's party ascended a steep mountain road, the defenders rolled huge boulders down the slope. At the eviction sites the police dispersed the hostile bystanders with truncheons and several volleys of buckshot. On the estate of George Twiss at Birdhill, County Tipperary, a crowd of two thousand people accompanied by brass bands gathered to protest evictions. With stones flying through the air the agent conferred with four priests and prudently postponed the operation. In sharp contrast, some of Lord Downshire's 250 tenants on the Blessington estate in County Wicklow were evicted for non-payment without resisting. The arrears lost on four of these farms averaged £89 not to mention legal costs.[17]

CLANRICARDE/WOODFORD

The 52,600-acre estate of Hubert George De Burgh Canning, 2nd Marquess of Clanricarde, soon became an agrarian combat zone that lasted for almost twenty years. The epitome of the absentee and miserly Irish landlord, Clanricarde visited his Irish property only once and even skipped his mother's funeral at Portumna in January 1876. Although a millionaire he used to take a homemade sandwich to the smoking room of his London club and consume it there to save money.[18] Following some evictions in 1882, his Catholic agent, John Henry Blake, and a servant were shot dead while driving to Sunday mass at Loughrea, a district synonymous with agrarian crime. This murder inspired Clanricarde's famous comment that he would not be intimidated into lowering his rents by the shooting of his agent.[19] Dubbed 'Lord Clan-rack-rent' by his myriad enemies in Ireland, he lived in splendid seclusion in the Albany, Piccadilly, surrounded by priceless paintings and china. There he wrote self-serving letters to the *Times* defending his treatment of tenants whom he regarded as terrorists. Singlehandedly, he did more to tarnish the reputation of his class than any other Irish landowner.

Clanricarde also inspired Ireland's two leading nationalist cartoonists, J. F. O'Hea and John D. Reigh, to produce some of their most scathing prints in the *Weekly Freeman* and *United Ireland* respectively. Exemplifying the 'age of mechanical reproduction', their weekly colour supplements greatly enriched the propaganda war by highlighting the contest between the forces of Good (Home Rule, freedom of speech, and tenant right) and those of Evil (coercion, the Union, landlordism, and eviction). Starting out as a painter, banner designer, and book illustrator in Cork, O'Hea soon found his métier as a comic artist for sundry humour magazines like *Zozimus*, *Zoz*, *Pat*, and *Tomahawk* using the pen name 'Spex'. In 1879 he joined the staff of the *Weekly Freeman* where he spent a highly productive decade. A fine example of his talent for demonising the enemies of Home Rulers may be seen in 'The Most Noble' (Plate 6) wherein Clanricarde lurks as the iconic rackrenting and evicting landlord.

Little is known about Reigh who also drew for *Zoz* before becoming the principal cartoonist of *United Ireland*. But taken together the combined political cartoons of these two artists along with those of Thomas Fitzpatrick would make a lively and amusing pictorial history of Irish political life during the 1880s and early 1890s. Blending social realism, melodrama, and caricature, their chromolithographs of eviction captured both the violence and the pathos. Occasionally displayed in shop windows, they were also affixed to the walls of Irish cottages. In fact, they reminded William O'Brien of the French revolution owing to their resemblance to the 'Journal-Affiche – Placard Journal of the Revolutionary Government'.[20]

In the autumn of 1885 Father Coen urged Clanricarde's 316 Woodford tenants to demand rent reductions of 25 per cent. The agent replied that his lordship would deal only with individual cases and not grant across-the-board abatements.[21]

Several months later most of them withheld their rent in a 'spontaneous' act of defiance. Infuriated by their slogan, 'No reduction, no rent', Clanricarde ordered his new agent, Frank Joyce, to proceed against those with arrears above £20. Not even the strenuous efforts of Chief Secretary Sir Michael Hicks-Beach and the moderate co-adjutor Bishop of Clonfert, Dr John Healy, could head off these evictions. The murder of a process server named Finlay set off more shockwaves. When multiple evictions began in the spring of 1886, the PDA sent emergency men to take over the vacant farms. On 20 May, some 5,000 people showed up at Woodford to hear speakers denounce Clanricarde and all forms of landlordism.

The subsequent evictions marked the first salvo in the second land war. Journalists from London as well as Dublin flocked to Woodford in search of newsworthy material. The *Pall Mall Gazette*'s 'special correspondent' used a melodramatic metaphor to describe Clanricarde's character and political significance. Irish landlordism, he wrote,

> is dead, but the stench of its decaying remains still pollutes the air. Its 'corpse crawls round unburied' – crying aloud, indeed, in dolorous accents of the vampire sort for decent burial – which, happily, will not be long delayed. And the whole story of it, from first page to last, is bound up with the Clanricarde estate.

Anticipating Bram Stoker's iconic bloodsucker, Count Dracula, he added that 'popular imagination has transformed the unknown, real Clanricarde into a veritable but invisible vampire, who lives and thrives on what he draws from the life blood of his tenants'. On this score R. F. Foster delivered the solemn verdict that 'if the post-Famine Irish landlords were vampires, they were not very good at it'. To which dismissal some anti-revisionist might well respond that it took only a little blood – or pound of flesh – to satisfy the appetite of indebted landlords for cash.[22]

The astute reporter also described the principal antagonists in this momentous conflict. Thus the tenants' champion was Father Coen, a 'modern Friar Tuck', president of the Woodford branch of the National League, and genial host. His adjutant, Father Egan, was a 'firebrand curate', the son of evicted parents, a great admirer of John Dillon, and a keen poacher who had organised illegal shooting parties on his lordship's land. On Clanricarde's side stood the agent, Joyce, a 'frank, good-natured man' and a convert to Protestantism, who was under constant police protection. The 'evictor-general-in-ordinary' was sub-sheriff John Redington of Prospect Hill, 'an honest straightforward land agent and public officer', who construed this fight as one 'between the National League and the Government'. Last but not least, there was the 'calm, resolute, courageous' Captain Edward C. Hamilton, the aggressive field director of the Property Defence Association and leader of the Protestant emergency men.[23]

The Woodford and Portumna tenants formed tight-knit, Irish-speaking communities west of Lough Derg where British laws were more often ignored than obeyed. Resolved to defend their homesteads as fiercely as any Kingston tenant had done years earlier, many families, inspired no doubt by local National League branches, barricaded their abodes with stones, logs, and thorny bushes. They also loopholed the gable walls so that they could thrust long poles or pikes at the foe. To counter these defences Sub-Sheriff Redington laid on an armed escort of two hundred police and two companies of the Somerset Light Infantry to protect his twenty bailiffs.

On the morning of 18 August this long 'siege train' left Portumna in forty horse-drawn cars and traps. Broken bridges and felled trees delayed their arrival at Dooris, where scouts on horseback and chapel bell ringers sounded the alarm. As the *Pall Mall Gazette* pointed out, Sheriff Redington's expeditionary force outnumbered the army led by Pizarro during the conquest of Peru. Among the observers were the agent and a gamekeeper armed with Winchester rifles. Despite the overwhelming display of force the evictors turned out only two tenants on the first day. After a tiring march on the following day, the police cordoned off old Pat Conroy's barricaded house at Looscaun where the defenders brought into play a hot liquid repellant that besmeared and scalded the attackers. Mixing water with meal, urine, and lime, the defenders heated this foul concoction in a large pot suspended over the fire. After retreating, the bailiffs returned and spent the next four hours trying to break through a gable wall. When they breached the wall and subdued the garrison, they wrapped Conroy in a sheet and carried him out. His daughter, 'a buxom sonsie girl in her teens', carried on fighting and had to be dragged out while the crowd cheered her pluck. The police conveyed all the resisters by train to Galway jail.[24] Determined to discourage further resistance, Redington called for reinforcements that raised the size of his army to seven hundred constables and soldiers.

Next on the sheriff's list was Patrick Fahey of Dooras, who kept the evictors at bay for five hours on 20 August. His family had lived on these 18 boggy acres for four generations. Wielding sharp sticks, iron hooks, and grape forks, they fought off the emergency men who had smeared their hair with oil in the hope of reducing the effects of hot stirabout. This siege finally ended after Redington handed Fahey a note promising to make no arrests if they gave up the fight. Assured by their priests that theirs would be an honourable surrender, the weary defenders filed out quietly. Several bailiffs and police took over the cabin to prevent re-entry. A day later the evictors tackled the garrisoned cottage of James Broderick, who seemed ready to negotiate. But when he learned that he would have to pay legal costs as well as some rent, he slammed the door shut and called on his 26 comrades to fight. The emergency men fell back before 'the lava of scalding limewater gruel [that] poured down on their devoted heads'. After an hour of fierce fighting the police charged with fixed bayonets, broke down an interior wall, and arrested the garrison. Three female defenders were released, but the male prisoners were taken to Galway jail in handcuffs. Severe boycotting soon enveloped the forces of law and order. After four days of heavy exertion they managed to evict only four or five families whose resistance strengthened communal solidarity and earned lavish publicity in the Home Rule press.[25]

SAUNDERS' FORT

The climactic siege on the Woodford estate began on 23 August at the heavily barricaded house of Thomas Saunders, who farmed 34 acres in Drummem having made some money in Australia. On this memorable occasion almost eight thousand supporters assembled from miles around to cheer on the garrison. From the chimney a green flag flew bearing the words 'No Surrender' and 'God Save Ireland'. This time Redington's escort comprised over 500 constables and soldiers as well as a squad of PDA emergency men led by Captain Hamilton. For three hours the defenders drove the bailiffs back with stones and 'a course of [hot] lime and tar [that] varied the savoury fare' adding a new chapter to the history of Irish siege warfare. The torrents of hot liquid prompted the *Freeman* and the *Times* to wonder rather mischievously if 'the Woodford mitrailleuse' had been patented and adopted by the War Office.[26] Thwarted by these tactics, Hamilton decided against sending for a battering ram owing to the inevitable delay. When the sheriff suspended operations to prevent more injuries, the crowd cheered lustily. Back at Portumna castle the police and bailiffs spent a rest-day cleaning their filthy clothes and restoring morale despite a stifling boycott by local shopkeepers. Hamilton ordered his men to build a mobile testudo or corrugated metal shed with a roof strong enough to repel stones and liquid, while Saunders's garrison reinforced their barricades and harvested some crops.

On 27 August the eviction party set out again for Drummem in a siege train comprising one hundred carts and wagons filled with armed men, wrecking tools, ladders, and the new testudo. A dozen magistrates accompanied the 'hangdog-looking crew' of twenty emergency men. Once again trees blocked their progress and scouts raised the alarm. Fathers Coen and Egan did their best to calm the boisterous crowd. The emergency men advanced under their protective shed, and the defenders threw two beehives out of an upper window. However, the bees failed to discriminate between friend and foe. Suddenly a local bailiff named Page handed his gun over to Father Coen and announced his resignation to tumultuous cheers from the crowd. Having failed to breach the walls with crowbars, the emergency men put up several ladders that were pushed away by the defenders' long forked poles. The crowbar brigade retired from the field and the police took over the siege, climbing onto the roof and opening a hole. Once inside the loft they drew their swords, fixed their bayonets, and arrested 22 men. Saunders wept at the sight of his ruined house and the tearing down of his green flag. For the forces of law and order this was a Pyrrhic victory because it had taken them four days to capture four dwellings.[27]

A print in the *Graphic*, entitled 'An Eviction of One of Lord Clanricarde's Tenants, Woodford, County Galway, Ireland', depicts the siege of Saunders' fort while the tight police cordon keeps spectators well away (Figure 5.4). The defenders upstairs are fending off the police (rather than emergency men) who have climbed up ladders only to be struck with implements and doused with hot water. The man wearing a top hat and brandishing a rifle on the left may well be the agent; and the gentleman in the front mounted on the sidecar could be either a magistrate or a priest.[28]

5.4 'An Eviction of one of Lord Clanricarde's Tenants, Woodford, County Galway, Ireland'. The police cordon keeps bystanders well away from Saunders' fort while the defenders repel the police with pitchforks, sticks, and buckets of hot liquid. The man brandishing a rifle on the left might be the agent, and the gentleman standing in the sidecar could well be a priest. (*Graphic*, 11 Sept. 1886)

Pondering all the turmoil around Woodford, the *Pall Mall Gazette*'s reporter felt as though he was in a war zone in some foreign land The four 'little fortresses' captured and occupied by the evictors, he noted, were surrounded by a hostile population and had to be supplied from Parsonstown by 'convoys of provisions periodically sent through the enemy's lines'. His account continued:

> No British outpost in Afghanistan or in Burmah is more cut off from all communication with the natives than these small garrisons. No one gives them so much as a drink of water for love or money… Seven hundred policemen and soldiers were employed in protecting the emergency men, and sixty peasants of the estate were marched off to Galway Gaol, there to be confirmed in their detestation of landlordism and of England, while their mothers and wives and sisters mourn sullenly for them at home. And over and above all this 'Saunders's Fort' becomes a rallying cry and a watchword for the Irish tenants all over the South and West.

The ever-boastful Captain Hamilton claimed to have saved the life of a district inspector from death. 'A thousand Galway heroes', he wrote, 'turned tail and ran away' at the mere sight of himself.[29]

Early in January 1887 Saunders and his comrades went on trial at the Sligo assizes for aggravated obstruction. After the inevitable guilty verdict, the judge, Chief Baron Palles, handed down some of the severest sentences ever imposed on resisters. Five defendants including Saunders received terms of 18 months and 26 others spent a year in jail. Upon their release they had to find sureties for good behaviour for three years.[30] S. T. Dadd's series of sketches entitled 'The Irish Land War' evokes the transformation of Woodford into an armed camp as the constabulary marches forth to protect process servers, bailiffs, and emergency men venturing out of the captured fort to obtain firewood (Figure 5.5).[31]

Hatred of both Clanricarde and Dublin Castle reached new heights after a young prisoner from Woodford, Thomas Larkin, died in Kilkenny jail on 2 October. In his funeral address William O'Brien told the 4,000 mourners that the judges, landlords, and prison officials were all guilty of 'legal murder'. To avenge this 'martyr' he called on them to carry on the war against landlordism. Father Egan also praised Larkin as a noble martyr to the cause of Irish freedom and tenant right.[32] Nationalist spokesmen hailed Saunders and his comrades as uncommon heroes who had cost the crown forces and the landlord dearly. No rent had been collected and the bill for removing these families approached £10,000 – two-thirds of which came from British and Irish ratepayers. The futility of this operation became all the clearer after the four families returned to their abodes illegally. The *Freeman* reckoned that Clanricarde would have to pay £700 just to keep caretakers on each farm for a year – a sum far above their rental value.[33]

SERVING SUMMONSES ON THE CLANRICARDE ESTATE, WOODFORD, COUNTY GALWAY.

MR. WHELAN, LORD CLANRICARDE'S BAILIFF, UNDER POLICE ESCORT.

EMERGENCY MEN, WITH POLICE GUARD, STARTING IN SEARCH OF FUEL · SAUNDERS' FORT IN THE BACKGROUND.

HOUSE OF AN EVICTED TENANT, PAT CONROY, FORTIFIED BY THE POLICE.

EMERGENCY MEN WITH POLICE GUARD, FELLING TREES FOR FUEL.

THE IRISH LAND WAR: SKETCHES BY OUR SPECIAL ARTIST IN GALWAY.

5.5   S. T. Dadd, 'The Irish Land War'. Dadd's sketches on the Woodford estate of Lord Clanricarde point up the dangerous state of the district as the police protect bailiffs and emergency men foraging for firewood. (*ILN*, 15 Jan. 1887)

Over the weekend more families were expelled on the adjacent estate of Mrs Hannah Lewis where the large crowd also jeered and threw stones. Three of the evicted were old or sickly widows who were readmitted as caretakers. At another house the heavily pregnant Mrs Spain, whose husband was in jail, grew so distraught over her pending eviction that she gave birth prematurely. After consulting a medical officer who advised against disturbing her, Redington allowed her to stay. The invalid wife of Thomas Coen fainted at the sight of the eviction party and had to be carried out and laid on the ground, while her daughters shrieked and cursed the evictors. Fathers Egan and Coen rushed forward to administer the last rites to their mother, and the entire family was then allowed back. Elsewhere a widow treated the bailiffs to a 'bath of scalding lime water'. Encouraged by the crowd four young girls taunted the besiegers from an upper window and dared them to come closer so that they could empty their buckets of hot liquid. Eventually, the crowbar brigade broke through a gable wall that almost collapsed. After pleas from the priests, the magistrate called a halt to the siege and the girls ceased discharging 'the watery element'. The police took down their names but did not arrest them; and the agent collected no rent from any of the tenants.[34]

After another visit to Woodford and Loughrea in November, Stead composed a bristling report entitled, 'Can Irish Rents Be Paid?' and answered his question with a resounding 'no'. As will be seen in the next chapter, Dillon and O'Brien chose Woodford as the launch site of their new offensive, the Plan of Campaign, in October. These evictions inspired O'Brien to compose a little ditty about a landlord who lived in 'a lordly hall'

> With rich treasures before him spread;
> Will make the peasant's cabin fall
> In ruins around his head.

Several years later negotiations for a settlement led by the Bishop of Clonfert collapsed and evictions resumed at Woodford early in 1889. By September over 110 families or 600 persons had been evicted and the remaining 800 tenants lived in dread of a similar fate.[35]

WINN/GLENBEIGH

In mid-January 1887 Irish evictions garnered even more notoriety at Glenbeigh near Brandon on the Dingle peninsula where house razing made headline news on both sides of the Atlantic. Strapped for cash and squeezed by his Jewish creditors in London, the Honourable Rowland Winn of Aghadoe

House sought to empty and then consolidate hundreds of small and uneconomic holdings into larger farms and pasturage. During the reign of his forebear, the late and indulgent Lady Headley, many tenants had paid little or no
rent. When Winn inherited the property, his rental income shrank from £1,690
in 1877 to a paltry £275 in 1880. By 1886 arrears had reached £9,000 and the
estate fell into chancery. The trustees ordered that 70 of the 300 tenants be
served with decrees – no doubt to encourage the others. After a county court
judge proposed that these tenants pay one year's rent and no arrears, the tenants' representatives, Father Thomas Quilter PP and J. D. Sheehan MP, urged
them to reject this offer and resist eviction 'at the point of the bayonet'. Despite
appeals for compromise from Dublin Castle, Winn and his agent, Langford
Roe, refused to call off the evictions.[36]

On a cold, wintry day, 11 January 1887, the deputy sub-sheriff of Kerry, Thomas
Goodman, led his little army into the remote glen of Droum. Among the bystanders was the outspoken radical MP from Cornwall, Charles A. V. Conybeare.
To prevent re-entry the agent ordered the bailiffs to burn down the cabins. Paddy
Reardon barely had time to remove some furniture before a bailiff poured paraffin
on his thatched roof and lit a match. Flames shot upwards and the rooftree and
walls soon collapsed to roars of anger from the crowd. Evidently, some 'gentle-
men' present restrained the crowd and averted a riot. Having failed to ignite the
rain-sodden roof of Thomas Burke's abode, the bailiffs broke through a wall
and the family emerged 'half-naked and emaciated by hunger'. The next cottage
tackled was occupied by two elderly brothers, Patrick (Paddy) and Thomas
Diggin, who had sixteen dependents between them. Evicted twice before, Patrick
and his wife watched their cottage being demolished. After she fainted, the
dazed husband grasped the hand of a grandchild and wandered away leaving
his wife behind. Several constables were so upset when they saw this family
shivering in a ditch that they handed over a few shillings; and Pierce Mahony
MP called the destruction of the Diggins's home 'a horrible atrocity'.[37]

Amédée Forestier's 'Scene at an Irish Eviction in County Kerry' (Figure 5.6)
leaves little doubt about the cruelty of the Glenbeigh evictions as a haggard old
man holding the hand of his barefoot granddaughter walks away from their
hovel followed by his daughter who cradles a baby. The tossed furniture, the
soaking ground, and the rocky, desolate landscape all underscore the harshness
of this proceeding.[38]

A much more innocuous print, 'The Rent War in Ireland: Agent and
Evicting Party Consulting Operations at Glenbeigh, County Kerry' (*ILN*, 5
February 1887), reveals a company of police waiting for the agent and the sheriff to decide on the location of their next target. This image lacks so much as a
hint of the arson attacks.[39]

5.6   Amedée Forestier, 'Scene at an Irish Eviction in County Kerry'. Amedée Forestier's rendering of
the Glenbeigh evictions features an old man leading his pretty little granddaughter away from their
hovel followed by his own daughter holding a baby. The broken furniture and the rocky, barren
landscape heighten the cruelty of these evictions. (*ILN*, 15 Jan. 1887)

As news of these evictions spread, over a dozen reporters – three of them
English – converged on Glenbeigh along with artists working for several London
illustrated weeklies. The sight of burnt out houses so upset Edward Harrington
MP for West Kerry that he called Roe a 'red-handed wretch, who preys on the
blood of the people'. 'Before God', he swore, 'I denounce him as the incendiary
who set fire to the roofs over your heads.' He exhorted the tenants to stand fast
because they would be around long after 'this scoundrel and his masters have
been hunted out'. Like Marcus Keane years before, he earned the epithet,
'exterminator-in-chief'. At a protest rally in Dingle Harrington and Conybeare
denounced Roe as an 'incendiary scoundrel'; and John Deasy, MP for West
Mayo, called the evictions akin to 'wholesale murder' and demanded the
prosecution of those responsible.[40]

Glenbeigh also made a lasting impression on the able army and police
officer, Colonel Alfred E. Turner, who commanded the sheriff's escort party.
This was his first taste of Irish evictions, and he was appalled by the expulsion
of half-starved men, women, and children whose 'only crime was that they
were poor'. Out of compassion he handed Father Quilter £5 for their relief.[41]

On 22 January, the *Penny Illustrated Paper* published a sketch of an old man and his family outside their burning cabin surrounded by police and bailiffs. Shock and despair are etched on the victims' faces in 'The Land War in Ireland: Barbarous Evictions at Glenbeigh, County Kerry'. A fortnight later, this weekly featured a blazing cabin surrounded by police in 'Reminder of the Savage Incendiary Evictions at Glenbeigh, in Ireland'.[42] One of the most searing prints to emerge from the ashes of Glenbeigh was Forestier's 'The Rent War in Ireland: Burning the Houses of Evicted Tenants at Glenbeigh, County Kerry', that appeared on the cover of the *ILN*'s 29 January issue (Figure 5.7). Here flames, sparks, and smoke dominate this act of arson backed up by the rifles and bayonets of the RIC.[43]

Images like this helped to raise funds for the victims at home and abroad.

The arrival of so many reporters, MPs, and 'foreign' observers moved

5.7 Amedée Forestier, 'The Rent War in Ireland: Burning the Houses of Evicted Tenants at Glenbeigh, County Kerry'. Forestier's dramatic cover illustration highlights the flames and smoke pouring out of an evicted cabin at Glenbeigh while the police keep the victims and onlookers well away. (*ILN*, 29 Jan. 1887)

Roe to call a halt to the burnings. However, the house levelling continued despite the menacing gestures of the crowds. Forty families were expelled during January amidst 'wails, witticisms, and imprecations' in Irish. Some protesters rolled boulders down Droum hill hoping to hit the sheriff's party marching along the road. The illness of Michael Reardon's wife led to a stay of execution, but his kinsman, Paddy Reardon, was driven out even though an infant child was sick. Smoking a cigar, Roe ignored the mother's plea for mercy. So she spent the night with her baby in a cold pigsty. While an emergency man was nailing Paddy's door shut, a 'buxom' young girl ran up and felled him with a shovel. She was arrested and then rescued from the clutches of the police by some bold bystanders. The officer in charge wisely decided not to attempt her recapture. At every house they visited the sheriff's party was jeered and cursed by the ubiquitous crowd amidst shouts of 'Roeneen the rat'.[44]

On 14 January one tenant finally fought back. Michael James Griffin and his garrison of 22 young men threw stones and burning turf at the bailiffs at Ballinakilla. After the crowbar gang had broken down the door, Deputy Sheriff Goodman dashed inside brandishing his revolver and the police who followed him beat the defenders with their batons. Several girls escaped through a rear window only to be caught and then released. Mrs Griffin swooned and had to be carried out. Word spread rapidly that she had died and the crowd fell silent and knelt in prayer. As *United Ireland* put it,

> Oh! The old faith of the Celt, the old refuge and sustenance of the Celtic breast through suffering centuries – down knelt the crowd then and there in the mire and the wet, and there was a momentary lull ... while hands were raised high in lamenting prayer.

Hoping to avert a riot the police commander ordered some of his men to load their rifles at which point Edward Harrington calmed the throng and averted a massacre. Mrs Griffin revived; and the police escorted the defenders in handcuffs to Rossbeigh barracks. At a 'monster meeting' in Killorgin eleven Home Rule MPs joined in denouncing Winn and Roe and hailing the heroic resisters.[45]

The evictions resumed in driving rain on 18 January, but this time the paraffin cans were left behind. Before reaching Coomasaharn (Coomasharen) the sheriff's party had to cross over the rain-swollen river Behy. The removal of the stepping-stones at the ford forced the police to choose between making a long detour upstream and wading across. Some local men and women volunteered to carry friendly reporters and visitors across on their backs. Even more impressive, both Conybeare and Harrington were honoured with a ride on two 'shaggy' Kerry ponies. As for the police, they had to roll up their trousers and carry their coats and weapons on their shoulders as they waded through the chilly waters. Roe reached the far side soaked and shivering to roars of laughter from the spectators on both banks.

Refusing Roe's offer of readmission, Maurice Quirke, who owed six years' rent, led his invalid wife and children outside while Pierce Mahony cried out: 'Is this really a Christian land?' Seventeen more people were then turned out and their homes reduced to rubble while the crowd groaned and jeered. Before the sheriff appeared Conybeare entered each abode, questioned the occupants closely, gave them legal advice, and then insisted on being driven out by the bailiffs. On their way back to camp the police had to re-cross the river. Once they had reached the other side, they vented their anger (and embarrassment) over all the taunts and jeers by unleashing a brutal baton charge against their tormentors. In the meantime the anti-nationalist *Times* reported that a woman had carried her half-naked infant outside to oblige an 'enterprising artist' who wanted to increase the dramatic quality of his sketch.[46]

On the next day a fierce storm halted the proceedings. Five Home Rule MPs sent a telegram to Hicks-Beach inviting him to visit Glenbeigh and see for himself Roe's 'inhuman' handiwork. Of course, they knew that the Chief Secretary would never travel so far to see 'mere Irish peasants' suffer. A leader in the *Freeman's Journal* on 19 January, entitled 'Shylock At Glenbeigh', castigated the London moneylenders for forcing Winn to order these 'barbarities' so that they could receive their pounds of flesh. The editor hoped that these atrocities against old men, dying women, and half-naked children would teach the English public what the enforcement of property rights meant in Ireland. By 21 January, Roe was offering to readmit any tenant who paid one gale's rent plus legal costs but he also threatened to raze the houses of anyone who refused this offer.[47]

The shrill outcries of Dillon, Conybeare, and other MPs as well as local priests soon reduced the number of final evictions. Thus five out of eight families ejected on 21 January were readmitted as caretakers. As Dillon pointed out, no Home Rule MPs had been present when the burnings began, but as soon as they appeared and the 'civilised world' learned what was transpiring, Roe had 'laid aside his oil cans and his torches' and become 'as mild as a sucking dove'. After being remanded and bailed, the Griffin garrison was tried by three magistrates in a coercion court at Killorglin. To the surprise and delight of their supporters all 23 men were acquitted and discharged. The joyous celebrations began with a speech by Father Thomas Quilter at a local hotel and ended with bonfires blazing all around Glenbeigh.[48]

From the *Daily News* to the *Pall Mall Gazette* Fleet Street sensationalised the Glenbeigh evictions. Stead called them 'infamously cruel' and predicted rightly that they would inspire widespread sympathy for the victims. Many of the *PMG*'s readers donated a few shillings or pounds that were forwarded to Father Quilter's relief committee that distributed over £300 to the homeless.[49] According to the *Standard* (17 January) the evictions were 'inhuman spectacles fit only for a barbarous country and a barbarous age'. The *Kerry Weekly Reporter* (22 January) described the crowbar brigade as 'about the most villainous looking individuals outside of a convict settlement, and whose duty is to knock down and burn the homesteads of the doomed tenantry'. This article continued:

> The pulse moves quicker, the blood runs cold, and the heart sickens in contemplation of those deeds, which must be written or referred to as the most powerful arguments that could ever be put forward against the systematical tyranny of landlordism in this country.

Faced with death or starvation, these tenants had every right to resist the evictors of 'the old and young, the prattling boys and frighted [*sic*] girls, the sick babes and the sick mothers'. 'It was inhuman and melancholy', he added, 'to see such deeds committed in this century of civilisation.'[50]

A song about the fate of an old Kerry farmer named McMahon might well have risen from the ashes of Glenbeigh:

The Agent said, you must go out, as lots have gone before;
The soldier and the police he brought around the cabin door;
The old man's eyes then filled with tears, the children got afraid,
He went up to the Agent, and in broken accents said:

Chorus
'For God's sake, let us stop, sir, for we've got no place to go!
I'm sure you wouldn't turn us out in all that blinding snow.
Ah, look at those poor children, sir, they'll soon be left alone;
For God's sake, don't evict us from our little Irish home!'

———

The Agent he stood coldly by, he didn't heed the plea,
The gold was all he wanted, for to satisfy his greed;
But if you let us stop, sir, your heart's not hard I know …
But then his scanty furniture they threw out in the snow
Then, with a cry of anguish, he sinks upon the ground,
While tears are being freely shed by everyone around;
A neighbour then came from the crowd, and gently raised his head –
His trouble's past, he'll speak no more, for poor McMahon was dead.[51]

J. F. O'Hea's 'The "Legal" Plan of Campaign' (*Weekly Freeman*, 22 January 1887) featured a demonic landlord holding a can of 'paraffin oil' while a mother and her children weep beside their burning abode. The villain of this graphic melodrama urges the police to continue their nefarious work: 'Well done! my gallant *Peace Officers*, I think we have pretty well roasted the Glen, and I find I have still paraffin enough left to burn out the old widow on yonder hill – By Jingo! it is as good as rat hunting.' J. D. Reigh's cartoon of the Glenbeigh evictions featured sympathetic English visitors denouncing 'robbery and murder' as an emergency man ignites the roof of a cottage. The evicted women and children weep while the learned legal authority, Chief Baron Palles, justifies this destruction: 'It is the Law. The Law must take its course.'[52]

On 20 January four more tenants were ejected after spurning Roe's terms of readmission. At each site the sheriff's party faced 'an incessant fire of imprecations both in English and Irish' from the hostile crowd. Roe did allow some tenants around Parkalassa to re-enter their 'wretched hovels' after making a token payment. But Tom Moriarty simply walked out because he could no longer earn money from odd jobs and selling periwinkles and carrageen seaweed. In vain Dillon protested the use of so many police to evict one poor peasant who had agreed to pay his rent but not the legal costs.[53]

Among the four tenants ousted and then readmitted at Ballinakilla on 25 January was Timothy Cahill, who lived in a shieling or cattle shed and was bereft of livestock and money. Timothy Sheehan owed £60 in rent and arrears but could offer no more than £5 – the remains of a marriage portion sent by two sons in Australia. Another tenant, who refused Roe's offer on the grounds that it would only postpone the inevitable scooped up his child, walked out into the rain followed by his weeping wife. While touring the estate two Parnellite MPs and a working-class Englishman came across a crude effigy of Roe built of turf sods and rags. A small stick resembling a cigar protruded from its mouth, and a wooden tablet hung from the neck bearing the words, 'Roe the Devil'.

Several days later the sheriff's party tackled James Quirke's abode at Coomasaharn. Obstacles placed on the road forced them to detour across moorland where they chased and beat several boys for blowing horns to warn the community. Women and girls cursed the bailiffs, who replied with 'grossly foul language'. Quirke threatened Roe with a reaping hook before being subdued. When his wife and daughter resisted, they were beaten and dragged outside kicking and screaming. His two brothers sobbed at the sight of the crowbar gang smashing the walls as Roe stood nearby smoking his pipe 'with callous indifference'. Suddenly, James's teen-age daughter, Mary, took a swing at Roe with a shovel but clobbered a bailiff instead. The cheering crowd surged forward to shield her from arrest. Nationalist papers praised Mary as 'the heroine of Glenbeigh', who had taken a 'noble stand' against 'the inhuman Roe and his Satanic satellites'. Admirers at home and abroad sent her money and medals; and Father Edward Hayes announced that if either Mary or her mother 'were my mother, so help me God, I would never rest until I had taken the life of Sir [*sic*] Rowland Winn'. A few years later this priest emigrated to Iowa where he offered to buy Mary's shovel for $25 so that he could donate it to the Youghal office of the National League in the hope that it would encourage others to resist.[54]

Forestier pointed up the absurdly unequal contest between the people and the police in his picture of a young woman wearing a shawl and apron resisting arrest in 'Attempting To Arrest a Girl for Assaulting an 'Emergency Man', at Glenbeigh, Kerry' (Figure 5.8).[55] Elated by the crowd's support, she appears to be on the verge of rescue by the two men wearing hats on her right.[56]

5.8   Amedée Forestier, 'Attempting to Arrest a Girl for Assaulting an "Emergency Man" at Glenbeigh, Kerry'. This sketch foregrounds a young woman resisting arrest by police bristling with rifles and fixed bayonets. Several men on the left are poised to rescue her from the clutches of the law. (*ILN*, 12 Feb. 1887)

After razing the cottage shared by Michael and John Quirke, the eviction party headed back to camp. Once again they had to ford the river Behy where volunteers carried sympathetic journalists on their backs. But the *Irish Times'* reporter named Dunlop did not qualify for any such favours given his Unionist leanings. A local man allowed him to climb up on his back and then suddenly dumped him in mid-stream to howls of derision from the onlookers. Moreover, the sight of half-dressed policemen wading in the stream with all their gear on their shoulders provoked more laughter and ribald remarks from the women on both banks. Once on shore the police batoned their hecklers with abandon.[57]

At a protest rally in Dingle Edward Harrington declared that the only way to prevent more such evictions was to abolish landlordism. 'In the blazing roof-trees of Glenbeigh', he added, 'a light had been cast upon the foul work of landlordism'. Conybeare called the landlords criminals who had robbed the tenants of their capital and labour. Every British MP, he asserted, should visit Ireland to see the realities. According to the *Pall Mall Gazette* such evictions were 'a thousand times more likely to be fatal to the prospect of peace and tranquillity in Ireland' than the renewal of the land war by means of the Plan of Campaign. In Parliament, Chief Secretary Hicks-Beach defended the Castle's efforts to dissuade Winn from evicting. Cries of 'Shame!' and 'No!' flowed from the Parnellite benches when Hicks-Beach stated that the only way to avoid more such evictions was to remove all the inhabitants from 'this poverty-stricken district'.[58] The story of Glenbeigh rapidly crossed the Atlantic by telegraph and appeared in such papers as the *New York Sun*, the *New York Tribune*, the *New York Times*, and the *Boston Herald, Globe,* and *Pilot.* The latter paper roundly denounced the brutality of Irish landlords and Castle officials beneath such headlines as 'THE LANDLORD PYTHON IN IRELAND'.[59]

Tensions remained high around Glenbeigh as some tenants re-entered their homes illegally and the sheriff's party had to return to deal with them. After Winn's death and Roe's resignation in 1888, Daniel Todd-Thornton, a trustee of the estate, assumed the role of agent and ordered the removal of James J. Griffin, secretary of the local branch of the National League, whose rent of £26 was twice the valuation. He owed three years' rent and had already been evicted twice before. The sheriff assembled a force of fifty police and proceeded to Lether East on 21 February to execute the decree. After the agent spurned Griffin's offer to pay one gale, the crowd grew menacing and Colonel Turner ordered Father Quilter to leave even though the priest was trying to calm his parishioners. The unnerved resident magistrate, Cecil Roche, warned that anyone who cheered or booed would be arrested, but the police refused to carry out this threat. Even though only Griffin and a sub-tenant were driven out, some nationalists labelled this 'Another Glenbeigh Campaign'.[60]

The novelist Rosa Mulholland (Lady Gilbert) evoked Glenbeigh briefly in her far-fetched romance, *Giannetta* (1889). The exotic plot involves a scheming uncle in an alpine district of northern Italy, who sells his niece, the eponymous and penniless orphan, to an elderly and benevolent Anglo-Irish tourist named Fitzgerald, who is convinced that she is his long lost daughter. This 'adopted' or bartered child accompanies her 'foster father' to England and thence Ireland where she inherits a large estate. Nearby a wicked absentee landlord, Sir Rupert Kirwan, plans multiple evictions while his idealistic nephew, Pierce Kirwan, falls in love with Giannetta. The two young lovers despise Sir Rupert who orders his bailiffs to burn down the cabins with paraffin oil. A few families try to fight back with stones and hot water. After being shot inside a fortified cottage, Pierce recovers and lands in jail for breaking the law. This fanciful tale of hidden identity, rags to riches, eviction, and teenage passion ends predictably with the joyous reunion of the two lovers.[61]

The prolific propaganda mill, the Irish Loyal and Patriotic Union, founded in 1885 by over a dozen ardent Church of Ireland landowners and Trinity College Dublin academics, insisted that no more than 760 out of the 1,233 evictions during the first half of 1886 could be attributed to non-payment of rent. All the other evictions involved town tenants, town parks, houseless farms, or tenant trespassers. Of those 760 evicted tenants, 250 had been reinstated, 377 had been readmitted as caretakers pending redemption, and 18 had sold their right to redeem leaving only 117 tenants homeless. By this partisan count only one out of every 3,000 holdings in the country stood in any danger of eviction.[62]

On the other hand nationalist spokesmen condemned 'the heartless brutality' of ousting tenants who could not afford to pay 'impossible rents'. Speakers at League rallies excoriated landlordism and tried to ban foxhunting wherever evictions had occurred.[63] The Home Rule press continued to fill columns with reports of families driven out and houses levelled. Thus the *Wexford People* described the ordeal of two tenants turned out in the fall of 1888 by a middleman. One of them, Patrick Kearney of Robinstown, was over seventy and sickly when the bailiffs entered and found him lying in a foetal position by the turf fire. His mind wandered as he reminisced about his youth, alluded to the rising of '98, and pleaded for a stay of execution. After the bailiffs carried him out and laid him on the ground, two constables placed some bedding beneath his body and someone gave him a dram of brandy. When told that he would have to enter the workhouse hospital, he sobbed: 'And so this is it after all – I'm to go to the poorhouse.'[64]

One unusual witness to the evictions on Lord Kingston's small Roscommon estate at Keadue in mid-April 1886 was the patrician English Tory radical, Wilfrid Scawen Blunt, who had been raised as a Catholic and whose diverse friendships ranged from George Wyndham and the Balfour brothers to Lady Gregory, Dillon, and Davitt. A philandering Arabophile and Celtophile, Blunt was an ardent Home Ruler and supporter of the Land League. He was so appalled by the 'brutal and absurd spectacle' of 250 armed men storming the cottages of 'half starved tenants' that he felt ill. He dashed off a damning letter to the *Freeman's Journal* and *Pall Mall Gazette* castigating the young 8th earl for allowing these proceedings and then had the gall to upbraid him at Kilronan castle. The evictions lasted several days and the victims' tales of hardship and loss deeply affected Blunt, who deplored the expenditure of £1,000 on the 'savage' expulsion of poor tenants in return for the collection of £20 in rent. This harrowing experience taught him that 'no one can understand what the Irish land question is till he has seen an eviction'.[65]

An apparently vindictive eviction occurred early in 1888 on Sir John Kennedy's estate near Dungarvan, County Waterford after Frank Mulcahy, a respectable farmer and sub-agent had objected to the removal of a desperately poor tenant with eleven children. For this insubordination the head agent, Royse, vowed that he 'would crush Mulcahy'. So he demanded the full rent due and a high price for the purchase of the farm. When Mulcahy failed to meet these terms, Royse hauled him into bankruptcy court. Later the sheriff arrived with seventy police and forced the tenant out along with his daughter.[66]

On Lord Carysfort's estate at Kilmurry, near Arklow, County Wicklow a crowd of 2,000 showed up in July 1888 to watch the expulsion of Bernard Rafferty whose family had lived there for seventy years. Two years behind with the rent he offered to pay one gale in August and another after the harvest. But the agent rejected these terms and gave orders to remove five nearly naked children, aged seven to one, who were asleep in one large bed. The bailiffs wrapped the children in bed clothing before carrying them out. One solicitous constable covered the infant with his cape. [67]

Not all evictions began or ended in blood, sweat, and tears. Occasionally, a bit of comedy or farce surfaced. In New Ross an elderly lady named Catherine Cavanagh locked the door of her town house, closed her shutters, and withdrew upstairs. From a window she threw basins of cold water as well as bottles, bricks, and flowerpots at two young bailiffs below. The crowd cheered as she belaboured them with a long pole. Evidently, the struggle to subdue her drove one bailiff into the nearest pub 'to drown his sorrow' with some 'J.J.' whiskey. [68] At Slievenue near Waterford the sub-sheriff had the unusual task of taking possession of not only a house but also the adjoining police barracks. After expelling the tenant, the bailiffs proceeded to evict the few constables to howls of delight from the onlookers. [69]

In September 1889 the siege of Monanimy Castle on the banks of the Blackwater River at Killavullen, County Cork, turned into farce. Owing more than three years' rent to her landlord, the widowed Mrs Thomas Barry and her supporters had barricaded the premises with timber and iron gates, removed all the furniture, broken much flooring, and felled trees across the road. For some time she and her children had been living in the dairy. When Sub-Sheriff Gale's party arrived with an escort of 100 police, they set up a tight cordon that excluded reporters but allowed a priest inside to reason with Mrs Barry. The so-called garrison consisted of her son and three workmen, who struck menacing postures on a balcony but failed to put up a fight. After climbing up two long ladders, the police gently apprehended the defenders and then released them. The bailiffs then tackled the dairy and carried Mrs Barry out in an armchair along with the furnishings while some local women wept. When the rumour spread that a cat had taken refuge in the crawl space under the roof, the bailiffs knocked down a ceiling but failed to find the feline. Several emergency men guarded by police took over the premises. [70]

When Walter Delahunty received his notice to quit on Count Edmund de la Poer's property at Island Tarsney, County Waterford, some 200 neighbours rallied to harvest and bag his corn crop before the bailiffs could seize it. Racing against time, they worked all night and then celebrated their achievement at a festive rally. This show of solidarity so impressed the landlord that he allowed Delahunty to name his own terms for reinstatement.[71]

DUNNE TO DEATH

Last but not least, what began as a minor eviction in County Louth became a major tragedy after a tenant died shortly after being expelled. Eighty-year-old James Dunne was a tenant of Captain Henry S. Singleton, and suffered from chronic bronchitis. For fifty years he had paid his rent faithfully, but old age had taken its toll and he had fallen far behind. Neither he nor his sons could come up with the £108 required for readmission as caretaker. On 11 October 1888 two Dublin agents with close ties to the PDA, Athol J. Dudgeon and Henry Emerson, who also managed the substantial estate of Lord Massereene, arrived at Belpatrick near Collon to preside over the operation. They watched the bailiffs carry Dunne outside wrapped in a thin blanket and heard him moan that he would not survive eviction. For several hours he sat on a stool in the cold coughing and trembling while family members and his priest, Father George Taaffe, tried to console him. For some unknown reason his sons failed to find him shelter. Finally, friends carried him into a barn and laid him down on a bed of straw where he expired before midnight.

Preceded by the similar death of an octogenarian, Bartley Geary, in Connemara in February, Dunne's fate caused a furore in the Parnellite camp. Even Gladstone alluded to this tragedy in a speech at Birmingham. The coroner's inquest at Ardee dragged on for nine sessions, and to the dismay of the landlord camp the nationalist jurors found both agents guilty of manslaughter on 9 November. The defendants were granted bail; their lawyers lodged an appeal; and on 22 January 1889 the judges in the Queen's Bench division quashed this verdict on the grounds of the jury's 'misconduct'. Absolved of any wrongdoing, Dudgeon and Emerson resumed their mission to make tenants pay dearly for withholding the rent.[72]

Dunne's demise inspired two colour prints by O'Hea and Reigh on 20 October. Reigh's cartoon in *United Ireland* revealed Dunne lying dead on a thin pallet of straw in a barn with the door wide open. Choosing the ironic title, 'The Vindication of the Law' (Plate 7), he omitted any mourners from the scene as a deathly bluish moonbeam suffuses the corpse. The caption contained Dunne's warning that his death would be on the agent's 'soul' if he were forced to forsake his warm hearth.

On the same day the *Weekly Freeman* carried O'Hea's tribute, 'Evicting to Death', that revealed the moribund Dunne reclining on a pile of boulders while in the background the sheriff's party marches past a ruined cottage. The accompanying doggerel pointed out that Dunne, who might not have perished had he been English, had toiled for eighty years 'to glut an idler's greed for gold' and to earn nothing but 'scorn and sneers'. When he could no longer ply his spade, he was 'cast from out his home – TO DIE!' If Christ was born in a stable, Dunne died in one; and the 'Sons of Albion' needed reminding that this oppression had to end and the 'despots' responsible for such horrors needed to be 'plucked down'.[73]

Two months later O'Hea produced an even more poignant indictment of eviction. In 'Two Christmas Hearths' (Plate 8), the juxtaposition of good and evil takes the form of a homeless three-generation family shivering on Christmas eve in the ruins of their cottage with only a few thin blankets to ward off the cold. The injured and despairing farmer gazes forlornly across the frozen field at the Yuletide festivities going on inside the Big House in the distance that glows with an orange-coloured warmth. The caption for this cartoon emphasised the acute suffering caused by eviction:

> Look at this scene – Two homes are pictured here,
> One full of comfort where the fire shines bright.
> The other, to its tenants once was dear;
> Squalid and bare to-night!
>
> Out in the cold, to famish, or to die,
> The parents and their little ones are sent.
> The man has worked, and toiled incessantly –
> But cannot pay the rent.
>
> He cannot pay – The sheriff won't forbear
> He pleads for time – the landlord will not wait.
> Father, and mother, children – all are there.
> Homeless, and desolate!
>
> Homeless! The very sound is like a knell!
> See in those faces sorrow is depicted –
> They know the meaning, which words cannot tell,
> Of that foul word – Evicted![74]

Contemplating the collective impact of so many evictions, the *Freeman's Journal* tried to articulate the evil of dispossession by invoking the iconic vampire: 'Yet this is but one of countless similar acts [evictions] which have been committed by the vampires who have for centuries been sucking the life blood and gnawing at the very vitals of the nation, and who have been guilty of crimes against suffering humanity which cry to Heaven for vengeance.'[75]

At least the *ILN* allowed a note of comedy to creep into one of its sobering pictures of the land war. On Christmas day 1886 their 'special artist' depicted himself wearing a loud tweed Ulster coat and deerstalker hat being chased away by villagers who have mistaken him for an agent or process server (Figure 5.9). And in the upper right-hand corner of 'Sketches in Ireland', a pig refuses to be evicted and runs back to his home hotly pursued by a squad of police.[76]

OUR SPECIAL ARTIST MISUNDERSTOOD BY THE CROWD.

REFUSING TO BE EVICTED.

TRIAL OF MOONLIGHTERS AT CORK: GUARD OUTSIDE THE JUDGE'S HOUSE.

OUR ARTIST VISITING THE LAND LEAGUE HUTS AT "COERCION HILL."

SKETCHES IN IRELAND: BY OUR SPECIAL ARTIST.

5.9 'Sketches in Ireland: By Our Special Artist'. A comic touch lightens two of the four small cuts in this print. In the upper left hand corner the *ILN*'s 'special artist' pictures himself being chased out of the village because he has been mistaken for an agent or process server. In the upper right-hand corner a pig runs back to his home despite the efforts of the police to capture him. And in the lower right hand corner, the artist visits a Land League hut built for evicted tenants at 'Coercion Hill'. (*ILN*, 25 Dec. 1886)

SIX

THE PLAN EVICTIONS
1887–90

*'If the police were taken away from their eviction work,
there would be nothing for them to do in the country.'*

WILLIAM REDMOND
House of Commons, 6 August 1889.

*'Habit is everything, your first eviction is
as hard to stomach as your first cigar.'*

F. MABEL ROBINSON
The Plan of Campaign: A Story of the Fortune of War
(London, 1888).

———

Taking advantage of the return of agricultural depression in 1885 and deeply dismayed by the defeat of Gladstone's first Home Rule bill, Tim Harrington, John Dillon, and William O'Brien decided to embark on a new offensive against landlordism during the fall of 1886 by advising tenants on selected estates to withhold their rent unless they received abatements of at least 30 per cent on non-judicial rents. Back in October 1885 Tim Healy broached the idea of lodging rents deemed too high in an escrow account; and Dillon, whose hatred of landlordism burned with a 'hard, gemlike flame', envisaged renewing the land agitation if evictions increased and if the Unionists at Westminster rejected Home Rule. Published in O'Brien's newspaper, *United Ireland*, on 23 October 1886, the Plan of Campaign was analogous in some respects to a closed-shop trade union insofar as it called on tenants to combine forces and demand a hefty abatement. Should the proprietor refuse, then they would pay the gale less the reduction into a 'war chest' held by trustees until the contest had been won. Any tenants evicted for embracing the Plan would be maintained by both the escrowed rent and National League funds.

Plan leaders constantly stressed both the significance and the propaganda value of eviction: 'Ejectment is the landlord's most common remedy. Every legal and constitutional obstacle, which could oppose or delay eviction must be used … The fullest publicity should be given to evictions. No landlord should get one penny on any part of his estate so long as he has one tenant unjustly evicted.'[1] They also insisted that tenants forced to pay a 'rack rent' were 'not morally bound' by their contract. Instead of paying 'impossible rents' and ending up beggars in the workhouse, the tenantry should insist on reductions of even their judicial rent. Predictably, the Plan provoked bitter disputes wherever landlords refused to yield. Besides badgering tenants who were slow to join, local organisers condoned the punishment of anyone who broke ranks by secretly paying their rent. Tenants evicted for adhering to the Plan often lived in cramped wooden huts for years and had to endure the pain of seeing their fields go to waste or, much worse, being farmed by a landgrabber.

After launching the Plan on the O'Grady's estate around Bruff, County Limerick on 9 November, Dillon and O'Brien moved on to the turbulent districts of Woodford and Portumna where they enlisted most of the Clanricarde tenantry. From there they proceeded to promote the Plan around the country backed by almost every Home Rule MP with the notable exception of Parnell who opposed reviving the land agitation. Although Davitt regarded the landlords as 'social brigands', he criticised the Plan preferring a No Rent campaign to abatements and hoping that the government would be forced to enact a giant land purchase scheme. In speech after speech the indefatigable O'Brien declared war on landlordism, insisting that it would never be smashed until the people made eviction 'an expensive and bitter job for the landlords'. Aided and abetted by the clergy, he and Dillon urged tenants to join the Plan despite police efforts to ban their recruitment rallies.[2]

Little agreement exists about the exact number of estates afflicted by the Plan. Estimates range from 203 (Geary) to 84 (Davitt). Between these poles fall Joseph O'Brien's count of 140 and Dillon's 116.[3] Whether or not these estimates included estates where landlords caved in at the very mention of Plan action is not known. In any event the Plan afflicted less than one per cent of all Irish estates and most of these lay in the south and west. Only two stubborn landlords in Ulster felt the sting of the Plan: Wybrants Olphert in western Donegal and Lord Annesley in County Cavan, where the tenants accepted the offer to buy their holdings at 14 years' purchase of the rent in August 1887. Wherever Protestant tenants predominated, the Plan leaders had a hard time mobilising farmers.

Any landowner who fought the Plan had to pay a steep price. Lord Lansdowne spent close to £10,000 trying to defeat this combination in Queen's County; George Brooke suffered almost as much loss on his Wexford estate; and the O'Grady, a widely respected resident owner, lost over £6,500 in rental income by holding out. Only outside help saved proprietors like William N. Leader of Currass, County Cork, Charles Talbot Ponsonby of Youghal, and Olphert of

Falcarragh from bankruptcy after defying the Plan. John Redmond compared the Plan to the sword of Damocles hovering over the heads of Irish landlords who refused to compromise until they faced ruin or the court of chancery.[4]

Among the landlords who surrendered to the Plan after watching their income dwindle were Lord Dunsandle and Richard Berridge in Galway, Colonel Sir Charles Knox-Gore in Mayo, and Lord Cork and Orrery in Kerry. At first Viscount Dillon of Ditchley Park Oxfordshire, owner of 89,000 acres in Mayo and Roscommon, could not wait to evict the Plan ringleaders. But his agent advised compromise because the income of £24,000 from some 5,000 tenants was needed to pay the interest on all the incumbrances. Following numerous evictions around Castlerea, O'Brien negotiated a settlement in January 1887 that included a 20 per cent abatement and reinstatement of the evicted. While the nationalist camp rejoiced, Irish officials groaned over Lord Dillon's 'humble submission'. J. D. Reigh hailed this 'glorious victory' for the Plan with a cartoon entitled 'Capitulation' (*United Ireland*, 15 January 1887) wherein Lord Dillon bows his coroneted head while handing over the sword labelled 'Rack Rents' to John Dillon. At a huge rally in Carracastle O'Brien extolled the tenants as 'heroes and soldiers' in the historic contest against land-lordism; and John Dillon boasted at a rally in Cork in February 1887 that what the government called 'an illegal conspiracy' had forced both the agent and his master to join the Plan.[5]

Many of the tenants on Sir Henry Burke's 25,000-acre estate around Marblehill, County Galway had worked long and hard to reclaim marginal land only to fall behind with the rent once prices fell. Pleading for reductions, they formed a defence association that prompted the owner to obtain 60 notices to quit. The tenants responded by holding a monster protest meeting, building huts for any tenants who might be evicted, and adopting the Plan once their demand for a 40 per cent abatement had been refused. Backed by the PDA multiple evictions set in motion the usual cycle of boycotting, arrests, and imprisonments. Burke managed to hold out until February 1888 when he granted a 25 per cent reduction conditional on payment of one year's rent.[6] Plan supporters celebrated this victory with torchlight processions, bonfires, brass bands, mass meetings, and fiery speeches. The nationalist press hailed this outcome as 'The Great Tenants' Victory'. Every week *United Ireland* published progress reports on Plan contests around the country culled from county newspapers and hailed each and every victory.[7]

As we will see, the Plan did suffer setbacks when and where landlords and the government combined forces to launch a counter-offensive. In June 1887 the Duke of Abercorn sent out a circular seeking to enlist the support of every-one with an interest in Irish land – from owners and mortgagees to insurance companies – in the newly formed Anti-Plan of Campaign Association that advised and assisted some beleaguered proprietors. Among those who resolved to fight the Plan on their estates were the O'Grady, Lord Ventry, Lord Lansdowne, the Countess of Kingston, the Earl of Massereene, Lord De Freyne, Charles Ponsonby, and Colonel O'Callaghan. Although few in number, they evicted as many Campaign ringleaders and rank and file members as possible while distraining chattels and then selling them at auctions that yielded no profit because local people were warned against bidding.[8]

Plan successes were often mixed. While landlords had to contend with sharp falls in income and the cost of eviction as well as boycotting, countless tenants lost their farms and the Plan executive had to pay for their housing and maintenance. The latter expenses severely strained the resources of the Parnellite party, and Parnell's clear disapproval did not help the cause. Nevertheless the publicity bestowed on this agitation by the nationalist press restored some of the morale lost after the stunning defeat of the Home Rule bill.[9]

Dillon's fondness for hyperbole moved him to proclaim the Plan as 'one of the greatest struggles that had ever marked the history of any country'. He went on to predict that it 'would undo the work of three centuries and reconquer the land of Ireland and hand it over to the people to whom it belonged'. In much the same vein O'Brien promised a Mallow audience that the Plan would turn 'a race of slaves into owners and rulers of this land'. The stress and strain of this agitation and the ordeal of imprisonment forged a strong bond between these two leaders that would last until the revival of the land war in the next century. Undaunted by arrests, trials, and imprisonment for their Plan activities, both leaders urged the tenantry to resist eviction by every 'reasonable' and 'honest' means. Their appearance at Plan rallies was almost guaranteed to attract crowds of several thousand despite the strenuous efforts of Dublin Castle to ban such meetings.[10]

Without the vigorous support of the Catholic clergy the Plan would have been a mere shadow of itself. All over the south and west priests helped to organise protest meetings, negotiated with the agent or owner over rent and arrears, and promoted the Plan at the risk of arrest. On numerous estates they served as trustees for the rent withheld, attended evictions, consoled the families affected, and showed up at the trials of resisters as well as their fellow priests. Because most of them came from farming stock they were well informed about such crucial matters as rent, valuation, terms of tenure, crops, and the land laws. Besides wielding 'enormous' parochial power they often regarded local landlords as rivals for the temporal control of their parishioners. As Tom Garvin has pointed out, their vision of the future included a prosperous and stable rural society filled with farm-owning and devout Catholics who had no intention of emigrating. At the height of the second land war proactive priests like

Fathers McFadden, Stephens, Keller, Murphy, Quilter, and Kennedy paid the price of prison time for promoting the Plan. Not only did they grace the platforms of Plan rallies but also at the 'great' National League convention in Cork on 23 July 1887, 150 of the 650 delegates were priests and canons along with a few 'church dignitaries'. [11]

In March 1888 Canon Keller PP reminded the Ponsonby tenants at Youghal that the brave 'soldiers' of the Plan had already forced 45 landlords to submit. 'When the history of this struggle will be written', he added, 'it will be difficult which more to admire – the persistent obstinacy of a rack-renting landlord or the justice and moderation and patient tenacity with which his tenants have resisted him for fifteen long months … Stand together, brothers all. We have passed the worst of it. Victory is within our grasp.' [12] Frustrated by the devotion of so many Catholic tenants to the Plan, Dublin Castle had a hard time curbing the agitation. The ordinary law proved powerless to curb this combination and the Castle's law officers badly bungled two state trials in the winter of 1886–7. Shortly after being acquitted, the defendants sallied forth from Dublin to promote the Plan. [13]

What the Plan leaders failed to anticipate, however, was the resilience and combativeness of Arthur James Balfour, who worked hard to subvert the Plan after becoming Irish chief secretary in March 1887. If he were an Irish landlord, he once declared, he would much rather beg for bread than yield to this 'criminal' combination. At first the Parnellites thought that this languid and seemingly effete nephew of the Conservative Unionist Prime Minister, Lord Salisbury, would not last six months in office. But his foppish and philosophical demeanour disguised a ruthless streak. Blunt deplored his 'scientific inhumanity in politics'; and a Cork priest opined that the man 'with the lank legs' was 'endowed … with feline malice'. [14] But insults never ruffled Balfour's fine feathers and his indifference to criticism infuriated his myriad enemies.

Besides passing a stringent coercion act designed to curb the agitation, he also orchestrated several secret syndicates composed of rich landed magnates in both Britain and Ireland that temporarily bought and managed half a dozen beleaguered estates and saved their owners from surrender. Among the wealthy peers whom Balfour recruited for this scheme were the Duke of Westminster and Lord De Vesci. To root out the Plan and prevent landlords from surrender he also tried to regulate evictions on certain estates depending on local conditions and the Castle's resources. Despite his myriad duties and concerns he kept an eye on the principal Plan estates and advised his under-secretary to dissuade harsh landlords like O'Callaghan and Clanricarde from purging every Campaigner. Because evictions required such large armed escorts the Irish administration had its hand on the throttle of the eviction machine. At times the conduct of callous or stubborn landlords caused Balfour almost as much annoyance as his nemeses in the nationalist camp. In any event a sure sign of the counterattack against the Plan was a spurt in the number of evictions from 3,127 in 1885 to 3,869 in 1887.[15]

The Plan offered landlords few attractive options. Suing a tenant in bankruptcy court for non-payment was not cheap; and proceeding for debt by distraint created its own set of problems. At shrieval auctions the agent was forced to buy up the farmers' interest and assets for nominal sums. In a few cases landlords used the Plan as an excuse to clear away their unprofitable tenants and replace them with strong farmers or graziers. Thus Arthur Pollock carried on his customary policy of removing cottiers and squaring their holdings during the Plan era.[16]

In the spring of 1888 the *Freeman's Journal* ran a series of feature articles on the Plan's origin and operation on over a dozen estates around the country. Among other landlords the reporter singled out Clanricarde, John C. Delmege of Glensharrold, County Limerick, and Sir Henry Burke of Marble Hill as chronic rackrenters and evictors who richly deserved the Plan. At the same time nationalist newspapers stepped up their coverage of evictions. Thus the *People* (Wexford) devoted a long article and editorial in June to the ejectment of Nicholas Boggan, his wife and seven children, from their hovel on Forth mountain near Larkinstown, in southeast Wexford. After a lyrical description of the landscape, this reporter denounced 'the hellish game of eviction and extermination' that 'vindictive landlords' had been playing for centuries. The editor called this eviction 'the best proof that can be found of the curse of landlordism'. Another article dealt with the ejectment of Laurence Connor at Oldtown, Ballygarret in August. Evidently, the sheriff escorted by droves of police had to march ten miles to deal with this one tenant. Connor and his family stood outside as the bailiffs smashed the furniture by tossing it out of a window. One headline, 'A DYING WOMAN THROWN ON THE ROADSIDE', signalled this paper's attitude towards the proprietor, Captain R. D'Olier George of Cahore House, Gorey, and his agent.[17]

To strengthen the government's hand against boycotting, intimidation, and the Plan of Campaign, Balfour introduced his notorious Criminal Law Amendment bill on 28 March 1887. Dubbed the 'Jubilee Coercion Act' by nationalists, this measure replaced trial by jury for political or agrarian crimes with 'star chamber' courts presided over by two magistrates or 'removables', whom Parnellites derided as 'half-pay Army officers, broken down sepoys', briefless barristers, and 'experienced cricketers as well as the sweepings of the Four Courts'. This act criminalised both the Plan and the National League, created a form of martial law in proclaimed districts, and facilitated the arrest of anyone who obstructed the sheriff, incited unrest, or attended banned rallies. Besides prosecuting those who resisted eviction or obstructed the sheriff, magistrates cracked down on public displays of support for the Plan. Thus two Kerrymen were jailed in April 1889 for six months because they had cheered for 'an illegal conspiracy' during a 'disorderly' rally following a football match at Killarney. And a Corkman was incarcerated for four months for blowing a horn at Towermore to annoy the Protestant caretaker of an evicted farm. Police detectives were assigned to 'shadow' local Plan leaders and take notes on any activities or words that could be construed as promoting the Plan. By January 1890 some 1,773 persons – mostly Land and National Leaguers as well as Plan of Campaign activists – had been imprisoned under this 'perpetual coercion act'. And upon their release crowds turned out to welcome many of them home with parades, bonfires, and banquets.[18]

Hoping to reduce the fierce opposition in Ireland to coercion, Balfour served up a measure of conciliation in the form of the Land Law (Ireland) Act of 1887 that enabled leaseholders to become judicial tenants and apply for fair rents in the same way as yearly tenants. Also, tenants served with writs for non-payment could submit their case to the land court and postpone eviction. Notices to quit could now be sent by registered letter and posted in public places thereby sparing process servers grievous harm. *United Ireland* denounced this latter provision on the grounds that it made eviction 'cheap, easy, safe, and private'; and nationalists called it 'the eviction-made-easy-clause'. This failed attempt at conciliation drew criticism from landlords and Liberal Unionists not to mention Home Rulers; and the Archbishop of Dublin, Dr William Walsh, pleaded in vain for the suspension of evictions while the measure was being debated.[19]

In August 1886 the sub-sheriff of Galway drove out four families on Hannah Lewis's property near Loughrea while angry bystanders hooted and jeered. Because three of these victims were old and sickly widows they were readmitted as caretakers. One pregnant woman, whose husband was in jail, grew so nervous at the evictors' approach that she gave birth prematurely and was allowed to stay on the advice of a medical officer. The invalid wife of a hard-working farmer fainted at the sight of the emergency men, who then carried her out and laid her on the ground amidst the shrieks of her daughter. Fathers Egan and Coen administered the last rites, but she suddenly recovered and the sheriff readmitted the family. At the 'tumbled down' abode of the widow Coen, four young girls gave the bailiffs a 'bath of scalding lime water'. After breaching a gable wall, the crowbar gang subdued the female garrison but the police released the girls. This landlord's refusal to grant a 50 per cent abatement resulted in the Plan's adoption on 13 December 1886.[20]

More evictions followed the decision of some 500 Woodford tenants to hand over their rent to Plan trustees in mid-November 1886. To resounding cheers Dillon told a packed meeting that 'if they beat Clanricarde, there was not a landlord in Ireland that would have the courage to face the tenants and try to smash them'. [21] It did not take the tenants long to establish their reputation as resolute Campaigners. Almost a year later the sheriff's party 'swooped down' on Martin Kenny's house at Clonmilan, County Galway. This wily tenant had dumped forty cartloads of stones inside his cottage along with agricultural tools. To avoid combat, he took his wife and seven children to an outhouse where they watched the bailiffs haul out all these obstacles. O'Brien arrived at Woodford on 21 October 1887 to celebrate the Plan's first anniversary with a huge illegal rally. With a flourish he held up and burned a copy of the police proclamation banning the meeting as bonfires blazed on the hillsides. The telegraph wires had been cut and a policeman's helmet dangled from one of them. [22]

With more ejectments looming Dillon urged Blunt to return to Woodford and denounce both Clanricarde and the new crimes act. Treated like semi-royalty by his new nationalist friends, Blunt defied the Castle's prohibition of Plan rallies by appearing before a large crowd on 23 October 1887. No sooner had he started to speak than divisional magistrate Byrne and several policemen dragged him off the platform. In the ensuing mêlée he fell several feet to the ground where the police pounced on him. When his brave wife, Lady Anne, tried to rescue him, the police roughed her up. Stones flew and the police beat members of the crowd before hauling Blunt and his friend, John Roche, off to Loughrea jail. After posting bail, Blunt returned to England amidst a blaze of publicity to await his trial. Back in Galway he was convicted of resisting arrest and sentenced to two months in jail where he suffered the usual deprivations, picked oakum, and wrote sonnets. Ardent supporters raised over £1,300 for his defence fund, and no less than eight MPs showed up at his appeal hearing in Portumna in January 1888. Released from Kilmainham prison on 6 March 1888, he was greeted like a hero-martyr. Within a year he had buried the hatchet with both Wyndham and Balfour. In the meantime O'Brien's arrest, trial, and imprisonment at the end of 1887 and again in the spring of 1888 made headline news in both British and Irish newspapers. [23]

Agrarian crime intensified around Woodford and Portumna after Clanricarde's agent threatened to carry out 1,600 evictions. When a crowd assembled in Loughrea on 10 February 1888 to hear the radical George Shaw-Lefevre MP condemn Blunt's mistreatment, the police dispersed them with brutal baton charges. More protest meetings condemning both Clanricarde and the Castle and supporting the imprisoned O'Brien drew huge audiences to Loughrea and elsewhere in May.[24] To emphasise the extent of the counter-campaign of eviction waged by some landlords, the *Pictorial News* (6 February 1888) carried Claude Byrne's dramatic sketch of a family of nine (including five children) being driven out. In 'The State of Ireland – Opening of the Great Eviction Campaign – The Crowbar Brigade At Work in the South' the sub-sheriff watches the family forsaking their home while the bailiffs hack a hole in the roof. On the far right a child clutches a birdcage signifying innocence and fragility (Figure 6.1).[25]

6.1   Claude Byrne, 'The State of Ireland – Opening of the Great Eviction Campaign – The Crowbar Brigade at Work in the South'. Byrne sketched the expulsion of a large family during a wave of evictions on Plan of Campaign estates. The sub-sheriff coolly surveys the siege as the bailiffs break through the roof. On the far right a child holds her precious birdcage. (*Pictorial News*, 6 Feb. 1888)

In January 1889 negotiations led by the Bishop of Clonfert broke down and Edward Tener, Clanricarde's agent, who had been assaulted at one eviction, applied for eighty more ejectment decrees while a brass band played patriotic airs outside Loughrea courthouse. At one point a policeman announced that he was fed up with the 'degrading' work of driving out poor families and gave three cheers for Dillon and O'Brien. Within minutes he was arrested and hurried away to the barracks. Clanricarde complained that he had received no rent for two years and ordered Tener to obtain more notices to quit. On one occasion the agent and a solicitor survived an ambush but the agent's horse suffered a fatal wound. In August 1890 the court at Woodford granted fifty more ejectment writs. A month later local papers carried advertisements soliciting farmers from Ulster willing to rent thirty farms ranging from ten to 100 acres. This blatant appeal for Protestant 'planters' raised tensions even higher as did the expulsion of 120 more families in November. The leading Campaigner in Portumna town, Edward Moloney, a prosperous wool and corn merchant as well as publican, risked losing all his property for refusing to pay arrears of £68. While Parnellite MPs complained about the cost to taxpayers of accommodating one hundred extra police on the Clanricarde estate, Tener continued to demand payment of at least three years' rent and arrears plus legal costs before any tenant could qualify for reinstatement. Fear of eviction hung over both estates like a dark cloud well into the next century.[26]

O'GRADY/HERBERTSTOWN

For years the O'Grady of Kilballyowen, County Limerick, had enjoyed friendly relations with his tenants as befitted the head of an ancient sept whose forebears had lived there for centuries. In 1885 he had conceded abatements of 15 and 20 per cent respectively on judicial and non-judicial rents. But this did not satisfy tenants made more militant by the low prices for butter and other produce. Father Matthew (Matt) Ryan CC of Hospital (Spiddal), known as 'the General', called for a 40 per cent reduction on non-judicial rents. O'Grady's refusal led to the Plan's adoption and soon the owner and his family were boycotted. Not even Madame Elizabeth O'Grady's faithful dressmaker would do her sewing. To the rescue rushed her uncle, the redoubtable Arthur Kavanagh, who arranged the estate's takeover by the Land Corporation. After more evictions the empty farms were stocked with £500 worth of cattle. But for the next few years Dillon and O'Brien kept whipping up support for the Plan with fiery speeches in the vicinity of Herbertstown and Bruff.

At the end of August 1887 the sub-sheriff backed by 200 police and soldiers executed six notices to quit. Resistance was sporadic. Some tenants felled big trees across the roads and stuffed their windows with prickly bushes and iron gates. Despite being hooted and jeered the O'Grady attended each eviction. Using a mixture of hot water and tar as well as stones and poles, Mrs Hanorah Cummins's garrison fought off the crowbar men who had climbed onto the roof. After the bailiffs breached a wall, the nine defenders were subdued. Old Margaret Moloney was confined to her sickbed when the sheriff knocked on her door. After she refused the offer of readmission, the bailiffs carried her out – bed and all – into the pouring rain despite a doctor's protest. Several soldiers were so upset by this 'inhuman shame' that they cursed the evictors. Finding shelter in her stepbrother's house, the widow admitted to a reporter: 'Ah, sir, didn't I ask them to lay me down outside the gate, and let them build any kind of shed over me, as long as I could even see the place.' Her death a week later prompted *United Ireland* to call this outcome one more link in 'the long chain of martyrs and victims to landlord cruelty'. At several sites the police dispersed crowds with their batons. When spectators came too close to one cottage undergoing eviction, the resident magistrate ordered his men to 'hunt the dogs'. Father Ryan was standing near another evicted cottage when a district inspector ordered him to leave with the cutting remark: 'Go away, you corner boy.' Later this priest spent several months in Limerick jail for his Plan activities.

Propped up by the Land Corporation, the O'Grady purged more Plan tenants until their subsidies petered out in 1891. Having lost well over £6,000, the O'Grady finally agreed to a settlement and in 1892 he started to sell farms to those willing to pay one and a half year's rent. However, the damage done to landlord and tenant relations on this estate took years to heal.[27]

KINGSTON/MITCHELSTOWN REVISITED

Reprising the conflicts of 1881, the Kingston estate became another battleground after the owner rejected the tenants' demand for a 20 per cent abatement in December 1886. This time the stakes were even higher because Anna the dowager countess now had the support of Dublin Castle. Even in good times she had a hard time paying the interest of £10,000 on a £236,000 mortgage loan from the Church of Ireland. By 1887 the arrears of interest amounted to £13,000 while her gross rental came close to £17,000. Pressed by her trustees and creditors, the widow of the last earl of Kingston ordered writs served on some 800 of the 1,200 tenants, many of whom were leaseholders ineligible to apply for judicial rents. Most of the tenants joined the Plan and hundreds turned out in January 1887 to help their decreed neighbours remove hay and other produce from their farms. Almost a thousand horses were used to cart away these assets before the bailiffs could seize them. A day or two later, the Campaigners rounded up a thousand head of cattle and sold them at a special auction held in Mitchelstown for £9,700. This fair ended with a parade and a rally complete with brass bands and speechmaking.[28]

At mass meetings in the summer of 1887 Home Rule MPs and local Plan leaders reminded the tenants that they were engaged in a fight for survival and were therefore justified in defending their homesteads. When the sheriff saw some of the formidable barricades, he decided to postpone the evictions. But the countess stood firm and refused to lower her rents. No doubt the arrest of both O'Brien and a local activist John Mandeville caused her some relief. O'Brien's subsequent trial provoked the protest meeting that culminated in the notorious 'Mitchelstown massacre' of 9 September. This 'riot' resulted from the effort of a police reporter to wade through some eight thousand peaceful protestors in order to reach the platform where Dillon was speaking. After the police responded to stone throwing by using their batons, they retreated to their barracks where they were besieged. Some of them opened fire at the crowd killing three men. The resulting fury of nationalists increased when a coroner's jury returned a verdict of murder against the resident magistrate and five constables. After O'Brien and Mandeville were convicted and imprisoned, the cry, 'Remember Mitchelstown', reverberated through the land and Balfour earned the epithet 'Bloody'. Although the land courts eventually reduced rents on the estate by up to 30 per cent, the Plan leaders demanded more. This impasse lasted until February 1888 when Webber and the trustees conceded a further abatement of 20 per cent and reinstatement.

Shortly after the Mitchelstown affray, the Unionist government lost several by-elections in England. Writing from Coole Park to his friend the Earl of Dufferin, Sir William Gregory blamed these losses on the impact of Irish evictions on the English electorate convinced as it was that the government was 'aiding and abetting' them:

> You cannot argue with an agricultural labourer on the sacredness of obligations, or convince him that four-fifths of these evicted tenants could and would settle with their landlords if allowed to do so. … Hodge sees the walls placarded with representations of old women dragged out of their homes by ferocious bailiffs, of children lying in ditches, of homesteads set on fire, and his sluggish nature is roused by the impassioned appeals of Irish orators, a kind of fervid eloquence so different from the humming and hawing of the candidate who tries to explain that all this is right, and so duly reflecting that he may also be evicted, he votes for those who denounce eviction. This feeling will turn the scale in many an English and Scotch election.

If Gregory exaggerated the impact of Glenbeigh and other evictions in Ireland on the British electorate, there was a grain of truth in his gloomy assessment. [29]

KENMARE/KILLARNEY

On Lord Kenmare's sprawling estate around Killarney the resourceful agent, Maurice Leonard, staved off the Plan for almost a year by means of negotiations and minimal evictions. Even though rents and arrears brought in an annual income of £28,700, the cost of improvements and heavy interest payments on mortgage loans kept profits low. Among the tenants evicted on 11 June 1887 was a popular Poor Law Guardian, Daniel Shea, who was sitting down to breakfast with his mother and sister when the bailiffs barged inside and proceeded to carry out the furniture including the dining table with the food and dishes on top. Sympathy for Shea and hatred of the 'ruffian' bailiffs incensed the crowd outside. At another house the bailiffs had a tug of war with a tenant over his household goods. Police restraint averted bloodshed. [30]

However, the Plan's adoption by the smallholders on the Rathmore estate in late October 1888 ushered in a year of turbulence and fitful violence. The expulsion of the leading Campaigners and O'Brien's castigation of Lord Kenmare as the worst example of callous landlordism kept Killarney and environs on edge for months. Attempts to distrain livestock proved futile because the farmers hid their cattle. By April 1889 the police were guarding him around the clock after he had obtained eighty more ejectment decrees that had to be posted because process servers were in such short supply. More negotiations over the summer resulted in a temporary truce pending negotiations.[31] After O'Brien's release from prison, arbitration by a judge and the Catholic Bishop of Kerry paved the way for a partial settlement on the Rathmore estate. In August Lord Kenmare and Leonard conceded a 25 per cent abatement and reinstated Plan tenants after they had paid one year's rent. This compromise brought the rental income back to pre-Plan levels even though arrears remained high. At the end of September two old men were driven out of their dwellings in the parish of Kilcummin. One of them, John Fleming, experienced his third eviction since 1881.[32]

MASSEREENE/LOUTH

The Plan also vexed the Louth estate of the 11th Viscount Massereene, who needed every pound of rent to pay for his heavy consumption of alcohol and luxuries as well as family charges. A convivial host and sportsman he was also determined to defeat this combination.[33] When half of his 230 tenants demanded abatements of 20 and 25 per cent on judicial and non-judicial rents respectively in 1886, the old agent, Alfred Wynne, advised compromise. But Massereene refused to meet a tenants' delegation and Wynne resigned. He was replaced by those two solicitors from Dublin, Athol J. Dudgeon and Henry Emerson, who were hardened veterans of the first land war.[34]

With their priests' blessings all the Catholic tenants joined the Plan in January 1887 while the 36 Protestant tenants continued to pay their rent. The agents then auctioned off the interest of 20 Plan tenants in their farms and served notices to quit. But these farmers outsmarted the agents by holding their own cattle fair and selling both livestock and crops. O'Brien and Dillon held frequent rallies at which they denounced tyrannical landlords and brutal bailiffs and promised that there would be no Glenbeighs in Louth. On 16 July 1887, O'Brien boasted in Drogheda that the Plan had made the landlords shudder at the very thought of evictions. Unlike the bad old days, evictions were no longer as cheap as 'shooting rabbits'. Besides inflicting much 'shame, misery, and the most ruinous loss and expense' upon individual landlords, they also shed 'the white light of publicity' on the evils of landlordism. The Tory government, he added, had good reason to fear Gladstone's return to power.[35]

After ten more evictions on 5 October, some tenants broke ranks and paid their rent in secret, prompting Dillon to hasten to Collon where he exhorted the tenants to act like men and stick to the Plan. After his arrest for this tirade, seven priests along with his friend Blunt attended his trial outside Drogheda in May 1888. Despite a noxious smoke bomb that forced a courtroom evacuation Dillon was found guilty of promoting the Plan and sentenced to six months in jail.[36]

On 27 October 1887 the crowbar brigade returned with 300 police and soldiers to stamp out what Unionists called this 'immoral conspiracy'. After the agents refused Father John Rock's offer to settle for a 20 to 25 per cent abatement, the bailiffs set to work on several barricaded cottages but were soon soaked and burned by buckets of boiling corn meal. When an old woman hit an army officer with a handful of mud, Captain Keogh RM read the riot act and the crowd jeered at this heavy-handed response to such a minor offence. On the next day some protesters trapped Keogh's car between two fallen trees on the road to Collon. For almost three hours the bystanders, many of them women, mocked and taunted him until emergency men arrived to remove the obstacles. Fierce resistance by Patrick Lawless's small garrison led to six more arrests. But the woman who had thrown hot liquid was released.

More evictions followed in the spring and autumn of 1888 with sporadic resistance. In September the garrison recruited by Francis Cooke, a respected poor law guardian and prominent National Leaguer, doused the emergency men with 'boiling gruel' and set loose a swarm of bees. Cooke stood in the yard encouraging his comrades inside and jingling some coins in his pocket to show that he could well afford to pay the rent. At James Downey's house a bailiff was felled by an iron bar and needed medical attention, and 'a local virago' threw some 'yard filth' in the face of a police officer. Two young men at the widow Bellew's cottage doused the bailiffs with hot liquid before being captured. In a nearby cabin old Laurence Bellew lay on his sickbed unable to move. With the consent of Dudgeon and Emerson, the sheriff handed Bellew a penny thereby converting him into a temporary caretaker.[37]

By May 1889 some 26 tenants had become caretakers, seven had redeemed, and seven farms remained vacant. The purge of Plan members continued. Expecting trouble, the sheriff arrived on 4 June with a battering ram, but his crew needed only crowbars to force an entry while two priests comforted the victims. Patrick Lawless and his comrades threw hot liquid and stones at the bailiffs until Father George Taaffe persuaded them to surrender. Charged with attempted murder they were remanded in custody. Other tenants tried and failed to impede the evictors. At least Margaret Lynch was spared. Aged 90, she received a medical certificate declaring her unfit for removal. Later arsonists set fire to a corn mill in Collon to punish the owner for having paid his rent. Of the twenty tenants facing eviction in June half settled, eight were turned out, and three others were reprieved. On 15 August, ten more tenants were forced out around Collon. And in September, 'two young ladies', Mary and Bridget Halligan from Monasterboice, tried and failed to repel the bailiffs. More distraining of chattel, more protest meetings, and more litigation over the Plan huts built to house evicted families kept this estate in turmoil well into 1890.[38]

Sectarianism reared its ugly head on this estate as soon as the agents planted Protestant Ulstermen on some thirty evicted farms. When rebuked for this action, Massereene vehemently denied that he was a bigot. His object, he stated, was to find solvent tenants with no ties to the Plan or the National League, and in practice this meant Protestants. Home Rulers like Shaw-Lefevre denounced the 'bribing' of northern farmers to take on evicted holdings for low rents; and Dr Logue, the Catholic Primate, along with the priests of Louth, warned that this kind of colonising would 'raise the demon of sectarian strife'.[39] Among the officials who worried about the consequences of planting 'the riff raff of Ulster' on this estate was the shrewd under-secretary in Dublin Castle, Sir Joseph West Ridgeway, who told Balfour that other landlords might follow suit and thereby trigger a disastrous 'religious war'. On the other hand the *Freeman's Journal* assured readers that 'the Orange Plantation' had failed because the landgrabbers from Ulster were paying little rent, were under-utilising their acreage, and suffering from boycotting.[40]

DE FREYNE/CASTLEREA

Evictions also created havoc on the 25,436-acre estate of Arthur, 4th Baron De Freyne of Frenchpark, near Castlerea, in County Roscommon. The cordial relations that had once prevailed between the tenants and their Catholic landlord had collapsed with the advent of the League. Family charges on the property that included a mortgage loan of £58,500 from St Patrick's College, Maynooth cramped his profit margin. The unpopular agent McDougall opposed a request for a 20 per cent abatement and obtained ejectment writs against those in arrear. Several months later, on 2 December 1886, the tenants endorsed the Plan and paid their adjusted rent to the trustee, Willie Redmond MP.[41]

Around midnight on 9 January 1887 three constables acting on suspicion of foul play crept up to John McNulty's cottage at Erritt where nine tenants were discussing Plan tactics. The eavesdropping Sergeant Wharton overheard McNulty boast that he wanted to 'cripple the landlords' by withholding rent. Without any warrant Wharton charged inside and ordered him to empty his pockets. But McNulty refused to allow any search of his person. The 'conspirators' were then escorted to the house of the high sheriff, who happened to be Lord De Freyne's brother, the Hon. Charles French. While the prisoners shivered on the steps in the bitter cold, another brother, the Hon. John French, who was a magistrate, agreed to charge them with an illegal conspiracy. Flaunting the warrant, Wharton emerged and thrust his hand into McNulty's pocket withdrawing £5 along with a rent receipt. When O'Brien learned of this flagrant abuse of authority, he rushed to Erritt and railed against both 'police thievery' and De Freyne's avarice. McNulty was tried and convicted of promoting an illegal organisation; O'Brien could only vow to make the county too hot for every landlord.[42]

When evictions began, McDougall caused more outrage by personally igniting the thatched roof of a cottage. After his departure in August 1887, the new agent, R. E. Blakeney, offered a 25 per cent reduction upon payment of one year's rent before 7 April 1888 and reinstated 56 tenants. Nevertheless, three hundred tenants remained loyal to the Plan while others paid only a fraction of what they owed. After more ejectment writs and evictions, De Freyne finally capitulated. His agent and a local priest reached a compromise whereby most rents were reduced by a whopping 55 per cent and legal costs were excluded. The threat of eviction did not disappear, however, and agrarian violence arising out of disputes over rents and grazing rights continued to plague this estate well into the new century.[43]

LANSDOWNE/LUGGACURREN

Lord Lansdowne's 9,000-acre estate around Luggacurren in Queen's County became a major Plan battleground while he was serving as governor general of Canada. Regarded by his peers as a lenient and improving proprietor, the 5th marquess was a stickler for property rights and aristocratic privilege. Heavy interest payments on the Irish estates made him amenable to the sale of tenanted land, but only at the 'right price' that tenants found exorbitant. Given his political prominence, Unionist convictions, and financial straits Dillon and O'Brien deemed him an ideal target for the Plan.[44]

In November 1886 the versatile agent, John Townsend Trench, rejected the tenants' demand for abatements of some 30 per cent, with the result that two prominent cattle ranchers, Denis Kilbride MP and John Dunne, along with Fathers Maher of Luggacurren and Andrew Dempsey, PP Ballinakill, launched the Plan.[45] Faced with rebellious tenants, Lansdowne dug in his heels. The ensuing struggle for the hearts and rents of the Luggacurren tenants was marked by futile negotiations, charges of bad faith, and visits by O'Brien as well as Liberal delegations from England. On 22 March 1887 the sheriff took possession of Kilbride's and Dunne's large houses and acreage. Adding insult to injury, he lodged 200 constables in Kilbride's mansion. Inaugurating the cluster of wooden huts built for evicted families, O'Brien accused Lansdowne of an 'outrageous' act of 'landlord perfidy'. According to Kilbride this was 'a fight of intelligence against intelligence … it was diamond cut diamond'.[46] This bitter dispute was aggravated by more evictions and made this county – among others – a fertile recruiting ground for the Gaelic Athletic Association (GAA) and the Irish Republican Brotherhood (IRB).[47]

On 19 April, the evictions resumed with scant resistance. Fathers Maher and Ryan consoled eight tenants who walked out. A swarm of bees sent the emergency men tumbling down the stairs and into the yard of one house to the crowd's delight. A few tenants were readmitted after paying a nominal sum, but when Thomas Mackey was asked if he wished to redeem, this eighty-year-old man replied: 'I'll go out and ye needn't bring all this crowd; we're slaves to Lord Lansdowne long enough, and we're ready to go out anytime.' Waving his stick aloft, he walked out amidst the cheers of his many supporters. Even those who had put up barricades left quietly. Edward Delaney, 'a fine, wild-looking man', shouted at the emergency men: 'The curse of God upon ye' and 'May the devil take you before night.' Referring to her husband Dennis, Mrs Shalloon declared that the bailiffs 'might evict him, but they could not evict God Almighty, and he would not be long wanting a place'. After Henry Mulhall refused the offer of readmission as a caretaker, he was driven out into the rain along with a 'very weak' ninety-year-old woman and six children. To prevent re-entry emergency men moved into some dwellings guarded by police. By 23 April, some 200 people had been ousted at a cost of over £500.[48]

In May O'Brien and Kilbride took their campaign to Canada where they accused Lansdowne of being a treacherous and rackrenting landlord. Their audiences ranged from hostile Orangemen in Ontario to adoring Catholics in Quebec. While some Loyalists threw stones and heckled them, Irish Catholics in Boston cheered them to the rafters. If they should lose the war against land-lordism, O'Brien asserted, then the countryside would become 'one vast Lugga-curren, one vast solitude of smokeless chimneys and of desolate homes'. He denounced landgrabbers and predicted that the 'rackrenter will howl for mercy and for quarter'. At a giant rally in Cork city on his return, he accused Lansdowne of pretending to negotiate when all he really wanted was to buy some peace before heading off to India. During regular visits to Luggacurren, O'Brien risked arrest by defying the ban on inflammatory language.[49] More evictions occurred in June and again in the autumn, when some Gladstonian Liberals showed up to express their solidarity. Shadowed by the police, they were warmly welcomed with brass bands, triumphal arches, and rallies. More tenants were turned out in the following spring after negotiations collapsed. Only one of the score of tenants evicted at the end of May 1889 resisted by throwing red pepper at the bailiffs. Father John Maher CC was found guilty of promoting the Plan and spent a month in Kilkenny jail. Returning to Luggacurren after his early release he was cheered by admirers along the way. So too was the defiant Kilbride, who had lost his 868-acre grazing farm back in March 1887 and was released in July after a three-month spell in the same prison.[50]

To make matters much worse, two Highland soldiers bored with eviction duty got drunk in Stradbally. While staggering back to camp at Luggacurren at night they accosted a young servant girl, Bridget Reilly, on the road to Timogue. They threw her into a ditch and, despite her screams and scratching, one of the soldiers raped or 'outraged' her while the other man held her down. She found shelter down the road and fainted. Both men were arrested and tried at Maryborough summer assizes where the victim courageously testified and the defendants offered no defence. The judge sentenced the guilty men to seven years in prison. As *United Ireland* put it, if these soldiers were found guilty, then 'a new and fearful import will be given the dread word eviction in the Irish peasants' mind, and a feeling aroused which we do not care to contemplate'. In Parliament O'Brien condemned the evictions; and Thomas Sexton asked Balfour for information about this 'outrage' while urging that the entire Highland unit be transferred to another camp.[51]

After a long pause the sheriff's party returned at the end of May 1889 to deal with thirty more tenants who had refused the offer to redeem. Although resistance was light, here and there the bailiffs had to contend with red pepper, cudgels, and fists. The defiance of the local tenantry remained strong, and on 7 July the (suppressed) Timahoe branch of the National League passed a resolution congratulating 'all the defenders … of the evicted tenants' living in Campaign Square on their 'victory' over his lordship. At a Plan rally on 23 September, O'Brien praised the unity and tenacity of the tenantry and condemned 'the fraud and dishonesty' of the owner. He called the agent 'a thimblerigger and an artful dodger'. In the House of Commons Balfour provoked a ripple of laughter by reciting an alleged exchange between two famous agents: 'Mr Samuel Hussey was asked … by Mr (J. Townsend) Trench:– "How is it, Hussey, that you have not got shot long ago?" And the latter replied: "Nothing so easy. I have warned them that if they shoot me you will be their agent."' Litigation over the cabins built for the evicted tenants at Luggacurren did not end until 1893 when a Dublin judge ordered their dismantlement. Despite their reinstatement the rancour of the tenants lasted until they were able to buy their farms under the Wyndham act in 1905–7.[52] Luggacurren thus joined Woodford, Bodyke, Coolgreany, and Coolroe, as another epic site of tenant defiance and landlord obstinacy.

PONSONBY/YOUGHAL

Charles William Talbot-Ponsonby, a retired naval officer who spent most of the year in Hampshire, fought the Plan vigorously on his 10,367-acre estate north of Youghal, County Cork. The tenants' dynamic leader, Canon Daniel Keller, demanded a 35 per cent abatement on the gross rental of some £7,000. To avoid eviction 200 of the 246 tenants sought rent reductions under the Land Act of 1887; but the landlord struck a pre-emptive blow by serving them with notices to quit thereby nullifying their applications. On 12 January 1887 he had to run a gauntlet of jeering people at Youghal petty sessions in order to obtain thirty decrees for non-payment. Some farmers harvested and sold cartloads of turnips to foil the distrainers.[53] Ponsonby's obstinacy and Keller's grit soon turned Youghal into another war zone and the adversaries braced for open conflict.

The commander of the eviction force, Colonel Alfred Turner, had no time for absentee or 'ruthless, cruel, and grasping' landlords. At the same time he could not abide politicised priests, snipers, vitriol throwers, and riotous crowds. Experience had taught him the deterrent effect of presenting an overwhelming display of force at eviction sites. Unfazed by all the death threats that came his way, he dismissed them as the Irish peasant's way of venting anger or passing time on the Sabbath when the priests forbade outdoor games. He once boasted that no one had ever been killed by the men under his command but overlooked the death of a young man from a bayonet thrust during a riot following Father Keller's arrest in March 1887. A few moderate Home Rulers may have found him approachable, but the Plan leaders heartily disliked his displays of overwhelming military force.[54]

Thirty decrees in the spring of 1887 resulted in the expulsion of seven families. This was the opening round in the uprooting of 250 Plan tenants over the next two years. Father Edward Murphy PP protested the futility of emptying farms that would 'lie there useless in the hands of the landlord or worked at a loss by Emergencymen'. And he predicted that the Campaigners would soon be 'driven from living on "stirabout" to feasting on beefsteaks (laughter and hear, hear). They were feeding like gamecocks, and were ready for the battle before them (hear, hear).'[55]

To avoid surrender and ease the stifling boycott Ponsonby turned to the Cork Defence Union that sent emergency men to work evicted holdings. Kate Mahony, a 70-year-old widow whose family had lived on the farm for 150 years, left quietly as her neighbours cursed the bailiffs. At Ed Flavin's holding the bailiffs chased two elusive goats around the yard; and the sheriff stopped the local brass band from playing at each site.[56]

Relations between the police and the people reached a new low during a banned rally addressed by O'Brien at Youghal on 24 March 1888. Upholding the right of free speech, he dared the police to arrest him. With the help of batons they forced their way through a crowd of five thousand to reach the platform where O'Brien and Keller refused to leave. A tussle broke out and

Captain Plunkett was felled by two blows from a hurley stick. Taking refuge in the priest's house, O'Brien called this clash another victory for the Plan despite all the cuts and bruises. Because some local shopkeepers refused to sell any food to the police, four of them were jailed on the charge of 'criminal conspiracy'.

On a visit to Youghal in April members of the Bradford Women's Liberal Association were shocked by the dissolution of 'the social fabric' following the removal of so many families. Canon Keller explained how the homeless tenants were being supported out of the funds held in escrow under the Plan. While touring the estate they could hardly believe the desolation and poverty they saw. Instead of a bed, one 87-year-old woman had nothing but a thin layer of hay covered by a piece of calico cloth. They listened to heart-breaking stories of industrious farmers reduced to idleness by eviction. The *Freeman* described this once flourishing property as a 'plague spot' overlain with a 'heavy cloud of depression'. More evictions loomed after the agent obtained 60 decrees in September.[57]

Weighed down with arrears, family charges, and legal costs, Ponsonby entrusted his estate to the Irish Land Corporation in the spring of 1889, composed of wealthy proprietors, who ordered a new round of evictions. Some tenants were prosecuted for ploughing up crops and emergency men were planted on vacant farms. Canon Keller dashed the last faint hope of a settlement by rejecting the Land Corporation's offer to sell evicted holdings at what he deemed an exorbitant price – some £118,000 – and by insisting on the reinstatement of every evicted tenant.[58]

THE SYNDICATES AND THE TEST ESTATES

Balfour's acute frustration over the Plan and resistance to eviction moved him to study the laws governing eviction in other countries. He then composed two memoranda in January 1889 setting forth the government's bleak choice between clearing the principal Plan estates and withholding the armed escorts that protected the sheriff's party from harm. Although he objected to conceding the demands of callous landlords like Clanricarde who wanted to purge every Plan member, he did not want to prohibit evictions just because the British public might deem them 'harsh and unnecessary'. At one point he went so far as to contemplate authorising a court-appointed receiver to administer the properties of absentees in districts proclaimed under the Crimes Act. However, he knew this would set a dangerous precedent and dropped the idea.

Eventually, he decided to create a half-dozen secret syndicates composed of rich landed magnates – from the Duke of Westminster to Arthur Hugh Smith-Barry MP – that would buy and manage beleaguered properties where surrender to the Plan would prove disastrous to the cause of law and order as well as the Union. Thwarted by Clanricarde's intransigence, Balfour focused on the Ponsonby estate at Youghal where the 'melancholy and pitiable' evictions were inflaming the district. The virtually 'broke' Ponsonby could not afford to hold out much longer. To avert surrender the chief secretary enlisted the help of Smith-Barry, the wealthy owner of estates in Cork, Tipperary, and Cheshire, in organising a syndicate to purchase and manage this property. This tough and combative leader of the Cork Defence Union and the Irish Unionist Alliance considered the Plan a 'communistic agitation' designed to expropriate the gentry and make Ireland ungovernable.[59]

At one point Balfour laid plans for the simultaneous eviction of the most active Campaigners on the major Plan estates. In his view this co-ordinated attack would avert the huge waste of time and resources involved in besieging fortified dwellings week after week. Such a strategy also appealed to him because Parliament could then debate all the evictions at one time instead of dragging out the discussion over a long period. Having scheduled this operation for the first week in April, he found that some landlords had developed cold feet; and his cabinet colleagues pointed out that this Castle-backed offensive would alienate public opinion in Britain. The dashing of his hopes for a knockout blow to the Plan moved Balfour to inform Ridgeway:

> I am sorry we cannot have all our evictions at the same time. Our plan for having an eviction campaign on all the Campaign Estates on the same date was certainly sound in principle. I fear that it is partly the landlords' fault that it has broken down. You do not provoke more rows by having eviction scenes simultaneously in five places than by having them in one! But if you have five acts in your tragedy, you will move your audience five times, have five adjournments of the House etc. etc.[60]

The millionaire Scottish businessman, Sir John Arnott, offered to buy the Ponsonby estate for £120,000 and reinstate the evicted tenants. But for some reason his offer was not accepted.[61] By the end of April Smith-Barry had arranged the estate's purchase under the Ashbourne act for £71,433. He then hired an agent and emergency men or caretakers to farm the land. The latter needed constant police protection. To Balfour's intense annoyance word of this syndicate soon leaked out and the nationalist camp erupted in a chorus of denunciations. The *Freeman's Journal* called the syndicate members 'selfish plu-tocrats' and accused Ponsonby of 'humbugging' his tenants while Smith-Barry was busy 'humbugging' Ponsonby.

Ignoring all the adverse publicity the syndicate spent thousands of pounds on stocking farms and saved Ponsonby from surrender. However, both sides paid a steep price for this outcome. The local National League branch imposed a crippling boycott on the nonconformist shopkeepers in Youghal because they refused to close their premises in protest over O'Brien's imprisonment. Although the syndicates provided fine grist for the nationalist propaganda mill, the Plan leadership had to bear the heavy cost of maintaining all the ejected tenants. Shortly after his release from prison, the sickly Dillon sailed off to Australia in March 1889 to raise money for this cause. He returned in April 1890 worn out but bearing £33,000 in relief funds. More Plan tenants were purged; and O'Brien was tried again, convicted of promoting the Plan, and imprisoned for four months in Clonmel jail.[62]

Five other syndicates took over the leading Plan properties that Balfour called the Test Estates. These comprised Luggacurren (Lansdowne), Coolgreany (Brooke), Falcarragh (Olphert), Kilrush (Vandeleur), and Ballycurry, Ashford (Tottenham). The Protestant farmers or 'planters' recruited in the north by the syndicates' agents required constant police protection. Balfour continued to urge the expulsion of the Campaign leaders on these estates and recommended that sheriffs make more use of the element of surprise to minimise resistance. At Youghal Canon Keller flatly rejected the syndicate's proposal to wipe out arrears and sell farms at 17 years' purchase of the rent. [63] The gap between the rival parties proved too wide to bridge. If Smith-Barry's exposure as the driving force behind the Ponsonby syndicate strengthened the resolve of some tenants to resist, it did not save them from the crowbar brigade.

On 3 July, fifteen prominent tenants on his Tipperary and Cork estates, led by Canon Cahill, travelled to Chelsea to present Smith-Barry with a memorial, published in some papers, that urged him to withdraw from the syndicate, stop the evictions, and submit to arbitration. In the presence of his new American wife and his agent, Smith-Barry told the deputation that the Youghal tenants could stop the evictions simply by paying one year's rent less 20 per cent on non-judicial rents plus three per cent interest on arrears and applying to the land courts for fair rents. In reply Cahill stated that it was 'a mockery' to tell tenants to enter the land courts – where the judges were allegedly landlord supporters – when their houses were being torn down. After more hostile exchanges, Smith-Barry abruptly announced that he had to leave for the House of Commons. In short, the long journey to Pont Street had been a complete waste of time and money. The *Freeman* deplored the 'ugly spirit' shown by Smith-Barry who could have saved the deputation much trouble by mailing his negative response. Later Canon Keller called the syndicate's terms 'preposterous'. He also accused Smith-Barry of preventing the tenants from applying to the land courts by invoking 'the eviction made easy' clause' of the Land Act of 1887 and serving notices to quit that would effectively confiscate all their improvements.

Meanwhile growing concern over the cost of maintaining the evicted Plan tenants forced Dillon and O'Brien to appeal to Parnell for help. But the leader refused to become involved even though he endorsed the newly founded Tenants Defence Association that collected £61,000 in its first year.[64] Smith-Barry's refusal to compromise and Keller's tirades against Ponsonby and the syndicate for opposing arbitration set the stage for two more waves of eviction in April and October 1890 when baton charges and arrests made matters worse. The *Cork Examiner* accused the authorities of 'exterminating' 1,600 souls and 'depopulating' 50 square miles. All told these Plan purges left only two of the original occupiers in place.[65]

On 15 April 1890 the sheriff's party set out again from Youghal to empty the houses of a dozen tenants who had paid no rent for at least six years. Shopkeepers pulled down their shutters and a black flag flew from the clock tower. Both *United Ireland* and the *Cork Examiner* condemned these 'miserable proceedings' with headlines like 'SMITH-BARRY'S EXTERMINATION SCHEME'.[66] Bagpipers accompanied the column of 50 Scottish soldiers, 100 police, emergency men, and assorted officials. A cart bearing a battering ram rumbled along at the rear. Five priests stood in the front of the huge crowd and welcomed a Liberal delegation from England that included J. T. Brunner MP and Lady Victoria Sandhurst, daughter of the 4th Earl Spencer. At a mass meeting Keller thanked the 'distinguished' English visitors for coming to see the 'brute force' being applied against the Irish people. Refusing the offer of readmission upon payment of a year's rent, eleven tenants carried their furniture outside and left quietly. Only one of the nine tenants evicted on the next day won a reprieve owing to sickly parents. Patrick Walsh cursed Smith-Barry and the syndicate and told the sheriff to go to the devil. The absence of resistance enabled the sheriff to reduce his escort to a mere eighty armed men.[67] A farmer named McMurphy recalled the good old days of friendly relations with the landlord and lamented that 'queer times' had arrived and 'the country had run wild'. Of the next 26 tenants ousted only Bridget Forrest was reinstated on the grounds of senility. To their surprise the bailiffs found a German countess, Gertrud von Guillaume-Schack, and her new friend, Mrs Leech from Yarmouth inside Mary Collins's house. A progressive activist and lecturer on the ethical treatment of workers, the countess had come all the way from Silesia to support the Plan tenants. Both ladies sauntered outside to resounding cheers from the crowd as the police looked on somewhat 'shamefaced'.[68]

On 19 April, Colonel Turner arrived at Ballyhobart astride his black charger and sporting a primrose in his lapel in honour of the late Lord Beaconsfield. Among the score of tenants expelled, William Egan owed six years' rent. Burdened with fourteen dependents, he left his squalid house cheering for the

Plan and damning Ponsonby. Inscribed above Anne Foley's door were the words: 'We'll have our own again when Smith-Barry is a thing of the past.' She left her house peacefully along with her 'fashionably dressed' schoolmistress daughter.[69] On 21 April, while a dozen tenants were being driven out, Countess Schack had a heated exchange with four Tory 'dames' from the Primrose League, whose membership had soared since 1881. These ladies had nothing but disdain for the Plan; and the countess responded that it was much better 'to shoot people than to starve them to death'. When one dame retorted that this was a most 'unchristian sentiment', the countess reminded her of Christ's maxim that the rich man should give to the poor. 'Do you not think', she asked, 'there has been enough starvation and enough of rags?' The Primrose ladies had no reply and failed to show up the next day.[70]

Lack of resistance moved Turner to reduce his police escort. Whistling and dancing a jig outside his cabin, Edmond O'Brien put on a brave face by bragging that he felt no sorrow in leaving. Another tenant had spent two years in a Plan-built hut and could not wait to return home. Edward Brennan had just buried his son and the agent had allowed him to return as a caretaker along with the gout-ridden Daniel McCarthy who lived in a 'charming' cottage built as a shooting lodge. Only Patrick Staunton resisted. Recently released from jail for having ploughed a grazing field, this young man had affixed an iron gate behind his door forcing the bailiffs to clamber through a window whereupon they wrested a shovel from his hands. He had covered the walls of his abode with *United Ireland* cartoons and pictures of prizefighters. For his defiance he wound up in Cork jail. While a few tenants were readmitted around Ballymacoda and Gortroe on grounds of poor health, the bailiffs placed Ellen Lee, a 'weak old woman', in a chair and deposited her on the roadside next to her husband in the driving rain.

By the end of the month more than 600 men, women, and children had vacated their homes to the horror of the Liberal delegates from England.[71] When the purge ended in October, the estate resembled 'a great wilderness of unoccupied and uncultivated land'. According to *United Ireland*, the syndicate had 'a wilderness on their hands – a beautiful tract of country made foul by the abomination of desolation'. What this paper did not mention was the move by the syndicates to stock the evicted farms on both the Ponsonby and Smith-Barry estates with several thousand cattle and sheep.[72]

On 21 June 1889, John Ellis, the Quaker and Liberal MP, who had just returned from Youghal, complained in the House of Commons that the evicted tenants had received no compensation for their improvements and that 23,585 persons had been forced out in 1886–7 alone. He compared those readmitted as caretakers to 'a man ... struggling for life on a raft at sea'. Not only had Gladstone's land act of 1881 failed to achieve dual ownership but the 'eviction made easy' clause had spawned 10,752 notices to quit. After condemning the syndicates, he insisted that 'the rights of property must be consistent with the rights of humanity'.[73] Balfour responded by blaming the Plan on outside agitators bent on promoting the Parnellite agenda at Westminster rather than helping tenants. For him the agitation boiled down to a question of law and order, and the syndicates offered the only way to defeat a criminal conspiracy run by paid agitators. Eviction, in short, was essential if the Plan was to be defeated.[74]

Another round of evictions began on 18 September 1890 after the court had granted 47 ejectment decrees. With only a few score of the 200 original tenants left, the sheriff encountered no resistance. In fact 10 out of 13 tenants on his list were declared too old or infirm to be removed from their hovels in the span of three days. Two years later some 147 of the evicted Plan members hoped to buy their farms back from the syndicate for a price approved by Smith-Barry but spurned by Keller. By that time the Plan's 'war chest' contained £5,000. Not until 1896 did some tenants start to buy their farms and many more followed suit after 1905.[75]

The bitter contest over the Plan at Youghal inspired Rosa Mulholland's melodrama, *Onora* (1900), in which the eponymous heroine survives eviction on the estate that had become a desert filled with 'the corpses of homes'. The inevitable absentee landlord is matched in his wickedness by the gombeen man, Rogan, whose lust for Onora drives him to foreclose on her fiancé, Joe the tenant farmer. The young couple plan to flee from penury and Rogan's clutches by emigrating to Iowa, but they are spared this fate by a gift of £1,000 from a remarkably altruistic woman who also loves Joe. After marrying, Joe and Onora pay off Rogan and settle down happily on their farm.[76]

Conflicts on the Test estates lasted for several more years and cost the adversaries untold thousands of pounds. In the long run dwindling rent receipts and a plethora of vacant holdings drove most owners to sell portions of their estates to the occupiers under the Land Act of 1903. Until that welcome day hundreds of evicted families had to live in austere and crowded Plan huts where storytelling and *céilidhes* fortified by porter and cakes helped to relieve some of their profound boredom and discomfort.[77]

SMITH-BARRY AND NEW TIPPERARY

The fallout from the syndicates soon embroiled Smith-Barry's 8,620-acre estate in Tipperary because of his role in rescuing Ponsonby from ruin. Plan spokesmen called him everything from 'a pernicious little noodle of a Cork landlord' to Jack the Ripper. Brushing aside this abuse, 'Black' Smith-Barry threatened to evict the tenants on both his Tipperary town and Cashel estates if they withheld their rent.[78] Canon Keller, Father David Humphreys, Dillon, O'Brien, and Archbishop Croke of Cashel all urged the tenants to defy their master. Anyone who paid his rent was branded a traitor and boycotted; and a small bomb exploded harmlessly near the estate office. Police reinforcements flooded the district after Smith-Barry vowed to oust the rebellious shopkeepers, and in early September 1889 rioting resulted in the arrest of fifty townsmen.

When Michael O'Brien Dalton, a prominent tradesman and Plan leader, faced eviction on 2 December 1889, all the shops were shuttered and Tipperary 'seemed like a town in mourning or struck by a plague'. The police beat back a crowd of Plan supporters and arrested several girls for 'riotous behaviour'. On the next day emergency men demolished Dalton's corn mill at Rossborough even though he had left the door wide open. After stripping the slate roof, they levelled this valuable structure. Two days later over forty leading citizens carried goods out of Miss King's shop in town before the sheriff could take possession and five priests supervised their storage. By 8 December, twenty shopkeepers had been forced out and most of the remaining shops closed in protest. Green handbills circulated calling on everyone to boycott Smith-Barry and his fellow 'murderers of our kith and kin'. In all some 55 town tenants and 75 rural tenants lost their premises during this dispute; the bill for all these evictions came to £16,213.[79]

Determined to punish Smith-Barry and help the evicted shopkeepers, O'Brien devised an ambitious scheme to construct a market village called New Tipperary on the fringe of town. On the festive opening day, 12 April 1890, hundreds of Campaigners and scores of dignitaries toured the 74 shops and houses that ran along Parnell and Davitt streets. Among the chief speakers were O'Brien, Davitt, and T. D. Sullivan. The English Home Rule delegation included the Hon. Ashley Ponsonby and his wife along with the 23-year-old daughter of a British army officer, Maud Gonne, who had fallen under the spell of both her French lover and John O'Leary. The latter tutored her in Irish history and literature; but he questioned her commitment to the Plan and in a patriarchal aside he confided to a friend: 'She is no disciple of mine; she went there [New Tipperary] to show off her new bonnet.'[80]

Despite all the fanfare and promise New Tipperary did not flourish. Some merchants yearned to return to their old premises; business declined; and rumours of a pending sale circulated within a year or two. A more pressing problem was the huge cost that exceeded £40,000. The financial crisis arising from the Parnellite split made matters worse, and some Plan tenants began to pay their rent despite being called 'rats', 'skunks', and 'traitors'. Gradually dissension and lack of funding loosened the Plan's grip; some thirty shopkeepers braved retaliation by returning to their old premises in town. In vain Dillon and O'Brien urged local shopkeepers and businessmen to use the new mart. In the meantime Archbishop Croke encouraged Smith-Barry's tenants to arrive at a provisional settlement.

On 25 September 1890 the trial began in Tipperary town of twelve Plan leaders including Dillon and O'Brien, who had been arrested several days earlier, for conspiring to deny Smith-Barry his rents until the Plan had triumphed on the Ponsonby estate. With swarms of police trying to control the angry crowd a fracas erupted at the gate leading to the courthouse when Colonel Caddell RM, the police commander, refused to admit the demonstrators. The pushing and shoving crowd prompted Caddell to order a baton charge to disperse the people rushing the gate. One of the victims was Henry Harrison, the newly elected MP for Mid-Tipperary and an Oxford undergraduate, who had recently won renown and a seat in Parliament (as will be seen in chapter 9) for defying the authorities during the Olphert evictions in Donegal. This intrepid young man was hit on the head while trying to assist another MP knocked to the ground. According to John Morley, who escaped injury by retreating to a safe distance, the constabulary had 'behaved most damnably'. The blood-spattered Harrison staggered into the courthouse where he received medical attention. When the police summonsed him for assault, he returned the compliment by charging a constable with the same offence.

Inside the packed courtroom the dozen defendants were charged with criminal conspiracy for their anti-rent efforts. The prolonged and tedious testimony ended with a verdict of guilty. But Dillon and O'Brien avoided jail by taking the night train to Dublin on 6 October and then sailing out of Dalkey harbour for France. Warrants were issued for their arrest but by then they were on their way to America to raise more funds. Upon their return they were arrested and imprisoned. In March 1891 they appeared in Cork city to testify at the trial of five men accused of inciting the 'alleged riot' outside the Tipperary courthouse. However, on the second day of this trial a chimney-fire spread to the roof and consumed the entire premises including most of the records. After the trial reconvened in a nearby building, the jurors could not agree on a verdict and the defendants were acquitted. When Harrison was prosecuted for assaulting a policeman, he failed to appear in court on the grounds of illness.

Of course, Irish newspapers followed every twist and turn of the turmoil in Tipperary and the trial in Cork city – depicting Smith-Barry and other principals as victims or villains depending on their editorial bias. For example, the *Irish Times* accused Harrison of having choked a policeman during the Tipperary mêlée while the Home Rule press reported that he had merely grabbed the constable's wrist to protect a fellow MP. At the outset of 1891, Unionist newspapers happily reported the collapse of the Plan on Smith-Barry's estate and the reinstatement of almost half of the 230 tenants upon payment of their rent despite the threat of intimidation. However, many of the evicted tenants did not return home until 1896.[81]

<h2>BROOKE/COOLGREANY</h2>

A fierce struggle took place on George F. Brooke's estate at Coolgreany, near Gorey, County Wexford, where 80 of the 108 tenants adopted the Plan on 15 December 1886. This wealthy and social-climbing Dublin wine merchant lived at Somerton, Castleknock, and Ballyfad House near Arklow. He chose his agent with care. Captain Edward Hamilton was the PDA's pugnacious field commander, who regarded the Plan as a political stratagem designed to make the country ungovernable. At a huge Plan rally in Enniscorthy, Dillon reminded his audience of their forefathers' heroism in 1798 and urged them to overthrow landlordism by withholding their rent. All but eight of the Catholic tenants joined the Plan and those who refused were 'ruthlessly' boycotted.[82]

After the interest in fifty farms had been sold, evictions began at the end of February 1887. One of the first to go was John O'Neill, a blacksmith, who had refused to work for a boycotted friend of Brooke's. O'Neill blocked his door with iron gates and recruited some defenders; but the bailiffs made short work of these defences and stormed inside. Another tenant, William Ford, took a donkey and cart into his cottage before leaving, and the crowd roared with laughter as the emergency men struggled to remove them.

Brushing aside pleas for compromise, Brooke ordered more evictions that *United Ireland* condemned as acts of 'perverse greed'. Backed by 250 police and soldiers, under the command of Captain Owen Slacke, the eviction party returned on 6 July to tackle the fortified house of Patrick Kavanagh who had paid no rent for over a year. Seven priests stood at the head of a jeering crowd as the crowbar men broke down the door only to find a barrier of logs that forced them to attack a blocked window. Once inside they subdued the garrison. To reach James Garvey's abode the sheriff's party had to march down a narrow lane lined with dry furze bushes that locals had set ablaze. The evictors had to run this fiery gauntlet before being doused with buckets of boiling liquid once they reached the house. Holding large shields, they charged inside and dragged out Garvey and five female defenders with such brutality that even a few officers muttered disapproval. They tore open the thatched roof and threw the furniture into the yard inflicting much damage. As the evictions continued, the crowd grew so restive that Daniel Crilly MP for North Mayo had to intervene to avert a riot. One of the cottiers expelled on 7 July, Thomas Kennedy, exclaimed on his way out: 'You may evict us from our homes, but you cannot evict the spirit of nationality from our hearts.' At this point the crowd sang 'God Save Ireland', and Captain Slacke ordered the police to push them back with their batons. Patrick Keogh's house was so well barricaded and the walls so thick that the bailiffs had to erect a giant scaling ladder to reach the roof. His daughter Lizzie was arrested for throwing a rotten egg at the head bailiff. [83]

During these evictions the crowds were led by priests and several MPs, while half a dozen Liberal observers from England deplored the 'savage and unmanly' conduct of the emergency men who dragged out the screaming female defenders. Around this time a Lawrence photographer captured five members of the Kavanagh family of Croghan outside their cottage (Plate 9). The body language of the towering son in the doorway spelled trouble for any would-be evictor. But the Kavanaghs won a reprieve because a Plan organiser had recently bought their house on behalf of the National League. [84]

While cottiers living in mud-walled hovels offered little resistance, stronger farmers like Patrick Darcy and Thomas Kinsella of Croghan fortified their stone-walled houses and stood their ground. The climactic siege took place on 11 July at Patrick Grennell's house where ramparts of tree trunks and branches had been built inside and outside. While John Redmond and Crilly watched, the evictors put up a ladder, hacked a hole in the roof, and entered. Finding Grennell hiding inside, they beat him senseless, carried him down the ladder, and hauled him through the barrier of trees. To save themselves the trouble of carrying all the furniture and farm equipment outside they set the dwelling on fire. In vain Redmond and two priests protested this wanton arson. Later Captain Hamilton denied that he had ordered his men to torch the premises. In the meantime the *Freeman*'s editor called on the Coolgreany tenants to fight 'the Jubilee Coercion Act' with all their might.

Elsewhere the evictors had to contend with sulphur and cayenne pepper sprinkled on turf fires that emitted 'noxious fumes' and caused delays. At Knockgreany on 14 July, the distinguished spectators included the daughter of Richard Cobden and two gentleman from University College Dublin – Count Stollberg, a German student, and Professor Pere Mallac. At Michael Green's barricaded cottage the crowbar gang were hacking away at a mud wall when it suddenly collapsed and almost crushed them. Later the Graham and Kinsella families held off the besiegers with scalding liquid until overwhelmed. At another house a swarm of bees forced the emergency men to postpone their assault. The defenders were arrested and taken to Wexford jail. And at Ballyfad, Davitt, who had been busy encouraging tenants to resist, watched the emergency men besieging Patrick Darcy's fortified house. After entering through a hole in the roof they rounded up the resisters and shouted obscenities at two young female defenders. They also smashed the furniture and crockery by throwing them through a hole in the roof. On 16 July Edward Byrne's garrison bombarded the bailiffs with stones and boiling gruel at Oulart, but they were soon overpowered and Byrne suffered a severe scalp wound. When this ten-day purge had ended, some sixty houses stood empty and 300 people were homeless.

On 22 July, Scawen Blunt showed up at Gorey courthouse in the company of Daniel Crilly to observe the trial of ten Coolgreany resisters one of whom was a 17-year old girl charged with throwing 'hot gruel'. Because the PDA's leader, Lord Courtown, chaired the hearing, and Captain Hamilton, who served as Byrne's agent, was present, the defendants' clever lawyer, Matthew Bodkin, made a great fuss about this conflict of interest. The chief prosecution witness was the head bailiff, Woods, who had been scalded and bruised in one of the sieges. Blunt described him and his fellow Protestant emergency men as 'great hulking blackguards' who carried revolvers into the courtroom and richly deserved to be in prison. In his view the otherwise peaceful people of the district so hated these 'evil visaged ruffians' from the north who were doing 'the land-lords' dirty work' that they leapt at the opportunity to resist. On the following day Courtown found the prisoners guilty but sentenced them to only six weeks – a lenient punishment given the nature of their offence. Blunt took some credit for the light sentences because the presence of English visitors like himself made all the difference. [85]

At a Plan rally in Arklow on 17 July, attended by eight priests and three Irish MPs, Dillon called Coolgreany a crucial battle in the war against the 'rob-ber' landlords. Defeat there, he warned, would turn the country into a waste-land filled with slaves rather than free men. Already the Plan had triumphed on sixty out of eighty estates and he thanked the people of Coolgreany for standing firm. Once again he praised the United Irishmen of Arklow who had sacrificed their lives in 1798 for 'the old cause'. But Davitt took a different line by scolding the men of Coolgreany for having shown so little courage in obstructing the sheriff's forces. He reserved his praise for the boys and girls who had risked imprisonment to defend their hearths. The adults, he averred, were better shouters and groaners than fighters. Only if they were prepared to face prison would they deserve the public's sympathy. Nevertheless, some of the male resisters were awarded medals 'For Bravery' in the shape of a Maltese cross inscribed with the words: 'Keep a Firm Grip on your Homesteads – Coolgreany–1887'. According to *United Ireland*, 'the Coolgreany Extermination Campaign' had 'poison[ed] the social life' of the district. [86]

Sixty emergency men from Cavan took over the evicted farms. Whether drunk or sober they swaggered around Coolgreany brandishing revolvers and bullying the populace. The evicted tenants were soon housed in huts built by the National League at a cost of £1,000. Although overcrowding and discomfort were acute, the location of these shelters so close to Captain Hamilton's residence offered its own reward. A banner over an arch proclaimed 'God Speed the Plan', and a green flag bore Dillon's name. After spending much time and money in Dublin courts seeking to remove these 'obnoxious' structures, Brooke and Hamilton finally obtained a judge's order in November 1888 for their dismantlement.[87]

On 28 September 1887 a party of emergency men shot and killed an evicted tenant named John Kinsella, aged 62, while trying to seize cattle at Croghan. When the head bailiff, George Freeman, refused to produce his warrant, angry words ensued and Kinsella raised his pitchfork in a menacing manner. Freeman then took aim with his revolver shouting: 'Drop that, or by God I'll shoot you'. When Kinsella failed to comply, Freeman opened fire and ordered his henchmen to do the same. Remarkably, Kinsella was the only victim of this fusillade. The nearest magistrate, Lord Courtown, who headed the PDA, promptly released the emergency men pending a court hearing. Coming so soon after the Mitchelstown 'massacre', this homicide added more fuel to the fire of nationalist outrage. The inquest ended with a verdict of 'wilful murder' against Freeman, Hamilton (who had been in Belfast on the fatal day), and the other shooters. But a grand jury in Wicklow soon acquitted all the defendants.[88]

Kinsella's death spurred Archbishop Walsh to visit Coolgreany on 2 October. Accompanied by six priests, he listened to the tenants' tales of woe, inspected a tumbled house, blessed the League huts, prayed at Kinsella's home, and blamed the shooting on 'cowardly wretches'. His initial sympathy towards the Plan and concern for the evicted tenants spurred him to urge Brooke to settle the dispute amicably. But the latter refused arbitration and kept on purging Plan tenants.[89] On a visit to Coolgreany in April 1888 an English lady, Isabella Bird, met Kinsella's daughter who was still in deep mourning. This 'quiet, feminine girl' showed her the old homestead and deplored 'the hellish' behaviour of the emergency men who had violated her bedroom before she could douse them with hot liquid laced with lime and pepper.[90]

Hamilton boasted that the Ulster Protestants whom he had planted on evicted farms were keen to 'exchange their inferior land for the fine land in the south'. His anti-Plan activities gave rise to the Cultivation of Derelict Land (Ireland) Trust, headed by Walter Gyles, secretary of the Irish Land Corporation, who recruited Ulstermen to farm evicted holdings with the help of subsidies for livestock and equipment.[91] Because Hamilton's glowing report of conditions around Coolgreany made the *Freeman*'s editor suspicious he sent a 'special commissioner' down to inspect conditions in 'leper land'. The latter found empty fields and sheep dying from scab and foot rot all of which he blamed on the Protestant planters. Hamilton angrily denied these charges and claimed that eight new and 'solvent' tenants were making a profit. But nationalists scoffed at his rebuttal and derided the landgrabbers as 'bogus' tenants or recycled emergency men planted there by Hamilton to create a 'Protestant colony'.

Dismissing the charge of sectarian bias, Hamilton made more news while taking a prospective tenant and his son around an evicted farm. Suddenly, 'a comely but sturdy band of women' appeared and denounced landgrabbing as a 'heinous crime'. Fearing for their safety, the men pulled out revolvers. At this point the former tenant arrived and swore that he would sooner die than allow anyone to 'rob him of the fruits of his industry'. Somewhat shaken, the male visitors withdrew leaving Hamilton and his gun dog to face the aggressive women. Holding his shotgun, Hamilton challenged them: 'You are a pack of cowards. I am not a match for the whole of you, but let any one of ye come forward and I'll fight her.' A plucky woman named Ellen O'Toole then stepped up and took a swing at the captain just missing his nose. At this point Hamilton chose flight over fight and 'the mob of exulting women' screamed and jeered at the retreating agent who later pressed charges. The women failed to appear before the magistrate and one of them told Father O'Neill that she was not afraid of the consequences: 'Faix to tell you the truth, your reverence, we'd like to get a taste of the jail.' In a public letter Hamilton denied the *Freeman*'s accusation that the farms were neglected and then justified the evictions. He also dismissed the story of his encounter with the 'Amazonian' women and declared that Mrs O'Toole belonged in a Charles Lever novel. Clearly, she was a figment of the reporter's 'mendacious' imagination. The *Freeman*'s reporter fired back insisting that the poisoned livestock and the derelict farms proved the 'grotesque and pitiful failure' of the evictions. As for Mrs O'Toole, far from being a myth she was the wife and sister of two tenants; and he urged Hamilton to visit Kavanagh's farm and challenge her to a fight – 'when, I venture to say, all his doubts on the subject will be speedily removed'. Hamilton continued to defend his action in the press and Coolgreany remained in turmoil for many months.

Not until the summer of 1891 were the League huts finally removed by court order. By the end of the year, Brooke was busy lobbying several Irish peers in his quest for a baronetcy as a reward for having fought the Plan. While appreciating Brooke's 'great public service', Balfour could not resist complaining to Lord Salisbury's private secretary that only an Irishman would consider himself deserving of honours on the grounds that he had resisted 'a lot of scoundrels who wished to pick his pocket'.[92]

O'KELLY/CLONGOREY

Another 'Glenbeigh' shattered the quiet around Clongorey, near Newbridge, County Kildare in March 1889. The heavily indebted and absentee owner, Peter de Penthony O'Kelly, possessed 500 acres of good grazing land and 500 acres of cut-away bog that barely sustained 72 poor tenants. The trustees had been pressing him to expel the tenants who had paid no rent for several years.[93] Thomas Ruttledge, the agent, attended the first round of evictions on 26 March when the bailiffs knocked down the mud-walls of a dozen cabins while a solicitor hired by the tenants followed the evictors from door to door and questioned each writ. When the sheriff came across piles of manure outside two dwellings, he applied the distraining order and sold them on the spot for 12 shillings. Disregarding a doctor's warning that a heart condition and dropsy might kill old Annie Kelly if she were evicted, the sheriff ordered her out. The parish priest denounced this 'most savage piece of blackguardism' and Ruttledge relented by postponing her removal. No such mercy was shown to Patrick Fullam, a bed-ridden cripple, whom the bailiffs wrapped in shawls and carried out as the crowd moaned and groaned.[94]

What provoked comparisons with Glenbeigh was the midnight burning of nine houses at the Bawn of Clongorey on 31 March. Ruttledge personally supervised this operation as the bailiffs sawed through rafters, doused thatched roofs with petroleum, and lit fires that could be seen for miles. Once the flames had died down, they knocked down the walls with crowbars. In his allegorical cartoon, 'Clongorey' (*Weekly Freeman*, 6 April 1889) (Plate 10), O'Hea portrayed the iconic female figure of Civilisation grieving over this callous act of destruction.

By contrast, Reigh's cartoon, 'A Triumph of Law and Order in Ireland' *(United Ireland*, 6 April 1889) (Plate 11), took a more realistic approach. As the flames consume their houses, the victims' faces reflect both rage and grief. As the caption reveals, the emergency men led by the agent 'were protected and encouraged by the Coercion Government'.[95] Shortly after this notorious episode a Lawrence photographer appeared on the scene and produced a stark image of Clongorey's fate in 'Eviction Scene, Ireland (Burnt Out)' (Plate 12). Here the leafless trees, the aimless observers, and the puddles of water reinforce the callousness of this deed. Apparently unchastened by the outcry, O'Kelly and his trustees ordered 18 more evictions in early June. But a judge refused to grant these decrees. Two old women who owed two years' rent were reprieved on doctor's orders. More evictions followed in September and some vacant farms were stocked with cattle from Wexford.[96] Another eviction photograph, also entitled 'Eviction Scene, Ireland. (Burnt Out)' (Plate 13), features the results of an assault by emergency men on a substantial cottage one half of which has been demolished by fire and crowbars. Several curious boys stroll around this site of destruction.

One benign by-product of the Plan of Campaign was a tedious and far-fetched novel with that title by F. Mabel Robinson filled with intrigues and

fractious love affairs in elite circles. Scenes of agrarian unrest and League rallies are interspersed with endless drawing-room chatter as the action shifts
from Cavan to the Georgian squares of Dublin, and then London. The hero,
Richard Talbot, loosely modelled on John Dillon, spends more time enjoying
life in high society than in working the Campaign trail. Murder and suicide
enliven the 'ludicrous' plot after the brutal bailiffs employed by the absentee
landlord, Roeglass, drive out Con Finnigan and three young women and set
their home on fire in the manner of Glenbeigh. Having read newspaper
accounts, Robinson describes the siege of barricaded houses in some detail.
One garrison uses slings to hurl stones and hot porridge at the evictors and a
little girl fights 'like a wild cat' until two constables drag her out amidst cries of
rage from the crowd of 5,000. Later an old man, two old women, a mother
with a baby and four other children suffer the same fate while bystanders shout
'Shame, shame!' Observing all this violence and suffering, one veteran
Campaigner calmly tells a naïve friend who is in a state of shock: 'Habit is everything, your first eviction is as hard to stomach as your first cigar.'[97]

George Moore's arresting short story about an eviction falls somewhere
between fiction, folklore, and reality. Here the wicked landlord is a woman,
Miss Barrett, whose features and traits make 'the Real Charlotte' of Somerville
and Ross seem almost virtuous. Fat, ugly, alcoholic, and lesbian she is a 'sewer
of debauchery' who emulates Mrs Gerrard by clearing her land of tenants to
make room for cattle. The familiar cast of characters includes the police, bailiffs,
innocent victims, and sinister schemers. In the climactic scene the inhabitants
of a wretched hovel fight the bailiffs, who pull down the rafters after the parents
and their six half-naked and wailing children have left. 'Bloated with drink',
Miss Barrett padlocks the door. One wonders if Moore ever witnessed some
such siege in his native county of Mayo.[98]

According to Joseph O'Brien the Plan had triumphed on 85 of 110 estates
by February 1891, although 20 owners still refused to reinstate their evicted
tenants. Despite the eviction of 7,000 individuals, hundreds of baton charges,
the death of 17 prisoners and the jailing of 5,000 people including 26 MPs, 9
clergymen, and 18 newspaper editors, the government, he contended, had
failed to crush the 'humble peasant communities' on the Test estates. Dublin
Castle's response to the widespread distress, moreover, had been 'ineffably
mean [and] ineffably stupid'.[99]

On the other hand Balfour could look back on his counteroffensive with
some satisfaction because the test estates had survived the conflict more or less
intact and the rescue efforts of the syndicates had forced his Irish adversaries to
drain the coffers of the National League in order to house and maintain all the
victims of eviction. Regarding eviction as a fact of life, he asserted: 'There have

always been evictions in Ireland (ironical cheers), and there always must be evictions in any country where either land or house property exists and where the tenants … refuse to pay their rents.'[100]

The Plan cost the Irish party and National League a great deal of money and effort, but it also weighed heavily on the government, the police, and rate-payers. According to a government return in 1893 the price tag for evictions on seventeen Plan estates amounted to £115,418 of which 83 per cent came out of national taxes and 17 per cent from local rates. The Clanricarde estate topped the list with £27,895 followed by Olphert (£15,847), Smith-Barry (£16,213), Massereene (£11,955), Cloncurry (£10,779), and Brooke (£7,663.) [101] Besides forcing many landlords to lower their rents the Plan also nudged some of them towards selling their tenanted land. At the same time the hardships caused by the Plan purges provided rich material for nationalist propagandists who reported countless stories of heroism by tenants who had defied the armed might of Dublin Castle and risked imprisonment to defend their homes.

SEVEN

RESISTANCE
1886-9

'There was nothing whatsoever in the laws of God
or in the laws of man to make it illegal or criminal
for a man to defend his home and his wife and children
against an invading force of the crowbar brigade'

WILLIAM J. LANE MP
speaking near Youghal, County Cork
14 August 1887

'When constabulary duty's to be done,
The policeman's lot is not a happy one!'

W. S. GILBERT
Pirates of Penzance, Act II

———

Organised resistance against eviction may have been the exception to the rule before 1879, but there was nothing new about vengeful acts directed against those held responsible for eviction, distraint, or any other transgression of 'the popular will'. As already noted, violence arising out of land disputes and conflicts with local authorities had a long history; and in the past agrarian secret societies had habitually punished enemies or violators of their codes of 'popular justice'. Such offences peaked during the early 1820s and then the tithe wars of the 1830s, when Catholic farmers, middle class-men, and even a few landowners refused to pay their dues to the Church of Ireland.[1]

One song, 'Johnny Grey', memorialised a Kilkenny man who died fighting the bailiffs after refusing to pay the tithe. When the 'treacherous crew' arrived at his door, Johnny grabbed his rifle and shot 'the Captain' dead.

> They surrounded the house and they held him at bay
> And soon our Young Johnny all bleeding he lay.
> With his last final shot, the Bailiff he did slay,
> And that was the ending of Young Johnny Grey.

9   The Kavanagh family of Croghan, near Coolgreany. Three generations of the Kavanagh family of Croghan, near Coolgreany, County Wexford, appear in this photograph taken in the latter 1880s. The fierce expressions on the faces of mother and eldest son suggest that they would not be easy prey for any eviction party. (NLI, TRAN 879, WL)

10   J. F. O'Hea, 'Clongorey'. O'Hea's revulsion over the arson attacks at Clongorey, County Kildare, inspired this allegorical image of Civilisation grieving over such wanton destruction. She declares: 'There has never been, in my time, anything more horrible than this. I blush as I have not blushed for many a year.' (*Weekly Freeman*, 6 Apr. 1889)

ABOVE

11   J. D. Reigh, 'A Triumph of Law and Order in Ireland'. Adopting a more realist approach than O'Hea, Reigh has drawn the burning of Clongorey village by emergency men 'protected and encouraged by the Coercion Government'. While several tenants sit or kneel in despair on the left, a woman attacks the agent. (*UI*, 6 Apr. 1889)

BELOW

12   'Eviction Scene. Ireland (Burnt Out)'. This photograph reveals the remains of the central square of the village without a single habitable dwelling. The roofless houses, bare trees, littered yard, and puddles of water combine to send a stark message about the violent death of a village. (NLI, R2159, WL)

15 'Eviction Scene. Ireland'.
In this Lawrence photograph the agent, sub-sheriff, and police mill around a barricaded cottage with furze or prickly bushes stuffed in the door and windows. The tenants' furniture and other belongings have been neatly piled outside.
(NLI, 1775 WL)

16   'Eviction Scene. Ready for Hot Water'.
Two emergency men pose for the camera holding
a wooden or wicker shield for protection against
any scalding liquid. (NLI, 1773 WL)

17   McNamara Family. The aged widow
Margaret McNamara sits defiantly in the window
of her barricaded house at Bodyke while family
members, friends, female servants, and two priests
pose outside. Father Peter Murphy stands next to
a basket of turf on the far right. (NLI, EBL 2662 WL)

ABOVE

18 'Praise The Lord ...'. In this Lawrence
picture some boys and men accompanied by
Father Peter Murphy parade a crude wooden
effigy of sub-sheriff McMahon past the widow
McNamara's house. The inscription reads:
'Praise the Lord, for Here the Tyrant's Arm Was
Paralysed.' (NLI, EBL 2655 WL)

BELOW

19 J. D. Reigh, *Bodyke Eviction Scenes*.
Reigh's action-filled portrayal of the Bodyke
evictions in June 1887 emphasises the extent of
tenant resistance and police brutality as female
bystanders are beaten and two young girls are
arrested. While one soldier aims his rifle, the
defender in the gable wall hole pours boiling
water on the bailiffs below. (By permission of NLI)

20   Henry Jones Thaddeus,
An Irish Eviction (1889).
The Cork-born artist, Henry
Jones Thaddeus, has represented
in a unique manner the fight for
possession inside a cottage. The
muscular tenant in the centre
with his back to the viewer is
poised to throw a bucketful of
scalding water, while his red-
haired wife stoops to his right
with a pitchfork in hand and
their frightened young daughter
clings to her mother's skirt. In
the background on the right
two men thrust a ladder at the
constables storming through
the door. (Private Collection)

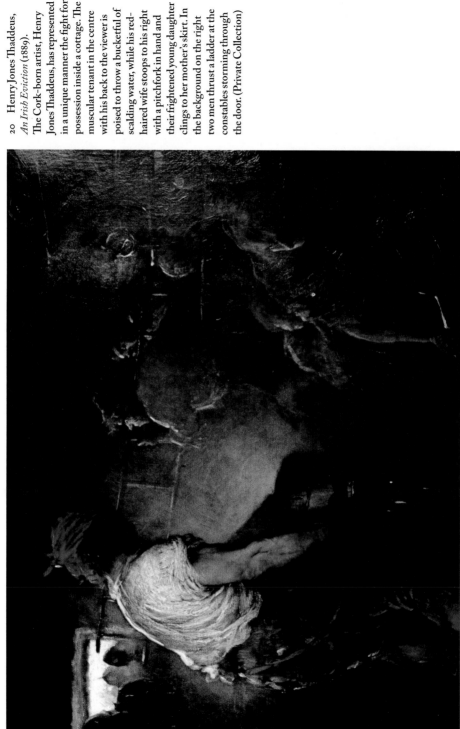

So come all you brave Irishmen wherever you may be:
Don't let them transport you all over the sea.
Stay in your own country and defend your own land
And soon we'll be free from this treacherous band.[2]

After the tithes war, obstruction of the sheriff's party tended to be sporadic and ineffective. The kind of violent resistance displayed at Ballykilcline in 1844, Kilcoosh in 1853, and Ballycohey in 1868 was an exception to the rule of submission with or without some hearty curses and shoving. One comic image of resistance to an urban eviction dates from 1840 when sub-sheriff Gabriel Whistler tried to oust a woman from her apartment on Constitution Hill in Dublin. Standing in the window, she empties the contents of a bucket or commode on this unhappy official. A squad of soldiers mocks her act of defiance and one of them takes aim with his rifle 'out of sport'. The artist, William Sadler, scion of a prominent artistic family, lived nearby and captured this amusing incident in full colour (Plate 14). What makes this scenario significant from the vantage point of the land wars forty years later was the presence of soldiers and the woman's resort to some kind of liquid to repel the sheriff.[3]

With a few notable exceptions most of the resistance to eviction during the famine years had involved more smoke than fire. Not until the advent of the Land League in the autumn of 1879 did tenants begin to barricade their abodes effectively, recruit garrisons, stockpile missiles, and organise huge crowds to harass the hereditary foe. For several good reasons we should treat newspaper accounts of resistance with some caution. Not only did reporters have their own biases, but the police also kept them well away from the contested site until the siege had ended. And in the heat of battle the latter could hardly obtain a panoramic view of the action outside not to mention inside. Small wonder then that local versions of the combat often diverged from those of reporters sent down from Dublin or London who knew little or nothing about the terrain, the landlord, the agent, and the people. Occasionally, a priest or a doctor would be allowed inside a cottage before the fighting began if an occupant was bedridden. On the whole only the bailiffs and constables along with the defenders knew exactly what transpired during these confrontations. Moreover, the divergent accounts of what transpired at Quinlan's 'castle' in 1881 should serve as a constant reminder that some accounts of resistance were highly exaggerated.

Because nationalist leaders and priests insisted that tenants had every right to defend their houses and farms from the crowbar brigade, the operative question during the 1880s concerned the kind and degree of violence to be used. Even

United Ireland set some limits on resistance by ruling out lethal weapons on the grounds that 'passive resistance'was much preferable to certain death. Firearms, this paper pointed out, were not only 'the counsel of despair'but also an invitation to 'massacre by a ruthless soldiery'. Aware that assaults on process servers were not sufficiently publicised, the Plan leadership encouraged tactics that would not only obstruct the sheriff's party but also draw more notice.[4] The sieges of fortified houses thus involved an element of political theatre designed to attract huge crowds and garner headlines. Paid organisers like John Kelly went about the country teaching tenants how to barricade their dwellings and foil the evictors without killing them.

A Lawrence photograph, entitled 'Eviction Scene. Ireland'(Plate 15), reveals the obstacles with which emergency men sometimes had to contend. Here the agent, sheriff, bailiffs, and police stand outside a cottage where the windows and doors as well as holes in the thatch have been stuffed with furze or prickly bushes. Fearing damage, the tenants have piled their belongings outside.[5]

This photograph came from the Dublin studio of William Mervyn Lawrence who had profited for years from buying and selling photographic images of Irish towns and landscapes, notably tourist sites like Killarney and Glendalough. This shrewd purveyor of stereographs and lantern slides was no Mathew Brady, let alone Alfred Stieglitz, but he had a sharp eye for consumer tastes. Like his precursor Frederick Mares, he understood the power and appeal of the camera. Aware that evictions were tailor made for photography, he sent out Robert French, a former policeman, to record these dramatic scenes. The resulting dry glass-plate negatives confirm Susan Sontag's insight that photographs are 'a grammar and, even more importantly, an ethics of seeing'.[6]

No matter how far removed from the physical act of forceful removal or siege warfare they may have been, Lawrence's eviction series still resonate with the violence of dispossession. The hybrid nature of photography – part art, part optics, part chemistry, and part technology – blurs the borders between art, illusion, and reality. As Jerry Thompson has observed, a photograph is 'a point of view' and not 'an embodiment of some absolute objective record of things as they are'. Liam Kelly rightly insists that these images require not only close reading, evaluating, and interpreting but also 'translating into the vernacular language'because they are the artistic constructions of the photographer rather than static records of reality. In particular, the eviction pictures raise more questions than answers owing to their posed nature after the operation has been completed as well as their highly political and emotional content. What the camera produces, in sum, is a mélange of the interpretive, the acquisitive, the appropriative, and the factual. And the Lawrence eviction photographs contain much more than a one-dimensional impression of the contest between the forces of landlordism and the Plan of Campaign.[7]

During the later 1880s Dublin Castle continued to dispatch hundreds of police reinforcements as well as regular soldiers to protect the sheriff's party from both the garrisons inside fortified dwellings and the surrounding crowds. And the police continued to violate their own rules and regulations by taking over siege operations after the emergency men had abandoned the field. Violence begat counter-violence; and nationalist spokesmen celebrated resistance with a steady drumbeat of rhetorical violence. Thus Dillon declared that if he were an Irish peasant, 'he would die on his own threshold rather than submit to eviction'. If only the people had arms, he added, little more would be heard about eviction parties.[8] But even he had to face the realities of unequal force. During the first land war the Land League's directors had exhorted tenants to hold on to their homesteads and not to pay rent except 'at the point of the bayonet' but they had failed to spell out either the tactics or the consequences of defying the sheriff. In fact, the systematic barricading of cottages and preparations for a protracted siege did not really begin until the summer of 1886.[9]

THE SECOND BATTLE OF WOODFORD

The skirmishes fought by a few determined tenants at Woodford in August 1886 marked, as we have seen, a new departure in defensive measures as Thomas Saunders and his neighbours raised the bar of resistance much higher. After that heroic stance National League 'organisers' started teaching tenants how to impede the evictors. In the meantime Dillon, O'Brien, and other Plan leaders went around the country urging tenants to resist the minions of Dublin Castle with all their non-lethal might. In short, from 1887 to 1889 resistance to eviction became the rule rather than the exception on many of the leading Plan estates.

On 29 August 1888 the sub-sheriff of Galway led his expeditionary force of 150 police and 200 Scots Fusiliers towards Clondegoff Castle, where an amphibious eviction force had landed several years earlier. In a lyrical passage the *Freeman's* reporter compared the lush landscape near the Shannon River to 'the sylvan, quiet beauty of Windermere'. The wailing bagpipes reminded him of 'the banshee fore-telling of the doom of some family' and RIC bayonets glittered in the sun. Braced for battle, the 'Pecksniffian' agent, Edward S. Tener, armed with a shotgun, advised the sheriff to bypass the barricaded houses and tackle five undefended targets elsewhere. At Clonmoylan James Callaghan and his comrades threw stones and hot liquid for two hours before his wall was breached. At Rossmore Mrs Page's defenders discharged hot liquid. With one blow she sent a policeman 'sprawling' into a dirty puddle for which offence she was arrested. John McDonnell's house contained an 80-year-old woman lying on her sickbed. After a doctor found her fit for removal, the bailiffs picked up the bed with its occupant and dropped both in the yard. Appalled by this act, the English visitors tendered her a few shillings.[10]

7.1   W. H. Overend, 'The Land War in Ireland: Sketches by Our Special Artist'. Engraved by
Overend, this print illustrates the kind of obstacles faced by the RIC on their way to eviction sites.
Logs, bogs, and rivers impeded their progress and often exhausted them on their long marches to
remote areas. (*ILN*, 22 Jan. 1887)

7.2   W. H. Overend, 'Peasants Firing the Hedges Between Woodford and Loughrea, Galway'. To
impede (or singe) eviction parties, local men sometimes set fire to the hedges on the approach roads or
boreens as this *ILN* print of an incident on the Clanricarde estate reveals. (*ILN*, 29 Oct. 1887)

Neither Parnellite MPs nor local priests were allowed to pass through the police cordon surrounding each targeted house. Spurning the offer of readmission if they paid one year's rent plus costs, eight families owing three or more years' rent were forced out after throwing stones and hot liquid. All the male resisters were arrested and remanded but the women were released pending a court appearance. Overcoming trees and boulders that blocked the road to Cloonoon, the sheriff's party expelled Michael Shaughnessy and Thomas Porter. One print, 'The Land War in Ireland: Sketches by Our Special Artist' (Figure 7.1), detailed some of the obstructions facing the RIC on their way to the next eviction site. Another delaying tactic involved setting fire to hedges along the route as the *ILN* print, 'Peasants Firing the Hedges between Woodford and Loughrea, Galway', made clear (Figure 7.2).

On 31 August the sheriff's party ran into token resistance from two tenants. At Douras, Tener ordered the bailiffs to carry out a young man, John Fahy, who was suffering from terminal tuberculosis. After an army doctor had pronounced him fit for removal, the agent ignored the parents' pleas for mercy and Fahy died three days later. Balfour's spokesman, George Wyndham, the future Irish chief secretary, justified the eviction on the grounds that Fahy suffered from epilepsy, not consumption, and could therefore be safely removed. He added for good measure that the youth had been treated 'in the very "spirit of humane and Christian forbearance"'. The authorities ignored the pleas of family and friends to hold an inquest.[11]

During one eviction a photographer posed two emergency men holding a wicker or wooden shield next to the furze-stuffed door as if to ward off any discharge of scalding stirabout (Plate 16).[12] The absence of an angry crowd and visible defenders may explain the light police presence. A day or two later, a battering ram made its first appearance on the Woodford estate but was not deployed.

Amidst much publicity thirty Woodford resisters were tried, convicted, and sentenced to prison terms ranging from one month to a year with hard labour. After being sentenced to two consecutive terms of six months, the defiant Francis Tully shouted from the courthouse steps: 'There will be no Tory Government when I am coming out, anyhow, or Clanricarde either. Hurrah for the Plan of Campaign'. More protest meetings followed this trial.[13]

A print in the *Graphic* based on a photograph showed some Woodford tenants proudly displaying their weaponry – buckets, bottles, pitchforks, loys, and cudgels – in front of a gate (Figure 7.3). The determination etched on their faces spoke louder than their primitive weapons.[14]

By the end of 1888, 40 more families had been uprooted around Woodford; 135 men had been imprisoned; and 90 families had been served with writs. Early in the new year bailiffs raided shops in Loughrea, whose owners had

7.3 'An Eye to Effect, from a Photograph Taken Just Before an Eviction on Lord Clanricarde's Estate, Woodford, Ireland'. Nine men, three women, and two children pose with their primitive weapons ready to fend off any evictors on the Clanricarde estate in 1888. This print derived from a photograph. (*Graphic*, 20 Oct. 1888).

supported the Plan. But the shopkeepers had concealed their goods to prevent their seizure. In the midst of a festive Plan parade a policeman proclaimed his disgust over the 'degrading work' of eviction. After cheering for Dillon, O'Brien, and the Clanricarde tenants, he vowed to resign. For this grave offence he was arrested and hustled back to barracks. In the meantime some ambushers tried and failed to shoot Tener on his way to Woodford petty sessions. Only the horse pulling the police escort cart was wounded.[15]

In the House of Commons Shaw-Lefevre denounced the 'vindictive' purge of almost a hundred Woodford tenants and predicted that 800 more would suffer the same fate if the rent strike continued. And on 12 January the *Freeman* credited Clanricarde with having 'done as much to break the back of landlordism as has the Plan of Campaign itself'.

On the Earl of Cork's estate in west Kerry eleven 'woebegone' tenants were evicted in mid-February 1887. Arrears had piled up after a bad fishing season and the meagre earnings from butter sales fell far short of what these Dingle tenants owed. Many of the thousand supporters carried clubs, pikes, and hooks as they greeted the evicted families; and Claude Byrne sketched some of the action for the *ILN*. The sheriff's party came up against stonewalls built across the road to impede their progress. At the first barrier, a protester shouted: 'Stand by your pikes men!' After some serious skirmishing, a police officer ordered his men to load their rifles with buckshot and fix bayonets. But this threat had little effect. At the next barrier the sheriff encountered some defiant girls standing on top of the wall. District Inspector Gray wisely retreated rather than risk bloodshed. Marching back to Dingle the police 'brutally batoned' some taunting girls and boys. A week later forty more families faced eviction. As soon as Colonel Turner saw the size and anger of the crowd, he consulted the parish priest, Father Egan, and persuaded the agent to accept the tenants' terms. Apparently Turner's peace-making effort prompted some local men to descend from the hillside and 'fraternise' with the police.[16]

VENTRY/DINGLE

At the end of July 1887 evictions took place on the estate of Lord Ventry, who owned over 93,600 acres on the Dingle peninsula. Conveyed in 21 wagons, the sheriff's party made its way to Ballyferriter where some tenants who were five years in arrears paid a fraction of what they owed. One strong farmer, Maurice Ferriter, scion of an old Dingle family, was the first to be driven out. Almost half of the thirty decreed tenants were reinstated after making a token payment. Apart from uttering curses and profanities, most of them left peacefully. Elsewhere, however, tenants blocked roads, knocked down bridges, barricaded doors and windows, and loopholed walls. Plan organisers like John Kelly, John Cullinane, and Michael Fleming had taught them well how to keep the enemy at bay at least for a few hours.[17]

London's illustrated weeklies continued to feature images of resistance. The *Graphic*'s influential French artist, Paul Renouard, sketched some eviction scenes in March 1888 while on a visit. The first image in 'Studies from Life in Ireland, IV' is entitled 'Barricading a House to Resist Eviction' (Figure 7.4), and foregrounds the heavy boulders and wooden gate being used to fortify the premises while chickens and pigs scrounge for food. The second image, 'The Eviction' (Figure 7.5), affords a rare glimpse of the action inside the cottage as two defenders wielding long cudgels brace for the charge by police through the huge hole in the wall. The debris on the floor includes a cornet – a favourite instrument of brass bands. On the far right a woman prepares to heave a pail of hot liquid at the enemy. Whether or not Renouard witnessed any of this action, this image bears a vague resemblance to Henry Jones Thaddeus's striking picture, *An Irish Eviction* (Plate 20), painted in the following year. In the third sketch, 'After the Eviction' (Figure 7.6), the agent or head bailiff surveys the extensive damage done to this slate-roofed dwelling.[18]

In many cases the resisters comprised family members, including wives and daughters, and close friends. But farmers' sons who lived nearby also volunteered their services. Apart from stones, pitchforks, and blackthorns, the weapon of choice was hot stirabout or water laced with everything from lime and tar to corn meal, urine, red pepper, and sheep dip. Here the women played a crucial role by heating this foul-smelling and sticky concoction and then throwing bucketfuls at the emergency men and police. Besides this weapon some women used farm tools and fists. At Rathduff near Cork city Eliza Forrest jabbed District Inspector Tyacke in the face with a pitchfork, while her brother held off the bailiffs with a scythe. Eliza also bit four constables 'severely' before being subdued.[19]

7.4   Paul Renouard, 'Studies from Life in Ireland, IV' (*Graphic*, 10 Mar. 1888). These three sketches (Figures 7.4 to 7.6) by the French artist, Paul Renouard, who visited Ireland in 1887–8, depict the before, during, and aftermath of an eviction. In 'Barricading a House to Resist Eviction', the defenders are 'scientifically' fortifying their cottage with boulders and a gate. They have stockpiled stones and are heating water, lime, and meal in a large pot to be thrown at the foe.

7.5   Renouard, 'The Eviction'. Inside the besieged cottage two defenders with long sticks prepare to repel the police. The woman on the far right aims a pail of hot liquid at the invaders. Amidst the litter on the floor lies a brass cornet. (*Graphic*, 10 Mar. 1888)

Here and there some ingenious weapons came into play. On Sir George Colthurst's property near Rathcool, County Cork, Timothy Leary hung an 'American hayrack' over his front door and attached ropes to this contraption. As soon as the bailiffs entered, he let go and the heavy rake fell on them. Leary also covered the deep well in his front yard with light boards and rushes in the hope that the evictors would break through. But this trap did not succeed. Once inside the bailiffs were pelted with stones and smeared with hot tar at the end of mops. One police officer ordered his men to load their rifles, but no shots were fired. After a seven-hour standoff the sheriff withdrew his men to loud hurrahs from the crowd.

When the police tackled the abode of John Trant, a Plan leader in the parish of Irramore, County Kerry, they ran into trouble. This tenant had retreated upstairs and locked himself inside a strong room behind a heavy door reinforced by an iron gate propped up by planks. After a three-hour struggle to break down this barrier, the police loaded their guns with buckshot and took aim at Trant, who bared his chest and shouted that he would rather meet his God than the agent. At length the gate gave way and he was arrested. A

few defenders threw sulphur or cayenne pepper into the fireplace hoping
to drive out the bailiffs, but the noxious
fumes soon dissipated and the evictors
resumed their task. In County Sligo a
tenant farmer chained himself to a
boulder buried deep in the ground
forcing the sheriff to send for a hack-
saw to sever the chain and secure the
premises.[20]

Miraculously no one was killed in
these sieges, but many of the combatants on both sides suffered cuts, burns,
and bruises, and at least a dozen aged
or sickly tenants died from 'natural
causes' after being expelled. Only on
rare occasions did the police fire buckshot over the heads of menacing crowds
preferring to drive them back with
batons and bayonets. Charges of

7.6   Renouard, 'After the Eviction'. An agent or
head bailiff surveys the extensive damage done to
this slate-roofed dwelling. (*Graphic*, 10 Mar. 1888)

police brutality usually followed on the heels of resistance; and Colonel Turner
had to deal with at least sixteen lawsuits accusing him of responsibility for bat-
tery and assault. But all of these charges were dismissed.[21] In the meantime
Plan leaders kept on denouncing the RIC for violating regulations by acting
like bailiffs after the latter had abandoned the siege. Resistance of course created a host of local heroes and heroines whose courage made priceless propaganda for the Plan. Their trials and imprisonment elevated them to the even
higher status of martyrs who had to endure hard labour, plank beds, cold nights,
awful food, lice, and abusive warders. Upon their release they were hailed by
admiring throngs and treated to lavish banquets.[22]

HURLEY'S MILL, CLONAKILTY

On 19 October 1886, the sheriff's party faced a determined garrison at Tim
Hurley's 50-acre farm at Castleview, three miles from Clonakilty, county Cork.
This tenant lived with his wife and five children on the upper floors of a five-storey
wool-carding mill. On the appointed day several thousand people marched
out of Clonakilty accompanied by brass bands as they conveyed a new wooden
shelter for the evicted family to a site near the mill.

As soon as the crowbar brigade drew near, they were pelted with stones,
brickbats, and scalding water thrown from the upper windows. Breaking through

a ground floor window, the bailiffs entered and found that the stairs had been removed. Suddenly large chunks of masonry and pieces of iron rained down on their heads from the floor above. One millstone dislocated a bailiff's shoulder. When an officer threatened to shoot, the defenders hurled more missiles and ignored priestly pleas to surrender. After a long standoff and more parleys, the sheriff agreed to withdraw his men. Several days later Hurley and six comrades were arrested for both obstruction and possession of dynamite. All but Hurley were released on bail pending their trial.[23]

An *ILN* print of this siege, 'Sketches of the Eviction Campaign in Ireland: Police and Bailiffs Besieging Tim Hurley's Mill at Clonakilty, County Cork'

SEIZING THE PROVISIONS BROUGHT FOR THE BESIEGED.

7.7   Anon, 'Police and Bailiffs Besieging Tim Hurley's Mill at Clonakilty, County Cork'. In Forestier's sketch of the siege of Hurley's mill at Clonakilty, County Cork, the police are protecting the crowbar gang from an angry crowd and the defenders in the top windows are throwing buckets of hot liquid on the besiegers below. In the upper left corner inset two constables apprehend a woman trying to deliver food to the garrison. (*ILN*, 27 Nov. 1886)

(Figure 7.7), shows the bailiffs storming the mill and the police fending off onlookers. In the upper left inset two constables are stopping a woman from delivering food to the defenders.[24]

A thrilling episode took place on Mrs Sarah Gabbett's estate near Caherconlish in eastern Limerick in January 1887. One of her tenants, Edmund or 'Big Ned' O'Grady, put up a Herculean fight against the crowbar brigade. Tall, powerful, and popular, he recruited two dozen friends to help him fortify and defend his premises at Ballybrood. They knocked down the stairway leading to the loft and covered the hole in the ceiling with heavy planks secured by nails and large stones. On the appointed day some 150 constables faced over a thousand hostile spectators. After the sheriff had read the decree aloud, O'Grady retorted from an upper window that he would sooner die than surrender. The defenders then pushed several bailiffs off a ladder and O'Grady felled another attacker with an iron bar. After the bailiffs hacked a hole in the roof, they were scalded by a mixture of hot water and urine. O'Grady shouted: 'Thry again begorra; ye're getting on finely; to Hell with the lot of ye.' The defenders then cut up a dead dog and flung the entrails down on the evictors with cries of 'Yez had a dhrink and maybe ye're hungry now; perhaps dog's mutton will put … more spunk into yez.' Once inside the emergency men pushed a ladder through the hole in the ceiling whereupon 'an avalanche of enormous stones' crashed down on their heads and shoulders. Here, too, several constables were ordered to load their rifles. But District Inspector Green kept his head and talked O'Grady into surrendering before any shots were fired. The garrison walked out with heads held high and were released in order to avoid a riot. A few emergency men and police were left behind to guard Hurley's premises.[25]

The Dublin poet, Carolan O'Carroll, celebrated 'noble' Ned O'Grady's gallant stand:

> Self-prisoned in the topmost room,
> The staircase torn away,
> With some brave ten of his kinsmen,
> The Giant stood at bay.

> Up scaling ladders, placed with care –
> The riflemen below –
> To drive the lion from his lair,
> The burly bailiffs go.

Trembling and bruised the bailiffs lie,
Nor can the armed men,
With rifles set and bayonet,
That desperate passage gain.

Now cheer aloud the gathering crowd –
The baffled bailiffs tire –
When from the hireling justice comes
The murderous order – 'Fire!'

'Fire then on me,' O'Grady cries,
'For I can stand till death!'
Oh, God! how nigh those fearless words
Had been his latest breath.

Then forth the giant stalks alone,
His eyes with wrath aflame –
'You've made your batons crowbars,
And you'll answer for the same.'
. . . .
He's cast the landlords from the land
And put the bailiffs down.[26]

On 27 September, a short but sharp fight took place on the farm held by
O'Grady's brother-in-law, Michael Lane, at Ardnacrusha near Parteen in
southeast Clare. For years Lane had been feuding with his landlord, Colonel
Thomas S. McAdam of Cuckfield, Sussex, over the rent. A 20 per cent abatement
granted in 1883 had failed to satisfy him. Father of nine or ten young children,
Lane resolved to defend his abode and asked Ned's brother, Thomas O'Grady,
to help him resist. When Sheriff Croker and Colonel Turner drew near, Lane
shouted: 'Come in, we will give it to you!' Once the crowbar gang attacked, the
muscular Lane and Thomas O'Grady flew out of the door flailing away with
'huge shillelaghs'. Several police suffered cuts and bruises before they managed
to fell the defenders 'like pigs' and beat them with rifle butts. Lane's wife,
Johanna, 'a powerful woman', joined in the mêlée and wielding a poker she
struck District Inspector O'Reilly's helmet so hard that he suffered 'an ugly
scalp wound' that bled profusely. The police had a hard time handcuffing the
two men while bystanders cheered until they were hoarse. When Lane's children
saw their mother being hauled away, they burst into tears. A week later the

magistrates sentenced both men to only one month in prison with hard labor because they had not resorted to hot tar. This coercion court called Mrs Lane's conduct 'the worst of all'.[27]

Not long after Glenbeigh, Irish landlordism earned even more notoriety on the estate of Lieutenant Colonel John O'Callaghan of Maryfort near Tulla, County Clare. Poor soil made life hard for smallholders on the Bodyke property; rents were widely regarded as exorbitant; and Dublin Castle classified this region as one of the most disturbed in the League-ridden west. Bitter quarrels between landlord and tenant erupted in 1881 over rent rises following tenant improvements. Abatements of 30 per cent in 1882–3 offered scant relief to tenants after agricultural prices plunged. Heavy incumbrances made O'Callaghan, who had few friends in Dublin Castle, an ideal candidate for the Plan. Major General Sir Redvers Buller considered him a 'driveller'; and Colonel Turner had no time for this 'harsh exacting landlord'.[28]

Led by their proactive priest, Father Peter Murphy, the Bodyke tenants requested a 30 per cent rent reduction in January 1886. But the agent, Stannard MacAdam, objected on the grounds that the Land Court had already crimped O'Callaghan's income. At a rousing rally on 29 January 1887 O'Brien urged the tenants to combine and defend their rights with more resolve than had been shown at Glenbeigh. He praised them as 'formidable customers … men of flesh and blood, and not worms. (Cheers)'. Warming to his task, he declared that 'if the Irish people had the power to meet the police man to man and rifle to rifle in the open field, I for one would cut short my speechmaking … and the next speech that the destroyers of the people's houses would hear would be a speech out of the mouths of the people's guns. (Loud cheers).' Such brave people, he added, would never allow their country to be 'turned into a howling wilderness, a vast Glenbeigh, one vast scene of misery, poverty and desolation'. Hoping to avoid serious trouble Buller advocated a temporary suspension of the evictions; but Balfour would have none of this because it would infuriate Unionist peers and endanger the passage of his new land bill. Nevertheless the evictions were postponed for a few months while O'Callaghan halfheartedly sought a settlement on his terms.[29]

Among the notables who made their way to Bodyke to witness the evictions were Davitt, Joseph Pease MP for York, and his good friend James Hack Tuke, who gave £300 to the Plan tenants. Another observer was the Harvard educated journalist and avid Home Ruler, Henry Norman, who later became a Liberal

MP. Hired by Stead in 1884 as a reporter, Norman telegraphed his articles about Bodyke to half a dozen British newspapers as well as the *Boston Advertiser*.[30] O'Callaghan insisted that the tenants, who owed at least £1,327 but offered £907, cover legal costs and accept a smaller abatement. Father Murphy and the Plan leaders rejected these terms; Davitt assured the tenants that they had the support of British workers; and the wheels of eviction began to turn.[31]

On 27 May Colonels Turner and Miller RM as well as sub-sheriff James McMahon led their task force out of Fortane (Fort Anne) escorted by 300 police and 150 Welsh Fusiliers. Chapel bells tolled and horns blew to summon a crowd that swelled to 5,000 including a dozen priests and five Home Rule MPs. Turner followed the Castle's advice to proceed with 'full military precautions'. Through the valleys marched the scarlet-clad soldiers and the police in their black-green uniforms. Norman deplored this invasion of a once peaceful district for the 'inglorious' purpose of demolishing the hovels of poor tenants. Father Murphy urged the crowd to refrain from stone throwing; but the elaborate barricading of cottages meant that the emergency men faced a hard day's work. With Davitt and four Home Rule MPs looking on, the evictors attacked the house of Margaret McNamara, an 80-year-old widow, who farmed 19 Irish acres with her three sons and two daughters. Two years behind with the rent, she posed obligingly for a photographer before the ejectment, sitting in the one open window looking like Whistler's mother (Plate 17). Among family members, friends, and retainers standing or sitting outside may be seen two priests including Father Peter Murphy on the far right.[32]

When the sheriff's party drew near, the women and girls inside began to shriek. Father Murphy ignored Turner's order to silence the crowd and the police beat them back with their batons. Just outside the widow's house, Sheriff McMahon suddenly suffered an epileptic fit and collapsed on the road. Loud cheers emanated from the crowd at this sign of 'divine Providence'. At first Turner was convinced that the sheriff had been hit by a stone given the 'evil reputation' of the local tenantry. An ambulance carted the unconscious sheriff away, and the evictions were suspended to the crowd's delight.[33] A day later a crude wooden effigy of McMahon appeared outside the McNamara house inscribed with the words: 'Praise the Lord, For Here The Tyrant's Arm Was Paralysed'. A photographer recorded this effigy being paraded through the village with a bunch of boys and the ubiquitous Father Murphy on the far right (Plate 18).[34] Throughout this turbulent fortnight protest meetings and brass bands sustained morale around Bodyke.

On 2 June, McMahon's replacement, Sub-Sheriff Edward William Croker of Ballinagar, took charge of operations backed by 300 well-armed men. Local people regarded this vainglorious official with the same contempt that the sheriff of Nottingham had inspired in Robin Hood's 'merrie band'. The first house tackled belonged to John Lyddy (Liddy) who held some 23 acres. Wearing a loud tweed suit and a shooting hat, Croker supervised the emergency men whom Norman described as 'gaol-birds' and 'cowardly ruffians' from the north with 'the hangdog, villainous faces one would expect to find among men' hired to perform such degrading work. Fifteen priests and curates along with Davitt stood at the head of the roaring crowd as the crowbar men stormed this house. As Norman put it, 'Anybody who has never heard an Irish yell may be interested to know that it is absolutely identical in key and cadence with an Indian war-whoop'. After two hours of pounding with crowbars the bailiffs breached the wall, charged inside, and hauled out Lyddy and his weeping family. They also smashed the furniture by throwing it into the yard. Father John Hannan CC carefully compiled a list of each broken item and handed it to Croker. Lyddy stared 'blankly' at the devastation around him, and tears welled up in Davitt's eyes. After the evictors left, a 'lean grey cat' jumped onto the roof and vanished through a hole thereby 'retaking possession of the deserted tenement'. When Davitt spotted the English Liberal visitors eating a picnic lunch with Turner and his 'burglar brigade', he lost his temper.[35]

Next on the sheriff's list was the widow McNamara's dwelling where the defenders unleashed a barrage of stones. The bailiffs' boss shouted at his men as they attacked a wall: 'Heave away my men; pitch the stones in on them, heave them in.' But they soon retreated and Croker ordered the police to replace them despite Davitt's protest. Three constables forced their way inside, and instantly 'all was babel'. As Norman put it, the defenders 'fought like tigers' and he expected 'to see the flash of firearms'. Several women grabbed the invaders' crowbars, and Davitt, standing nearby, told the widow in Irish to lie down so that the bailiffs would have to carry her out. Norman risked arrest by tackling a bailiff who had struck young Kate McNamara's breast. During the siege one McNamara daughter offered the agent an egg in lieu of rent, and her 'plucky' sister Kate jumped up on some rocks and shouted: 'Three cheers for the Plan of Campaign!' In Turner's eyes these girls were 'unsexed furies'. As soon as the eviction party left, Mrs McNamara re-entered and 'smoke was seen curling up merrily from the chimney'. All the way back to town Croker's forces were groaned and jeered. At a protest rally that night Davitt declared that 'the chief criminals in Ireland are the landlords and the[ir] only crime the crime of eviction (loud cheers)'. He also accused O'Callaghan and the government of hiring mercenaries to make war on a three-year-old child. He expressed regret for having opposed the use of physical force to defend homesteads and insisted that never again would he censure any Irishman for fighting the 'diabolical' evictors. How absurd it was, he pointed out, to spend £1,000 of taxpayers' money on ousting two families now safely back in their homes. Invoking John Mitchel's exhortation to 'make every house a fortress', he urged his audience to meet force with force short of an armed rising that was bound to fail. He also took the men of Bodyke to task for having shown less courage than the women. His tirade so upset the English delegates – several 'ladies' and Sir Wilfrid Lawson MP – that they walked out in a huff.[36]

On the next day Colonel Turner allowed a few reporters, priests, and MPs to pass through the police cordon and confer with James Lyddy, father of sixteen children, who called Croker a 'thief' and a 'blackguard'. When the siege began, the women threw hot liquid at the bailiffs before being subdued. A soldier rudely pushed Norman away when he tried to enter the cabin. One daughter hit a police inspector with an iron hoop. At Martin McNamara's house Croker was almost bowled over by a bucket of cow-dung. A burly bailiff hurled his crowbar like a javelin through a loophole hoping in vain to impale a defender. After a wall collapsed the police charged inside and rounded up the wife and eight children including an imbecile girl who screamed while stumbling over the rubble. In a moment of comic relief several constables tried to capture a pig, a goat, a donkey, and some ducks and geese while the crowd laughed and yelled 'whisht' and 'hurrish' to speed the animals on their way. Eventually, the pig escaped and returned to 'his own domestic ditch'. Davitt and his English friends handed three sovereigns to this family.

Michael Hussey's two sons and a daughter named Maggie repelled the bailiffs with a mixture of hot gruel and dung along with stones, sticks, and bottles while several bands played patriotic tunes. Undaunted, Croker picked up a crowbar and helped the emergency men breach a gable wall; and Maggie invited them inside with 'a radiant, exultant smile' all the while cheering for the Plan. Without warning a 'douche' of hot liquid sent one constable sprawling and scalded Croker's face. This 'perfect broadside' spurred the bailiffs to retreat. Thoroughly annoyed, Turner ordered some riflemen to load and aim their weapons at the resisters whereupon a frantic Father Murphy shouted: 'You won't do that! you won't murder them!' One son appeared at an upstairs window and yelled: 'Fire away, fire away, you scoundrels.' Eventually Turner calmed down and told the firing party to back off. When the gable wall collapsed, the bailiffs charged inside to be greeted by a swarm of bees that flew up the chimney and stung a defender on the roof badly enough to require medical attention. Exhausted, bruised, and bereft of ammunition, the garrison surrendered and Norman shook their hands on the way out. He ended his vivid account with a tribute: 'The names of Hussey and Macnamara – Kate, Maggie, and all the boys – will be honoured in Clare for many a long year.'[37]

On 6 June the evictors returned with canvas umbrellas to ward off hot liquid.

Croker strutted about with a silk handkerchief wrapped around his scalded cheek and head. Davitt talked Thomas Fahy of Ballymacduagh out of using a pitchfork on the bailiffs and loaned his own umbrella to Fahy's wife as she cuddled her baby on a makeshift bed in the pouring rain. At another house a young girl was arrested for throwing hot water mixed with some kind of acid that singed Turner's uniform. At Pat McNamara's house three girls scalded the emergency men with hot yellow gruel. A baseless rumour flew that he had thrown either red cayenne pepper or a mixture of vitriol and salt into his fireplace in order to drive the bailiffs away. In the ensuing struggle a policeman choked Johanna Kennedy exclaiming: 'Ye devil, ye haven't had half enough.' Under arrest the defenders hailed the Plan and shouted 'God Save Ireland'. [38]

Forcing their way into John Cooney's barricaded cottage, the crowbar gang found his young son lying on a mattress suffering from chronic heart disease. Although a doctor pronounced him too sick to be disturbed, the agent insisted on his removal. So his sisters wrapped him in blankets and overcoats and helped their 'dying' brother outside 'tottering and crying'. When several army officers overheard the doctor say that the boy might 'drop dead any minute', they muttered words so disparaging that Norman would not quote them. This 'act of incredible and indescribable cruelty', he wrote, went far to explain 'why Irishmen hate England's rule and English rulers'. But he did not stop there: 'The spectacle [of the son's removal] was simply paralysing in its inhumanity… If that lad dies, his blood will be upon the agent Hosford's head, as clearly as ever man's blood lay upon a murderer on the scaffold.' No sooner had the evictors left than some kindly neighbours carried the invalid back inside, replaced the furniture, rebuilt the wall, and relit the fire. At a subsequent rally Davitt denounced 'the hellish work' of the British government and praised the 'Irish heroines' for their valiant defiance. On 7 June, three women threw hot water and lime out of Henry Murphy's house, but the emergency men prevailed. 'Purple with passion', Mrs Murphy emerged holding an infant while five young children trailed behind her. Shoving her 'half-naked baby' in the agent's face, she shouted: 'Hosford, did ye ever get a child, ye cruel murderer!' Davitt advised her not to accept the chair brought by a police sergeant saying: 'Sit on the grass, Mrs Murphy, don't take anything at their hands.' [39]

Canvas shields and umbrellas failed to block all the hot liquid aimed at the emergency men who were trying to knock down a wall on top of four combative women at Pat Tuohy's house. One defender yelled: 'Come on, come on, and I will give it you yet.' Despite the wall's collapse the women forced the foe back with more torrents of liquid. At last these 'determined Amazons' were overpowered and dragged outside kicking and screaming. During the trial in Ennis the scalded policemen described their ordeal and the magistrate sentenced mother and daughter to a month in prison with hard labour. Elsewhere Pat Wall's eighty-year-old mother, Bridget, was sitting in a chair when a policeman struck her in the eye with his baton. News of this 'outrage' reached Westminster where infuriated Irish MPs deplored this abuse of force. After their discharge from prison, the resisters returned home. [40]

The climactic siege took place on 10 June at John O'Halloran's farm in Lisbareen. This strong farmer and father of six children had spent over £200 on a new house and land reclamation and he deeply resented the rent increases that followed these improvements. [41] Having blocked the windows and doors and loopholed the gable ends, O'Halloran and his comrades dug a deep trench and built a steep embankment around the house. Davitt surveyed the defences and approved of everything except the pitchforks, which he confiscated. In another lyrical passage the *Freeman's* reporter described Turner's army marching through the countryside with the scarlet uniforms of the soldiers giving 'a warmth of tone which set off a picture as lovely as ever the eye of the artist rested upon'. Croker's siege train reminded him of 'some huge serpent of many hues traveling [*sic*] in search of its prey'; and he wondered how anyone could justify sending 400 heavily armed men to capture one small cabin defended by an old woman, two boys, and four teenage girls. As usual the police set up their cordon and the soldiers formed skirmishing parties in case of any guerrilla attacks. [42]

The O'Halloran women heated up a big pot of water mixed with mud and meal, and the men held long poles to push back ladders. One daughter threw boiling liquid at the foe shouting: 'Come now if you dare.' Foiled by the thick walls, the crowbar gang, aided by some constables, shifted their assault to the roof but were pushed off their ladders and fell to the ground. After Turner ordered several riflemen to load their weapons and threatened to shoot any resisters, two sons appeared in a window and refused to back away when the soldiers took aim. Another son, Frank, cut a hole in the roof to fend off the police who then climbed through an upstairs window. As bayonets clashed with shillelaghs, the women screamed, the police shouted, and the crowd cheered lustily for the garrison. One daughter, Honoria, grabbed Constable Norton's 'sword-bayonet' and would have cut her hand had not her brother Frank felled him with a single blow. She held off the invaders with the bayonet, while her brothers dragged the unconscious Norton upstairs. They were about to throw him out of the window when Father Hannan hastened up the ladder and talked them into surrender. [43] After the fort fell, several enraged policemen chased a group of hecklers through a field and batoned one lad severely. Crying out for revenge some local men rushed down the hillside ready to do battle. But Father Glynn intervened and averted a bloodbath. Another priest persuaded Turner to release the O'Halloran girls pending their trial. After the evictors had left, the family returned home.

This contest produced many cuts and bruises but fortunately no fatalities. For their defiance of the law the O'Halloran men spent three months in Limerick jail with hard labour, while their women were sentenced to one month. In the House of Commons Parnellite MPs denounced the RIC for their brutality and deployment as surrogate bailiffs.[44]

Reigh highlighted the O'Halloran siege in his colourful cartoon, 'Bodyke Eviction Scenes' (*United Ireland*, 18 June 1887) (Plate 19). Here one of the sons is dumping hot liquid on the umbrella-toting bailiffs below as a soldier takes aim with his rifle; a young woman in the window shoves two constables off a ladder; a policeman 'bludgeons' a woman; and three children are made 'Prisoners of War'.[45] The *Penny Illustrated Paper* also foregrounded the battle with a cover print, 'Ireland's Land War: Fight for a Cottage at Bodyke' (18 June 1887) wherein two women are discharging hot liquid and knocking policemen off their ladder while the sheriff's party huddles pathetically beneath umbrellas.[46]

On 11 June, four more families were expelled around Lisbareen. Three 'pretty girls' inside the mud-walled cottage of Peter and Ellen Wall bombarded the bailiffs with hot stuff. A girl tried to hook a bailiff with a salmon gaff at the end of a pole, but he snatched it out of her hands. Evidently, it took nine constables to subdue the defenders. Michael O'Callaghan's three daughters were arrested for throwing hot stirabout. At Thady Collins's home a daughter lay dying from consumption. The father's tears moved the agent to check her medical record and then grant a temporary reprieve. However, Captain Welch ordered his men to bludgeon the unruly crowd, and two English observers joined Davitt in denouncing these 'horrors' and contributed to the Bodyke Defence Fund. On Sunday Davitt addressed a banned meeting at Feakle calling the evictions 'criminal' and congratulating the people of Bodyke for 'rivetting the attention of the civilised world'.[47]

On 15 June, the tranquillity of the valley was shattered again by the cries of homeless women and children forced out of their homes. Michael McNamara lay on his sickbed, and an army doctor predicted fatal consequences if he were disturbed. This tenant refused Hosford's offer of readmission in return for possession of the holding. Uncharacteristically, the agent handed him a penny in token payment thereby converting him into a caretaker. Later the crowbar brigade emptied the cabins of Jeremiah Walsh and Patrick McNamara. The latter's bedridden old father left moaning and groaning followed by his son, daughter in law, and seven children.[48]

Davitt honoured his pledge to stay so long as the evictions lasted. At indignation meetings he railed against the police and the 'extermination' brigade and urged tenants to fight back even if this meant jail rather than the workhouse. All told these thirty evictions cost between £3,000 and £5,000 including the wages paid to the armed escort. In addition O'Callaghan had to pay £500 to the sheriff's party and lost at least £1,350 of arrears and £200 in lawyers' fees.[49]

Because most of the evicted tenants returned illegally or were readmitted, this 'victory' over the Plan could hardly have been more Pyrrhic. *United Ireland* (11 June 1887) called the purge both 'ludicrous' and 'savage', not least because it had cost more than one hundred times what the tenants owed. The *Freeman's Journal* vilified O'Callaghan as a vengeful and miserly rackrenter who had bled his tenants white before evicting them and praised all the brave women and girls being prosecuted for assault. Dillon likened Colonel Turner to a Turkish pasha and called him a turncoat for having professed to be an ardent Home Ruler until Balfour came into power at which point he began to do 'the dirty work of the landlords'. In the long run, however, Turner's growing distaste for evictions and anger over his dismissal by John Morley moved him to abandon the Unionist cause.[50]

In the House of Commons C. A. V. Conybeare denounced Mrs Wall's black eye as a classic case of police brutality. Dillon deplored this 'cruel and brutal' example of landlordism and accused O'Callaghan of having told a tenant seeking an abatement: 'You must pay it or go out; and I care no more of pitching one of you out than of shooting a bird on the roadside.' Several Liberal MPs who had just returned from Bodyke also condemned the 'atrocities' they had seen. The unflappable Balfour responded that charges of police brutality arose from 'the usual fertility of resource and perfervid imagination' of journalists.[51]

On his return from a fund-raising tour for evicted tenants, Davitt and his American wife addressed a festive rally at Bodyke on 24 July. They hailed the O'Halloran women as 'heroines of the whole countryside' and awarded them silver medals in the shape of a Celtic cross along with £5 and new dresses. Three boys fresh from prison were promised similar medals as well as Waltham watches. English and Scottish sympathisers had paid for these prizes that were designed to remind all and sundry of the momentous struggle to free their country from British rule. At another mass meeting Davitt averred that peace would never come to Ireland so long as Irish landlords carried out these 'infamous outrages' against their poor tenants.[52]

Norman ended his account of the Bodyke evictions with a diatribe against the legal system that gave 'one man the power of life and death over hundreds of others'. Reckoning that over half a million people had been evicted between 1849 and 1885, he asked how any Englishman could contemplate this figure 'without a shudder of shame'. The blatant cruelty of eviction and the recent passage of 'the cruellest Coercion Bill of all the eighty-seven' made it clear to him why Ireland had bred so many rebels.[53]

Visiting Bodyke in September, Samuel Laing, the English railway magnate and former Liberal MP, found that twenty evicted families had reoccupied their homes, repaired the damage, rounded up their livestock, and harvested the potato crop. Although local industry was paralysed, O'Callaghan had 'shot his bolt' and could not possibly purge every Plan tenant without employing a small army. Laing was moved to recommend that every British MP – regardless of party – spend at least a month in the west of Ireland so that they could see for themselves all the injustices. Bodyke, in short, joined Woodford, Glenbeigh, and Coolroe as one more epitome of landlord callousness, police brutality, and tenant heroism.[54]

After the battles of Bodyke, Sheriff Croker continued to lead his forces against the Plan. Having survived more blows and hot liquid with the help of a wicker shield during Michael Lane's eviction at Parteen in County Limerick in September 1887, he remained one of the toughest sub-sheriffs in the west.[55]

In January 1888 Colonel Turner helped to negotiate a partial settlement whereby the O'Callaghan tenants paid £1,000 in rent and the owner covered legal costs and reinstated the evicted families. A jubilant O'Brien called this a great victory for the Plan following evictions that 'would write the blackest chapter in the annals of Irish landlordism'. 'The Bodyke tenants are saved', he exulted, 'and the black chapter is wiped out (loud cheers).' But this was not the end of O'Callaghan's troubles. Plan activists and protest meetings led to more arrests and imprisonments in the spring; and disputes over rents and arrears put an end to the truce in 1893.[56]

LEADER/CURRASS

Because William Leader's tenants around Currass (also Curraghs) and Meelin, near Buttevant in north Cork seemed less enthusiastic about the Plan than the O'Callaghan tenantry, Dillon and O'Brien made frequent visits to keep them up to the mark. Many of them had toiled long and hard to reclaim swampland, and resentment over rent increases drove them to adopt the Plan in mid-December 1886. With the battle lines drawn, ejectment writs followed in short order. At rallies in January 1887 Dillon urged the tenantry to fight for their rights and Father R. P. Collins held aloft a sheaf of writs collected around Currass and set them on fire to roars of approval from four thousand supporters.[57]

Notices to quit culminated in evictions on 9 August 1887 that provoked a boycott and labourers' strike. Leader responded by importing men from his Dromagh estate to reap the crops at Currass. During this harvesting operation he audaciously appeared with a police escort and exhorted the labourers to complete their task despite all the harassment. When a tenant's delegation approached to plead their case, Leader refused to talk to them or the parish priest who bore his surname. After lighting his pipe, he threw the match at Father Leader's back as he walked away. Five tenants were prosecuted for obstructing the sheriff and three of them were jailed for a month.

Tensions remained high. The distraining of crops a year later brought out a thousand Plan supporters to curse and harass the emergency men. When evictions resumed on 5 September 1888, Sub-Sheriff Gale took one tenant, Tim Connors, by surprise by arriving before dawn. The bailiffs dumped his furnishings on the manure heap and then moved on to the farm of Cornelius O'Connor (or Connor), who had paid no rent for three years. Despite the pitchfork in his hand the police collared him and the bailiffs drove out his wife and ten daughters. The evictors then marched to Knockardfree where John Field had reclaimed much land. Preparing for their unwelcome visit, he had filled the downstairs with white thorn bushes. A poster portrait of William O'Brien hung from a window. Upstairs the two sons and their mother hurled hot liquid and stones while the father paced anxiously in the yard. When the emergency men threw the stones back, the crowd howled in derision. Scalded by hot liquid, they attacked a gable wall with crowbars. After a brief fight, the police arrested and handcuffed the sons and made them march over ten miles to Buttevant before entraining for Cork prison. Several hours later the sheriff's party had to return because the youngest son, William, had hidden inside and his presence nullified the eviction. Two priests persuaded the lad to leave and he walked out cheering loudly for the Plan. A coercion court sentenced James and John Field to two and six weeks in prison respectively.[58]

A third round of evictions began on 5 July 1889 when sheriff Gale and his bailiffs expelled four substantial tenants who had refused to settle. Michael O'Brien and his family were asleep when the evictors arrived early in the morning and forced them out half clothed. John Field endured a second ejectment, but this time his sons were not there to resist. Struggles on this estate dragged on owing in part to Smith-Barry's promise to plant northern Protestants on evicted farms. Finally, after almost five years of turmoil, Leader settled with his tenants in the spring of 1891 by accepting two years' rent, reinstatement, and the sale of farms at 14 years' purchase of the rent.[59]

HILL/GWEEDORE

Fierce clashes over eviction also took place in west Donegal where impoverished cottiers subsisted on mollusks, sprats, and corn meal after the potato crop had failed. Outside one hovel a mound of empty shells attested to a diet of limpets or mussels supplemented by meal. Their meagre cash came from the earnings of children in domestic service. Captain Arthur George Sandys Blundell Hill inherited his Gweedore estate from his father, Lord George Hill, the noted philanthropist and souper who had spent thousands of pounds on improvements since 1838.[60]

Failure to pay rent led to the eviction of dozens of cottiers in mid-August 1886. Although these tenants offered no resistance, the sheriff recruited some 700 police and soldiers to protect his bailiffs. Half of the evicted tenants were readmitted as caretakers. Inside Mary Gallagher's abode a bailiff brushed a few tea leaves off a dresser. When she told him to pick them up, he refused and she punched him. All her belongings were thrown outside and the door nailed shut. Charles Gallagher's wife and six children sent up 'a heartrending, piteous, shrieking cry' as the bailiffs dropped a stone on their turf fire. Some eighty families were driven out in one week and the agent collected only £4 out of £290 owed. 'Is the game worth the candle?' asked one reporter who followed the sheriff from house to house.[61]

At Father James McFadden's bidding the tenants adopted the Plan in December. Disputes over the £3,400 in unpaid rent and arrears culminated in the ejectment of 130 more tenants in the autumn of 1887. This time some tenants had prepared a hot reception and the eviction party had to contend with barricaded dwellings and trees felled across the road. The Castle sent reinforcements and Gweedore soon 'bristled' with the spiked helmets and bayonets of the 250 police and soldiers on guard duty.

On 4 October 1887, the agent, Colonel Dopping, rode up to the cottage of Manus Roarty armed with a Winchester rifle and demanded possession while the police cordon kept the crowd well away. The bailiffs broke through a barrier of tree trunks, withstood a shower of hot liquid, and drove out Roarty and his wife who subsequently re-entered. At Ardnagappery, the defenders of bed-ridden Mary Bonar's abode resorted to hot liquid and stones. Dopping pointed his rifle at a boy who had thrown a stone but did not shoot. Father McFadden attended each eviction hoping to prevent violence and defending the tenants' right to resist. When he tried to stop the crowbar brigade from damaging one house, some bystanders rushed to his side but were beaten back by batons. After the magistrate read the riot act, a half-naked 'idiot boy' suddenly leapt through a hole in the wall throwing stones, screaming in Irish 'in a paroxysm of frenzy and terror', and jumping up and down. The police hustled him away. The collapse of a gable wall and the roof did not deter the defenders but they were soon overwhelmed and dragged outside bruised and bloodied. The frail Mary Bonar pummelled a policeman on her way out. Much the same scenario occurred two days later at Margaret Boyle's bog-cabin where the crowbar men were scalded and stoned and a police officer ordered his men to load and aim their rifles. One distraught constable defied this order, threw down his rifle, and announced that he would not fire on his own people. For this act of insubordination he was promptly arrested. [62]

A print in the *Penny Illustrated Paper* (8 October 1887), 'Eviction by Force in Ireland', features two men trying to repel the police and bailiffs while a woman in the doorway strikes a constable's helmet with a poker. Strong resistance prevented the evictors from emptying more than four houses in the course of three days. Realising the cost to his own pocket and reputation, Hill acceded to the Plan's demands by lowering rents by 30 per cent, reinstating 130 evicted tenants, paying legal fees, and remitting half the arrears. This surrender did not endear the owner to Dublin Castle or those combative landlords who yearned to defeat the Plan. But Father McFadden rejoiced over this resounding victory. [63]

Similar sieges, skirmishes, and confrontations took place from Donegal to Waterford. At Elton, County Limerick, Alice and Julia Barry along with four men fended off the invaders with stones and pitchforks wounding a district inspector who was leading his men through a hole in the mud wall. On Lord Bandon's estate outside Clonakilty, County Cork, a lone defender, Dan Connor, turned the uniforms of several policemen white with a 'shower of lime and dirty liquid'. After throwing missiles at the invaders, he retreated upstairs where he was beaten into submission.

On the Ponsonby estate at Youghal a wily brick-maker cum farmer, John Fleming, heated some pokers and tongs and left them near the fireplace of his factory. When the invaders picked up these tools to extinguish the fire, they howled in pain. Fleming also greeted the police with a blast of high-pressure steam when they entered his pottery.[64] At the end of October 1887, David Foley and his son Laurence fought off a dozen crowbar men on Colonel Tottenham's property at Ballykerogue, County Wexford. Drenched with hot liquid thrown from the loft, two furious emergency men took aim with their revolvers while their boss shouted: 'Shoot him, shoot him.' But the resident magistrate rushed forward and ordered them to put their weapons away. Under fire from stones and scalding water, the crowbar gang took two hours to bore a small hole in the rear wall. When ordered to surrender, Foley replied: 'No Sir; we refuse to stir or budge an inch while life remains in our bodies to defend our homes. We will continue to defend this house against the robbers outside; and if necessary we will die here. Let the scoundrels come on now.' The siege continued after sunset despite the illegality of executing a *habere* decree this late in the day. After the evictors withdrew, the defenders sang the old Fenian tune 'God Save Ireland' and bonfires lit up the night sky. Before dawn, however, the garrison surrendered owing to lack of water and ammunition. A month later they were tried and sentenced to prison terms ranging from three to six months with hard labour. They were hailed as heroes on their way back from the courthouse to prison.[65]

A single eviction on the Marquess of Waterford's estate in November 1887 caused quite a stir. William Shanahan of Scrahan near Kilmacthomas had fortified his house and recruited twenty defenders. Led by a much hated head bailiff, John Kirwan, eight emergency men walked alongside a battering ram protected by 120 constables under the command of Captain Slacke and County Inspector Whelan. While the unruly crowd booed and jeered, the bailiffs broke through the door without using the ram and entered along with two priests. They drove out the garrison and smashed the furniture by throwing it out of a hole hacked in the roof. Next door stood a barricaded barn around which the crowd swarmed. There the police unleashed a baton charge inflicting many cuts and bruises. The garrison inside scalded the besiegers with hot liquid and shoved torches in their faces. When Kirwan shouted 'burn them out', his men obliged by igniting the furze blocking the windows and the defenders had to leave. Among those treated by doctors was Shanahan whose weak heart barely withstood all this stress.[66]

FIGHTING PRIESTS

Fathers James McFadden and Daniel Stephens of Gweedore were not the only priests who played pivotal roles in Plan operations. High on the list of clerical activists were the Reverends Patrick Coen, Thomas Doyle, John Fahy, David Humphreys, Matthew Ryan, John Maher, M. B. Kennedy, and Daniel Keller to name a few. Supported by their curates, many parish priests defied the coercion act and paid the price of protracted trials and harsh imprisonment for promoting the Plan and chairing banned meetings. At Arthurstown in County Wexford, for example, in July 1889 the state prosecuted the Very Rev. Canon Thomas Doyle, parish priest of Ramsgrange, along with his curate and 22 parishioners for having promoted the Plan on Colonel Tottenham's estate. For more than a week this town resembled an armed camp as the authorities brought in 450 police and soldiers to protect the courthouse against any rioting.

One fearless priest, Father Robert Little of Killaloe and Birr, earned renown by helping a parishioner, John Frost, to stave off the evictors near Sixmilebridge, County Clare. Burdened with a family of twelve, Frost had paid no rent for four years. When the sheriff's party arrived on 11 January 1887, they found Father Little chained to an iron gate outside the cabin door. The chains led inside where they were held by Frost's supporters. Breathing defiance, Father Little told the bailiffs that they would have to trample on his body to gain entry. When the crowd surged forward to protect their spiritual leader, the police beat them back and then took Frost's cottage by storm. To avert a riot the sheriff persuaded the landlord to allow the tenants to buy their farms for 18 years' purchase of the rent. However, this agreement collapsed after Frost was arrested and imprisoned for re-entering his house. The *ILN* recognised Father Little's bravery in 'The Rent War in Ireland: Priest Chained to Gate to Prevent Entrance of Evicting Party' where he is pictured bound in chains and defying the sheriff and the police (Figure 7.8).[67]

7.8   W. H. Overend, 'The Rent War in Ireland: Priest Chained to Gate to Prevent Entry of Evicting Party'. Bound in chains to a gate in front of the Frost cabin, Father Robert Little defies the police and agent to remove him. This bold priest has warned the sheriff's party that they will have to trample on him if they intend to complete their task. (*ILN*, 19 Feb. 1887)

Near Bandon in County Cork a resourceful tenant and his friends removed part of his ceiling, hoisted a cart and donkey up into the loft, nailed the wheels to the joists, and replaced the flooring leaving some fodder for the beast. The crowd roared with delight as the bailiffs toiled all day to extract the donkey and cart.[68]

Another harmless form of resistance involved reaping crops before they could be distrained. For example, in August 1888 Count Arthur Moore expelled Malachy O'Neill of Kilross, County Tipperary because he wanted to merge the latter's large holding with his home farm. On eviction eve O'Neill's friends showed up with ten mowing machines and began to cut the grass. The estate steward alerted the police who chased the mowers over hill and dale. Three priests converged and calmed the crowd. On the morrow eight emergency men returned with a mower protected by forty constables. But spikes driven into the ground ruined the blades of the machine leaving some thirty acres uncut.[69]

All this resistance took a heavy toll on tenants and their adversaries. The elderly and infirm as well as young children were often exposed to the violence of siege warfare as well as the elements after their removal. Rumours persisted of mothers driven insane by this rupture in their lives and ending up in the local lunatic asylum. With no little pride some defenders bore the scars of batons and bayonets. Balfour, of course, dismissed resistance to eviction as part and parcel of the Parnellite plan to destabilise government and attain Home Rule. The thought that tenants might be defending their homes for personal rather than political reasons never seems to have crossed his mind.

On a lighter note, a bizarre charge arose out of one eviction near Woodford where a woman accused a constable of cannibalism. According to *United Ireland*, Mrs Page of Tierascragh was wrestling with a 'peeler' when he bit her arm. Balfour asked his private secretary to look into the matter and he concluded that Mrs Page had indeed shoved a constable into the cesspool outside her cottage. The notorious bias of *United Ireland*, he contended, was reason enough to dismiss her 'extraordinary' charge; and he deplored all the 'filth, offensive matter, and …lime' thrown at policemen trying to do their duty.[70] No doubt Lord Courtown would have agreed. In his annual report to the PDA he accused the Plan leaders of forcing emergency men to act like 'fighting men. …[They] had to storm fortified positions; they had been bruised, scalded, and injured in many ways; but they have all been uniformly victorious (hear, hear.).' And he praised Captain Hamilton's 'heroic' efforts to defend property rights.[71]

PORTRAYING RESISTANCE

Most eviction paintings depicted either the exteriors of dwellings under siege or the exodus of the occupants. Along with reporters, priests, and relatives of the tenants the police did not allow artists near houses under siege. A rare exception to the rule of exterior perspectives was the painting executed by the Cork artist, Henry (or Harry) Jones Thaddeus in 1889. Born Henry Thaddeus Jones, he changed his surname because the common Welsh name of Jones did not appeal to someone keen to cultivate rich and famous patrons in London and Florence. By 1886, this precocious artist had earned high praise from connoisseurs and art patrons for his stunning portrait of Pope Leo XIII painted from life in the Vatican. Commissions from Gladstone, Pius X, and other notables of church and state followed in short order.[72]

Venturing well beyond impressive likenesses of the social and political elite, Thaddeus produced two striking pictures of veiled and direct violence. In *The Wounded Poacher* (1881), the victim of a gamekeeper's gun returns to his cabin where his adoring wife tries to deal with a serious chest injury. His far more dramatic, arresting, and overtly political picture, *An Irish Eviction, County Galway, Ireland* (1889) reveals the fierce combat inside a cottage being stormed by the police (Plate 20). This rare painting of a cottage interior under siege may not merit the accolade of a 'great masterpiece', but it certainly deserves to be counted as one of the finest images of resistance ever painted. And it merits comparison with Rembrandt's masterly play with light and shadow.[73]

Exhibited at the height of the Plan agitation, this picture evokes the heat and fury of the second land war as the muscular protagonist, illuminated by a shaft of light, prepares to hurl a bucket of boiling water at the police. Standing beside him his red-haired wife stoops to pick up a pitchfork while her terrified young daughter clings to her skirt. In the rear two men – one well endowed with the prognathous mouth and snub nose of a stereotypical Paddy – keep the constables at bay with a ladder. Here Thaddeus's brush has captured both the violence of eviction and the fierce resolve of tenants to defend their homes.

As Joseph O'Brien has rightly noted, 'gruel and hot lime do not a revolution make'.[74] Sooner or later the eviction parties captured almost all these fortified abodes and their defenders usually spent months in jail. Nevertheless resistance paid some handsome dividends for the nationalist cause. The publicity accorded these sieges drew some notable visitors from Britain and encouraged League or Plan activists to carry on the fight against landlordism and the Union. The Parnellite propagandists, in sum, deserve credit for portraying resistance as a contest between stone-throwing peasant Davids and the well-armed Goliaths of Dublin Castle.

In one of his many anti-landlord harangues Dillon told an audience in Leicester that 17,000 people had been evicted in County Kerry alone between January 1871 and December 1886.[75] Such exaggerated figures should not blind us to the amount of organisation and determination behind this resistance. Fortifying cottages, stockpiling missiles, recruiting garrisons, and summoning huge crowds required a tremendous amount of effort as well as community solidarity. One remarkable feature of this siege warfare was the absence of any immediate fatalities despite all the violence. Admittedly, Dan Curtin came perilously close to dying on Arthur Langford's estate near Kanturk at the end of May 1889 after an emergency man struck him on the head with a hatchet in response to a blow from a hurley stick. And Kinsella died at the hands of a trigger-happy emergency man in September 1887.[76] From the government's point of view, resistance to eviction cost tens of thousands of pounds for the transport, food, shelter, and supplies of the police and military escorts between 1886 and 1890. In the absence of any precise 'spreadsheet' for these expenditures, Davitt's figure of £960,000 for the years 1887–94 exclusive of landlords' expenses must remain in the category of a partisan guesstimate.[77]

Few reports of resistance emanated from Ulster, where landlord and tenant relations had become less contentious after the end of the first land war and where relatively few Protestant tenants had joined the Plan. Unfortunately, little is known about the attitudes of the police and military assigned to protect the eviction parties. Apart from the two or three constables who dared to 'down their rifles' in public, we have few clues about how they regarded baton charges, the siege of fortified dwellings, and the arrest of resisters. Years later Colonel Turner, hardly an impartial source, admitted that the men under his command found the expulsion of impoverished families more than distasteful: 'We all loathed the work, and most of us deeply sympathised with the poor ejected ones.' In retrospect he could write that the Plan evictions 'ought never to have taken place; no one gained, but every one concerned lost, by them'. And Sir Redvers Buller deplored the Castle's historic enforcement of unjust rents: 'For 120 years British bayonets have backed up landlords in extracting excessive rents, and have supported them in grossly neglecting their tenants.'[78]

Last but not least, resistance gave women and girls a chance to prove that they could fight just as courageously – if not more so – as their menfolk. When not throwing stones, they 'stir/red the boiling pot' – literally and figuratively. And they earned high praise from Davitt for hurling more than hearty curses at the evictors. Their efforts to defend hearth and home received lavish attention in nationalist papers and raised tenant morale all over the country. Imprisonment, moreover, added more lustre to their martyrdom in the cause of tenant right. In the long run this kind of defiance sowed some of the seeds of rebellion that would eventually bear lethal fruit in the next century.

EIGHT

THE BATTERING RAM
1887–90

*'It will never again come to that state of things when
the Irish tenantry will be content to be ragged, trembling,
famished creatures who were crushed underneath
the lash of the Vandeleurs and Turners (loud cheers.)'*

WILLIAM O'BRIEN
speaking at Tullycreen, County Clare, 19 September 1888.

*'The battering-ram may be good for hunting children
from their homes, but it fills no pockets and pays none of the
evictor's debts – debts that will go on accumulating till the
crack of doom, if he does not consent to do justice (cheers).'*

CANON DANIEL KELLER OF YOUGHAL
speaking at a Plan of Campaign rally near Youghal, County Cork
on 4 March 1888 (*Cork Examiner*, 5 March 1888).

———

During the second land war Dublin Castle adopted a new and mighty weapon
to overcome resistance, namely, that ancient tool of siege warfare, the battering
ram.[1] Frustrated by the fusillades of stones and hot liquid that drove the bailiffs
and police back time and again, some sub-sheriffs procured and deployed rams
to break into heavily fortified houses. Not only did they want to shorten sieges
but they also hoped to avoid the carnage of rifle fire. Despite its destructive power
and propaganda value, hardly any historian has recognised the significance of
this formidable instrument of law enforcement.

What some called a 'military engine', the ram boasts a history older than the
Old Testament. For centuries before the invention of gunpowder and cannon it
broke down gates and poked big holes through the walls of towns and castles.
With or without a giant ram's head affixed to the front end this weapon enjoyed a
long run in the early annals of siege warfare. Among numerous cultural critics
Terry Eagleton has construed the land of Ireland as 'a sexual subject, as the torn
victim of imperial penetration'. And an obvious symbol of that political rape was

the (phallic) ram forcing its way into the (feminine) domicile. Along the same lines Seamus Heaney invoked a sexual trope in his poem, 'Act of Union', wherein an English naval ship serves as the ram that breaks the boom across Lough Foyle ending the epic siege of Derry and beginning the Protestant re-conquest of Ireland. Here the act of ramming serves as a metaphor for rape and colonisation:

And I am still imperially
Male, leaving you with the pain,
The rending process in the colony,
The battering ram, the boom burst from within.
The act sprouted an obstinate fifth column
Whose stance is growing unilateral.[2]

Following the passage of his stringent coercion act, Balfour proposed that battering rams be used to break through the barricades of defiant tenants on Plan estates in order to prevent long sieges. Evidently, Under-secretary Ridgeway persuaded the commander of the RIC to adopt this weapon in November 1887. In vain Parnellite MPs and local Campaigners denounced what they regarded as a brutal and unfair weapon that was designed to uphold landlordism rather than justice. Suspended on a chain from a long-legged tripod (or bipod) made of logs, the ram proved an awesome addition to the basic tools of the crowbar brigade.

At least one ram, made in Derry for evictions on a Donegal estate, had iron poles bolted together to support a heavy fourteen-foot beam that was 'shod with an iron shoe' at the business end. To move this instrument into position the builder constructed a two-wheeled 'trolley'. Protruding from an iron band in the middle was a ring to which the chain running from the apex of the triangle was attached. Even when kept in reserve, the ram made some tenants think twice before resisting. In their attack on Hurley's mill near Clonakilty in October 1886 the bailiffs had thrust a tree trunk against a window. But this simple device required heavy lifting and hauling for want of a tripod and, as the *ILN*'s print, The Battering-Ram at the Barricaded Window' (Figure 8.1), reveals, this log was much too slender to dent a reinforced window or door.[3] Bombarded by bricks and sticks, the rammers failed to breach Hurley's defences and they had to return the next day to complete their task.

Because Plan tenants improved their defensive tactics with bigger logs and pumps and syringes to squirt hot liquid, sheriffs realised the need for a more efficient ram with an iron-sheathed head and a tall tripod. They also taught Protestant emergency men how to set up and heave the ram with ropes. Part and parcel of what Michel Foucault has called the politics and physics of power, the ram was not just a 'punitive mechanism', a disciplinary agent of the state, and an example of the technology of power. It was also a public spectacle designed to intimidate tenants and discourage resistance. Protected by droves of constables and soldiers, the ram exuded an aura of invincibility that riveted the attention of bystanders including reporters and artists.[4]

8.1 'The Battering Ram at the Barricaded Window'(Hurley's Mill). Here the bailiffs are using a tree trunk to break inside Tim Hurley's mill near Clonakilty, County Cork, in October 1886. This primitive ram proved too slender to make an impression on any blocked window or wall. (*ILN*, 27 Nov. 1886)

Between 1887 and 1890 battering rams made dramatic appearances on estates belonging to Major Bunbury (Bansha, Tipperary), James Byrne (Coolroe, Wexford), Lord Clanricarde (Woodford, Galway), Michael Cormack (Modeshill, Tipperary), Lieutenant Colonel John O'Callaghan (Bodyke, Clare), Wybrants Olphert (Falcarragh, Donegal), Charles W. Talbot Ponsonby (Youghal, Cork), Valentine Ryan (Cappawhite, Tipperary), Colonel Charles J. Tottenham (New Ross, Wexford), and Captain Hector Vandeleur (Kilrush, Clare). Although held in reserve, rams also showed up on the estates of Lord Waterford (November 1887), William Leader (September 1888), Wybrants Olphert (January 1889), the Endowed Schools Commissioners (March 1889), George Brooke (April 1889), Lord Massereene (May 1889), and Lord Lansdowne (May 1889).[5] On occasion the same ram would be used at different but nearby sites. Balfour, of course, justified the ram as a device designed to spare lives, but Parnellites denounced it as a cruel and terrifying addition to the Castle's arsenal, and they made much political capital out of this awesome 'engine' of destruction.

TOTTENHAM/BALLYKEROGUE

According to the radical English politician, George Shaw-Lefevre, the new model tripod ram made its first appearance in July 1888 when sub-sheriff Croker deployed one on the Vandeleur estate at Kilrush. Later, Colonel Turner contended that Croker and not the RIC had obtained this contrivance. But who actually paid for this ram – Dublin Castle or the PDA – remains a mystery.[6] Shaw-Lefevre was mistaken, however. In fact, the ram made its debut on 29 November 1887 at Ballykerogue, eight miles from New Ross, County Wexford where the tenants had adopted the Plan after Lieutenant Colonel Charles G. Tottenham's rejection of their demand for an abatement. Two of the local Plan leaders, David and Laurence Foley, who had fought the sheriff's party a month previously, had painstakingly fortified their cottage with iron gates and logs. Again they recruited a garrison of over twenty farmers' sons. Anticipating a tough fight, sub-sheriff Connor arranged for a ram – 'a long and heavy pole capped with iron' – as well as a steam-powered fire engine with which to douse the defenders. For good measure he procured an escort of two hundred police and soldiers.

When called on to surrender, the garrison sang 'God Save Ireland' and cheered for the Plan. They then repelled the emergency men with stones and scalding liquid discharged through a 'garden syringe' that soaked the besiegers even though they were carrying wicker and canvas shields. At first the ram made little headway and the streams of cold water from the fire engine had no effect. Exhorted by their boss, two emergency men pulled out revolvers and threatened to shoot a defender who was about to throw a bucket of hot stuff. However, the resident magistrate ordered the emergency men to put their weapons away and blamed Tottenham for all this trouble. Eventually, the rammers breached the rear wall and some rafters collapsed. The fighting continued into the night as Foley insisted that his men would fight to the death despite priestly pleas to surrender. The police broke the rules of engagement at evictions by launching an attack after sunset when half the house was in ruins. Charging inside they overpowered the garrison and escorted them to New Ross jail.

The version of the divisional police magistrate in charge of the southeast division, Captain Slacke, differed in almost every respect. In his telegram to the Inspector General of the RIC Slacke proudly announced that the rammers

8.2 J. F. O'Hea, 'The Tory Idea of "Conciliation"'. O'Hea mocks the siege of the Foleys' cottage at Ballykerogue, County Wexford. Thuggish rammers are trying to break through the shattered door while two terrified occupiers huddle inside. A fireman pours a stream of water through the roof to drive out the defenders; and a buffoonish officer holding a broom directs the operation. (*WF*, 10 Dec. 1887)

8.3　Claude Byrne, 'The State of Ireland – With the Emergency Men at the Eviction Campaign – Fixing the Battering Ram (On the Tottenham Estate)'. Byrne's sketch of resistance on the Tottenham estate in Wexford features a ram suspended on a bipod hard at work on a barricaded window. At the top two emergency men hold shields to ward off missiles (*Pictorial News*, 9 June 1888)

took only eight minutes to penetrate the defences and capture the garrison that had laid in provisions for a ten-day siege. With evident delight Ridgeway relayed this good news to Balfour whom he credited with having suggested the ram in the first place. All the resisters were tried and found guilty of obstruction and received prison sentences ranging from three to six months with hard labour.[7]

J. F. O'Hea's parodic cartoon, 'The Tory Idea of "Conciliation"' (Figure 8.2), reconstructed the siege of Foley's little fort. Here five brutish emergency men, two policemen, and a soldier heave and haul the ram suspended from a bipod, while two terrified occupiers pray for deliverance inside the shattered door. A fireman pours a stream of water through the broken roof. The absurdity of this operation is underlined by the buffoonish army officer armed with a besom.[8]

Claude Byrne sketched an eviction scene near Arklow for the *Pictorial News* (9 June 1888) that faintly resembled the siege of Foley's fort. The principal image in 'The State of Ireland – With the Emergency Men at the Eviction Campaign' (Figure 8.3) reveals several emergency men hauling away on chains attached to a huge ram suspended between two short posts. Presumably they made short work of the barricaded window.[9] This ram apparently returned to Ballykerogue on 22 May but was not deployed again owing to lack of resistance.[10]

CORMACK/MODESHILL

Wherever the ram appeared, hostile crowds led by priests and other local notables gathered to jeer the evictors and support the tenants, while reporters and foreign visitors took note of the confrontation. For example. the *Freeman's Journal* (10–12 May 1888) covered the expulsion of 17 tenants on the property of an absentee landowner, Michael Cormack, at Modeshill, County Tipperary, in some detail. After the appointment of a hated land agent and farmer named Hanly, the tenants refused to pay their rents and demanded abatements of 30 per cent. Negotiations broke down; cattle were seized; writs were obtained; and the tenants adopted the Plan at the end of May 1887. A year later the sub-sheriff set out from Mullinahone with 150 police and soldiers to uproot the Plan activists. Felled trees and boulders delayed their arrival. Upon seeing the ram lashed to a wagon the crowd jeered and groaned. After entering and securing Mrs Mulally's cottage through a hole cut in the roof, they moved on to Patrick Funcheon's barricaded and 'neat little cottage' next door. After the emergency men erected their weapon, they punched a hole big enough for them to crawl through and capture the defenders.

On the following day the ram gang was joined by an eager Hanly as well as the son of a local magistrate and the brother of the estate solicitor. Close to a thousand spectators heckled and cursed them as they pounded the walls of several houses one of which belonged to Edmund Cody who walked out supporting his 89-year-old father and cheering for the Plan. However, the ram failed to pierce the wall of Patrick Tobin's abode because he had built an interior cross wall that forced them to move their weapon elsewhere.

The crowd's mood grew ugly after the resident magistrate threatened to strike a 'young lady' with his stick for mocking his accent. The police then charged some unruly onlookers with their batons. The emergency men moved on to Michael Neary's fortified house where they set up the ram. When this tenant refused to open his door, one rammer exclaimed: 'Oh, let us have a shot at the house now, after our trouble in putting it up.' And the gang proceeded to demolish a wall with 'fiendish pleasure'. After three days of besieging cottages, the agent called a halt to avoid serious violence. At Father Cahill's trial on 18 May for inciting resistance seven fellow priests and curates showed up in court while the police drove back the crowd outside with their rifle butts. His acquittal for lack of evidence brought joy to all his supporters.

VANDELEUR/KILRUSH

The ram also loomed large on Captain Hector Vandeleur's estate around Kilrush, where so many ghosts from the famine clearances haunted the barren fields and deserted clachans. After some rent rises during the 1870s, the gross rental came close to £12,000. But arrears by 1888 exceeded £30,000. More evictions culminated in the tenants' demand in mid-December 1886 for a reduction of 40 per cent on non-judicial rents and the abolition of arrears. Vandeleur countered with an offer of one year's rent to be paid with a clear receipt up to March 1888. The tenants' leaders were not impressed and adopted the Plan despite the efforts of several priests and Colonel Turner to break the impasse. The agent then obtained ejectment decrees against 114 tenants some of whom owed over four years' rent.[11]

In October 1887 the eviction of some town tenants in Ennis and Kilrush set off disturbances and baton charges. But the real struggle began on 18 July 1888 when Sub-Sheriff Croker and Colonel Turner, mounted on his favourite black charger, led some 300 hussars, dragoons, and constables towards Moyasta. The emergency men strutted proudly alongside their brand new ram. Although Turner had no love for Vandeleur, he assembled this small army because he expected fierce resistance and wanted to overawe the crowd. Balfour personally found Vandeleur 'stupid, obstinate, and selfish', but he attached great importance to the outcome of this struggle.[12]

For the next fortnight the tolling bell of Kilrush chapel signalled the departure of Croker's 'feudal' army of 'exterminators'. Shops were shuttered and one reporter likened Kilrush to 'a city of the dead'. Among the spectators were

Davitt, Lady Victoria Sandhurst, and four or five Home Rule MPs. Turner kept the priests outside the cordon because he considered them to be the prime movers of the Plan as well as trustees of the rent. Later he admitted that ejecting poor tenants, especially little children, was 'a horribly trying ordeal' and 'a graphic picture of the evils of unmitigated landlordism'. Like most evictions, he wrote later, this was 'a battle of Kilkenny cats, in which all were injured and none benefited'. While he struggled between obedience to the principle of law and order and compassion for such helpless people, he also accused some tenants of feigning resistance in order to impress local Plan leaders. More than once he endured hot stirabout during an eviction.[13]

Robert French photographed one disassembled ram lashed to a two-wheeled cart (Plate 21). Protruding from the legs are iron spikes to ensure a firm grip in the soil; and on top lies a wooden trestle to support the beam while being attached to the tripod's long chain.[14]

After storming two barricaded houses around Killimer, Croker's men arrived at Michael Cleary's farm at Carrowdotia. This farmer had blocked all the apertures and then put his two sons and two daughters in charge of the fighting. The police cordon fended off the vast crowd while a bailiff up on the roof stuffed straw down the chimney in order to smoke out the occupants. This tactic failed and torrents of hot liquid forced the besiegers away. Croker ordered the rammers to set up their weapon; and their boss shouted: 'Back, away with them; away with them'. The whole house shuddered from the heavy blows. But an interior stonewall thwarted the rammers who were soon drenched with scalding stirabout. The ram gang then attacked a gable wall that crumbled to Turner's delight. In fact, he called this outcome a 'tip-topper'. Fearing bloodshed, however, he stopped the police from dashing inside with swords and bayonets at the ready. After a long parley, Cleary's children surrendered and stumbled out over the rubble to lusty cheers from the crowd. The sons were arrested and jailed, while the daughters were charged and released on recognizance. The agent then ordered the emergency men to demolish the house.[15]

This siege inspired a song, 'Cleary Abu', that celebrated Cleary's heroism:

Cleary Abú
The first house they came to
He acted 'no man'; he opened
His door to the Battering Ram.
But the next house they came to
Was Cleary Abú: he showed to
The Saxons what the Irish could do.
He barred up the doors

He defended the 'Plan'
He Defied all the Blows
Of the Battering Ram.[16]

A sketch of the ram at work on Cleary's house appeared in the *Graphic* (4 August 1888), entitled 'Under the Plan of Campaign – On the Vandeleur Estate' (Figure 8.4). Under the watchful eyes of the sheriff and agent the ram penetrates a wall. In the top right corner the Spellisseys [*sic*] pose next to their few worldly possessions; and in the top left corner Colonel Turner's little army marches back to base camp.[17] This scenario was repeated wherever crowbars and sledgehammers failed to do the job. Bruised by stones and smeared with hot liquid, the evictors would charge inside and beat the resisters before hauling them out to groans and curses from the ever-present crowd.

8.4   Anon, 'Under the Plan of Campaign – On the Vandeleur Estate'. The sub-sheriff and the agent observe a ram smashing through a wall on the Vandeleur estate. In the top right corner the Spellissey [*sic*] family poses next to their few belongings. And in the top left corner Colonel Turner's armed escort marches back to base camp. (*Graphic*, 4 Aug. 1888)

On 19 July at Derha, Croker's men tackled the fortified cabin of Patrick Spellissy (Spellacy), who had paid no rent for four years. To put a stop to the streams of stirabout the rammers burst through the back door and subdued the resisters while the crowd vilified Vandeleur. The same fate awaited James and

Patrick Spellissy who threw rocks and 'dirty water' at the bailiffs before the ram and the crowbars broke through the barricades. Having run out of ammunition, the defenders surrendered.[18]

On the next day a strong farmer, Michael Connell of Carrowdotia walked out of his fortified house on a hillside overlooking the Shannon leaving his young children in charge of the defence. Heaving their ram against a wall, the emergency men were soon soaked with hot gruel. This bombardment enraged Turner who commanded two riflemen to take aim at the house. But he soon calmed down and rescinded the order. All this time Connell sat nearby smoking his pipe. When the wall was breached, the colonel called on the children to leave. Three little girls and a boy then walked out followed by five adolescent boys. The English delegates present were shocked to see how young these defenders were. Always keen to belittle tenant resistance, the *Times* derided this 'theatrical display' as 'supremely ridiculous' and designed to impress the local Plan leaders.

Four days later the ram gang captured three defended houses around Caravana. When Inspector Hill clambered through the hole in Margaret Higgins's battered house at Leadmore, a volley of stones drove him back. The rammers enlarged the breach allowing the police to rush inside where they were hit by stone-throwers in the loft. Hand to hand combat culminated with the arrest of two young men.[19]

Near Clooneylissaun (Cloonyhissane) in the parish of Killimer, Simon Connell and his comrades squirted boiling water mixed with corn meal and lime at the foe on 26 July. Wearing his signature monocle, Croker lent a hand to the rammers. Two police inspectors then entered through the hole made by the ram, struck Connell, and arrested him for assault. On orders from the agent the rammers knocked down the front wall as an object lesson for anyone contemplating resistance. At Bryan Connell's house the bailiffs used sledgehammers to gain entry and soon subdued him along with his belligerent wife. To no avail Pat Leo's fearless daughter warned Croker that she would douse him with hot water if he did not go away. After the rammers finished their task, the police arrested her and a young brother and the house was levelled. Some of these resisters received jail terms of up to four months with hard labour.[20]

On the same day the ram showed up at Mathias McGrath's fortified house at Moyasta. Owing almost three years' rent, he too had built an inner wall of stones behind the door and blocked the windows. Putting his powerful son Pat in charge of the defences he retired with his ailing wife Bridget to a nearby cowshed to watch the siege unfold. Backed by an armed escort the bailiffs approached warily. Croker rapped on a window with his blackthorn demanding possession. Pat replied that he would yield only to 'superior force' and hurled a bucket of 'filthy stuff'. Turner sent for the ram and Pat yelled: 'Come on Croker, and do your worst.' Despite the torrents of hot liquid, the emergency men pounded away until they had opened a hole through which Pat challenged District Inspector Dunning: 'In with you now, and meet me.' He refused to allow any of his female defenders to leave and shouted: 'I'll fight for them, thank you: come on now, and do your best ... I will die here if I must, but I won't come out till I am taken.' Dashing through the opening with a wicker shield Inspector Hill tripped over one of the ram's legs and fell headlong into the kitchen. Pat pounced on him and some constables came to his rescue. Soon 'the air was filled with the screams of women, the cries of the combatants and the crash of batons'. Pat 'fought with the courage of a lion', until the police beat him senseless and dragged him out dazed and bleeding over the rubble. The sight of her beloved son being pummelled was too much for his mother, Bridget, to bear. She screamed and wailed being convinced that he was dead. While a constable sat on Pat's chest another handcuffed him. The fighting continued because three plucky girls in the loft kept on scalding the invaders and outside the police beat back the unruly crowd. With one wall crumbling from the ram's strokes, Turner called a halt to allow a photographer to take some pictures.[21] One photograph, 'Eviction Scene (Battering Ram)' (Plate 22), captures sheriff Croker posing proudly close to the ram that has opened a huge hole in the wall. He holds a wicker shield as though some defenders still lurked inside.[22]

When the cameraman called out 'Steady Please', Mrs McGrath groaned with concern for Pat who was carefully guarded by two constables. After finishing his 'shoot', the photographer – possibly Robert French – graciously thanked everyone, and the rammers resumed their work. On the march back to Kilrush Pat McGrath was greeted by an old woman on the roadside. Despite his injuries he broke his handcuffs as though they were made of tin, kicked them away, and embraced her to loud hurrahs from bystanders. This time the police cuffed his wrists behind his back and resumed their procession singing or whistling British patriotic tunes. Both McGraths were soon convicted and sentenced in a coercion court.

Reigh's cartoon of the Moyasta evictions appeared in *United Ireland* (4 August 1888) under the title, 'The Vandeleur Eviction Campaign' (Plate 23). Here six rammers have breached a wall and one defender is poised to throw a bucket of hot liquid through the hole. The peripheral images show the cabin in shambles, a policeman dragging out a wounded defender, and on the lower right Pat with a bloody bandage around his head snapping his handcuffs between two constables.[23]

Pat's mother suffered a sad fate. Convinced that the police had killed her son and in despair over her ruined house, she 'pined away' and died of pneumonia a fortnight later. The family demanded an inquest into her death because she had been in good health before the eviction. Several Home Rule MPs wanted to charge Turner with murder or manslaughter. But the coroner's jury blamed her death on overexcitement caused by the eviction and anxiety about Pat's condition. Subsequently, several Moyasta tenants sued Colonel Turner, Croker, and the agent for 'unlawfully breaking and entering' their houses, but this case was dismissed. The criminal law was less forgiving towards the resisters. After rebuking Pat for his 'unmanly' defiance of the law, the magistrate sentenced him to two months in jail with hard labour.[24]

On 30 July the rammers withstood streams of hot liquid from the five children of Thomas Considine at Tullycrine, who left his house cheering loudly for Dillon and the Plan. John Flanagan carried his furniture outside to save it from being smashed, removed the door and windows, and walked out quietly. Showered with boiling liquid, the bailiffs broke through a window stuffed with thorns and captured the defenders. Mrs Considine refused to pay 'tuppence ha'penny' to settle her account and cheered for the Plan. Her daughter looked forward to 'better times outside than inside' and hailed the Plan as 'the best plan that ever was invented, and though the Army is strong, the Plan of Campaign is stiffer'. Three years in arrears, Mary O'Dea refused to redeem for £15 and carried out her belongings before the sheriff arrived. Joanna O'Dea had a little daughter confined to bed with a spinal problem. Although described as an 'idiot', she was certified fit for removal, and the bailiffs hoisted her up and out. Her mother refused readmission for a token payment declaring that she would 'not pay ten farthings, no, nor ten buttons'.[25]

During this grim fortnight fourteen houses were emptied and several were demolished after the tenants had rejected another offer to settle. Some of them moved into wooden huts built by the National League branch on the adjoining estate of Vandeleur's brother-in-law. Despite all their hardships they did not lose faith in O'Brien who assured an audience at Tullycrine that 'the Irish tenantry will [never again] be content to be ragged, trembling, famished creatures who were crushed underneath the lash of the Vandeleurs and Turners'.[26]

Captain Vandeleur returned to Kilrush in the spring of 1889 at the urging of Shaw-Lefevre and the Vicar General of Kilrush, the Very Rev. Dr Dinan. Hard pressed for cash he offered to reinstate the evicted tenants and reduce non-judicial rents by 20 per cent. But the Plan leaders held out for 36 per cent. When word spread that he was contemplating a major clearance if his offer was rejected, an old friend and Unionist MP, Henniker Heaton, talked him into arbitration by the noted Liberal lawyer, Sir Charles Russell, MP. Backed by the Archbishop of Dublin, Russell proposed a 20 per cent abatement upon payment of one year's rent along with reinstatement. To the Castle's dismay

Vandeleur accepted these terms. At the same time he had the nerve to request compensation for the ram's destruction of several farmhouses; and he also grumbled about the damage done to Kilrush House by the emergency men who had been quartered there. Despite some last-minute hitches Russell's settlement prevailed and most tenants were back in their homes and paying the lower rent by 1891.[27] However, peace on this estate proved more than elusive.

The nationalist propaganda mill made Vandeleur look like a small-time Clanricarde, and Shaw-Lefevre accused the government of failing to promote arbitration and 'terrorising' people with the ram. Animosity towards Vandeleur flared up again in May 1891 when he ousted a number of town and rural tenants around Kilrush who had paid no rent for at least five years. Although loyalty to the Plan faded away, some dissatisfied tenants demanded more compensation money than the valuator had recommended, and further litigation imperilled the settlement.[28]

CLANRICARDE/WOODFORD REVISITED

During the renewed eviction campaign at Woodford in the autumn of 1888 the sub-sheriff of Galway brought a new battering ram into play. The target was the two-storey, slate-roofed house at Looscaun belonging to Francis Tully a prominent Plan leader, who had earned the nickname of 'Dr Tully' for prescribing 'leaden pills' as the best cure for landlords. Tully had paid no rent for his 17-acre farm since 1884 and had gone to great pains to fortify his sturdy premises including a wide trench around the house that created a rampart of earth. The windows and doors were blocked with logs and bushes; the walls had been loopholed; and two green flags fluttered from the roof.[29]

On 1 September, the massive eviction party arrived with scaling ladders, a battering ram, and a portable shed with a metal roof to ward off missiles. Among the observers kept beyond the police cordon were Viscount Avonmore, Fathers Coen and Egan, Matthew Harris the outspoken MP for Galway East, and several Americans. The emergency men had been practising on their new-fangled weapon and could not wait to try it out. However, the steep slope rendered the ram useless. Some crowbar men attacked a wall under cover of the shed while the police swarmed up the ladders only to be repelled by long forked poles that pushed them down to cries of delight from the crowd. The roof became the main combat zone as the defenders repelled the besiegers with all their might. Several constables entered the loft and used their bayonets and swords against the garrison's blackthorns and pikes. During the final assault both Tully and his sister were injured; and a policeman burned his hands after grasping a pike at the heated end. After surrendering, the defenders descended the ladders bloodied but unbowed. Because Tully could barely stand he was carried down in handcuffs while his green flags were removed. Determined to send a clear message, Tener ordered his bailiffs to destroy the abodes of resisters including Tully's fine house.[30]

Lawrence's photograph of the ruined fort, 'Dr Tully's House after Eviction, Woodford' shows emergency men posing on or near the roof while the police, some soldiers, and a doctor with his black bag and bowler hat look on (Plate 24).[31] 'Still' pictures of the ram obviously lack the dynamic impact of a moving film but they reveal clearly enough both its dimensions and destructive force. Although the ram gang and other officials are carefully posed, these images do reveal something about the barricading and the ramming operation. One picture entitled 'Battering Ram' (Plate 25) underscores its destructive power as bailiffs and police stroll near the gaping hole in the wall. Here the sheriff or agent consults with an officer while the emergency men gloat over their conquest. Lastly, in 'Eviction Kilrush' (Plate 26) a woman, flanked by nine children, stands defiantly with arms akimbo in front of her battered cottage.[32]

Much impressed by the ram's early successes, Balfour composed a memorandum for his uncle in January 1889 urging the RIC to procure 'a suitable battering ram with a testudo arrangement' to deflect missiles and liquid. The ram, he contended, would shorten sieges and eliminate the need to fire on obstinate garrisons. Lord Salisbury approved the scheme but advised him to rely more heavily on the element of surprise. He also posed one pressing question: who would foot the bill? Would the cost fall on British taxpayers or would landlords hire the ram at so much an hour? [33] Needless to say, nationalist MPs raised the same question in the House of Commons. But the Irish administration kept the source of funding a secret. Anxious to avoid more vituperation about the Castle's role in evictions, Balfour had originally hoped that the landlords would pay for this 'interesting machine'. Failing this option, he agreed with Undersecretary Ridgeway that the PDA should provide more rams since it had already paid for one. Acting on his own initiative, however, David Cameron, Divisional Commissioner in the northwest, bought a ram from a Derry firm to speed up evictions around Gweedore and charged it to the secret service fund. This move nettled Balfour who had to parry pointed questions in Parliament from hostile Home Rule MPs about a weapon they so heartily despised. During a debate on conditions around Gweedore in April 1889, Balfour deflected Swift McNeill's protest over the use of a weapon that 'terrorised' the people. The sole purpose of the ram, Balfour insisted, was to protect the lives and limbs of the police in the course of performing their duty. By expediting the capture of barricaded houses, the ram would minimise their exposure to danger. To distance the government from any formal involvement the cost of rams did not appear in the annual

RIC budget. At the same time Balfour ordered the police take a more proactive stance at sieges. Instead of standing around with their rifles at their sides while the bailiffs were being assaulted, the police should threaten to open fire if garrisons refused to surrender. What really annoyed him were 'misrepresentations' in nationalist newspapers that accused the government of colluding with the landlords to deploy rams at evictions. Lack of evidence does not, of course, preclude the possibility that the PDA co-operated closely with Dublin Castle in procuring rams.[34]

BYRNE/COOLROE

In the summer of 1888 the ram suffered another humiliating defeat at Coolroe some ten miles from New Ross in County Wexford. The Castle's investment in this weapon meant that any defeat was bound to cause embarrassment while delighting the nationalist camp. The man responsible for this stunning turn of events was a strong farmer and local Plan leader, Thomas Somers, whose landlord was an eighty-year-old bachelor and devout Catholic named James E. Byrne. Known locally as 'The Hermit of Burkestown' and 'Jemmy the Wig', Byrne lived with his unmarried brother at Rosemount. During the famine Byrne's forebear had evicted at least thirty tenants. The *People* described him as a miserly old misogynist who allowed only one female – a charwoman – inside his decrepit house. He would fine tenants for the slightest breach of their contracts and walk several miles to Ballycullane to buy a penny bun. His small estate adjoined that of the wealthy and popular Colcloughs of Tintern Abbey. Scorning judicial rents, Byrne had offered some tenants a 25 per cent abatement if they paid promptly. But arrears piled up after they insisted on paying no more than Griffiths valuation. After they adopted the Plan, Byrne obtained decrees against the better-off tenants and spurned appeals from the authorities to compromise.[35]

Preparing for a long siege, Somers, his brother, brother-in-law, and nine local men dug a five-foot deep trench around the sturdy, slate-roofed house. The resulting rampart of sod and clay covered the ground-floor windows. They barricaded the upper-floor windows with iron bars, gates, and chains, and filled a deep pit inside with water. They also stockpiled tar and rotten eggs. On 16 August 1888, Sub-Sheriff Connor and resident magistrate Heffernan Considine headed for Coolroe with a ram and scaling ladders lashed to a wagon escorted by 200 police.

Arriving at the farm, they encountered over a thousand jeering spectators led by the Redmond brothers and six priests. Somers and his comrades scoffed at the order to surrender and started throwing stones and squirting boiling liquid spiked with paraffin, tar, and sheep-dip through large syringes. After repeated charges the emergency men had nothing to show for their exertions except scalded faces and blackened clothing. A rotten egg just missed Byrne. Standing in a hole in the roof Somers used his long iron-tipped pole to send constable Finegan tumbling down the muddy slope. The ram gang tried to set up their 'great engine' on the steep slope. Once again an earthen rampart foiled this instrument. The foreman lost his temper and damned his men for abandoning it. When several defenders on the roof toppled the ram with a grappling hook, the crowd roared with delight

One defender accused Byrne of being a second Clanricarde and a hypocrite who would have to answer to God for all his 'devilish work'. After several hours of futile assaults, the demoralised emergency men retreated. The sheriff then ordered the police to fix their bayonets and draw their swords before charging up the embankment. Four times they stormed the fort and four times they were driven back by stones and scalding liquid to shouts of 'No surrender!' Some constables fell down the slope as their ladders were shoved away by the long poles. Struck by a stone, the head rammer, James Woods, pulled out his revolver and threatened to shoot, but a police inspector told him to put it away. Several policemen threw the stones back. The conflict continued until six o'clock and the police suffered most of the injuries. When a visitor from Kansas tried to force his way through the cordon only to be shoved back, he shouted: 'No wonder the Irish are rebels when such work is allowed.'

Thoroughly frustrated by the garrison's tenacity, Considine threatened to use some 'cold stuff' – meaning a volley of rifle fire – even though one gable end was ablaze. Alarmed by the prospect of gunfire, the Redmond brothers conferred with Canon Doyle who persuaded the garrison to yield 'with all the honours of war'. The weary defenders walked out with heads held high to loud cheers from the crowd. Placed in handcuffs they were taken off to Wexford jail. At the end of this strenuous day Byrne offered the emergency men nothing more than potatoes and buttermilk for supper; but they declined this paltry fare and made straight for New Ross where they quenched their thirst with 'good Rhine wine'. [36]

A vivid image of the ram's defeat appeared in the *Penny Illustrated Paper* (25 August 1888). In 'Landlord v. Tenant in Ireland: Deplorable Eviction Scene at Burkestown, Near New Ross' (Figure 8.5), the intrepid defenders are driving the police off the roof with stones, pikes, and boiling liquid, while the ram lies defeated on the ground beneath the toppling tripod. On the far right the landlord and several officials look on glumly as the tight police cordon in the distance prevents the crowd from approaching. [37] Claude Byrne's sketch of this epic siege appeared in the *Pictorial News* (25 August 1888). In 'Desperate Eviction Struggle in Wexford' (Figure 8.6), several constables mount a ladder only to be squirted with hot liquid through small holes in the thatch. One policeman is

8.5 'Landlord *v.* Tenant in Ireland: Deplorable Eviction Scene at Burkestown, Near New Ross'. In this sensational print, the defenders of Somers fort, Coolroe, drive the police off the roof with stones, long poles, and hot water. The ram lies useless on the ground as a defender topples the tripod with a grappling hook. On the far right the landlord and several officials look on glumly while the police cordon keeps the crowd at a distance. (*Penny Illustrated Paper*, 25 Aug. 1888).

8.6 Claude Byrne, 'Desperate Eviction Struggle in Wexford'. Claude Byrne's sketch of the battle at Somers fort shows the repulse of the police by means of crowbars and hot stirabout squirted through syringes. In the lower left corner sub-sheriff Connor takes refuge behind a wicker shield. There is no sign of the ram in this print. (*Pictorial News*, 25 Aug. 1888)

being thrown off the roof. On the far right the boss of the emergency men draws his revolver. And in the lower left corner sub-sheriff Connor wearing an Ulster coat takes shelter behind a large wicker shield.[38] Lastly, French photographed the scene after the eviction when several constables pretended to charge their adversaries inside the empty house.In a photograph entitled 'Somer's [*sic*] Fort, Coolroe', the extent of the damage attests to the ferocity of this siege (Plate 27).[39]

Despite the garrison's surrender the nationalist camp treated the conflict like a great victory. As the *Freeman's Journal* observed, the evictors 'retired from the spot, baffled and beaten, and in some cases badly wounded…. Fortune favoured the brave', and Somers's men 'had displayed the most marvellous and heroic courage' by defeating 'that eviction machine of modern growth.' At a rally in Ballycullane John Barry MP said that he could not believe that Byrne 'this wretched old man, out of sheer malice and vindictiveness, would try to exact his pound of flesh from the rack- rented tenantry (cheers)'. Alluding to the famous siege during the Russo-Turkish war, the *People* called Somers's resistance 'The 'Plevna' of Wexford'. On 17 August, Byrne attended six more evictions with police protection. Tenants cursed him vigorously and cheered for the Plan. At one house a young girl rushed up and smeared him 'from head to foot' with a rotten goose egg. The enraged 'Hermit' demanded her arrest, but the police refused to oblige lest they provoke a riot.[40]

On 6 September, the Somers garrison arrived at Arthurstown for their trial. No less than six thousand supporters hailed their heroes as they passed by arches of evergreens and green banners emblazoned with 'God Save Ireland'. Brass bands played with gusto. The police cordoned off the town centre and used their batons and rifle butts freely to keep the people back. When the New Ross brass band began to serenade the prisoners outside the police barracks, they were bludgeoned by the constabulary one of whom drove his bayonet through the big drum. The bandsmen tried to defend themselves with their instruments but this unequal contest ended with bent brass, bruises, and arrests. Only the intervention of Canon Doyle and several Parnellite MPs averted a riot. A week later Somers and seven comrades were convicted of obstruction and assault and jailed for four to six months with hard labour. The *People* called these sentences 'savage and vindictive'. Soon the Redmond brothers were arrested for having encouraged the Coolroe resisters, and Willie Redmond had to spend three months in prison. Refusing to lodge an appeal, he called on every tenant to defend his home against 'unjust eviction'.[41]

The 'despised and rejected' Byrne could not leave his demesne without a police escort. After Sunday mass parishioners booed and hooted him and his brother. Even the tough emergency men hired to harvest his crops required police protection. Somers's 'fearless' defenders were greeted like conquering heroes on their release from Wexford jail. When Byrne ordered another round of evictions in April 1890, the chapel bells rang to summon resistance. At least three cabins were filled with prickly brush or gorse. Perched on his thatched roof one Plan tenant flailed away at an effigy of 'the Hermit'. Several bystanders snatched a rifle from a constable who had struck a young woman with the butt after being hit by a stone. The enraged defenders chased the agent and the undermanned police escort away with sticks, stones, clods of earth, and rotten eggs; and the bailiffs were lucky to escape with only bruises as they retreated to New Ross.[42]

GLASCOTT/WHITECHURCH, WEXFORD

On 10 April 1888, a sheriff's party took a ram to Whitechurch, six miles from New Ross, where Bryan Berney (or Bierney), had worked one day a week for many years as a blacksmith for William Madden Glascott of Alderton and Pilltown. In February 1887 this landlord granted his regular tenants an abatement of 25 per cent, hoping to avoid the Plan. Anxious about his own security of tenure, Berney requested and was denied a change from a weekly to a yearly tenancy. The resulting quarrel put him at odds with the other tenants despite Father O'Sullivan's efforts to mediate the dispute. Served with an ejectment writ in February 1888, he installed iron gates, bars, and chains in his cottage. When the ram gang approached, Berney and his comrades threw hot liquid and rotten eggs at the enemy; and some women in the crowd made taunting remarks about the sexual peccadilloes of Glascott's son. After persistent ramming the emergency men entered through the hole followed by the police who arrested the garrison. This eviction marked the start of a purge of 150 Plan tenants and sub-tenants that lasted until April 1890.[43]

PONSONBY/YOUGHAL

The rammers were thwarted again on the Ponsonby estate where the landlord's syndicate was determined to purge every active Campaigner. When evictions resumed on 23 February 1888, Captain Hamilton planned a dawn attack in order to take the house of Maurice Doyle of Inchiquin by surprise. This strong farmer had fortified his house and then moved to an outhouse before the crowbar brigade arrived. When the sheriff showed up at dawn, only two labourers were present. Doyle had painted the words 'Plan of Campaign' in big black letters on a gable wall and a sign over the door read: 'Exterminators come on'. Word of the eviction spread rapidly and six priests arrived at the head of a small crowd.[44]

21 'On the Road for Eviction'. In this photograph of a disassembled ram lashed to a cart the wooden table or trestle lying on top is designed to support the beam when the rammers attach it to the chain hanging from the tripod. (NLI, 1766 WL)

ABOVE

22 'Eviction Scene (Battering Ram)'. Wearing a
bowler hat, sub-sheriff Croker poses with a wicker
shield near the ram's head pretending to fend off
scalding water or stones. The size of the hole reflects
the awesome power of this 'engine' of destruction.
(NLI, 1779 WL)

BELOW

23 J. D. Reigh, 'The Vandeleur Eviction
Campaign – The Ram at Work'. The central image
in Reigh's cartoon features the ram 'at work' on the
Vandeleur estate in July 1888. The police are
arresting a gentleman in the lower left corner and
mistreating a wounded defender in the upper right
hand corner. Below this image the muscular Pat
McGrath breaks his handcuffs. (UI, 4 Aug. 1888)

24 'Dr Tully's House After Eviction. Woodford'.
Emergency men pose triumphantly on the slate roof
of Dr Tully's house having entered through the attic.
On the ground police, soldiers, and officials survey
the scene. (NLI, 2482 WL)

25 'Battering Ram'. The ram lies at rest after demolishing part of a wall. In the foreground the agent or sub-sheriff consults with an army officer. (NLI, 1769 WL)

26 'Eviction Kilrush'. Surrounded by children and two men, a woman stands defiantly outside her ruined home at Kilrush. Part of the roof has collapsed under the ram's blows. (NLI, 4918 WL)

27 'Somer's Fort. Coolroe'. Several constables assume positions of attack in the aftermath of the siege and fall of Somers fort. The height of the earthen rampart and the extent of the damage to the house can be clearly seen. (NLI, 2491 WL)

28 J. F. O'Hea, 'Balfour's Holiday'.
A foppish Balfour accompanies his
robotic 'Maiden' on their Irish
vacation in this cartoon. The sledgehammer and axe-like arms and the
iron-sheathed head bespeak her trade.
A thuggish emergency man or porter
conveys the minister's baggage labelled
'Insolence', 'Eviction Writs', 'Batons',
and 'Dynamite for Blowing up Tenants'.
(*WF*, 29 June 1889)

29 J. F. O'Hea, 'Balfour's 'Plan of
Campaign' Mounted on a rocking-
horse and clad in the uniform of a
cavalry officer Balfour reviews his
army of cannon-like rams or 'Notices
to Quit' in this cartoon.
(*WF*, 6 Oct.1888)

30   J. D. Reigh, 'Black Smith-Barry Finds a Difficulty in Raising the Wind'. In this Reigh cartoon, Arthur Hugh Smith-Barry, the architect of the Ponsonby syndicate, toils as a blacksmith forging the crow-bar of 'Coercion'. On the left stand such leading opponents of the Plan as Olphert, Lord Clanricarde, the Duke of Abercorn, and Ponsonby – all identified as 'Land Grabbers'. They want Smith-Barry to repair or improve their eviction tools. The looming ram bears the label, 'Balfour's Maiden'. On the right a rebellious Tipperary tenant abandons his post at the bellows exclaiming: 'I'm hanged if I blow the bellows for this devil's work any longer.' (*UI*, 6 July 1889)

After pounding away at a thick wall for half an hour, the rammers opened a hole large enough to reveal a second stone wall and thickets of prickly bushes inside. So they abandoned the ram and climbed up a ladder onto the roof. Ripping away some slates they dropped into the attic stuffed with hawthorn branches. When Doyle rushed up the stairs, an emergency man swung at him with a hatchet but missed. He was then throttled and thrown down the stairs. Only the arrival of the police saved him from grievous harm. After the eviction of his widowed mother next door, Doyle took the whole family to the Imperial Hotel in Youghal, for the night, a sure sign that he could afford to pay the rent. To prevent re-entry the sheriff installed six constables and two emergency men in Doyle's house.[45]

TOTTENHAM/BALLYKEROGUE REVISITED

After a long hiatus, the ram returned to Ballykerogue on 22 May 1888. But this time it lay idle because the three tenants scheduled for removal did not resist. Describing the march to Stokestown, the *People's* reporter dwelled on the striking contrast between the beauty of nature and the ugliness of eviction:

> The morning was a glorious one, and high above the tramp of the 'black army' could be heard the joyful song of the lark as he rose merrily in the morning air. The joyous song of the birds, singing their praise to Almighty God, appeared in strange contrast to the dull tread of Colonel Tottenham's evicting party, at the rere [*sic*] of which a number of young boys were whistling the 'Dead March in [*sic*] Saul' – a dismal marching tune.

Some trees and boulders on the road delayed the evictors' arrival. Apart from their usual heckling the crowd remained peaceful as the emergency men went to work. When Mrs James Costello asked permission to retrieve the rosary beads she had left behind in her cottage, one of them told her to go to hell.[46]

On 7 January 1889, the crowbar brigade led by sub-sheriff Connor and Colonel Miller RM appeared again along with two hundred police and soldiers. Their arsenal included a battering ram and a large shed mounted on wheels with a hinged zinc roof to ward off liquid and missiles. Negotiations had collapsed after the Campaigners spurned the agent's offer of a 15 per cent abatement on rent and arrears. However, lack of resistance enabled the sheriff to leave both 'machines' behind and the crowd was denied the thrill of a fierce siege. Only James Howlin fought back with boiling water spiked with lime until the bailiffs broke down his door. An emergency man kicked a little girl who had assaulted him. Although the Howlins were allowed to re-enter owing to the ill health of one member, they lost their farm. Later the widow Walsh and her family left their Duganstown home without a fight. In the span of three days the bailiffs emptied over a dozen households. Four more families were driven out on 24 April. The sheriff's party marched back to New Ross and stored the ram and testudo in the market house owned by Tottenham. By May, 200 more people had been driven out.

The crown made an example of resistance to both rent and eviction by prosecuting Canon Doyle, his curate, and 22 respectable parishioners for their active engagement in the Plan. In early July 1889 the nervous authorities sent some 450 police and soldiers to Arthurstown to protect the courthouse where the defendants were being tried. After a prolonged hearing the magistrates found the priest guilty of inciting tenants to withhold their rent. The *Freeman* covered this trial in great detail; and *United Ireland* hailed the 'brilliant success' of the Tottenham tenants in their long and arduous struggle against landlordism.[47]

OLPHERT/FALCARRAGH

On 8 January 1889 the sub-sheriff brought a ram onto the Olphert estate at Falcarragh where the rocky and boggy soil barely sustained the Irish-speaking populace. Since this bitter conflict on the one Plan estate in Donegal will be dealt with in the next chapter, suffice to say here that this ram suffered another humiliating defeat at a barn fortified by the tenant James Curran. Hoping to shorten the siege, the sub-sheriff had ordered a ram from a firm in Derry but this instrument proved too slender to penetrate the stone wall. Singing 'God Save Ireland', Curran and his comrades manned the barn's defences. In the words of the *Freeman*, they were prepared to 'throw themselves upon the bayonets or expose themselves to the bullets of the soldiers even if it is only to hold one inch of their home. Tomorrow will tell its tale.'

Such martyrdom proved unnecessary because the ram failed to perform and showers of stones and slates routed the rammers. Hoping to salvage victory from this setback, the resident magistrate, Ulick Bourke, ordered several riflemen to load their weapons and advance while yelling at the defenders: 'Come out of it. You are defying the law here and you are stoning those men who come here under a legal process. I should give the military orders to fire if you stone anybody. It is a very serious thing and I advise you strongly to come out.' After he read the riot act, the garrison responded with another chorus of 'God Save Ireland'. Curran challenged Bourke to 'put up that big stick'– meaning the ram – because they would rather die than surrender to the emergency men. Major Mends then renewed his threat to shoot if the resistance continued. As the *Freeman* noted, 'It was certainly a striking spectacle to find five Donegal peasants enclosed behind the walls of an ordinary barn defying all the power of the forces of the Crown.' Father Peter Kelly, parish priest of Dunfanaghy, then passed through the police cordon and assured Curran that it was no disgrace to yield to the police. Heeding this appeal, the defenders climbed down a ladder and submitted to arrest and handcuffs. Convicted of obstruction, they were sentenced to five months in prison with hard labour. Tim Healy lodged an appeal and the judge reduced the term to three months. Upon their release from Derry jail on 12 July the garrison enjoyed a triumphal reception. What had begun as an epic siege ended with some bruises, a useless ram, an honourable surrender, many arrests, and, as we will see in the next chapter, the illegal and brief return of many evicted families to their homes in mid-April.[48]

BUNBURY/BANSHA

At the end of May 1889 the sheriff deployed a ram on the small estate of Major Bunbury at Bansha in southeast Tipperary. With the help of his children, Edmond Keating had dug a deep moat and barricaded his cabin. Hurling stones and hot liquid, they held off the evictors for an entire day while the police beat anyone who tried to break through their cordon. The ram's failure to breach the wall forced the emergency men to climb up on the roof where they dumped some burning and noxious material down the chimney. The five defenders had to make a quick exit coughing and choking. Arrested and hand-cuffed, they were taken off to Clonmel jail. With tongue in cheek the *Cork Examiner* urged bailiffs to make more use of 'noisome' fumes because Balfour's maiden had lost its punch.[49]

The ram also appeared briefly on two other properties in Tipperary. In May 1889 a tenant of Valentine Ryan at Cappawhite lost one mud wall to the ram even though his family was readmitted owing to a child's illness. And in December a ram arrived on the estate of Smith-Barry, who, as we have seen, was determined to punish Michael O'Brien Dalton for orchestrating the Plan. The destruction of the corn mill so angered local people that they boycotted Smith-Barry's new butter factory.[50]

The *Cork Examiner's* reporter described the Rossborough ram in almost loving detail:

It was a touching sight to see the tenderness with which Balfour's interesting 'maiden' was handled. That 'maiden', with the iron-bound extremities, was borne in a four-wheeled vehicle on springs, with leather suspenders to the trestles which contributes much to the comfort of her repose when not out on active duty. The bailiffs surround that vehicle after the manner of pall-bearers at a funeral, and with

a strong body of police in front and in rere, they march along to the scene of operations, a most ludicrous procession.

But there was nothing ludicrous about either the ram's handiwork or the
baton charges launched by the police against hecklers lining the road.[51]

At indignation meetings around the country Parnellite MPs railed against
the ram and police brutality. T. P. Gill MP told the Youghal tenantry that
whenever he asked English audiences how they would react if the ram gang
appeared at their doorstep, they invariably replied: 'We would shoot them.' But
he judiciously advised against any such course of action on the Ponsonby estate
because victory seemed so near.[52]

CRITICS OF THE RAM IN PARLIAMENT

News of the ram spread fast across the Irish Sea provoking outbursts from both
English and Irish Home Rulers in Parliament. On 8 April 1889 John Morley
asked Balfour to reveal who had procured and paid for the Falcarragh ram – that
'extraordinary machine'. Balfour explained that the Assistant-Commissioner
of the RIC had requested this device in order to overcome the 'perfectly disgrace-
ful' resistance of tenants to eviction. Several days later J. G. Swift MacNeill, the
flamboyant Protestant nationalist MP for South Donegal, ignited a heated
debate about the multiple evictions around Gweedore. He accused the police
of terrorising the peasantry with not only summary arrests but also the ram
that was being deployed to enforce landlords' rights.[53] After Arthur O'Connor
lashed out against the RIC's 'reign of white terror' in their pursuit of D. I. Martin's
murderers, Balfour coolly justified the ram as an instrument designed to protect
bailiffs and police from injury. When Henry J. Wilson asked about the cost of
the Falcarragh ram and other eviction gear, the Irish Solicitor General replied
that the bill came to £48 18s 2½d. The House greeted his mention of the ha'pence
with ripples of laughter.

Thomas Sexton wanted to know if the notorious Falcarragh ram would be
used again and whether or not MPs would be allowed to inspect it over the holi-
days. Balfour replied that he preferred not to 'answer the question offhand'
insisting that the ram was not a tool of landlordism – whatever that word might
mean – but a purely defensive device designed to protect the enforcers of law
and order. Nationalists hated the ram, he added, because they knew it would
shorten sieges and diminish the suffering caused by resistance. Sexton scoffed
at the argument that the ram was 'an engine of self-defence' when it was being
used to collect the private debts of landlords and wreak vengeance on tenants.

In vain Home Rulers tried to discover who was paying for these rams and they condemned the destructive impact of this weapon on both the houses and morale of the tenantry. Having seen the Falcarragh ram, MacNeill asked his fellow members how he could obtain a scale model to be shown to English audiences. Unionist MPs erupted in laughter at this request. In another tirade against the ram on 5 August he called Balfour's regime 'a gross, wicked, villainous, sordid system of tyranny'. In reply Balfour pointed out that the ram had hardly been used on the Olphert estate and was a benefit to all concerned.

Almost a year later MacNeill surprised the House of Commons by producing a miniature ram. In the midst of a speech on 10 July 1890 condemning police brutality in Donegal he pulled out this model from his overcoat and held it up to derisive laughter from the government benches. He declared that the ram had destroyed countless cottages in Ireland and wondered if Olphert had received any rent from the 300 tenants whose houses had been 'unroofed'.[54] Later he expressed his hope that Balfour 'would not exercise any maidenly reserve' when explaining why the Donegal ram had not appeared in the RIC estimates. Ignoring the pointed allusion to 'maidenly', Balfour praised the ram's efficacy. Despite all its notoriety the Falcarragh ram remained in storage throughout the subsequent evictions.[55]

RAM CARTOONS

Both Reigh and O'Hea had great sport with the ram because it served so well as an epitome of Balfourian coercion and the landlords' anti-Plan campaign. In over a dozen colourful and semi-serious cartoons these artists mocked 'Balfour's Maiden' – an epithet that implicitly questioned his masculinity. In 'Balfour's Holiday' (*Weekly Freeman*, 29 June 1889) O'Hea depicted the chief secretary foppishly dressed in holiday attire arriving at a train station en route to Ireland (Plate 28). Wearing a straw boater, Balfour is accompanied by his robotic 'Maiden' with a sledgehammer and axe for arms and a slender, iron-sheathed ram for a head. The brutish emergency man is pushing a trundle laden with baggage marked 'Insolence', 'Eviction Writs', 'Batons', and 'Dynamite for Blowing up Tenants'. Nearby a can of 'Petroleum' sits in a wicker basket. The caption contains Balfour's exclamation: 'Ta! Ta! Bye! Bye! I'm off to Ireland to have a real good time of it – This is the sort of Fun I like!'

Reigh also exploited the ram as a symbol of landlord tyranny and Castle brutality. In 'The Judgment of Solomon – The Rackrenters Repudiate Arbitration' (*United Ireland*, 20 April 1889), he pilloried the landlords and Balfour for refusing to concede the demands of the Plan. Waving a green flag above a homeless mother and infant, William O'Brien urges blindfolded Justice to approve the tenants' demand for a fair rent on the estate of Lord Lansdowne – 'The Viceregal

Exterminator of Luggacurran [*sic*]'. The latter holds a crowbar marked 'EVICTION' and a can of 'PETROLEUM', while a fearful Balfour wearing a RIC uniform clutches the ram's tripod.

In an artful and satirical allusion to Lord Lansdowne's appointment as Viceroy of India, Reigh invoked Hindu mythology by casting this eminent landlord as 'Siva The Destroyer', the omnipotent and phallocentric god (better known as Shiva), in 'The Most Noble and "Humane"' (Figure 8.7). Seated on a plinth and wearing a tunic, Lansdowne, the resolute adversary of the Plan at Luggacurren, holds a crowbar and a can of paraffin surrounded by burnt-out cabins and weeping women and children. The priapic ram, now labelled 'Eviction Made Easy', lies between the legs of both the tripod and his lordship.[56]

Another O'Hea cartoon, 'A Fellow Feeling' (*Weekly Freeman*, 8 September 1888) features a portly John Bull rebuking Lord Clanricarde, whose coat pockets are stuffed with writs, for his 'extortionate rents' and callous evictions. Through a gaping hole in the wall and above the head of this notorious landlord appear the phallic ram and the Union Jack. O'Hea also mocked the ram in his

8.7 J. D. Reigh 'The Most Noble and "Humane" the Marquis of Lansdowne as "SIVA THE DESTROYER" – The Idol of Coercionists'. Reigh casts Lord Lansdowne as 'Siva the Destroyer', the omnipotent and phallic Hindu god. The recently appointed Viceroy of India holds a crowbar and a can of paraffin while surrounded by weeping women and children and burnt out homes. Labelled 'Eviction Made Easy', the giant ram lies appropriately between the legs of the tripod and his lordship. (*UI*, 8 June 1889)

'Balfour's Plan of Campaign' (*Weekly Freeman*, 6 October 1888) (Plate 29), wherein the chief secretary wearing the uniform of a cavalry officer and mounted on a rocking horse reviews a legion of cannon-like rams or 'Notices to Quit' interspersed with flags symbolising the defeat of Irish rebellions.

Reigh found another use for the ram's tripod in 'Giving the Evictors a Free Hand' (Figure 8.8). Here the sadistic Clanricarde flogs a handsome tenant farmer while his wife and child watch this punishment in anguish. On the far left another ram appears with a pennant inscribed 'Ponsonby Estate'. Slung around Balfour's waist is a bag marked '£33,000,000 for Irish Rack Renters'. In one hand he holds an olive branch of 'rack rents' while behind his back he grasps the bloody truncheon of 'Coercion'. The demonic Clanricarde asks Balfour why he is wearing the 'ridiculous costume' of the angel of 'Peace'. In the distance more Plan members are being whipped in the same manner that recalls the triangular flogging device used by loyalists and Crown soldiers against suspected United Irishmen during the era of martial law in 1797–8.[57]

8.8   J. D. Reigh,'Giving the Evictors a Free Hand'. Reigh demonises Lord Clanricarde, who is exercising his 'legal rights' by whipping a tenant bound to the tripod of a ram in front of the distraught wife and child. On the left Balfour appears in the guise of the angel of peace. In one hand he holds out an olive branch but behind his back he carries a bloody truncheon while assuring his lordship that he has no wish to stop his 'little amusement'. On the far left looms the Ponsonby battering ram; and on the hill to the right more Plan members are being flogged in the same manner. (*UI*, 24 May 1890)

In 'Black Smith-Barry Finds a Difficulty in Raising the Wind' (*United Ireland*, 6 July 1889) (Plate 30), Reigh ridiculed the leader of the Ponsonby syndicate by placing him in his smithy. Four distinguished enemies of the Plan – Olphert, Lord Clanricarde, the Duke of Abercorn, and Ponsonby – stand behind the ram labelled 'Balfour's Maiden', asking for help in improving or repairing their eviction tools. The bearded blacksmith uses a hammer labelled 'Eviction Syndicate' to forge the crowbar of 'Coercion'. However, his handiwork has been halted by the rebellious Tipperary tenant (on the far right) who refuses to blow the bellows any more.

One of Reigh's last ram cartoons reversed the deployment of this weapon. In 'Back! Away with Them; Or the Last Eviction in Ireland' (*United Ireland*, 1 September 1888), the allegorical figures of the Home Rule electorate in England, Scotland, Ireland, and Wales haul away on the ram marked 'General

Election' at the entrance to Dublin Castle. Looking out fearfully from a tower window are the beleaguered Unionist leaders (Salisbury, Balfour, Chamberlain, Goschen, and Hartington) waving the flag of 'Perpetual Coercion'. This clever inversion of realities places the ram in the hands of voters in the Celtic Fringe who are destined to free Ireland from British misrule.

MR PUNCH AND THE RAM

That quintessential Englishman, Mr Punch, could not resist poking fun at the ram. During the Falcarragh evictions *Punch* published a splendid piece of satire attributed to the political diarist, 'Toby MP', whose weekly column, 'Essence of Parliament', delighted so many readers. On 20 April 1889, this witty observer noted that 'Windbag Sexton' had questioned the use of the Letterkenny ram and Swift MacNeill had declared that since 'this bathering-ram has been bought out of public funds', Balfour should 'lay a model of it on the table'. Toby then concocted the following scenario for a vaudeville show at Westminster:

> Promises to be the greatest Variety Entertainment of this or any other age; lift House of Commons at one bound into the front rank of morning performances. Open every day, wet or shine. … Full-size model of battering-ram, with clanking chains, iron-shod poles, boat-hooks, and scaling-ladders, on view on table, side by side with astonished Mace. Chairs and tables cleared out of Library; model of Irish cottage set up. John O'Connor, disguised as struggling tenant, regularly evicted at 3 p.m. and 7 p.m. (No extra charge.).

To add to the merriment Edward Sheil MP South Meath will play the role of a young boy who hands a pitcher of hot water to his parent so that the latter can pour it over Colonel J. P. Nolan MP North Galway wearing a policeman's uniform. Every fifteen minutes Shaw-Lefevre will walk through the House in prisoner's garb, and every ten minutes Joseph Biggar MP West Cavan, cast as a Resident Magistrate, sentences Balfour to six months in prison. A week later *Punch* (27 April 1889) published Harry Furniss's satirical sketch of Balfour encased in a suit of armour and riding a ferocious ram with huge horns (Figure 8.9). With sword in hand he charges his well-armed questioners in the House of Commons.[58] By mid-1890, almost all the rams had been mothballed and the flow of ram cartoons had virtually ceased.

After Swift McNeill displayed his model ram in Parliament, Toby MP noted: 'shows it in working order; Committee much interested; inclined to encourage this sort of thing; pleasant interlude in monotony of denunciation of Prince Arthur [Balfour] and all his works.' Magic-lantern shows on the riverside

8.9　Harry Furniss. 'Balfour on His Battering-Ram'. Harry Furniss mocks both Balfour and the
battering ram by placing the chief secretary in a suit of armour. Mounted on a woolly ram and with
sword in hand he charges his many questioners or adversaries in Parliament. (*Punch*, 27 Apr. 1889)

terrace were all very well in good weather, Toby added, but on rainy nights the
ram should be exhibited indoors.[59]

In the spring of 1893 John Tenniel used a formidable ram, labelled 'Opposition',
in a *Punch* cartoon about the impending defeat of the second Home Rule bill
in the House of Lords. In 'The Assault!!' the Unionist leaders are hauling away
at the ram with Lord Salisbury's head attached to the business end. Dressed
like Roman soldiers, they are about to break down the huge wooden door of
the 'Home Rule Bill' in the castle while Gladstone peers fearfully through a
donjon window.[60]

Despite all the publicity about the ram, considerable ignorance of this tool
prevailed in England. Take the case of the learned Sir James Charles Mathew,
who presided over the Evicted Tenants Commission appointed by the new
Liberal government in October 1892 to reinstate 'the wounded soldiers of the

land war'. A graduate of Trinity College Dublin, and a nephew of the temperance crusader, Father Theobald Mathew, he spent almost all his distinguished legal career in London. At the outset of the commission hearings he crossed swords with Edward Carson by refusing to allow the cross-examination of witnesses. When questioning Canon Keller of Youghal, about the Ponsonby clearances, he asked: 'What is the battering-ram? (Laughter). I suppose every one here knows what it is, but I do not.' To this remarkable query Keller replied succinctly: 'It is a long pole, mounted with iron, and swung from a triangle. There are ropes attached, and some men catch it, pull it back, and knock it against the wall.'[61] Here ended the lesson.

By the summer of 1890, the hue and cry over the ram had died down and few tenants were mounting serious resistance to the sheriff's party. The ram may have had a relatively short shelf life, but it left an indelible impression on many Irishmen and it served nationalist spokesmen admirably as living proof of the failure of the Balfourian regime. Maud Gonne revived memories of 'Balfour's Maiden' in the mid-1890s by enlivening her harangues against Irish landlordism and British imperialism with some of Lawrence's eviction slides long after the rams had been put in cold storage.

As for the long shadow cast by the ram in the countryside, one old man was standing outside his cottage in the late 1880s when he saw an English yachtsman and amateur photographer approach and set up his large camera on top of a tripod. The panic-stricken peasant exclaimed: 'Oh! begor! and is it the battering-ram you have brought against me?' Evidently, he had never seen either a ram or a camera before.[62] Even Jules Verne took note of the ram in his only Irish novel, wherein he attributed 'this instrument of savage social war' to 'the scientific ingenuity of a distinguished statesman'. Known as 'Balfour's Maiden', the ram 'demolishes everything' after being 'reared against the house' and leaves only the walls standing.[63]

As we have seen, the ram made rich propaganda for the leaders of the Plan and National League at a time when Balfour was anxious to keep eviction news and his own role in this weapon down to a dull roar. Any defeat for the ram was worth its weight in gold to the Campaigners. An editorial in *United Ireland* lamented that 'the whole forces [*sic*] of Government in Ireland seem consolidated into one huge battering-ram to crush the people. The cry of "Back, away with them" echoes from one end of Ireland to another. Eviction is the object, and Coercion the means' to ensure the collection of rack-rents. The time had come, the editor continued, to persuade English workingmen to join forces with the Irish people and 'swing the great engine of their power with a will. With the first united stroke the hateful edifices of a Coercion Government comes [*sic*] tumbling to the ground crushing the CLANRICARDES under its ruins.'[64] The

Freeman (21 May 1889) deplored the terror caused by the ram during the centenary of the French revolution: 'Thank God, numbers of honest Englishmen have come over to see for themselves the shocking work of the Chief Secretary's "Maiden", which goes about the country, like the guillotine during the French Revolution, marking its hideous track with innocent blood.'

Whether or not one favours a Freudian interpretation of Balfour's delight in the ram (after all, like the proverbial cigar, a ram is a ram) some nationalists made great sport of this unmanly bachelor's embrace of the mechanical 'maiden'. No doubt, their shrill rants against the ram at Plan rallies helped to raise more money for the newly founded Tenants' Defence Association that supported the evicted tenants.[65] The ram further tarnished the already unenviable reputation of Irish landlords while serving as a powerful reminder that the British government for all its pious professions of due process, trial by jury, and freedom of speech could not govern Ireland without resorting to brute force.

NINE

FALCARRAGH:
THE OLPHERT ESTATE
1888–90

'I am the law in Gweedore.'

FATHER JAMES MCFADDEN
*PP of Gweedore, speaking at Doe (Doagh),
County Donegal in January 1888.*

*'Tomorrow or next day the miserable scenes which
had made Gweedore and Falcarragh words of horror
through the civilized world would be repeated,
when 250 families will be driven from their rooftrees,
homeless, desolate, famished on the world.'*

J. G. SWIFT MACNEILL
*speaking at Gweedore, 9 November 1890
(Freeman's Journal, 10 November 1890).*

———

Long synonymous with dire poverty and subsistence farming on rock-strewn holdings, the coastal region of northwest Donegal became a vortex of Plan activism and evictions after 1886. According to the American journalist, W. H. Hurlbert, Gweedore had been in a state of absolute 'barbarism' until the arrival of Lord George Hill who allegedly transformed the district after the 1830s. The impoverished and mostly Gaelic speaking tenants had grown so accustomed to ejectment that this term was one of the very few English words 'understood by young and old' alike. On a tour of western Donegal in the spring of 1889 J. H. Tuke found widespread distress, owing to partial failures of the potato crop and the scarcity of employment for young men who depended on seasonal labour in England and Scotland for survival. Many families subsisted on tiny holdings of bogland or 'rock and black turf' with only a little milk from the cow to supplement their meagre diet of corn meal and molluscs. Numerous press reports of Wybrants Olphert's disputes with his tenants around Falcarragh, just north of Gweedore, afford insights into the fierce struggle between this seasoned old landlord and his tenants.[1]

9.1 'The State of Ireland: Armed Peasants Guarding the House of Father Stephens at Falcarragh, Donegal'. An unruly crowd of Olphert tenants armed with shillelaghs and pitchforks protect the house of their beloved priest, Father Stephens, whom the police are trying to arrest for promoting the Plan of Campaign around Falcarragh. (*ILN*, 11 Feb. 1888)

Descended from a Dutch Protestant who had bought land in the barony of Killmacrenan in 1661, Olphert had resided there for more than sixty years and was the longest serving magistrate in the country. Seated atop a sloping lawn, Ballyconnell House enjoyed a splendid view of the sea and Bloody Foreland. Apart from protests against rent increases following improvements to their holdings and poor potato harvests, tenant rancour had been minimal up to July 1884 when scores of families were ousted for non-payment. The successful effort of the parish priest of Gweedore, Father James McFadden, to raise £150 enabled these tenants to pay their arrears and costs and achieve reinstatement. But in 1885 the depression resulted in arrears of £1,200 that prompted Olphert's creditors to demand the removal of delinquent tenants. According to the Duke of Abercorn, 'foolish agents' had caused most of 'poor old Olphert's' difficulties by mishandling the issue of arrears on his 18,133-acre estate around Falcarragh and Ardsmore.[2] In January 1888, the tenants eagerly embraced the Plan.

Olphert had to contend with a formidable adversary in the charismatic parish priest, Father James McFadden (also spelled MacFadden), who was both loved and feared by his parishioners. He had the support of an equally courageous curate, Canon Daniel Stephens, who shared his penchant for provoking the police and the magistracy. On 11 February 1888, the *ILN* highlighted Stephens's popularity in a print filled with well-dressed parishioners armed with sticks and pitchforks and preventing his arrest (Figure 9.1). McFadden advised the tenantry to demand an abatement of 25 per cent on judicial rents and 40 per cent on non-judicial rents. Since Olphert's rent receipts came close to McFadden's annual income of almost £1,000, he baulked at this request. Once again his creditors pressed him hard for more ejectment decrees in the (vain) hope of squeezing some money out of the tenants who were rapidly joining the Plan.[3]

In January 1889 Olphert embarked on a purge of his rebellious tenants that inflamed townlands all around Falcarragh while eastern Donegal remained tranquil. Besides reporters these evictions attracted Liberal delegates from the English midlands keen to see for themselves the baneful effects of Irish landlordism and to reaffirm their faith in Home Rule. McFadden's arrest for promoting the Plan led to a stifling boycott of the Olphert family, and police patrols guarded the demesne night and day. Olphert's son and heir always carried a revolver while strolling around the grounds. T. W. Russell MP and delegates from the Manchester Liberal Association were soon joined by Balfour's private secretary, Hugh Fisher MP, who had been sent to keep his master informed about the latest developments.[4] Hurlbert stayed for a few days relishing the hospitality of landlord and priest alike. Less than impartial he defended Olphert's decision to fight the Plan and denied that the cottiers were distressed because they could still afford the 'luxury' of tea. While the local women impressed him as hard workers, he found the men lazy. When he remarked to Olphert's son, Robert, that seeing him so well armed reminded him of 'the Far West' in America, the latter laughed: 'And we are as far in the West as we can get.'[5]

Emulating Father Lavelle, McFadden declared war on landlordism, the Castle, the courts, and Olphert. But his devotion to the Plan soon exposed him to the heavy hand of Balfour's crimes act. Convicted in January 1888 for inciting tenants to withhold their rent, he spent three months in jail. When he lodged an appeal, the judge doubled the sentence. Shortly thereafter Canon Stephens was arrested on the same charge while attending his superior's trial. A month later fifteen fellow priests showed up in court to console him before he went off to prison for three months. Upon McFadden's release in mid-October, five thousand people turned out at Letterkenny along with six brass bands to welcome him home, and the hills around Gweedore glowed at night with bonfires. Stephens received much the same triumphal reception when freed in August.[6]

The unrepentant McFadden went to England to promote the Plan and returned to Donegal in December to face another prosecution. Dreading both trial and imprisonment, he evaded arrest by staying inside his house and slipping out at night to celebrate Mass in Derrybeg church. But the police caught up with him after Mass on Sunday morning 3 February 1889. Brandishing his sword, District Inspector William Martin pushed his way through the dense crowd of parishioners and grabbed the priest by his soutane shouting: 'Come on sir'. A woman cried: 'He is killing the Priest!' and other women began to wail and sob. Some men then rushed forward to free McFadden from Martin's grasp. Although the priest implored the crowd to go home in both English and Irish, stones flew and several constables were injured. One man picked up a fence-post and dealt Martin a blow that fractured his skull. McFadden and his sister carried the unconscious officer into the parish house where he soon expired. This homicide provoked a police rampage and McFadden along with 46 other suspects were arrested in brutal fashion and charged with murder. The police hauled all their captives off to Derry jail and launched a reign of 'white terror' around Gweedore.[7]

Charged with complicity in Martin's murder, McFadden was tried at both Lifford and Letterkenny along with the other suspects, 21 of whom were discharged at the end of March. Refusing to abandon his fellow defendants, he appeared at the summer assizes in Maryborough where the Irish Attorney General, Sir Peter O'Brien, led the prosecution. Eventually, the crown dropped the murder charge but prosecuted McFadden for advocating the Plan. However, the jury failed to reach a verdict and he was released on his own recognizance. In the meantime the remaining defendants were tried at Maryborough assize at the end of October. Convicted of complicity in Martin's murder, Willliam Coll was sentenced to ten years' penal servitude and his thirteen co-defendants received prison terms ranging from seven years to two months with hard labour for riotous conduct.[8] All these trials received full coverage in the Irish and British press.

After touring Falcarragh in January 1889, T.W. Russell concluded that Olphert's tenants were not badly off because they had judicial rents and were living on wages earned from seasonal labour in Great Britain. He went further by rhapsodising about the benefits of fresh sea air and the beautiful coastal scenery that made them so much better off than the 'hopeless, joyless, Godless' slum dwellers in the East End of London: 'They look out on a fair landscape – Errigal and Muckish looking down on them and their troubles, the Atlantic making music at their very doorsteps.' Dismissing 'the cry of exceptional distress' as 'a complete and entire fraud', he concluded that if potatoes were scarce, 'money was not'. Falcarragh became a hive of Plan activism; and once again Balfour intervened on a landlord's behalf by sponsoring a syndicate that evicted scores of tenants and operated the vacant holdings like a grazing ranch.[9] While supporters raised money for the Olphert Defence Fund, the proprietor presided over the expulsion of several hundred families or almost 1,600 individuals.

O'DONNELL'S FORT

To counter this eviction campaign John Kelly, a leading Plan organiser, taught Olphert's tenants how to fortify their houses. On the bitterly cold morning of 2 January 1889, sub-sheriff John McCay, Ulick Bourke RM, County Inspector Lennon, and Major Mends led 250 police and soldiers on a seven-mile march to a tiny village named Bedlam near Gortahork. Most of the bailiffs were muscular 'headmen' who belonged to a quasi-mafia that 'mediated between owners and occupiers' while working for the local authorities.[10] As the *Freeman*'s reporter put it, 'A wilder and more isolated district it is impossible to conceive. Remote from all communication with the civilised world, living upon the Atlantic air, potatoes, and Indian meal, the inhabitants lead simple but healthy lives, under the care of their devoted clergy.' The *Freeman* took note of the physical signs of distress: 'The faces of the women, who look prematurely aged, the drooping shoulders of the men, and the wistful eyes of the pale-cheeked children, made up a picture *in petto* of the Irish tenants at the present moment.'[11]

On the march to Bedlam the sheriff's party had to repair three bridges that had been knocked down. At the abode of a local blacksmith, Patrick (Paddy) O'Donnell, who had paid no rent for two years the police used their batons and bayonets to push a crowd of almost 2,000 up a hill. The women were clad in traditional red skirts and white blouses while the men wore 'bright coloured tunics [making] …a splendid show of muscle and physique'. Fathers McFadden and Stephens were much in evidence. O'Donnell had barricaded his windows with large stones and built a stone wall inside the doorway. Equipped with ladders, saws, sledgehammers, axes, crowbars, and revolvers, the emergency men stormed the front door only to be repulsed by stones and pointed poles. Dropping their tools, they threw the stones back at the garrison. After three hours of back and forth bombardment the bailiffs withdrew and left the field to the police. Mounting a ladder Sergeant McComb was stabbed in the lip and thigh by a pitchfork, fell to the ground, and had to be carried to an aid station. The defenders hauled the ladder inside singing 'God Save Ireland'. In vain McFadden rebuked Bourke for allowing the police to act like bailiffs. During a lull in the fighting the defenders 'lolled lazily out of their port holes' and greeted the crowd. After Bourke warned the garrison of the dire consequences of further resistance, he read the riot act and the impetuous Major Mends sent for some riflemen. How absurd it was, the *Freeman*'s reporter noted, to see '200 armed men standing round a miserable hovel defended by men whose only arms were stones and pitchforks.' Despite bayonet charges and scaling ladders the police failed to capture the garrison. 'To say the least', it was 'a humiliating position for a section of the British army, and the soldiers seemed to feel it as such.' Although Bourke threatened to shoot any stone throwers, he also urged Father Stephens to use his influence on the resisters. While the riflemen were loading their weapons, Stephens passed through the cordon and persuaded the garrison to surrender. One of the dozen defenders who climbed down a ladder was a ten-year old boy. Cheered lustily by hundreds of supporters, the prisoners were escorted to Derry jail.[12]

J. D. Reigh's 'The Fight for Bare Life on the Olphert Estate' (*United Ireland*, 12 January 1889) suggests the excitement, violence, and fear of these sieges (Plate 31).[13] This pictorial narrative begins in the upper left corner with Paddy O'Donnell and his wife and son peacefully engaged in digging up rocks outside their cabin. In clockwise order the tenant's family and friends prepare for a siege by blocking the windows with boulders; the O'Donnells pose at night outside their roofless house having lost 'the battle'; and the eviction party flees from volleys of stones and hot liquid 'in the thick of the fight'. In the centrepiece Father McFadden shouts at Major Mends, who has drawn his sword and ordered his riflemen to fire: 'For God's sake spare my poor people.' Behind him Canon Stephens urges the garrison to end their resistance.

More evictions sparked more unrest. While the police tightened their grip on the district, shopkeepers refused to deal with either them or the emergency men. One of the latter had to admit that the houses around Falcarragh were 'better fortified, protected, and garrisoned' than any he had encountered on other Plan estates.[14] On 3 January, the emergency men tackled less fortified houses like John Doogan's abode in Ardsmore after surrendering their revolvers to a police officer. Both sides indulged in stone throwing until District Inspector Lennon negotiated surrender. At Owen Ferry's cottage the crowd howled with laughter when the household cat refused to leave. Whenever an emergency man tried to scoop him up, the creature escaped and darted inside. On the fourth attempt the cat found a small hole in the wall and disappeared for good. At this point the sheriff's party gave up and left. When Shane Doogan's defenders threw stones, Bourke ordered some soldiers to fix bayonets and the bailiffs blocked the chimney to smoke out the defenders. Suddenly two young girls opened the door and threw stones carried in their aprons. They withdrew only to reappear with a large stone in each hand. They ran fearlessly towards the besiegers, who parted ranks to let them pass and friends in the crowd embraced them to 'wild plaudits'. Returning to their house, they retrieved the furniture thrown out by the bailiffs. Two more evictions followed before Bourke called it a day.[15]

Back in Bedlam on 4 January, the sheriff's party laid siege to Neal (or Neill) Doogan's well-fortified two-storey house. This tenant had made money from mining in Montana and had reputedly spent £500 on his new abode near the sea. To foil the evictors Doogan and his comrades dug a trench across the boreen, blocked windows, bored loopholes, and built two stonewalls inside the door. The police cordon prevented even reporters, priests, and MPs from approaching the premises. When Bourke demanded possession, Doogan retorted that he was an American citizen and would 'claim the protection of the United States if I am hurt'. He also declared that he cared as little for the Queen as the devil. Both sides threw stones at each other and Doogan shouted: 'I will show you a real Irish fight' and his garrison sang 'God Save Ireland'. After a rumour spread that the defenders were armed with rifles, the cagy Doogan refused to confirm or deny this report. Several of his men taunted the besiegers by waving loaves of bread out of a window to show that they could hold out for days. District Inspector William Heard mounted a ladder brandishing his sword but a stone knocked him to the ground unconscious. After Bourke read the riot act, Doogan shouted: 'I was born here and I will die here' adding that he had earned his money 'in the bowels of the earth' in 'the land of the free and the home of the brave'. The splenetic Major Mends then ordered ten men to advance with loaded rifles and warned that he would end this defiance if he had to shoot everyone inside. At length Father Stephens persuaded the garrison to abandon the fight and thirteen weary defenders filed out. To ensure harsh punishments the magistrates transferred the case to Fermanagh assizes, where the garrison was convicted of riot, assault, and resistance and sentenced to five months in prison with hard labour. Doogan himself received a harsher sentence: eight months with hard labour. Every defendant had to give sureties for good behaviour upon release.[16] Bourke's report to his superiors about this siege prompted Castle officials to recommend more forceful measures and ban any future stone-throwing by the forces of law and order.

At Drumnatinney only five of the twenty tenants on the sheriff's list offered resistance. On 5 January, James McNulty's garrison held off the enemy with volleys of stones. After the riot act was read, several riflemen were ordered to aim their weapons. But no shots were fired because the defenders took Stephens's advice to surrender to the police rather than the heartily despised emergency men. James Doogan's garrison comprised a young girl and her brother who hurled stones and hot water before being subdued and arrested. While the elderly Francis Ferry left quietly, the barricades at Ned Curran's cottage were so formidable that the sheriff postponed the assault.[17]

While some constables and bailiffs nursed their injuries, the agent Hewson demanded possession from 26 tenants who had been readmitted as caretakers. After sheriff McCay's men had finished practising on the battering ram procured from a firm in Derry, they ousted James McHugh, who had paid no rent for four years. They then climbed up a steep hill to drive out the bedridden Dan Magee whose garrison hurled stones, bottles, and hot water. The bailiffs broke a hole in the roof, entered, and captured one woman and her elderly mother who cursed them in Irish.[18]

Bourke's task force also expelled some tenants in arrears on the adjoining estate of Mrs Ann Stewart, a widow who lived in Dalkey and owned 7,274 acres around Bloody Foreland. The poorest tenants shared their hovels with the livestock; and the valuable midden lay just outside the door. After surmounting granite boulders rolled onto the approach roads, the sheriff's party ran into showers of stones that caused more injuries and ended with a police baton charge. To avert a riot Father McFadden 'threw himself boldly between the opposing forces'. Forced out on 18 January, Pat Gallagher and his five children retook possession illegally despite the presence of the police and the agent. In July a jury found him guilty of 'forcible re-entry' but recommended mercy. Next the crowbar gang tackled the abode of Owen Coyle, who had recently died. Here the sheriff wisely withdrew when he learned that the wake was in progress. Two days later the Parnellite MP, John O'Connor, praised the local people for their 'scientific obstruction of eviction' that would resound all the way to Glenbeigh. Ending his speech with a flourish, he declared: 'Landlordism is dying hard. It is on its [*sic*] legs and it is kicking violently. It is doomed to die and it is our duty to hasten its departure.'[19]

Among the tenants evicted on an adjacent estate was Denis McClafferty whose wife had borne five children aged from 11 down to a nursing infant. These 'wretched creatures' were thrown out on a cold winter's day. At another site Lieutenant Pixley of the 60th Rifles was so moved by the sight of eight 'squalid' children running about in rags that he paid the tenant's arrears on the spot.[20]

These evictions inspired the *Penny Illustrated Paper* to reprise R.C.Woodville's poignant print from the *ILN* in March 1880. Under a new title, 'A Poor Peasant's Prospect in Ireland: Eviction', this image features a homeless family stranded on a snowy road by the collapse of their old nag. As the caption explains, 'the full tide of poor Paddy's misfortune' revealed here should 'impress the British public and have a humanising effect upon the callous landlords who permit such atrocities to be committed in the Sister Isle.' More damning still was a letter to the *Freeman's Journal* (12 January 1889) from Archbishop Croke of Cashel calling these evictions 'scandalous, heartrending, and unchristian'. Sending 'the armed forces of the Crown …and a gang of ruthless desperadoes… to demolish the humble dwellings of the poor for the benefit of a pampered few', he opined, was a sin beyond redemption. Balfour's reaction was almost predictable. The evicted tenants could have paid the rent but opted for the Plan instead, and Croke's letter was 'one of the most monstrous … ever penned by an ecclesiastic'.[21]

The arrest, trial, and imprisonment of Father McFadden and 19 co-defendants for Martin's murder, the resilience of the Plan leaders, and recurrent evictions kept Falcarragh and environs in turmoil for the next two years. Constables swarmed over the countryside chasing suspects and shadowing visitors from abroad. On a visit in mid-March, the English Liberal MP, H.J. Wilson, deplored the ban on public meetings as well as the dire poverty of so many tenants. In his article, 'The Reign of Terror in Donegal', he called the conduct of the police 'ludicrous'.[22]

En route to Falcarragh court on 15 January, Paddy O'Donnell's defenders were hailed as heroes by five priests and hundreds of supporters. Their trial at the assizes for assault and riot ended with guilty verdicts and sentences of five to eight months with hard labour. Castle officials were anxious about the condition of Gweedore where the dense population enabled a crowd of over three thousand to assemble in half an hour just by blowing a horn from a hilltop. The police crackdown continued as Father McFadden was tried for involvement in Martin's murder. Although acquitted on this charge he was found guilty of promoting the Plan and jailed along with Father Stephens for six months without hard labour. Another victim of the Crimes Act, John Kelly, spent six months in prison for organising the Plan and teaching tenants around Gweedore how to resist. [23]

In the meantime the *Derry Journal* (17 April 1889) mocked the Falcarragh ram by quoting a parodic version of a song from Gilbert and Sullivan's *Patience* published in the *Pall Mall Gazette*. The author composed a witty dialogue between Olphert and the ram that began:

Landlord
Prithee, pretty maiden, prithee tell me true.
(Hey but I'm doleful, spite of women wailing!)
Shall I get my rack-rents slightly overdue?
Hey women wailing O!
Olphert Rent Collector!
          .   .   .   .

Battering-ram
Gentle sir, I truly hope that it may be.
(Hey, why be doleful, all the men are ailing?)
I'm Coercion's Daughter, put your trust in me.
Hey women wailing O!
Through resistance crashing,
Wall and roof-tree smashing!
Hey women wailing O!'

Early in April Olphert and his syndicate managers proceeded against 44 caretaker-tenants whose redemption period had expired. The loss of two potato crops in succession had caused great distress among the cottier class; some seventy families now faced eviction in this 'war of extermination'.[24] In the meantime Swift MacNeill complained in Parliament about the 122 ejectment decrees recently obtained by Donegal landlords. Given the number of people forced to subsist on Indian meal, he asked Balfour if the government had any plans to prevent starvation. The chief secretary disputed the number of decrees and denied that any tenants were starving.

Olphert's purge of the Plan resumed on Thursday 11 April while McFadden languished in Derry jail. Led by Father Boyle, several local priests took his place to boost tenant morale. With military precision Sub-Sheriff McCay and Bourke deployed their escort of police and soldiers but the absence of strong barricades enabled them to leave the ram behind. Nevertheless, the *Derry Journal* (15 April 1889) charged Balfour and the Castle bureaucracy with relying on this 'instrument of barbarism' in order to 'expound the sweet Gospel of extermination'. Surrounded by a police cordon, Pat (or Paddy) McGinley and his eight young children walked out after removing the windows and opening the door of his abode. James Gallagher and his nineteen children followed suit. But when the bailiffs broke down Chas McGinley's door at Drumnatinney, the women threw bottles and boiling water that scalded one bailiff. Upstairs McGinley used a long pole to dislodge a bailiff from a ladder. Leaning out of a window, he complained that Olphert had raised the rent every time he improved his 'worthless land'. His offer to surrender in return for £100 as compensation for all his improvements went unheeded. After forcing their way inside, the police arrested him and his female defenders. Daniel Ferry, who had built his house after returning from America, fought fiercely but proved no match for scaling ladders and crowbars.

Incensed by the sight of two emergency men beating a woman into submission, Patrick O'Brien MP for North Monaghan and his young companion, Henry Harrison, who had just arrived from Oxford, approached a magistrate and swore depositions concerning this brutality. Four days later McGinley re-entered his house and relit the turf fire. When a bailiff asked him what he was doing there, McGinley replied: 'I have come back to the walls that I built. It is better for me to die here than in the ditch.' A second arrest landed him back in Derry jail along with seven other resisters who were charged with obstructing the sheriff. One bedridden woman was allowed to remain until she could be conveyed to the workhouse. Apart from some 'filthy' hot liquid, the emergency men encountered light resistance. Upon seeing a mother and child dragged outside, Patrick O'Brien rushed forward and gallantly carried her baby to safety and assured the woman that her infant 'might become another Davitt, evicted at such an early age'. On 13 April, Owen Coyle's defenders showered the enemy with stones, one of which struck the agent Hewson who bled profusely from a head wound that required medical treatment. After a long struggle, two women walked out holding babies and submitted to arrest. Nearby, the widow Coyle won a reprieve because her daughter lay 'dangerously ill'.

As at Coolgreany some of the women and girls showed more courage than their menfolk. When the emergency men reached Neal Doogan's house, his wife stood in the doorway and grappled with two emergency men who struck her on the face and breast before subduing her. Pat Doohan's female defenders also fought like tigresses, hurling stones and boiling water from the attic until soldiers charged upstairs with drawn swords and fixed bayonets. The besiegers broke holes in the roof only to be shoved away by poles. But once they gained the upper hand they beat the defenders. In another barricaded house only one of the twelve defenders was male. To prevent any more reoccupations the police posted men inside half a dozen houses. By this time a diluted form of martial law had descended on Falcarragh, and lurid press reports of the sieges and arrests were attracting more 'foreign' observers including Maud and May Gonne and three Oxonians.[25]

THE OXONIAN INVASION

The leader of the Oxford contingent was the maverick and militant MP for Camborne in Cornwall, C. A. V. Conybeare, who had graduated from Christ Church before becoming a barrister. An ardent Home Ruler and critic of Balfour's regime he wanted to expose the harshness of these evictions. He soon ran into two young men from Balliol College – Godfrey R. Benson and his pupil, Henry Harrison. Born near Alresford, Hampshire in 1864 and educated at Winchester, Benson had taken a first class degree in classics that led to his appointment as a college lecturer in philosophy. Whether or not he ever studied under Professor Thomas Hill Green, the beloved godfather of the new liberalism, who died much too young in 1882, Benson must have been imbued with the principles of 'political obligation' and collectivism that inspired so many of his students and readers. Constructing an English variant of German idealism out of evangelical and secular components, Green rejected laissez-faire individualism in favour of voluntary action combined with state intervention to achieve the common good. And he infused pupils like Arnold Toynbee and A. C. Bradley with a mission to become useful citizens and address the profound inequities of capitalism.

Henry Harrison, whom we last encountered after his beating by a policeman in Tipperary, came from an affluent northern Irish family that boasted an Irish judge. Born in Holywood, County Down, in 1867, he moved with his mother to Mayfair, London following the death of his father in 1873. A talented athlete, he captained the cricket and football teams at Westminster School. Matriculating at Balliol in January 1887, he excelled at sports, was tutored by Green's devoted disciple and later memoirist, R. L. Nettleship, and became secretary of the Oxford Home Rule Club.[26] During the spring 'vac' of 1889 he and Benson embarked on a walking and reading tour of Donegal. Upon reaching Gweedore they heard about the evictions and headed straight for Falcarragh in search of some excitement and a just cause.

During a lengthy interview in Ballyconnell House on 16 April, Conybeare told Olphert rather disingenuously that he belonged to no party and wanted to hear both sides of the dispute. Olphert complained bitterly about the severe boycott that denied him even 'a particle of fuel' and made him 'the worst treated landlord in Ireland' despite his sixty years' residence. Incensed by the tenants' defiance, he threatened to clear out all the Plan tenants and destroy their abodes if they rejected his offer to reduce non-judicial rents by 25 per cent and judicial rents by 10 per cent. Their refusal would doom the last chance of an amicable settlement. Admitting that he had never witnessed an eviction, he blamed any suffering on the tenants.[27] Later Conybeare joined two Parnellite MPs in requesting an inspection of the battering ram stored in the police barracks. After being rebuffed by the chief police officer, they telegraphed Balfour reminding him of his pledge to allow an inspection of the 'engine constructed at the expense of English taxpayers'. Once again they were denied permission. In the words of the *Freeman's Journal*, 'It is not quite clear whether they [the police] are ashamed of the unpatented invention, or whether they imagined that some members of Parliament might blow it up or put it in their pockets.' Late at night Conybeare, Harrison, and Benson sneaked into the barracks to have a peek at the ram. Suddenly out of the darkness loomed burly Sergeant Kenny who ordered them to leave. Conybeare retorted that he wished to God all the police and soldiers were out of the country' because that would usher in 'good times'. Frustrated by this failure, they telegraphed Balfour protesting their treatment and reminding him of his pledge to allow this inspection. On 14 April, the three Oxonians wandered around Falcarragh urging evicted families to return home. At Bessie Ferry's cottage they gave the agent a pound in order to wipe out her five years' arrears and ensure readmission. Relying on his few words of Irish, Harrison conversed with some of the homeless tenants. That night fifty families returned to their dwellings expressing a preference for prison rather than sleeping rough or entering the workhouse.[28]

Infuriated by this defiance, Olphert demanded that the police, who had just left the village, return and drive out the trespassers. In the meantime Hewson appeared in Lifford court wearing a bandage over his scalp wound and seeking seventy more ejectment decrees scattered over six townlands. Instead of repeating the eviction process, however, the police posted two armed guards outside each reoccupied abode and threatened to arrest anyone who tried to leave or enter. To ease the hunger of the trapped tenants the three 'English' Samaritans, as they were called, bought loaves of bread, little cakes, tea, and sugar and wrapped them in small parcels to be slipped through doors before the police could pounce. When a constable asked what they were doing, Benson coolly replied that they were only feeding cats. Where the doors were strongly barricaded Harrison tied the bundles to a long string and lowered them down the chimney.

Shortly before midnight on 16 April Harrison approached Manus McGinley's house and asked the occupants to open the door. Losing patience he lifted it off the hinges in order to deposit a food packet inside. When Head Constable Mahony ordered him to cease and desist, he refused. Despite Conybeare's effort to impede him Mahony arrested Harrison, who allegedly refused to give his name, and hauled him off in handcuffs to the barracks, where he was denied visitors. Both Conybeare and Benson offered to share their friend's fate, but Mahony refrained from arresting the former because he was a man of 'social substance'. Charged with assisting the illegal return of evicted tenants, Harrison spurned bail and spent two nights in police custody before being transferred to Derry jail. In the meantime his two companions continued their mission of mercy around Drumnatinney.[29] On assignment in Gweedore Reigh sketched several eviction scenes. Using the ironic title, 'Triumph of Law and Order in Gweedore' (Plate 32), he depicted a police sergeant collaring Harrison wearing a tweedy (and almost orange) Ulster overcoat in the act of handing a loaf of bread to a mother with her infant. Opposite Harrison's cameo portrait in the upper left corner a woman with two babies has been arrested during the 'Midnight Police Raid'. Below this image appears the ram, labelled 'Balfour's Modest Maiden'; in the lower left hand corner the evictors have just torched a cottage ('Police Arson').[30]

On the morning of Harrison's transfer to Derry jail Conybeare exhorted the large crowd to cheer for his friend and the Plan of Campaign. The noise of the bystanders so upset the horse pulling the police cart with Harrison on board that it refused to budge. Angry and embarrassed by the crowd's jeers and laughter, Mahony summoned another horse and cart and then ordered his men to 'get your batons and knock the devil out of them'. The police obeyed by beating and shoving Conybeare, one old man, several priests and Irish MPs, and a *Daily News* reporter. According to the *Freeman's Journal*, the RIC acted with 'relentless savagery'.[31] For another day Conybeare and Benson distributed their packets to the 'starving' tenants. At one point the Cornishman wheeled around and called the policeman shadowing him 'Balfour's booby'. Outside one evicted house he exclaimed: 'This is some of Balfour's hellish work.' These remarks were duly recorded by the constable and used against him at his trial. Soon both men were arrested and charged with obstruction, inciting illegal reentry, and promoting the Plan.

Around 3 a.m. on 17 April the reinforced police and bailiffs launched a surprise attack on the reoccupied houses. Wielding sledgehammers and hatchets, they broke down doors and arrested the occupants. Among the victims were the crippled widow Coyle who was carried out in a chair and placed on the roadside, a 90-year old man, and a woman with twin babies. In an unusual move policemen were ordered to occupy some of the empty houses, one of which they used as a barracks. Awakened by news of this attack, Conybeare arose and rushed to the lodging house where Deputy Divisional Magistrate David Cameron was staying. Brushing aside the landlady, he knocked on the door and then burst into the officer's bedroom fulminating against the police attack. He demanded that Harrison be treated like an 'English gentleman' and granted bail or a solicitor. Equally incensed Cameron jumped out of bed shouting: 'Get out or I'll arrest you. By God, if I had my clothes on I'd arrest you.' Conybeare thanked him sarcastically for his 'gentlemanly and magisterial demeanour' and withdrew. He then led one poor constable on an exhausting foot race around the village.[32]

Conybeare visited Harrison in Derry jail before the latter left for Falcarragh coercion court on 22 April along with eight handcuffed tenants, who had been jailed for resisting eviction. Clad in a brown serge suit and plus fours, the young Oxonian shivered from the cold during the ride from Letterkenny through the mountains. Conybeare was also charged with participating in a 'criminal conspiracy' and inciting evicted tenants to repossess their holdings, and he handled his own defence. Edmund Leamy MP defended Harrison, whom the magistrates released without bail. Although named a co-conspirator, Benson was not indicted and prosecuted for reasons unknown. As soon as the trial ended, he was advised to return to Oxford before the authorities changed their minds.

During the trial Conybeare provoked the magistrates with verbal parries and thrusts. Denying any involvement in the Plan, he mocked the police for hindering the mission of mercy and grilled Olphert relentlessly about his eviction campaign. The prosecution witness, Sergeant Kenny, accused him of having shouted 'To Hell with Balfour' and cheering for the Plan. When Conybeare called Kenny a spy, the magistrate rebuked him for using such an offensive word. And the defendant retorted: 'I have not the slightest desire to wound the tender susceptibilities of the police force, but spy has only one syllable and detective has three, and I used the shorter term to save time. (Laughter.)' Denouncing the trial as a 'miserable parody of Continental tyranny', Leamy praised the compassion of Harrison who had been charged with 'an illegal conspiracy' for handing out bread to starving people. In his opinion Sergeant Kenny was 'a lynx-eyed omniscient sergeant' who invented conspiracies whenever he saw Englishmen talking to local 'ladies'. The *Derry Journal* (22 April) extolled Harrison as an altruistic 'English gentleman' whose 'generosity and humanity' had now transformed him into 'a manacled culprit'.

After six days of testimony and more protests from Conybeare and Leamy about the miscarriage of justice, Harrison was acquitted on 3 May along with the tenant resisters. However, Conybeare was not so fortunate. Convicted of promoting a criminal conspiracy, he was sentenced to three months' hard labour. Before leaving town he urged a throng of supporters to cheer for the Plan, and the Parnellite MPs present sang 'God Save Ireland'.[33] Both the trial and the ongoing evictions drew more Liberals from Lancashire and Edinburgh. Because Cameron denied their request to see the ram, they toured the eviction sites instead dogged by the police. But on 19 April some Mancunians and reporters were finally allowed to inspect but not photograph the ram as well as the scaling ladders, iron shields, pickaxes, and metal netting stored in the barracks. British Home Rulers donated £50 to relieve the homeless. In the wake of the trial both Conybeare and Harrison received numerous invitations to address Home Rule rallies in England; and the Cornishman had a heated exchange with T. W. Russell in the press over the origins of their Olphert dispute.[34]

By 1 May, seventy more families had been forced out and further ejectments were pending. Father McFadden dismissed rumours of a settlement declaring that Olphert would never yield. In a public letter (9 April), the landlord's daughter who lived in England painted an idyllic picture of the tenants (presumably the Protestant ones) who had seemed content and well-fed during her recent visit. Denying the presence of distress, she insisted that her father had always treated them kindly. Now, however, they lived in fear of their Plan neighbours. She dismissed the tenants' plea of poverty as an excuse to join the Plan. In the meantime the Duke of Abercorn, chairman of the Donegal Central Committee of the Olphert Defence Fund, urged Ulster loyalists to donate money to save this proprietor from a 'monstrous and cruel conspiracy'. A cheque for £1,500 from English sympathisers may have alleviated Olphert's financial woes but did nothing to settle the dispute.[35]

The third wave of evictions began on Friday 24 May, when 250 police and soldiers under Cameron's command set out to clear the Glasserchoo estate. A tight police cordon prevented Irish MPs, priests, reporters, and the Liberal delegates from approaching each dwelling. But Balfour's private secretary, Hugh Fisher MP, was allowed to pass through the armed ranks. At several sites women and girls led the resistance with stones, bottles, and hot liquid. Bryan McFadden's female garrison pelted the enemy with missiles until an emergency man climbed through a hole in the roof and started throwing stones, supplied by a comrade on the ground, at the resisters downstairs. Father McFadden, who was standing inside the cordon, cried out: 'this is murder'. On the first day a dozen families lost their homes and the police made thirteen arrests.

On Monday 27 May, the sheriff arrived at the sturdy two-storey house of James McGinley, aged 70, who had paid no rent for two years. In vain Cameron had urged him to accept Olphert's terms; but McGinley refused to abandon either his protest or the Plan and vowed to fight to the death with the help of his son and nephew. On the appointed day Cameron rode up to the house and ordered reporters to stand outside the cordon. From an upstairs window the old man shouted at the sheriff that Olphert had fixed the rent 'by fraud behind my back' making him ineligible for any rent reduction in the Land Court for

fifteen years. He also called Hewson the son of a landgrabber. McCay supervised the siege while members of the Olphert family stood watching on a
nearby hill. Streams of hot liquid and volleys of stones forced the emergency
men back at which point District Inspector Heard ordered his constables to
advance. This bold officer then mounted a ladder and broke through the slate
roof with a sledgehammer helped by a muscular emergency man. The defenders'
long poles pushed the police off their ladders with painful effects, and one
officer lost his sword in the struggle. Finally, superior force prevailed. A defender
sustained a sword-cut on his cheek and an emergency man gashed McGinley's
head with a hatchet. The three blood-smeared defenders were beaten and
dragged out. At another barricaded house five Irish-speaking men and women
fought fiercely until overpowered, arrested, and handcuffed. A number of
besiegers also received cuts and bruises. Later five women were convicted of
obstruction and sent to prison for up to a month.[36]

A photograph taken near Derrybeg shows an evicted family of eight posing
outside their sod-and-thatch roofed cottage (Plate 33). The belongings tossed
into the yard include a large dresser, a butter churn, a wicker basket, two spades,
and a few plates and dishes. A long table lies on its side against the wall. To
prevent re-entry two boards have been nailed to the doorframe.[37]

In a biting cartoon O'Hea used the Tories' recent electoral defeat at Rochester
to convey the horrors of the Falcarragh evictions. In 'A Set Off Against Rochester',
a sadistic policeman and an emergency man strut out of a ruined cottage holding
two doll-like infants aloft in triumph (Plate 34). The thuggish faces, sharp tools,
and bayonets of the evictors accentuate the inhumanity of this operation.
According to the caption, 'To compensate for the loss of Rochester the Tories
determined to do something notable – and they do – They send an army of
Balfour's Braves to besiege a Cabin at Falcarragh, which, after a general assault,
they capture and take the garrison, consisting of two, into custody – the said
two being of the respective ages of 6 and 8 months.'[38]

THE DONEGAL DEBATES

After his release from jail Conybeare returned to Westminster where he
recounted his harrowing experiences in Donegal and Derry prison. He accused
the RIC of harassing visitors to Falcarragh, smashing tenants' belongings, and
committing 'atrocious assaults on women and children'. In reply Balfour
applauded the brave enforcers of law and order in 'a country practically in a
state of revolution' and defended the MP's arrest. Continuing evictions and arrests
around Gweedore provoked more acrimony in the House as Irish and British
Home Rulers accused the government of using the police and magistracy to prop
up landlordism at the expense of destitute tenants.[39]

During a debate in the House of Lords on 15 July the Duke of Argyll dispar-
aged the peasants of Donegal for obeying the criminal orders of the Land League.
He described Olphert as a 'quiet country gentleman' and called the struggle
there typical of 'the whole agrarian history and condition of Ireland'. Blaming
the woeful condition of the peasantry on 'native Irish habits' rather than British
misrule, he rebuked McFadden and Stephens for promoting the Plan and
upheld the right of landlords to evict tenants who refused to pay their rent.[40]
In the summer two of the 21 Falcarragh resisters died of typhus and typhoid
fever shortly after their release from jail. The *Cork Examiner* attributed their
demise to Balfourian coercion as well as unsanitary conditions and demanded
an end to the 'death-trap' of Derry prison.[41]

Before the Plan purge resumed in October the sheriff's party had to remove
eight impoverished families on the nearby estate of Benjamin Joule, a British
businessman from Manchester. The principal victim there was Bridget McGinley
whom the agent sought to expel even though she offered to pay all arrears and
costs. In fact, she had walked 22 miles to the agent's house back in October
with the money owed – all to no avail. Not only H. J. Massingham, the radical
representative of the *Star*, but also Cameron and the sheriff urged her reinstatement but the agent grew irate admitting that he wanted the holding and not
the money. When asked for Joule's address so they could send him a telegram, he
refused to comply and McCay reluctantly handed over possession.[42]

Returning to Ardsmore on 23 October, the eviction party laid siege to the
widow Coyle's (Coll's) barricaded house. Singing patriotic songs, four girls inside
threw stones while women in the crowd heckled the aggressive estate bailiff.
Several burly policemen dragged the old woman outside the police cordon.
Because they were kept well away from the house the reporters could only hear
piercing screams after the emergency men stormed the abode. Struck by a
crowbar, Bridget Conaghan bled profusely from a head wound that had to be
treated by an army surgeon. Two English visitors from Northampton were
incensed by this brutal attack as well as the refusal of the police to allow Father
Boyle to attend to her. Following arrest the four young defenders were released
pending their trial. Several evicted farmers complained of rent increases after
thay had improved their holdings. At John Doogan's farm his mother threw
one small stone before the bailiffs emptied the premises. Evidently, his rent had
almost doubled after spending £300 on an embankment to prevent flooding.
Four more evictions took place before the sheriff called it a day.

On the morrow Hewson observed the eviction of Daniel Magee and 19
relatives at Drumnatinney. Among the victims were twin babies who were
being turfed out for the third time. Keeping the mother inside the cordon, the
emergency men carried the twins outside in their cradles exposing them to the
frosty air. After a half-hour's separation their mother became so frantic that she

slapped a constable in the face.[43] Manus Ferry offered no resistance. At the cottage of Manus McGinley, who had been hit in the head by a bailiff's hatchet back in June and had just finished four-months' imprisonment, the frail health of his mother did not stop an emergency man from dragging her outside. After she fainted, a priest administered the last rites. But the authorities would not allow her 70-year-old husband to assist her. When Cameron learned that the doctor feared she might die from the strain, he arranged transportation to her son's house. As soon as sheriff McCay granted the old couple several days' respite to put their affairs in order, Hewson rebuked him for interfering in the rights of property.

Ten more evictions took place around Bedlam and Gortahork (Gortahorte) on 25 October bringing the total to almost thirty in less than a week. Apart from a few buckets of hot liquid mixed with red bog scrapings that stained Cameron's riding breeches there was little resistance. Conybeare's mother expressed her sympathy by sending £10 to the evicted tenants fund.[44] On the next day Ned Gallagher's female garrison threw some stones and hot water mixed with 'red bog ore' at the emergency men, who broke through the thatched roof and captured four girls. Among other victims of the crowbar gang were four adults and their 16 children as well as Charles Harkin aged 100 who was carried out and placed in a chair.

Hewson saved the worst for last. Determined to teach the remaining Plan tenants a lesson, he arranged an arson attack on the dwellings of four leading resisters around Drumnatinney including James McGinley and Dan Ferry. With due deliberation he waited until all the reporters and English visitors had left before setting out on Saturday night, 26 October, with his five-man 'paraffin brigade' to destroy these houses. In fact, he set fire to the thatch himself. Angry protests over this incendiarism had no effect. In the meantime the Plan leaders supervised the building of forty wooden cabins for the evicted tenants on land belonging to Father McFadden.[45]

A year later, on 6 November 1890, Balfour arrived at Gweedore on an inspection tour of the northwest with economic development in mind. To his credit he had been studying conditions in the congested districts in search of ways to alleviate the chronic distress and he had shunned police protection. Among his advisers was J. H. Tuke. Convinced that most local officials were utterly corrupt when it came to disbursing relief, he wanted to invest government as well as private funds in light or narrow-gauge railway construction through Mayo, Donegal, Galway, and Kerry on the assumption that this ambitious scheme would provide jobs and have a multiplier effect. Personally he was pleased to discover that none of the proposed railway lines crossed Plan of Campaign estates.

The timing of the chief secretary's visit could not have been worse because more evictions were pending around Falcarragh. After conferring briefly with

Olphert and Hewson in the Gweedore hotel, Balfour was accosted by MacNeill who upbraided him over the ram as well as the evictions and arrests. The latter asked if he planned to inspect the ram and some of the cottages it had demolished. With his usual sangfroid Balfour brushed aside these barbed questions, retired to his room, and left Gweedore early the next morning.

Three days later at a rousing rally in Derrybeg MacNeill accused Balfour of pretending to alleviate distress in Donegal through railway construction when he was helping to knock down houses with the ram. He described Balfour as arriving with a light railway scheme in one hand and a battering ram in the other, and instead of consulting Father McFadden he had 'slunk away like a thief in the night'.[46]

A whimsical cartoon by Reigh commemorated Balfour's presumed relief mission. In 'Light Railway Disaster at Gweedore' (Plate 35), the mighty ram derails a small locomotive driven by an alarmed Balfour who is about to be ejected. The coal tender behind the chief secretary contains canvas bags stuffed with such supposedly conciliatory offerings as 'Fraudulent Promises' and 'Bunkum Hypocrisy'.[47]

On the eve of the final Plan purge in November the Irish Catholic hierarchy issued a joint pastoral letter denouncing the eviction of tenants who had lost their potato crop and could not possibly pay the rent. In vain local priests backed by Patrick O'Donnell, Bishop of Raphoe, urged Olphert to accept arbitration and avoid evicting 250 families. But the latter demanded that the tenants pay some arrears as well as legal costs and renounce the Plan before any settlement could occur. Of course, McFadden and his fellow priests scorned these conditions.[48]

The last wave of Plan evictions began on 11 November 1890 after gale force winds and rain had pelted the district. Under the command of the sub-sheriff and Captain Slacke of the RIC the crowbar brigade and its escort of 300 police and soldiers arrived at remote Ardsbeg on the rocky coast below Errigal Mountain. They set up a double cordon around Neal Ferry's premises and allowed only MPs, priests, and the English Liberal delegates to stand between the two rings. Once again the battering ram remained back in Falcarragh barracks. Among the English observers were Sir John Swinburne, Bart MP for Staffordshire, several English ladies, and the Gonne sisters who had trudged over hill and dale to reach the site. The cruelty of this operation stunned them all. Most of the tenants carried their pitiful belongings outside to prevent damage. At the old widow Herraghty's cabin her daughter-in-law lay sick in bed cradling a newborn baby. In vain her husband Hugh appealed for help from the priest, crying 'soggarth' repeatedly. But the police kept the priest well away; and a surgeon certified that she was fit for removal. Obeying a county inspector's order to 'turn him out, turn him out', the police drove the three adults and eight young children into the rain. Swinburne was so upset by this scene that he declared that if he had perpetrated one-tenth of this 'cruelty' on his Staffordshire tenants, they would have strung him up at his own door and 'the country would have said, "Serve him right"'.[49]

On the next day Bishop O'Donnell, accompanied by seven priests, arrived in Falcarragh and consulted the agent while the evictions were in progress. He watched in despair as fifteen more families were removed from their hovels. Maud and May Gonne returned to the scene along with three Home Rule MPs including Swift MacNeill. The reverential crowd knelt down in the mud to receive the bishop's blessing. Among the evicted were 'babies in arms, octogenarians, the feeble, the halt, and even the blind' as well as a woman named Olphert. By far the oldest victim was Darby Curran, aged 105, who had been expelled back in June and had found refuge with a friend. His delirious condition and a doctor's certificate enabled him to return as a caretaker. Foul weather prevented the sheriff from completing this round of evictions. When Swift MacNeill tried to break through the police cordon, a constable pushed him away. The angry MP took a piece of chalk from his pocket and marked the policeman's coat so that he could identify him later and he vowed to mark the uniform of every other constable who treated him roughly. For this 'offence' he was charged with assault.[50]

The evictions dragged on for eight more days. Bridget McGinley's defenders threw stones at the police who hurled them back with a vigour unbecoming officers of the law. Despite volleys of stones some constables climbed up a ladder, broke through the slate roof, and subdued the defenders. Two days later, emergency men beat and kicked Owen Doogan, aged 90, who refused to leave; and his enraged daughter broke an earthenware basin over the head of an assailant. After Doogan stumbled out on two sticks singing 'a mournful croon like a funeral dirge', he was arrested along with his daughter and taken to Derry jail, where both were charged with obstruction and assault, and then released on remand. After completing their destructive work, the 'exterminators' marched back to camp singing 'Glory, glory alleluia'.[51]

In 'The Triumph of "Law and Order" at Falcarragh' (Plate 36), Reigh produced another graphic narrative of eviction. In each corner appear miniatures of Swift MacNeill, James Dalton, Norma Borthwick 'an English sympathiser', and Maud Gonne 'an Irish sympathiser' all of whom supported the Plan. Around the central portrait of the moderate Home Rule Bishop Patrick O'Donnell appear images of the siege of Bridget McGinley's two-storey house, the arrest of two boyish defenders, and the eviction of the young Mrs Hegarty (or Herraghty) with her newborn baby. At the bottom the crowd kneels in the mud to receive the bishop's blessing. Indulging in some artistic licence, Reigh placed a ram in the rear of this print.

By the end of December 1890, almost four hundred families or over two thousand individuals had lost their homes around Falcarragh and Ardsmore since 1888. Only around 50 families had been readmitted as caretakers. The *Freeman* reckoned that another 130 'firesides remain to be extinguished'. According to one estimate this purge cost taxpayers £15,847. Like Marcus Keane, Olphert challenged these figures insisting that only 166 persons had been evicted while an additional 146 faced the same fate.[52] Hardly any Plan tenants remained by the end of 1890 and most of the evicted families were living in small wooden huts. Not until the early 1900s did most of them return home.

MAUD GONNE

On 9 November 1890, Maud Gonne made her official debut on a political platform by addressing several thousand enthusiastic listeners at a Plan rally in Falcarragh. Frustrated by the exclusion of women from every nationalist society including the National League, growing tired of polite literary salons in Dublin, and hungering for adventure, she took Tim Harrington's advice and embarked on a riding expedition through Donegal with her cousin May to witness evictions. Describing herself as both a sister and an Irishwoman, this rebellious daughter of an English army officer stationed at the Curragh in the wake of the Fenian uprising announced that she was prepared to risk imprisonment in the fight against landlordism. After railing against the 'doubly cruel law of eviction', she urged her rapt audience to defend their birthright because such basic necessities as food and clothing took precedence over rent. Her political inexperience belied her natural talent for audacity and publicity. 'Balfour's vile coercion government and Olphert's atrocious deeds', she stated, must not be allowed to remain cloaked in secrecy. The more resistance to eviction the better 'so that our friends from England will have time to come and see with their own eyes what coercion government in Ireland means.'

The Falcarragh evictions accelerated her evolution from a keen Home Ruler to a radical republican filled with fantasies of shooting landlords, agents, and bailiffs. To reach Gweedore she endured a chilly ride with her Great Dane from Letterkenny to Dunfanaghy where Father Peter Kelly, a Fenian sympathiser, greeted her with a hot rum toddy to relieve her chill. When she asked about the usefulness of resistance, Kelly told her that it had to be well organised and backed to the hilt by the tenants' leaders. 'Stones and boiling water', he added, 'are no match for guns'. Brushing off several lusty suitors, she met Father McFadden who impressed her as the best kind of 'fighting priest' because his peasant background made him care more about the land question and the well-being of his parishioners than Home Rule. When Father Stephens took her to a petty sessions trial of six 'mountainy' tenants accused of stealing some of Olphert's turf, she discovered that the presiding magistrate was Olphert himself and the chief witness was 'the foxy agent' Hewson. Needless to say, all the defendants were found guilty.

At one eviction site she watched the bailiffs carry out an old woman on a mattress clutching her rosary and a statuette of the Virgin Mary. Later she saw a young mother with her day-old infant driven out into the rain. Father Stephens paid for this family to spend the night in a local hotel. Filled with fury after observing six evictions, she admitted later to wishing that the bailiff would die 'since he was an essential cog in the British war machine'. Her pacifist views did not prevent her from wanting to see men like Olphert, Balfour, and Lord Salisbury die because in time of war it made more sense 'to kill generals than private soldiers… and the first principle of war is to kill the enemy'. [53]

Not even the grave illness of her infant son in Paris and her own pulmonary problems stopped her from returning to Gweedore in July 1891 against her doctor's advice and helping some evicted tenants to re-enter their old homes illegally. Her ardent suitor Yeats could never come close to matching either her audacity or her republican separatist leanings. When Olphert pressed Castle officials to issue a warrant for her arrest, both Patrick O'Brien MP and Father McFadden urged her to leave the country immediately. Aware that her frail constitution could not endure the rigours of prison, she headed north to Larne and then sailed to France.[54]

In 1891 over a hundred Olphert tenants paid three years' arrears and legal costs as the Plan withered away. The imminent death of the old landlord did not prevent a dozen 'squatter families' from being expelled. Eventually the syndicate returned the property to the son and heir and the evicted tenants received some relief from English sympathisers. However, the damage had been done and rancour over the Plan doomed any chance of reconciliation.[55]

Whether or not Conybeare's experiences in Derry jail curbed his appetite for defying the law, he resumed his parliamentary duties in 1890, backed Keir Hardie, married a Theist, embraced women's suffrage, and failed to hold his seat at the election of 1895. On the other hand both Harrison and Benson went on to enjoy distinguished careers in journalism and politics respectively.

Legend has it that Harrison felled three constables with his fists while resisting arrest at a Plan rally in Tipperary. Whatever the truth of this tale there can be no doubt that he suffered a serious head wound from a baton in Tipperary town on 25 September 1890. Nevertheless the story of his pugilistic prowess gained momentum and earned him enduring fame in Irish eyes.[56] His uncontested election as the Parnellite MP for Mid-Tipperary in 1890 did not result in a long tenure, however. Unwavering loyalty to Parnell cost him his seat in 1892 and he lost two subsequent elections. This keeper of the Parnell flame defended 'the Chief's' reputation against all the slings and arrows of the anti-

Parnellite majority. After working as a banker in London, he enlisted in the Royal Irish Regiment in 1915 and won the Military Cross for bravery on the Western Front. Returning to London, he devoted his journalistic skills to supporting the Free State government during the 1920s and then the de Valera regime. His best-known book, *Parnell Vindicated: The Lifting of the Veil* (1931), argued that Captain William O'Shea actively connived in his wife's liaison with Parnell for political and financial gain. Most of his newspaper articles and books dealt with Irish politics and British imperial affairs. By contrast the affluent and well-connected Benson pursued a successful career in politics and public service. After a stint at Westminster as the Liberal MP for Woodstock (1892–5), he became a political and charitable activist earning a peerage as Baron Charnwood in 1911.

A Limerick man, Michael McDonagh, evoked the land war around Falcarragh in a gloomy poem, 'A Voice From Gweedore', that reverberated with wails of 'dire distress' arising from the 'evil, tyranny and malice' lurking there. Paying tribute to those martyred 'noble priests' Fathers McFadden and Stephens, who had been hunted down and imprisoned for delivering their flock from evil and for upholding Christian laws, the poet dwelled on the 'dark, heart-rending tales' of a 'savage landlord' and a brutish Balfour who used a 'battering ram and vile police and soldiers' to terrorize the weak, the young, and the aged. Although 'brutal, base, and bad' laws had sent too many 'worthy sons and daughters' to jail, the anguished cries of the Donegal peasantry would soon be heard and 'dark vengeance' would fall 'on tyrants' heads'. [57]

What McDonagh tried to convey in verse, O'Hea strove to capture in a compelling cartoon, 'What Our English Visitors Saw' (Plate 37). In a scenario that might have come straight out of Falcarragh, a 'Countryman' is serving as a guide for some English visitors keen to see the scars of the land war. Pointing to a row of demolished stone cottages, he explains that hundreds of people used to lived thereabouts until the government 'sent down the sojers and pollis with battering-rams and petroleum – and look at the place now. Shure there isn't a house standin' for miles about except the polis-barracks up there.'

TEN

'PLUS ÇA CHANGE'
1890–1900

'I shall have to knock down some houses
when I carry out the next batch of evictions but I don't
like to do it just yet, it would cause a commotion.'

MAURICE F. HUSSEY
agent to Lord Dillon, 3 Jan. 1898.

'Nothing good comes of turning the decent people out.'

ELIZABETH BOWEN
Bowen's Court (1965), p. 88.

———

The bitter feud that tore asunder Parnell's party over his liaison with Mrs O'Shea sounded the death-knell of the Plan of Campaign and splintered the National League. Thousands of evicted tenants were directly affected by the quarrel over the Paris Funds that amounted to over £40,000 lodged in a Parisian bank, of which Parnell was one trustee. This sum was the residue of his successful money-raising tour of North America at the outset of 1880 aimed at financing the Land League and the Irish parliamentary party. By the end of 1890 his enemies were insisting that this money should be spent on the evicted tenants on Plan estates. But Parnell strongly objected because his loyalties lay with the 'wounded soldiers' of the first land war rather than the casualties of the Plan that he had scorned. After their release from Galway jail, Dillon and O'Brien demanded that the beneficiaries of this money should be the most recent victims of eviction. During the party summit negotiations at Boulogne early in 1891 Parnell managed to procure £8,000 for the homeless Land Leaguers. But that marked the end of his withdrawals. Once Tim Healy had stooped low enough to accuse his former chief of embezzling this money in an article entitled, 'Stop, Thief' (*Weekly National Press*, 11 June 1891), the feuding only intensified.[1]

As Frank Callanan has made clear, the Plan of Campaign became a huge bone of contention on which the adversaries gnawed vigorously. During 1891 Parnell denounced 'the tragic farce' of New Tipperary and accused Dillon and

O'Brien of having launched the Plan simply to appease the British Liberal Party. He also held them responsible for providing relief to every tenant evicted under the Plan's auspices.[2] Through 'virulent' editorials and articles in the *Weekly National Press*, the anti-Parnellites heaped abuse on Parnell accusing him not only of adultery but also of betraying the Home Rule cause and abandoning the evicted tenants who had sacrificed their homes after 1886. In his biting cartoon, 'A Startling Contrast' (*Weekly National Press*, 18 July 1891), Thomas Fitzpatrick pilloried Parnell as a selfish sinner. Here the jaunty Parnell has left Ireland with a padlocked bag containing the Paris Fund. Wearing a boater and smoking a cigar, he waves a cynical goodbye to a well-dressed evicted tenant farmer and his family outside their ruined cottage as he heads for the comforts of married life at Eltham with the buxom Mrs O'Shea seated in a fancy brougham on the left. To heighten the stark contrast between the haves and the have-nots the artist inserted a battering ram next to the razed cabin in the upper right hand corner.[3]

For several years nationalist newspapers were filled with polemical articles and letters about the Boulogne negotiations and the Paris funds. Dillon's two top priorities were party unity and the evicted tenants, and he knew that all the wrangling over this money was harming both causes. Not until the summer of 1894 did a Parisian court finally decide to entrust the funds to Justin McCarthy who distributed them among the homeless Plan tenants. Following their arrest in London and imprisonment in February 1891, Dillon and O'Brien called for the reinstatement of over a thousand tenants evicted on Plan estates. While denouncing John Redmond and his fellow Parnellites, they raised funds for the Plan victims and demanded a bold land purchase act that would enable the Estates Commissioners to acquire land compulsorily for distribution among the homeless tenants. County associations donated thousands of pounds to relieve their hardships but maintenance costs drained the party's assets. In 1891 alone these payments amounted to £45,220. According to Dillon £234,000 had been raised for this purpose between November 1886 and December 1893 with Irish donors providing £129,000 while £62,000 came from America and Australia. In addition, the 'war chests' on each Plan estate allegedly held £42,000. O'Brien's wealthy American wife donated £500 to this cause. Other contributions included £83,000 from the Tenants Defence League, £18,000 from the National Fund, and £29,000 from the Paris funds.[4]

A Dublin Castle survey in 1892 contended that most of this money was being spent on evicted families on the Test estates with Olphert coming first (365 families), followed by Clanricarde (169), Ponsonby (114), Brooke (64), O'Kelly (45), Lansdowne (43), Massereene (39), Tottenham (17), and O'Grady (13). By the summer of 1896 many of Smith-Barry's evicted tenants in Tipperary had been reinstated. Of the 783 unlet evicted farms in seven western counties in November 1895, 419 were derelict, 39 had been retaken by either old or new tenants, and 27 were 'temporarily' relet to evicted tenants. By this time 28 per cent of the 626 tenants evicted on six Plan estates had been reinstated. But 99 of the 105 new tenants planted on four of them remained firmly in place.[5]

In the meantime many landlords struggled with contumacious tenants and declining rental income, often resorting to seizures of chattels for non-payment. In his notebook for 1891 the agent of Lord Rathdonnell (who owned 13,265 acres in seven different counties) kept tabs on tenants some of whom had bought their holdings under the Ashbourne Act. Grading them from 'poor, miserable, and troublesome' to 'decent and respectable', he naturally focused on those who had fallen behind with the rent or deserved to be ejected for non-payment if not League activity. Because Margaret McMann was 'constantly at law' with her neighbours in Mullinavannog, County Monaghan, her eviction would bring 'general blessings'. The widow Sarah McCann of Mullinderg, also of County Monaghan, had taken 'forcible possession' of her house following her eviction in the 1880s. After the premises were torn down to prevent re-entry, the local League branch built her 'a large Sentry Box'-like abode that she moved around her holding to foil the agent. When the Board of Guardians ordered its removal, she had it transported to the cemetery. The authorities demolished this structure and the League installed her in a sod and board hut that was razed while she was in prison. Refusing Lord Rathdonnell's offer of £20 to leave, she 'haunted the place' with the help of friends and the League. After her death in 1890, no neighbour dared to use her coveted land for fear of League retribution. Maria Bell of Knocknastaken, County Fermanagh, was 'a very poor decent respectable old widow' whom the agent provided with a pair of shoes to prevent her from going barefoot. Francis Hamilton had bought his 42-acre holding for £390 in 1889. He was a 'cross cantankerous man' who blocked his neighbour's access to the bog on his land. Last but not least, there was Patrick McGuiggan of Coyagh, County Tyrone, who farmed his widowed mother's land. A 'coarse ill-conditioned man', he was 'the chief of the land league and has been the chief instrument in giving annoyance' to two tenants who had taken over an ejected farm. The time had come to warn Patrick that if he failed to pay the overdue rent, then the land would be cleared and the house dismantled.

On the other hand the new agent on the Cosby estate in Queen's County reported that rents and arrears received fell from £6,443 in 1893 to £6,074 between 1893 and 1894 and then rebounded to £6,494 in 1897. Despite arrears of almost £200 in 1892, two tenants on the Downshire estate in Wicklow managed to avoid eviction and were still there in 1902 paying judicial rents and owing only £35 in arrears. On the Clonbrock estate in Galway, however, arrears averaged £4,433 on a rental of £10,900 in 1890–4; and in the early 1900s the annual deficit came close to £1,500.[6]

William O'Brien's appeals for funds to help 'the wounded soldiers' of the Plan drew huge audiences. Speaking at Castlebar in 1893, he asserted that 25,000 farmers had recently been 'stripped' of the interest in their farms and now faced eviction. And at Youghal in June 1894, he urged support for the 900 people living in League huts. Irishmen, he declared, would never allow the veterans of the land war to be 'butchered to make a holiday for Mr Smith-Barry's syndicate, to see them as a piece of mere barbarous vengeance, offered up as victims on the unholy altar of Irish landlordism'. Equally active in fundraising, Dillon had some very good news for his supporters: the landlords, those hereditary enemies of 'our race', were doomed to perish. Unfortunately, Clongorey came back into the news in 1892 when ten families were driven out of the wooden huts built for them after the notorious arson attack in March 1889. Deeply concerned about the plight of the evicted tenants, Davitt boasted that 'the Irish race' at home and abroad had donated the staggering sum of £1,200,000 to advance the cause of Irish freedom since 1879, of which £300,000 had gone to their relief. In the meantime the provincial press encouraged readers to give by publishing the names of even the smallest contributors.[7]

Embers of the Plan continued to glow on a dozen estates after January 1891 when Shaw-Lefevre's motion for government arbitration to end these disputes was soundly defeated in Parliament. A Castle estimate in May 1892 put the total cost of the Plan at £194,000 with over £13,000 remaining in the 'war chests' on fourteen Plan estates. But these figures were rough estimates based on the monthly reports of the Special Crimes Branch of the RIC.[8] In the first three months of 1892, county courts approved 320 notices to quit as landlords pressed their tenants to pay rent and arrears. So long as the Parnellite party feud continued, evicted tenants had good reason to worry about their future despite the return of Gladstone to power in August 1892 that raised their hopes for reinstatement.

THE EVICTED TENANTS QUESTION

For more than two decades the evicted tenants question pervaded the discourses of nationalist politicians who worried about how much money and legislation would be required to resolve this problem. A major impediment to success, of course, was the need for land on which to settle the dispossessed with or without compulsory purchase orders. In the early 1890s the government offered little or no relief to evicted families. Section 13 of the Land Purchase Act of 1891 had promised reinstatement for tenants evicted since 1879 provided that the landlord wished to sell the holding to the former occupier. But this provision became a dead letter and Balfour's unpopular measure failed to revive the flagging land market. On the other hand the act did create the valuable Congested Districts

Board that went far to improve the lives of countless impoverished occupiers of uneconomic holdings in the west who were known as 'congests'.[9]

In the autumn of 1892, the three-man Evicted Tenants Commission, chaired by Dillon's father-in-law, Sir James Mathew, gathered evidence about tenants who had lost their farms during the land wars. However, the Irish Landowners' Convention accused the commissioners of bias and refused to participate. The commission's report (25 February 1893) stressed the social and economic losses arising from vacant farms and idle farmers and expressed regret over all the pain caused by the Plan. Pointing out that settlements had been achieved on 99 out of the original 116 Plan estates and that the cost of eviction had far exceeded the rents due, the tribunal recommended that the Land Commission be empowered to resolve any lingering disputes. If the owner refused to settle, then the Land Commissioners should negotiate reinstatement with or without purchase. Any new occupier of an evicted holding, moreover, would be compensated for his removal.[10]

P. A. McHugh's abortive bill to reinstate Plan tenants by compulsion also relied on section 13 of the Land Purchase Act of 1891. As he explained, new tenants were occupying 1,533 of the 3,676 evicted farms while 1,442 were in the hands of landlords or the Land Corporation and the remainder were derelict. His bill would have forced landlords to settle with their former tenants. Determined to defeat this measure, Smith-Barry condemned any attempt to compel landlords to take back tenants who had withheld rent and thereby invited their eviction. He would refuse to give up any farms that were now in his own hands. Other landlords attacked the principle of abolishing the cherished right of eviction for non-payment that was for them the very foundation of landlord and tenant relations.[11]

Morley's Evicted Tenants bill of 1894 raised many of the same hackles among landowners and landgrabbers, but at least it survived the Commons before being defeated on 14 August. A rash of evictions on the Aran Islands did not endear the chief secretary to the nationalist camp, however. In fact, *United Ireland* accused him of protecting landgrabbers by banning protest meetings within a mile of their farms. In February 1896, J. J. Clancy launched a third attempt to deal with reinstatement; but once again the landlord lobby blocked the compulsory purchase clauses and railed against preferential treatment for ex-tenants who had caused so much trouble. In addition there was the vexing problem of what to do with those industrious farmers who had taken over and improved evicted holdings and who refused to surrender them despite all their harassment. They had invested too much money and labour to walk away from their farms even with compensation.

Ejectments continued to decline – from 1,880 in 1896–8 to 1,211 in 1899–1901 and then down to a mere 165 in 1907. In February 1896 Gerald Balfour, the new chief secretary, boasted that 'actual' evictions had dropped from 5,201 in

1882 to only 671 in 1895, while the number of reinstated tenants on Plan estates had risen from 429 in 1893 to 732. On the other hand at least a third of the 1,400 tenants evicted on the major Plan estates remained homeless in 1895 and not until 1907 did the government address this festering grievance by means of the Evicted Tenants Act.[12]

Throughout the 1890s the Irish Landowners Convention kept pressing for government money to compensate all the proprietors who had lost income through the fair rent clauses of the Land Act of 1881. They accused the land courts and assistant commissioners of having deprived them of almost one quarter of their gross rental incomes and half of their net rents. Equally futile were their pleas for state help in dealing with the interest payments on their heavy incumbrances. Hoping to revive the land market, the Balfour brothers cooked up the anaemic Land Purchase Bill of 1896 that vexed right-wing Unionists and appealed only to strong farmers keen to buy their holdings at an acceptable price.[13]

Before becoming eligible to buy his farm the evicted tenant had to be reinstated by paying a portion of the rent and arrears due. But the real stumbling block to readmission was the lack of compulsory purchase because so many landlords refused to part with their lands voluntarily except for high prices. Nevertheless, some evicted tenants did accept the terms offered by their landlords or an arbitrator. Thus by 1894, 221 of Olphert's 323 evicted tenants had made purchase agreements; and the numbers on the Clanricarde and Smith-Barry properties were 70 and 62 respectively. Here and there litigation over the huts built for the evicted tenants caused friction and cost money. As we will see in the next chapter, the refusal by many landowners to sell their tenanted land as well as strong resentment of the cattle ranching system in the west provoked serious unrest in parts of Munster and Connacht after 1900.

In the meantime agents of the PDA and CDU worked hard to break up boycotting conspiracies against farmers who had taken over evicted holdings. In June 1891 a tenant punched Lord Ely's agent for having called him a 'rogue'; and in November 1892 the garrison at Tim Murphy's fortified house on Lord Egmont's estate at Kanturk held off the evictors with red-hot iron bars, spiked tree branches, and boiling water. After two hours the bailiffs broke into the house and forced their way from one barricaded room to another until they captured the defenders upstairs. Several bailiffs and police suffered burns. And on Lord Bantry's estate at Castletown-Berehaven the police had a hard time protecting the bailiffs from harm as they tried to serve 300 writs. Tenants threatened with distraint continued to hide their livestock and crops. When emergency men tried to distrain crops on an evicted farm near Errigal in September 1895, a large crowd gathered, shots were fired, and the harvesting operation ended abruptly.[14]

The forays of moonlighters nursing grievances or grudges as well as the strength of the IRB in both Clare and Galway, where nominal membership stood at 900 and 4,500 respectively, continued to perturb the police. Moreover, a relatively new association, the Herds' League, was growing bolder around Carron, Corofin, and Lisdoonvarna. Police inspectors considered this society 'very dangerous' because members had already mutilated a few cattle, plotted at least one murder, and committed other outrages in order to redress their grievances. In the East Riding of Galway, officials predicted that if Clanricarde's evicted tenants were not soon reinstated, the lives of the 'planters' and the agent Tener would be 'in great danger'. Loughrea remained a centre of political extremism with constant meetings of IRB activists. In the spring of 1892 a police pensioner, who had taken an evicted farm there, found that nocturnal marauders had broken the legs of forty ewes. At Listowel and Castleisland in Kerry, moonlighters forced two tenants to surrender their evicted holdings at gunpoint and left after firing several shots into the roof. A much worse fate befell James Donovan, a caretaker hired by the CDU on Lord Cork's estate near Newmarket in north Cork. In April 1894 two men armed with shotguns broke into his house after his police guard had left for the night. In front of his young son they beat him in bed, dragged him outside, renewed their assault, and then shot him. Despite his grave injuries he crawled back inside before expiring.[15]

In the spring of 1894 Mrs Nano O'Connor of Valentia Island, the litigious widow of a leading local nationalist, escaped eviction after neighbours rallied to her support. She was promptly reinstated as a caretaker. In County Armagh several prominent landlords including the Earl of Gosford and the Countess of Charlemont obtained almost fifty ejectment decrees at Markethill quarter sessions in April 1895.[16] Another sign of continuity was the shameless quest of George Brooke of Coolgreany for a baronetcy. He pestered several Irish peers with requests to plead his case for honours with Lord Salisbury on the grounds that he had fought so hard to defeat the Plan. As he informed Lord De Vesci in March 1897, his 'struggle with socialism' had cost him more than £25,000 and he fondly hoped that the lord lieutenant would persuade the prime minister to bestow a baronetcy that finally came his way in 1903.[17]

BODYKE REVISITED

Disputes over rent and tenure continued to agitate Colonel O'Callaghan's estate in Clare. The Special Crimes Branch reported a good deal of republican activity around Bodyke in 1892 when notices to quit were inspiring some young men to join the IRB and nominal membership stood at around 900 compared with 4,500 for Galway. Although most tenants were paying their rents reasonably well, the poorest ones faced distraint and ejectment. Several landgrabbers had received death threats, and moonlighters or IRB members fired the occasional volley at their enemies. In July 1892, hillside snipers opened fire at Sheriff Croker's party after repossessing a deserted cottage, but hit no one. The police shot a few rounds with equal futility. Trouble flared up again at the end of February 1893 when the agent Macadam along with the sheriff and some bailiffs seized the cattle of tenants who had refused to pay rent unless granted abatements of 25 to 30 per cent. When an angry 'mob' tried to free these animals from the Tulla pound, the police beat them with batons and rifle butts. Some tenants paid up on the next day to regain their livestock. The same scenario occurred on 10 April, when bailiffs rounded up Lyddy's sheep and took them to the pound. At Martin Molony's farm a belligerent crowd threw stones at the distrainers and the police fixed bayonets. A fusillade of shots between Plan snipers and the police injured no one. In September Macadam walked into petty sessions court to obtain more decrees with a revolver stuck in his belt. And in November ten ejectments took place, three of which resulted in readmission.[18]

Although the *Times* was fond of pronouncing the demise of the Plan, the troubles at Bodyke were far from over. Police patrols could not prevent boycotting; and in April 1894 shots were fired at the caretakers on Molony's farm. During the summer a dozen cattle died from arsenic poisoning on two evicted farms. At Ballinahinch printed notices signed 'Vengeance' warned locals not to buy any hay from one of O'Callaghan's sons. In January 1896 the agent narrowly survived an ambush while on his way to examine some poisoned cattle and he drove the shooters away with a few rounds from his repeating rifle.[19] The prospects for peace on this troubled estate seemed further away than ever.

ARAN ISLANDS/DIGBY

On 4–5 April 1894 evictions shook the Aran Islands, where the parish priest Father O'Donoghue had done much to stimulate the fishing industry by arranging subsidies from the Congested Districts Board. Acting on orders from the three absentee owners, the Digby ladies, who lived in or near Dublin, the agent Henry Robinson of Roundstone, uprooted two-dozen impoverished families on Inishmore and Inishmaan. Although the recent loss of half the potato crop meant that 'hunger was stamped on every face', these ladies had lost patience over all the unpaid rent. The evicted tenants included two widows with 18 children between them, a blind boy, and a woman of 84 with a broken leg. The *Irish Daily Independent*'s 'special commissioner' witnessed the 'atrocities' inflicted on these Irish-speaking peasants who subsisted on fishing and the meagre produce of fields that had been created by the arduous ferrying of soil from the mainland. He blamed these 'callous' expulsions on the government.

Even greater poverty prevailed around Killeany where a few tiny hovels contained two large families. And to make matters worse, the Poor Law Union official in charge of relief also held the job of bailiff.

Protected by fifty constables, Robinson refused to allow Michael Derrane's family to occupy the pigsty after being driven out of their home. Somehow the wife borrowed enough money to return as a caretaker. In vain Father McDonald CC protested the expulsion of blind Thomas McDonagh and his octogenarian parents. One defiant son had to be dragged out. Mrs McDonagh limped back to her house and kissed the door and windows before taking refuge in a son's house. The sight of a homeless mother caressing her baby so upset Father McDonald that he fainted and fell on some rocks injuring his arm. Several families with young children had to spend the night outside. Among the few allowed to re-enter were Mrs McDonagh, a widow, along with her seven wailing children and two families with sons dying from consumption. The bedridden Bartley Connolly was carried out on a pallet of hay and laid on the ground.

Five more dwellings were emptied on Inishmaan as a policeman photographed some of these painful scenes. All the publicity prompted questions in Parliament and gave rise to a relief fund. These evictions moved the editor of the *Connaught Telegraph* (5 May 1894) to ask how 'such horrors [could] be perpetrated in a Christian land' and denounce the 'heartless cruelty... unfeeling tyranny... selfishness and oppression' of 'rapacious landlordism' over the centuries. Only Home Rule would put an end to all the house-wrecking and misery.[20]

To publicise these evictions O'Hea's gifted successor, Thomas Fitzpatrick, produced 'Arran [*sic*] Isles – 1894' (Plate 38). In this bleak cartoon, the grim reaper attends a lifeless tenant sprawled on some rocks next to the dreaded ejectment decree. Opposite them a rack-renting and fiendish landlord is busy counting the coins in his hand with a can of paraffin oil and house-wrecking tools lying at his feet. In the background an evicted family gives vent to grief. J. D. Reigh also condemned these evictions in 'The Liberal Alliance in Arran [*sic*] Island' (*United Ireland*, 21 April 1894). Here the bailiff who doubles as the relieving officer holds a notice to quit and presides over the removal of a three-generation family. Trouble returned to the islands in 1904 after the potato crop failed once again. Mounting arrears moved the tenants to accept Father Farraher's advice and seek to buy their holdings. But the trustees demanded payment of some rent first. Faced with this impasse, Robinson resigned as the agent in July and the owners applied for 120 ejectment decrees to expel the unprofitable islanders whom the *Freeman's Journal* hailed as dignified and courteous Gaelic speakers.[21]

LOUGHGLYNN/DILLON

In 1894 rent disputes rumbled across Lord Dillon's estate in Roscommon where the landlord had already conceded the Plan's demands. Several ejectments around Loughglynn in late March caused a furore. On 1 April Willie Redmond reminded a raucous audience that Roscommon's brave voters had 'struck the great blow against landlordism' by defeating the O'Conor Don at the general election of 1880. Condemning these evictions, he added that party unity was essential to the defeat of landlord tyranny. After the rally some neighbours broke into two of the locked evicted houses and Redmond joined in the effort to reinstate the families and carry their furniture back inside.[22]

Evidently Lord Dillon had had his fill of conflict and irregular rent payments because he took his agent's advice and sold his Irish properties to the Congested Districts Board (CDB) in 1899–1900 for £290,000. This sale enabled him to pay off mortgages of £68,000, and the new owner-occupiers welcomed the advent of land annuities significantly lower than their judicial rents.[23]

CASTLEREA/DE FREYNE

Defying reports of the Plan's imminent collapse, many of the 1,700 tenants on the De Freyne estate continued to withhold rent and expressed their envy of Lord Dillon's nearby tenants, who were busy buying their farms on favourable terms. Resentment of 'the diehard' Lord De Freyne was rife around Castlerea where the bulk of the tenantry – like those in western Donegal – subsisted on smallholdings and a meagre diet by means of seasonal work in Britain. Disputes over cattle ranching and rent increases flared up in the early 1890s and continued for years.[24] Back in October 1888 Thomas and Bridget Barrett had lost their farm near Frenchpark demesne for want of four years' rent. Returning illegally, they were evicted again on 14 February 1892. After their third reoccupation De Freyne ordered that their cottage be torn down in September 1893. On this occasion the bailiffs apparently set fire to several cottages with one or two children still inside. No one died but nationalists had another field day by comparing this arson to Glenbeigh. Evidently, Patrick O'Brien MP took some pictures of the ruins and promised to display them at Westminster. At protest meetings around Castlerea, Plan leaders called De Freyne a callous rackrenter who had 'kindled a flame' in the 'hearts of the people' as well as in the thatch of cabins. Tensions mounted even higher after a sickly old man, Peter Hunt, died only a fortnight after losing his home. The Barretts' supporters built a small wooden house for them and imposed a ban on stag hunting so long as the landlord and his agents rode to hounds. Three Plan ringleaders were prosecuted for trying to boycott anyone who refused to help build this shelter. Determined to purge the Barrett family, De Freyne caused more anger by obtaining a court order in Dublin to demolish their house.

Another partial failure of the potato crop moved the county court judge at Castlerea to deny the agent's request for more ejectment decrees on title in October 1894. The judge also urged him to accept the tenants' offer to pay two years' rent even though they owed twice that amount. De Freyne refused to compromise and rejoiced when Patrick O'Brien, John Fitzgibbon, an influential local draper, and nine other local men were prosecuted for promoting the Plan. After the 'Frenchpark eleven' were acquitted, celebrations accompanied by bonfires broke out all over the countryside.[25]

In April 1894 De Freyne's enemies raised a ruckus about the £45,000 mortgage loan he had received from Cardinal Cullen and the trustees of St Patrick's College at Maynooth. But the Archbishop of Dublin refused to heed the demand of some 'wild' and 'fanatical speakers' that the college should foreclose on De Freyne pointing out that the interest on this mortgage supported destitute children. Despite De Freyne's offer to lower non-judicial rents by 30 per cent, Fitzgibbon accused him of wanting 'to smash the tenants' combination by refusing every reasonable concession'. Following more evictions in the autumn of 1894, Davitt and O'Brien declared that even worse than the potato blight was the blight of the rent office and the landgrabber and they urged the tenants to stay strong in their fight against landlordism.[26]

In 1901 Fitzgibbon, by now chairman of Roscommon County Council, landed in jail for leading another anti-rent protest on this estate. Although a third of these tenants avoided eviction by paying their rents, those who had recently joined the United Irish League refused to pay and demanded the same terms of purchase as those prevailing on Lord Dillon's estate. De Freyne replied that they would have to pay their arrears before any sales could take place. By selling the interest of 30 more tenants in 1902 he nullified their judicial rents and set the wheels of eviction in motion. On the nearby Murphy estate much the same resistance to rent culminated in evictions followed by the boycotting of caretakers installed on the evicted farms.[27]

Ejectment decrees issued in Dublin saddled the non-compliant De Freyne tenants with legal costs three or four times higher than what they owed. Speakers at a protest rally on 26 December at Fairymount roundly condemned the landlord and defended the rent strike. Fitzgibbon's exertions on behalf of the United Irish League landed him in prison for four months. On 7 July 1902 a dozen families owing three years rent were evicted and only one of these was readmitted. When the sheriff's party returned with sixty policemen mounted on cars and bicycles, a young girl shoved District Inspector Hetreed, and a farmer's wife knelt down outside her front door surrounded by forty girls and keened over the loss of her home. Mrs Devine threw cow dung in the agent's face explaining that she did not care if she was sent to prison because she had to satisfy herself. The price of that satisfaction was a fortnight in jail. At every dwelling the agent was pelted with mud or manure and cursed with profanities. A touch of comic relief was provided by the refusal of a goat and a pig to leave the premises and they ran the emergency men ragged. Persistent death threats forced the police to guard these caretakers night and day.[28]

Among the evicted tenants were Martin Doherty and his wife, who carried their infant child out in a cradle into the pouring rain. He complained bitterly that the agent was not there to see his handiwork. Pat Sharkey's five little girls sobbed as they left with their 78-year-old grandfather. The widow Morrisroe tried and failed to re-enter her abode in Cortown (or Corthoom Beg). Thomas Freeman won a reprieve by allowing the bailiffs to seize his two cows, while the ubiquitous crowd cursed the sheriff's party. F. C. Dickinson's picture in the *Graphic* entitled 'The Land War in Ireland: An Eviction on the De Freyne Estate' depicts an old woman sitting in a chair and sunk in despair while the bailiffs carry her furniture outside (Figure 10.1). The top-hatted agent or landlord perched on the table and his well-dressed companion on the far right present a striking contrast to the impoverished victim of this proceeding.[29]

10.1   F. C. Dickinson, 'The Land-War in Ireland: An Eviction on the De Freyne Estate'. A despairing old woman sits in a chair while the bailiffs carry her few belongings outside. A goat is tethered to the table on which the top-hatted agent is seated. (*Graphic*, 13 Sept. 1902)

Beleaguered by the local United Irish League (UIL) branch, Lord De Freyne sued the leaders for damages in 1903 and the latter countered by serving the Irish Land Trust and the PDA with a writ from the High Court of Justice. In July the Irish Court of Appeal granted their request for a jury trial. The owner appealed this verdict and in April 1904 the law lords dismissed his case. But the tenants were saddled with legal costs they could ill afford. In the meantime 30 more ejectment decrees were granted for non-payment of rent since 1902. The report of a police informer about a plot to blow up De Freyne's manor house and shoot his agent spurred the police to increase their vigilance around Frenchpark.[30]

Early in October 1903 the sheriff's party forced out more destitute families around Errit while most of the younger men were away harvesting crops in England. A few women threw sods, cabbages, and dung at the evictors. While some tenants came to terms, others refused to settle in the hope of forcing De Freyne to sell. Purchase negotiations resumed in 1904, and with Fitzgibbon's help many of the Sligo and Roscommon tenants finally bought their farms. Two decades later the Land Commission acquired 1,100 acres of this estate through a compulsory purchase order under the Land Act of 1923.[31]

CLARE ISLAND

On Clare Island in Clew Bay, County Mayo, the cottiers were steeped in arrears; and the ancient rundale system with its patchwork of scattered and fenceless plots of poor soil hampered productivity. The *ILN* had highlighted evictions there back in April 1886 by means of Claude Byrne's image of a police constable cuddling a barefoot girl outside her shanty. Five years later, in November 1891, many tenants received notices to quit. Rising to the occasion, they held a protest meeting that led to the prosecution of eighty men for unlawful assembly. The prolonged trial forced them to walk miles back and forth to Louisburgh and Westport, and they had a hard time posting bail. Decrees and ejectments followed in April 1892 after a partial failure of the potato crop. Some modest relief efforts prevented starvation. O'Brien moved to adjourn debate in the House of Commons on 8 April to condemn the 'harsh and unconstitutional' use of police to evict these destitute families. This was 'a matter of life and death', he insisted, and the conflict of interest that enabled the agent to double his income by serving as the sub-sheriff in charge of evictions was 'a tenfold scandal and a shame.' Years later the islanders' prospects improved dramatically after the CDB bought the property and transformed the maze of smallholdings into profitable farms purchased by the occupiers.[32]

Landlord and tenant disputes erupted into open conflict near Clonmel in April 1895 when a widow named Fahey and her small female garrison fought off the evictors on Samuel Perry's estate. Confronted with barricades and streams of hot water mixed with lime, the emergency men abandoned their assault to resounding cheers from the crowd. Not to be denied, the sheriff's party returned the next day and arrested the widow and her three sisters for obstruction.[33]

DURSEY ISLAND/LEIGH-WHITE

At the same time several families lost their homes in a remote corner of Edward Egerton Leigh-White's estate in southwest Cork. Dursey Island contained around 25 small farms on semi-arable soil and rocky pasturage. In stormy weather the island was virtually inaccessible. In 1894 the owner had rejected the CDB's offer to buy the property and help the tenants who had paid no rent for at least four years. Led by Sub-Sheriff John Gale the eviction party sailed with 160 police on board the admiralty tender, *Stormcock*. Upon arrival they were greeted by volleys of stones thrown by eighty islanders from the top of a cliff. The police scrambled up the hill and dispersed their assailants with batons. They then pitched their tents in the pouring rain and laid in a week's supply of provisions. At a protest rally Father Barton and James Gilhooly, MP for West Cork, denounced both the landlord and the use of an admiralty vessel to transport the evictors. Negotiations broke down, however; Leigh-White refused to sell his property for the price offered by the CDB and evictions continued.[34]

THE RETURN OF MAUD GONNE

Having made her political debut at Gweedore and New Tipperary, Maud Gonne continued to champion the cause of the evicted tenants with all the bravura and passion that made her the iconic embodiment of an avenging Erin or Hibernia. Aware of the rich propaganda value of the Lawrence eviction pictures, she used them to thrill audiences in England and France while recounting the destructive handiwork of the crowbar gang and the rammers. Determined to counter all the patriotic pageantry surrounding Queen Victoria's Diamond Jubilee visit to Dublin, she skilfully arranged a 'magic lantern-slide' show of evictions on Plan estates in Rutland (now Parnell) Square on the night of 22 June 1897. Accompanying photographic images of the battering ram, ruined cottages, and the burnt-out village of Clongorey were numerical estimates of famine victims over the years and pictures of nationalist martyrs. Gonne's clever propaganda stunt from a window of the National Club struck a distinctly discordant note amidst all the celebrations of the royal visit.

As Fintan Cullen has noted, Gonne was well ahead of her time in making such 'dramatic use of [these] atrocity scenes'. In sum, she relied on 'the well-worn nineteenth-century trope of the destroyed home as a means not just to

PREPARING FOR THE BATTLE

PEACE

Major Mends — Fire.
Father McFadden — 'for God's sake spare my poor people.'

31 J. D. Reigh, 'The Fight for Bare
Life on the Olphert Estate'. Reigh limns
the fierce conflict over the Plan on the
Olphert estate as Paddy O'Donnell
and his family evolve in clockwise order
from contented tenants to resolute
Campaigners barricading their cabin
with boulders. In the lower left hand
corner the evictors flee from stones and
scalding water; and in the opposite
corner the homeless O'Donnells mourn
the loss of their home. In the centrepiece
Father McFadden exhorts Major Mends
to rescind his order to open fire. Behind
him Canon Stephens urges the garrison
to surrender before any blood is shed.
(*UI*, 12 Jan. 1889)

ABOVE

32   J. D. Reigh, 'Triumph of Law and Order in
Gweedore'. In this pictorial narrative Reigh depicts
a police sergeant collaring Harrison in his tweedy
Ulster overcoat. The young offender has been caught
supplying bread to a mother with an infant and other
family members who have re-entered their cottage
illegally. Opposite the cameo portrait of Harrison
two constables have driven out a young mother with
two babies. Below this image looms the ram or
'Balfour's Modest Maiden' (*UI*, 27 Apr. 1889)

BELOW

33   'At Derrybeg. Co. Donegal'. An evicted family
poses outside their crude cottage near Derrybeg in
County Donegal. Among the belongings thrown
outside are a large dresser, long table, butter churn,
wicker basket, spades, and a plates or dishes. To
prevent re-entry the bailiffs have nailed two boards
to the doorframe. (NLI, R 1367 WL)

34   'A Set Off Against Rochester'. In this
melodramatic cartoon O'Hea plays off the Tories'
recent defeat at a by-election in England to
emphasize the inhumanity of the Falcarragh
evictions. Here a brutish constable and emergency
man strut out of a ruined cottage holding aloft in
triumph their prisoners – two infants less than nine
months old. (*WF*, 27 Apr. 1889)

35   J.D. Reigh, 'Light Railway Disaster at Gweedore'. Reigh uses the battering ram to poke fun at Balfour's 'relief' mission to boost the economy of northwest Donegal. Here the chief secretary panics as his little locomotive pulling a tender filled with 'Bunkum Hypocrisy', 'Soft Soap', and 'Fraudulent Promises' suffers derailment by the mighty ram at Gweedore. (*UI*, 15 Nov. 1890)

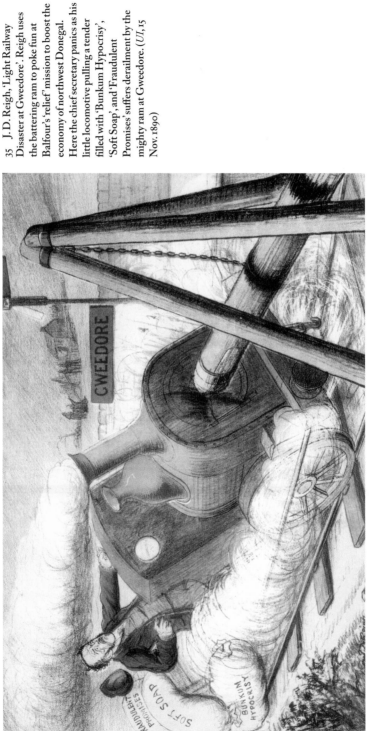

ABOVE

36 J. D. Reigh, 'The Triumph of "Law and Order" at Falcarragh'. Small cameos of Swift MacNeill, James Dalton, Norma Borthwick, and Maud Gonne appear in the corners of this Reigh cartoon that pays tribute to the champions of the Plan at Falcarragh. The central portrait of Bishop Patrick O'Donnell is surrounded by the siege of Bridget Mc Ginley's barricaded house, the arrest of two boys, and the eviction of Mrs Hegarty (or Herraghty) with her newborn baby. At the bottom the crowd kneels in the mud to receive the bishop's blessing. Behind his grace appears a battering ram. (*UI*, 22 Nov. 1890)

BELOW

37 J. F. O'Hea, 'What Our English Visitors Saw'. In O'Hea's biting cartoon a local guide explains the effects of the land war in Donegal to some English tourists. He points out that hundreds of people used to inhabit all these ruined cottages. But then the government sent down soldiers, police, battering rams, and petroleum cans to destroy the village. Only one building has been left standing – the police barracks on the hill. (*WF*, 21 Sept. 1889)

38   Thomas Fitzpatrick, 'Arran [sic] Isles 1894'.
O'Hea's successor, Thomas Fitzpatrick, has drawn
the grim reaper hard at work on the Aran Islands.
This skeletal figure sits next to a dead tenant with
the notice to quit by his side. Opposite them a rackrenting and fiendish landlord squats in front of an
empty house counting coins like Shylock. A can of
paraffin oil and house-wrecking tools lie at his feet,
while an evicted mother bemoans her fate in the
background. (*WF and National Press*, 21 Apr. 1894)

39   Lady Butler, *Evicted* (1890). In this celebrated
painting by the notable English military artist, Lady
Butler, a tall and handsome woman stands alone on
a bleak mountainside in County Wicklow near the
still smoking remains of her home. Wearing the
traditional dress of the Connemara peasantry –
full-length red skirt, white blouse, and black sash –
she looks towards the sky in sorrow, resignation, and
defiance. (National Folklore Collection, UCD)

40 'Royal Constabulary [*sic*] at the Eviction in Kerry, 1909'. The eviction of Richard Walsh from his fortified house near Castleisland, County Kerry in 1909 attracted much local publicity. And the presence of so many police constables reflects the sheriff's correct assumption that Walsh would put up a stiff fight. (From Hugh Sutherland, *Ireland Yesterday and Today* (Philadelphia, 1909))

41 'The Captured House After the Eviction in Kerry, 1909'. Relatives, friends, local labourers, and curiosity seekers swarm over the exposed rafters and walls of Walsh's ruined house and pose obligingly for the photographer. (From Sutherland, *Ireland*)

represent Irish domestic difference from England but to beat the empire'. In lecture halls and assembly rooms she performed like the prima donna she would soon play in *Cathleen ni Houlihan*, composed in 1902 by Lady Gregory and Yeats. She held Irish landlordism and British imperialism responsible for 'horrors' akin to those of 'savages' rather than 'civilised' Englishmen, and she deplored the harsh treatment of Irish political prisoners in Portland jail. Many of her harangues appeared subsequently in *United Ireland*. Filled with frustration over his spurned advances and disapproval of her radical politics, Yeats called her 'the idol of the mob & deserves to be'.[35]

Gonne returned to Donegal in 1898 when she denounced the government's failure to relieve starving cottiers. Her article in the *United Irishman* lamented the plight of evicted tenants:

> In the cold, in the damp, in the hunger, with the gnawing sense of hopeless impotency under wrong, the evicted tenants yet must say, 'Liberty is sweet', or else why do they hesitate. Why do not those who are living in such conditions … take forcible possession of the land? Why do they not rekindle the fire in the old hearth? What do they risk?

During the Boer war she urged Irishmen not to enlist in the British army but to stay at home and fight for their own country. On the eve of Queen Victoria's last visit to Ireland in April 1900 she wondered if the monarch ever thought about 'the countless Irish mothers who, shelterless under the cloudy Irish sky, watching their starving little ones, have cursed her before they died'. Such cruelties, she added, had been carried out in the Queen's name; even worse, eviction had forced countless poor and innocent peasant girls to emigrate overseas where they were falling into the hands of male predators who seduced them and then turned them into prostitutes. Her rants against the Boer war drew the attention of Special Branch policemen who shadowed her and reported her 'revolutionary' speeches and activities to the Inspector General. However, the Castle's law officers decided not to prosecute her for sedition on the grounds that she was 'half-demented'.[36] After her marriage to the pro-Boer warrior, John MacBride, she embraced republican separatism and launched the militant women's association, Inghinidhe na hÉireann.

AN EVICTION PAINTING

Ironically, the most romantic image of an Irish eviction in the late Victorian era came from an English artist, Lady Butler, in 1890. Born into an affluent English family, she earned renown as a painter of British military scenes or battles even though she abhorred violence and rarely painted soldiers engaged in combat. Her rebellious streak also led her to marry a distinguished army officer of Anglo-Irish and Catholic origins and she soon converted to both Roman Catholicism and Home Rule.[37]

After running into an eviction party near Glendalough in County Wicklow, Lady Butler reached the 'smouldering' ruins they had left in their wake. Setting up her easel, she began to paint, when suddenly the evicted woman appeared in search of any valuables left in the rubble. In the words of the artist, she seemed 'very philosophical and did not rise to the level of my indignation as an ardent English sympathiser'.[38] Evidently she proved the ideal model for Lady Butler who produced this noble, dignified, and barefoot symbol of loss in her justly famous painting, *Evicted* (Plate 39). The barren mountainous terrain resembles the later work of the Pre-Raphaelite painter, John Brett, who combined realism and impressionism in his evocative land-and-seascapes. Standing alone on a bleak mountainside devoid of trees near the smoking ruins of her former abode, she wears the traditional dress of a western countrywoman – full-length red skirt, white blouse, and black sash. A wedding ring and the absence of any man suggest widowhood. The ambiguous expression on her face as she gazes skyward combines sorrow, resignation, and defiance. In the middle distance the eviction party marches down the road. Despite her crushing loss she refuses to weep or bow her head in despair. In Margaret Kelleher's felicitous phrase this iconic woman epitomises the feminisation of eviction.

Lady Butler had good reason to fear that her painting would not prove 'very popular' at the Royal Academy exhibition in May 1890. At the annual academy banquet graced by royals, aristocrats, art patrons, and two former Irish chief secretaries (Balfour and Hicks Beach), Lord Salisbury delivered a post-prandial speech. Referring to this painting, the prime minister coolly observed: 'I will only say with respect to it that there is such an air of breezy cheerfulness and beauty about the landscape which is painted, that it makes me long to take part in an eviction whether in an active or a passive sense.' The audience greeted this remark with 'loud laughter'. When told of this remark, Lady Butler remarked: 'How like a Cecil.'[39]

PLAN CARTOONS

Cartoons about the Plan and evictions faded rapidly after 1892. Fitzpatrick's 'Protecting the Wounded' (*Weekly Freeman*, 16 December 1893) featured a miserly landlord wielding a crowbar and a satchel full of ejectment writs. He threatens a Pallas Athena-like Erin who represents the anti-Parnellite Irish National Federation while brandishing the sword of the 'Irish Party' and the shield of the 'Evicted Tenants Fund'. Next to her stand several thuggish emergency men equipped with pickaxes and a battering ram. An injured farmer and his family appear outside their derelict home as a crowd approaches bearing a banner inscribed 'Reinstatement to the Rescue'. Fitzpatrick's cartoons in the early 1890s contained a number of wicked landlords allegorised as voracious tigers or wolves.[40]

An ominous reminder of the menace of eviction surfaced in a letter written by Lord Dillon's agent in Roscommon that coincided with the launch of the United Irish League in January 1898: 'I shall have to knock down some houses when I carry out the next batch of evictions but I don't like to do it just yet, it would cause a commotion.'[41] So long as the rent nexus remained in place such old habits died hard in estate offices as did the instinct of tenants to defy the eviction party. Two photographs of an eviction at Castleisland, County Kerry, prove that some tenants were ready and willing to defend their homes as late as June 1909 (plates 40 and 41). While police surround the doomed house, local men pose in front and on top of the skeletal remains. These graphic images could have come right out of the 1880s.[42]

ELEVEN

THE THIRD LAND WAR
1900–10

*'The desire for ownership is doubtless very strong, but tenants
are tolerably prudent men and will not, I think, be inclined
to rush into improvident bargains nor are landlords the least likely
to take advantage of them. On the contrary I am sure they
will make every possible effort to meet the legitimate requirements of
their tenants for I am convinced that the great majority of
them are men sincerely anxious to put an end to this everlasting
quarrel and to see what may be accomplished if Irishmen
for the first time in the history of their country pull together.'*

LORD DUNRAVEN *to* WILLIAM O'BRIEN
11 September 1903 (NLI, O'Brien MSS 8554/2.)

*'The demands of the landlords...were either insanely grasping or
showed a determination to defeat the Act ... Unquestionably the grasping
landlords have played into their [our critics'] hands and in the people's
desperation anything is possible. .... For the present I can see no prospect except
anarchy or less general hell. The tragedy of the thing is that we were
all so near giving a new life and soul to the country.'*

WILLIAM O'BRIEN *to* LORD DUNRAVEN
29 December 1903 (NLI, O'Brien MSS 8554/2.)

——

However few and far between they may have been, the evictions occurring
after 1900 deserve a context – namely, the third land war that disturbed many
counties outside Ulster during the Edwardian era. When that indefatigable
agitator, William O'Brien, launched the United Irish League in January 1898,
he hoped to complete the unfinished agenda of the old Land League paying
particular attention to the stark disparities between the impoverished cottiers
and affluent graziers of Connacht not to mention the gentry. He aspired to break
up the cattle dealers' virtual monopoly of ranchland in the west so that cottiers or
'congests' could own farms carved out of all the fertile pasturage. The deprivations
of the peasantry around Clew Bay where he was living at the time drove him to

tackle 'the Western Problem' by 'undoing the unnatural divorce between the people and the land'. Quite apart from commemorating the centenary of the 1798 uprising, he conceived the UIL's mission to be the elimination of the rent nexus by voluntary means. As he put it bluntly, the landlords 'will have to go'– a consummation devoutly to be wished by nationalists of all hues but one that took almost three decades of struggle and legislation to achieve.[1]

To promote the new agitation O'Brien launched the *Irish People* as the UIL's official voice. Determined to reunite the parliamentary party after years of acrimonious feuding, he wanted to enable smallholders and evicted tenants to own their farms through state-aided land purchase, assuming rather naïvely that every landlord would be willing to sell for a reasonable price. On the other hand John Redmond, the new leader of the party, gradually distanced himself from O'Brien because his priorities lay with Home Rule as befitted a prosperous Catholic property owner. On the left wing of the parliamentary party, Davitt, Dillon, and Sexton distrusted O'Brien's intentions and sought a more radical solution to the land question.[2]

Like the Land League, the UIL began operating in western Mayo where small farmers had long chafed against the cattle grazing system that denied them access to the rich pasturage or callow land around them. Back in 1880 Parnell had been an outspoken critic of the eleven-month letting system. UIL branches spread rapidly from west to east reaching 1,000 in August 1901 with almost 100,000 members in Ireland and Scotland. Emulating its forebear, the UIL evolved into a combined agrarian and political movement more than capable of punishing those who disobeyed its orders. In Fergus Campbell's view this campaign was 'the most serious outbreak of agrarian conflict in twentieth century Ireland' aggravating landlords, graziers, and the police in over a dozen counties. The third land war may not have been as violent and widespread as the first and it may have lacked multiple evictions, but it lasted three times longer and caused Dublin Castle endless headaches.[3] The UIL's leaders had three main goals: forcing landlords to lower their judicial rents, turning tenant occupiers into owners at 'fair' prices, and abolishing the eleven-month leasing system that had profited graziers and landlords alike. They began their campaign rather modestly with protest meetings where speakers denounced cattle ranching, the lack of rent abatements, and the reluctance of landlords to sell both their tenanted and untenanted land. Since the UIL was not highly centralised, some branches devoted more time and energy to fundraising for the parliamentary party than withholding rents and harassing graziers.

Much of the momentum behind this agrarian unrest derived from widespread resentment of the grazier class that dominated rural society in many parts of the west and midlands. Although graziers came in various shapes and sizes and some were Protestants, they comprised a rural bourgeoisie in charge of millions of acres of pasturage in nine western counties. By letting this land for just under a year, the landowners avoided the fair rent clauses of the Land Act of 1881 and could therefore charge higher rents. Most graziers were absentees who lived in substantial houses with ranches scattered far and wide. Their unpopularity was clearly expressed in an undated ballad, 'The Grazier Tribe', that dwelled on their infestation of the countryside:

> Oh, ye men in name have you no shame
> To see this beauteous land,
> Turned into one vast wilderness
> By a cursed grazier band;
> This land so kind was ne'er designed
> By providence on high
> To keep John Bull with mutton full
> While the natives starve and die.
>
> Oh ye men of honest labour,
> If ever you're be free,
> Now take your stand upon the land
> And strike for liberty;
> Commit no crime, now is the time,
> To burst your galling chains,
> And drive this band clean off the land,
> As Brian drove the Danes.
>
> So ye valiant sons of labour
> Wherever you are found,
> To seek a home you need not roam
> But quietly look around;
> There may be seen fine meadows green,
> And bullocks sleek and grand,
> Just get your pole and take a stroll
> And clear them off the land.[4]

As David Jones has made clear, these town and country entrepreneurs made good profits whenever beef prices were high. After raising young cattle for a year or two they sold them to farmers in east Leinster who finished the fattening process before selling the animals to English or Scottish buyers who then shipped them to British ports. Besides cattle dealing what distinguished the graziers from the strong farmer class was their urban presence. Many were also shopkeepers and moneylenders, who bridged the traditional gap between town and country. Petty and aggressive capitalists, they dominated small towns on the strength of owning several houses, lending money at usurious rates, and selling goods on credit to small farmers.[5] Sheep-ranching had already acquired a bad name in the wake of the famine clearances and the activities of Pollock and Adair, and the advent of cattle ranches on the plains of Connacht and Munster had much the same alienating effect. On his travels through Mayo in October 1880 Bernard Becker had heard people complain about their loneliness owing to depopulation. Evidently, the countryside had been reduced to a 'desert' let in large blocks to English and Scottish graziers where once a thousand poor smallholders had lived 'after a fashion'. The *Western News* blamed Connacht's population loss not on the landlords but on cattle ranching that was 'the root crime against Ireland'.[6]

Ironically, the veteran Leaguer, James Daly, who held several ranches himself, declared in 1898 that the grazier class deserved to be killed. Fortunately for all concerned his exhortation went unheeded. Every spring landowners would advertise untenanted lands for let, and this seasonal ritual often resulted in the intimidation of bidders by those who coveted this land. As Jones contends, these 'speculators in livestock and land' were also agile 'social climbers' anxious to distance themselves as far as possible from the peasantry. Ensconced in handsome two-storey houses, they emulated the gentry by indulging in horseracing, foxhunting, and shooting. They employed servants and sent their sons to elite secondary schools en route to prestigious professions. Cattle-ranching landowners like Lord Ashtown championed the graziers' cause and hailed them as 'the backbone of the country'. Their social aloofness did not prevent many of them from engaging in both local and national politics. In fact, men like Daly, John Hayden, and John Fitzgibbon were devout Home Rulers and tenant-righters.[7]

Unlike the first two land wars in which large and small tenant farmers as well as labourers had coalesced to fight a common foe the anti–grazier movement divided the rural middle class from plebeians. Landlords may have been ultimately responsible for the ranching system but the prime target of the agitators was the grazier. With his eye set on reuniting the parliamentary party, Redmond could not afford to ignore the anti-ranching imperatives of his radical followers. As F. S. L. Lyons put it, the 'fortunes' of both the UIL and the parliamentary party remained closely 'intertwined' until the end of the constitutional movement in 1918.[8]

During 1900, county inspectors of the RIC reported generally good relations between landlords and tenants except on the Dunsandle and Clanricarde estates in east Galway and the Murphy and De Freyne estates in north Roscommon as well as parts of Cork, Sligo, Tipperary, Leitrim, and Kerry where boycotting and intimidation made life miserable for some law-abiding tenants. The monthly reports of these inspectors, duly summarised and forwarded to the inspector general, the under-secretary, and other high-ranking officials, contain much useful information about political activism, agrarian crime, membership of secret societies, evictions, and 'unlet' as well as 'derelict' holdings. Agrarian outrages reached 194 in December 1900, rose to 217 in January 1902, declined to 195 in the following year, and then soared to 576 in 1908.[9]

At first overt hostility to graziers was confined mainly to Sligo and the east ridings of Galway and Cork where UIL branches were most active. One of the 400 persons receiving police protection was the irascible Ashtown, whose dismissal of several herdsmen and plan to replace them with 'Scotchmen' caused 'bad feeling' around Ballinasloe. The absence of major unrest did not, however, stop the Inspector General from warning his superiors about the power of the UIL and the existence of 'very serious undercurrents of sedition' in some places. While evictions reached 59 in June 1901, the number of unlet farms stood at 2,221 of which 926 were derelict. Outside the 'disturbed' counties rents were being paid more or less regularly. On 7 July the venerable Father McFadden, now the parish priest of Glenties, returned to the fray by urging 500 supporters in Gweedore to carry on the fight against 'British misrule'. They should boycott the courts, land agents, landlords, and land grabbers until such time as Ireland could have its own police force and army and be rid of the English altogether.[10]

By March 1902 the anti-rent and anti-grazier campaign was shifting into higher gear in half a dozen counties where 'violent' speeches as well as boycotting and intimidation were on the rise. Warned about increasing unrest, the lord lieutenant, Lord Cadogan, urged that the most disturbed counties be proclaimed under the Crimes Act. Shortly thereafter some of the UIL's 'professional agitators' were arrested, tried, and imprisoned along with several outspoken newspaper editors. The combination of coercion and better harvests helped to improve landlord and tenant relations outside the turbulent triangle of Athenry, Craughwell and Loughrea in east Galway as well as north Roscommon, and parts of Clare, Cork, and Tipperary. In these areas the county inspectorate worried about the UIL's ability to 'terrorise' local people by means of intimidation that often went unreported owing to fear of retaliation. By the autumn 'peaceable' conditions were prevailing in all but seven or eight counties where the UIL had tightened its grip. However, one important casualty of the government's combination of coercion and conciliation was the once unbreakable bond between O'Brien and Dillon. Viscerally opposed to any overtures to the landlords, Dillon had held aloof from the UIL; and even though O'Brien had finally accepted the necessity of compulsory purchase to achieve his goals, the breach continued to widen.[11]

At the end of 1902 some moderate Redmondites supported O'Brien's decision to join a few liberal landlords in a round-table discussion about a new departure in land purchase. At the prompting of Captain John Shawe-Taylor, an idealistic young landlord from Galway, Lord Dunraven and several liberal gentry friends embarked on a risky attempt to break the impasse in the land market and convert the remaining tenantry into peasant proprietors through a bipartisan approach. Hoping to abolish landlordism and reinstate 'the wounded soldiers of the land war' by voluntary measures, Dunraven invited O'Brien and several other tenant representatives to take part in the famous Land Conference in December. One bad omen, however, was the exclusion of Dillon. Although sympathetic to many tenant grievances, Dunraven believed that the state had badly mistreated the landlords and should compensate them for all their losses since 1881. Convinced that the Irish 'race' possessed fortitude, chivalry, kindness, honesty, and 'prudence' along with a few minor defects, he wanted to put right the 'centuries of misgovernment' that had 'warped and twisted the natural [*sic*] character'.[12]

Within a fortnight the conferees had reached a consensus about the necessity of creating 'an occupying proprietary' that would satisfy 'the just claims of both owners and occupiers'. The state's role would be limited to proof of title and rentals as well as providing subsidies. The price of land would be based on an average of 18½ years' purchase of first-term rents or 22½ years' purchase of second-term rents. To promote sales the vendors would receive a 'sweetener' in the form of a 12 per cent bonus on the purchase price. The conferees also concurred that the land question could never be resolved without relief for the evicted tenants. Jubilant over this consensus Dunraven and O'Brien looked forward to implanting the 'spirit' of conciliation in a new land purchase bill. Even the Landowners Convention placed its blessing on the report. The brilliance and 'boundless ambition' of George Wyndham, who succeeded Gerald Balfour as chief secretary at the end of 1900, worried perceptive subordinates like Sir Horace Plunkett who found these qualities a recipe for failure because they seemed to be aimed at transforming not only Ireland but also his own political career. In any event the visionary Wyndham incorporated many of the Conference's proposals in his draft land purchase bill. However, Davitt, Dillon, and Sexton dogmatically opposed any deal supported by even the liberal wing of the landlord class.[13]

The Land Conference accord led to a lull in the land war as O'Brien urged UIL branches to cool their ardour pending the bill's passage. Nevertheless small farmers in the west chafed against the graziers' monopoly of grassland and their protests spread rapidly to Roscommon, Leitrim, Clare, and Sligo. The weather did not help farmers as heavy rains ruined crops and hurricane force winds in February felled many trees and damaged dwellings in the midlands. In the meantime county inspectors were calling conditions unusually 'peaceable' in most of Galway, Mayo, and Sligo. Although tensions remained high on the De Freyne and Murphy estates, the overall improvement so impressed Wyndham and his astute under-secretary, Sir Antony MacDonnell, that they rebuked the Inspector General for producing a pessimistic summary and made him revise his report.[14]

From 1902 to 1905 two-thirds of the country remained relatively peaceful, with evictions averaging 31 per month and unlet holdings fluctuating between 2,081 and 1,523. Sporadic outbreaks of agrarian crime, however, beset most of the western counties and Tipperary where tenants were withholding rent in order to compel their landlords to sell or subdivide untenanted land. Wherever negotiations for sale ended in agreement disturbances declined. One example of the pervasive hostility to graziers came from the Clanricarde estate where Harry Persse, a retired Indian police officer, had invested in two grazing ranches at Kilcreest. Death threats, vandalism, and boycotting brought him to the brink of surrender in 1905. When his cry for help reached the Castle, the Law Officers advised against prosecution on the grounds of insufficient evidence. Eventually Persse found a few graziers willing to take up his leases, but three constables were assigned to guard him and his manor house around the clock.[15]

THE WYNDHAM ACT, 1903

It took a good deal more than the UIL's agitation to produce and pass the Land Purchase Act of 1903. Designed to enshrine 'the mutual good feeling and self-sacrifice evidenced in the Land Conference', in Dunraven's words, the Wyndham act was intended to be a 'friendly' and final settlement of the land question.[16] Besides the UIL agitation, this measure owed much to the stagnant land market and the willingness of the O'Brienites to co-operate with a handful of landlords. Among other major contributors were the overweening ambition and idealism of Wyndham as well as the expertise and political connections of MacDonnell. The latest round of judicial rent revisions brought many land-lords on board because they feared the loss of even more rental income if these reductions continued. However, abiding resentment of the 'infamous' Land Act of 1881 made proprietors hold out for a high price for their land – between 23 and 25 years' purchase of the rent. All these factors combined to push the government towards a measure that dwarfed the Ashbourne act of 1885. The coolness of the Liberal leaders towards this measure did not discourage Wyndham, who entertained high hopes for a personal and political triumph. 'Ireland', he exclaimed in one of his manic moods, 'is going to revolutionise America, and America the World'.[17]

During the drafting of this bill MacDonnell travelled back and forth to

London arranging private talks between Wyndham and the Irish leaders. His experience as a colonial governor in India had taught him much about relations between landlords and peasants as well as land law but he was unprepared for the ferocity of partisan politics at home. As a Catholic and closet Home Ruler, MacDonnell was trusted by O'Brienites as much as he was distrusted by rabid Unionists. And he enjoyed the powerful support of the king as well as Lord Lansdowne and the Irish viceroy, Lord Dudley. Given all his contributions this measure deserved to be called the Wyndham–MacDonnell act.

The revised bill called for the sale of whole estates as distinct from individual holdings by means of Treasury funding and annual instalments (annuities) paid by the purchasers over 68½ years at 3.5 per cent interest that were less than the current judicial rents. The 12 per cent bonus on the purchase price – (Dunraven and O'Brien preferred 15 per cent) – proved irresistible to many cash starved landlords, who were also allowed to sell their demesnes to the Estates Commissioners and pay annuities like any other purchaser. Thus Lord Carysfort raised £20,000 by selling his demesne to the Estates Commissioners in July 1905. Unfortunately, the measure offered no relief to evicted tenants.[18]

The inflationary effect of the bonus and the complex zones system raised the price of land by more than four per cent above that prevailing under the Ashbourne act. The malcontents in the nationalist camp suspected Dunraven and Wyndham of having struck a secret deal with Redmond that favoured the landlords and would derail Home Rule. In a strident speech at Swinford the diehard Dillon denounced both the measure and landlordism thereby deepening the gulf between himself and O'Brien. For his part Sexton made sure that the *Freeman's Journal* joined in the chorus of criticism.[19]

Regarding voluntary purchase as more of 'a palliative than a cure', these radicals feared the loss of appetite for independence among the new owner-occupiers who would succumb to the Unionist strategy of 'killing Home Rule with kindness'. They also accused the landlords of demanding exorbitant prices. Redmond distanced himself from the Dunravenites lest he alienate the radicals and complained about the plight of smallholders in Connacht where the CDB could not break up the ranches without compulsory purchase powers.[20]

Bureaucratic delays also bedevilled this measure. The originating applications for sales moved slowly through the Estates Commission because the under-manned staff could not cope with all the paperwork required from the owners, agents, and solicitors. Providing proof of title, marriage settlements, and incumbrances or charges on the lands to be sold proved more than burden-some. By 1904 applications to buy and sell were pouring in even though many proprietors held back in the (vain) hope of obtaining a better price later. Some shrewd agents were advising their employers to sell as soon as possible even though this meant their own loss of income.[21] Landlords who put off selling until after 1909 lost some of the bonus and had to settle for payment in depreciating land stock. In addition, the cap placed on the amount of money allocated annually by the Treasury to finance the act hindered the operation.

Despite all these obstacles many tenants managed to shuffle off the coils of landlordism. But as Campbell points out, sales under the act amounted to only 12 per cent of tenanted land up to 1908. At this point almost one third of all tenanted land had been sold since 1870 amounting in all to 7.3 million acres for £28 millions. By then roughly 70 per cent of agricultural land remained unsold. By 1909 almost 270,000 sales had been completed and pending agreements amounted to £36 millions in Treasury advances.[22]

This act failed in short to achieve Wyndham's dream of converting every tenant farmer into an owner; and years passed before the recommendation of Lord Dudley's Royal Commission on Congestion that the CDB be empowered to acquire land compulsorily took effect. Eventually, however, the act opened the gates to a socio-economic transformation that improved the well-being of many rural people. To add to the burdens of ownership some of the new owners found themselves saddled with loans from local shopkeepers that one official described as 'the never-dying worm of peasant proprietorship'.[23]

Among the first to take advantage of this measure were the Duke of Leinster, Lords Dunraven and Rossmore, MacDonnell, and Redmond. However, within a few years purchase transactions began to slow down and thousands of keen buyers were left in the lurch. The neglect of the evicted tenants troubled Dunraven who lamented that their hopes for reinstatement had been 'dashed to the ground'. And yet he knew full well that his fellow landlords would never allow the measure to become 'a tenants' relief act'.[24]

Here and there disputes over purchase ended in eviction after tenants withheld their rent and negotiations broke down. Thus on the Ballyduff estate of Isabella Thompson and Helen Orpen in County Waterford, the tenants wanted to buy at 20 years' purchase of first-term and 22 years' purchase of second-term rents. But the owners held out for a higher price and the agent obtained writs against three strong farmers who were in arrears in the hope of teaching the others a lesson. As the sheriff's party approached on 3 April 1905, horns and chapel bells summoned a crowd. The parish priest berated a police sergeant for daring to enter his church in order to silence the bell-ringer. After the agent spurned the offer of two tenants to pay their rent, they walked out. But the third tenant had barricaded his house and the bailiffs had to smash a window to gain entry whereupon they drove out eight adults and three children. No sooner had the evictors left than all three families repossessed their dwellings to deafening cheers from the crowd. A week later the owners obtained more notices to quit.[25]

Land purchase may have banished the spectre of eviction for tenant purchasers but most smallholders were not so fortunate. As Frederick Wrench, the well-informed estates commissioner, advised Arthur Balfour in 1907, compulsory powers were essential in order to convert ranch land into tillage farms without 'interfering with the pastoral wealth of the country'.[26] Despite the grandiose vision of its architects the Wyndham act failed to usher in any 'golden age' and often gave rise to more friction than closure and more envy than satisfaction among thousands of smallholders. By 1907 many of the UIL's 139,283 members were frustrated over the state's continuing failure to break up the cattle ranches.[27]

THE ANTI-RENT AGITATION

In the early 1900s tenants on the neighbouring estates of Lord De Freyne and Thomas Wills-Sandford were complaining vigorously about their rents and inability to buy their farms. After more than a dozen evictions, serious strife broke out in the summer of 1903 around Castlerea. Recapitulating the Plan, the Wills-Sandford tenants withheld their rent until their landlord caved in and sold their farms. Castle officials feared that his surrender would encourage other tenants to launch their own no-rent campaign to achieve the same goal.[28] Early in 1904 local UIL leaders and two priests urged Lord Dunsandle's tenants to withhold their rent pending a purchase agreement. Tense meetings, abortive negotiations, and threats of ejectment culminated in Captain Denis St George Daly's decision to sell 2,500 acres of untenanted land. These two victories boosted the UIL's morale and spurred ten other Galway landlords to follow suit. If sales on the De Freyne estate cooled the ardour of the rebellious tenants, discontent affected other parts of Mayo as well as Galway, Kerry, and Sligo. Wyndham deplored this 'interference with the liberty of the subject', but voluntary land purchase could do nothing to allay the anger of farmers whose landlords refused to sell. To add to the Castle's woes, Protestant landgrabbers planted on evicted holdings around Portumna in the 1880s required constant police protection. As the county inspector for the East Riding of Galway reported, 'the people seem to be possessed by an insatiable craving for land'. Rent strikes averaged 35 per month and reached a peak of 63 in ten counties in January 1908. Depending on the presence of moonlighters and IRB activists acts of intimidation and boycotting oscillated from month to month and tended to soar in the spring when grazing leases were up for renewal.[29]

Directed mainly against landlords who refused to sell their grasslands, these anti-rent protests shattered the optimism of Dunraven and O'Brien, who maintained an amicable relationship despite the odds, while striving to remove the financial constraints that hampered land purchase. However, disillusionment and stress eroded O'Brien's morale. A combination of quarrels with the Dillonites who scorned 'Dunravenism', dismay over the 'unreasonable' prices demanded by the landlords, and the loss of Redmond's support moved him to resign his seat and withdraw from public life in November 1903. Clinging to the shards of hope, he wrote to Dunraven in October 1905: 'It is an uphill battle, but the only real enemy is Ignorance, and I think we shall beat it down.'[30]

THE CATTLE DRIVING CAMPAIGN

There is no need to relate the particulars of the ranch war carefully set forth in the works of Jones, Bew, and Campbell. Suffice to say that cattle driving and boycotting marked this stage of the war against landlords who refused to sell their ranch lands and graziers who were in no mood to part with such a valuable source of income. While Bew argues that the anti-ranching campaign bore all the hallmarks of a class war between graziers and small farmers, Campbell contends that it resembled the land wars of the 1880s insofar as the owners of the grazing land were the landlords. Some of the UIL branches in Clare, Galway, Mayo, and Kerry had been radicalised by IRB activists; and if there were no moderate priests to restrain them, they were ready to use the violent tactics of the old Land League against landgrabbers and bailiffs. At the same time the Dillonites sought to abolish not just the grazing system but also landlordism. The abiding hostility between smallholders and absentee graziers was in Campbell's words 'a subsidiary aspect of this broader struggle' to force landlords to part with all their land. While O'Brien now accepted the necessity of compulsory purchase in order to dissolve the ranches, he did not approve of the cattle drives orchestrated by the radical barrister and MP for North Westmeath, Laurence Ginnell, and his comrade in arms, David Sheehy MP for South Meath.[31]

By May 1905 the anti-grazing campaign was causing the Castle more concern than secret societies like the IRB, the GAA, and the Ancient Order of Hibernians (AOH). In chronically disturbed east Galway, where the IRB had infiltrated some of the UIL's 52 branches, the police had a hard time protecting law-abiding citizens from harm. In October the agitators in Roscommon adopted a new tactic – namely, cattle driving that spread rapidly to Galway and eight other counties in 1906. UIL speakers vilified the eleven-month letting system and the graziers and justified the scattering of herds as the best way to convince the Estates Commissioners and the CDB that they should acquire and divide the grasslands among deserving tenants. The 'policy of fight', in short, expressed the frustration of smallholders over the failure of the landlords and the Wyndham act to redress their grievances. Paid UIL 'organisers' taught people how to stampede a herd and evade arrest, and 'drumming parties' as well as beaters began to disperse cattle on selected estates. Occasionally shots were fired into the dwellings of non-compliant cattle ranchers or herdsmen. [32]

The losses arising from beasts injured or gone astray drove 45 graziers in eastern Galway to surrender their leases. Although county inspectors reported 'satisfactory' conditions in most of the country during 1906, cattle driving spread to the once tranquil counties of eastern Leinster reaching a peak of 681 in 1908. Over the three-year period 1907–9 the police recorded 1,271 cattle drives and at least 2,000 cases of boycotting while between 200 and 300 persons were under police protection. These drives did not exactly please ratepayers who had to foot the bill for wounded or lost animals as well as extra police. Walking a political tightrope between the militants and moderates in his party, Redmond advocated compulsory purchase and urged his followers to risk imprisonment for the cause of Home Rule.[33]

For almost five years the war against graziers embroiled parts of counties Galway, Mayo, Clare, Kerry, Mayo, Roscommon, Leitrim, Sligo, Longford, Tipperary, and Westmeath. Sporadic cattle drives also occurred in the King's and Queen's counties as well as Kilkenny, Longford, and Meath. If the number and intensity of outrages remained far below the levels of 1880–2, Dublin Castle could not cope with all the overt and covert intimidation. Land hunger and hostility to graziers forced the police to run from pillar to post in pursuit of the elusive foe.

In the meantime Lord Ashtown raised more hackles around Ballinasloe by evicting several Catholic herdsmen and replacing them with Protestants. He also tried to buy a cattle ranch coveted by local farmers. Frequent skirmishes with poachers on his north Waterford estate must have contributed to the small incendiary bomb that rocked his shooting lodge at Glenahiry on the night of 14 August 1907. Although no one was injured, this crude 'infernal machine' caused a mighty row in the Castle and inspired nationalists to accuse Ashtown of planting the bomb so that he could blame it on the AOH and all his other nationalist enemies.[34]

REINSTATING THE EVICTED TENANTS

In speech and pamphlet Laurence Ginnell kept up a steady stream of invective against the landlords for their 'capricious' evictions and 'callous' rackrents while demanding full restitution for all the 'martyrs' of the land wars. As he put it in 1917, the claim of these 'wounded soldiers of the land war' and their descendants had to be 'the strongest and most urgent of all the victims of the English garrison. The failure to satisfy those claims is the greatest blot on land legislation, and the greatest disgrace to the representatives who acquiesced in that most ungrateful neglect.'[35] Other UIL leaders backed the cause of reinstatement with frequent denunciations of all those allegedly evicting and rackrenting landlords. In July 1905 Denis Kilbride, the veteran Plan activist, who now lived in Dublin, was reinstated on one tenth of the 868 acres he had once held at Luggacurren; and he immediately demanded the return of all his grazing land.[36]

Preferring to accentuate positive gains, the Irish government published a survey in 1906 of the 4,950 evicted tenants who had applied for reinstatement. Of this cohort 41 per cent came from Munster and 20.5 per cent from Connacht. County Cork topped this chart with 665 claimants, followed by Kerry (444), Galway (364), Mayo (282), Limerick (279), and Tipperary (234). Of the 1,158 evicted holdings still in landlords' hands some 44 per cent lay in Munster. In addition 108 holdings were either vacant or unoccupied. This report contained the names of the evicting landlords along with the location, size of holding, rent, and arrears on each tenancy.

The commissioners also compiled data about the circumstances and character of each applicant in order to ascertain the merit of his or her case. Thus Bridget and John Waters had been evicted by Robert H. Metge from their 76-acre farm near Dunboyne, County Meath on 1 August 1891. Described as people of good character they were living in 'poor circumstances' in a labourer's cottage. Joseph Whelan, on the other hand, had emigrated to Burlington, New Jersey after being forced out of his 48-acre farm on the Cosby estate at Ballymaddock, Queen's County, owing arrears of £75. Some of the claimants were eminently respectable. Lord Longford's land steward, William Ievers of Castle Ievers, Athlacca, County Westmeath, was a man of 'good character' who had been ejected in April 1902 owing two years' rent. M. Blood Smyth was a 'Lady' of good character who had been expelled by Lord Leconfield from her 372-acre farm near Croom, County Limerick in June 1888 owing arrears of £1,778. Helena R. Lloyd of Doon West, Portrinard in the same county, was a 'lady in fair circumstances' who had been expelled by a kinsman in May 1899 after running up arrears of £940. By contrast R. F. Hannigan, of Clonmel, an ex-tenant on the Ormonde estate, was a 'bad' character with convictions for cattle theft and forgery. For some years his uncle, a parish priest, had supported him. Frederick Mulcahy of Knockgrafton, County Tipperary, had accumulated arrears of £1,105 before being turned out in September 1893. Apparently, he was 'affected in his mind'. Martin Maher of Ballyphilip, County Tipperary, had lost his 235-acre farm in June 1887 with arrears of £540. Although a man of 'good character' he was 'a politician and given to agitation'.

Another respectable claimant, Richard Parker, was a bank manager from Ballymote, County Waterford, who owed two years' rent. Mary MacDonnell, the wife of Dr M. A. MacDonnell the anti-Parnellite MP for Queen's County, had been evicted from the Knight of Glin's estate even though she was 'well off'. Michael Mansfield, a sergeant in the RIC and a man of 'good character', had lost his 287-acre farm in County Waterford in 1879. Another policeman, ex-Head Constable Robert McFarland, had been evicted at Templetuohy, County Tipperary, in July 1903 after telling his landlord, Mrs K. L. Morgan, that he wished to surrender the holding because the rent was too high. Later he reneged and expressed his wish to stay. Refusing to relent, the landlord sent him a notice to quit even though he owed no arrears. The local UIL branch spurned his plea for help and a county court judge ruled that he had broken his contract by proposing to leave. Phillip McDonnell had lost his 105-acre farm at Boulick, County Tipperary back in July 1882, since when he had become an active United Irish Leaguer. The assessor gave him a low score: 'bad character … and agitator'.[37]

Evidently 129 of the Plan evictees belonged to Lord Clanricarde, 68 to Lord Lansdowne, 51 to George Brooke, 46 to Lord Massereene, 36 to Lord Kenmare, 27 to A. L. Tottenham, 21 to Hanna Lewis, 19 to Captain Hector Vandeleur, 19 to Lord Ventry, 15 to the Countess of Kingston, and 14 to Lord Dillon. This survey also documented the arrears and rent outstanding. Thus 49 of the Luggacurren tenants owed Lord Lansdowne £5,112; and 36 of Brooke's ex-tenants around Coolgreany owed £2,443. The rental of the unlet holdings on this property came to £323.[38]

Bowing to heavy pressure from UIL radicals, Chief Secreary Augustine Birrell steered his Evicted Tenants (Ireland) Act through parliament on 28 August 1907. This measure enabled the Estates Commissioners to acquire untenanted land compulsorily and sell the divided holdings to 'fit and proper persons'. The planted occupiers or 'land grabbers' would be compensated with land elsewhere. Tenanted land and demesnes were excluded and those who refused the offer could be compensated for their interest in the holding.

By June 1908 one third of the 5,700 registered evicted tenants had taken advantage of this measure – a substantial increase over the 284 reinstatements during 1903–6. And by 1914 some 3,581 evicted tenants had been reinstated on old or new holdings. The number of fraudulent claims for reinstatement, however, complicated the commissioners' task. For example, when a Dublin city councillor declared that only 19 per cent of the 12,398 claimants had been reinstated by the end of March 1911, one of his colleagues pointed out that some of the successful petitioners were not former tenants at all but simply men with good connections to the Redmondite party.[39] In the meantime the dispossessed found another champion in the French journalist, Louis Paul-Dubois, who extolled the UIL and censured the landlords for their 'odious record' of 'gratuitous evictions', reckless consumption, and rampant corruption over the years.[40]

During the early 1900s the fragile craft of Irish Party unity threatened to founder on the reefs of O'Brienism, Dillonism, Dunravenism, and Ginnellism. To keep on board colleagues who backed the cattle drives Redmond, ever the centrist politician, promised a 'vigorous agitation'. But his courtship of O'Brien alienated Dillon and after much anti-Semitic abuse aimed at his Jewish wife, O'Brien resigned from the party for the last time in 1909. By then the Royal Commission on Congestion in Ireland, headed by Lord Dudley, had recommended endowing the CDB with the power to deal with ranching, the 'congests' or families that could not make an 'adequate' living on their holdings, and the compulsory purchase of untenanted lands. [41]

Although one anxious county inspector in eastern Galway warned in August 1909 that 'terrorism governs everything', even there intimidation was on the decline. The growth of Sinn Féin caused some officials as much concern as cattle driving, but conditions in the country were steadily improving owing in large part to such political issues as the budget crisis, the new land act, and the approaching general election. By the end of 1910 the third land war had run out of steam. [42]

If the anti-grazing campaign failed to eliminate the grazier class, it did take some heat off the landlords and served as a distraction from evictions. Nevertheless vestiges of the old hostility towards the landlords remained and the shortcomings of the Wyndham act kept agrarian unrest alive. On the other side of the great divide Dunraven deplored 'the pig-headed fighting policy' that had shattered his dream of seeing 'Irishmen [both landlords and tenants] for the first time in the history of their country pull[ing] together.' At the same time he endorsed the landlords' claim for state compensation as well as higher prices for their land because the government had treated them so shabbily since 1881. He yearned to recapture the conciliatory 'spirit' of the Land Conference in order to deal with higher education and the restructuring of local self-government through a conciliar scheme. But lingering antagonism between landlord and tenant proved too strong. O'Brien shared the dismay of Redmondites over the neglect of the evicted tenants and Dillon continued to rant against 'Dunravenism'. Then came the devolution controversy of 1904–5 orchestrated by Dunraven, MacDonnell, and a handful of liberal landlords in the Irish Reform Association that infuriated Ulster Unionists, riled Balfour's cabinet, and forced the complicit Wyndham to resign. Although the tenacious MacDonnell defied his Unionist enemies and retained his post, this major crisis hammered the last nail into the Unionist coffin of conciliation. [43]

THE LAND ACT OF 1909

No matter how fierce its opposition to compulsory purchase, the landlords' lobby could not prevent the passage in December 1909 of Birrell's long awaited bill that refinanced the Wyndham act and offered some relief to the 'congests'. Future sales would be paid for with excess stock backed by the Exchequer and the bonus was now based on a sliding scale. Critical of the 12 per cent bounty to vendors, Birrell wondered why the Duke of Leinster, for example, deserved to line his 'breeches pocket' with £80,000 just for agreeing to sell his well-managed estate. Besides increasing the annuities paid by purchasers, this statute empowered the CDB to buy, improve, and redistribute untenanted land to smallholders in the west. In the House of Lords irate peers tried but failed to eliminate the compulsory purchase clauses. Up until 1923, however, some owners of ranch lands in the west refused to sell on the grounds that the UIL had deliberately driven down their value through agrarian outrages. Clanricarde reacted to this measure by cleverly converting the graziers and planters on his estate into 'permanent tenants' who could not be removed by the Board. These 'bogus tenancies' allowed graziers in at least seven parishes to hold on to their ranches until 1916 when his lordship finally died and the CDB was able to buy and redistribute the grasslands by both voluntary and compulsory methods.[44]

As Dooley has pointed out, the 'plight' of the evicted tenants formed a large plank in Sinn Féin's platform in 1917. By then Ginnell had become an enthusiastic Sinn Féiner and published a pamphlet about the sufferings of the 'victims of the English garrison'. Redmondite MPs were also pressing for the reinstatement of the remaining evicted tenants. The Irish Convention of 1917 gave the proponents of land purchase the chance to boast that monies advanced for this purpose since 1870 amounted to almost one hundred million pounds. Under the various statutes 308,833 tenants had bought 10,202,910 acres of land; and pending sales came to £23,936,053. However, contrary to Campbell's assertion that 'by 1921, the lives of smallholders in the west of Ireland had been transformed by a series of land reforms', not even the Land Act of 1923 satisfied the land hunger of many landless men who insisted that their experience of rackrents and evictions entitled them to good farmland.[45]

EVICTION PROTESTS

During the third land war some UIL branches mounted large and loud protests at eviction sites. Thus in May 1901 the threat of rioting by tenants facing eviction on Inishturk off the coast of Mayo moved Lord Lucan's agent to negotiate a settlement after a British gunboat had landed the sub-sheriff and his armed escort on the island. One month later a serious fracas broke out on the insolvent estate of Charles Gore Tottenham in County Leitrim. For some years this property had been tied up in chancery and in September 1897 the court approved 28 decrees for non-payment. Negotiations over purchase delayed the execution of these writs until January 1898 when several thousand UIL members assembled and tore down some empty cottages to prevent the emergency men or 'caretakers' from occupying them. The sub-sheriff returned on 25 June 1901 with an escort of 100 police to execute 16 more decrees. Led by Denis Kilbride, the protestors tried and failed to stop the bailiffs from expelling several families near Kiltyclogher. But the menacing crowd forced the sheriff to withdraw. When the evictors returned on July 18, they were attacked by 250 men wielding sticks and stones. A nervous police officer ordered his men to load their weapons, and the crowd backed away in time to avoid another Mitchelstown. [46]

FELL/WATERGRASSHILL

In County Cork an eviction in the autumn of 1904 caused a major ruckus on the small estate of Richard L. Fell near Watergrasshill or Mitchelsfort. This dispute began in 1900 when a litigious UIL activist, Edmond Murphy, failed to pay £97 for the rent of his 100-acre farm. Strapped for cash and burdened with five years' arrears, he tried to sell the interest for £800. However, the long-suffering absentee Fell blocked the sale by exercising his right of pre-emption. This litigation did not stop Murphy from harvesting the crops. Exasperated by all the bother and lost rent, Fell's son and agent moved to repossess, whereupon Murphy heavily fortified the premises and recruited a garrison of 21 men. Anticipating a serious fight, Sub-Sheriff John Gale sent for reinforcements. Once he saw the barricades and a crowd of one thousand he postponed the assault and Murphy's supporters spent the day listening to bands playing patriotic music and cheering speakers who denounced wicked landlords. [47]

The real battle began on 12 October when Gale returned with forty constables and three bailiffs accompanied by William Hanna, the secretary of the Cork Defence Union. Awed by the size and ugly mood of the crowd, Gale approached cautiously. As soon as he started to read the writ aloud, he was drenched with a mixture of hot water, mud, and lime. A defender shouted: 'Ha! Ha! Gale – was the water hot?' Armed with a revolver and a flask of whisky, Hanna threatened to shoot a man in an upstairs window if he threw any stones. But a 'perfect storm' of stones, bricks, and bottles flew out of the house wounding dozens of police who vented their anger by batoning bystanders. A UIL leader exhorted the garrison: 'Hold the fort, boys ... We don't want to interfere with the police; if we did, we could eat up the few constables that are here before our breakfast.' After the bailiffs retreated, the constabulary advanced with rifles and crowbars at the ready only to be driven back. When two Irish MPs arrived and mounted a wagon to get a better view, the police rudely shoved them off.

Delayed by felled trees and harassed by spectators, the police reinforcements finally arrived. Several men and women approached the house with loaves of bread for the garrison, but the police drove them away while the crowd shouted 'Hold the fort!' Jeremiah Delany appeared in a window sharpening his scythe and then waved it tauntingly. After the police put up ladders and climbed onto the roof, the defenders drove them back with stones, pikes, and pitchforks. Some constables picked up the stones and threw them back. One of those wounded during these assaults was Sean O'Faolain's father, PC Denis Whelan, who hurled some stones at the house before being hit on the head and shoulder by a huge stone. To make matters worse he grabbed a red-hot crowbar thrust through a window and suffered a nasty burn. These injuries moved Mrs Whelan to scold her heavily bandaged husband for having tried to play the hero – the 'foolah to catch the blow and snatch the bar!' Sean vividly recalled this incident in his memoir, *Vive Moi!* [48]

As soon as the police broke through a rear wall and secured the ground floor, the defenders withdrew upstairs and held off the invaders with long poles and crowbars along with more stones and hot water. The likelihood of more serious injuries led to a ceasefire and Father O'Leary talked Murphy into surrendering 'honourably' on the condition that the garrison be granted bail. With heads held high they walked out and submitted to arrest. Despite the lateness of the hour – it was 2.30 in the morning – the crowd paraded around the village accompanied by a brass band. The sheriff left behind a dozen constables to guard the lone emergency man in charge of the farm. At a rally next day in Cork city, O'Brien praised Murphy and denounced landlords like Fell who yearned for the good old days of the 'pitch cap and the (flogging) triangle' of the '98 insurrection. [49]

When Murphy's defenders were tried at Riverstown on 18 October for riot and unlawful assault, hundreds of supporters turned up sporting green rosettes and carrying laurel branches. Several brass bands serenaded the defendants while scores of police blocked the road leading to the courthouse beating anyone who came too close to their cordon. Captain A. J. C. Donelan MP for East Cork saved one man from serious injury and denounced this 'murderous … cowardly, brutal' baton charge on peaceful citizens. During the trial O'Brien was listening to testimony unaware of the mêlée outside when a man rushed into the courtroom shouting that the police had just killed a demonstrator. O'Brien hastened outside, appealed for calm, and returned with several comrades supporting one of the defendants, John Mulcahy, who had left to find drink and food. Blood flowed profusely from a deep scalp wound. Appalled by this brutal attack, O'Brien demanded an explanation from County Inspector Rogers. The court then adjourned and the police withdrew from the town centre. At a rally in

Glanmire O'Brien accused the police of 'atrocious' misconduct and insisted that Rogers rather than the resisters be put on trial. One Home Rule MP hailed Murphy's garrison for mounting 'one of the bravest defences ever made by any people in the assertion of their liberties (cheers)'. On 19 October, the *Cork Examiner* devoted over eleven columns to the courthouse riot.

When the court reconvened on 29 November, several hundred police restrained the crowd and three nationalist MPs and five priests were searched before being allowed inside. During the protracted trial counsel for the defence cross-examined the police witnesses about the weight of the stones thrown. Convicted of rioting and unlawful assembly, Murphy was sentenced to six months with hard labour while his comrades received three months. The defendants' appeal led to a second trial in March 1905 when the verdict was upheld. In October Mulcahy charged Inspector Rogers with assault during the Riverstown riot and the Castle dispatched Lord O'Brien, lord chief justice, to preside over this trial in Cork city. Not even the sharp cross-examination by Mulcahy's lawyer, Tim Healy, could win this case for the plaintiff; and the government brushed aside nationalist accusations of jury packing.

In April the Cork branch of the UIL along with town and county councillors, priests, and the *Cork Examiner* promoted the Riverstown and Fort Murphy Defence Fund Committee to raise money for the prisoners' families. Meetings were held and thirty neighbours volunteered to sow oat seeds on the farm of one prisoner. This episode proved that even a single eviction could still become a *cause célèbre* given a little bit of help from the UIL and a sympathetic press.[50]

FORT WALSH, 1909

Another instance of siege warfare erupted near Castleisland, County Kerry, in June 1909. On this occasion a combative farmer named Richard (Dick) Walsh and his fourteen-man garrison fought tooth and nail against eviction. Four years behind with the rent, he refused the offer of his landlord, Pierce Gun Mahony of Kilmurry house, scion of an old gentry family, to buy the holding owing to disputes over turbary and the purchase price. After Mahony's trustees acquired the interest in the farm in 1906 and served a notice to quit, Walsh took them to court thereby delaying his removal for over two years. Emulating Somers of Coolroe, he and his friends dug a moat and built a rampart around the sturdy stone house, blocked the boreen with trees and barbed wire, and stuffed the windows and doors with tree stumps and prickly bushes. Alerted to the likelihood of a 'hot reception', sub-sheriff Redmond Roche ordered a brand new battering ram with ladder-like rungs that could be grasped without the need for a tripod (Figure 11.1).

11.1 'Battering Ram at an Eviction in Kerry, 1909'. Several policemen guard the brand new ladder-like ram commissioned by the sub-sheriff to deal with Richard Walsh's fortified house near Castleisland in 1909. Mounted on a cart, this ram has rungs that obviate the need for a tripod given an ample supply of manpower. (From Hugh Sutherland, *Ireland Yesterday and Today* (Philadelphia, 1909))

Dublin Castle showed its concern by assigning the Assistant Inspector General of the RIC, F. I. Ball, to take charge of the assault accompanied by six police inspectors. After two attacks on 'Walsh's Fort' had failed, Roche returned on June 22 with an escort of 300 police and soldiers drawn from surrounding counties and Dublin. Summoned by horns and chapel bells, a crowd of several hundred materialised. Because the moat and embankment rendered the ram useless, the besiegers had to resort to the crowbar and the pickaxe. For four hours the defenders kept the evictors at bay by means of a pump spraying hot water mixed with lime and tar. Besmeared with this 'obnoxious' liquid, the bailiffs harnessed a horse to the tree stumps and pulled them out. But the defenders fought on in the pouring rain. Finally, the police took over the siege from the weary bailiffs, put up ladders, and tried to climb through holes in the roof. Ignoring the pleas of John Murphy MP for East Kerry to end their resistance, the garrison soaked Ball and his men with the sticky stirabout. In vain Murphy urged Ball to restrain his forces because Walsh's 83-year-old and sickly mother lay inside. After the police broke through a gable wall, Ball charged inside with sword drawn. The invaders subdued and handcuffed the garrison and hauled them off to jail. One eyewitness, the American journalist, Hugh Sutherland, could not believe that so much military force had been brought to bear on one farmhouse in a time of relative peace. The sheriff allowed Mrs Walsh to remain and some solicitous neighbours attended to her needs.

At a protest meeting held that night speakers praised the defenders and roundly condemned the RIC for acting like bailiffs. Sutherland found the siege both exciting and 'sordid' and admired 'the savage obstinacy' of the garrison. No sooner had the caretaker and his police guard left behind by the sheriff disappeared than the Walshes quietly 'recaptured' their house. Friends and neighbours helped them to repair all the damage. At Westminster nationalist MPs also deplored the use of police to evict tenants; and the Liberal Chief Secretary Birrell sounded just like Arthur Balfour defending the constabulary.[51]

Last but not least, an insolvent shopkeeper named John Shanahan faced eviction by a bankruptcy court at Creggs in northeast Galway on 10 November 1911. Too sick to fight he hired his yardman to defend the premises. This lone defender threw buckets of hot water, gruel, and lime-wash at the bailiffs until they subdued him. Mrs Shanahan walked out with her three children. Ignoring a doctor's diagnosis that her husband was too sick to be removed, the bailiffs swept him up from his bed and carried him outside where he lay in the rain until neighbours conveyed him to a cottage.[52]

The longer that landowners held on to their tenanted and untenanted lands the larger the target they presented to UIL activists determined to advance 'the Cause'. According to Campbell the ranch war was just as important as the land war and the Plan of Campaign in 'the broader struggle between landlord and tenant'. By then serious outrages were few and far between and the shooting death of a police constable at Craughwell in the previous year while chasing some men who had fired at labourers repairing the wall of an evicted holding was an exception. Slowly but surely many of the scars left by the ranch wars began to heal and Redmond promised to deliver a third Home Rule bill to his followers despite the ominous rumblings of militant Ulster Unionism.[53]

If the wheels of the Wyndham act ground slowly, they could not grind finely enough to abolish the inequities inherent in a capitalist agricultural economy. Clearly, the gradual transfer of ownership to the occupying tenants failed to spoil their appetite for Home Rule, as the Dillonites had long feared. Land purchase in short may have realised some of Parnell's and Davitt's hopes of a non-violent end to landlordism but the amicable partnership of ancient foes envisaged by the Land Conferees never came to pass. In fact, the unity of the Redmondite party, as Bew rightly contends, depended on maintaining 'a double standard' or calculated ambiguity about the resolution of the 'land question'.[54]

THE LAND QUEST

—

Years ago Estyn Evans, that wise Welsh 'scientist, humanist, and poet' of Irish geography and material culture, pointed out the central significance of land (and locality) to the Irish people:

> It is to the land that you Irish are bound: this is the one enduring fact. Who will pretend to analyse the emotional and spiritual bonds which tie people to the place of their childhood and to its local environment, and which influence them all their lives in ways they hardly suspect?

In the same address he invoked George Russell (AE)'s pronouncement that the gombeen men or moneylenders in the countryside 'had the power to evict people; and they did so more than many landlords. The landlords owned the land; the Gombeen men owned the people.' But then AE was a devoted co-operativist, mystic, and idealist.

Unpacking the oft-invoked phrase 'land hunger' reveals more than the simple desire to own a few acres of good grazing land and a potato field. Called an indenture, the legal instrument for renting an agricultural holding spelled out clearly the obligations or responsibilities of the signatory. In particular, the tenant was required to keep 'the Demised Premises ... in right, good, perfect order, repair and condition'. He or she also had to maintain all the buildings, fences, ditches, drains, gardens, hedges, and other 'improvements'. Failure to comply with these provisions could cause serious trouble including the necessity of paying for any needed repairs. Tenants were thus caught in a tight web of strictures that must have chafed sorely except on estates where the agent or sub-agent was incompetent, dishonest, or absent for long periods. No wonder then that so many tenants could not wait to possess and manage their own land free at last from the tentacles of landlordism. Accompanying the psychological and material satisfaction of ownership – including an annuity paid to the state that was less than the old rent – was an end to the fear of eviction and relief from the aggravating sense of being 'cabin'd, cribb'd, and confin'd' by landlordism.

When land purchase operations ground to a halt during the Great War, thousands of would-be buyers and sellers were left in the lurch. In the aftermath of Armageddon, Ireland was wracked by both a guerrilla war against the Crown forces and a civil war over the terms of the treaty of 1921. In these troubled times the old land question became quite simply a quest for land whether by legal or other means. With near anarchy prevailing in parts of the south and west farmers' sons and other landless men seized land without the approval of either the Land Commission or the local IRA. They considered this form of land grabbing the undoing of the Cromwellian conquest and plantation. Such seizures occurred despite the sale to tenants of almost nine million acres under the land acts of 1903 and 1909 for a total of £83 millions in 1920 by which time some three million acres remained unsold.

Resentment of landlordism and its practitioners as well as land hunger fuelled the fourth land war that disturbed parts of the country from 1917 to 1923 when Sinn Féin launched a campaign on behalf of smallholders and land-less men. Protestant landlords and strong farmers were ostracised, farms were seized, and graziers as well as 'loyalists' received death threats. Festering anger over the state's failure to break up and reapportion the ranch lands agitated the countryside; and not until the passage of the Land Act of 1923 did compulsory purchase orders begin to improve the lives of thousands of 'congests' who had run out of patience in their long wait for more than a few acres of 'cow's grass' and tillage in the east.[1]

Recapitulating the previous land wars, this new agitation began in Connacht and spread rapidly into parts of Leinster. The Land League's long-term goal of universal peasant proprietorship continued to inspire landless men to expropriate the remaining landlords while extremists espoused insurrection against Castle rule in the wake of the Easter Rising. Thus Eamon de Valera, that resilient survivor of rebellion, urged Sinn Féin members in Clare in February 1918 to join the Volunteers and 'help divide the land evenly'. And in May 1920 the newly established Dáil revived the UIL courts in the name of the nascent 'republic' to arbitrate disputes over land and other issues.

The grievances arising out of the grazing system and the refusal of land-lords to sell their best farmland continued to disturb the peace while the Land Commission struggled to cope with the seemingly endless demand for land. As Peter Hart has made clear, the guerrilla war of 1919–21 and its fratricidal sequel reopened some old wounds from the land wars. Towards the end of April 1922, several days after the IRA's occupation of the Four Courts in Dublin, some landless men shot and killed eight men including a Church of Ireland clergyman around Dunmanway and Clonakilty in west Cork. All the victims were Protestants and their lands were seized. Besides land hunger the motives behind this 'massacre' apparently ranged from retaliation for the pogrom against Catholics in the north to hatred of loyalists or informers and an atavistic resentment of Protestants.[2]

Not even the compulsory powers acquired by the Land Commission under the Land Act of 1923 ended the turmoil over who should own the land. What Dooley has called this 'most important piece of social legislation' charged the commissioners with the arduous task of taking over the duties of the now defunct CDB and redistributing land to the 'deserving' poor. After buying up the unsold acreage at prices much lower than those prevailing in 1903–4, the commissioners parcelled it out to applicants both west and east.

The radical Land Act of 1933 authorised the Land Commission to bestow small farms in Leinster on congests, landless men, unemployed labourers, and other 'deserving' candidates in the western counties. This radical measure did not eliminate the grazier class; and the influx of 'primitive' peasants from the Gaeltacht caused deep dismay among the elitist strong farmers of Meath, whose political representatives called it 'the purest of communism'. Nevertheless the 25,802 allottees who received some 353,000 acres up to March 1937 had good reason to thank de Valera and his party for such a benefaction, whether or not they had enough capital to turn a profit. The relatively few evicted tenants who qualified for these land grants reflected the paucity of *bona fide* evictees. Ironically, these 'internal migration schemes' to end the chronic poverty in the west represented a solution that the prescient Parnell had recommended back in 1880. De Valera's ambitious and costly resettlement programme brought about a modest social revolution in a country where just under one quarter of the rural population belonged to the farmer class.[3] By harnessing the land question to the pursuit of independence in the time-honoured tradition of the New Departure, de Valera also greatly enhanced the appeal of Fianna Fáil.

In the spring of 1922, while IRA units were skirmishing with Provisional government forces and sectarian murders were scarifying northeast Ulster, armed 'hooligans' forced eighteen Protestant families off their farms on the former Lansdowne estate at Luggacurren, County Laois. The victims had apparently been planted there during the Plan evictions three decades earlier. A similar raid by armed men took place on the Cosby property at Stradbally where four Protestant families were expelled from farms they had held since the 1880s. Local people dared not give the victims shelter for fear of reprisal. Following the violent sectarian evictions around the Cosby estate in Laois came the seizure of over eight farms in west Cork and the murder of their Protestant owners who were apparently suspected of being loyalists if not informers.[4]

Last but not least an unusual eviction occurred on the outskirts of Dublin on 15 May 1924. On that morning an under-sheriff arrived at Killakee Castle, Rathfarnham, with orders from a bank to repossess the ancestral house of the thirty-year-old Hon. Hugh Hamon Massy. This son and heir of the 7th Baron Massy lay in bed upstairs in an alcoholic stupor. A doctor arrived and certified that he was fit for removal. Massy refused the offer of an ambulance so the bailiffs carried him out on a mattress and laid him on the roadside while the sheriff took possession. Attended by his wife he lay there for several hours to the amusement of the villagers who had gathered to gawk at this strange sight. Finally, some friends conveyed him in their car to a hotel in town. (In marked contrast to the *Freeman's Journal*, the *Irish Times* chose not to report this incident.) After the eviction Massy returned to the demesne and set up quarters in the gatehouse or Beehive cottage. With no money to his name and incapable of holding a job, he lived off his wife's earnings as a secretary in Ballsbridge and spent the days foraging for firewood in Massy Woods. When his father died in 1926, he succeeded to the barony and became known as 'the penniless peer'.[5] In such microcosmic ways was the 'conquest' of Ireland gradually undone – rood-by-rood and acre-by-acre.

So the cynical and dyspeptic George Moore was right after all when he predicted that the bankers and moneylenders would replace the landlords as the principal evictors in Ireland once the peasantry had conquered the lords of the soil. 'Centuries of inherited idleness and filth' and 'infamous moral teaching', he asserted, had made the Irish peasant what he was.[6] However, Moore missed a crucial point. Paddy's so-called hereditary idleness and immorality applied with equal force to his own class. In short, what was sauce for the plebeian goose was also sauce for the aristocratic gander.

CONCLUSION

The cumulative impact of the realities and images of eviction on contemporaries cannot, of course, be weighed and measured. Nevertheless we may safely assume that burning resentment of eviction pervaded not just Davitt and Dillon but also many of their contemporaries and successors during and after the last days of British rule in the twenty-six counties not to mention Northern Ireland. No matter how parochial they may have appeared, evictions had as many repercussions on the national as well as local level as did agrarian crimes. They affected both the political conscious and unconscious of the Irish populace. However legal any given eviction may have been, questions of an ethical nature were bound to arise over the act of severing the taproots of tenant domesticity and livelihood whether in rain or sunshine. Whatever their justification evictions not only enraged and demoralised communities but also perturbed successive generations of nationalist or republican persuasions who could never forgive the state or Dublin Castle for having backed the landlords to the hilt in these operations.

According to Terry Eagleton, '"Land" in Ireland is a political rallying cry as well as a badge of cultural belonging, a question of rents as well as roots.' One might add that unlike the British experience Irish land proved a constant source and site of contestation. Given the nature of Ireland's so-called conquest and colonisation the descendants of the dispossessed had good reason to ask who were the rightful owners of the land. Margaret O'Callaghan's shrewd contention that the remit of the Irish administration – from the Land Commission to the Local Government Board and beyond – 'provided a dynamic connection between high and low politics' could be applied equally well to the subject of ejectment.[7] Evictions, then, were not just parochial affairs of concern only to the victims and their immediate neighbours. As we have seen, they became major media events in the Dublin and London press after 1879 as well as in newspapers circulating in Greater Ireland overseas. They intruded into ministerial discussions, royal commissions, parliamentary questions and debates, as well as the daily deliberations of the Castle and county officers of the RIC. And in the long run they helped immeasurably to drive more nails into the coffin of Irish landlordism.

Memories of eviction persisted among the people most affected and passed down from one generation to another through anecdotes, folklore, ballads, and songs. During his tour of the 'disturbed' west in 1880 Bernard Becker's jarvey driver regaled him with 'many heartrending and more or less truthful stories of evictions' in Mayo that had depopulated much of that county. Evidently, these destructive acts had 'filled the hearts of the people with revenge, and, rightly or wrongly, they not only blame the landlord but the occupier of the land'. This driver accused Lords Sligo and Lucan of having swept away hordes of cottiers and replacing them with one or two large farmers or graziers from Scotland and England who were paying a lower rent – one pound per Irish acre – than all of the evicted because the landlords knew that they would get their money regularly. However, these evictions had provoked so much hostility that the graziers feared for their lives and returned home leaving all their acres in the landlords' hands. Thirty years after the fact, local people were still 'speak[ing] sorely' about the famine clearances and Becker was shown 'the graveyards which alone mark the sites of thickly populated hamlets abolished by the crowbar'. In fine, the jarvey driver mourned 'the desolation of the land and the ravages of the so-called "crowbar brigade" as if they were things of yesterday'.[8]

Even though the nationalist stereotype of the rackrenting, evicting, and predatory landlord of the Clanricarde ilk gradually receded into the background, it did not disappear. Most country people forgot that some landlords – whether rich or poor – had tolerated arrears of three or more years before proceeding to evict. As Dooley has noted, land hunger lasted long after 1923 and preoccupied ministers and other politicians during the Cosgrave and de Valera regimes. So long as cattle ranches lay undivided and cottiers lived in miserable conditions so long would the land question deserve to be known simply as the quest for land.[9]

However rare actual ejectment may have been after the 1850s – except on the contested Plan of Campaign estates – we must wonder about the psychic toll that the mere threat of eviction took on the sensibilities of tenants at will who failed to pay the rent due for whatever reason. All the apprehensions, tensions, and resentments arising from a writ or *habere* decree go far to explain the mass support for the aims of the Land, the National, and the United Irish Leagues, all of which employed ostensibly non-violent tactics in order to end 'the tyranny' of landlordism and eventually achieve the promised land of both peasant propri-etorship and Home Rule. As Ball rightly points out, the ubiquitous crowds at evictions in the 1880s 'drew on an older tradition of peasant resistance which was defensive and often violent but which was vital in carrying forward a semi-revolutionary programme to permanently alter the social and economic relations of rural Ireland'.[10]

One can only guess at the reactions of British readers who perused newspaper accounts of all those tense confrontations between the sheriff's task force and unruly onlookers at eviction sites. Such reports must have confirmed their belief that Ireland was indeed a foreign country utterly different from England's rural and peaceful countryside. For most Irish Catholics, on the other hand, the images and realities of eviction fostered a victim mentality that sustained both the land agitation and the Home Rule movement.[11] Eviction in short enabled the tenants' advocates to wrap themselves in the mantle of martyrdom while reinforcing their case for returning the land to its rightful owners.

Whatever the legal grounds for the dreaded *habere* decree, the notice to quit was bound to strike tenants and their allies in the towns as morally wrong and living proof of the iniquity of landlordism. The awesome sight of heavily armed police and soldiers parading through the district and aiding and abetting the bailiffs in their 'callous' work could hardly be forgotten by those who bore witness. In Campbell's view, 'land played a critical role' in both the 'social revolution' that began in the 1880s and the 'political revolution' that followed in 1916–23. One may well quibble about the extent of the so-called social revolution that occurred outside the imaginations of the former landowning elite. But there can be no doubt about the extent of the political revolution that gave birth to the flawed democracy known as the Irish Free State.[12]

Besides creating a massive grievance for the tenantry and their political representatives, the mere threat of ejection gave the Catholic clergy a splendid opportunity to enhance their already formidable authority. Priests often stood at the head of angry crowds, helped to dissuade the police from shooting resisters, consoled the homeless, presided over indignation meetings, and attended trials in the coercion courts. They constantly represented their parishioners in negotiations with the agent or owner over rent and arrears, and many of them risked arrest for promoting the League and the Plan. Following in the giant footsteps of Fathers Lavelle and McFadden, a younger generation of priests defied the law by engaging wholeheartedly in 'the struggle for the land'. In sum, they propagated the faith in tenant rights and Home Rule as well as God; and their contributions to these 'noble causes' proved invaluable even when their vision of an independent Ireland differed from that of the 'lay patriots'.[13] Women often played a leading role in resisting eviction and mobilising the community against the forces of law and order. Not only did they fight alongside their husbands and brothers to obstruct the sheriff's party but they also at times surpassed the men in courage and stamina.

In a cultural sense eviction caused not only emotional trauma and material loss but also an ominous absence. Elizabeth Bowen expressed this lack in a haunting passage about the death of once lived-in and lively houses:

> This is a country of ruins. Lordly or humble, military or domestic … ruins feature the landscape – uplands or river valleys – and make a ghostly extra quarter to towns … Fallen-in farms and cabins take only some years to vanish. Only major or recent ruins keep their human stories; from others the story quickly evaporates. Some ruins show gashes of violence, others simply the dull slant of decline. … Not all these are ruins of wars: where there has not been violence there has been abandonment. Mansions, town houses, farmhouses, cottages have often been left to die – and very few people know the story of the bitter necessity.

With profound insight she added: 'We have everything to dread from the dispossessed.'[14]

One obvious reason for that dread involved the highly emotive association of eviction with 'extermination' – the coinage that dominated tenant-right discourses during the famine. Dispossession triggered painful thoughts of the original 'conquest' by English or Anglo-Norman-Welsh invaders and the planting of 'foreign' settlers on the 'native' soil. The leitmotif of loss played powerfully into the struggle for independence and memories of eviction doubtless inspired some 'bitter and violent men' to burn down over two hundred 'ancestral houses' during the Troubles in the name of undoing 'the Cromwellian conquest' and purging the country of the 'ould oppressors'.[15]

Kevin Whelan's reading of Paul Ricoeur serves as a reminder that memory is neither static nor monolithic. The selective and subjective nature of memory, he asserts, can help us to 'liberate ourselves from the ligatures of the past through the capacity for forgiveness'. One wonders, however, if the nationalist habit of demonising the landlords left much room for either forgiving or forgetting. One of those who fell into this category was the intelligent and articulate Home Ruler, William J. O'Neill Daunt of Kilcasan, County Cork. A minor landowner who had converted to Catholicism in his youth and helped O'Connell to found the Repeal Association, Daunt had no time for the 'brawlers' and 'spouters' of the Land League including Davitt. Nevertheless he too blamed the land war on the tyranny of the landed elite. A lifelong opponent of the Union, he condemned the narrow-minded, selfish, and sectarian attitudes of the (Protestant) landlords who had 'mercilessly scourged the unfortunate people by intolerable rents and capricious evictions'. In the eyes of this thoughtful old warhorse, the 'insatiable West British landlords' in their 'heartless greed' had done everything in their power to enslave rather than emancipate 'their native land'. And by nationalist standards of the day, Daunt was a moderate.

In his classic study, *Passing the Time in Ballymenone*, the 'existential' and empathetic ethnographer, Henry Glassie, recorded the daily and nightly routine and mentalities of a predominately Catholic community in the parish of Cleenish near Lough Erne just inside the border of Northern Ireland. Among many discoveries during his sojourn in 1972 was the lingering hostility to the land-lords, agents, middlemen, and bailiffs who had once ruled this society. Memories of the bad old 'days of the landlords' persisted. According to one trusted respondent the landlords had once possessed the power to evict tenants just for cutting down a tree. Because a tenant could not make a will as soon as he or she died, the family 'could be out on the road in a week'. Here and there a decent proprietor might be found. But in general 'you could be evicted any time. And they did it. They did it.' Given their exposure to rack rents and arbitrary eviction, the tenants rebelled by founding the Land League and forcing the government to lower their rents.

Eventually, the state bought out the landlords and sold the farms to the occupiers. As one local Fermanagh man exclaimed, 'It was the first great victory ever they got was to get rid of the landlords.' Paraphrasing another informant, Glassie reported that even though the landlords were Christians, they did not 'treat their fellows well'. Some of them made their labourers feel 'like slaves out of Africa'. One old widow walked forty miles to Ballyconnell to pay her rent on time. She saved thereby one shilling that she spent on enough oats and sugar to make a 'noggin' of gruel. The landlords, in short, 'depressed us' and 'racked us'. Landlordism, then, 'was a system, but … it was a system dependent on indi-viduals. Even if the landlords were absent, the middlemen, agents, and bailiffs were not. They lived right here.' For these reasons 'they could be opposed, fought and justly murdered'.

Such utterances constitute far more perceptions than lived realities. The aversion of so many tenants for the rent nexus was, of course, greatly exacerbated by the profound differences of religion, ethnicity, class, and history between 'them' and 'us'. Bombarded by rancorous or satirical denunciations of the landed elite in Land League or nationalist speeches, newspapers, and cartoons, the Catholic tenants of Anglo-Irish proprietors could hardly be expected to respect the right of their masters to own the land. Whatever the justification for their diatribes against the old Ascendancy, Glassie's friends in Ballymenone serve as living proof that the demonisation of the landlords thrived well into the twentieth century.[16]

Accusations of callous evictions and 'extortionate' rents were not confined to the plebeian votaries of the Land League. One is reminded of Yeats's immortal phrase, 'great hatred, little room'. To cite two other prominent examples of unburied axes, neither Davitt, who had personally tasted the bitter aloe of eviction, nor Dillon, whose grandfather had been evicted in Roscommon, showed much inclination to forgive.

As for Irish-American mentalities, Kevin O'Neill contends that the 'social memory' of famine emigrants contained vivid 'images of failure, devastation, and pain' many of which derived from eviction.[17] Not only did the collective memory of the clearances and forced emigration refuse to go away; it also became a highly politicised threnody in Irish Catholic communities at home and abroad. In the aftermath of the Great Famine the twin grievances of dispossession and forced emigration formed an essential part of Irish Catholic identity. On the same score Kerby Miller has argued that most Irish-American Catholics saw themselves 'not as voluntary, ambitious emigrants but as involuntary, nonresponsible "exiles" compelled to leave home by forces beyond individual control, particularly by British and landlord oppression'. To the extent that these immigrants suffered from a sense of exile, epitomised by 'the American wake' with its traditional songs of lament sung on the eve of parting, there can be little doubt that eviction – whether actual or threatened – played a vital role in shaping this mentality of alienation.[18]

Ian McBride's emphasis on the 'social' nature of memory, moreover, applies directly to eviction because it seared the minds of not just the families affected but also the crowds that gathered to support the victims and bear witness.[19] In familial or communal settings memories of eviction – what Raymond Williams called 'structures of feeling' – were 'reconstructed over and over again' for the emotional benefit of all concerned.

During the first decade of the twentieth century a younger generation of militants, many of whom were urban Gaelic Leaguers, embraced the radical ideals of Sinn Féin and Republicanism in the quest for a more Gaelic and independent nation free from the two great banes of landlordism and British rule. The leaders of the movement for cultural as well as political separatism –

ranging from D. P. Moran to Patrick Pearse, and Arthur Griffith – had not forgotten about Kilrush, Glenveagh, Partry, Glenbeigh, Woodford, Bodyke, Coolroe, Coolgreany, Clongorey, Falcarragh, and Youghal, let alone the famine clearances. Many of their followers in towns as well as rural areas took pride in the feats of such heroes and heroines as Thomas Saunders, Ned O'Grady, Thomas Somers, Mary Quirke, the McNamara women, and the O'Halloran sisters. Then there is the case of Dan Breen, the indestructible guerrilla fighter who fired the opening salvo of the Anglo-Irish war at Soloheadbeg, County Tipperary, in January 1919 that killed two constables who were escorting a wagon filled with dynamite. Born in 1894, Breen could never forget 'the last eviction' one mile from his home at Grange where the bailiffs had driven out a relative and left him to die by the roadside. Apparently, this event made an 'indelible impression'.[20]

To sum up, if there is any truth in Laurence M. Geary's assertion that 'the representation and deconstruction of any historical event, the ways in which it is perceived, and remembered, are often as important as the event itself', then the long and painful story of rural evictions played a vital part in nurturing Irish nationalism during its formative period.[21]

POSTSCRIPT

The refusal of the land question to disappear from Irish mentalities and the reductionist nature of political memory came home to me forcibly one night during a visit to Derry in August 1971. Returning from a late-night excursion across the border into Donegal, my companion (a young early modern Irish historian transplanted from Trinity College Dublin to Magee College) and I heard the muffled but booming sound of a bomb in the Bogside. We prudently waited half an hour before descending cautiously into town. After parking the car we walked down William Street – the site of so many confrontations – in the pitch dark. We soon found ourselves in a surreal scene ankle-deep in broken glass from the blasted warehouse. Under floodlights workmen were already busy nailing plywood panels into the empty window frames. I approached a grizzled old man standing in a doorway opposite the bombsite who told me that he was the last resident of this street. When I tried to offer words of commiseration, he muttered emphatically and without any prompting: 'It's all the fault of the landlords.'

L.P.C. jr
21 August 2010

Notes

PREFACE

1   L. Perry Curtis, Jr, '"The land for the people": post-famine images of eviction', in Vera Kreilkamp (ed.), *ÉIRE/LAND* (Boston, McMullen Museum of Art, Boston College, 2003), pp. 85–92.

INTRODUCTION

1   Hayden White, *Tropics of Discourse: Essays in Cultural Criticism* (Baltimore, 1978), pp. 121–34; J. P. Mahaffy, 'The Irish landlords', *Contemporary Review* 41 (Jan. 1882), p. 160.

2   James Godkin, *The Land-War in Ireland: A History for the Times* (London, 1870), p. 411.

3   Barbara L. Solow, *The Land Question and the Irish Economy, 1870–1903* (Cambridge, MA, 1971); W. E. Vaughan, *Landlords and Tenants in Mid-Victorian Ireland* (hereafter, *LTMVI*) (Oxford, 1994), esp. pp. 21, 24–9, 126–37, 215–28; Mahaffy, 'Irish landlords', pp. 160–76. Cormac Ó Gráda, *Ireland: A New Economic History, 1780–1939* (Oxford, 1995), pp. 255–6. See also David Vallone and Christine Kinealy (eds), *Ireland's Great Hunger* (Lanham, 2002), p. 143; and Tim P. O'Neill, 'Famine evictions' in Carla King (ed.), *Famine, Land and Culture in Ireland* (Dublin, 2000), p. 54.

4   O'Neill, 'Famine evictions', pp. 29, 58.

5   Robert J. Scally, *The End of Hidden Ireland: Rebellion, Famine, and Emigration* (New York, 1995), p. 112.

6   Stephen Ball, 'Crowd activity during the Irish Land War, 1879–90' in Peter Jupp and Eoin Magennis (eds), *Crowds in Ireland, c.1720–1920* (Basingstoke, 2000), pp. 212–41.

7   Quoted in F.S.L. Lyons, *John Dillon: A Biography* (London, 1968), p. 38. William Gladstone called eviction a 'death sentence'. *Freeman's Journal* (hereafter *FJ*), 12 Nov. 1888.

8   Brian P. Kennedy, 'The traditional Irish thatched house: image and reality, 1793–1903' in Adele M. Dalsimer (ed.), *Visualizing Ireland: National Identity and the Pictorial Tradition* (Winchester, MA, 1993), esp. pp. 165–6.

9   Quoted in Mic Moroney, 'Postcards from the edge', *Cara* 32: 2 (Mar.–Apr. 1998), p. 21.

10   Christopher Morash, *Writing the Irish Famine* (Oxford, 1995), p. 175.

11   Brian P. Kennedy and Raymond Gillespie (eds), *Ireland: Art into History* (Dublin, 1994), pp. 8–9.

12   Fintan Cullen, 'Art history: using the visual' in Laurence M. Geary and Margaret Kelleher, *Nineteenth-Century Ireland: A Guide to Recent Research* (Dublin, 2005), p. 162.

13   See Father Lavelle's indictment of English imperialism and Irish landlordism in *The Irish Landlord Since the Revolution* (Dublin, 1870), esp. pp. 5–36.

14   Michael Davitt, *The Fall of Feudalism in Ireland* (London, 1904), p. xvii.

1 DISPOSSESSION AND IRISH LAND LAWS

1   Sarah S. Gibson and Paul G. Kuntz, 'Expulsion', *Encyclopedia of Comparative Iconography* (Chicago, 1998), vol. 1, pp. 299–305; Sir George Nicholls, *A History of the Irish Poor Law* (Dublin, 1856; New York, 1967), pp. 160–1.

2   Gustave de Beaumont, *Ireland: Social, Political, and Religious* ed. and trans. W. C. Taylor (Cambridge, MA. 2006), pp. 30–1; Terry Eagleton, *Heathcliff and the Great Hunger* (London, 1995), pp. 42–3.

3   Rev. T. O'Rorke, *History … of … the Parishes of Ballysadare and Kilvarnet* (Dublin, 1878), pp. 164–7; Sir William Butler, 'They were a great people, Sir', *The Light of the West, 1865–1908* (Dublin, 1933), pp. 145–8, 152.

4   Quoted in Declan Kiberd, *Inventing Ireland* (London, 1995), p. 172.

5   Hugh Sutherland, *Ireland: Yesterday and Today* (Philadelphia, 1909), p. 63. He was a staff writer for the *North American*.

6   *People*, 11 Aug. 1888.

7   Solow, *Land Question*, pp. 51–7, 203; Vaughan, *LTMVI*, pp. ix, 21; O'Neill, 'Famine evictions', pp. 55–7.

8   Ó Gráda, *Ireland: A New Economic History*, p. 256; Michael Turner, *After the Famine: Irish Agriculture, 1850–1914* (Cambridge, 1996), p. 167; Vaughan, *LTMVI*, pp. 21–4; and K. Theodore Hoppen, *Elections, Politics, and Society in Ireland 1832–1885* (Oxford, 1984), pp. 127–8.

9   Vaughan, *LTMVI*, pp. 67–102. Compensation for disturbance usually caused much more aggravation than compensation for improvements.

10   James S. Donnelly, Jr, *Captain Rock: The Irish Agrarian Rebellion of 1821–1824* (Madison, 2009), pp. 228–9, 347–48, 434–35, n. 11. For the 'feigned lessee' and the 'casual evictor', see O'Neill, 'Famine evictions', pp. 32–8 as well as Thomas de Moleyns and Albert W. Quill, *The Landowner's and Agent's Practical Guide* (7th edn, Dublin, 1877), pp. 165–6.

11   O'Neill, 'Famine evictions', pp. 41, 46–7; De Moleyns and Quill, *Landowner's Practical Guide*, pp. 163–4; Robert B. MacCarthy, *The Trinity College Estates: 1800–1923* (Dundalk, 1992), esp. pp. 65–6, 112–13.

12   O'Neill discusses the various legal procedures governing eviction and the incidence of agrarian crime in 'Famine evictions', pp. 32–9, 41–2.

13   For the Landlord and Tenant Law Amendment Act (Ireland) 1860, see Francis Nolan and Robert R. Kane, *The Statutes Relating to the Law of Landlord and Tenant in Ireland* (Dublin, 1878), pp. 2–114. See also O'Neill, 'Famine Evictions', pp. 33–8.

14   For the Landlord and Tenant Act (Ireland) 1870, see Nolan and Kane, *Statutes Relating to the Law of Landlord and Tenant in Ireland*, pp. 1–xix, 125–296; R. R. Cherry, *The Irish Land Law and Land Purchase Acts, 1860 to 1891* (2nd edn, Dublin, 1893), pp. 88–110, 156–77; Robert Donnell, *Practical Guide to the Law of Tenant Compensation and Farm Purchase under the Irish Land Act* (Dublin, 1871); E. D. Steele, *Irish Land and British Politics: Tenant-Right and Nationality, 1865–1870* (Cambridge, 1974); and Vaughan, *LTMVI*, pp. 93–102.

15   A. M. Sullivan, *New Ireland* (London, 1878), pp. 371–2.

16   Vaughan, *LTMVI*, p. 22.

17   De Moleyns and Quill, *Landowner's Guide*, pp. 163–96; W. E Vaughan, *Landlords and Tenants in Ireland, 1848–1904* (Dundalk, 1984), pp. 15–16, 24, and Vaughan, *LTMVI*, pp. 21–5, 31, 43; Cecil R. Roche and Thomas D. Rearden, *The Irish Land Code and Labourers Acts* (Dublin, 1896), pp. 384–402; Nolan and Kane, *Statutes Relating to the Law of Landlord and Tenant*, p. 4; Cherry, *Irish Land Law*, pp. 99–114, 383–5; and W. F. Bailey, *The Irish Land Acts, A Short Sketch* (Dublin, 1917), pp. 14–15.

18   The hanging gale was eliminated under the Land Purchase Act of 1896. Gerard J. Lyne, *The Lansdowne Estate in Kerry Under the Agency of William Steuart Trench 1849–72* (Dublin, 2001), pp. 184–92; Vaughan, *LTMVI*, pp. 113–14.

19 Hoppen, *Elections*, pp. 33–42, 73, 125–7, 145–6; J. H. Whyte, 'Landlord influence at elections in Ireland, 1760–1885', *English Historical Review* LXXX (Oct. 1965), pp. 743–4.

20 De Moleyns and Quill, *Landowner's Guide*, pp. 125–39.

21 Vaughan, *LTMVI*, pp. 31, 92; De Moleyns and Quill, *Landowner's Guide*, pp. 180–8; and Nolan and Kane, *Law of Landlord and Tenant*, pp. 71–4, 90–2.

22 James S. Donnelly, Jr, *The Great Irish Potato Famine* (hereafter, *GIPF*) (Thrupp-Stroud, 2001), pp. 152–3; De Moleyns and Quill, *Landowner's Guide*, pp. 164–7; *Times*, 6 Feb. 1882.

23 Vaughan, *LTMVI*, pp. 22, 29–30.

24 The Land Act of 1870 empowered a tenant to file a claim for compensation for improvements if he could prove that he had been 'disturbed' unjustly. *Rules for Proceedings Under Part I of the Landlord and Tenant (Ireland) Act, 1870* (Dublin, 1870), pp. 4–6.

25 Vaughan, *LTMVI*, pp. 20–9.

26 See Tables 1 and 2 in Solow, *Land Question*, pp. 54–7.

27 See Vaughan's cautionary comments about eviction data in Appendix I, 'Eviction Statistics, 1849–1887', *LTMVI*, pp. 229–31.

28 NLI, Leitrim Papers, Rental for 1856–7, MS 3804. Vaughan considers the high rents on the Leitrim estates exceptional.

29 Vaughan, *LTMVI*, pp. 44–66, 84–7, 119–30 and Vaughan, 'An assessment of the economic performance of Irish landlords, 1851–81' in F. S. L. Lyons and R. A. J. Hawkins (eds), *Ireland Under the Union: Varieties of Tension* (Oxford, 1980), pp. 189–98; *Times*, 13 Oct. 1860.

30 Griffith was testifying before the Select Committee on General Valuation etc. (Ireland). See Report, *HC 1868–9* (362), IX, 1, pp. 60–1. Thomas Nelson, *The Land War in County Kildare* (Maynooth, 1989), pp. 15–16.

31 Hoppen, *Elections*, pp. 127–9.

32 Vaughan, *LTMVI*, pp. 29–31.

33 Vaughan, *LTMVI*, pp. 141–64, 177–9; L. Perry Curtis, 'Landlord responses to the Irish Land War, 1879–87', *Éire-Ireland* 38: III & IV (2003), pp. 156–8.

34 W. H. Hurlbert, *Ireland Under Coercion*, vol. II (Edinburgh, 1888), p. 200.

35 Vaughan, *LTMVI*, pp. 35, 230–1; Donnelly, *GIPF*, pp. 111–16. Father Lavelle reckoned that 270,000 houses were destroyed between 1841 and 1861, and 1.3 million people were 'driven to the workhouse, exile, or death'. Lavelle, *Irish Landlord*, p. 266.

36 Kevin Whelan, 'An underground gentry? Catholic middlemen in eighteenth-century Ireland', in James S. Donnelly and Kerby A. Miller (eds), *Irish Popular Culture, 1650–1850* (Dublin, 1998), pp. 118–72; Donnelly, *GIPF*, pp. 132, 134–6, Vaughan, *LTMVI*, pp. 256–58; and Ó Gráda, *Ireland*, pp. 31, 33, 124–7; MacCarthy, *Trinity College Estates*, passim.

37 Vaughan, *LTMVI*, p. 21.

38 'Decline of the Celtic Race', quoted in *Times*, 14 Sept. 1854.

39 Kevin Whelan, 'Eviction', in W. J. Mc Cormack (ed.), *The Blackwell Companion to Modern Irish Culture* (Oxford, 1999), p. 204.

40 O'Neill, 'Famine evictions', pp. 41–2.

41 *Waterford News and General Advertiser*, 4 July 1889. William Pembroke Mulchinock (1820–64) was the author of 'The Rose of Tralee'.

2 THE FAMINE EVICTIONS

1   Davitt used the incendiary term 'holocaust' in his epic work, *The Fall of Feudalism*, p. 50. Lady Gregory's comment is quoted in Valone and Kinealy (eds), *Ireland's Great Hunger*, p. 143. See also Ó Gráda, *Ireland: A New Economic History*, pp. 178–87; O'Neill, 'Famine evictions', pp. 39–48; W. E. Vaughan, *Sin, Sheep and Scotsmen* (Belfast, 1983), p. 27; David S. Jones, 'The cleavage between graziers and peasants in the land struggle, 1890–1910', table 10.4 in Samuel Clark and James S. Donnelly, Jr (eds), *Irish Peasants: Violence and Political Unrest, 1780–1914* (Manchester, 1983), p. 393. See also Joel Mokyr, *Why Ireland Starved* (London, 1983), pp. 262–7.

2   Davitt, *Fall of Feudalism*, p. 68; O'Neill, 'Famine evictions', pp. 29–32. Davitt based his estimate for the famine years on Michael G. Mulhall who greatly exaggerated the numbers in his *Dictionary of Statistics* (London, 1886), where he asserted that 363,000 families suffered final eviction between 1849 and 1882 equivalent to 1,815,000 individuals (p. 175). He placed readmissions at 25 per cent. See also Vaughan, *LTMVI*, p. 21.

3   Scott Brewster and Virginia Crossman, 'Re-writing the famine: witnessing in crisis', in *Ireland in Proximity: History, Gender, Space*, ed. Scott Brewster et al. (London, 1999), pp. 42, 44.

4   Ó Gráda, *Ireland, A New Economic History*, p. 480, n. 27. Raymond D. Crotty, *Irish Agricultural Production* (Cork, 1966), pp. 44–6. For a revisionist study of famine relief efforts, see Robin Haines, *Charles Trevelyan and the Great Irish Famine* (Dublin, 2004).

5   Vaughan, *LTMVI*, p. 138; A. M. Sullivan, *New Ireland* (London 1878), p. 59.

6   For the varying estimates of excess deaths during the famine, see Cormac Ó Gráda, *Ireland, A New Economic History*, pp. 178–87, *Ireland before and after the Famine* (Manchester, 1988), pp. 82–8, and *Black '47 and Beyond: The Great Irish Famine* (Princeton, 1999), pp. 4, 38–43 as well as Mokyr, *Why Ireland Starved*, esp. pp. 264–8. Besides Donnelly, *GIPF*, pp. 169–78, see Cecil Woodham-Smith's *The Great Hunger* (London, 1962), the dated anthology edited by R. Dudley Edwards and T. Desmond Williams, *The Great Famine* (New York, 1957), Christine Kinealy, *This Great Calamity* (Dublin, 1994), and Cathal Pórtéir (ed.), *The Great Irish Famine* (Cork and Dublin, 1995).

7   Donnelly, 'The administration of relief, 1847–51', chapter XVI in W. E. Vaughan (ed.), *A New History of Ireland*, V, *Ireland Under the Union*, I: *1801–70* (Oxford, 1989), pp. 318–19; Donnelly, *GIPF*, pp. 92–112; Woodham-Smith, *Great Hunger*, pp. 310–20; and *Clare Journal* (hereafter, *CJ*), 6 May 1847.

8   For the amended Irish Poor Law Act of 1847 and the Gregory clause, see Donnelly, *GIPF*, pp. 102, 110–12. Canon John O'Rourke called the Gregory clause a 'complete engine for the slaughter and expatriation of a people'. *The History of the Great Irish Famine of 1847* (Dublin, 1874 and 1989), p. 171. See also *FJ*, 28 Dec. 1847. For Lord Clarendon's 'firm' views on dealing with Irish pauperism, see Peter Gray, *Famine, Land and Politics* (Dublin, 1999), esp. pp. 168–72, 307–10.

9   Kevin Whelan, 'Pre and post-famine landscape change' in Pórtéir, *Great Irish Famine*, pp. 19–33; Peter Gray, *The Irish Famine* (London, 1995), pp. 69, 71, and Donnelly, 'Mass eviction and the Great Famine' in Pórtéir, *Great Irish Famine*, pp. 155–6.

10   'The outcry against evictions', *CJ*, 28 May 1849 and *Cork Examiner* (hereafter, *CE*), 27 Aug. 1849, and Donnelly, *GIPF*, pp. 123–4; *FJ*, 13, 17 Jan. and 25 Mar. 1846.

11   Michael de Nie analyses famine reportage in the British press in *The Eternal Paddy: Irish Identity and the British Press, 1798–1882* (Madison, 2004), pp. 82–143. For a classic example of the Anglo-Saxonist case against the 'savage' Irish Celt, see the *Economist*, quoted in *CJ*, 8 May 1848.

12   John Mitchel, *The Last Conquest of Ireland (Perhaps)* (Dublin, 2005), esp. pp. 66–9, 118–21, 126–34, 195–209 and his compilation, *The History of Ireland from the Treaty of Limerick to the Present Time being a Continuation of the History of the Abbé MacGeoghegan* (London, n.d.), vol. 2, p. 215.

13   De Nie, *Eternal Paddy*, pp. 84–94, 118–32; Woodham-Smith, *Great Hunger*, p. 156; Gray, *Famine*, pp. 227–83; Brewster and Crossman, 'Re-writing the famine', *Ireland in Proximity*, p. 46.

14   Lavelle, *Irish Landlord*, pp. 262–3, 280–2. For British official ideology and practices during the famine see Gray, *Famine, Land and Politics*, passim.

15   Irish Poor Law Inquiry, Appendix II (22 Mar. 1849), *BPP 1849*, vol. xvi. No. 507, pp. 51–2. Donald Jordan, *Land and Popular Politics in Ireland* (Cambridge, 1994), p. 107 and Woodham-Smith, *Great Hunger*, pp. 298–9.

16   *Times*, 24 Mar. 1846.

17   See the debates in the House of Lords on 5, 12, Feb. and 12 Mar. 1846. *Times*, 6, 13 Feb. and 13 Mar. 1846.

18   Sir William P. MacArthur, 'Medical history of the famine' in Edwards and Williams, *Great Famine*, pp. 263–315.

19   For Skibbereen in 1847, see Lord Dufferin and the Hon. G. F. Boyle, *Narrative of a Journey from Oxford to Skibbereen During the Year of the Irish Famine* (Oxford, 1847), pp. 1–23. See also Woodham-Smith, *Great Hunger*, esp. pp. 143–205; Roger J. McHugh, 'The famine in Irish oral tradition', in Edwards and Williams, *Great Famine*, pp. 391–436; Cathal Póirtéir (ed.), *Famine Echoes* (Dublin, 1995); Brendan Ó Cathaoir, *Famine Diary* (Dublin, 1999); *Limerick and Clare Examiner* (hereafter, *LCE*), 13 Dec. 1848, 14 Feb., 30 May 1849 and *CJ*, 6 May 1847.

20   Osborne's letters to the *Times*, signed 'S.G.O.', were published under the title, *Gleanings in the West of Ireland* (London, 1850). See also *The Letters of S. G. O.*, ed Arnold White, 2 vols, (London, 1891), esp. vol. I, pp. 223–82 and vol. II, pp. 294–5 as well as *Oxford DNB*, vol. 42, pp. 23–4.

21   Asenath Nicholson, *Annals of the Famine in Ireland*, ed. Maureen Murphy (Dublin, 1998), pp. 27, 72–7, 108–11, 114–16, 132 and *Ireland's Welcome to the Stranger* (New York, 1847). See also Gordon Bigelow, 'Asenath Nicholson's new domestic economy', in Marilyn Cohen and Nancy J. Curtin (eds), *Reclaiming Gender: Transgressive Identities in Modern Ireland* (New York, 1999), pp. 145–60.

22   Quoted by Davitt, *Fall of Feudalism*, p. 223. See also Lady Wilde's ('Speranza') poignant poem, 'The Famine Year' (1847) quoted in Gray, *Irish Famine*, pp. 167–8. For more famine horrors, see Póirtéir, 'Folk memory and the famine: in Póirtéir, *Great Irish Famine*, pp. 221–30 and *Famine Echoes*, pp. 50–131, 182–96, 229–43 as well as O'Rourke, *Great Irish Famine*, pp. 269–75, 365–6, 388–90, 403–7, 418, 482–504.

23   See Lalor's letters to the *Nation* and the *Irish Felon* quoted in L. Fogarty, *James Fintan Lalor: Patriot and Political Essayist* (Dublin, 1919), esp. pp. 12–13, 37, 57–66, 93–102.

24   Woodham-Smith, *Great Hunger*, pp. 157–9, 188–205. The Society of Friends raised £242,000 for the needy. James Hack Tuke, *A Visit to Connaught in the Autumn of 1847* (London, 1848), esp. pp. 18–27 and Tuke, *A Memoir*, comp. Sir Edward Fry (London, 1899), pp. 40–71; *Oxford DNB*, vol. 55, pp. 528–30; and Gray, *Famine*, pp. 191–2, 261.

25   Evidently, 131 families had found berths in Ballina poorhouse by February 1848. Tuke, *Connaught*, pp. 18–27, 62–8 and *Memoir*, pp. 146–8, 256–65; Gray, *Famine*, p. 191 and Jordan, *Land and Popular Politics*, p. 111.

26   David Seth Jones, *Graziers, Land Reform, and Political Conflict in Ireland* (Washington, DC, 1995), pp. 90–106; Donnelly, *Cork*, p. 57; Donnelly, 'Captain Rock: the origins of the Irish agrarian rebellion of 1821–24', *New Hibernia Review* II: 4 (Winter 2007), pp. 47–72; and Donnelly, *Captain Rock*, pp. 225–66.

27 Sullivan, *New Ireland*, pp. 42–5; Fitzpatrick, 'Emigration, 1801–70', *NHI*, v, p. 596; and W. J. O'Neill Daunt, *Eighty-Five Years of Irish History* (London, 1888), pp. 169–70.

28 Emigrating to western Pennsylvania, the Molly Maguires enforced their brand of 'popular justice' against coal mine managers and agents. Far more reliable than Trench's version of events on the Shirley estate and their aftermath in *Realities*, pp. 30–40, are Kevin Kenny, *Making Sense of the Molly Maguires* (New York, 1998), pp. 13–44 and Wayne G. Broehl, Jr, *The Molly Maguires* (Cambridge, Mass., 1964), pp. 21–32, 41–70. For evictions in Queen's county, see J. W. H. Carter, *The Land War and its Leaders in Queen's County, 1879–82* (Portlaoise, 1994), Appendix 11, pp. 299–300.

29 Gray, *Famine, Land and Politics*, pp. 181–2, 186–91; O'Neill, 'Famine evictions', pp. 53, 59–61; Donnelly, *GIPF*, p. 158; Donnelly, 'Mass evictions and the Great Famine: the clearances revisited', in Póirtéir, *Great Irish Famine*, pp. 155–6; Sir Francis B. Head, *A Fortnight in Ireland* (London, 1852), pp. 140–2; Donnelly, *Cork*, p. 118; Vaughan, *LTMVI*, pp. 24–7, 229–30, 297–8; Haines, *Trevelyan*, p. 164; James Quinn, 'The exterminator', *History Ireland* (Sept./Oct. 2009), p. 66; Gray, *Irish Famine*, p. 68; Ó Gráda, *Black '47 and Beyond*, pp. 44–5; Ciarán Ó Murchadha (ed.), *County Clare Studies* (Ennis, 2000), pp. 253–6.

30 For scalps and scalpeens, see Woodham-Smith, *Great Hunger*, pp. 72, 226, 277; Donnelly, *GIPF*, pp. 113, 155. See also Scally, *End of Hidden Ireland*, p. 112; Jonathan Bell and Mervyn Watson, *A History of Irish Farming, 1750–1950* (Dublin, 2008), pp. 37–40; and William Nolan et al. (eds), *Donegal: History and Society* (Dublin, 1995), p. 481.

31 S. Redmond, *Landlordism in Ireland: Letters on the Eviction of the Gerrard Tenantry* (Dublin, 1846), pp. 14–28, 46–50. See also *FJ*, 27–28, 30 Mar., 2 Apr. 1846 and *LCE*, 4 Apr. 1846; Mitchel, *Last Conquest*, pp. 109–10. For Londonderry's speech, see *Times*, 20, 24, 31 Mar. 1846. See also Woodham-Smith, *Great Hunger*, pp. 71–2 and Gray, *Famine, Land and Politics*, pp. 90–1, 132. See also McHugh, 'The famine in Irish oral tradition', Edwards and Williams, *Great Famine*, pp. 428–9.

32 Padraig G. Lane, 'The management of estates by financial corporations in Ireland after the famine', *Studia Hibernica* 14 (1974), pp. 70–6. Almost three-quarters of all the holdings in Mayo ranged between one and five acres. Jordan, *Land and Popular Politics*, pp. 67–70, 112–13, 116. See also Head, *Fortnight in Ireland*, pp. 158–9.

33 Lavelle, *Irish Landlord*, p. 270.

34 For Father Matt McQuaid's verdict on the Farnham estate evictions in Cavan in 1847–8, see Marianne Elliott, *The Catholics of Ulster* (New York, 2001), pp. 310–11.

35 Marcus Keane (also spelled Kean) managed almost 40 per cent of the land in Kilrush poor law union. See Donnelly, *GIPF*, pp. 144–56; Ciarán Ó Murchadha, '"The exterminator general of Clare" – Marcus Keane of Beech Park' in Ó Murchadha, *County Clare Studies*, esp. pp. 169–77; and Monsignor Ignatius Murphy, *A People Starved: Life and Death in West Clare, 1845–1851* (Dublin, 1996), pp. 33–83.

36 *LCE*, 3 Nov. 1847, 11, 25, 29 Mar., 12 Apr. 1848, and 13 June, 11, 18 Aug. 1849; Donnelly, *GIPF*, pp. 144–56.

37 Ó Murchadha, '"Exterminator general"', pp. 178–81, 187–90. For the controversy over Keane's evictions, see Donnelly, *GIPF*, pp. 144–9; Woodham-Smith, *Great Hunger*, pp. 319, 336, 364–5, 368; *CJ*, 3 Apr. 1848, 16, 20 Aug. 1849, 11 Nov. 1850; and *LCE*, 8 Apr. 1848, 13 June, 19 Sept., 13 Oct. 1849.

38 Scrope's letter to the *Morning Chronicle* also appeared in the *CJ*, 4 Oct. 1849. See also Donnelly, *GIPF*, pp. 146–53; Ó Murchadha, 'Exterminator General', pp. 175–6, 187–9, 196; and *LCE*, 2, 6 Sept. 1848, 14 Feb., 2, 16, 30 May, 13 June, 11, 17, 18 Aug., 19 Sept. 1849.

39 *LCE*, 16 May, 19 Sept., 13 Oct., 8 Dec. 1849.

40 *LCE*, 13, 17 Jan., 7 Feb. 1849.

41 *LCE*, 25, 29 Mar., 5, 12, 5, 19 Apr., 2, 6, 30 Sept., 11, 29 Nov., 2, 6 Dec. 1848.

42 A Celtic high cross marks the mass grave at Kilrush overlooking Scattery Island with the inscription: 'In enduring memory of the numerous heroes of West Clare who died of hunger rather than pervert [*sic*] in the Great Famine and who were buried here coffinless in three large pits.' E. J. McAuliffe, *Notes on the Parishes of Kilmurry McMahon and Killofin, Co. Clare* (Dublin, 1989), p. 21. See also Noel J. Mulqueen, *The Vandeleur Evictions and the Plan of Campaign in Kilrush* (Ennis, 1988), pp. 14–18.

43 Sullivan, *New Ireland*, pp. 120–1.

44 UCD, National Folklore Collection (hereafter, NFC) 407/176.

45 See the mild resistance of a few families at Kilmurry, Ibrickane near Miltown Malbay, County Clare, *CJ*, 16 Apr. 1849.

46 In 1845, when Major Mahon acquired this 27,000-acre Crown estate, arrears amounted to £13,000 exclusive of the poor rates. Scally, *End of Hidden Ireland*, pp. 82–6, 95, 100–4. See also the website: www.ballykilcline.com/evicted_f.html.

47 As for 'Molly Maguirism' around Ballykilcline, see the murder of an alleged informer in Scally, *End of Hidden Ireland*, pp. 96–104.

48 Scally, *End of Hidden Ireland*, pp. 38–40, 95, 105–29; Donnelly, *GIPF*, pp. 141–3, Woodham-Smith, *Great Hunger*, pp. 324–5; Gray, *Famine*, pp. 182–3, 186–7; Ó Cathaoir, *Famine Diary*, pp. 137–8; and David Fitzpatrick, 'Emigration, 1801–70', in Vaughan (ed.), *New History of Ireland*, v, *Ireland Under the Union*, 1, *1801–1870*, p. 596; Gray, *Famine*, pp. 182–7.

49 *FJ*, 14, 16–17 Jan. 1846; Ó Cathaoir, *Famine Diary*, p. 25.

50 *LCE*, 24, 28 Feb. 1849 and Ó Murchadha, 'Exterminator General', pp. 185–7

51 Gerrard of Gibstown, County Meath had recently bought this property in the Incumbered Estates Court. Vaughan, *LTMVI*, pp. 20–2, 24, 26, 39, 183; Donnelly, *GIPF*, p. 159.

52 Póirtéir, *Famine Echoes*, pp. 230–1.

53 Ó Cathaoir, *Famine Diary*, p. 41. Fr Cathal Stanley, comp., *Castles and Demesnes: Gleanings from Kilconieran and Clostoken* (Loughrea, 2000), p. 47. *LCE*, 30 Sept., 2 Dec. 1848; Scally, *End of Hidden Ireland*, pp. 111–12; and Ó Murchadha, 'Exterminator General', pp. 179, 183–5. Of 37,286 estimated 'actual evictions' in 1846–9, some 16,400 (or 44 per cent) resulted in house levelling. The comparable figures for 1850–9 were 38,639 evictions and 12,926 (or 33 per cent) house razings. Vaughan, *LTMVI*, Appendix I, p. 230.

54 Scully did not patent his invention 'but gave it freely for the general good of his fellow landlords'. Sullivan, *New Ireland*, p. 122; Gray, *Famine*, pp, 13–14, 275–8; Thomas E. Jordan, *Ireland and the Quality of Life: The Famine Era* (Lewiston, 1997), p. 57. For Head's dismay over unroofed cottages, see *Fortnight In Ireland*, pp. 116, 128, 130, 145, 172, 186, 214–15.

55 Sir William Butler, *An Autobiography* (London, 1911), pp. 11–12.

56 Vaughan, *LTMVI*, pp. 230–1, 279–80. Dublin Castle included threatening letters under the heading of agrarian outrages.

57 Davitt, *Fall of Feudalism*, pp. 47–50, 222–3; T. W. Moody, *Davitt and Irish Revolution 1846–82* (Oxford, 1981), pp. 4–22.

58 For Mitchel's indictment of the British government, see Donnelly, *GIPF*, pp. 18–21, 233. Besides Mitchel's *The Last Conquest of Ireland (Perhaps)* (Glasgow, n.d., Dublin, 1861), see MacGeoghegan and Mitchel (comp.), *History of Ireland*, vol. 2, pp. 212–13.

59   For the post-eviction murder of a farmer see *FJ*, 20 Mar. 1846.

60   Thomas Davis contended that art was 'superior to writing'. See 'National Art' in *Essays Literary and Historical by Thomas Davis*, ed. D. J. O'Donoghue (Dundalk, 1914), quoted in Cullen, *Sources in Irish Art*, pp. 65–8.

61   Peter Murray, 'Realism versus romanticism in framing national identity', *Whipping the Herring: Survival and Celebration in Nineteenth-Century Irish Art* (Cork, 2006), pp. 11–23; Claudia Kinmonth, *Irish Rural Interiors in Art* (New Haven and London, 2006); Sighle Bhreathnach-Lynch, 'Framing the Irish: Victorian paintings of the Irish peasant', *Journal of Victorian Culture* (Autumn 1997), 2: 2, pp. 246–50 reprinted in *Ireland's Art Ireland's History*, pp. 52–71; and Brian P. Kennedy, 'The traditional Irish thatched house: image and reality, 1793–1993', in Adele M. Dalsimer (ed.), *Visualizing Ireland* (Winchester, 1993), pp. 171–4.

62   Allen Staley, 'George Frederic Watts: 1817–1904', *Victorian High Renaissance* (Minneapolis, 1978), p. 63. This painting appears on the cover of the Penguin edition of Cecil Woodham-Smith's *The Great Hunger* (Harmondsworth, 1991) and is also reproduced in Donnelly, *GIPF*, facing p. 85.

63   Goodall's *An Irish Eviction* (1850). See Gray, *Irish Famine* pp. 70–1.

64   Walter G. Strickland, *A Dictionary of Irish Artists* (Dublin, 1913), vol. 1, pp. 572–3. See also Curtis, '"The land for the people": post-famine images of eviction', in Kreilkamp (ed.), *Éire/land*, pp. 87–8. A sepia image of Kelly's painting graces the cover of volume v of W. E. Vaughan (ed.), *A New History of Ireland, Ireland Under the Union* 1: 1801–70.

65   For Nicol's origins and career, see Bhreathnach-Lynch, 'Framing the Irish', *Journal of Victorian Culture* (Autumn 1997), pp. 247–59; Brian P. Kennedy, *Irish Painting* (Dublin, 1993), pp. 20, 77; *Whipping the Herring*, pp. 15–16, 116–17, 200–1; and David and Francina Irwin, *Scottish Painters at Home and Abroad, 1700–1900* (London, 1975), pp. 304–5. See also *Times*, 11 Mar. 1904. This painting appears on the jacket cover of Donnelly, *GIPF* and in Gray, *Irish Famine*, pp. 72–3. Kinmonth alludes in passing to Nicol's 'An ejected family', in *Irish Rural Interiors in Art*, p. 134.

66   Catherine Marshall, 'Painting Irish history: the famine', *History Ireland* (Autumn 1996), pp. 46–7. Bhreathnach-Lynch also discusses Nicol in *Ireland's Art*, pp. 55–8, 62–5.

67   For Daniel MacDonald's 'The eviction', see *Whipping The Herring*, pp. 134–5.

68   For the early Victorian wood-block process see Simon Houfe, *The Dictionary of British Book Illustrators and Artists, 1800–1914* (Woodbridge, 1978), pp. 26–7, 49–53; Eric de Maré, *The London Doré Saw: A Victorian Evocation* (London, 1973), p. 17; and Robert L. Patten, *George Cruikshank's Life, Times, and Art*, vol. 1, 1792–1835 (New Brunswick, 1992), pp. 2–6, 307–8, 324–6, 403.

69   Peter W. Sinnema, *Dynamics of the Pictured Page: Representing the Nation in the Illustrated London News* (Aldershot, 1998), esp. pp. 2, 46–9. See also Peter Sinnema, 'The work of art in the age of mechanical reproduction' in Hannah Arendt (ed.), *Illuminations* (New York, 1969), pp. 51, 223. A useful survey of the *ILN* may be found in Simon Roufe, *Dictionary*, pp. 67–75.

70   Peter Murray discusses Mahoney's famine pictures in *Whipping The Herring*, pp. 90–1, 231–4, 238–40. See the illuminating essay by Margaret Crawford, 'The Great Irish Famine 1845–9: Image versus reality' in Raymond Gillespie and Brian P. Kennedy (eds), *Ireland: Art into History* (Dublin, 1994), pp. 75–88. The sketch of Moveen (*ILN*, 22 Dec. 1849) appears in Donnelly, *GIPF*, p. 153 and Noel Kissane, *The Irish Famine: A Documentary History* (Dublin, 1995), p. 145.

71   Donnelly, *GIPF*, pp. 123–6, 148 and Murray, 'Realism versus romanticism in framing national identity', *Whipping the Herring*, pp. 21–3; Margaret Kelleher, *The Feminization of Famine: Expressions of the Inexpressible?* (Cork, 1997), esp. pp. 21–5.

72 *ILN*, 15 Dec. 1849, p. 393. See also 'Destitution in Ireland – failure of the potato crop', *Pictorial Times*, 22 Aug. 1846, reproduced in Kissane, *Irish Famine*, p. 23.

73 'Eviction: the last look' (n.d.) in NLI, C. W. Cole's Sketchbook, Department of Prints and Drawings, p. 53.

74 *ILN*, 16 Dec. 1848, vol. 13, p. 380. Both prints appear in Woodham-Smith, *Great Hunger*, pp. 276–7 and Kissane, *Irish Famine*, pp. 141–2. See also Murray, 'Representations of Ireland in the *Illustrated London News*', *Whipping the Herring*, pp. 235–6.

75 Lord Dufferin, *Contributions to an Inquiry into the Present State of Ireland* (London, 1866), pp. 28–9. W. N. Hancock, *Report on the Supposed Progressive Decline of Irish Prosperity* (Dublin, 1863), pp. 15–16. For eviction and outrage data see Vaughan, *LTMVI*, Appendix 1, pp. 230–1 and Appendix 19, pp. 279–80.

76 According to Kerby Miller, 100,000 Irish emigrants sailed to the Antipodes. *Emigrants and Exiles: Ireland and the Irish Exodus to North America* (New York, 1985), pp. 291, 569–70. By 1861 there were over 600,000 Irish-born immigrants in England. Fitzpatrick, 'Emigration, 1801–70', in Vaughan, *A New History of Ireland*, v, 1, p. 654; and Donnelly, *GIPF*, pp. 178–86.

77 Gerard Moran, *Sending Out Ireland's Poor: Assisted Emigration to North America in the Nineteenth Century* (Dublin, 2004), esp. pp. 35–90, 123–91; Oliver MacDonagh, 'Irish emigration to the United States of America and the British Colonies during the Famine' in Edwards and Williams, *Great Famine*, pp. 332–40; and Donnelly, *GIPF*, pp. 140–4.

78 Jim Rees, *Surplus People: The Fitzwilliam Clearances, 1847–1856* (Cork, 2000). One ship carrying Palmerston tenants sank off the coast drowning 87 passengers. Woodham-Smith, *Great Hunger*, pp. 227–30; MacDonagh, 'Irish Emigration to the United States' in Edwards and Williams, *Great Famine*, pp. 338–40; and Gray, *Famine*, pp. 192, 300.

79 Moran, *Sending Out Ireland's Poor*, esp. pp. 95–116. Lyne, *Lansdowne Estate in Kerry*, pp. xvii–xxx., l–lvi, 25–68, 195–201, 444–5, 716 as well as Trench, *Realities*, pp. 63–76, 103–32. 137–9, 167–96; and for the Prior Wandesforde estate in Kilkenny, see William Nolan, *Fassadinin: Land, Settlement and Society in South-East Ireland, 1600–1850* (Dublin, 1979), pp. 204–8. Woodham-Smith, *Great Hunger*, pp. 276–84; Oliver MacDonagh, *A Pattern of Government Growth: The Passenger Acts and their Enforcement* (London, 1961), esp. pp. 66–70, 81–4, 180–6, 222–7, 246–50, 266–70; and Miller, *Emigrants and Exiles*, pp. 252–62.

80 Moran, *Sending Out Ireland's Poor*, pp. 43–58, 63–68, 102–9. For the Pomona legend, see Dermot James, *The Gore-Booths of Lissadell* (Dublin, 2004), pp. 22–5, 31–9; Anne Marreco, *The Rebel Countess: The Life and Times of Constance Markievicz* (Philadelphia, 1967), pp. 6–7, 305; Jacqueline Van Voris, *Constance de Markievicz in the Cause of Ireland* (Amherst, 1967), pp. 18–20; Mary Lee Dunn, 'An agenda for researching the famine experience of Kilglass parish, County Roscommon', Valone and Kinealy, *Ireland's Great Hunger*, p. 116.

81 Miller, *Emigrants and Exiles*, pp. 305–7.

82 Moran, *Sending Out Ireland's Poor*, pp. 40–1, 46–7, 58–67, 94–7, 219–23.

83 Quoted in the *People*, 13 Oct. 1888.

84 James Clarence Mangan, *Selected Writings*, ed. Sean Ryder (Dublin, 2004), p. 318.

85 *The Poetical Works of Aubrey De Vere*, vol. 1 (London, 1884), pp. 238–9, 242.

86 O'Neill, 'Famine evictions', pp. 56–8.

87 Foster, *Modern Ireland*, pp. 318–31, 334; Mokyr, *Why Ireland Starved*, pp. 99–102; O'Neill 'Famine Evictions', pp. 52–3, 56–8.

3 INTERLUDE, 1855–78

1 Jones, 'Cleavage' in Clark and Donnelly, *Irish Peasants*, esp. pp. 374–80; *NLI*, Bruen Papers, Survey of the Bruen Estate, 1871, MS 19,801; Crotty, *Irish Agricultural Production*, pp. 72–92; Turner, *After the Famine*, pp. 69–77.

2 Bell and Watson, *A History of Irish Farming*, esp. pp. 230–42.

3 NLI, Leitrim Rentals and Accounts, MS 3804.

4 Carter, *Land War*, pp. 11, 299–300; Ó Gráda, *Ireland, A New Economic History*, p. 256; Jones, Table 10.4 in 'Cleavage', Clark and Donnelly, *Irish Peasants*, p. 393.

5 Vaughan, *Sin, Sheep and Scotsmen*, p. 34; and Vaughan, *LTMVI*, pp. 138–76, 279–86.

6 Vaughan, *LTMVI*, pp. 11, 23, 27, 230–31. During the depression of 1863–64 evictions rose from 1,522 to 1,590; and reported house razings plunged from 5,285 in 1850 to 20 in 1870.

7 Trench also evicted two 'genteel' tenants one of whom was an Anglo-Irish baronet. Lyne, *Lansdowne Estate*, pp. 187–9, 201–20.

8 Padraig G. Lane, 'An attempt at commercial farming in Ireland after the famine', *Studies* (Spring 1972), pp. 54–66; *Times*, 30 Apr., 2 May 1856; *FJ*, 1 May 1856; Vaughan, *LTMVI*, pp. 27, 36. For the origins of the Pollock (or Pollok) estate, see *FJ*, 31 May 1888.

9 'Evictions and cultivation in Ireland', *Pall Mall Gazette* (hereafter, *PMG*) 7 Feb. 1868, quoted in *Times*, 8 Feb. 1868.

10 *Nation*, quoted in *Times*, 29 Oct. 1860 and *Galway Press* (hereafter *GP*), 25 May 1861.

11 Donnelly, *Captain Rock*, pp. 119–22, 130–9, 342–45.

12 Brian Girvin, *From Union to Union: Nationalism, Democracy and Religion in Ireland* (Dublin, 2002), pp. 7–17; Rev. Henry Seddall, *Edward Nangle: The Apostle of Achill* (London, 1884), esp. pp. xvi, xxviii; Lyne, *Lansdowne Estate*, p. 647. See also David Hempton and Myrtle Hill, *Evangelical Protestantism in Ulster Society, 1740–1890* (London, 1992); Irene Whelan, *The Bible War in Ireland: The 'Second Reformation' and the Polarization of Protestant-Catholic Relations 1800–1840* (Madison, 2005); Patrick Hickey, *Famine in West Cork: The Mizen Peninsula, Land and People, 1800–1852* (Dublin, 2002), p. 251

13 For the activities of Dallas and other 'soupers', see Desmond Bowen, *Souperism: Myth or Reality* (Cork, 1971), esp. pp. 88–106, 157–75, 186–9, 217–34; Bowen, *The Protestant Crusade in Ireland, 1800–70* (Dublin, 1978), esp. 208–29, 244–56; Donal A. Kerr, *A Nation of Beggars? Priests, People, and Politics in Famine Ireland, 1846–1852* (Oxford, 1994), pp. 210–14; Irene Whelan, 'Edward Nangle and the Achill Mission, 1834–1852' in Raymond Gillespie and Gerard Moran (eds), *'A Various Country': Essays in Mayo History, 1500–1900* (Westport, 1987), pp. 113–34. Head not only praised the new and clean Protestant churches he found in the west but also blamed the destitution and 'moral degradation' of the peasantry on the priesthood. *Fortnight in Ireland*, pp. 239–400.

14 *Times*, 29 Jan. 1847. For souperism in Ulster folk tradition, see Elliott, *Catholics of Ulster*, p. 310.

15 The thin gruel or soup provided by these missionaries occasionally bore the surname of the local landlord – as in 'Benson's gravy' or 'Downshire's porridge'. See also Póirtéir, *Famine Echoes*, pp. 166–81, 200, 278–9 and Elliott, *Catholics of Ulster*, pp. 310–11.

16 The previous owner of Balllyovey parish or Partry was Sir Robert Lynch-Blosse. Gerard P. Moran, *The Mayo Evictions of 1860* (Cathair na Mart, 1986), pp. 26–7. See also Lavelle, *Irish Landlord*, pp. 272–3, 430 and Nicholson, *Annals of the Famine*, p. 132.

17 A leading Protestant fundamentalist, W. S. Trench's son, John Townsend Trench, joined the Plymouth Brethren and preached eccentric sermons in Dublin and elsewhere. Lyne, *Lansdowne Estate*, pp. 647–81.

18 Father P. Lavelle, *The War in Partry, or Proselytism and Eviction* (Dublin 1861), reprinted in *Irish Landlord*, pp. 504–35. E. R. Norman discusses Lavelle's conflicts with his ecclesiastical superiors in *The Catholic Church and Ireland in the Age of Rebellion, 1859–73* (Ithaca, 1965), esp. pp. 43–4, 97–108, 111–12, 127–30 as does Tomás Ó Fiaich in '"The patriot priest of Partry": Patrick Lavelle, 1825–1886', *Journal of the Galway Archaeological and Historical Society* 35 (1976), pp. 129–48. See also *FJ*, 18 Nov. 1886; *DIB*, vol. 5, pp. 340–2.

19 *Mayo Constitution*, 31 July, 7 Aug., 27 Nov. 1860; Ó Fiaich, 'Patriot priest', pp. 136–7; *Daily Express*, 23 Nov. 1859; Moran, *Mayo Evictions*, pp. 50–98, and Bowen, *Souperism*, pp. 165–72.

20 According to J. F. Maguire MP, Plunket had evicted 165 people by 1861. Bowen, *Souperism*, pp. 168–9.

21 Quoted in *Times*, 24 Nov. 1860.

22 Lavelle, *Irish Landlord*, pp. 497–9, 526–7.

23 *MC*, 1, 8, 15, 22 Jan. 1861; *GP*, 1 May 1861; Lavelle, 'War in Partry' in *Irish Landlord*, pp. 504–35. See also Lavelle's letter to the *Times* (5 Dec. 1860) quoted in the *GP*, 12 Dec. 1860.

24 For Dr Cullen's disapproval of Lavelle's clericalism, see Norman, *Catholic Church*, pp. 43–4, 99–108, 111–12, 127–30, 389, and Jordan, *Land and Popular Politics*, pp. 243, 252–3; Lex, *Doings in Partry: A Chapter of Irish History in a Letter to the Rt Hon. the Earl of Derby, KG* (London, 1860), p. 31.

25 *Times*, 24 Oct., 22, 24, 26–27, 30 Nov., 4, 8 Dec. 1860; *GP*, 1, 5, 8 Dec. 1860, 23 Jan., 1 June 1861; Moran, *Mayo Evictions*, pp. 76–109; Lavelle, 'War in Partry' in *Irish Landlord*, pp. 504–35; and Lex, *Doings in Partry*, pp. 1–48.

26 *Times*, 1 Jan., 16 Feb. 1861. For Plunket's letter to Earl Cowley at the British Embassy, see the pamphlet, BL 3940.cc. 81, pp. 1–3. A small image of Nicol's 'Notice to quit' appears in Kinmonth, *Irish Rural Interiors in Art*, pp. 133–4 and fig. 136.

27 Abraham and Joseph Mitchell [*sic*] of Tournakeedy [*sic*], Ballinrobe, were listed as the owners of 14,179 acres valued at only £1,164. De Burgh, *LOI*, p. 318. See also Vaughan, *LTMVI*, pp. 26–7.

28 Plunket, *Irish Landlord*, p. 367.

29 Mary L. Meaney, *The Confessors of Connaught: or, The Tenants of A Lord Bishop – A Tale of Our Times* (Philadelphia, 1865). For these and other tales involving eviction, see the invaluable compilation of Rolf and Magda Loeber, *A Guide to Irish Fiction, 1650–1900* (Dublin, 2006).

30 Alice Nolan, *The Byrnes of Glengoulah: A True Tale* (New York, 1869).

31 See the editorial and letter from 'A Moycullen man' in *GP*, 19 Dec. 1860.

32 A. M. Sullivan, *New Ireland*, pp. 218–31; Liam Dolan, *Land War and Eviction in Derryveagh 1840–65* (Dundalk, 1980); and Vaughan, *Sin, Sheep and Scotsmen*, esp. pp. 11–28.

33 *GP*, 13 Apr. 1861 quoting the *Londonderry Standard*; *FJ* and *CE*, 11–13 Apr. 1861; *Northern Whig*, 12 Apr. 1861; Vaughan, *Sin, Sheep and Scotsmen*, pp. 44–8.

34 *GP*, 17, 24 Apr., 25 May, 1 June 1861. At the Dublin banquet Father McFadden tried to console the grieving Glenveagh tenants by pointing out that they were heading for a country free from tyrants. Sullivan, *New Ireland*, pp. 228–31.

35 *GP*, 17, 24 Apr., 29 June 1861 and *CE*, 26 Apr., 1, 24 May, 3 June 1861; Vaughan, *Sin, Sheep and Scotsmen*, pp. 20–2, 46–7.

36 *Times*, 25 June 1861 and Vaughan, *Sin, Sheep and Scotsmen*, pp. 44–6; W. H. Hurlbert, *Ireland Under Coercion* (Edinburgh, 1888), vol. 1, pp. 71–2.

37 Patrick Sarsfield Cassidy, *Glenveigh, Or the Victims of Vengeance – A Tale of Irish Life in the Present* (Boston, 1870); Vaughan, *Sin, Sheep and Scotsmen*, pp. 40–1.

38 Cassidy, *Glenveigh*, pp. iv–v; Dolan, *Land War*, pp. 202–3.

39 For the Cormack saga, see the two editorials, 'More exterminations', *GP*, 8, 25 May 1861 and the leading article and letters from Daniel W. Welply JP, *CE*, 1, 20 May 1861.

40 When the parish priest rebuked him for devising this new lease, Scully took his entire family to the nearest Protestant church. Sullivan, *New Ireland*, pp. 363–73 and Vaughan, *LTMVI*, p. 34.

41 Homer E. Socolofsky, *Landlord William Scully* (Lawrence, Kansas, 1979), pp. 1–23, 39–64 and Paul W. Gates, *Landlords and Tenants On the Prairie Frontier* (Ithaca, 1973), pp. 20–38, 266–97; *CE* and *FJ*, 15–18 Aug. 1868; A. M. Sullivan, *New Ireland*, pp. 363–73; Vaughan, *LTMVI*, 35–6; *DIB*, vol. 8, pp. 819–20.

42 For an informed discussion of the Ulster custom, tenant right, and the Land Act of 1870, see Vaughan, *LTMVI*, pp. 67–102, 213–14, 232, 273–6, and also Robert W. Kirkpatrick's valuable study, 'Landed estates in Mid-Ulster and the Irish Land War, 1879–85' (PhD thesis, Trinity College Dublin, 1976), pp. 110–34. Godkin, *Land-War*, pp. vi–vii; Paul Bew, *Ireland: The Politics of Enmity, 1789–2006* (Oxford, 2007), pp. 277–8; R. Donnell, *Reports of One Hundred and Ninety Cases in the Irish Land Courts* (Dublin, 1876), pp. 17–19, 457–8; Robert Donnell, *Practical Guide to the Law of Tenant Compensation and Farm Purchase Under the Irish Land Act* (Dublin, 1871), passim. NLI, W. S. O'Brien Papers; Peter Fitzgerald, *Address of the Knight of Kerry To The Tenants of the Townland of East and West Ballyherney, In the Island of Valencia* (London, 1872), pp. 1–16.

43 Powell spent most of his career in New York painting portraits and historical pictures. In 1871 Powell's *The Eviction* was converted into a colour print. NLI, DPD 4291 TD.

44 Peter H. Falk (ed.), *Who Was Who In American Art, 1564–1975* (Madison, CT, 1985), vol. III, p. 2651.

45 'Erigena' (J. G. Barrett), *Evelyn Clare: Or, The Wrecked Homesteads: An Irish Story of Love and Landlordism* (London, 1870).

46 William C. Upton, *Uncle Pat's Cabin, Or Life Among the Agricultural Labourers* (Dublin, 1882).

47 Mrs Lorenzo Nunn, *Heirs of the Soil* (London, 1870)

48 Georges Denis Zimmermann, *Songs of Irish Rebellion: Irish Political Street Ballads and Rebel Songs 1780–1900* (2nd edn, Dublin, 2002), pp. 1–2.

49 'A new song called the emigrant's farewell to Donegal', *c.*1846, Zimmermann, *Songs of Irish Rebellion*, pp. 236–7.

50 'The Irish tenant farmers lament from eviction from his native home', *A Collection of Irish Broadside Songs* (Dublin, n.d.). BL, Rare Books Collection.

51 Kickham's prison ballad appeared first in the *Kilkenny Journal* under the pseudonym of Darby Ryan, Junior. Zimmermann, *Songs of Irish Rebellion*, pp. 245–7.

52 There are several contrasting versions of 'The General Fox Chase' (1862). In one Hayes is the 'ruthless bailiff' who has evicted thousands on orders from Braddell. After his own expulsion, he shoots the agent and goes on the run. In another version 'Farmer Hayes' is the innocent victim of the knavish agent who has served him with an ejectment decree. After slaying this treacherous 'fool', Farmer Hayes flees west to Mayo before shipping out from Dublin. In 1865 a man was arrested in Dublin for singing this ballad on the grounds that it celebrated fugitive Fenians. Zimmermann, *Songs of Irish Rebellion*, pp. 257–9 and *CE*, 1 Aug. 1862. See also the informative documentary about Hayes entitled 'Meirligh', shown on TG4 in 2005. For this information I am indebted to Mic Moroney.

53 Quoted by Father Lavelle, *Irish Landlord*, p. 278.

54 For glimpses of his life and friendships, see *William Allingham, A Diary*, ed. H. Allingham and D. Radford (London, 1908), esp. pp. 79–96. He began writing 'Laurence Bloomfield' while stationed in Ballyshannon, County Donegal.

55 William Allingham, *Laurence Bloomfield* (London, 1893), esp. pp. 69–70.

56 Robert Burke, *The Eviction; Or the Plundered Homes* (Dublin 1868), esp. pp. 17–25.

57 Mic Moroney and Terry Moylan kindly found this ballad, attributed to O'Donovan Rossa, in *Songs of the Gael*, compiled by An t-Athair Pádraig Breathnach (Dublin and Belfast, 1922).

4 THE FIRST LAND WAR, 1879–83

1 Ó Gráda, *Ireland*, pp. 256–63; Moody, *Davitt*, pp. 271–85, 328–9; Vaughan, *LTMVI*, pp. 208–13; Clark, *Social Origins*, pp. 225–45; and L. Perry Curtis, 'Incumbered wealth: landed indebtedness in post-famine Ireland', *American Historical Review* 85: 2 (Apr. 1980) pp. 332–67. The ten estates in this sample belonged to Lords Downshire, Erne, Gosford, Inchiquin, Meath, and Ormonde, as well as Deane Drake and Sir George Hodson. For Abercorn's arrears see PRONI, Abercorn MSS, DOD 623.

2 The nature of rents, valuations, arrears, and tenant right as well as the responses of landlords to the agricultural crisis and the land war in mid-Ulster are thoroughly explored by Robert W. Kirkpatrick in his PhD thesis, TCD (1976), 'Landed Estates in Mid-Ulster and the Irish Land War, 1879–85', pp. 1–60, 105–12, 141–68. In County Kildare only 23 evictions occurred between 1877 and 1880; and the 13 evictions carried out in 1879–80 represented a tiny fraction of the 9,000 agricultural holdings there. Nelson, *Land War*, pp. 15–16. For Trinity College's vast property holdings, see MacCarthy, *Trinity College Estates* as well as TCD Library, MUN/P/22/207 (1) and MUN/P/28/156–250 for protests over rent increases in 1876 and troubles on the small Killanny estate in County Louth.

3 See NLI, the Knight of Kerry's printed letter 'To The Tenant Farmers' of Valencia island, 20 Oct. 1879; Howth Castle, William Rochfort's Letter Book, Howth Papers, 1 May 1879, pp. 33, 35; Kirkpatrick, 'Landed estates in Mid-Ulster', pp. 47–78; and R. W. Kirkpatrick, 'Origins and development of the land war in mid-Ulster, 1879–85' in F. S. L. Lyons and R. A. J. Hawkins (eds), *Ireland Under the Union* (Oxford, 1980), pp. 201–3, 213–24.

4 For Parnell's perceptive political and economic visions, see Donal McCartney, 'Parnell, Davitt and the land question' in Carla King (ed.), *Famine, Land and Culture in Ireland* (Dublin, 2000), pp. 71–82 and Liam Kennedy, 'The economic thought of the nation's lost leader: Charles Stewart Parnell', *Colonialism, Religion and Nationalism in Ireland* (Belfast, 1996), pp. 75–102. For the New Departure and causes of the land war, see Vaughan, *Landlords and Tenants in Ireland*, pp. 27–35 and *LTMVI*, pp. 208–16.

5 The extensive literature on the New Departure and the Irish National Land League includes first and foremost Moody, *Davitt*, esp. pp. 122–6, 133–4, 250–66, 325–81, followed by Paul Bew, *Land and the National Question in Ireland, 1858–82* (Dublin, 1978), pp. 46–73; Bew, *Ireland*, pp. 309–14; Lyons, *Ireland Since the Famine* (hereafter, *ISF*), pp. 154–62; Philip Bull, *Land, Politics and Nationalism* (Dublin, 1996), pp. 69–93; Donnelly, *Cork*, pp. 251–307; Alvin Jackson, *Home Rule: An Irish History, 1800–2000* (London, 2003), pp. 38–48; Samuel Clark, *Social Origins of the Irish Land War* (Princeton 1979), pp. 182–304; F. S. L. Lyons, *Charles Stewart Parnell*, pp. 79–92, 98, and Lyons, *John Dillon*, pp. 28–60. See also John Devoy, *The Land of Eire* (New York, 1882), quoted in Terence Dooley, 'The Land for the People': The Land Question in Independent Ireland* (Dublin, 2004), p. 26 and Margaret

O'Callaghan, *British High Politics and A Nationalist Ireland: Criminality, Land and the Law Under Forster and Balfour* (Cork, 1994), esp. pp. 153–4.

6 Moody, *Davitt*, pp. 271–327 and Donald E. Jordan, *Land and Popular Politics in Ireland* (Cambridge, 1994), pp. 199–248.

7 Bull, *Land*, pp. 69–99; *Connaught Telegraph* (hereafter, *CT*), 21 June 1879.

8 Vaughan, *LTMVI*, pp. 52–3, 208–16.

9 Ball, 'Crowd activity', p. 224; David N. Haire, 'In aid of the civil power, 1868–90', in Lyons and Hawkins, *Ireland Under the Union*, esp. pp. 127–43.

10 See *CT*, 21, 28 June, 5 July 1879 and Becker, *Disturbed Ireland*, p. 37.

11 Vaughan, *LTMVI*, pp. 44–66, 238–40 and *Times*, 23 June 1880. While the term 'rack-rent' denoted the full letting or market value of a tenancy, Irish nationalists and tenant-righters regarded it as a highly exploitative or unjust rent.

12 Rath House, Termonfeckin, Dillon Papers, Dillon estate office announcement, 28 Sept. 1879, and tenants' letters to Lord Dillon, 20 Oct. 1879 and Charles Strickland (n.d.).

13 Becker, *Disturbed Ireland*, pp. 74–9; Bew, *Land and the National Question*, pp. 54–6.

14 *CT*, 14, 21 June 1879.

15 *CT*, 21 June, 19 July 1879.

16 *CT*, 21 June, 19 July 1879; Davitt, *Fall of Feudalism*, pp. 147–50; Moody, *Davitt*, pp. 290–1, 310–11, 342, 360, 479; Bew, *Land and the National Question*, p. 74. Plunkett House, Oxford, Diary of Sir Horace Plunkett, 7 Jan. 1903. For the violence of Dillon's rhetoric, see Lyons, *Dillon*, pp. 37–8, 73–4 and *Times*, 24 Aug. 1880, 4 Oct. 1888.

17 Davitt, *Fall of Feudalism*, p. 120; *CE*, 14–17 Dec. 1879; *Times*, 15 Dec. 1879; PRONI, Annesley Papers, Lord Annesley to William Shaw, 8, 13 Dec. 1881 and 13 Mar. 1882, D. 1854/6/8 and Charlemont Papers, Lord Charlemont to Hugh Boyle, 20, 26, 27 Nov., 5 Dec. 1880, D.266/367/50–6, by permission of PRONI.

18 Donations to 'the Blake Fund' ranged from £200 to a few shillings. See the four police intelligence files: NAI, Crime Branch Special (hereafter CBS), 1893, 6846/S. Terence Dooley, *The Decline of the Big House in Ireland* (Dublin, 2001), p. 216.

19 For death threats in the pre-famine era that peaked in 1821–3 and 1831–4, see Stephen R. Gibbons, *Captain Rock, Night Errant: The Threatening Letters of Pre-Famine Ireland, 1801–1845* (Dublin, 2004), passim and Donnelly, *Captain Rock*, esp. pp. 51, 84–8, 91–7, 228–32. And for the counter-offensive of many wealthy landlords, see L. Perry Curtis, 'Landlord responses to the Irish land war, 1879–87', *Éire-Ireland* 38: III & IV (2003), pp. 134–88.

20 Threatening letters rose from 553 in 1879 to 1,576 in 1880. Moody, *Davitt*, pp. 303–6 319–21, 420, 565–8. Vaughan, *LTMVI*, pp. 141–63; Bew, *Ireland*, pp. 314–52; and Haire, 'In aid of the civil power, 1868–90' in Lyons and Hawkins, *Ireland Under the Union*, pp. 126–32. For evictions and outrages in mid-Ulster, see R. W. Kirkpatrick, 'Origins and development of the land war in mid-Ulster, 1879–85' in ibid., pp. 208, 222–4. See also Davitt, *Fall of Feudalism*, pp. 152–5 and *FJ*, 9 June 1879.

21 Kirkpatrick, 'Landed estates in Mid-Ulster and the Irish land war', pp. 143–51; Moody, *Davitt*, Appendix D1–D2, pp. 563–4. For outrages and evictions from 1878 to 1883, see Moody, *Davitt*, pp. 562–68. See also W. E. Forster's speech on law and order in Ireland, *Times*, 4 Mar. 1881 and TNA, Birrell's cabinet memorandum, 13 Feb. 1909, CAB 37/98.

22 Carter, *Land War*, pp. 58–62, 138.

23 Kirkpatrick, 'Landed estates in Mid-Ulster and the Irish land war', pp. 73, 167–70. Fintan Lane, 'Rural labourers, social change and politics in late nineteenth-century Ireland' in Fintan Lane and

Donal Ó Drisceoil (eds), *Politics and the Irish Working Class 1830–1945* (Basingstoke, 2005), pp. 113–39.

24   *CE*, 9 June 1881. For the origins and extent of Rockite violence, see Donnelly, *Captain Rock*, esp. pp. 37–83, 222–89, 337–54.

25   Davitt, *Fall of Feudalism*, pp. 311–13; Samuel M. Hussey, *The Reminiscences of an Irish Land Agent* (London, 1904), pp. 215, 222–4. See also Hussey's letter, *Times*, 22 June 1881 and G. C., *George Cruikshank's Irish Satires and Caricatures* (London, 1914), p. 16.

26   Moody, *Davitt*, pp. 425–30, 449–54; *Times*, 23 Dec. 1880, 4, 9 June, 4 July, 12 Oct, 1881, 20 Feb. 1882; *CE*, 6 June 1881.

27   *Times*, 25 Nov. 1879; Moody, *Davitt*, pp. 351–2.

28   'The Land League's advice to the tenant farmers of Ireland' (*c*.1881), Zimmermann, *Songs of Irish Rebellion*, p. 274.

29   For examples of 'execution sales' and hostile crowds, see *CE*, 7 Apr., 30 May, 1 June 1881 and *FJ*, 1 June, 18 Aug. 1881.

30   Moody, *Davitt*, Appendixes D and F, pp. 562–3, 567–8.

31   Vaughan, *LTMVI*, p. 232; Carter, *Land War*, pp. 23–4, 58, 86–7, 192–3.

32   Rath House, Termonfeckin, Dillon Papers. Charles Strickland to Alfred Markly, solicitor, 9 June 1881; anonymous letter to Strickland, 8 Mar. 1882; tenants' address to Strickland, 7 Mar. 1882; and sub-agent Blake to Lord Dillon, 12 Mar. 1882, 'List of Tenants at rentals of £20 upwards … in arrear at 1st November 1880' (1881). For conditions in counties Kerry, Roscommon, and Mayo, see *Times*, 17, 30 Mar. 1881. Vaughan, *LTMVI*, Appendix I, p. 231. The number of families evicted between 1849 and 1880 came to 90,107 according to the RIC. *Return by Provinces and Counties … of Cases of Evictions which have Come to the Knowledge of the Constabulary…1849 to 1880, inclusive*. HC 1881 (185), LXXVII. 725. See also Carter, *Land War*, pp. 127–8; *FJ*, 30 May 1887 and Davitt, *Fall of Feudalism*, p. 220.

33   Jordan, *Land and Popular Politics*, pp. 241–56; *Times*, 14 Oct., 24 Dec. 1880. Contrary to some reports, the Tory government of Lord Beaconsfield (and not Chief Secretary Forster) introduced buckshot to the RIC in Mar. 1880. *Times*, 9 Apr. 1881.

34   Ball, 'Crowd activity', pp. 213–26; Niamh O'Sullivan, 'Through Irish eyes: the work of Aloysius O'Kelly in the *Illustrated London News*', *History Ireland* (Autumn 1995), pp. 10–16 and also Niamh O'Sullivan, *Aloysius O'Kelly: Art, Nation, Empire* (Notre Dame, 2010), esp. pp. 1–12, 34–77.

35   Ball, 'Crowd activity', pp. 216–20, 222–4, 240. For the simianisation of Irish rebels in British and American comic weeklies, see Curtis, *Apes and Angels: The Irishman in Victorian Caricature* (rev. edn, Washington DC, 2001).

36   See Janet K. TeBrake, 'Irish peasant women in revolt: the Land League years', *Irish Historical Studies*, XXVIII: 109 (May 1992), pp. 63–80 and Niamh O'Sullivan, 'The iron cage of femininity: visual representation of women in the 1880s land agitation' in Tadhg Foley and Seán Ryder (eds), *Ideology and Ireland in the Nineteenth Century* (Dublin, 1998), pp. 189–96.

37   TeBrake, 'Irish peasant women in revolt', pp. 66–77; Ball, 'Crowd activity', pp. 225–6, 232–8.

38   Ball, 'Crowd activity', p. 228.

39   For an amusing account of the so-called battle of Pallas, see Becker, *Disturbed Ireland*, pp. 195–206; Ball, 'Crowd activity', pp. 229–30, 236–8.

40   Ball, 'Crowd activity', pp. 238–41.

41   *Times*, 24 Nov., 13 Dec. 1879 and *CE*, 24 Nov., 13, 15 Dec. 1879; Jordan, *Land and Popular Politics*, pp. 250–3; Davitt, *Fall of Feudalism*, pp. 179–80, Bew, *Land and the National Question*, pp. 91–2, Clark, *Social Origins*, p. 311, and Moody, *Davitt*, p. 349.

42 For the 'Battle of Carraroe', see Davitt, *Fall of Feudalism*, pp. 213–19; *FJ*, 5–8 Jan. 1880; Ball, 'Crowd activity', p. 224.

43 Ball, 'Crowd activity', pp. 216–18, 238–41.

44 Seán na Ráithineach, 'On the murder of David Gleeson, bailiff' (1737) in Kenneth H. Jackson, *A Celtic Miscellany* (New York, 1971), p. 224. H. O. Arnold-Forster, *The Truth About The Land League* (London, 1882), p. 67. See also the partisan pamphlet of the Irish Loyal and Patriotic Union, *1879–1888, The Sanction of a Creed* (Dublin, 1888).

45 Davitt, *Fall of Feudalism*, pp. 213, 219; W. Steuart Trench, *Realities of Irish Life* (London, 1966), pp. 30–3; *FJ*, 9–10 Jan. 1880, 26 May 1881; Bernard H. Becker, *Disturbed Ireland: Being the Letters Written During the Winter of 1880–81* (London, 1881), pp. 195–206; *Times*, 17 Sept. 1880, 2 May, 9, 11, 16 June 1881; *CE*, 4 June, 1 Sept. 1881; Ball, 'Crowd activity', pp. 232–3.

46 *FJ*, 4, 26 Apr. 1881; *CE*, 5 Apr. 1881; *Times*, 4, 26 Apr. 1881.

47 For other attacks on process servers, see *Times*, 15 Apr., 2, 25–26, 30–31 May 1881; *CE*, 28 May, 1–2 June 1881.

48 *CE*, 9, 30 May, 1–2 June, 27 Aug. 1881.

49 *Times*, 28, 31 Jan., 22 Mar., 4, 15 Apr., 2, 30, 31 May, 4, 9, 11, 16 June 1881, 9 Oct. 1883, 3 Oct. 1885. See also *FJ*, 6 Jan. 1880, 30 May 1881.

50 *Return of the Number of Police Employed in Protecting Process-Servers from 1st January 1880 to 30th June 1880*, HC 1880 (280), lx, p. 451 and *Return of the Number of Cases Reported by the Constabulary in which Resistance was offered to the Police, … from the 1st day of February 1880 to the 30th day of June 1880.* Ibid., (327), Part III, p. 293. *FJ*, 10 Jan. 1880.

51 *ILN*, vol. 78, (14 May 1881), p. 477.

52 *ILN*, vol. 78 (21 May 1881), p. 493.

53 Moody, *Davitt*, pp. 393, 397, 398–9, 417; Bew, *Land and the National Question*, pp. 119–21.

54 For the Land Law (Ireland) Act, 1881 see *FJ*, 18 Aug. 1881, *Times*, 26 Apr. 1881; Roche and Rearden, *Irish Land Code*, pp. 1–246; Cherry, *Irish Land Law*, pp. 217–343; Moody, *Davitt*, pp. 454–6, 483–9, 498–9, 528–9; Lyons, *ISF*, pp. 164–5; Dooley, *'The Land for the People'*, p. 9.

55 Bull, *Land, Politics, and Nationalism*, pp. 90–1, 109; Kennedy, *Colonialism, Religion and Nationalism in Ireland*, pp. 79–83. For the illusory nature of dual ownership, see E. M'Causland's letter, *Times*, 1 Jan. 1881 as well as Gladstone's defence of his measure, *Times*, 12 Apr., 17 May 1881.

56 For the first, second, and third cycles of rent revisions, see Bailey, *Irish Land Acts*, pp. 15, 18–20. Lord Waterford's speech in the House of Lords appears in *Hansard, Parliamentary Debates*, 3rd series, vol. 266 (1882), pp. 39–41. See also Jones, 'Cleavage' in Clark and Donnelly, *Irish Peasants*, pp. 377–92.

57 For the ambivalence of Irish nationalist leaders towards political violence, see L. Perry Curtis, 'Moral and physical force: the language of violence in Irish nationalism.' *Journal of British Studies*, 27: 2 (Apr. 1988), pp. 150–89.

58 Curtis, 'Landlord responses to the Irish land war', pp. 156–8. For these three landowning victims, see *Times and FJ*, 27–30 Sept., 1–5, 13, 19 Oct. 1880, 1–5, 7–9, 12, 23 Apr. 1882, and 8, 18–19, 23 Apr. 1884. See also William Barlow Smythe, *The Tale of Westmeath: Wickedness and Woe* (Dublin, 1882) as well as Becker, *Disturbed Ireland*, p. 243.

59 *Times*, 24 Dec. 1879. Jordan, *Land and Popular Politics*, pp. 194, 209–10, 244, 274–5.

60 The Arrears Act empowered the Land Commission to pay landlords roughly one-half of what they were owed. Dooley, *Decline of the Big House*, p. 96. Moody, *Davitt*, pp. 494–6, 534, and Davitt, *Fall of Feudalism*, p. 364.

61 T. P. O'Connor, *Memoirs of an Old Parliamentarian* (London, 1929), vol. 1, p. 199. This figure exceeds the official count of 3,221 evicted families in 1881. Vaughan, *LTMVI*, Appendix I, p. 231.

62 Redpath denied that he had ever said that Irish landlords 'should be shot down like dogs'. *Times*, 29 June, 6 Oct. 1881; Moody, *Davitt*, pp. 367, 386, 396.

63 'Up, men, and at them', *Parnell's Land League Songster* (New York, 1881), p. 11.

64 'Poor Pat must emigrate', ibid., p. 14.

65 Patrick Galvin, *Irish Songs of Resistance* (Dublin, 1962), p. 46.

66 *FJ*, 28, 30 May, 6 June 1881; *CE*, 30 May 1881; and *Times*, 15 Apr., 28, 31 May, 4, 7 July 1881. See also Webber's self-serving letters to the *Times*, 7 June, 19 Sept. 1881. For the official hearing on the 4th Earl of Kingston's lunacy, see *Northern Whig*, 12, 15 Apr. 1861.

67 *Times*, *FJ*, and *CE*, 15–20 Aug. 1881; Donnelly, *Cork*, pp. 278–82.

68 *FJ*, 25 May 1881.

69 *FJ*, 1, 3–4, 6, 10 June 1881; *CE*, 3, 4, 10 June 1881; John S. Kelly, *The Bodyke Evictions* (Scariff, 1987), pp. 24–6, and *CJ*, 24 Dec. 1880. O'Callaghan owned 4,842 acres valued at £1,919 around Maryfort.

70 *Times*, 14 Oct. 1880.

71 *FJ*, 8–9 June 1881; *Times*, 2 Apr. 1881.

72 The term 'caretaker' applies here only to tenants legally reinstated for six months or more after making a token payment at the time of eviction. *Times*, 4 June 1881.

73 *Times*, 23, 25 May, 6 June 1881.

74 For the 'siege' of Quinlan's castle, see *Times*, 23, 25, 31 May, 4 June 1881; *FJ*, 23, 30–31 May, 4, 6 June 1881; *CE*, 23 May, 4, 6 June 1881; Davitt, *Fall of Feudalism*, p. 319.

75 This reporter called the 'mob's' behaviour 'an insurrectionary movement' and praised the authorities for suppressing such a display of (hereditary) violence. *Times*, 6 June 1881.

76 *Times*, 4 June 1881; *FJ*, 9 June 1881.

77 *CE*, 15, 19 Aug. 1881; *FJ*, 30 May 1881; Carter, *Land War*, pp. 139–41.

78 *Times*, 4 June 1881; *FJ*, 21–22 Apr. 1882.

79 Moran, *Sending Out Ireland's Poor*, pp. 166–76; Tuke, *Memoir*, pp. 147–9, 152–221; Baron E. De Mandat-Grancey, *Paddy at Home ('Chez Paddy')* (London, 1887), pp. 107–12 and Dooley, *Decline*, pp. 36, 55, 60, 97, 103, 119.

80 Peter Murray, 'Representations of Ireland', *Whipping the Herring*, pp. 248–53; O'Sullivan, *Aloysius O'Kelly*, pp. 67–8; Simon Houfe, *The Dictionary of 19th Century British Book Illustrators and Caricaturists* (London, 1998), pp. 84, 140–1; Benezit, *Dictionary of Artists* (Paris, 2006), vol. 10, p. 739.

81 *ILN*, vol. 76, 7 Feb. 1880, p. 132.

82 W.C.M., 'The condition of Ireland', *Graphic*, 25, 7 Jan. 1882, p. 5

83 After George Thomas's premature death, William managed the *Graphic*, with the help of another brother, Lewis Samuel, who died in 1872. Twenty years later William published the first illustrated English daily called the *Daily Graphic*. *Graphic* 5: 120 (16 Mar. 1872), p. 243; *DNB, Supplement*, vol. III (London 1901), pp. 379–80; and *Who Was Who, 1897–1915* (London, 1935), p. 704.

84 Brief biographies of the *Graphic*'s leading artists may be found in Simon Houfe, *Dictionary of British Book Illustrators*. See Julian Treuherz, *Hard Times: Social Realism in Victorian Art* (London, 1987), esp. pp. 9, 53–63.

85 *ILN*, vol. 78, pp. 288–9, 19 Mar. 1881; Niamh O'Sullivan, *Aloysius O'Kelly Re-Orientations: Painting, Politics and Popular Culture* (Dublin, 1999).

86 *ILN*, vol. 76, pp. 288–9, 20 Mar. 1880. This image was reprinted under a different title in the *Penny Illustrated Paper* (hereafter *PIP*) on 12 Jan. 1889, p. 21.

87 NLI, HP (1880) 4. 'Irlande – La land-league – Expulsion d'un fermier par la police anglaise', *Le Monde*

illustré, no. 1237, p. 356 (11 Dec. 1880), NLI. Charles Auguste Loye (1841–1901) adopted the name of his birthplace. Montbard, *Dictionary of British Cartoonists and Caricaturists, 1730–1980*, comp. Mark Bryant and Simon Heneage (Aldershot, 1994), p. 142; Benezit, *Dictionary of Artists*, vol. 9, pp. 1294–5.

88 *FJ*, 6 Dec. 1881.

89 Davitt, *Fall of Feudalism*, pp. 212–20; Moody, *Davitt*, pp. 290–2; Carter, *Land War*, pp. 61–2; *FJ*, 28 May 1888; *Times*, 24 May 1881, 1 Oct. 1888. See also UCD, NFC 437/373–80.

90 Zimmermann, *Songs of Irish Rebellion*, p. 60.

91 'A New Song Entitled The Kerry Eviction (1880s?)', Zimmermann, *Songs of Irish Rebellion*, pp. 286–7.

92 UCD, NFC 407/262.

93 W. G. Lyttle, *Sons of the Soil: A Tale of County Down* (Bangor, 1886).

94 Ellis Carr, *An Eviction in Ireland and its Sequel* (Dublin, 1881).

95 Jules Verne, *The Extraordinary Adventures of Foundling Mick* (new edn, Dublin, 2008).

96 *Times*, 30 May 1881; *FJ* and *CE*, 30–31 May, 1 June 1881. Dempsey left behind four young children and a pregnant wife. Attributed to Patrick Dempsey, this ballad appears in Cathal Stanley compiler, *Castles and Demesnes* (Loughrea, 2000), p. 191.

97 Because the grave robbers did not know which coffin contained Keane's body they dragged both coffins away and buried them together. Ó Murchadha, 'The exterminator general of Clare', *County Clare Studies*, pp. 169, 193–4.

98 Hussey, *Reminiscences*, pp. 235–6; Curtis, 'Landlord responses', *Éire-Ireland*, p. 164; *Times*, 15 Dec. 1884.

99 For the League's decline and fall in Queen's County, see Carter, *Land War*, pp. 117–18, 163, 177–82. Borris House, Kavanagh Papers, Arthur McMurrough Kavanagh to Lady Harriet Kavanagh, 22 Nov. 1882. Quoted in Donald McCormick, *The Incredible Mr Kavanagh* (London, 1960), p. 193.

100 Ball, 'Crowd activity', p. 239.

5 THE SECOND LAND WAR, 1886–90

1 Ó Gráda, *Ireland: A New Economic History*, pp. 250–61. The average rent reductions by the Land Court rose from 22.1 per cent to 29.5 per cent in the first three months of 1886. W. T. Stead, 'Can Irish rents be paid?' *PMG*, 8, 11, 16, 17, 24 Nov. 1886; Davitt, 'The distress in the Western Islands', *FJ*, 1–4 Feb. 1886; 'Life in West Donegal', *FJ*, 2 Feb. 1886.

2 Vaughan, *LTMVI*, Appendix 1, pp. 230–1; Solow, *Land Question*, p. 55. Stradbally Hall, Cosby Papers, Reports of J. T. Trench, 31 Dec. 1884 and 31 Dec. 1886. See also the letter-book of Gilbert Hodson, agent on the Hodson estate, in the 1880s and 1890s. NLI, Hodson MS 16501.

3 Vaughan, *LTMVI*, Appendix 19, pp. 279–80; *Times*, 25 May 1887; *People*, 3 Mar. 1888; TNA, CAB 37/98. Kirkpatrick, 'Landed estates in Mid-Ulster', pp. 2–14. See also 'Letters from Ireland, 1886' quoted in John P. Harrington (ed.), *The English Traveller in Ireland* (Dublin, 1991), pp. 291–304; *FJ*, 22 Jan. 1887.

4 *Times*, 3 Oct. 1885; *FJ*, 1 Feb. 23 Oct. 1886; *CE*, 22–23 Oct. 1886.

5 *FJ*, 22 Jan. 1876

6 For the 'semiotic' ritual aspect of 'monster meetings' in 1843–5, see Gary Owens, 'Constructing the repeal spectacle: monster meetings and people power in pre-famine Ireland', *People Power*, ed. Maurice R. O'Connell (Dublin, 1993), pp. 80–93; Ball, 'Crowd activity', pp. 228–30, 238–41. For reports of anti-eviction rallies at Athlone, Oldcastle, and Woodford, see *FJ*, 6, 8 Feb. 1886.

7   *FJ*, 17–18 Aug. 1886.

8   *Waterford Daily Mail* (hereafter, *WDM*), 14 Feb. 1887. For other examples of eviction news from Counties Monaghan and Wexford, see *WDM*, 18 Feb., 30 Mar. 1887 and *People*, 13 June 1888.

9   *FJ*, 27 Sept. 1887.

10   *ILN*, 3, 10, 17, 24 Apr. and 8 May 1886, vol. 88. For some rollicking tales of sailing around the western islands in British gunboats, see Sir Henry Robinson, *Memories: Wise and Otherwise* (London, 1924), pp. 58–70 and Robinson, *Further Memories of Irish Life* (London, 1924), p. 130.

11   *ILN*, 10 Apr. 1886, vol. 88, p. 375 and 1 May 1886, p. 468. Byrne arrived in Westport on 15 March along with the *Irish Times* correspondent to report on distress on Achill Island. See *Irish Times*, 17, 25 Mar. 1886.

12   *ILN*, 17 Apr. 1886, vol. 88, p. 399. Photograph by Francis Guy, 'Hut at present occupied by evicted tenant (10 in family)', NLI, Lawrence Collection, EBL 2659

13   *ILN*, 1 May 1886, vol. 88, pp. 466–7.

14   *Donegal Independent* (hereafter *DI*), 23 July 1887.

15   For the Fribbs dispute, see NLI, letters of Lord Arthur Butler from 2 Sept. 1880 to 19 Jan. 1881, Ormonde Papers, MS 23,578, pp. 908–9, 912, 932–3, 937–40, 965, 972–4.

16   *Times*, 21, 26 Feb. 1887; *DIB*, vol. 2, pp. 309–10.

17   *Times*, 17, 26 Feb. 1887; PRONI, Downshire Papers, D. 671/R2/108, 115, 117.

18   Clanricarde's 53,00 acres valued at £21,000 stretched from the Shannon river to Galway town and embraced eight townlands. See T. W. Russell's articles, *Times*, 26, 29 Jan., 1 Feb 1889 and the Duke de Stacpoole, *Irish and Other Memories* (London, 1922), pp. 2–4.

19   The widows of these two victims were compensated with £4,600 levied on three baronies. *Times*, 30 June, 1 July 1882, 14 Jan. 1889, 9–10 Nov. 1892.

20   See the entry for O'Hea by Carmel Doyle in *DIB*. *Weekly Freeman*, 17 Dec. 1887; *People*, 11 Apr. 1888. Curtis, *Apes and Angels*, pp. 68–72, 76–7; Theo Snoddy, *Dictionary of Irish Artists: 20th Century* (Dublin, 2002), pp. 481–82.

21   To the Castle's dismay, Clanricarde's neighbour, Sir Henry Burke of Marble Hill, reduced his rents substantially. *FJ*, 23–24 Aug. 1886 and 3 Jan. 1889 and *Times*, 26 Jan. 1889, 7 Oct 1890.

22   For the origins of the Plan see the eight articles in the *PMG*, 19, 22 Oct., 8, 11, 16, 18, 24, 25 Nov. 1886 and the five articles about the Woodford evictions, *PMG*, 29 Nov., 2, 7, 8, 10 Dec. 1886, reprinted in the pamphlet, '*No Reduction, No Rent': The Story of the Woodford Evictions and the Plan of Campaign*, Extra Number 30 (London, 1886). Foster, *Modern Ireland*, p. 375. See also Shaw-Lefevre's two letters to the *FJ*, 19 Dec. 1887 and 17 Jan. 1888 and 3 Jan. 1889.

23   *PMG*, *Woodford Evictions*, pp. 36–8 and 2 Dec. 1886. In letters to the *Times* (2, 5 Feb. 1887) Clanricarde denied that he had refused to lower rents in the fall of 1885 and decried other 'inaccuracies' in the press. See also George Shaw-Lefevre's letter to the *Times*, 19 Dec. 1887, *FJ*, 3 Jan. 1889. See Captain Edward C. Hamilton, *The Woodford Evictions* (Dublin, 1886) and 'The land war in Ireland', *ILN*, vol. 90, p. 64.

24   *FJ*, 23–24 Aug. 1886; *Times*, 28 Oct. 1886. This was one of the earliest applications of hot stirabout towards an eviction party.

25   *PMG*, *Woodford Evictions*, pp. 41–2; *FJ* and *Times*, 23–26 Aug. 1886; Hamilton, *Woodford Evictions*.

26   *FJ* and *Times*, 30 Aug. 1886.

27   *PMG*, *Woodford Evictions*, pp. 42–50, *FJ*, 26–28, 30 Aug. 1886.

28   *Graphic*, vol. 34, p. 265 (11 Sept. 1886).

29   PMG, *Woodford Evictions*, pp. 42–50, *FJ*, 26–28, 30 Aug. 1886; Hamilton, *Woodford Evictions*, pp. 11–12. See also Hamilton's testimony before the Cowper Commission on 6 Dec. 1886. *BPP 1887*, vol. 26, C. 4969, pp. 794–97.

30   *FJ*, 6 Jan. 1887.

31   *ILN*, vol. 90, p. 62 (15 Jan. 1887).

32   *UI*, 8 Oct. 1887, *FJ*, 31 Aug., 1 Sept. 1886, 3 Oct. 1887; *Times*, 26, 28, 30 Oct. 1886; Laurence M. Geary, *The Plan of Campaign, 1886–1891* (Cork, 1986), pp. 6–7, 15–21, 55–8.

33   *FJ* and *Times*, 23–28, 30–31 Aug. 1886.

34   *FJ*, 30–31 Aug. 1886.

35   *Times*, 14 Jan. 1889; 9 Nov. 1892; *CE*, 10 Apr. 1888, 23 Sept. 1889.

36   The grandson of the first Baron Headley of Aghadoe, Rowland Winn owned almost 14,000 acres in west Kerry plus property in Yorkshire. His ancestors included the Blennerhassetts of Ballyseedy. *Burke's Peerage* (London, 1894), p. 704. *FJ*, 18 Nov. 1886, 12–13, 17, 27, 31 Jan., 7 Feb. 1887; *Times*, 8 Feb. 1887; Pierce Mahony, *The Truth About Glenbeigh* (London, 1887); Curtis, *Coercion*, pp. 131, 149–50, 154–58, 164–65; and *KWR*, 29 Jan. 1887.

37   *FJ*, *CE*, and *Times*, 12–14 Jan. 1887.

38   *ILN*, 15 Jan. 1887, vol. 90, p. 63. See also *CE*, 12 Jan. 1887; *FJ*, 17 Jan 1887,

39   *ILN*, 5 Feb. 1887, vol. 90, p. 150. For the Belgian born Forestier's career, see Houfe, *Dictionary*, p. 307.

40   *Times*, 24 Jan. 1887. *FJ*, 17–18, 20, 22, 26 Jan. 1887, *CE*, 12–15, 17 Jan. 1887, *New York Times*, 18 Jan. 1887.

41   Colonel Sir Alfred E. Turner, *Sixty Years of a Soldier's Life* (London, 1914), pp. 198–9. Later promoted to Major General and knighted, Turner spent six years with the RIC (1886–92). In 1886 he succeeded General Sir Redvers Buller as commander of the crown forces in the southwest.

42   *PIP*, vol. 52 (22 Jan., 5 Feb. 1887), pp. 56–7 and p. 92. The fragile condition of this volume at the British Newspaper Library, Colindale prevents any reproduction.

43   *ILN*, 29 Jan. 1887, vol. 90, p. 111. Five years later Maud Gonne reproduced this print in her article for the *Journal des Voyages* (Paris). Fintan Cullen, 'Marketing national sentiment: lantern slides of eviction in late nineteenth-century Ireland', *History Workshop Journal* 54 (Autumn 2002), pp. 168–9.

44   *FJ*, *CE* and *Times*, 14–18, 21 Jan. 1887, and *Pilot*, 22 Jan. 1887.

45   *FJ*, 17–19, 23, 25 Jan. 1887, *CE*, 25 Jan. 1887, *UI*, 22 Jan. 1887, and *Times* 15, 17–19 Jan. 1887; *Boston Globe*, 15 Jan. 1887.

46   *FJ*, 18–21 Jan. 1887, *UI*, 22 Jan 1887, *KWR*, 22 Jan. 1887; Mahony, *Glenbeigh*, pp. 10–16; *Times*, 18 Jan. 1887.

47   *CE*, *FJ*, and *Times*, 19–20, 22 Jan. 1887; *KWR*, 22 Jan. 1887; Mahony, *Glenbeigh*, pp. 12–14.

48   *FJ* and *CE*, 21–22, 24–26 Jan. 1887.

49   *PIP*, 5 Feb. 1887, *FJ* and *CE*, 26–27, 31 Jan. 1887. A working-class rally in Finsbury raised over £13 for the Glenbeigh victims.

50   'Resisting the Evictor' and 'The Glenbeigh Horrors', *KWR*, 22 Jan. 1887.

51   'The Kerry Eviction' (n. d.) quoted in Zimmermann, *Songs of Irish Rebellion*, pp. 286–7.

52   J. D. Reigh, 'The law must take its course', *UI*, 22 Jan. 1887.

53   *FJ* and *Times*, 21, 22, 24, 26 Jan., 8 Feb. 1887.

54   *FJ* and *Times*, 29, 31 Jan. 1887; *CE*, 26–28 Jan. 1887; *KWR*, 12, 19 Feb. 1887; *Boston Pilot*, 5 Feb. 1887.

55   *ILN*, Feb. 12, 1887, vol. 90, p. 180.

56   Forestier may well have had Mary Quirke in mind when he sketched this woman being pursued by a large contingent of heavily armed police.

57 *FJ*, 15, 17, 24–25, 29–31 Jan 1887, *KWR*, 22, 29 Jan. 1887, *Times*, 31 Jan. 1887.

58 *KWR*, 22 Jan. 1887, *CE* and *FJ*, 24–26, 29 Jan. 1887, *UI*, 15, 22 Jan. 1887, *PMG*, 13, 17, 19 Jan. 1887, *Times*, 29 Jan. 1887; Curtis, *Coercion*, pp. 165–7.

59 *Boston Pilot*, 22, 29 Jan., 12 Feb. 1887; *New York Times*, 15, 18–22, 26 Jan. 1887; *New York Tribune*, 19–22 Jan. 1887; *Boston Herald*, 12–13 1887. *Boston Globe*, 15 Jan. 1887.

60 Sixteen tenants settled their rent disputes over the summer. *FJ*, 23–24 Feb., 15, 26 Sept. 1888; *CE*, 22–23, 28 Feb. 1888; *Times*, 24 Feb., 15 Sept. 1888.

61 Rosa Mulholland, *Giannetta, A Girl's Story of Herself* (London 1901).

62 Patrick Buckland, *Irish Unionism: One: The Anglo-Irish and the New Ireland, 1885–1922* (Dublin, 1972), pp. 1–3, 302–8; ILPU [Irish Loyal and Patriotic Union], *Evictions In Ireland* (Dublin, 1886), pp. 5–7 and *Times*, 31 Jan. 1887.

63 At a 'monster' meeting at Crecora, County Limerick on 17 October 1886, 'the manhunting and foxhunting gentry were roundly condemned'. *Times*, 19 Oct. 1886.

64 *People*, 13 Oct. 1888.

65 For the evictions at Arigna, near Keadue in County Roscommon on 13–15 April 1886 and their aftermath, see W. S. Blunt, *The Land War in Ireland* (London, 1912), pp. 46–9, 72–5. *FJ*, 20 Apr. 1886. For Blunt's arrest at Woodford, trial at Portumna, and imprisonment in Galway jail, see Blunt, *Land War*, pp. 367–410.

66 *Waterford News*, 13 Jan. 1888.

67 *People*, 18 July 1888.

68 *People*, 31 Mar. 1888.

69 *CE*, 28 Sept. 1888.

70 *Times* and *CE*, 25 Sept. 1889.

71 *Waterford News*, 5 Oct. 1888.

72 For the Dunne saga, see L. Perry Curtis, Jr, '"Killed by eviction": a case study in Co. Louth, 1888' in Felix M. Larkin (ed.), *Librarians, Poets and Scholars* (Dublin, 2007), pp. 140–55. See also *FJ*, 13 Feb., 12 Oct. 1888.

73 J. F. O'Hea, 'Evicting to death', *Weekly Freeman,* 20 Oct. 1888 and J. D. Reigh, 'The vindication of the law', *UI*, 20 Oct. 1888.

74 *WF*, 18 Dec. 1886.

75 *FJ*, 16 June 1887.

76 *ILN*, 25 Dec. 1886, vol. 89, p. 693.

6 THE PLAN EVICTIONS, 1887–90

1 Plan of Campaign Manifesto, *UI*, 23 Oct. 1886; Lyons, *Dillon*, pp. 74–5. See also *The Plan of Campaign: Its Origin, Progress, and Present Aspect*, n.d., NAI, C.O. 903/1, No. 11.

2 *FJ*, 11, 20 Jan. 1887; *UI*, 15 Jan. 23 July 1887; *CE*, 10 Sep. 1888.

3 Joseph V. O'Brien, *William O'Brien and the Course of Irish Politics 1881–1918* (Berkeley, 1976), pp. 47–8; Lyons, *Dillon*, pp. 86, 109–10; Davitt, *Fall of Feudalism*, p. 520; *Times*, 3 Feb. 1891, Report of the Commissioners appointed to inquire into the Estates of Evicted Tenants in Ireland, H.C. (c. 6935), 1893–1894, xxxi, p. 422. Laurence M. Geary, *The Plan of Campaign, 1886–1891* (Cork, 1986), pp. 153–79.

4 Geary, *Plan*, pp. 38–41; Samuel Laing, *The Plan of Campaign* (London, 1887); Lyons, *Dillon*, pp. 73–5, 105–6; O'Brien, *O'Brien*; pp. 58–86; Sally Warwick-Haller, *William O'Brien and the Irish Land War*

(Dublin, 1990), pp. 84–98; Curtis, *Coercion*, pp. 147–60, 236–63; Dooley, *Decline*, pp. 96–8; *Times*, 5 Mar. 1887, 3 Feb., 22 Apr. 1891; *FJ*, 20 Apr. 1887, 30 May 1888.

5 The *Freeman* reported that Lord Dillon had conceded a 30 per cent reduction. *FJ*, 30 Nov. 1887. Rath House, Termonfeckin, Dillon Papers. The gross rental in 1880 was £24,085. *FJ*, 10–11 Jan 1887, 24 May 1888; *UI*, 15 Jan., 5 Feb., 2, 9, 16 Apr. 1887; Geary, *Plan*, pp. 3, 41–4, 64.

6 *FJ*, 23–24 Feb., 28 May 1888; Geary, *Plan*, pp. 15–16, 40–7, 107, 158.

7 *UI*, 22 Jan., 27 Apr., 14 May, 4, 11 June, 30 July 1887.

8 *UI*, 30 July, 20 Aug., 3, 10 Sept. 1887. For the Anti-Plan of Campaign Association, see the circular sent by the Duke of Abercorn to the O'Conor Don, 18 June 1887, Clonalis, O'Conor Don Papers, 9.4 HS 216.

9 Geary, *Plan*, pp. 15–16, 41, 42, 44, 47, 64; Frank Callanan, *T. M. Healy* (Cork, 1996), pp. 172–8. For T. P. Gill's articles, see *New York Tribune*, 15 Jan., 24–25 Feb. 1888.

10 *FJ*, 17, 19, 26 Oct. 1886, 10–13 Aug., 10–11 Sept. 1887, *UI*, 17, 24 Sept. 1887. O'Brien, *O'Brien*, pp. 53–4 and William O'Brien, *Ireland Under Tory Rule* (London, 1888), pp 4–5.

11 Tom Garvin, 'Priests and patriots: Irish separatism and fear of the modern, 1890–1914', *IHS*, 25: 97 (May 1986), esp. pp. 68, 78–81; 'Balfour's war on the priesthood', *FJ*, 24 Feb., 13 Sept. 1888, 1 Jan. 1889; *CE*, 7 Apr. 1888; *UI*, 23 July 1887.

12 *CE*, 5 Mar. 1888.

13 Geary, *Plan*, pp. 60–6.

14 Wilfrid Scawen Blunt, *My Diaries, 1888–1914*, Part I (New York, 1922), pp. 69–70; Father Edward Murphy PP Killeagh, *CE*, 5 Mar. 1888.

15 For Balfour's resilience, anti-Plan tactics, and the secret syndicates on the Ponsonby and other Test Estates, see Curtis, *Coercion*, pp. 148–53, 179–86; Geary, *Plan*, pp. 72–7, 110–14; and BL, Balfour to Sir Redvers Buller, 7 May, 2, 7 Aug. 1887, Balfour to Sir West Ridgeway, 10, 14 Dec. 1888, and Balfour to De Vesci, 25 Jan. 1889, Add MSS. 49826–7.

16 'Campaigning in Ireland', *Times*, 1 Apr. 1887. *FJ*, 23 Feb., 31 May 1888.

17 *FJ*, 23, 28–29 May 1888; *People*, 13 June, 11, 18 Aug. 1888.

18 Davitt, *Fall of Feudalism*, pp. 522–8; *Times*, 10 Aug. 1889; *People*, 26 Oct. 1887; *UI*, 27 Aug. 1887; *CE*, 13 Apr., 7 Dec. 1889; Lyons, *Dillon*, pp. 87–90; Curtis, *Coercion*, pp. 179–87.

19 See Sections 6 and 7, Land Law (Ireland) Act, 1887, in Cherry, *Irish Land Law and Land Purchase Acts*, pp. 381–3. *FJ*, 18 July 1887, 18 Sept. 1888; Curtis, *Coercion*, pp. 243, 257, 336–42. 'Extermination in the dark', *UI*, 23 July 1887; *Times*, 17 May 1892.

20 *Times* and *FJ*, 30 Aug. 1886.

21 *FJ*, 23 May 1888; *Times*, 20 Nov. 1886.

22 *FJ* and *UI*, 22 Oct. 1887.

23 Blunt, *Land War in Ireland*, pp. 351–410; Curtis, *Coercion*, pp. 205–7; *FJ* and *Times*, 24–25 Oct. 1887, 3–4, 9, 11 Jan. 1888; *CE*, 4–5, 9 Jan 1888; *LRTV*, 25 Oct. 1887.

24 *FJ*, 4 Jan., 8, 11, 24, 29 Feb., 9, 30 Apr., 4, 18, 23 May 1888.

25 *Pictorial News*, 6 Feb. 1888, p. 5.

26 *FJ*, 9 Jan. 1889, 13, 19–20 Nov. 1890, *Times*, 11 July 1890, 20 Jan. 1891, 9 Nov. 1892; Paul Manzour, 'The Land War in Loughrea', Parts I and II, 1879–1916, in Joseph Forde et al. (eds), *The District of Loughrea* (Loughrea, 2003), pp. 397–402.

27 *UI*, 3, 10 Sept. 1887; *People*, 30 Mar. 1887, *FJ*, 3 Jan., 28 Apr., 23 May 1888; *CE*, 30, 31 Aug., 1 Sept. 1887,

28 Apr. 1888; Geary *Plan*, pp. 47–8, 59, 102–3, 139, 141.

28 *FJ*, 19, 21 Jan. 1887.

29 *UI*, 30 July, 20 Aug., 10 Sept., 1 Oct. 1887; *FJ*, 7, 11 July 1887, 17 May 1888; *CE*, 10, 12–13 Sept., 13 Oct. 1887; Geary, *Plan*, pp. 76, 141–2, 167; Donnelly, *Cork*, pp. 278–82, 341–7; Curtis, *Coercion*, pp. 197–200; PRONI, Sir William Gregory to Lord Dufferin, 26 Sept. 1887, Dufferin MSS.

30 Donnelly, *Cork*, pp. 167, 338, 362; *CE*, 13 June 1887; *KWR*, 30 Apr. 1887; Hussey, *The Reminiscences of an Irish Land Agent*, p. 221.

31 *CE*, 14 Jan., 22 Apr. 1889; *UI*, 1, 15 June 1889; *Times*, 11, 14, Jan., 2 Feb. 1889; and Geary, *Plan*, p. 98.

32 James S. Donnelly, Jr, 'The Kenmare estates during the nineteenth century', Part III, *Journal of the Kerry Archaeological and Historical Society* 23 (1990), pp. 20–45; *CE*, 12 Aug., 1 Oct. 1889; *Times*, 5, 31 Aug., 10 Sept.1889.

33 Lord Rossmore, *Things I Can Tell* (London, 1912), pp. 135–8. In the 1870s Massereene borrowed £120,000 from the Representative Body of the Church of Ireland. Geary, *Plan*, p. 45; Larry Conlon, *The Heritage of Collon, 1764–1984* (no. loc., 1984), pp. 9–18; and *Times*, 26 Aug. 1888.

34 Dudgeon survived an ambush in 1880 when working for the Orange Emergency Committee. The perpetrator spent 12 years in Mountjoy jail before being released in poor health and packed off to America. *Times*, 10 Apr. 1889, 11 Nov. 1892.

35 *FJ*, 29 Jan., 3 June, 18–19 July 1887; *UI*, 4 June, 3 July, 15 Oct. 1887; O'Brien, *O'Brien*, p. 46.

36 *FJ*, 5, 10 Oct. 1887, 10–12, 14 May 1888; *Times*, 25 June, 26 Aug. 1888 and *Dundalk Democrat* (hereafter *DD*), 29 Jan. 1887. See also the ILPU's pamphlet, *The Plan of Campaign Illustrated: An Account of the Massereene Estate* (Dublin, 1888); *Times*, 26, 27 Aug., 12, 14, 19, 22, 26, Sept., 8, 16, 20 Oct. 1888.

37 *CE*, 28 Oct. 1887; *FJ*, 28–29 Oct. 1887, 13, 15 Oct. 1888; *Times*, 19 Sept. 1888, 8, 10 Apr., 12 June 1889.

38 *DD*, 23 Mar. 1889; Conlon, *Collon*, pp. 51–4; *UI*, 5 Nov. 1887, 20 Oct. 1888, 8 June 1889; *FJ*, 8, 10, 15–16 Apr., 15 May, 4–7 June, 25–26 Sept., 5 Dec.1889; *DV*, 17 Aug. 1889; *Times*, 8, 10 Apr., 5, 12 June, 17 Sept. 1889.

39 *MHCA*, 4 May 1889. *Times*, 10 Apr., 3, 24 May 1889. Geary, *Plan*, pp. 103–5.

40 BL, Ridgeway to Balfour, 30 Apr. 1889, Balfour Papers, Add. MS 49810; Curtis, *Coercion*, pp. 186–87, 190, 193–94. See also *Times*, 25 June, 26 Aug., 1, 12 14, 19, 22, 26 Sept., 8, 15 Oct. 1888, 8 Apr., 24 May, 12 June 1889; *FJ*, 12 July 1889, 25–26 Nov. 1891.

41 Geary, *Plan*, pp. 45, 161; Dooley, *Decline*, p. 96; *FJ*, 1 June 1888.

42 *FJ*, 3, 11, 14, 27, 31 Jan. 1887. *Times*, 4 Oct., 30 Nov. 1888; *UI*, 15 Jan. 1887; *ME*, 5 May 1888.

43 *FJ*, 23, 27 Jan., 9 Apr., 5–6 May, 1 June 1888, 4 Jan. 1889; 11 Jan. 1891; Geary, *Plan*, pp. 37, 45, 136, 161.

44 Despite owning 143,000 acres in Ireland, England, and Scotland, Lansdowne was strapped for cash. For both prestige and monetary reasons he became viceroy of Canada (1883–8) and then India (1888–93). Lyne, *Lansdowne Estate*, pp. xl–xliii. See also Hurlbert, *Ireland Under Coercion*, vol. I, pp. 182–3.

45 Besides preaching for the Plymouth Brethren, Townsend Trench invented a tubeless bicycle tire. Lyne, *Lansdowne Estate*, pp. xlvii–lvi. For a sympathetic view of Lansdowne, see Hurlbert, *Ireland Under Coercion*, vol. II, pp. 219–42.

46 *FJ*, 30 Mar., 26 Sept. 1887; *UI*, 15, 22 Jan., 30 July 1887; *Times*, 25, 28 Apr., 6 June 1887; Geary, *Plan*, pp. 48–9, 73.

47 See Pádraig G. Lane, 'Government surveillance of subversives in Laois, 1890–1916' in P. G. Lane and William Nolan (eds), *Laois – History and Society* (Dublin, 1999), pp. 602–4.

48 *FJ* and *Times*, 20–23, 25 Apr. 1887; *UI*, 16 Apr. 1887.

49 *Pilot*, 4 June 1887. See also O'Brien, *O'Brien*, pp. 41, 44; *Times*, 29–30 Apr., 2–3 May 1887, 18 Sept. 1888; *FJ*, 30–31 May, 3, 7, 16 June 1887, 13, 22 Sept. 1888; *UI*, 11, 25 June, 30 July 1887.

50 *FJ*, 26 Sept. 1887; *UI*, 8 Oct. 1887, 22 Oct. 1888, 15–16 Apr., 28–31 May, 1, 3, 6 June, 4 July 1889; *WI*, 1 June 1889.

51 *WI*, 1, 4 June 1889; *FJ*, 1, 4 June, 6, 8 July 1889; *UI*, 8 June 1889; *CE*, 3–4 June 1889; *Times*, 4 June 1889.

52 *Times*, 28 May 1889; *FJ*, 24 Sept. 1888, 29 May 1889; *UI*, 4 Nov. 1893; Geary, *Plan*, p. 168; Dooley, *Decline*, pp. 103–4. NLI, Land League (Ireland), Minutes of the suppressed Timahoe branch of the Irish National League, 7 July 1887, MS 41720.

53 Talbot Ponsonby of Langrish House, Petersfield owned 10,367 acres in southern Cork. In 1886, his 246 tenants paid close to £7,000 in rent. Canon Daniel Keller, *The Struggle for Life on the Ponsonby Estate: A Chapter from the History of Irish Landlordism* (Irish Press Agency, n.d.), reprinted in the *FJ*, 29 Sept. 1887, pp. 15–16; Donnelly, *Cork*, pp. 355–60; Curtis, *Coercion*, 250–2. See also the Castle report on the Plan, TNA, CO 903/1, 17 June 1889, pp. 22–36 and *FJ*, 29 Sept 1887, 21, 29 May 1888, 3 June 1889, 6 Feb. 1891; *CE*, 13 June, 30 Sept. 1887, 24 Feb., 13–14 Apr., 30 May 1888, 22 Apr. 1890, and *Times*, 6 Feb. 1891.

54 Turner, *Sixty Years*, pp. 198–201, 206–19, 230–33, 259–60, and Curtis, *Coercion*, pp. 131, 133, 138–42, 147, 155–8, 167–73, 196–7; O'Brien, *O'Brien*, p. 43; and Keller, *Struggle for Life* and *The Ponsonby Estate and Mr Smith-Barry, M.P.: A Reply* (London, 1889). In November 1888, Patrick Ahern died from a bayonet wound inflicted during a riot at Midleton, County Cork. *Times*, 5–6 Nov. 1888. See also *CE*, 23 Apr. 1888.

55 *UI*, 16 Apr., 4 June 1887 and *CE*, 13 June 1887, 5 Mar. 1888.

56 *FJ* and *Times*, 27 May 1887.

57 *People*, 28 Mar. 1888; *CE*, 24 Feb., 1 June 1888; *FJ*, 13 Apr., 21 May, 9 Sept. 1888.

58 Castle officials worried lest Keller's counter-offer of £104,000 drive land values down all over the south. Donnelly, *Cork*, p. 358, *CE*, 15–16 Apr., 29–31 May 1889; *FJ*, 29 May 1889; *Times*, 17 Apr., 5 Aug. 1889; *Times*, 3 Sept. 1890.

59 See Balfour's two memoranda on eviction strategy in Hatfield House, Salisbury Papers, Balfour to Salisbury, 8 Jan. 1889 and BL, Balfour Papers, 30 Jan. 1889, Add. MS 49827. Arthur Hugh Smith-Barry, later first Baron Barrymore (1843–1925), owned 21,510 acres in Counties Cork and Tipperary valued at £27,791 plus 5,000 acres in England. Curtis, *Coercion*, pp. 56–7, 244–52 and *DIB*, vol. 1, pp. 318–19.

60 BL, Balfour Papers, Balfour to Ridgeway, 5 Mar., 18, 20 Apr., 30 May 1889, Add. MS 49827–28; Curtis, *Coercion*, pp. 246–7.

61 Michael J. F. McCarthy, *Five Years in Ireland, 1895–1900* (Dublin, 1903), pp. 124–5, 138.

62 *Times*, 27 Apr. 1889; *CE*, 15 Apr. 1890; Lyons, *Dillon*, pp. 100–6; Curtis, *Coercion*, pp. 246–52. BL, Ridgeway to Balfour, 21, 25 Feb., 2, 6, Mar. 1889, Balfour Papers, Add. MS 49809. For the sale of the Ponsonby estate to Smith-Barry, Walter Morrison, and others on 2 April 1889, see NAI, Irish Land Commission records, vol. 17, no. 406.

63 Ian d'Alton, 'Keeping faith: an evocation of the Cork Protestant Character, 1820–1920' in Patrick O'Flanagan and Cornelius G. Buttimer (eds), *Cork – History and Society* (Dublin, 1993), pp. 771–5. *CE*, 30 May, 1 June 1888. For the syndicates and Test estates, see Curtis, *Coercion*, pp. 239–55, 248–52 and Geary, *Plan*, pp. 109–21; Donnelly, *Cork*, pp. 355–60; *FJ*, 14–15 Apr., 7 June 1889; Keller, *Struggle for Life*; *FJ*, 28 Feb., 17, 19, Mar., 1 Apr., 27 May, 16 Aug. 30 Sept., 1887, 6 Mar., 15 Apr., 14, 24, 29 May, 3, 7 June 1889; *CE*, 30 Sept. 1887, 22 Apr. 1890; *Times*, 15 Mar., 31 May 1889, 12 July 1890.

64 Lyons, *Dillon*, pp. 106–8; *FJ*, 4, 11 July 1889; *CE*, 4, 5, 8 July 1889.

65 Donnelly, *Cork*, pp. 359–60; Geary, *Plan*, pp. 108–14, 120.

66 *CE*, 17 Apr. 1890.

67 *CE, FJ*, and *Times*, 16–19, 21 Apr. 1890; *UI*, 19 Apr., 3 May 1890.

68 Gertrud Gräfin von Guillaume-Schack (1845–1903) published several lectures on British-European human rights. Thanks go to Charles Wardell and Michael Ermarth for this information. See also *CE*, 16–19 Apr. 1890.

69 At Edmund Foley's house an emergency man was reprimanded for threatening Mrs. Leech from Yarmouth. *FJ, CE*, and *Times*, 21 Apr. 1890.

70 *FJ*, 22–23 Apr. 1890. For the Primrose League in Cork, see d'Alton, 'Keeping faith', *Cork – History and Society*, pp. 769–71.

71 Out of 152 evictions in April 20 involved farms without houses and 14 tenants remained as caretakers owing to illness or old age. *FJ, CE*, and *Times*, 22–26, 28–29 Apr., 1 May 1890; *UI*, 26 Apr. 1890.

72 *CE*, 24–25 June 1889, 22 Apr. 1890; *UI*, 26 Apr. 1890; *Times*, 19, 22–23 June, 15, 18–19, 30 July, 5 Aug. 1889, 12 Sept. 1890, 6 Feb. 1891.

73 A colliery owner and ardent Home Ruler, Ellis opposed British imperialism in both Ireland and South Africa. *Oxford DNB*, vol. 18, pp. 241–2.

74 'Evictions in Ireland', House of Commons, *Times*, 22 June 1889. See also Balfour's speech at Portsmouth, Hampshire, *Times*, 6, 22 June 1889.

75 Geary, *Plan*, pp. 138–9, 173; Donnelly, *Cork*, 376; *FJ*, 19–20, 22 Sept. 1890; *Times*, 27, 30 Sept., 16 Nov. 1892, and 4 Mar. 1896. See also NAI, CBS 4697/S.

76 Rosa Mulholland, *Onora* (London, 1900).

77 Maud Gonne, *The Autobiography of Maud Gonne: A Servant of the Queen*, eds A. Norman Jeffares and Anna McBride White (Chicago, 1995), p. 116.

78 Geary, *Plan*, pp. 119–21. Smith-Barry's agent was Horace H. Townsend, who also managed the Ponsonby estate for the syndicate. See the Liberal Union of Ireland pamphlet, *The Smith-Barry Estate, Tipperary* (Dublin, 1890) and *Times*, 1, 9 July, 17 Aug., 5–6, 9, 11–12, 16 Sept., 19 Oct. 1889.

79 *FJ*, 3–4 Dec. 1889; *Times*, 19, 22 Oct., 7, 9–10, 18, 31 Dec. 1889; *CE* and *FJ*, 1 Oct., 2–7, 9, 12 Dec.1889; Geary, *Plan*, p. 120.

80 Marcus Bourke, *John O'Leary: A Study in Irish Separatism* (Tralee, 1967), p. 207; Gonne, *Autobiography*, p. 92.

81 *FJ*, 7 Dec. 1889, 11, 14, 16, 21 Apr., 24–27, 29 Sept., 2 Oct. 1890; *CE*, 24–27, 29 Sept. 1890, 24–28, 30 Mar. 1891; *Irish Times*, 24–27, 29 Sept, 2 Oct. 1890; *UI*, 12, 19 Apr. 1890; *Times*, 24 Sept. 1889, 11 July, 26–27, 29 Sept., 6–7, 11 Oct., 6 Nov. 1890, 15, 20, 22 Jan., 10 Feb., 3, 22 Apr., 23 May, 1, 6, 30 June 1891, 6 Apr. 1896; O'Brien, *O'Brien*, pp. 75–9; Donnelly, *Cork*, pp. 374–5; and Geary, *Plan*, pp. 112–14, 128–29. For the Tipperary show trial and the escape of Dillon and O'Brien, see Lyons, *Dillon*, pp. 108–12, 253–4. See also Curtis, *Coercion*, pp. 254–5, 327.

82 *Times*, 16 Mar. 1889; *FJ*, 17 Jan., 22 Oct. 1887; Peggy Doyle, *The Coolgreany Evictions 1887* (1986), pp. 15–17, 21, 38–40, 56–7; *WI*, 17 Oct. 1888.

83 *FJ*, 3 Jan., 6–8 July 1887; *UI*, 9 July 1887; Doyle, *Coolgreany*, pp. 15–17.

84 Sarah Rouse, *Into the Light* (Dublin, 1998), pp. 20–1. This photograph of the Kavanagh family appears in NLI, WL, TRAN 879. The fragility of the *Cooolgreany Evictions* album has led to restricted access. See also Doyle, *Coolgreany*, pp. 24, 41, 44; *FJ*, 8 July 1887; *UI*, 16 July 1887.

85 *FJ*, 9, 11–16 July 1887; *UI*, 9, 16, 23 July, 1 Oct. 1887; *CE*, 18–19 July 1887; Doyle, *Coolgreany Evictions*, pp. 15–38, 40; Geary, *Plan*, pp. 75–6; W. S. Blunt, *Land War*, pp. 278, 282–5.

86 *CE*, 18–19 July 1887; *FJ*, 16 July 1887; Doyle, *Coolgreany Evictions*, pp. 39–41.

87 *WI*, 9, 13, 20 June, 18 July, 28 Nov. 1888; *Times*, 25 Oct. 1887, 17 July, 26 Nov. 1888; *People*, 20 June, 18 July 1888.

88 Doyle, *Coolgreany*, pp. 42–7; *FJ*, 18 May, 29–30 Sept., 1, 4–5, 13, 24, 27, 29 Oct. 1887; *LRTV*, 4, 11 Oct. 1887; *CE*, 29 Sept., 5–7, 13–15, 26, 27 Oct. 1887; *UI*, 1, 8 Oct. 1887; *People*, 31 Oct. 1888; *WI*, 27 May 1889.

89 *FJ*, 24 Oct. 1887, 30 May, 4 June 1889; *UI*, 29 Oct. 1887. For Archbishop Walsh's efforts to end the Plan at Coolgreany, see his article, 'Arbitration or the Battering-Ram?' *Contemporary Review*, vol. 55 (June 1889), pp. 197–214 and two letters to the O'Conor Don, Clonalis, O'Conor Don Papers, 23, 28 Dec. 1889, 9.4 HE 079.

90 *People*, 11 Apr. 1888; *WI*, 4 July 1888; *Times*, 26 Oct. 1888.

91 Geary, *Plan*, pp. 103–4, 111, 157; *FJ*, 25 May, 9 Dec. 1889; *Times*, 16 Mar., 24 Sept. 1889.

92 The *Freeman* sent E. Dwyer Gray, the young son of the recently deceased owner, to ascertain the facts. *FJ*, 22 Oct. 1888, 2, 4, 6, 9 Dec. 1889, 27 Feb. 1891. See also *Times*, 31 Dec. 1889; *People*, 17, 20 Oct. 1888; *Times*, 13 June 1891; Curtis, *Coercion*, pp. 399–400.

93 O'Kelly lived in Lusk, County Dublin and owned a total of 3,152 acres in Kildare. *Kildare Observer* (hereafter *KO*), 6 Apr. 1889; *FJ*, 2 Apr., 4 June 1889; *Times*, 20, 22, 24, 26 Jan., 8 Feb., 28 Apr. 1887.

94 *KO*, 30 Mar. 1889.

95 *UI*, 6 Apr. 1889.

96 *FJ*, 3–4 June, 26 Sept., 30 Nov. 1889; *UI*, 8 June 1889, 26 Apr. 1890; *Times*, 11 Nov. 1892. For the Lawrence photograph, see NLI, R 2159 WL.

97 F. Mabel Robinson, *The Plan of Campaign: A Story of the Fortune of War*, 2 vols (London, 1888). A critical review of this novel appeared in *FJ*, 5 Jan. 1888.

98 George A. Moore, 'An eviction', *Parnell and His Island* (London, 1887), pp. 189–211.

99 *Times*, 3 Feb. 1891; O'Brien, *O'Brien*, p. 253.

100 Balfour speaking in the House of Commons. *Times*, 22 June 1889.

101 These estimates were compiled by the Evicted Tenants Commission in 1892–3 and excerpted from the parliamentary blue book no. 69 in a leaflet, 'What some Irish evictions have cost the country'. Bodleian Library, John Johnson Collection, n.d. (*c*.1893).

7 RESISTANCE, 1886–9

1 James S. Donnelly, 'The Rightboy movement', 1785–8', *Studia Hibernica* 17 & 18 (1977–8), pp. 120–202; 'Hearts of oak, hearts of steel', *Studia Hibernica* 21 (1981), pp. 7–73; 'Captain Rock: the origins of the Irish agrarian rebellion of 1821–24', *New Hibernia Review* 11: 4 (Winter, 2007), pp. 47–72 and Oliver MacDonagh, 'The economy and society, 1830–45' in Vaughan (ed.), *A New History of Ireland*, v, *Ireland Under the Union*, 1, pp. 222–5.

2 Galvin, *Irish Songs of Resistance*, pp. 37–8.

3 Many thanks go to Honora Faul of the National Library of Ireland for discovering this print. NLI, DPD 3176 TX 18.

4 *UI*, 11 June 1887.

5 NLI, Lawrence Collection, 1775 WL.

6 Susan Sontag, *On Photography* (New York, 1977), pp. 3–4, 55–7, 85–9, 155.

7 Only around 60 of the 1,200 landscape negatives advertised for sale in 1890 dealt with evictions. Rouse, *Into The Light*, pp. 54–5; Liam Kelly, *Photographs and Photography in Irish Local History* (Dublin, 2008), pp. 85–102; Edward Chandler, *Photography in Ireland: The Nineteenth Century*

(Dublin, 2001); Jerry Thompson, *Truth and Photography* (Chicago, 2003), pp. 3, 7; Fintan Cullen, 'Marketing national sentiment: lantern slides of evictions in late nineteenth-century Ireland', *History Workshop Journal* (hereafter *HWJ*), 54 (Autumn, 2002), pp. 164–79.

8   For Dillon's speech at Dundalk, see *Times*, 4 Oct. 1888.

9   T. W. Moody cites no examples of serious resistance to eviction in *Davitt*, pp. 317, 320–2, 345–9, 418–19.

10   *FJ* and *Times*, 29–30 Aug. and 1 Sept. 1888.

11   *Times*, 29 Sept. 1888; *FJ*, 30–31 Aug., 1, 8 Sept. 1888; *CE*, 1 Sept. 1888.

12   NLI, Lawrence Collection, 1773 WL.

13   *CE*, 4 Sept., 3 Oct. 1888; *Times*, 4 Oct. 1888.

14   'An eye to effect – from a photograph taken just before an eviction on Lord Clanricarde's estate, Woodford, Ireland', *Graphic*, 20 Oct. 1888, vol. 38, p. 416.

15   *FJ*, 3, 7, 9, 12 Jan. 1889; *Times*, 13, 21 Aug., 12 Oct. 1889. For the small bomb or 'infernal machine' found inside an empty cottage at Woodford, see *Times*, 6 Dec. 1889.

16   The tenants agreed to pay one gale's rent and Father Egan covered the legal costs. *KWR*, 19 Feb. 1887; *FJ*, 16 Nov. 1886, 23, 25–28 Feb. 1887. Turner, *Sixty Years*, pp. 199–200.

17   *CE*, 22–23 July 1887; *UI*, 30 July 1887; Geary, *Plan*, p. 27. Kelly's arrest, trial, and sentencing are covered in *FJ*, 13, 15 Apr. 1889.

18   *Graphic*, 10 Mar 1888, vol. 37, pp. 264–5. For Renouard's career at the *Graphic* after 1884, see Houfe, *Dictionary of British Book Illustrators*, pp. 86–7, 431.

19   *Times*, 16 Nov. 1888, 26 June 1889.

20   *KWR*, 12, 26 Feb. 1887; *Times*, 26 Feb., 24 Aug. 1887; Doyle, *Coolgreany*, pp. 34–8.

21   Turner, *Sixty Years*, pp. 253–4.

22   The release from prison of three tenants on the Leader estate in Cork inspired celebrations. *CE*, 15 Oct. 1887.

23   *Times*, 20 Oct. 1886; *FJ* and *CE*, 20–21 Oct. 1886.

24   *ILN*, 27 Nov. 1886, vol. 89, p. 578. The caption derived from the *Times*, 20 Oct. 1886.

25   *FJ* and *Times*, 19 Jan. 1887. In his memoir, *In the Royal Irish Constabulary* (London, n.d. [*c*.1904]), pp. 163–85, District Inspector G. Garrow Green described O'Grady as 'a fine specimen of the well-to-do Irish peasant' and called Plunkett 'the Hon. Captain Bunkum.' A clever lawyer and a sympathetic jury resulted in O'Grady's acquittal. See also *New York Times*, 18 Jan. 1887 and the *New York Tribune*, 19 Jan. 1887.

26   'Hurrah for Ned O'Grady!', *UI*, 29 Jan. 1887.

27   *Limerick Reporter and Tipperary Vindicator* (hereafter, *LRTV*), 27, 30 Sept., 4 Oct. 1887; *Times* and *FJ*, 28 Sept. 1887; *UI*, 1 Oct. 1887.

28   Geary, *Plan*, pp. 73–4; Curtis, *Coercion*, p. 155; BL, Balfour Papers, Balfour to Colonel A. E. Turner, 8 Sept. 1887, Add. MS 49826. See also Samuel Laing, *A Visit to Bodyke: Or, The Real Meaning of Irish Evictions* (London, 1887), pp. 6–7, 11 and Kelly, *Bodyke Evictions*; *FJ*, 28 Sept., 8 Oct. 1887, 25 May 1888; *CE*, 28 Sept., 8 Oct. 1887.

29   *FJ* and *Times*, 31 Jan. 1887; *UI*, 5 Feb. 1887; BL, Balfour Papers, Balfour to Buller, 7 May 1887, Add. MS 49826.

30   Tuke, *Memoir*, pp. 256–7. Norman's articles appeared in *Bodyke: A Chapter in the History of Irish Landlordism* (London and New York, 1887). *Oxford DNB*, vol. 41, p. 15.

31   *Times*, 2 Feb., 2, 8 July 1887.

32   NLI, Lawrence Collection, EBL 2662.

33   *FJ* and *Times*, 28 May 1887 and *UI*, 4 June 1887.

34   NLI, Lawrence Collection, EBL 2665. See also *KWR*, *FJ*, and *Times*, 31 May, 4 June 1887. Sheriff

M'Mahon recovered from his seizure but played no part in subsequent evictions. Kelly, *Bodyke Evictions*, p. 75; *FJ* and *Times*, 27, 30, 31 May and 1 June 1887.

35 *FJ* and *PMG*, 1–4 June 1887; *UI*, 11 June 1887; *Pilot*, 11 June 1887. Norman photographed Davitt standing next to Lyddy's wife and three-year-old child. Norman, *Bodyke*, pp. 27–9; Kelly, *Bodyke Evictions*, pp. 76, 139, and Turner, *Sixty Years*, pp. 209–12.

36 *KWR*, 11 June 1887; *Pilot*, 11 June 1887; *FJ*, *PMG*, and *Times*, 3–4, 6, 11 June 1887; *UI* and *CE*, 11 June 1887; Kelly, *Bodyke Evictions*, pp. 76–80; *WDM*, 6 June 1887.

37 Hussey's sons ended up in Limerick jail. Norman, *Bodyke*, pp. 34–41; *WDM*, 6 June 1887; *FJ*, *PMG*, and *Times*, 4, 7 June 1887; *UI*, 4, 11 June 1887; Turner, *Sixty Years*, pp. 212–13; Kelly, *Bodyke Evictions*, p. 84.

38 *FJ* and *Times*, 7 June 1887; Norman, *Bodyke*, pp. 47–50.

39 Norman, *Bodyke*, pp. 42–6, 51–2; *FJ*, *PMG*, and *Times*, 7–8 June 1887.

40 Norman, *Bodyke*, pp. 52–4, 71–3; Kelly, *Bodyke Evictions*, pp. 107–9; *PMG*, *Times*, and *FJ*, 8–10 June, 16 July 1887.

41 By 1880 O'Halloran (also spelled Halloran) was paying £33 for 18 Irish acres valued at £16 15s. But the Land Commissioners lowered his rent to £23 10s in 1882. *FJ* and *PMG*, 11 June 1887. Laing, *Visit to Bodyke*, pp. 7–8; *Irish Times*, 15 June 1887; Kelly, *Bodyke Evictions*, p. 141.

42 Only clergymen and reporters were allowed to pass through this police cordon. *FJ*, 11 June 1887 and *CE*, 10 June 1887.

43 The accounts of the siege of fort O'Halloran differ slightly in *FJ*, *PMG*, and *CE*, 11 June 1887; Turner, *Sixty Years*, pp. 214–15.

44 Kelly, *Bodyke Evictions*, pp. 101, 165; Norman, *Bodyke*, pp. 55–63. See also the first-hand account of the siege by Frank O'Halloran in the *Irish Times*, 15 June 1887, reprinted in Kelly, *Bodyke Evictions*, pp. 90–4; *Times*, 17 June 1887; *CE*, 13 June 1887 and also http://www.clarelibrary.ie/eolas/cocclare/history/ bodyke_evictions/bodyke. index.htm/·

45 *UI*, 18 June 1887.

46 The fragility of volume 52 prevents reproduction of this striking image. *PIP*, 18 June 1887, p. 385.

47 *Times*, *PMG*, *FJ*, and *CE*, 13 June 1887; *Pilot*, 18 June 1887; Norman, *Bodyke*, pp. 64–7.

48 Turner, *Sixty Years*, pp. 222–3, and *FJ*, *PMG*, and *Times*, 14, 16 June 1887.

49 *CJ* as quoted in Kelly, *Bodyke Evictions*, pp. 102–3; Norman, *Bodyke*, p. 76; *FJ*, 13, 16 June 1887.

50 *UI*, 11 June 1887; *FJ*, 9, 16 June 1887, 7 May 1888. Some 22 out of the 26 resisters charged with obstruction on 18 June (and later released) were women or girls. Kelly, *Bodyke Evictions*, p. 165.

51 Dillon's motion to adjourn was defeated by 246 to 165 votes. *Times*, 10–11, 16–18 June 1887 and *UI*, 25 June 1887.

52 The reverse side of these medals bore the inscription: 'For Defending the Homes of Bodyke, 1887'. *FJ*, 16 July 1887; *UI*, 18 June, 30 July 1887; *CE*, 11 June, 25 July 1887. French photographed the O'Halloran sisters, who eventually emigrated.

53 Norman, *Bodyke*, pp. 76–8. According to Turner, respect for Mrs O'Callaghan saved her husband from being murdered. *Sixty Years*, pp. 215–16.

54 Laing, *Visit to Bodyke*, esp. pp. 8–12. See also *Daily News*, 8 Oct. 1887 and Kelly, *Bodyke Evictions*, pp. 65–106. In 1987 President Patrick Hillery unveiled a stone memorial at Bodyke marking the centenary of the tenants' resistance.

55 *FJ*, 28 Sept. 1887; *LRTV*, 30 Sept., 7 Oct. 1887; *UI*, 1 Oct. 1887.

56 Geary, *Plan*, p. 171; Turner, *Sixty Years*, pp. 239–42; Tuke, *Memoir*, p. 257; *CE*, 9, 21, 23 Apr. 1888; *Times* and *FJ*, 20 Sept. 1888.

57 *FJ*, 31 Jan. 1887; *UI*, 15 Jan. 1887.

58 *FJ*, 25, 29 Aug., 7, 16 Sept. 1887, 6–7 Sept. 1888; *CE*, 6, 13, 19 Sept. 1888; *UI*, 5 Feb., 15 Sept. 1888.

59 *FJ*, 21 May 1889; *CE*, 6, 8–9 July 1889; *Times*, 23 Feb. 1891; Geary, *Plan*, p. 168.

60 Captain Hill owned 24,200 acres valued at £1,308 with a rental of roughly £798. See also Nicholson, *Annals of the Famine*, pp. 64–72; Hurlbert, *Ireland Under Coercion*, vol. I, pp. 73–89; Proinnsias Ó Gallchobhair, *The History of Landlordism in Donegal* (Ballyshannon, 1962), pp. 22–9; and Vaughan, *LTMVI*, pp. 30, 45, 221.

61 *DI*, 21, 28 Aug., 13 Nov. 1886.

62 *FJ*, 27 Sept., 5–8, 10 Oct. 1887; *UI*, 8 Oct. 1887; *DI*, 1, 8 Oct. 1887.

63 *PIP*, 8 Oct. 1887, pp. 222–3; *FJ*, 8, 10 Oct., 25 Nov. 1887; Geary, *Plan*, pp. 29, 166; *Times*, 19 Dec. 1888, 6 June 1889.

64 *DI*, 22 Jan. 1887; *WDM*, 19 Nov. 1887; *Times*, 30 July 1888; *FJ*, 17 Aug. 1888; *CE*, 13 Aug. 1889; *UI*, 12 Feb., 13 Aug. 1887.

65 *UI*, 29 Oct. 1887.

66 *WDM*, 18 Nov. 1887.

67 *ILN*, vol. 90, pp. 201–2, 19 Feb. 1887; *FJ*, 12 Jan. 1887; *UI*, 15 Jan. 1887. Frost's landlord was Henry Vassall D'Esterre JP. For Frost's joyful release from prison, see *CE*, 4 Oct. 1887; *New York Daily Tribune*, 12 Jan. 1887.

68 UCD, NFC437/ff. 376–7.

69 *CE*, 24–25 Aug. 1888.

70 *FJ*, 30 Aug. 1888 and *Times*, 29 Sept., 1 Oct. 1888.

71 Lord Courtown's praise of Captain Hamilton appears in the annual *Report of the Property Defence Association* (Dublin, 1888), pp. 1, 4–6, 10.

72 Anne Crookshank and the Knight of Glin, *Ireland's Painters, 1600–1940* (New Haven and London, 2002), pp. 261–3. See also *Whipping The Herring*, p. 137, and the Gorry Gallery, *An Exhibition of 18th–20th Century Irish Paintings* (Dublin, Mar. 2008), pp. 34–42.

73 Brendan Rooney alludes to 'the claustrophobic intensity' of this picture in *Whipping the Herring*, p. 136. See also his biography, *The Life and Work of Harry Jones Thaddeus, 1859–1929* (Dublin, 2003). *The Wounded Poacher* may be seen in Brian P. Kennedy, *Irish Painting* (Dublin, 1993), p. 94.

74 O'Brien, *O'Brien*, p. 36.

75 While the exact number of final evictions during the Plan era remains moot, the figure of 2,375 between 1887 and 1890 appears in a parliamentary return. *Times*, 13 June 1887, 14 Nov. 1890; O'Brien, *O'Brien*, p. 253.

76 *FJ* and *CE*, 1 June 1889; *UI*, 15 June 1889.

77 Davitt, *Fall of Feudalism*, p. 520.

78 Turner, *Sixty Years*, pp. 252, 257; Haire, 'In aid of the civil power, 1868–90' in Lyons and Hawkins, *Ireland Under the Union*, p. 142.

8 THE BATTERING RAM, 1887–90

1 This chapter is a revised version of my article, 'The battering ram and Irish evictions, 1887–90', *Éire-Ireland* 42: 3 & 4 (Fall/Winter 2007), pp. 207–48, for which I owe thanks to the editors.

2 Terry Eagleton, *Heathcliff and the Great Famine* (London, 1995), p. 4. Seamus Heaney, 'Act of

Union', *Poems, 1965–1975* (New York, 1982), p. 204.

3 BL, Ridgeway to Balfour, 29 Nov. 1887, Balfour Papers, Add. MS 49808; *Derry Journal* (hereafter, *DJ*), 15 Apr. 1889; 'Hurley's Mill, Clonakilty, County Cork', *ILN*, 27 Nov. 1886, vol. 89, p. 578.

4 For Michel Foucault's discourse on the technology and 'micro-physics of power', see *Discipline and Punish: The Birth of the Prison* (New York, 1979), pp. 23–8, 47–54, 195–223, 306–8.

5 *WDM*, 19 Nov. 1887; *FJ*, 10–11 May, 3, 7 Sept. 1888, 16, 20 Apr., 10–13, 15, 30 May, 3 June 1889; *DV*, 23 Mar. 1889; *Times*, 3 June 1889; 'Ireland – The Clanricarde evictions – determined resistance', *Pictorial News*, 8 Sept. 1888, no. 576, p. 8.

6 Shaw-Lefevre's letters about the Kilrush evictions appeared in the *Times*, 1, 8 June 1889. Ball mistakenly identifies Bodyke as the first ram site. 'Crowd activity', p. 239.

7 *Times* and *FJ*, 24 Oct., 30 Nov. 1887; *People*, 28 Jan., 23, 30 May 1888; *UI*, 29 Oct. 1887, 12 Apr. 1890; *WDM*, 25 Oct. 1887; BL, Ridgeway to Balfour, 29 Nov. 1887, Balfour Papers, Add. MS 49808.

8 *Weekly Freeman*, 10 Dec. 1887; *WI*, 10 July 1889.

9 *Pictorial News*, 9 June 1888, no. 563.

10 *FJ*, 23 May 1888, 24–25 Apr. 1889; *People*, 23, 30 May 1888.

11 *FJ*, 15 Nov. 1886, 10–12, 19 May 1888; *CE*, 14, 16, 18–19 July 1888; *Times*, 8 Aug. 1887, 16. 23, 26 July 1888, 1 June 1889; *PMG*, 16 July 1888; and Geary, *Plan*, p. 93.

12 Turner, *Sixty Years*, pp. 250–1; Mulqueen, *Vandeleur Evictions*, pp. 33–57; *CE*, 19 July 1888.

13 Turner, *Sixty Years*, pp. 251–3.

14 NLI, Lawrence Collection, 1766 WL.

15 *CE* and *Times*, 19 July 1888.

16 Quoted in Mulqueen, *Vandeleur Evictions*, p. 30.

17 *Graphic*, 4 Aug. 1888.

18 Spellacy (or Spellissy) farmed some 25 Irish acres at a judicial rent of £23, *CE*, 18–21, 23–28, 30–31 July, 1–2 Aug. 1888. Mulqueen, *Vandeleur Evictions*, pp. 44–5, 88–9; *Times*, 20–21 July 1888.

19 *CE* and *Times*, 20–21, 25, 27 July 1888.

20 *CE* and *FJ*, 26 July, 1–2 Aug. 1888.

21 *CE* and *CJ*, 26–27 July 1888; *FJ* and *Times*, 27 July 1888.

22 NLI, Lawrence Collection, 1779 WL. The *Cork Examiner* (27 July 1888) called this photographic session 'contemptible and insulting'.

23 *UI*, 4 Aug. 1888.

24 Mulqueen, *Vandeleur Evictions*, pp. 45–9, 82–6; J. B. Hall, *Random Records of a Reporter* (London, 1928), pp. 35–8; Turner, *Sixty Years*, pp. 253–4; *FJ* and *CE*, 27, 31 July, 18, 24–25 Aug., 25 Sept. 1888; *CJ*, 27 July 1888; *Irish Times*, 18, 21 Aug. 1888; *Times*, 27 July, 6, 16–18, 22 Aug. 1888, 1, 6, 8 June 1889.

25 Mulqueen, *Vandeleur Evictions*, pp. 44–7; *FJ*, *CE*, and *Times*, 31 July, 1–2 Aug., 26 Sept. 1888.

26 *Times*, 20 Sept. 1888; *CE*, 25 Sept. 1888; *Irish Times*, 20 Aug. 1888; Mulqueen, *Vandeleur Evictions*, pp. 55–6.

27 *FJ*, 10 Jan., 1–2, 4, 11, 17 Apr. 1889, 14–17, 19, 22–23 Apr. 1890, 11 Feb., 24 May, 17 Oct. 1891; *Times*, 9 Jan., 17 Apr., 6 May, 1 June 1889; *CE*, 4 June 1889, 14–17, 19, 22–23 Apr. 1890; Geary, *Plan*, pp. 135, 177.

28 Mulqueen, *Vandeleur Evictions*, pp. 50–5; *FJ*, 9 Jan. 1891; *Times*, 9 Jan., 25 Apr., 8 June, 25 July 1889, 22 May 1891; David Fitzpatrick, *Politics and Irish Life 1913–1921* (Dublin, 1977), p. 51.

29 *CE* and *FJ*, 30–31 Aug., 1 Sept. 1888.

30 *FJ*, 3–4, 8 Sept. 1888; *CE* and *Times*, 3–4 Sept. 1888.

31 NLI, Lawrence Collection, no. 2482.

32 For these three photographs, see respectively NLI, Lawrence collection, R1779, R1769, and CAB4918.

33 Curtis, *Coercion*, pp. 244–5.

34 *Times*, 8, 12 Apr. 1889; Curtis, 'Battering ram', *Éire-Ireland*, pp. 218–19.

35 *People*, 10, 31 Mar. 1888.

36 *Irish Times*, 17, 20–21 Aug. 1888; *People*, 18 Aug., 3 Nov. 1888; *PMG*, 17 Aug. 1888; *Times* and *FJ*, 17 Aug. 1888; *CE*, 7– 8, 10–13, 15 Sept. 1888.

37 *PIP*, 25 Aug. 1888, pp. 120–1.

38 'Desperate eviction struggle in Wexford', *Pictorial News*, 25 Aug. 1888, no. 574, pp. 8–9.

39 NLI, Lawrence Collection, R2491.

40 *FJ*, 17 Aug. 1888; *People*, 25 Aug. 1888.

41 *FJ*, 7–8, 12–13, 15 Sept 1888; *CE*, 7, 10, 12, 14–15 Sept. 1888; *People*, 8, 12, 15 Sept., 6 Oct. 1888; *WI*, 15 Sept. 1888.

42 *People*, 14 Apr., 25 Aug., 1 Sept., 3 Nov. 1888; *FJ*, 11–12 Apr., 18 Aug. 1888; *CE*, 8 Oct. 1888, 12, 16–18, 21–26, 29 Apr. 1890; *Times*, 12, 25 Apr. 1890; *UI*, 19 Apr. 1890.

43 *People*, 3 Mar., 14 Apr. 1888.

44 *FJ*, 23–24 Feb. 1888.

45 Keller, *Struggle for Life*, pp. 4–8; *FJ*, 23–24 Feb. 1888; *CE*, 28–30 Sept. 1887, 24 Feb. 1888; *Mayo Examiner* (hereafter, *ME*), 5 May 1888.

46 *People*, 23, 30 May 1888; *FJ*, 23 May 1888, 24–25 Apr. 1889.

47 *FJ*, 9–11 Jan., 24–25 Apr., 5–6, 8–10, 1889; *WDM*, 25 Oct. 1887; *Waterford News*, 6 July 1889; *WI*, 12 Jan., 10 July 1889; *People*, 28 Jan. 1888; *Nation*, 10 July 1889; *UI*, 12 Apr. 1890.

48 *FJ* and *Times*, 23, 26, 28 Aug. 1888, 9, 11–13 Jan., 11–13 Apr., 15 May, 13 July 1889, 10, 12–15, 17–21 Nov. 1890; *Northern Whig* (hereafter, *NW*), 9 Jan. 1889; *DI*, 12 Jan. 1889; and *Donegal Vindicator* (hereafter, *DV*), 20 Apr. 1889.

49 *FJ*, *CE*, and *Times*, 3 June 1889; *UI*, 8 June 1889.

50 *FJ*, 13 May, 2–5, 10 Dec. 1889; *Times* and *CE*, 2–5, 10 Dec. 1889. See also Curtis, *Coercion*, 250–5; Geary, *Plan*, 52, 107, 111–21, 129; O'Brien, *O'Brien*, pp. 75–9, 82; Lyons, *Dillon*, 107–10, and the ILPU pamphlet, *Mad Tipperary* (Dublin, 1890).

51 *CE*, 3–5 Dec. 1889.

52 *CE*, 2 Dec. 1889.

53 *Times*, 9 Apr. 1889. Educated at TCD and Oxford, John Gordon Swift MacNeill (1849–1926) was a brief-less barrister who served as MP for South Donegal from 1887 to 1918. *Oxford DNB*, vol. 35, pp. 960–2.

54 See the debate on Donegal, *FJ*, 11, 12, 17 Apr. 1889 and *Times*, 6, 7 Aug. 1889, 11 July 1890. A fine caricature of MacNeill appears in Henry W. Lucy, *A Diary of the Unionist Parliament, 1895–1900* (London, 1901), p. 93.

55 *Times*, 8, 10 May, 6, 7 Aug. 1889, 11 July 1890; *FJ*, 11–12 July 1890. Mr. Punch mentioned MacNeill's model ram in 'The essence of Parliament', *Punch*, 17 Aug. 1889, vol. 97, p. 76 and 19 July 1890, vol. 99, p. 36. See also MacNeill's memoir, *What I Have Seen and Heard* (London, 1925), p. 249. In 1994 the artist and designer, Yanny Petters, created a miniature battering ram for a scale-model village or clachan in the 'Model World' exhibition in Newtownmountkennedy, County Wicklow. This ram stood outside a cottage with a big hole in the front wall. Entitled 'Famine eviction scene', this

anachronistic scenario enlivens the cover of Fintan O'Toole's book, *The Ex-Isle of Erin: Images of Global Ireland* (Dublin, 1996).

56 Reigh also invoked Indian mythology while demonising landlords in 'The Irish Juggernaut', *UI*, 22 Sept. 1888.

57 For the wooden flogging triangle used at Athy, County Kildare (and elsewhere), see Thomas Pakenham, *The Year of Liberty* (London, 1969), pp. 71–3.

58 *Punch*, 20 Apr. 1889, vol. 96, p. 192 and 27 Apr. 1889, vol. 96, p. 193.

59 *Punch*, 19 June 1890, vol. 99, pp. 35–6.

60 *Punch*, 18 Mar. 1893, vol. 104, p. 127.

61 *Times*, 16 Nov. 1892. Scion of a minor Catholic gentry family in County Cork, Mathew had the additional distinction of being John Dillon's father-in-law after 1895. *Oxford DNB*, vol. 37, pp. 288–9; *DIB*, vol. 6, p. 425.

62 This Englishman also terrified some women cottagers, who mistook him for a process server and fled inside. John Bickerdyke, *Wild Sports in Ireland* (London, 1897), pp. 25–26. I am grateful to Peter Beirne of Clare County Library for this reference.

63 Jules Verne, *The Extraordinary Adventures of Foundling Mick* (Dublin, 2008), p. 103.

64 *UI*, 15 Sept. 1888.

65 For T. P. Gill's denunciation of the ram in a speech at Drogheda, see *UI*, 15 June 1889.

9 FALCARRAGH: THE OLPHERT ESTATE

1 Hurlbert, *Ireland Under Coercion*, vol. i, pp. 73–123. For Tuke's influential ideas on Irish economic development, see *Times*, 22, 28 May and 29 June 1889; Tuke, *Memoir*, pp. 259–65; and Tuke, *The Condition of Donegal* (London, 1889), pp. 16–24.

2 See the report on Gweedore by the *Freeman*'s special correspondent *FJ*, 8 Apr. 1889; 'Historicus', *DV*, 27 Apr. 1889; the Rev. James McFadden's pamphlet, *The Present and The Past, or The Agrarian Struggle in Gweedore* (Londonderry, 1889). The Olphert estate was valued at only £1,802. PRONI, Duke of Abercorn to Lord Dufferin, 11 July 1888, Dufferin Papers.

3 *FJ*, 22 Jan 1887, 8 Apr., 20 May 1889, 14 Nov. 1890; *DI*, 25 Aug. 1888; *Times*, 26 Apr. 1889; *ILN*, 11 Feb. 1888, vol. 92, p. 135. For Father McFadden, see Brendán MacSuibhne, 'Soggarth Aroon and Gombeen-Priest: Canon [sic] James MacFadden [sic] (1842–1917), in Gerard Moran (ed.), *Radical Irish Priests 1660–1970* (Dublin 2008), pp. 149–84 and Ó Gallchobhair, *Landlordism in Donegal*. The militant McFadden should not be confused with the moderate Father James McFadden, parish priest of Tullaghbegley East, Raymunterdony, Glena, Cloughaneely, and Falcarragh in the same diocese of Raphoe. *Thom's Irish Almanac and Directory*, 1880, pp. 943, 966. *DIB*, vol. 5, pp. 1001–3.

4 T. W. Russell's views on the Olphert dispute appeared in the *Times* on 27 Oct. 1888 and 14 Jan. 1889. After denouncing the Plan, he called 'the cry of exceptional distress ... a complete and entire fraud.' See also Geary, *Plan*, pp. 30–4, 109, 139.

5 Hurlbert found Olphert congenial, handsome, and 'charming'. *Ireland Under Coercion*, vol. i, pp. 90–123 and vol. ii, p. 305. See also *Times*, 18 Aug. 1888 and *DI*, 25 Aug. 1888.

6 *FJ*, 20–21, 23, 28, 30–31 Jan., 15–16 Feb. 1888; Ó Gallchobhair, *Landlordism in Donegal*, pp. 72–82.

7 Ó Gallchobhair, *Landlordism in Donegal*, pp. 86–106; *FJ* and *Times*, 4, 6, 8, Feb., 1, 3 Apr. 1889; *DI*, 16 Mar. 1889.

8   Ó Gallchobhair, *Landlordism in Donegal*, pp. 150–80; MacSuibhne, 'Soggarth Aroon', pp. 167–9; Geary, *Plan*, pp. 29–32; *FJ*, 17 Oct.1888, 2–5, 30–31 Jan., 6 July 1889; *DJ*, 1 Nov. 1889; *Times*, 4, 6, 8, 25–26 Feb., 1, 3, 8 Apr., 25 Dec. 1889.

9   *Times*, 14 Jan. 1889; Geary, *Plan*, pp. 30–4, 109, 139; Helmingham Hall, Stowmarket, Ridgeway Papers, Balfour to Ridgeway, 26 Nov. 1889.

10   *FJ*, 3–4 Jan.1889. Hurlbert found the people of Bedlam 'very civil.' *Ireland Under Coercion*, vol. i, pp. 111–12. For the Donegal 'headmen', see Hugh Dorian's description in Brendán MacSuibhne and David Dickson (eds), *The Outer Edge of Ulster: A Memoir of Social Life in Nineteenth-Century Donegal by Hugh Dorian* (Dublin, 2000), pp. 3–4.

11   *FJ*, 3, 12 Jan 1889; *NW*, 3 Jan.1889.

12   *FJ* and *NW*, 2, 3 Jan. 1889; and *DI*, 5 Jan.1889.

13   'The fight for bare life on the Olphert estate', *UI*, 12 Jan.1889.

14   *FJ* and *Times*, 11, 12, 18, 26 Apr., 3 May 1889.

15   *NW* and *FJ*, 4–5 Jan.1889.

16   *FJ*, 4, 5 Jan., 16, 18, 21, 26 Apr. 1889; *DV*, 16 Mar.1889; *DI*, 12, 26 Jan., 16 Mar. 1889; *DJ*, 29 Apr., 3 May 1889.

17   *FJ*, 7 Jan. 1889, *DI*, 12 Jan. 1889; *NW*, 7 Jan. 1889.

18   *DI*, 12 Jan. 1889; *FJ*, 8 Jan. 1889.

19   *FJ*, 20, 22 Jan. 1887; *DI*, 23 July 1887.

20   *FJ*, 9–11 Jan., 13 Apr. 1889; *NW*, 9 Jan. 1889; *DI*, 12 Jan. 1889; *DV*, 20 Apr. 1889; *Times*, 9, 14 Jan. 1889.

21   The original title of Woodville's print was 'The State of Ireland – Evicted: A Sketch on the Road in Connemara', *ILN*, vol. 76, pp. 288–9 (20 Mar. 1880); *PIP*, 12 Jan. 1889, p. 21. See also BL, Balfour Papers, Add. MS 49808, Balfour to Major Ross, 15 Jan. 1889.

22   *DV*, 18 May 1889; *FJ*, 23 Oct. 1889.

23   *DI*, 19 Jan., 16 Mar. 1889; *FJ* and *NW*, 16, 18, 21 Jan., 13 Apr. 1889; *DV*, 20 Apr. 1889; *DJ*, 12, 15, 17, 19 Apr. 1889. BL, Balfour Papers, Add. MS 49809, Ridgeway to Balfour, 12 Feb. 1889. In the House of Lords, the Duke of Argyll called Father Stephens 'a perfect firebrand'. *Times*, 16 July 1889.

24   *FJ*, 10, 12 Apr. 1889; *DJ*, 8, 10 Apr. 1889. See also Shaw-Lefevre's letter about the Olphert estate, *Times*, 1 June 1889.

25   *FJ*, 11–12, 15 Apr. 1889; *Times*, 12, 15 Apr. 1889; *DI*, 20, 27 Apr. 1889; *DJ*, 15, 17, 24, 26 Apr. 1889.

26   For Benson's career, see also *Oxford DNB*, vol. 5, pp. 184–5. And for Harrison, see *Oxford DNB*, vol. 25, pp. 502–3; *DIB* (Cambridge, 2010); Henry Harrison, *Parnell Vindicated: The Lifting of the Veil* (London, 1931), p. 88; *FJ*, 23–24 Apr. 1889; *Times*, 15–18, 24, 26, 27, 29, 30 Apr., 1–4 May 1889. For T. H. Green, see Melvin Richter, *The Politics of Conscience: T. H. Green And His Age* (Cambridge, MA, 1964), esp. pp. 13–96, 222–66, 344–76. One of Harrison's teachers at Balliol was R. L. Nettleship, Green's devoted student who compiled and edited *The Works of T. H. Green*, 3 vols (London, 1885–8).

27   *CE* and *FJ*, 17 Apr. 1889; *DJ*, *FJ*, and *Times*, 3 May 1889.

28   *FJ*, 15–19, 26 Apr. 1889; *DJ*, 17, 29 Apr., 3 May 1889; *Times*, 23, 26–27 Apr. 1889; *CE*, 16 Apr. 1889.

29   *FJ*, 16, 18 Apr. 1889; *Times*, 12–13, 16–17, 26–27 Apr. 1889; *DI*, 20 Apr., 4 May 1889; *CE*, 18–19 Apr. 1889; *DJ*, 15, 17, 19, 22, 26, 29 Apr. and 1 May 1889.

30   *UI*, 27 Apr. 1889.

31   *FJ*, 18, 23 Apr. 1889; *Times*, 18, 19, 23 Apr., 2 May 1889.

32   *FJ*, 18–19 Apr. 1889; *Times* 19, 22 Apr. 1889; *WI*, 24 Apr. 1889.

33 *Kerry Sentinel*, 10 July 1889; *UI*, 13 July 1889; *DJ*, 19, 22, 24, 26, 29 Apr., 1, 3 May 1889; *CE*, 19, 23 Apr. 1889. Conybeare's protests over conditions in Derry prison drove Ridgeway to call him a 'mean, dirty, little cur'. Curtis, *Coercion*, p. 229.

34 *FJ*, 19–21, 26 Apr. 1889; *Times*, 18, 22–27, 29, 30 Apr., 3–4, 7 May 1889; *WI*, 24 Apr. 1889; *CE*, 18 Apr. 1889; *DJ*, 22, 24, 26, 29 Apr., 6, 8 May 1889. After the trial Harrison denied that he had refused to give his name to Head Constable Mahony. See also Conybeare's aspersions towards T. W. Russell, *DJ*, 23 May 1889.

35 See Florence Kettlewell's letter, *Times*, 17 Apr. 1889 and also 14–16, 20, 23 May 1889; *DJ*, 25 Nov. 1889.

36 *FJ*, 24, 25, 28 May, 5 June 1889; *CE*, 28 May, 5 June 1889; *UI*, 1 June 1889; *DV* and *DI*, 1 June 1889; *Times*, 23–26 Apr., 25 May, 1 June 1889.

37 NLI, 'At Derrybeg. Co. Donegal', Lawrence Collection, 1367 WL.

38 At Rochester on 16 April, the Gladstonian Liberal candidate, the Hon. Edward Knatchbull-Hugessen narrowly defeated his Unionist opponent. *FJ*, 12, 17 Apr. 1889.

39 *Times*, 7 May, 6–8 Aug. 1889, 3 Dec. 1890.

40 *Times*, 17–19, 24–27, 29–30 Apr., 3, 25 May, 16 July, 2, 6 Dec. 1889; *FJ*, 18, 19, 23 Apr., 15, 20 May 1889.

41 John McGee died on his way home. A third prisoner also fell ill. The *Cork Examiner* (12–13 Aug. 1889) described the jails as 'hot-beds of disease'.

42 *FJ*, 24–26 Oct. 1889; *DJ*, 23, 25 Oct. 1889.

43 *FJ*, 24–26 Oct. 1889; *DJ*, 25 Oct. 1889.

44 *DJ*, *FJ*, and *Times*, 25 Oct. 1889.

45 *FJ*, 28–29 Oct. 1889; *DJ*, 28, 30 Oct. 1889; *Times*, 28 Oct. 1889.

46 *FJ*, 7–8 Nov. 1890; BL, Balfour Papers, Add. MSS 49828–30, A. J. Balfour to W. L. Jackson, 20 Aug. 1890; Balfour to J. H. Tuke, 25 Aug. 1890; Balfour to Sir Henry Robinson, 2 Sept. 1890; Balfour to Ridgeway, 1 Oct. 1890.

47 *UI*, 15 Nov. 1889. For Balfour's tour of Donegal and Connemara in November 1890, see *FJ*, 5–8 Nov. 1890; Curtis, *Coercion*, pp. 362–71; Robinson, *Memories: Wise and Otherwise*, pp. 98–9.

48 For Bishop O'Donnell's peace mongering, see *FJ*, 4, 20 Nov. 1890 and *Times*, 23 Nov. 1890.

49 *FJ*, 10, 12–14 Nov. 1890.

50 *FJ*, 13–15, 17 Nov. 1890; *Times*, 3 Dec. 1890. Father Stephens had become the Bishop of Raphoe's secretary. *FJ*, 10 Nov. 1890.

51 *FJ*, 17–21, 24, 27 Nov. 1890.

52 *Times*, 21 Nov. 1890. T. W. Russell contended that Olphert had evicted 330 of his 450 tenants since 1887 mostly for non-payment. *Distressed Ireland* (London, 1891).

53 *FJ*, 10, 12 Nov. 1890; Karen Steele (ed.), *Maud Gonne's Irish Nationalist Writings, 1895–1946* (Portland, OR, 2004), esp. pp. xxi–xxii; Gonne, *Autobiography*, pp. 95–8, 104–17; *DIB*, vol. 5, pp. 733–9; Kelleher, *Feminization of Famine*, pp. 112, 118–25.

54 Gonne, *Autobiography*, pp. 140–4; Karen Steele, *Women, Press, and Politics During the Irish Revival* (Syracuse, 2007), pp. 66–105; *Oxford DNB*, vol. 22, p. 726; R. F. Foster, *W. B. Yeats: A Life: I – The Apprentice Mage* (Oxford, 1997), esp. pp. 91–3, 113–14; Margaret Ward, *Maud Gonne: A Life* (London, 1990), pp. 22–9; Samuel Levenson, *Maud Gonne* (New York, 1976), pp. 48–55, 66–7, 73–5.

55 *Times*, 23 June 1891, 12 Apr. 1892. After Olphert's demise, Major Henry Irvine succeeded Hewson as agent. *FJ*, 20 Oct. 1891, 12–13, 18 Apr. 1892.

56 Owen McGee, 'Henry Harrison', *DIB*; Lyons, *Dillon*, pp. 113–15; Lyons, *ISF*, pp. 188–90.

57 Michael M'Donagh, 'A voice from Gweedore', *DV*, 4 May 1889.

10 'PLUS ÇA CHANGE'

1 Lyons, *The Irish Parliamentary Party, 1890–1910* (London, 1951), pp. 15–32; Lyons, *Fall of Parnell*, pp. 151–4, 251; Lyons, *Parnell*, pp. 531, 568, 572, 587; Lyons, *Dillon*, pp. 109–10, 132–3, 142, 145, 147. See also Davitt's five public letters concerning the Paris funds, *FJ*, 18, 20, 23, 29, Sept. 2 Oct. 1893 and *CE*, 6 July 1894.

2 For Parnell's 'blistering attack' on the Plan and Dillon in September 1891 and the virulent campaign waged by the anti-Parnellites, see Frank Callanan, *The Parnell Split, 1890–91* (Syracuse, 1992), esp. pp. 110–34, 139–56, 251, 287–90.

3 This cartoon appears in Callanan, *Parnell Split*, p. 134.

4 Evicted families received £125,000 in monthly allowances excluding grants for building cottages and legal defence. Geary, *Plan*, p. 141; NAI, 'The Paris funds', Chief Secretary's Office, no. 13,300/S, 20 Mar. 1897, CBS 1897, 13491/S, and 'Cost of the Plan of Campaign', 13 May 1892, 4697/S; *FJ*, 9–10 Jan. 1891, 18 Mar. 1897, 21 Dec.1904; Lyons, *Dillon*, pp. 102–10, 142, 147; *Times*, 6 Nov. 1893. Henry Harrison greeted Dillon and O'Brien at Euston Station on 14 February 1891 before the police escorted them to an Irish jail.

5 Some 978 evicted tenants were receiving £1,325 in February 1892. NAI, CBS, 1892 4925/S and 'Return of Evicted Farms Unlet on 1st Nov. 1895', CBS, 1895, 10734/S. See also Dillon's letter to the *Weekly National Press*, 26 Jan. 1892 and *Times*, 14 Mar. 1896.

6 For seizures of cattle on the Kenmare estate, see *CE*, 4 Mar. 1891. Stradbally Hall, Cosby Papers, Reports of Charles P. Hamilton, December 1893, 1894, and 1897. The majority of evicted tenants belonged to the Ponsonby (219) and Clanricarde properties (198). TNA, *Return as to Evicted Tenants…on Certain Plan of Campaign Estates. Miscellaneous Notes*, xxxv, p. 32, CO 903/4. PRONI, Downshire MS, D.671/R2/117, 125. For the Rathdonnell estate, see NAI, Irish Land Commission, Agent's Notebook (*c*.1891), pp. 130, 133, 163, 170, 198, 204, 206–7, 215.

7 *Times*, 27 Nov.1893; *Connaught Telegraph*, 27 Jan. 3, Feb., 2 June 1894; *FJ*, 29 July, 2 Aug. 1892.

8 For examples of these Special Crime reports see NAI, Western Division: Monthly Confidential Reports to the Inspector General RIC, Crime Branch Special (hereafter, IGMCR/CBS), 1895, 10784/S and 1897, 13491/S. Geary, *Plan*, pp. 134–5.

9 For section 13 of the Purchase of Land (Ireland) Act, 1891, see Cherry, *Irish Land Law and Land Purchase Acts*, pp. 442–3; *Times*, 25 Mar., 3 Dec. 1890, 6 June, 6 Aug. 1891; Curtis, *Coercion*, pp. 350–6.

10 *Times* and *FJ*, 10 Mar. 1893.

11 *Times*, 31 Jan., 27 June 1891, 17 May, 8, 12 Nov.1892, 30 Mar. 1893, 29 Jan., 7, 16 Aug. 1894, 27 Feb. 1896. 'The Mitchelstown Estate', NAI, CBS 1893, 6815/S; *UI*, 24 Feb. 1894.

12 Andrew Gailey, *Ireland and the Death of Kindness* (Cork, 1987), pp. 35–40, 93–6; Catherine Shannon, *Arthur J. Balfour and Ireland, 1874–1922* (Washington, 1988), pp. 88–91; *Times*, 19 Mar. 1896; 'Farmers and the Land Bill: Extracts from Reports of Crime Special Sergeants for April 1896.' NAI, CBS, 1896, 11862/S. *FJ*, 26 Apr. 1890, 15 Apr. 1892, 29 Sept.1893; *Times*, 27 Oct. 1892, 30 July, 10 Dec. 1894.

13 *FJ*, 28 Jan. 1896; *CE*, 29 Jan. 1896; *Times*, 13 Apr., 5–6 July, 20 Aug., 20 Oct. 1894. 28 Jan. 1896.

14 *Times*, 1 Oct., 19 Nov. 1892, 11 Sept. 1895.

15 *Times*, 23 Apr. 1884; *CE*, 26 Apr. 1894.

16 *FJ*, 2 Apr. 1895.

17 Hatfield House, Salisbury Papers, Lord Castletown to Lord Limerick, 21 May 1892; George F. Brooke to Lord de Vesci, 13 Mar. 1897.

18 *Times*, 30 July 1892, 28 Feb. 1893, 11 Apr., 15–16, 20 Nov. 1893; *CE*, 15–16 Nov. 1893.

19 *Times*, 13 Apr., 5–6 July, 20 Aug. 1894, 28 Jan. 1896.

20 The Digby estate comprised 11,000 acres on the Aran Islands. Two of the Digby sisters had married aristocrats (Lords Ardilaun and Howth). Oliver J. Burke, *The South Isles of Aran* (London, 1887), pp. 66–70; Sean Spellissy, *Window on Aran* (Ennis, 2003), pp. 36–38; *FJ*, 4, 6, Apr. 1894; *Irish Daily Independent* (hereafter, *IDI*), 10–14, 16, Apr. 1894; *UI*, 12, 14, 21 Apr. 1894; *CT*, 5 May 1894; *Times*, 26 Apr. 1894.

21 *FJ*, 29–30 Nov., 1 Dec. 1904.

22 *IDI*, 2 Apr. 1894; *UI*, 23, 30 Sept. 1893, 7 Apr. 1894. According to Hugh Sutherland, the Dillon estate rental rose from £5,000 to £26,000 in 80 years. *Ireland*, pp. 50–9, 64–6, 69–70.

23 After selling his Irish estate, Lord Dillon's net annual income (excluding his English property) came close to previous average receipts of £8,480. Rath House, Termonfeckin, Dillon Papers, Charles P. Johnson, solicitor, to Lord Dillon, 21 June 1900.

24 Paul Bew, *Conflict and Conciliation in Ireland, 1890–1910* (Oxford, 1987), pp. 34, 89, 92, 165, 208; *Times*, 6 Feb. 1891.

25 *FJ*, 2, 18 Oct. 1893; *UI*, 4 Nov. 1893, 17 Mar., 7 Apr. 1894; *Times*, 3–4, 6 Nov. 1893, 26 Feb. 1894; NAI, IGMCR/CBS, 1895, 10784/S.

26 *UI*, 7, 14 Apr., 2 June 1894; Geary, *Plan*, pp. 37, 136–7, 161; *FJ*, 18, 22–23 Oct. 1894; *Times*, 17, 20, 25 Oct. 1894; NAI, IGMCR/CBS, 1895, 19784/S. For Maynooth's risky mortgage loan to the 7th Earl of Granard, see Dooley, *Decline of the Big House*, pp. 80–90.

27 *Roscommon Journal* (hereafter, *RJ*), 22 Feb., 3 May, 2 Aug., 13 Sept 1902; *FJ*, 28 Nov. 1904; Michael J. F. McCarthy, *Priests and People in Ireland* (Dublin, 1902), pp. 166–72.

28 Sutherland, *Ireland*, pp. 60–4; *RJ*, 12 July, 16, 30 Aug., 4 Oct. 1902; NAI, IGMCR/CBS, 5 Apr., 16 Aug., 15 Sept., 16 Oct. 1902, 26674/S, 27491/S, 27730; TNA, CO 904/75–6.

29 F. C. Dickinson, 'The land war in Ireland: an eviction on the De Freyne estate', *Graphic*, vol. 66, 13 Sept. 1902, p. 354.

30 NAI, IGMCR/CBS/4 (Jan. to Mar. 1903), CBS, 28217/S, 28288/S, 28290/S.

31 *RJ*, 12, 26 July, 2 Aug., 13 Sept. 1902, 11 July, 10 Oct. 1903, 30 Apr., 22 Oct. 1904; *Times*, 22 Nov. 1904; *FJ*, 5 Dec. 1904; NAI, IGMCR/CBS, 28217/S.

32 O'Brien's motion to adjourn was defeated by 188 to 156. *FJ*, 9, 15 Apr. 1892; *Times*, 8–9 Apr. 1892; Sutherland, *Ireland*, pp. 72–6, 133–5.

33 *FJ*, 22, 24 Apr. 1895; *Times*, 22 Apr. 1895.

34 Leigh-White of Bantry House, the maternal nephew and heir of the 4th and last Earl of Bantry, owned 69,500 acres in County Cork valued at £14,561. *CE*, 27–29 Apr. 1905; *Times*, 28–29 Apr. 1905.

35 Cullen, 'Marketing national sentiment', *HWJ*, pp. 165–70, 175–6; *Maud Gonne's Irish Nationalist Writings*, p. xxii; *UI*, 20 May 1893, 31 Mar. 1894; Antoinette Quinn, 'Cathleen ni Houlihan writes back: Maud Gonne and Irish nationalist theater' in Anthony Bradley and Maryann G. Valiulis (eds.), *Gender and Sexuality in Modern Ireland* (Amherst, 1997), pp. 39–47; and Foster, *Yeats*, vol. 1, p. 181.

36 Gonne, 'The evicted tenants', *UI*, 9 Dec. 1899 and 20 Apr. 1900; Steele, *Gonne*, pp. 55, 57, 129. For police reports on Gonne's activities, see TNA, CBS, 12 Dec. 1900, 903/7, p. 29 and ICR, 25 Mar. and 13 June 1905, CO 904/11.

37 In 1877 Elizabeth Thompson married Lieutenant-General Sir William Francis Butler whose reli-

gion as well as anti-imperial and Home Rule convictions did not endear him to his fellow officers.

38 Elizabeth Butler, *An Autobiography* (London, 1922), p. 199, quoted in Bhreathnach-Lynch, 'Framing the Irish', p. 255. For Lady Butler's artistic career, see J. W. M. Hirchberger, *Images of the Army … The Military in British Art, 1815–1914* (Manchester, 1988), pp. 75–83.

39 Thompson, *Autobiography*, pp. 199–200; Marshall, 'Painting Irish history: the famine', p. 49. For Lord Salisbury's address, see *Times*, 5 May, 8 July, 5 Dec. 1890 and Bhreathnach-Lynch, *Ireland's Art*, pp. 63–6.

40 See 'The latest victim', *Weekly Freeman and National Press*, 18 Aug. 1894, 'The wolf from the door', ibid., 22 Sept. 1894, and 'Reductions', ibid., 8 Dec.1894 respectively.

41 Rath House, Termonfeckin, Dillon Papers, Maurice F. Hussey to Lord Dillon, 3 Jan. 1898.

42 Sutherland, *Ireland*, facing pp. 234 and 226 respectively.

11 THE THIRD LAND WAR

1 Bew, *Conflict*, pp. 17–18; Fergus Campbell, *Land and Revolution: Nationalist Politics in the West of Ireland, 1891–1921* (Oxford, 2005), pp. 8–18, 25–30, 35–41; Dooley, *'Land for the People'*, p. 60.

2 Bew, *Conflict*, pp. 35–72; Campbell, *Land and Revolution*, pp. 26–47; Lyons, *Dillon*, pp 180–6, 222–6.

3 Kennedy, *Colonialism*, pp. 86–89. Philip Bull's assertion that the third land war 'culminated' with the Wyndham Act of 1903 is far from the mark. In fact the agrarian agitation continued well into 1910. Bull, *Land, Politics, and Nationalism*, pp. 95–6.

4 Campbell, *Land and Revolution*, pp. 17–21; Jones, *Graziers*, pp. 15–23. For the conversion of 130 holdings into 50 grazing farms occupying over four thousand acres on the Clanricarde estate in the 1890s, see the testimony of the agent, Edward S. Tener, before the Fry Commission, *BPP, 1898*, vol. 34, C.9107, Appendix B, pp. 91–92. 'The Grazier Tribe' in *Irish Street Ballads,* comp. Colm O Lochlainn (Dublin, 1978), p. 154. Thanks go forth to Terry Moylan via Mic Moroney for finding this ballad. See also Galvin, *Irish Songs of Resistance*, pp. 21–2.

5 Jones, 'Cleavage' in Clark and Donnelly, *Irish Peasants*, pp. 374–417.

6 Crotty, *Irish Agricultural Production*, p. 354. Anon., 'Evictions in Galway', *Galway Press*, 6 Apr. 1861; *Times*, 31 Dec.1894. See also Thomas O'Neill Russell, *Is Ireland A Dying Nation?* (Dublin, 1906), pp. 34–52. Becker, *Disturbed Ireland*, pp. 36–7; *Western News* (Ballinasloe), 25 May, 8 June, 14 Sept. 1901.

7 Jones, 'Cleavage' in Clark and Donnelly, *Irish Peasants*, pp. 404–13; Jones, *Graziers*, pp. 139–75; Bew, *Conflict*, pp. 206–8.

8 Lyons, *Ireland Since the Famine*, p. 258.

9 For agrarian crime data from 1899 to 1908, see TNA, Jan 1901, CO 904/72 and Lord Cadogan's memorandum on Irish crime. CAB 37/98.

10 TNA, Miscellaneous Notes, W. Series, Chief Secretary's Office, CO 903/7 and I. G. reports to Undersecretary, 12 Feb., 12 Mar., 10 Apr., 11 May, 12 July 1901, CO 904/72.

11 Bew, *Conflict*, pp. 35–95; Lyons, *ISF*, pp. 213–16; Campbell, *Land and Revolution*, pp. 42–50, 60–63; TNA, Report of the I.G. to the Undersecretary, 26 July 1901, CAB 37/57 No. 72, and 10 Mar. 1902, CAB 37/61/58. See also NAI, IGMCR/CBS/2– 28217/S. Reports of county inspectors during 1902 – (especially Clare, Cork, Galway, Kerry, Leitrim, Limerick, Roscommon, and Sligo).

12 Representing the tenants were O'Brien, John Redmond, T. C. Harrington, and T. W. Russell. For the

Land Conference, see the Earl of Dunraven, *Past Times and Pastimes* (London, 1922), vol. 2, pp. 3–20, 179–85; Lyons, *Dillon*, pp. 227–30; and NLI, Dunraven to O'Brien, 4 June 1904, O'Brien Papers, 8554/4.

13 Lyons, *Irish Parliamentary Party*, pp. 100–1, 238–40; Lyons, *Dillon*, pp. 227–30; Bull, *Land*, pp. 143–52. For Sir Horace Plunkett's concern over Wyndham's vaulting ambition, see his diary, Plunkett House, Oxford, Plunkett Papers, 11 Nov. 1900, 5, 9 Jan., 27 May, 23 1901, 28 Feb., 23 Aug., 24 Sept. 1902, 28 Feb., 15 Oct. 1904, 10 Jan., 24 Feb. 1905. Gailey, *Ireland*, pp. 161–72. According to Davitt, 'the Dunraven Treaty…spoiled a radical and final settlement of the land question.' *Fall of Feudalism*, p. 29.

14 NAI, IGMCR/CBS/2–28217/S (Jan. 1902), 26321/S, 26674/S, 27730/S, 29177/S 28290/S (Feb. 1902 to Dec. 1903) and TNA, CO 903/7, 904/73–7, NAI, IGMCR/CBS/4/5, 15 Aug., 12 Sept., 14 Nov. 1901, 16 Jan., 19 Feb. 1902. See also Lyons, *Dillon*, pp. 227–30. The 164 agrarian crimes reported for 1903 included 87 threatening letters, 32 acts of arson, 10 cases of property damage, 9 assaults, and 7 cattle maimings. Among the 72 individuals receiving constant police protection were Lords Ashtown and De Freyne. NAI, IGMCR/4–5, 18 Dec 1903 and 8 Jan. 1904; Wyndham to MacDonnell, 30 Dec. 1903, Memorandum on Reports of County Inspectors, n.d., and Return of Serious Offences for the first eleven months of 1903, 16 Dec. 1903, CBS 29177/S.

15 The average figures for evictions are based on the county inspectors' reports for 41 months in this four-year period. NAI, IGMCR/CBS, 2–8. For the Persse episode, see TNA, Irish Crime Records, CO 903/11(1905). pp. 164–8.

16 Campbell, *Land and Revolution*, p. 286; NLI, Dunraven to William O'Brien, 2 Apr. 1904, O'Brien Papers, 8554/3.

17 Wyndham to Sidney Cockerell, 14 May 1903, *Life and Letters of George Wyndham*, eds. J. W. Mackail and Guy Wyndham (London, 1925), vol. II, p. 456.

18 Dunraven, *Past Times*, pp. 20–5; Lyons, *Dillon*, pp. 227–35; Campbell, *Land and Revolution*, pp. 69–73, 78–84; Bew, *Conflict*, pp. 96–104; Bew, *Ireland*, pp. 362–3; Gailey, *Ireland*, pp. 188–96; Dooley, 'Landlords' in King, *Famine*, pp. 129–32. Bodleian Library, MacDonnell to his wife, 26, 27 Mar., and n.d. 1903, MacDonnell Papers MS e. 216, ff. 37–40, 43–8. The *Daily News* (4, 26 Mar. 1903) gave MacDonnell much credit for this measure. See also ILC Report, Cmd. 1150, *BPP, 1921*, vol. 14, p. xiii.

19 Lyons, *Dillon*, 228–42; Bull, *Land*, pp. 165–7; Bew, *Conflict*, pp. 101–3.

20 For farm sales see Birrell's speech on 30 Mar. 1909. *Hansard, Parliamentary Debates* (1909), vol. III, p. 189. Elizabeth R. Hooker, *Readjustments of Agricultural Tenure in Ireland* (Chapel Hill, 1938), p. 225.

21 Thus Colonel John Lopdell, the agent, told Sir Henry Grattan-Bellew to proceed with sales to tenants totalling £57,206 (excluding the bonus) and not to worry about the UIL's objections or threats. NLI, Bellew Papers, Lopdell to Bellew, 14 Apr. 1908 and James Robinson to Bellew, 20 Jan. 1912, MSS 27,248 and 27,290 (2).

22 By 1911 some 43 per cent of all tenanted land had been sold since 1881. For the acreage and percentage of land sold to tenants between 1881 and 1920, see Table 3 in Campbell, *Land and Revolution*, pp. 90–1. See also Bew, *Conflict*, pp. 134–40.

23 See the report of the Royal Commission on Congestion in Ireland (5 May 1908), *BPP, 1908*, vol. 42, Cd. 4097, esp. pp. 43, 91–3.

24 For another example of the trouble caused by land purchase, see Abbeyleix, Lord De Vesci to his agent, Arnold Fitzherbert, 14 July 1911. De Vesci Papers. See also NLI, Dunraven to O'Brien, 2

Apr., and O'Brien to Dunraven, 6 Sept. 1904, O'Brien Papers 8554/3/5 and BL, Wyndham to Balfour, 24 Sept. 1903, Balfour papers, Add. MSS 49804, ff. 184–5.

25 *CE*, 4–5, 12 Apr. 1905.

26 BL, Frederick S. Wrench to Balfour, 12 June 1907, Balfour Papers, Add. MS 49816, ff. 173–75.

27 For UIL membership and branches see TNA, Irish Crime Records, 1905, CO 903/12, and Campbell, *Land and Revolution*, pp. 104–5.

28 NAI, IGMCR/CBS/4 (Aug. 1903) and CBS/12 (February 1908); Campbell, *Land and Revolution*, pp. 93–4.

29 According to the Special Crime Branch, membership in the IRB in counties Clare, Galway, Mayo, and Kerry came close to 10,000 in May 1892. NAI, CBS, 1893, 6317/S. See also NA, IGMCR/CBS/7 (Feb. and Mar. 1905) and CBS/13 (Jan. and Feb. 1908); Campbell, *Land and Revolution*, pp. 86–99.

30 NLI, O'Brien to Dunraven, 12 Nov.1903 and 20 Oct. 1905, O'Brien Papers 8554/2 and 8554/6. See also Bew, *Conflict*, pp. 111–23; Lyons, *ISF*, pp. 241–4; Campbell, *Land and Revolution*, pp. 93–8.

31 Bew, *Conflict*, pp. 122–76; Campbell, *Land and Revolution*, pp. 85–105, 145–8; Bull, *Land*, pp. 172–5; Jones, 'Cleavage', pp. 381–7; Jones, *Graziers*, pp. 176–208.

32 NAI, I. G. to Undersecretary, Apr. 1907, IGMCR/CBS, 11; Bew, *Conflict*, pp. 122–64; Campbell, *Land and Revolution*, pp. 99–105, 145–8.

33 NAI, IGMCR/CBS, 7–11 (1905–7); Campbell, *Land and Revolution*, pp. 99–105, 146, 296–9; Jones, 'Cleavage' in Clark and Donnelly, *Irish Peasants*, pp. 382–4; Jones, *Graziers*, pp. 188–9; and Bew, *Conflict*, pp. 151–8, 173.

34 L. Perry Curtis, 'The last gasp of Southern Unionism: Lord Ashtown of Woodlawn', *Éire-Ireland* 40: 3 & 4 (Fall/Winter 2005), pp. 140–88.

35 Quoted in Dooley, *'Land for the People'*, p. 75.

36 Campbell, *Land and Revolution*, pp. 106–7, 45–50; NLI, *Return of Persons Claiming Reinstatement as Evicted Tenants, or Representatives of Evicted Tenants* (Dublin: HMSO, 1906).

37 Most reinstatement seekers came from Cork (665), Kerry (434), Galway (364), Mayo (282), Limerick (279), Tyrone (178), and Queen's (177). NLI, *Return of Persons Claiming Reinstatement As Evicted Tenants*.

38 Ibid.

39 *Times*, 25 Nov. 1911. Dooley, *'Land for the People'*, pp. 74–5; NAI, *List of Persons Who Have Lodged Applications with the Estates Commissioners As Evicted Tenants or Representatives of Evicted Tenants* (ILC, Dublin Nov. 1907). See also *Returns Under Section 3 of the Evicted Tenants (Ireland) Act, 1907*, Cd. 4093, Cd. 41171, Cd. 4344, and Cd. 4425, *BPP, 1908*, vol. 90, pp. 1297–1371. See also *CE*, 29 June 1909, 11 Nov. 1911; *Times*, 30 July, 3, 22, 28 Aug. 1907.

40 Lyons, *Dillon*, p. 298; Bew, *Conflict*, pp. 145–46; L. Paul-Dubois, *Contemporary Ireland* (Dublin, 1908), pp. 242–4.

41 For the report of the Royal Commission on Congestion in Ireland (5 May 1908) and Sir Antony MacDonnell's dissenting minute, see *BPP, 1908*, vol. 42.

42 The number of agrarian offences spiked at 576 in 1908. Of these 233 were threatening letters. In 93 per cent of these offences no one was brought to trial and only 20 of those tried were convicted. NAI, IGMCR/CBS/9–15. (Monthly reports from Jan. 1906 to Dec. 1912.) See also Birrell's cabinet

memorandum on the state of Ireland, TNA, 13 Feb. 1909, CAB, 37/98/31; Bew, *Ireland*, 363–67; Campbell, *Land and Revolution*, pp. 100–3.

43 See the letters between Dunraven and O'Brien from 14 September 1903 to 19 December 1905, NLI, O'Brien Papers 8554/2–5. For the devolution scheme of the Irish Reform Association and the bitter backlash by Ulster Unionists, see Lyons, *ISF*, pp. 215–18; Gailey, *Ireland*, pp. 185, 221–3, 235–54; Bew, *Conflict*, pp. 118–21.

44 Bew, *Conflict*, pp. 183–8. Lyons, *Dillon*, pp. 307–8; Lyons, *ISF*, pp. 307–8. For Birrell's speech on the second reading of his land bill (30 Mar. 1909), see *Hansard, Parliamentary Debates*, 1909, vol. III, pp. 188–99. For Clanricarde's struggles to retain his property, see *BPP, 1898*, I, (74), p. 273, *Times*, 24 Apr., 3 May, 6 June 1913, and *Hansard*, 5th series, 28 Sept 1915, vol. 74, pp. 749, 21 Mar. 1916, vol. 81, pp. 78–80, and 2 Nov. 1916, vol. 86, pp. 1838–9. And for the landlords' response to this measure, see the *24th Report of the Executive Committee of the Irish Landowners' Convention. 1908–9* (Dublin, 1910), p. 46 as well as the *21st Report of the Congested Districts Board for Ireland* (1913), Cd. 7312, *BPP. 1914*, vol. 16, pp. 12–13. Fitzpatrick, *Politics and Irish Life*, pp. 48–9, 303; and Campbell, *Land and Revolution*, p. 146.

45 For land purchase data from 1870 to 1917, see Bodleian Library, MacDonnell MS Eng. Hist. C. 371, Confidential Memorandum of the Irish Convention, No. 8 (1917), ff. 7–22, the report of the sub-committee on land purchase, and Appendix IX, no. 25 (22 Mar. 1918), ff. 63–84 and 220–31; Dooley, '*Land for the People*', pp. 74–81; Campbell, *Land and Revolution*, p. 286.

46 TNA, Miscellaneous Notes, W. Series, CSO 903/ 7. The Tottenham estate comprised 14,561 acres in Leitrim valued at £3,656. Kilbride spent eight months in prison for an 'incendiary' speech in Westmeath. See the UIL pamphlet, '*Stand Aside' – Trial By Jury in Ireland* (Dublin, 1903).

47 Richard Fell owned 1,330 acres valued at £818; and his son, William, held some 400 acres. *CE*, 12 Oct. 1904.

48 *CE*, 13–14, 17–20 Oct., 30 Nov., 15, 20–22 Dec. 1904. Sean O'Faolain, *Vive Moi!* (Boston, 1964), pp. 28–39. Constable Whelan of Cornmarket Street, Cork testified at the trial of the Murphy garrison on 20 Dec. 1904.

49 *CE*, 19 Oct., 30 Nov., 15, 20–22 Dec. 1904, 12, 19 Jan., 24–25, 27–28 Mar. 1905; *FJ*, 29–30 Nov. 1904.

50 *CE*, 25, 28–30 Mar., 1, 3, 6, 10–11 Apr. 1905.

51 *FJ*, 19 Dec. 1908, 21, 23, 25, 30 June, 1909; *CE*, 22, 23, 24 June, 14 July 1909; *Times*, 23 June 1909; Sutherland, *Ireland*, pp. 118–22.

52 Campbell, 'The hidden history of the Irish land war: a guide to local sources' in Carla King, *Famine, Land and Culture*, pp. 140–52. *FJ* and *Times*, 10–11 Nov. 1911; Bew, *Conflict*, pp. 35–80, 139–45; Campbell, *Land and Revolution*, p. 146.

53 Campbell, *Land and Revolution*, pp. 85–165; Bew, *Conflict*, pp. 134–58, 167–92; *Times*, 8 May 1908; *CE*, 9 Apr., 7 May 1908; *FJ*, 9 May 1908; Jones, 'Cleavage' in Clark and Donnelly, *Irish Peasants*, pp. 381–7; Lyons, *ISF*, pp. 299–305.

54 Bew, *Conflict*, pp. 205–10.

EPILOGUE: THE LAND QUEST

1 Dooley, '*Land for the People*', pp. 26–56; Campbell, *Land and Revolution*, pp. 238–57; Jones, *Graziers*, pp. 209–28. For Evans 'the springs of true patriotism' and the forgers of 'the most genuine bonds' came from small regions like 'the Kingdom of Mourne' or West Cork. Emyr Estyn Evans, *Ireland*

and the Atlantic Heritage: Selected Writings (Dublin, 1996), pp 31–41. Henry Glassie pays a fine tribute to 'Prof.' Evans in the Foreword, pp. ix–xiii.

2   Dooley, *Decline*, pp.127–33; Dooley, '*Land for the People*', pp. 26–49, 99–116, 228–32; Peter Hart, *The I.R.A. and its Enemies* (Oxford, 1999), pp. 273–92; Campbell, *Land and Revolution*, pp. 301–4; *CE* and *Irish Times*, 28–29 Apr., 1–2 May 1922.

3   Dooley, '*Land for the People*', pp. 2–3, 12–13, 17–20, 57–116, 132–55, 206–7; Kennedy, *Colonialism*, pp. 85–9.

4   Dooley, '*Land for the People*', pp. 42–4; Hart, *I.R.A.*, pp. 273–92; *Times*, *CE*, and *Cork Constitution*, 27–29 Apr., 1–2 May 1922.

5   Hugh Massy's mother disinherited him for converting and marrying his Catholic nurse, who was a widow with three children. For the rise and fall of the Massy family see Frank Tracy, *If Those Trees Could Speak: The Story of an Ascendancy Family in Ireland* (Dublin, 2005), esp. pp. 57–71. Charles Shackleton kindly alerted me to this incident. *FJ*, 16 May 1924. No mention of the Massy saga appeared in the *Irish Times*.

6   George Moore, *Parnell and his Island*, p. 247.

7   Eagleton, *Heathcliff and the Great Famine*, p. 7; O'Callaghan, *British High Politics*, p. 154.

8   Becker, *Disturbed Ireland*, pp. 36–40.

9   Dooley, '*Land for the People*', esp. pp. 228–30. For the failure of the CDB to buy Lord Sligo's estate in 1899, see NLI, O'Brien Papers, O'Brien to Dunraven, 6 Sept. 1904, 8554/5.

10   Ball, 'Crowd activity', p. 240.

11   For the 'grievance culture' among the Catholics during the late twentieth-century 'Troubles' in Northern Ireland, see Elliott, *Catholics of Ulster*, pp. 440–3.

12   Campbell, *Land and Revolution*, pp. 303–4. For the political revolution after the Great War, see Peter Hart, 'Definition: defining the Irish revolution' in Joost Augusteijn (ed.), *The Irish Revolution, 1913–1923* (Basingstoke, 2002), pp. 17–33.

13   Garvin, 'Priests and patriots', *IHS* 25, pp. 67–81; Jim MacLaughlin, 'The politics of nation-building in post-famine Donegal', in Nolan et al., *Donegal*, pp. 583–624.

14   Elizabeth Bowen, *Bowen's Court* (London, 1964), pp. 15–16, 455.

15   Dooley, *Decline*, pp. 171–97, 286–7.

16   Kevin Whelan, 'Between filiation and affiliation: the politics of postcolonial memory' in Clare Carroll and Patricia King (eds), *Ireland and Postcolonial Theory* (South Bend, 2003), p. 93. TCD, Lecky Papers, W. J. O'Neill Daunt to W. E. H. Lecky, 10 Feb., 2 Mar., 21 Sept. 1880, nos 188, 192, 203. Henry Glassie, *Passing the Time in Ballymenone: Culture and History in an Ulster Community* (Philadelphia, 1982), pp. 11–34, 502–11.

17   Kevin O'Neill, 'The star-spangled shamrock' in Ian McBride (ed.), *History and Memory in Modern Ireland* (Cambridge, 2001), p. 121.

18   Miller, *Emigrants and Exiles*, esp. pp. 455–62, 556–7.

19   McBride, *History and Memory*, p. 12.

20   Dan Breen, *My Fight For Irish Freedom* (Tralee and Dublin, 1964), p. 12.

21   Laurence M. Geary, 'Introduction', *Rebellion and Remembrance in Modern Ireland* (Dublin, 2001), p. 9.

Select Bibliography

MANUSCRIPT SOURCES

National Library of Ireland (NLI)
Bellew Papers
Hodson Papers
Inchiquin Papers
Leitrim Papers
William O'Brien Papers
Ormonde Papers

Trinity College Library (TCD)
Trinity College Muniments – Letter Books and Rentals
Lecky Papers

National Archives of Ireland (NAI)
Chief Secretary's Office, Registered Papers
Crime Branch Special – Monthly Reports of County Inspectors to the Inspector
General, RIC (1900–11)
Irish Land Commission Records

Public Record Office of Northern Ireland (PRONI)
Annesley Papers
Charlemont Papers
Downshire Papers

The National Archives (Kew) (formerly Public Record Office) (TNA)
Colonial Office Papers – Dublin Castle records, Inspector General RIC Monthly
    Confidential Reports, Reports of the Inspector General to the Undersecretary,
    and Miscellaneous Notes, W. Series – CO 903 and 904 (1900–9).

British Library (BL)
Balfour Papers

Others
Cosby Papers, Stradbally Hall, County Laois
De Vesci Papers, Abbeyleix, County Laois
Viscount Dillon Papers (formerly at Rath House, Termonfeckin)
Howth Papers, Howth Castle, County Dublin
O'Conor Don Papers, Clonalis, County Roscommon
Sir Horace Plunkett Diary, Plunkett House, Oxford
Salisbury Papers, Hatfield House, Hertfordshire

British Parliamentary Papers

Return by Provinces and Counties … of Cases of Evictions which have Come to the Knowledge of the Constabulary…1849 to 1880, inclusive. HC 1881 (185), lxxvii, p. 725.

Return of the Number of Police Employed in Protecting Process-Servers from 1st January 1880 to 30th June 1880, HC 1880 (280), lx, p. 451.

Return of the Number of Cases Reported by the Constabulary in which Resistance was offered to the Police … from the 1st day of February 1880 to the 30th day of June 1880. Ibid. (327), Part III.

NEWSPAPERS AND MAGAZINES

Clare Journal

Connaught Telegraph

Cork Examiner

Donegal Independent

Donegal Vindicator

Freeman's Journal

Galway Press

Graphic

Illustrated London News

Irish Daily Independent

Irish Times

Kerry Weekly Reporter

Kildare Observer

Limerick and Clare Examiner

Londonderry Sentinel

Mayo Constitution

Mayo Examiner

Northern Whig

Pall Mall Gazette

Penny Illustrated Paper

The People (Wexford)

Pictorial News

Pictorial Times

Punch

Roscommon Journal

Times (London)

United Ireland

Waterford Daily Mail

Waterford News

Weekly Freeman

Wexford Independent

CONTEMPORARY BOOKS AND ARTICLES

Allingham, H. and Radford, D. (eds), *William Allingham, A Diary* (London, 1908).

Allingham, William, *Laurence Bloomfield* (London, 1893).

Anon, *A Collection of Irish Broadside Songs* (Dublin, n..d.).

Anon, *Parnell's Land League Songster* (New York, 1881).

Arnold-Forster, H. O., *The Truth About The Land League* (London, 1882).

Bailey, W. F., *The Irish Land Acts, A Short Sketch* (Dublin, 1917).

Barrett, J. G. ('Erigena'), *Evelyn Clare: Or, The Wrecked Homesteads: An Irish Story of Love and Landlordism* (London, 1870).

Beaumont, Gustave de, *Ireland: Social, Political, and Religious*, ed. and trans. W. C. Taylor (Cambridge, MA, 2006).

Bickerdyke, John, *Wild Sports in Ireland* (London, 1897).

Blunt, W. S., *My Diaries, 1888–1914*, Part I (New York, 1922).

Blunt, W. S., *The Land War in Ireland* (London, 1912).

Bowen, Elizabeth, *Bowen's Court* (London, 1964).

Breathnach, An t-Athair Pádraig, *Songs of the Gael* (Dublin and Belfast, 1922).

Breen, Dan, *My Fight For Irish Freedom* (Tralee and Dublin, 1964).

Burke, Robert, *The Eviction; Or the Plundered Homes* (Dublin 1868).

Butler, Elizabeth, *An Autobiography* (London, 1922).

Butler, Sir William, *An Autobiography* (London, 1911).

Butler, Sir William, *The Light of the West, 1865–1908* (Dublin, 1933).

Carr, Ellis, *An Eviction In Ireland And Its Sequel* (Dublin, 1881).

Cassidy, Patrick Sarsfield, *Glenveigh, Or the Victims of Vengeance – A Tale of Irish Life in the Present* (Boston, 1870).

Cherry, R. R., *The Irish Land Law and Land Purchase Acts, 1860 to 1891* (2nd edn, Dublin, 1893).

Daunt, W. J. O'Neill, *Eighty-Five Years of Irish History* (London, 1888).

Davis, Thomas, *Essays Literary and Historical by Thomas Davis*, ed. D. J. O'Donoghue (Dundalk, 1914).

Davitt, Michael, *The Fall of Feudalism in Ireland* (London, 1904).

De Stacpoole, Duke, *Irish and Other Memories* (London, 1922).

De Vere, Aubrey, *The Poetical Works of Aubrey De Vere* (London, 1884).

de Moleyns, Thomas and Quill, Albert W., *The Landowner's and Agent's Practical Guide* (7th edn, Dublin, 1877).

Donnell, Robert, *Practical Guide to the Law of Tenant Compensation and Farm Purchase under the Irish Land Act* (Dublin, 1871).

Donnell, Robert, *Reports of One Hundred and Ninety Cases in the Irish Land Courts* (Dublin, 1876).

Dufferin, Lord and Boyle, the Hon. G. F., *Narrative of a Journey from Oxford to Skibbereen During the Year of the Irish Famine* (Oxford, 1847).

Dufferin, Lord, *Contributions to an Inquiry into the Present State of Ireland* (London, 1866).

Dunraven, Earl of, *Past Times and Pastimes*, 2 vols (London, 1922).

Godkin, James, *The Land-War in Ireland: A History for the Times* (London, 1870).

Gonne, Maud, *The Autobiography of Maud Gonne – A Servant of the Queen*, ed. A. Norman Jeffares and Anna McBride White (Chicago, 1995).

Gonne, Maud, *Maud Gonne's Irish Nationalist Writings, 1895–1946*, ed. Karen Steele (Portland, OR., 2004).

Green, G. Garrow, *In the Royal Irish Constabulary* (London, n.d. [*c.*1904]).

Hall, J. B., *Random Records of a Reporter* (London, 1928).

Hamilton, Edward C., *The Woodford Evictions* (Dublin, 1886).

Hancock, W. N., *Report on the Supposed Progressive Decline of Irish Prosperity* (Dublin, 1863).

Hurlbert, W. H., *Ireland Under Coercion*, 2 vols (Edinburgh, 1888).

Hussey, Samuel M., *The Reminiscences of an Irish Land Agent* (London, 1904).

Irish Loyal and Patriotic Union, *The Plan of Campaign Illustrated – An Account of the Massereene Estate* (Dublin, 1888) and *Mad Tipperary* (Dublin, 1890).

Keller, Canon Daniel, *The Struggle for Life on the Ponsonby Estate: A Chapter from the History of Irish Landlordism* (Irish Press Agency, n.d.).

Laing, Samuel, *A Visit to Bodyke: Or, The Real Meaning of Irish Evictions* (London, 1887).

Laing, Samuel, T*he Plan of Campaign* (London, 1887).

Lavelle, Father Patrick, *The War in Partry; or, Proselytism and Eviction* (Dublin 1861).

Lavelle, the Rev. Patrick, *The Irish Landlord Since the Revolution* (Dublin, 1870).

Lex, *Doings in Party: A Chapter of Irish History in a Letter to the Rt Hon. the Earl of Derby, KG* (London, 1860).

Lucy, Henry W., *A Diary of the Unionist Parliament, 1895–1900* (London, 1901).

Lyttle, W. G., *Sons of the Soil: A Tale of County Down* (Bangor, 1886).

McCarthy, Michael J. F., *Five Years in Ireland, 1895–1900* (Dublin, 1903).

McCarthy, Michael J. F., *Priests and People in Ireland* (Dublin, 1902).

McFadden, Rev. James, *The Present and The Past, or The Agrarian Struggle in Gweedore* (Londonderry, 1889).

MacNeill, J. G. Swift, *What I Have Seen and Heard* (London, 1925).

Mahaffy, J. P., 'The Irish landlords', *Contemporary Review*, vol. 41 (Jan. 1882).

Mahony, Pierce, *The Truth About Glenbeigh* (London, 1887).

Mandat-Grancey, Baron E. De, *Paddy At Home ('Chez Paddy')* (London, 1887).

Mangan, James Clarence, *Selected Writings*, ed. Seán Ryder (Dublin, 2004).

Meaney, Mary L., *The Confessors of Connaught: or, The Tenants of A Lord Bishop – A Tale of Our Times* (Philadelphia, 1865).

Mitchel, John, *The Last Conquest of Ireland (Perhaps)* (Dublin, 2005).

Mitchel, John, *The History of Ireland from the Treaty of Limerick to the Present Time being a Continuation of the History of the Abbé MacGeoghegan* (London, n.d.).

Moore, George A., 'An eviction', *Parnell and His Island* (London, 1887), pp. 189–211.

Mulholland, Rosa, *Onora* (London, 1900).

Mulholland, Rosa, *Giannetta, A Girl's Story of Herself* (London 1901).

Nicholls, Sir George, *A History of the Irish Poor Law* (Dublin, 1856; New York, 1967).

Nicholson, Asenath, *Annals of the Famine in Ireland*, ed. Maureen Murphy (Dublin, 1998).

Nolan, Alice, *The Byrnes of Glengoulah: A True Tale* (New York, 1869).

Nolan, Francis and Kane, Robert R., *The Statutes Relating to the Law of Landlord and Tenant in Ireland* (Dublin, 1878).

Norman, Henry, *Bodyke: A Chapter in the History of Irish Landlordism* (London and New York, 1887).

Nunn, Mrs. Lorenzo, *Heirs of the Soil* (London, 1870).

O'Connor, T. P., *Memoirs of an Old Parliamentarian*, 2 vols (London, 1929).

O'Rorke, Rev. T., *History… of… the Parishes of Ballysadare and Kilvarnet* (Dublin, 1878).

O'Rourke, Canon John, *The History of the Great Irish Famine of 1847* (Dublin, 1874; 1989).

Osborne, Sidney Godolphin, *Gleanings in the West of Ireland* (London, 1850).

Osborne, S. G., *The Letters of S. G. O.* ed. Arnold White, 2 vols (London, 1891).

Robinson, Sir Henry, *Memories: Wise and Otherwise* (London, 1924).

Robinson, Sir Henry, *Further Memories of Irish Life* (London, 1924).

Paul-Dubois, L., *Contemporary Ireland* (Dublin, 1908).

Robinson, F. Mabel, *The Plan of Campaign- A Story of the Fortune of War*, 2 vols (London, 1888).

Rossmore, Lord, *Things I Can Tell* (London, 1912).

Russell, Thomas O'Neill, *Is Ireland A Dying Nation?* (Dublin, 1906).

Smythe, William Barlow, *The Tale of Westmeath: Wickedness and Woe (*Dublin, 1882).

Sullivan, A. M., *New Ireland* (London, 1878).

Sutherland, Hugh, *Ireland: Yesterday and Today* (Philadelphia, 1909).

Tuke, James Hack, *A Visit to Connaught in the Autumn of 1847* (London, 1848).

Tuke, J. H., *The Condition of Donegal* (London, 1889).

Tuke, J. H., *A Memoir*, comp. Sir Edward Fry (London, 1899).

Turner, Col. Sir Alfred E., *Sixty Years of a Soldier's Life* (London, 1914).

Upton, William C., *Uncle Pat's Cabin, Or Life Among the Agricultural Labourers* (Dublin, 1882).

Verne, Jules, *The Extraordinary Adventures of Foundling Mick* (new edn, Dublin, 2008).

SECONDARY WORKS

Ball, Stephen, 'Crowd activity during the Irish Land War, 1879–90' in Peter Jupp and Eoin Magennis (eds), *Crowds in Ireland, c. 1720–1920* (Basingstoke, 2000).

Bell, Jonathan and Watson, Mervyn, *A History of Irish Farming 1750–1950* (Dublin, 2008).

Bew, Paul, *Land and the National Question in Ireland, 1858–82* (Dublin, 1978).

Bew, Paul, *Conflict and Conciliation in Ireland, 1890–1910* (Oxford, 1987).

Bew, Paul, *Ireland: The Politics of Enmity, 1789–2006* (Oxford, 2007).

Bhreathnach-Lynch, Sighle, 'Framing the Irish: Victorian paintings of the Irish peasant', *Journal of Victorian Culture* 2: 2 (Autumn 1997), pp. 246–50.

Bourke, Marcus, *John O'Leary: A Study in Irish Separatism* (Tralee, 1967).

Bowen, Desmond, *Souperism: Myth or Reality* (Cork, 1971).

Bowen, Desmond, *The Protestant Crusade in Ireland, 1800–70* (Dublin, 1978).

Brewster, Scott and Crossman, Virginia, 'Re-writing the Famine: Witnessing in crisis', in Scott Brewster et al. (eds), *Ireland in Proximity: History, Gender, Space* (London, 1999).

Broehl, Wayne G., Jr, *The Molly Maguires* (Cambridge, MA, 1964).

Bryant, Mark and Heneage, Simon (comp.), *Dictionary of British Cartoonists and Caricaturists, 1730–1980* (Aldershot, 1994).

Buckland, Patrick, *Irish Unionism: One: The Anglo-Irish and the New Ireland, 1885–1922* (Dublin, 1972).

Bull, Philip, *Land, Politics and Nationalism* (Dublin, 1996).

Cahalan, James M., *'Great Hatred, Little Room': The Irish Historical Novel* (Syracuse, 1983).

Callanan, Frank, *T. M. Healy* (Cork, 1996).

Callanan, Frank, *The Parnell Split, 1890–91* (Syracuse, 1992).

Campbell, Fergus, *Land and Revolution: Nationalist Politics in the West of Ireland, 1891–1921* (Oxford, 2005).

Campbell, Fergus, 'The hidden history of the Irish land war: a guide to local sources' in Carla King, *Famine, Land and Culture* (Dublin, 2000), pp. 140–52.

Carter, J. W. H., *The Land War and Its Leaders in Queen's County, 1879–82* (Portlaoise, 1994).

Chandler, Edward, *Photography in Ireland: The Nineteenth Century* (Dublin, 2001).

Clark, Samuel, *Social Origins of the Irish Land War* (Princeton, 1979).

Clark, Samuel and Donnelly, James S. Jr (eds), *Irish Peasants: Violence and Political Unrest, 1780–1914* (Manchester, 1983).

Conlon, Larry, *The Heritage of Collon, 1764–1984* (no. loc., 1984).

Crawford, Margaret, 'The Great Irish Famine 1845–9: image versus reality' in Raymond Gillespie and Brian P. Kennedy (eds), *Ireland: Art into History* (Dublin, 1994), pp. 75–88.

Crookshank, Anne and Glin, the Knight of, *Ireland's Painters, 1600–1940* (New Haven and London, 2002).

Crotty, Raymond D., *Irish Agricultural Production* (Cork, 1966).

Cullen, Fintan, 'Marketing national sentiment: lantern slides of eviction in late nineteenth-century Ireland', *History Workshop Journal*, Issue 54 (Autumn 2002).

Cullen, Fintan, 'Art history: using the visual' in Geary, Laurence M. and Kelleher, Margaret, *Nineteenth-Century Ireland: A Guide to Recent Research* (Dublin, 2005).

Curtis, L. Perry, Jr, *Coercion and Conciliation in Ireland, 1880–92* (Princeton, 1963).

Curtis, L. Perry, Jr, *Apes and Angels: The Irishman in Victorian Caricature* (Washington, D.C., 1971; rev. edn. 2001).

Curtis, L. Perry, Jr, 'Incumbered wealth: landed indebtedness in post-famine Ireland', *American Historical Review* 85: 2 (Apr. 1980), pp. 332–67.

Curtis, L. Perry, Jr, 'Moral and physical force: the language of violence in Irish nationalism', *Journal of British Studies* 27: 2 (Apr. 1988), pp. 150–89.

Curtis, L. Perry, Jr, 'Landlord responses to the Irish land war, 1879–87', *Éire-Ireland* 38: 3 & 4 (2003), pp. 134–88.

Curtis, L. Perry, Jr, '"The Land for the people": post-famine images of eviction' in Vera Kreilkamp (ed.), *ÉIRE/LAND* (Chestnut Hill, MA, 2001), pp. 87–8.

Curtis, L. Perry, Jr, 'Landlord responses to the Irish land war, 1879–87', *Éire-Ireland* 38: 3 & 4 (2003).

Curtis, L. Perry, Jr, 'The last gasp of southern unionism: Lord Ashtown of Woodlawn', *Éire-Ireland* 40: 3 & 4 (Fall/Winter 2005), pp. 140–88.

Curtis, L. Perry, Jr, 'The battering ram and Irish evictions, 1887–90', *Éire-Ireland* 42: 3 & 4 (Fall/Winter 2007), pp. 207–48.

Curtis, L. Perry, Jr, '"Killed by eviction": a case study in Co. Louth, 1888' in Felix M. Larkin (ed.), *Librarians, Poets and Scholars* (Dublin, 2007), pp. 140–55.

D'Alton, Ian, 'Keeping faith: an evocation of the Cork Protestant character, 1820–1920' in Patrick O'Flanagan and Cornelius G. Buttimer (eds), *Cork: History and Society* (Dublin, 1993), pp. 771–5.

de Nie, Michael, *The Eternal Paddy: Irish Identity and the British Press, 1798–1882* (Madison, 2004).

Dolan, Liam, *Land War and Eviction in Derryveagh 1840–65* (Dundalk, 1980).

Donnelly, James S., Jr, *The Land and the People of Nineteenth-Century Cork* (London, 1975).

Donnelly, James S., Jr. 'The Kenmare estates during the nineteenth century', Part iii, *Journal of the Kerry Archaeological and Historical Society* 23 (1990), pp. 20–45.

Donnelly, James S., Jr, 'The rightboy movement', 1785–8, *Studia Hibernica* 17 & 18 (1977–8), pp. 120–202.

Donnelly, James S., Jr, 'Hearts of oak, hearts of steel', *Studia Hibernica* 21 (1981), pp. 7–73.

Donnelly, James S., Jr, *The Great Irish Potato Famine* (Thrupp-Stroud, 2001).

Donnelly, James S., Jr, *Captain Rock: The Irish Agrarian Rebellion of 1821–1824* (Madison, 2009).

Dooley, Terence, *The Decline of the Big House in Ireland* (Dublin, 2001).

Dooley, Terence, 'Landlords and the land question, 1879–1909' in Carla King (ed.), *Famine, Land and Culture in Ireland* (Dublin, 2000), pp. 117–39.

Dooley, Terence, '*The Land for the People': The Land Question in Independent Ireland* (Dublin, 2004).

Doyle, Peggy, *The Coolgreany Evictions 1887* (1986).

Eagleton, Terry, *Heathcliff and the Great Hunger* (London, 1995).

Edwards, R. Dudley and Williams, T. Desmond (eds), *The Great Famine: Studies in Irish History, 1845–52* (New York, 1957).

Elliott, Marianne, *The Catholics of Ulster* (New York, 2001).

Fitzpatrick, David, 'Emigration, 1801–70', *A New History of Ireland*, v, *Ireland Under the Union*, 1, *1801–1870* (Oxford, 1989), pp. 562–622.

Fitzpatrick, David, *Politics and Irish Life 1913–1921* (Dublin, 1977).

Fogarty, L., *James Fintan Lalor: Patriot and Political Essayist* (Dublin, 1919).

Foster, R. F., *Modern Ireland, 1600–1972* (London, 1988).

Foster, R. F., *W. B. Yeats: A Life: I – The Apprentice Mage* (Oxford, 1997).

Foucault, Michel, *Discipline and Punish: The Birth of the Prison* (New York, 1979).

Gailey, Andrew, *Ireland and the Death of Kindness* (Cork, 1987).

Galvin, Patrick, *Irish Songs of Resistance* (Dublin, 1962).

Gates, Paul W., *Landlords and Tenants On the Prairie Frontier* (Ithaca, 1973).

Geary, Laurence M., *The Plan of Campaign, 1886–1891* (Cork, 1986).

Geary, Laurence M., 'Introduction', *Rebellion and Remembrance in Modern Ireland* (Dublin, 2001).

Girvin, Brian, *From Union to Union: Nationalism, Democracy and Religion in Ireland* (Dublin, 2002).

Gray, Peter, *Famine, Land and Politics: British Government and Irish Society 1843–1850* (Dublin, 1999).

Gray, Peter, *The Irish Famine* (London, 1995).

Haines, Robin, *Charles Trevelyan and the Great Irish Famine* (Dublin, 2004).

Haire, David N., 'In aid of the civil power, 1868–90', in Lyons and Hawkins, *Ireland Under the Union*, pp. 115–47.

Hart, Peter, *The IRA and Its Enemies* (Oxford, 1999).

Hart, Peter, 'Definition: defining the Irish revolution' in Joost Augusteijn (ed.), *The Irish Revolution, 1913–1923* (Basingstoke, 2002), pp. 17–33.

Heaney, Seamus, *Poems, 1965–1975* (New York, 1982).

Hempton, David and Hill, Myrtle, *Evangelical Protestantism in Ulster Society, 1740–1890* (London, 1992).

Hirchberger, J. W. M., *Images of the Army … The Military in British Art, 1815–1914* (Manchester, 1988).

Hooker, Elizabeth R., *Readjustments of Agricultural Tenure in Ireland* (Chapel Hill, 1938).

Hoppen, K. Theodore, *Elections, Politics, and Society in Ireland 1832–1885* (Oxford, 1984).

Houfe, Simon, *The Dictionary of British Book Illustrators and Artists, 1800–1914* (Woodbridge, 1978).

Hussey, Samuel M., *The Reminiscences of an Irish Land Agent* (London, 1904).

Irwin, David and Francina, *Scottish Painters at Home and Abroad, 1700–1900* (London, 1975).

Jackson, Alvin, *Home Rule: An Irish History, 1800–2000* (London, 2003).

James, Dermot, *The Gore-Booths of Lissadell* (Dublin, 2004).

Jones, David Seth, *Graziers, Land Reform, and Political Conflict in Ireland* (Washington, DC, 1995).

Jones, David Seth, 'The cleavage between graziers and peasants in the land struggle, 1890–1900' in Clark and Donnelly, *Irish Peasants*, pp. 374–417.

Jordan, Donald, *Land and Popular Politics in Ireland* (Cambridge, 1994).

Jordan, Thomas E., *Ireland and the Quality of Life: The Famine Era* (Lewiston, 1997).

Kelleher, Margaret, *The Feminization of Famine: Expressions of the Inexpressible?* (Cork, 1997).

Kelly, John S., *The Bodyke Evictions* (Scariff, 1987).

Kelly, Liam, *Photographs and Photography in Irish Local History* (Dublin, 2008).

Kennedy, Brian P., 'The traditional Irish thatched house: image and reality, 1793–1993', in Adele M. Dalsimer (ed.), *Visualizing Ireland* (Winchester, 1993), pp. 171–4.

Kennedy, Brian P., *Irish Painting* (Dublin, 1993).

Kennedy, Brian P. and Gillespie, Raymond (eds), *Ireland: Art into History* (Dublin, 1994).

Kennedy, Liam, 'The economic thought of the nation's lost leader: Charles Stewart Parnell', *Colonialism, Religion and Nationalism in Ireland* (Belfast, 1996), pp. 75–102.

Kenny, Kevin, *Making Sense of the Molly Maguires* (New York, 1998).

Kerr, Donal A., *A Nation of Beggars? Priests, People, and Politics in Famine Ireland, 1846–1852* (Oxford, 1994).

Kiberd, Declan, *Inventing Ireland* (London, 1995).

Kinmonth, Claudia, *Irish Rural Interiors in Art* (New Haven and London, 2006).

Kirkpatrick, R. W., 'Origins and development of the land war in mid-Ulster, 1879–85' in Lyons and Hawkins (eds), *Ireland Under the Union*, pp. 201–35.

Kissane, Noel, *The Irish Famine: A Documentary History* (Dublin, 1995).

Lane, Fintan, 'Rural labourers, social change and politics in late nineteenth-century Ireland' in Fintan
    Lane and Donal Ó Drisceoil (eds), *Politics and the Irish Working Class 1830–1945* (Basingstoke, 2005),
    pp. 113–39.

Lane, Pádraig G., 'The management of estates by financial corporations in Ireland after the famine',
    Studia Hibernica 14 (1974).

Lane, Pádraig G. 'Government surveillance of subversives in Laois, 1890–1916' in P. G. Lane and
    William Nolan (eds), *Laois – History and Society* (Dublin, 1999).

Lane, Pádraig G., 'An attempt at commercial farming in Ireland after the famine', *Studies* (Spring
    1972), pp. 54–66.

Levenson, Samuel, *Maud Gonne* (New York, 1976).

Loeber, Rolf and Magda, *A Guide to Irish Fiction, 1650–1900* (Dublin, 2006).

Lyne, Gerard J., *The Lansdowne Estate in Kerry Under the Agency of William Steuart Trench 1849–72*
    (Dublin, 2001).

Lyons, F. S. L., *The Irish Parliamentary Party, 1890–1910* (London, 1951).

Lyons, F. S. L., *John Dillon – A Biography* (London, 1968).

Lyons, F. S. L., *Ireland Since the Famine* (London, 1971).

Lyons, F. S. L., *Charles Stewart Parnell* (London, 1977).

Lyons, F. S. L. and Hawkins, R. A. J. (eds), *Ireland Under the Union: Varieties of Tension* (Oxford, 1980).

McAuliffe, E. J., *Notes on the Parishes of Kilmurry, McMahon and Killofin, Co. Clare* (Dublin, 1989).

McBride, Ian (ed.), *History and Memory in Modern Ireland* (Cambridge, 2001).

MacCarthy, Robert B., *The Trinity College Estates: 1800–1923* (Dundalk, 1992).

McCartney, Donal, 'Parnell, Davitt and the land question' in Carla King (ed.), *Famine, Land and
    Culture in Ireland* (Dublin, 2000), pp. 71–82.

McCormick, Donald, *The Incredible Mr Kavanagh* (London, 1960).

MacDonagh, Oliver, 'Irish emigration to the United States of America and the British colonies during
    the famine' in Edwards and Williams, *Great Famine,* pp. 319–88.

MacDonagh, Oliver, *A Pattern of Government Growth: The Passenger Acts and their Enforcement*
    (London, 1961).

MacDonagh, Oliver, 'The economy and society, 1830–45' in Vaughan (ed.), *A New History of Ireland*, v,
    Ireland Under the Union, i, pp. 218–41.

McGee, Owen, 'Henry Harrison', *Dictionary of Irish Biography* (Cambridge, 2010).

McHugh, Roger J., 'The famine in Irish oral tradition' in Edwards and Williams, *Great Famine,* pp.
    391–436.

MacSuibhne, Brendán and Dickson, David (eds), *The Outer Edge of Ulster: A Memoir of Social Life in
    Nineteenth-Century Donegal by Hugh Dorian* (Dublin, 2000).

MacSuibhne, Brendán, 'Soggarth Aroon and gombeen-priest: Canon James MacFadden (1842–1917)'
    in Gerard Moran (ed.), *Radical Irish Priests 1660–1970* (Dublin 2008).

Manzour, Paul, 'The land war in Loughrea', in Joseph Forde et al. (eds), *The District of Loughrea*
    (Loughrea, 2003).

Marreco, Anne, *The Rebel Countess: The Life and Times of Constance Markievicz* (Philadelphia, 1967).

Marshall, Catherine, 'Painting Irish history: the famine', *History Ireland* (Autumn 1996), pp. 46–7.

Miller, Kerby, *Emigrants and Exiles: Ireland and the Irish Exodus to North America* (New York, 1985).

Mokyr, Joel, *Why Ireland Starved* (London, 1983).

Moody, T. W., *Davitt and Irish Revolution, 1846–82* (Oxford, 1981).

Moran, Gerard P., *The Mayo Evictions of 1860* (Cathair na Mart, 1986).

Moran, Gerard, *Sending Out Ireland's Poor: Assisted Emigration to North America in the Nineteenth Century* (Dublin, 2004).

Morash, Christopher, *Writing the Irish Famine* (Oxford, 1995).

Moroney, Mic, 'Postcards from the edge', *Cara* 32: 2 (Mar./Apr. 1998).

Mulqueen, Noel J., *The Vandeleur Evictions and the Plan of Campaign in Kilrush* (Ennis, 1988).

Murray, Peter, 'Realism versus romanticism in framing national identity' in Peter Murray (ed.), *Whipping the Herring: Survival and Celebration in Nineteenth-Century Irish Art* (Cork, 2006).

Nelson, Thomas, *The Land War in County Kildare* (Maynooth, 1989).

Nolan, William et al (eds), *Donegal: History and Society* (Dublin, 1995).

Norman, E. R., *The Catholic Church and Ireland in the Age of Rebellion, 1859–73* (Ithaca, 1965).

O'Brien, Joseph V., *William O'Brien and the Course of Irish Politics 1881–1918* (Berkeley, 1976).

O'Callaghan, Margaret, *British High Politics and A Nationalist Ireland: Criminality, Land and the Law Under Forster and Balfour* (Cork, 1994).

Ó Cathaoir, Brendan, *Famine Diary* (Dublin, 1999).

O'Faolain, Sean, *Vive Moi!* (Boston, 1964).

Ó Fiaich, Tomás, '"The patriot priest of Partry": Patrick Lavelle, 1825–1886', *Journal of the Galway Archaeological and Historical Society*, vol. 35 (1976), pp. 129–48.

Ó Gallchobhair, Proinnsias, *The History of Landlordism in Donegal* (Ballyshannon, 1962)

Ó Gráda, Cormac, *Ireland: A New Economic History, 1780–1939* (Oxford, 1995).

Ó Gráda, Cormac, *Ireland Before and After the Famine* (Manchester, 1988).

Ó Gráda, Cormac, *Black '47 and Beyond: The Great Irish Famine* (Princeton, 1999).

Ó Murchadha, Ciarán, *Sable Wings Over the Land: Ennis, County Clare* (Ennis, 1998).

Ó Murchadha, Ciarán, '"The exterminator general of Clare" – Marcus Keane of Beech Park' in Ó Murchadha (ed.), *County Clare Studies* (Ennis, 2000), pp. 169–200.

O'Neill, Kevin, 'The star-spangled shamrock' in Ian McBride (ed.), *History and Memory in Modern Ireland* (Cambridge, 2001).

O'Neill, T. P., 'Famine evictions' in Carla King (ed.), *Famine, Land and Culture in Ireland* (Cork, 2000), pp. 29–70.

O'Sullivan, Niamh, *Aloysius O'Kelly: Art, Nation, Empire* (Notre Dame, 2010).

O'Sullivan, Niamh, 'The iron cage of femininity: visual representation of women in the 1880s land agitation' in Tadhg Foley and Seán Ryder (eds), *Ideology and Ireland in the Nineteenth Century* (Dublin, 1998), pp. 189–96.

Owens, Gary, 'Constructing the repeal spectacle: monster meetings and people power in pre-famine Ireland', in Maurice R. O'Connell (ed.), *People Power* (Dublin, 1993), pp. 80–93.

Pórtéir, Cathal (ed.), *The Great Irish Famine* (Cork and Dublin, 1995).

Póirtéir, Cathal (ed.), *Famine Echoes* (Dublin, 1995).

Rees, Jim, *Surplus People: The Fitzwilliam Clearances, 1847–1856* (Cork, 2000).

Richter, Melvin, *The Politics of Conscience: T. H. Green And His Age* (Cambridge, MA, 1964).

Rouse, Sarah, *Into the Light* (Dublin, 1998).

Scally, Robert J., *The End of Hidden Ireland: Rebellion, Famine, and Emigration* (New York, 1995).

Shannon, Catherine B., *Arthur J. Balfour and Ireland, 1874–1922* (Washington, 1988).

Sinnema, Peter W., *Dynamics of the Pictured Page: Representing the Nation in the Illustrated London News* (Aldershot, 1998).

Snoddy, Theo, *Dictionary of Irish Artists: 20th Century* (Dublin, 2002).

Socolofsky, Homer E., *Landlord William Scully* (Lawrence, Kansas, 1979).

Solow, Barbara L., *The Land Question and the Irish Economy, 1870–1903* (Cambridge, MA, 1971).

Sontag, Susan, *On Photography* (New York, 1977).

Spellissy, Sean, *Window on Aran* (Ennis, 2003).

Stanley, Cathal (comp.), *Castles & Demesnes* (Loughrea, 2000).

Steele, Karen, *Women, Press, and Politics During the Irish Revival* (Syracuse, 2007).

TeBrake, Janet K., 'Irish peasant women in revolt: the Land League years', *Irish Historical Studies* XXVIII: 109 (May 1992), pp. 63–80.

Thompson, Jerry, *Truth and Photography* (Chicago, 2003).

Tracy, Frank, *If Those Trees Could Speak: The Story of an Ascendancy Family in Ireland* (Dublin, 2005).

Treuherz, Julian, *Hard Times: Social Realism in Victorian Art* (London, 1987).

Turner, Michael, *After The Famine: Irish Agriculture, 1850–1914* (Cambridge, 1996).

Steele, E. D., *Irish Land and British Politics: Tenant-Right and Nationality, 1865–1870* (Cambridge, 1974).

Vallone, David and Kinealy, Christine (eds), *Ireland's Great Hunger* (Lanham, 2002).

Vaughan, W. E., *Sin, Sheep and Scotsmen* (Belfast, 1983).

Vaughan, W. E. (ed.), *A New History of Ireland, V, Ireland Under the Union, I, 1801–70* (Oxford, 1989),.

Vaughan, W. E., *Landlords and Tenants in Mid-Victorian Ireland* (Oxford, 1994).

Vaughan, W. E., *Landlords and Tenants in Ireland, 1848–1904* (Dundalk, 1984).

Voris, Jacqueline Van, *Constance de Markievicz in the Cause of Ireland* (Amherst, 1967).

Ward, Margaret, *Maud Gonne: A Life* (London, 1990.

Warwick-Haller, Sally, *William O'Brien and the Irish Land War* (Dublin, 1990).

Whelan, Irene, *The Bible War in Ireland: The 'Second Reformation' and the Polarization of Protestant-Catholic Relations 1800–1840* (Madison, 2005).

Whelan, Kevin, 'An underground gentry? Catholic middlemen in eighteenth-century Ireland', in James S. Donnelly and Kerby A. Miller (eds), *Irish Popular Culture, 1650–1850* (Dublin, 1998).

Whelan, Kevin, 'Between filiation and affiliation: the politics of postcolonial memory' in Clare Carroll and Patricia King (eds), *Ireland and Postcolonial Theory* (Notre Dame, 2003), pp. 92–108.

Whelan, Kevin, 'Eviction' in W. J. Mc Cormack (ed.), *The Blackwell Companion to Modern Irish Culture* (Oxford, 1999).

White, Hayden, *Tropics of Discourse* (Baltimore, 1978).

Whyte, J. H., 'Landlord influence at elections in Ireland, 1760–1885', *English Historical Review* lxxx (Oct. 1965).

Woodham-Smith, Cecil, *The Great Hunger* (London, 1962).

Zimmermann, Georges Denis, *Songs of Irish Rebellion: Irish Political Street Ballads and Rebel Songs 1780–1900* (2nd edn, Dublin, 2002).

UNPUBLISHED THESES

Kirkpatrick, Robert W., 'Landed Estates in Mid-Ulster and the Irish Land War, 1879–85' (PhD thesis, University of Dublin, 1976).

Vaughan, W. E., 'A Study of Landlord and Tenant Relations between the Famine and the Land War, 1850–78' (PhD thesis, University of Dublin, 1974).

Index